KU-018-120

Contemporary Russian Politics

Contemporary Russian Politics

A reader

Edited by Archie Brown

OXFORD

UNIVERSITY PRESS

OXFORD
UNIVERSITY PRESS

Great Clarendon Street, Oxford OX2 6DP

Oxford University Press is a department of the University of Oxford.
It furthers the University's objective of excellence in research,
scholarship, and education by publishing worldwide in

Oxford New York

Athens Auckland Bangkok Bogotá Buenos Aires Cape Town
Chennai Dar es Salaam Delhi Florence Hong Kong Istanbul Karachi
Kolkata Kuala Lumpur Madrid Melbourne Mexico City Mumbai Nairobi
Paris São Paulo Shanghai Singapore Taipei Tokyo Toronto Warsaw
with associated companies in Berlin Ibadan

Oxford is a registered trade mark of Oxford University Press
in the UK and in certain other countries

Published in the United States
by Oxford University Press Inc., New York

© Editorial material and selection OUP 2001

The moral rights of the author have been asserted

Database right Oxford University Press (maker)

First published 2001

All rights reserved. No part of this publication may be reproduced,
stored in a retrieval system, or transmitted, in any form or by any
means, without the prior permission in writing of Oxford University
Press, or as expressly permitted by law, or under terms agreed with the
appropriate reprographics rights organizations. Enquiries concerning
reproduction outside the scope of the above should be sent to the
Rights Department, Oxford University Press, at the address above

You must not circulate this book in any other binding or cover
and you must impose this same condition on any acquirer

British Library Cataloguing in Publication Data
Data available

Library of Congress Cataloging in Publication Data
Data available

ISBN 0–19–829999–0

10 9 8 7 6 5 4 3 2

Typeset in Minion and Meta
by RefineCatch Limited, Bungay, Suffolk
Printed in Great Britain by
The Bath Press, Bath

Preface

This book brings together some of the best analyses of contemporary Russian politics. It combines edited versions of important journal articles with newly written chapters. The latter were commissioned either because no suitable article existed or because none of those in print covered especially significant recent developments. Additional material is provided by the volume editor in the form of introductory and concluding chapters and brief introductions to all of the twelve sections into which the book is divided. It is hoped that the book will, thus, give readers access to valuable analyses which until now were available—if at all—only in a very wide range of periodicals. In an era of expanding titles and shrinking library budgets, there are many students (and some of their teachers) who will have had extremely limited access to this material. The chapters specially commissioned from authorities on their particular subjects, together with the editorial matter, round off the volume. It should, accordingly, be useful for a variety of courses which look at Russian politics today as well as for readers who simply wish to know more about the major successor state to the Soviet Union.

University teachers of Russian politics emphatically endorsed the view that a book such as this was needed. When the table of contents was circulated by Oxford University Press to eight anonymous reviewers (all I know of their identity is that four were based in Britain and four in the United States) they got very positive responses. One of the reviewers noted: 'There is a crying need for a reader such as this. It collates a wide variety of excellent contemporary articles from an impressive range of sources, covering some of the most important themes and issues in Russia today.' And another pleaded: 'please bring it out soon!' Since that request was made in the spring of 2000, it is fair to say that it has been heeded both by me and by Oxford University Press.

One reviewer in particular, though, said that my initial plan of the book was too ambitious and that the resulting work would be far too long. He or she was partly right, though the cuts I made were less stringent than the assessor proposed. That was, not least, because other reviewers stressed that the breadth of coverage was one of the book's major advantages and urged, for example, that I should 'avoid reducing the overall volume too much', since 'Russian politics is a vast subject'! The original proposal had, however, significantly more entries than the work which is now published and was divided into sixteen sections rather than twelve. Partly in response to the peer group reviewers, I amalgamated some sections and applied still more stringent selection criteria within them. As noted above, I also took the opportunity to fill gaps in the available literature relating to important recent developments by commissioning articles from scholars with particular expertise in the relevant subject. The invited authors responded, in almost every case, with commendable speed and in all cases with work of quality. The final product is still by no means a slim volume, but none the worse for the process of review and compression it underwent.

In my original plan, extensive though the coverage was, I had confined myself to Russian domestic politics. More than one assessor, however, called for an additional section on

Russian foreign policy. Even without that viewpoint receiving the wholehearted endorsement of my OUP editors, I would have been persuaded that such a section was highly desirable, though clearly a volume could be compiled on foreign policy alone. (That, however, goes for most sections of the book, selection within all of which involved hard choices.) I am particularly grateful to Roy Allison and Margot Light for the chapters they wrote specially, thus helping to make the section on 'Russia and the World' as valuable as any in the book and to Margot Light, additionally, for drawing my attention to the perceptive article by Vladimir Baranovsky in what was at the time the current issue of the Chatham House journal, *International Affairs*, and which now completes the foreign policy section of the Reader.

At a much earlier stage Oxford doctoral students Tomila Lankina and Craig Weller were among those who helped me draw up very long lists of articles which were candidates for inclusion in the Reader. I continue to be indebted also to the Secretary and Librarian of the Russian and East European Centre of St Antony's College, Jackie Willcox, for cheerfully, and with great skill, doing two jobs which at one time occupied two people. In visits to Russia in April and September 2000 I had the opportunity to discuss their chapters with the numerous Russian contributors to the book. Some of these articles had been previously published and, in common with the Western contributors, those based in Russia kindly and readily agreed to my proposals for cuts in the interests of keeping the whole book within a viable length. Five of the Moscow-based contributors (St Petersburg is represented by two articles by Vladimir Gelman) wrote important pieces in their area of expertise specially for the volume and did so, quite rightly, in Russian. I am grateful not only to them but also to Polly Jones for combining speed with accuracy in skilfully translating them.

The contributors include some of the most renowned political scientists and specialists on Russia as well as outstanding younger scholars in the early stages of their career. All have been remarkably cooperative and have made work on what has undoubtedly been a complicated book to produce a much more agreeable task than it might have been. I should say a particular word of thanks to Eugene Huskey since he is the author of no fewer than three of the forty chapters in the volume, two of them previously published and one, at my request, freshly written on the institutional inheritance of Vladimir Putin and the new Russian president's innovations. I am grateful, too, to the copyright owners who have granted Oxford University Press permission to republish, whether in whole or in part, the articles and extracts from books which appear in the pages that follow.

That brings me to the editors at OUP who have worked with me on this volume. If Tim Barton must take primary credit for seeing the need for a Reader on Russian politics and kindling my enthusiasm for compiling it, Angela Griffin and Miranda Vernon, the editors I have subsequently dealt with on a regular basis, have made sure that my enthusiasm for the project was sustained. They have been understanding of some slippages on deadlines in the case of a multi-author book of this degree of complexity, while, nevertheless, ensuring that the book remained on a fast-track schedule. Their efficiency and helpfulness have made working with the Press a pleasure.

I am also extremely grateful to a colleague who is also one of the contributors, Paul Chaisty, for his editorial assistance—in particular, in the compilation of the glossary and in helping to check the articles which had been electronically scanned, not a process that reproduces the original as automatically as some might imagine. In that work of editorial checking, I have received similarly generous and efficient help from my wife, Pat, and I am particularly indebted to her for compiling the index within the confines of a tight schedule.

Many people have played a role in bringing the work to fruition, but above all the international group of authors of the chapters that follow. It is their hope and mine that this book will provide for a wide readership both fresh insight and significant information on Russian politics and that it will stimulate interest in the subject. Understanding what is happening in a major nuclear power, which is also resource-rich and the world's largest country, clearly matters. What occurred in Russia during the twentieth century had a profound impact on developments elsewhere in Europe and in the world as a whole. And Russia still has the potential to be a major player in international politics as the twenty-first century unfolds. To what extent that will be for the benefit of her own citizens and her neighbours depends upon the foundations on which the post-Communist system is built. Furthermore, on an analytical level, Russia constitutes a fascinating and important case-study for all who are interested in comparing transitions from authoritarian rule, a process which is not unilinear and whose destination is not predetermined.

ARCHIE BROWN
St Antony's College, Oxford

Contents

The Contributors

ROY ALLISON is Head of the Russia and Eurasia Programme at the Royal Institute of International Affairs (Chatham House), London.

VLADIMIR BARANOVSKY is Deputy Director of the Institute of World Economy and International Relations (IMEMO), Moscow.

LAURA BELIN took her first degree at Harvard and Master's in Russian and East European Studies at Oxford before spending five years working for the Open Media Research Institute and, subsequently, Radio Liberty. She is now completing a doctorate at Oxford on the Russian mass media.

GEORGE BRESLAUER is Dean of Social Sciences and Chancellor's Professor of Political Science at the University of California at Berkeley and also Editor of *Post-Soviet Affairs*.

ARCHIE BROWN is Professor of Politics at the University of Oxford and Director of the Russian and East European Centre, St Antony's College.

YITZHAK M. BRUDNY is a Senior Lecturer in Political Science and Russian Studies at the Hebrew University of Jerusalem, Israel.

VALERIE J. BUNCE is Professor of Government at Cornell University.

PAUL CHAISTY is a Research Fellow at St Antony's College, Oxford.

ALLA CHIRIKOVA is a Research Fellow at the Institute of Sociology of the Russian Academy of Sciences, Moscow.

JOHN DUNLOP is a Senior Fellow at the Hoover Institution, Stanford.

RICHARD E. ERICSON is Professor of Economics, Columbia University, New York, and former Director of the Harriman Institute.

OKSANA GAMAN-GOLUTVINA is Professor of Political Science at the Russian Academy for Public Administration, Moscow.

VLADIMIR GELMAN is Lecturer in Russian Politics in the Faculty of Political Science and Sociology of the European University at St Petersburg.

KATHRYN HENDLEY is Associate Professor of Law and Political Science and Director of the Center for Russia, East Europe, and Central Asia at the University of Wisconsin-Madison.

EUGENE HUSKEY is Professor of Political Science and Director of Russian Studies at Stetson University, Florida.

JEFF KAHN, currently at University of Michigan Law School, has a doctorate in Politics from Oxford University and is the author of a forthcoming book on Russian federalism.

TERRY LYNN KARL is Professor of Political Science at Stanford University, Director of Stanford's Center for Latin American Studies and a Senior Fellow of the Institute for International Studies.

IGOR KLYAMKIN is Director of the Institute of Sociological Analysis, Moscow.

NATASHA KOGAN graduated from Wesleyan University, worked for McKinsey & Co. in New York, and is now with Cybersettle.com.

TOMILA LANKINA, currently at Stanford University, recently completed an Oxford doctorate on the institutional dimension of ethnic mobilization in Russia.

GAIL LAPIDUS is a Senior Fellow of the Institute for International Studies, Stanford University.

NATALYA LAPINA is a Research Fellow at the Institute for Scientific Information in the Social Sciences (INION), Moscow.

YURY LEVADA is Director of the All-Russian Institute for the Study of Public Opinion (VTsIOM), Moscow.

MARGOT LIGHT is Professor of International Relations at the London School of Economics and Political Science.

ALEXANDER LUKIN is Associate Professor (*dotsent*) of Political Science at the Moscow State Institute of International Relations (MGIMO) and currently a Visiting Fellow at the Brookings Institution, Washington, DC.

ROBERT G. MOSER is Assistant Professor of Political Science in the University of Texas at Austin.

PETER ORDESHOOK is Professor of Political Science at the California Institute of Technology.

SERGEI PEREGUDOV is a Professor at the Institute of World Economy and International Relations (IMEMO), Moscow.

RICHARD ROSE is Director of the Centre for the Study of Public Policy, University of Strathclyde, Scotland.

PETER RUTLAND is Professor of Political Science at Wesleyan University, Connecticut.

PHILIPPE C. SCHMITTER is Professor of Political and Social Sciences at the European University Institute in Florence.

LILIA SHEVTSOVA is a Senior Research Fellow at the Carnegie Center, Moscow.

NODARI SIMONIA is Director of the Institute of World Economy and International Relations (IMEMO), Moscow.

DARRELL L. SLIDER is Professor of Government and International Affairs at the University of South Florida, Tampa.

WILLIAM SMIRNOV is head of the Department of Political Science, Institute of State and Law of the Russian Academy of Sciences, Moscow.

RONALD GRIGOR SUNY is Professor of Political Science at the University of Chicago.

VERA TOLZ is a Reader in the Department of Politics and Contemporary History, University of Salford.

STEPHEN WHITEFIELD is Tutor in Politics and a Fellow of Pembroke College, Oxford.

Abbreviations and Glossary

ABM	Anti-Ballistic Missile Treaty
apparat	apparat (apparatus), bureaucracy
apparatchik	apparatchik, bureaucrat, full-time official (especially Communist Party official in Soviet era)
arbitrazh	arbitration courts dealing with commercial disputes
ASSR	Autonomous Soviet Socialist Republic
BBC SWB	British Broadcasting Corporation Summary of World Broadcasts
blat	blat, informal relationship of exchange based on mutual favours
CEC	Central Electoral Commission
CFE	Conventional Forces in Europe Treaty
CIA	Central Intelligence Agency (United States)
CIS	Commonwealth of Independent States
Comecon	Council for Mutual Economic Assistance
CPD	Congress of People's Deputies (Russia)
CPSU	Communist Party of the Soviet Union
CTBT	Comprehensive Test Ban Treaty
DPR	Democratic Party of Russia
dvoevlastie	dual power, dyarchy
DVR	DCR, Democratic Choice of Russia (political party)
EBRD	European Bank for Reconstruction and Development
Ekho Moskvy	Echo of Moscow (radio station)
EU	European Union
FSB	Federal Security Service (successor to KGB)
GKOs	Russian Government Bonds
glasnost'	glasnost, openness, transparency
Golos Rossii	Voice of Russia (electoral bloc)
Goskomstat	State Committee for Statistics
guberniya	provincial administrative unit (Tsarist Russia)
IMEMO	Institute of World Economy and International Relations
IMF	International Monetary Fund
KFOR	NATO Kosovo Force
KGB	Committee of State Security (political police)
kompromat	compromising material often used to blackmail
Komsomol	Communist Youth League
KPRF/CPRF	Communist Party of the Russian Federation
krai/kray	kray, territory
LDPR	Liberal Democratic Party of Russia
MFA	Ministry of Foreign Affairs
MGIMO	Moscow State Institute for International Relations

MVD	Ministry of the Interior
NACC	North Atlantic Cooperation Council
NATO	North Atlantic Treaty Organization
NDR	OHR, Our Home is Russia (political party)
NGO	Non-Governmental Organization
NMD	National Missile Defence
nomenklatura	nomenklatura, Communist system of appointments; also used to refer to the people appointed by this system as an especially privileged social stratum
NTV	Independent Television Channel
obkom	Regional Committee of the Communist Party of the Soviet Union
oblast'	oblast, region
okrug	circuit, large territory or district
OMON	Ministry of Interior Special Police Force
OMRI	Open Media Research Institute
ORT	Russian Public Television
OSCE	Organization for Security and Cooperation in Europe
Otechestvo	Fatherland (electoral bloc)
OVR	Fatherland-All Russia (electoral bloc)
perestroyka	perestroika, reconstruction (or restructuring)
PfP	Partnership for Peace Agreement
Politburo	Political Bureau of the Central Committee of the Communist Party of the Soviet Union
PR	Proportional Representation
pravovoe gosudarstvo	law-governed state, state based on the rule of law
PRES	Party of Russian Unity and Accord
RF	Russian Federation
RSFSR	Russian Socialist Federative Soviet Republic
RTR	All-Russian Television and Radio Company
siloviki	power ministries (those controlling means of coercion)
Spetsnaz	Special Forces Unit (Defence and Interior ministries)
SPS	Union of Rightist Forces (electoral bloc)
START II/2	Treaty on the Further Reduction and Limitation of Strategic Offensive Arms (also Start I and III)
svyazy	connections
TV6	television company owned by the Moscow Independent Broadcasting Corporation
ukaz	decree, edict
USSR	Union of Soviet Socialist Republics
VGTRK	All-Russian State Television and Radio Company
Vsya Rossiya	All Russia (electoral bloc)
VTsIOM/VCIOM	VTsIOM, All-Russian Centre for the Study of Public Opinion
Yabloko	Political party led by Grigory Yavlinsky
Yedinstvo/Edinstvo	Yedinstvo, Unity (political party)

Note on Spelling and Transliteration

In the chapters which have been specially written for this book British-English spelling is adopted. Where previously published articles from a wide variety of journals or (in two cases) books constitute the chapters, the original spelling, whether American or British, is retained. The same goes for transliteration of Russian words; the transliteration used in the original English-language source (unless misprinted there) is preserved. There are several different ways of transliterating a number of the letters in the Cyrillic alphabet into English, and so inconsistency in this respect—a consequence of producing a multi-author book on a brisk publishing schedule—by no means necessarily connotes error. Uniformity has, however, been the aim for the specially commissioned articles which are appearing in print for the first time. Given the customary dilemma between familiarity and linguistic rigour in transliteration from Russian, a compromise is adopted in those chapters. When a Russian word is in italics (as, for example, in the titles of Russian-language publications in the footnotes), it is transliterated strictly according to the British Standard System in the fifteen chapters published here for the first time. In the main body of the book, however, familiarity is given precedence over consistency—thus 'Sergei' rather than 'Sergey' and 'Gusinsky' rather than 'Gusinskiy' or 'Gusinskii'. Likewise, Boris Yeltsin appears, spelled thus (rather than as 'Yel'tsin') in the text of the book, with the soft sign in his name acknowledged only in footnotes.

Introduction to Contemporary Russian Politics

Archie Brown

Russian politics has been in continuous flux ever since Mikhail Gorbachev became leader of the Communist Party of the Soviet Union in 1985. Whereas, however, the Gorbachev era has been the subject of a voluminous literature, including books which analyse that period as a whole,[1] the literature on post-Soviet Russia, while extensive, has been less consolidated. Now that the presidency of Boris Yeltsin has come to an end and significant changes are being initiated, for better or worse, by his successor, Vladimir Putin, the time is certainly ripe for a broadly based examination of the new Russian politics. Much of what is happening is not within the control of individual leaders and this book ranges well beyond national leadership and, indeed, politics in the narrower sense of the term to examine also changes in the Russian economy and society.

The volume can lay claim to be unusual in a number of ways. In the first place, it is the *only* Reader on post-Soviet Russian politics. That is to say, it is the only book which brings together many of the most illuminating published articles of recent years on a variety of major aspects of Russian political life. Second, as noted in the Preface and uncommonly for a Reader, it combines the best of the recent with the newest of the new. Fifteen of the volume's forty chapters have been written specially for this work. The resultant book is, therefore, as up to date as a substantial volume can be, with such developments as the presidential election of 2000, the 'new Russian federalism', and foreign policy under President Putin analysed by authoritative scholars. A third distinctive feature of this collective work is that if the largest single category of authors consists of those based in the United States (as might be expected, given the quantitative and qualitative strength of American political science), Russians working in Russian institutes or universities run them a very close second. The book, accordingly, reflects the increasing interaction between Russian and Western scholars engaged in the study of politics. A conscious effort has, indeed, been made to bring to a Western readership—not least, to students in the English-speaking world—Russian analyses and perspectives with which they are unlikely to be familiar.

The authors themselves, of course, whatever their nationality, espouse a variety of viewpoints. What the contributions included in the book share is an attempt to get beneath the surface of Russian politics and to avoid the glib oversimplifications which have become all too

[1] See e.g. Archie Brown, *The Gorbachev Factor* (Oxford: Oxford University Press 1996); Anthony D'Agostino, *Gorbachev's Revolution, 1985–1991* (London and Basingstoke: Macmillan, 1998); Jerry F. Hough, *Democratization and Revolution in the USSR, 1985–1991* (Washington: Brookings Institution, 1997); John Miller, *Mikhail Gorbachev and the End of Soviet Power* (London and Basingstoke: Macmillan, 1993); and Stephen White, *After Gorbachev* (Cambridge: Cambridge University Press, 1993).

familiar in Western political and, to a lesser extent, scholarly discourse. Russian politics in the post-Soviet period have been poorly understood and greatly oversimplified. Much Western commentary has veered between, on the one hand, the premature conclusion that Russia has established both democracy and a market economy and, on the other, a fatalistic gloom about inevitable authoritarianism and corrosive corruption. The complexity of the real world of Russian politics has been reduced to a Manichean struggle between 'democrats' or 'reformers', on the one hand, and 'Communists' or 'reactionaries', on the other. The few Russian politicians and social scientists given a regular hearing in the West have, quite disproportionately, been those who can be relied upon to reinforce such images, while the writings of the most serious and objective of Russian scholars remain, with few exceptions, known only to relatively restricted circles of Western specialists.

While the book conveys a good deal of important and fresh information, it is not primarily a compilation of facts. Articles have been chosen on the basis that they contribute significantly to understanding and conceptualizing post-Soviet political developments. The word 'comprehensive' must be a relative term when it refers to the variety of areas and facets of Russian politics which can be examined within the covers of a single book. However, the extent of the coverage is unusually broad, embracing analysis of political institutions; leaders and leadership styles; the rule of law versus informal networks and rules of the game; political behaviour; public opinion; the role of the mass media; federalism and regional politics; the politics of economic reform and the influence of economic interests; Russia's sense of national identity; and its evolving foreign policy, among other areas of study. The large penultimate section of the book is devoted to a lively debate on the Russian transition in comparative perspective, while the final section deals with the large issue of the scope, limitations, significance, and even desirability of democratization in Russia.

Although the Reader is divided into twelve sections (each of which has some internal coherence and contains three or more chapters), a political system is an interconnected whole and, therefore, it is natural that themes and problems cross sectional boundaries and are approached from different angles in a variety of contexts. Thus, reflections on the extent to which Russia can be fitted into generalizations about transition, based on comparative study, are not confined exclusively to Section 11. Furthermore, the central issue of democratization in Russia bulks large in chapters on the executive and legislature as well as in the studies of political parties and elections and not merely in the concluding section of the book. Similarly, the development of a new form of interest-based politics in Russia is a theme which is addressed not only in Section 6—that which is most explicitly devoted to the topic—but in, for example, the chapters on political finance and on the mass media.

The book begins with the institutional design of the Russian political system. Its earliest institutions were a legacy of the late Soviet period and, though the focus of the volume is very much on Russian politics *after* the collapse of the USSR, a number of authors note the imprint of Soviet institutions, and the influence of Soviet practices and networks, on the structure and functioning of the post-Communist polity. While several authors trace a path-dependence from Soviet times, Peter Ordeshook (in Chapter 2) argues that Russian democrats were insufficiently conscious of the need to develop incentives that would underpin democracy and he offers proposals to remedy what he sees as a failure of institutional crafting. In a later section, Richard Rose (Chapter 20) documents 'antimodern' patterns of behaviour in Russian society and provides a more culturally based explanation of political problems with which Russia still has to come to grips.

In the ordering of sections, the executive takes precedence over the legislature, for it has been the dominant partner, though the post-Soviet era has seen periods of acute conflict between the legislature and the presidency, particularly in the First Russian Republic (1992–3). Following the adoption of a new Constitution in December 1993, the Second Russian Republic (1994 to the present day) has witnessed a more complex relationship between president, government, and parliament in which the legislature was at times bypassed by a combination of presidential disdain and presidential decree and at other times cajoled or (in the case of some deputies' votes) bought. It came to be more subtly managed and assuaged by Prime Ministers Primakov and Putin—and by Putin again after he became president.

Although discussion of elections clearly overlaps with that of parties, the section on the former precedes the latter, and this corresponds with Russian political reality. Contested elections came into existence only in the late Soviet period. There were competitive elections for a union-wide legislature in 1989 (with more than one candidate contesting a majority of seats in the newly created Congress of People's Deputies), but this was not yet a multi-party election. Nor was the election for the Congress of People's Deputies of Russia the following year. Boris Yeltsin became president of Russia after his victory in the June 1991 election, during which he did not embrace a political party, having resigned from the Communist Party of the Soviet Union a year earlier. Indeed, even in 1996 when he won his second term of office, Yeltsin remained ostentatiously 'above party', as did Vladimir Putin in 2000, though Putin signalled his closeness to the electoral bloc, Unity (Yedinstvo) which had been formed partly to pave his way to the Kremlin. The first multi-party, as distinct from multi-candidate, election in Russia was in December 1993, though it would be odd to accord it the special status of a 'founding election'. Following as it did Yeltsin's controversial, unconstitutional, and ultimately violent dispersal of the previous legislature, it exemplified apathy and disenchantment, attracting by far the lowest turnout of all Russian elections at the national level between 1989 and 2000.

Whether Russia is in transition to a market economy or has come to rest at what Joel Hellman, in an important comparative study of transitions, has called 'partial reform equilibrium', is one of the major themes addressed and elucidated in the Reader.[2] The links between economic and political power are an important subject for analysis in any country and their complete fusion in the Soviet Union was one of the defining characteristics of that system. In post-Soviet Russia the linkages differ both in form and substance from the Soviet era, while remaining different again from those to be found in a Western democracy with a market economy. Argument continues about how the Russian system should be characterized. In his contribution to this Reader Richard E. Ericson, a distinguished economist and strong supporter of transitions to a genuine market, conceptualizes the Russian economic system today as 'feudal' and sees parallels with medieval rather than contemporary Europe. Sergei Peregudov argues that the system is a form of oligarchical corporatism, while Nodari Simonia holds that it should best be understood as 'bureaucratic capitalism'. Another Moscow-based author, Oksana Gaman-Golutvina, gives reasons why elites as well as the mass of the people

---

[2] Joel Hellman, 'Winners Take All: The Politics of Partial Reform in Postcommunist Transitions', *World Politics*, 50/2 (Jan. 1998), 203–34.

in Russia should have become disillusioned with the idea of 'development', but calls for a new commitment to modernization as a societal goal.

One of the most traumatic issues facing Russian politicians after 1991 was the fact that their state, while still the world's largest country, had lost territory which had been part of a greater Russia (whether Imperial Russia or the Soviet Union) for well over a century and, in some cases, for several centuries. A major consequence was that twenty-five million Russians now found themselves living 'abroad'—in republics which had been part of the USSR but which, following its collapse, had become independent states. This produced the 'identity crisis' discussed by more than one author in the pages that follow and a worry that Russia might follow in the footsteps of the Soviet Union and itself break up. However, two of the contributors who are leading Russian specialists on politics in the regions, Alla Chirikova and Natalya Lapina, argue that the dissolution of Russia is highly unlikely and point to many of the advantages which the central authorities enjoy. Other contributors, while not arguing that Russia is in danger of disintegration, emphasize the degree of autonomy enjoyed by republican and regional authorities in the post-Soviet era—certainly in sharp contrast with their lack of independence in the unreformed Soviet Union. Indeed, it is possible to argue that contemporary Russia contains a multiplicity of polities within the boundaries of a single state. There are relatively democratic regions, at one extreme, and local despotisms at another. Most of the units (or, in the official Russian terminology, subjects) of the federation which enjoy republican status are very much at the authoritarian end of that spectrum.

In the sphere of foreign policy Russia has undergone, and is still undergoing, a very difficult adjustment from a superpower, which before 1985 was feared, to the Gorbachev era, when its every move was front-page news in the West, to being a country which is frequently ignored. When Russians say that 'there would have been no NATO bombing of Yugoslavia if there had still been a Soviet Union', they are almost certainly correct in that supposition. That is to leave entirely aside the issue of the intrinsic merits or demerits of the NATO operation—whether over the longer run it did more good than harm—but simply to note that Soviet political weight and military power, aligned to Soviet hostility to such measures, would have weighed heavily in the deliberations of NATO members, including, not least, those taking place in Washington. The overwhelming probability is that Soviet opposition would have dissuaded NATO from military intervention in the absence of an explicit mandate from the Security Council of the United Nations. In the late 1990s, in contrast, the opposition to the NATO bombing on the part of President Yeltsin, of the Russian government and parliament, and, indeed, of Russian public opinion more broadly was discounted. With 'the end of the bipolar division of Europe', writes Vladimir Baranovsky in Chapter 31, 'Russia unexpectedly found itself pushed to the periphery of the continent'. Margot Light, in the same section of the book, argues that Russian foreign policy under Yeltsin was incoherent, but that it is likely to acquire a greater coherence under Putin. This, as Roy Allison notes, will probably mean a stronger promotion of Russian national interests vis-à-vis the new states of Eurasia (the former republics of the Soviet Union) as well as in relations with the West. Yet the policy will be modified, on the one hand, by the hard facts of scarce economic and military resources and, on the other, by the present Russian leadership's pragmatic preference for dialogue and active diplomacy rather than confrontation.

The last two parts of the book are much concerned with the issue of the democratization of Russia in a comparative context. The second last section, in particular, explicitly addresses the question of how far the conceptual advances and theoretical insights of the general body of 'transitological' literature can illuminate not just the Soviet transition but transitions from Communist rule more generally. Two leading comparativists, much of whose work has focused on Latin America or southern Europe, Philippe C. Schmitter and Terry Lynn Karl, cross swords with Valerie Bunce on the value of the branch of political science which has become known as transitology. Bunce makes clear that she is far from being opposed to comparison but argues that greater illumination is likely to emerge from intra-regional comparisons of states which have emerged from Communist rule than from cross-regional comparisons. Schmitter and Karl hold that 'both intra-regional and cross-regional comparisons are essential to the process of theory-building, but cross-regional comparisons which incorporate the experiences of eastern Europe have some distinct advantages for addressing many of the theoretical issues predominant in the study of democratization today'. In the same section of the book, a Russian scholar with a thorough knowledge of Western political science writing on democratization, Vladimir Gelman, applies concepts drawn from the transition literature (including earlier writings of both Schmitter and Karl) to political developments in the Russian regions.

The theme of democratization is the major preoccupation also of the concluding section of the book. The authors address the question whether Russia is becoming a democracy and also discuss the criteria for making such an assessment. One of the most senior of Russian political scientists, William Smirnov, notes advances which have been made but argues that much of what has been described as 'democracy' has been little more than a façade. He does not, however, call into question the necessity of democratization, arguing a case, indeed, for further constitutional and political reform. A younger Russian scholar, Alexander Lukin, takes a more sceptical view of the assumption that speedier democratization is what Russia most needs. Development of the fundamentals of liberalism, a market economy and a rule of law, he holds, should have a prior claim over democratization which is likely—in the absence of those building blocks—to remain in Russia a far cry from democracy worthy of the name. A final chapter by the editor discusses the requirements of democracy in general, evaluates Russia's experience in particular, and draws together some of the numerous analyses and viewpoints which have been presented in the earlier parts of the book.

Institutional Design

Section 2

Institutional Design

Introduction

Archie Brown

The institutional design of early post-Soviet Russia closely reflected the reforms which were introduced in the last years of the Soviet Union. As a prelude, therefore, to the discussion in the chapters which follow, attention needs to be paid to the Russian polity's institutional inheritance from the Soviet state. Prior to 1989 the Soviet Union had been run primarily by the officials of the Communist Party of the Soviet Union, although ministries also wielded real power within their respective domains. The CPSU was organized hierarchically with the general secretary at the top and a Politburo—the functional equivalent of the Cabinet in a Western democracy—as the highest collective decision-making body. The supposedly representative bodies, the soviets (with the Supreme Soviet of the USSR at the top of that particular hierarchy), were far less powerful. At the local level, soviets had many practical functions to perform, but they were subordinate to the top party official in their locality, whether district, town, or region. At the highest level the Supreme Soviet was, at best, a pseudo-parliament, meeting for only a few days in the year and rubber-stamping decisions taken elsewhere.

At the Nineteenth Conference of the Soviet Communist Party in the summer of 1988, Mikhail Gorbachev, the last General Secretary of the CPSU, and holder of that office from 1985 to 1991, pushed through a number of radical reforms to the institutional structure of the Soviet, and hence Russian, political system. A new system of representative organs was created and the principle of competitive elections accepted. In a sharp break with the Soviet past, elections took place in March 1989 for an entirely new body, the Congress of People's Deputies of the USSR. Two-thirds of the seats were filled on the basis of election in territorial constituencies, in a majority of which there were several candidates. In a compromise between reformers within the Communist Party and conservative Communists (for this institutional design emanated from within the political elite) a third of the seats were reserved for the representatives of 'public organizations'. This, on the one hand, ensured that a hundred senior members of the Communist Party were able to enter the legislature from that 'public organization' without the inconvenience of fighting a contested election, but, on the other, it produced some very high-calibre deputies from the creative and scientific unions and, above all, from the Academy of Sciences. Those elected from the Academy included the distinguished physicist and leading dissident in the country, Andrei Sakharov; the head of Soviet space research, Roald Sagdeev; and the person who topped the Academy's poll, Nikolai Shmelev, who was both a prominent economic reformer and a creative writer.

The Congress of People's Deputies, while accorded great powers, nevertheless was not in permanent session. Instead, it elected an inner body, bearing the same name as the previous discredited legislature, the Supreme Soviet, but very different from its namesake—in the first instance because it met for as many as eight months of the year. This two-tier system was again a political compromise. It would have been surprising if Russia had gone from centuries of authoritarian rule, including seventy years of Communist Party domination in the Soviet Union, to Western-style parliamentarism in one move. The shift from uncontested 'elections' to competitive elections and from a largely decorative 'legislature' to a legislative assembly in which debate took place and ministers and political leaders could be called to account was a fundamental one. Yet, the reform included palliatives for hard-liners inasmuch as, while radicals might be elected to the Congress of People's Deputies, the fact that the deputies themselves had to choose the membership of the smaller but more regularly functioning Supreme Soviet meant that the boldest critics among them were unlikely to be chosen by a majority of their fellow-deputies in the Congress to take seats in the Supreme Soviet. With all its limitations, however, the new legislature—whose debates and interrogations of the executive were initially recorded live on television and radio—meant that Russia had, at last, become a country in which public political argument was accorded legitimacy.

Divisions within the Communist Party of the Soviet Union, to which one in ten of the working population (and a far higher proportion of those with professional qualifications) belonged, had until the second half of the 1980s been suppressed, but with the creation of a new legislative assembly the real diversity of view within the ruling party came more clearly into the open than ever before. The elections from the Congress, 87.8 per cent of whose deputies were members of the Communist Party,[1] to the Supreme Soviet further illustrated the point. The Supreme Soviet was itself a bicameral body with a lower house called the Soviet of the Union and an upper house named the Soviet of Nationalities. Nominations for the two houses of the Supreme Soviet were made by Congress deputies on a region-by-region basis. Thus, for example, the three Baltic states of Latvia, Lithuania, and Estonia were able to get deputies who would pursue national independence elected to the Supreme Soviet as well as to the Congress of People's Deputies by presenting the latter body with a list of nominations for the former which was exactly the same number as their allocation of seats in the Supreme Soviet, thus leaving their fellow deputies with no choice but to endorse them. In contrast, the Moscow group of deputies allowed the Congress to cast their votes among fifty-five candidates for its allotted twenty-nine places in the Soviet of the Union and from twelve candidates for its eleven seats in the Soviet of Nationalities. This, however, gave the relatively conservative majority of deputies the opportunity to make sure that Boris Yeltsin came twelfth out of twelve in that election, even though, when the public as a whole had had their say, he had achieved an overwhelming victory in the March 1989 election for a constituency comprising the whole of Moscow. Since his exclusion from the Supreme Soviet would have helped to discredit the new legislature from the very outset, Gorbachev—who was chairing the proceedings—was glad to rule as legitimate the resignation of one of the elected members, Aleksei Kazannik, a Siberian lawyer, in favour of Yeltsin.

One year after this legislature was created at the level of the entire Soviet Union, separate legislatures for the country's fifteen union republics were set up. The institutional design varied from one to another, but in Russia it followed closely the all-Union arrangements. In other words, there was again a Congress of People's Deputies and a smaller body elected by the Congress, the Supreme Soviet, which would be in session more frequently. Since,

---

[1] *Izvestiya*, 6 May 1989, p. 7.

however, over the previous year, the reservation of a third of the seats in the all-Union Congress for representatives of particular associational interests had been criticized as undemocratic, the Russian legislature reflected public opinion (which had become a force to be reckoned with) and did not adopt that device. All deputies were elected from territorial constituencies.

Another aspect of institutional design which was adopted for Russia after having been worked out within the highest echelons of the Soviet political elite, but again with an important difference, was the creation of a presidency. Gorbachev was elected president of the Soviet Union by the Congress of People's Deputies of the USSR in March 1990. This event was long preceded by private debates within the political elite as well as by discussion in the mass media of the desirability or otherwise of creating a presidency and, if so, what kind of presidency. Gorbachev himself was initially resistant to the idea of becoming president on the grounds that his opponents might argue that he had begun the whole reform process merely with that aim in view. There was also resistance to the idea of a presidency from conservative Communists who believed, with some reason, that a Gorbachev who became an elected president would be even freer of the constraints which they attempted, with only limited success, to place upon him in his role as party leader. Again there was a compromise. It was agreed that the presidency of the Soviet Union should be a post to which the incumbent was elected by the whole people, but on this first occasion the election to it would be indirect—that is to say, by the members of the Congress of People's Deputies.

There was never to be a second time, for the Soviet Union itself disappeared at the end of 1991. A decision in favour of indirect election rather than general election by all the citizens was essentially taken for tactical reasons. On the one hand, it was more reassuring for the majority of party officials from whose standpoint the idea of Gorbachev becoming even further out of their control was intolerable. On the other, it saved Gorbachev from putting his position at serious risk, for in the first months of 1990 his popularity was in decline and that of Boris Yeltsin rising. A presidential election in which they would have been the two leading candidates would not have been a foregone conclusion (though the data of the leading public opinion polling organization in Russia and the Soviet Union, VTsIOM, indicated that it was not until May 1990 that Yeltsin actually overtook Gorbachev in the polls). This decision to opt for indirect election, taken as one of Gorbachev's allies later put it 'more for pragmatic than for principled motives',[2] was a short-term tactical success but a long-term strategic error. If Gorbachev had won the presidency in a vote involving the whole citizenry of the Soviet Union, he would have acquired the legitimacy of being the first leader in Russian history to owe his position to the ballot-box. Moreover, the Union itself would have acquired substantially more legitimacy and the possibility of its becoming a democratic federation, or looser confederation, in which perhaps all but the Baltic states would have remained members, would have been greater.

The fact that popular elections for presidential office first took place on a republican rather than all-Union basis strengthened the legitimacy of those republican leaders who sought independence from the Soviet Union.[3] Boris Yeltsin, in particular, benefited from becoming the

[2] Vadim Medvedev, *V komande Gorbacheva: Vzglyad iznutri* (Moscow: Bylina, 1994), 111.

[3] In terms of sequencing, I see this as much more important than the distinction in degree of democracy between the elections for the all-Union legislature in 1989 and the legislatures of the union republics in 1990. Juan Linz and Alfred Stepan are right in principle in pointing out that the chances of democratization on a union-wide level, as against disintegration of the USSR, were affected by the fact that more democratic elections occurred

first Russian leader to be directly elected by the people in June 1991. This also put him in a strong position to resist the reactionary members of the Soviet elite who staged a coup in August 1991, put Gorbachev under house arrest in the Crimea, and attempted to turn the clock back to the pre-reform Soviet Union. Their claim to be representing the popular will rang hollow so soon after Yeltsin's resounding victory over all his opponents in the presidential election, including one of the active putschists, General Albert Makashov.

Other institutional arrangements in Russia—such as the dual executive, whereby there is a prime minister as well as a president—reflect the conscious institutional design of *Soviet* reformers. Within Gorbachev's inner circle, once the idea of moving to a presidency had been accepted, there was serious discussion of institutional variants, the main alternatives being seen as the American presidency and that of the Fifth French Republic. Within both the Presidium of the Supreme Soviet and the Institute of State and Law of the Academy of Sciences studies of the American and French models were undertaken. Eventually, the view which prevailed was that espoused by one of Gorbachev's senior aides, Georgy Shakhnazarov who for many years had been president of the Soviet Association of Political Sciences and an active participant in international gatherings of political scientists, even though he was a deputy head of a department of the Central Committee of the CPSU. Shakhnazarov argued that the French system of having a government headed by a prime minister would save Gorbachev, in the difficult conditions of 1990, from being submerged in detailed decision-making. The dual-executive system—in which, however, the prime minister was clearly of subordinate rank to the president—was duly adopted for the Soviet Union and subsequently for Russia. As in France, so in Russian experience, prime ministers have frequently made useful scapegoats for policy failures and their average tenure is much briefer than that of the presidents.

In the chapters that follow in this section Igor Klyamkin and Lilia Shevtsova likewise emphasize the respects in which Russia's institutional structures were the outcome of short-term tactical considerations. The particular form of dual power which resulted from the conflicting claims to legitimacy of the Congress of People's Deputies and the president in the 1992–3 period was resolved in favour of the presidency with the adoption of the December 1993 Constitution, but other types of institutional conflict occurred later, including at times tensions arising from the dual executive, an institutional legacy of the late Soviet period which, as already noted, still persists. Peter Ordeshook, in Chapter 2, suggests that Russian democrats have not thought sufficiently clearly about 'building a sensible incentive structure to support stable democratic institutions', though there may also be a question as to whether genuine democrats were ever in a majority within the post-Soviet government or

---

earlier at the republican than at the all-Union level. They focus, however, on the difference between the 1989 and 1990 elections for the legislatures. These differences were not, in my view, so fundamental; in both years the elections were essentially contested but in neither year were they multi-party as distinct from multi-candidate. Indeed, the elections which constituted the great break with the Soviet past—consolidating political pluralism, though not yet democracy—were those of March 1989. The argument of Linz and Stepan on the importance of sequencing could, however, be applied—and more tellingly—to the distinction between the indirect election for the presidency of the entire Soviet Union in 1990 and the popular elections for the presidencies of its constituent republics in 1991. Cf. Juan J. Linz and Alfred Stepan, *Problems of Democratic Transition and Consolidation: Southern Europe, South America, and Post-Communist Europe* (Baltimore: Johns Hopkins University Press, 1996), 378–86.

parliament.[4] A number of Ordeshook's proposals, including the simultaneous holding of presidential and parliamentary elections, would surely, however, serve the cause of democratization, including the consolidation of political parties and the links between the presidency and a parliamentary majority. Eugene Huskey's study of institutional design in Russia (Chapter 3), written like the two previous chapters, while Yeltsin was still president, examines, *inter alia*, the question of whether Russia should be regarded as a 'delegative democracy' of the kind identified by Guillermo O'Donnell in a number of Latin American countries.

It remains to be seen how long-lasting will be the political structures formed, first, under the influence of late Soviet reforms and, then, with a conscious tilt in a presidential direction, by the 1993 Constitution. In later sections of this volume attention will be paid to what is happening to these institutions during the presidency of Vladimir Putin.

---

[4] Holding on to power and newly acquired property has been for many office-holders a higher priority than democratic institution-building. Moreover, even those who consciously thought of themselves as 'democrats' did not necessarily embrace a value-system in accordance with Western ideas of democracy. As Alexander Lukin has pointed out, in an important study of the beliefs of those who saw themselves as democrats in Russia in the late 1980s and beginning of the 1990s, '"democratic" activists viewed democracy not as a system of compromises among various groups and interests, or as the separation of powers, but as the unlimited power of the "democrats" replacing the unlimited power of the Communists.' See Lukin, *The Political Culture of the Russian 'Democrats'* (Oxford: Oxford University Press, 2000), 298. Lukin notes also that one of the most influential members of Yeltsin's team in the early post-Soviet period, Gennady Burbulis, who was a leading light within its supposedly *democratic* wing, professed his admiration on a number of occasions for General Pinochet's achievements in Chile (ibid. 296).

1 The Tactical Origins of Russia's New Political Institutions

Igor Klyamkin and Lilia Shevtsova

The transformation of Russia's political system after the fall of Communism, like the earlier transformation of the Soviet Union itself, was determined exclusively by the logic of the political battle being fought at the time, and not by any long-range plans for state-building or by strategic agreements among the main political actors. The fundamental problems of how to create a new set of political institutions for a radically new Russian system of government were treated largely as tactical questions, rather than strategic ones, a fact that could not fail to influence the future course of events.

The nature of Yeltsin's—and Russia's—confrontation with the central Union authorities was transformed at the beginning of 1991 into a sharp public conflict within the old Russian Republic parliament, and a split within its leadership. In the resulting situation Yeltsin, whose legitimacy was to a large extent determined by this very structure, was forced to seek other ways of gaining the support of society and additional legitimacy. Thus, the post of the Russian presidency did not grow merely out of Yeltsin's struggle with Gorbachev (who had earlier created a Soviet presidency), but was also a result of the split within the new Russian political class and the attempt on the part of Yeltsin's team to secure power through the creation of the post of president elected directly by the population. The presidency was a completely new institution in Russia's political tradition, but still, by a circuitous route, through the twisted paths of the political struggle, it led right back to the autocratic tradition.

In short, the idea of the presidency was a new one, even a revolutionary one, in terms of the means of constituting supreme power and the sources of its legitimacy, where the former sources of legitimacy (hereditary monarchy and ideology) had exhausted their historical potential. But at the same time this was a movement in a direction typical for Russia, towards a system where power is personified completely and embodied in one person. This marriage of the new with the traditional found its reflection in the conflict between two tendencies—democratic and autocratic—which has still not been resolved.

The presidential system that arose in Russia as a result of the political struggle, and directly influenced by the nature of that struggle, was at the same time a response to the legacy of the Communist Party of the Soviet Union (CPSU)—the impotence of parliamentary-type soviets, deprived of government support. It is here we find the peculiar

This chapter is extracted from Igor Klyamkin and Lilia Shevtsova, *This Omnipotent and Impotent Government: The Evolution of the Political System in Post-Communist Russia* (Moscow: Carnegie Moscow Center, 1999), 10–13. Reproduced by kind permission of the authors and Carnegie Moscow Center. © Carnegie Endowment for International Peace.

nature of the formation of the Russian presidency. Not only did it fail to overcome the fundamental contradiction characteristic of the soviets, it actually resurrected it, although in modified form.

Formerly the essence of this contradiction lay in the fact that the legal power of the soviets ran up against the Communist Party's claims to a monopoly on power; but after the latter had exited the political stage, the line of conflict shifted to a different plane: the Supreme Soviet vs. the president. The conflict also, inevitably, took on an even sharper character, since this time it was not a question of a split between legitimate (the popularly elected soviets) and illegitimate (CPSU) power, but of a conflict between two government institutions—the parliament and the president—both legitimized by popular elections.

Their fierce confrontation, which lasted for close to two years, exposed the lack of readiness on the part of the Russian political class—as opposed, for example, to the political class of the countries of Eastern Europe—to reach agreement on the division of power and on the observance of democratic norms in the political game. It became clear fairly quickly that each side intended to use democratic legitimization procedures in order to perpetuate the kind of monopoly on power more traditional for Russia, or at the very least to erect a political system in which the division of power would be part of a hierarchy of institutions in which one would dominate over all the others. In short, democracy was used in the struggle for a monopoly on power. And this mental predisposition, which has its roots in the centuries-old traditions of Russian government, was perpetuated and actively stimulated by the power configuration of 1991–1993.

The parliamentary-style soviets, in full accordance with national tradition, at first tried to affirm their own omnipotence as a counterweight to the omnipotence of the CPSU. At the same time Russia, to a greater extent than the other union republics, was perpetuating the old model, since the union structure had been preserved in the Congress of People's Deputies—an unwieldy organ, able to function only in a populist, mass-rally type of regime. It had been granted almost unlimited powers and created in order to aid the CPSU in gaining hegemony in the democratization process. This goal was not attained. But the very existence of this structure, on the strength of its monopoly on power, to a large extent predetermined the peculiar nature of Russia's political development vis-à-vis the other republics of the former USSR. And if many Russian deputies supported the introduction of the presidency, it was only because the Congress of People's Deputies was still legally the supreme organ of power in the Russian Federation.

However, in spite of its unlimited powers, the authority of the Congress lacked one component that was absolutely necessary within the context of Russia's political culture. It was not personified—it had no charismatic figure to compete with Yeltsin. Even speaker Ruslan Khasbulatov, who aspired to usurp Yeltsin's dominance over Russian politics, paled in comparison to Yeltsin's populist appeal. Moreover, in the eyes of the public, supreme power was vested in Yeltsin, who had become the symbol of the victory over Communism in August 1991. For this reason a seemingly paradoxical situation arose: the Congress of People's Deputies, which was defending the populace from the unpopular economic reforms that began in January 1992, inspired even less trust among the people than the president, whose name was, to a significant extent, associated with those reforms.

As for Yeltsin, the only way he could handle the Congress of People's Deputies and the Supreme Soviet was through unconstitutional measures, using the political capital that had been acquired through the referendum of April 1993 on trust in the president and support for his reform program. As shown by the events of September 21–October 4, 1993, which began with Yeltsin's decree dissolving the Supreme Soviet and the Congress of People's Deputies, and ended with the armed storming of the building where the deputies were meeting, this capital proved to be more than sufficient.

And so a historical line was drawn, putting an end to the political system of parliamentary-type soviets. This system, which was a continuation of the Communist period, provided a relatively painless way to overcome the omnipotence of the CPSU. But its inability to function and to endure made it necessary to add the institution of a popularly elected president, which was new for Russia, and which resulted in a duality of power—a dyarchy, and a concomitant degradation of the fledgling system of statehood. But the new system, which arose after the violent eradication of this dyarchy, could not free itself of the traces of the old: symptoms of dyarchy are constantly making themselves felt, although in a completely different context and in more subtle ways.

2 Re-examining Russia: Institutions and Incentives

Peter C. Ordeshook

Can Russia become a stable liberal democracy? Are there ways to end the conflicts that seem a permanent feature of Russian politics? Will the new constitution adopted in December 1993 bring order to relations between the executive and legislative branches and to the making and enforcement of law? Does the bloody strife in Chechnya, where Soviet flags once again fly from tanks and armored personnel carriers, presage a repeat of Russia's historical experience with political reform, with democrats once again driven into authoritarianism's iron embrace?

At present, pessimistic answers to these questions seem better grounded than optimistic ones. Democratic reformers, stunned by their poor showing in the December 1993 parliamentary elections, seem unable to coalesce, while nationalists and fascists marshal their forces to seize power through Russia's infant democratic institutions. Political maneuvering proceeds in a manner barely contained by law; even some of those once counted among democracy's staunchest defenders have resorted to undemocratic tactics when it suited their purpose. No longer are people concerned with lofty democratic ideals: instead they focus on mere survival, with those able to do so grabbing all the wealth they can. The anarchy of day-to-day business dealings is tempered only by the *mafiya*, whose contract-enforcement capability, though based on criminal violence, goes unchallenged by the state. With plummeting production fueling demands for subsidies to inefficient industry, comparisons with Weimar Germany are not entirely far-fetched.

Indeed, the marvel of the December 1993 elections is not that democratic reformers did so badly while Vladimir Zhirinovsky did so well, but that the fascists, ultranationalists, and hard-core antireformists somehow failed to secure outright control of the new legislature.[1] Is Russia trapped in some terrible equilibrium that can only be escaped by a passage through more dangerous turmoil or a retreat from liberal democracy? Even the possibility should be enough to impel democrats in Russia and abroad to start looking for another way out.

Although most of those concerned with ex-Soviet states pay lip service to the proposition that economic reform and political reform are tightly interdependent and must proceed

This chapter was first published as an article (under the same title) in *Journal of Democracy*, 6/2 (Apr, 1995), 46–60. Reproduced by kind permission of the author and Johns Hopkins University Press.

[1] If we look only at those seats in the Duma filled by national party-list PR, Zhirinovsky's party, in combination with the Communists and Agrarians, secured 43 percent of the vote while the ensemble of reformist parties (at least one of which failed to surpass the 5 percent threshold) received a total of 34 percent.

together or not at all, the two are in fact often dealt with as though different principles guide each. This is a grave mistake, for the same basic principle must guide both.

The economic reformer formulates strategy in terms of laws regarding private property, banking, and contracts, as well as government policies regarding tariffs, taxes, privatization, borrowing, and subsidies. Economic reformers of every stripe understand that changes in law and policy must be guided by a common principle—namely, that socially desirable outcomes cannot be wished into existence, but depend on the ways in which governmental actions and the structure of economic institutions channel individual self-interest. Decrees and exhortations cannot make people work, save, invest, or invent. Instead, they need incentives (Adam Smith's 'invisible hand') to do these things in natural and self-sustaining ways. Intelligently designed public policies and economic institutions are needed if reform is to give people an immediate self-interest in working, saving, investing, and inventing.

The significance of self-interest

Although the methods for best applying the principle of self-interest in economics may be imperfectly understood, they seem pellucidly clear when compared to knowledge of political reform. Like the transition to markets, the transition to democracy depends on the design and handling of institutions—in this instance, rules of legislative representation, electoral laws, and constitutional allocations of power—that give people an immediate self-interest in pursuing certain types of actions and outcomes. For a democracy to be stable, moreover, its institutions must be crafted to give those who might destroy them an incentive not to do so.

The framers of the United States Constitution had a keen sense of the political (to say nothing of the economic) significance of self-interest that contemporary Russian leaders would do well to emulate. James Madison displayed this famously in *Federalist* 51 when he wrote that 'the great security against a gradual concentration of the several powers in the same department, consists in giving to those who administer each department, the necessary constitutional means, and *personal* motives to resist encroachments of the others . . . Ambition must be made to counteract ambition. The interest of the man must be connected with the constitutional rights of the place.'[2]

This principle of prudently deployed self-interest has so far been the great missing ingredient in Russian political reform. Instead of building a sensible incentive structure to support stable democratic institutions, Russia's democrats have opted for a naive, populist version of democracy featuring crude demarcations of power between Moscow and federal subjects, a simplistic view of presidential leadership, and parliamentary-election procedures that try to be all things to all people.

Perhaps this is not surprising, for while the known economic laws of supply and demand, market efficiency, and market failure compel a daily appreciation of their relevance, fewer such laws have revealed themselves so forcefully in politics. Economic errors allow for continuous refinement and adaptation of both theories and practices, whereas political mistakes often become manifest too late or under circumstances too complex and exigent to allow for learning and correction. This fact, coupled with the burden of an antidemocratic past, has

[2] Jacob E. Cooke, ed., *The Federalist* (Middletown, Conn.: Wesleyan University Press, 1961), 349 (emphasis added).

meant that political reform in Russia is all too often viewed through the old lens of command and control, and that political power is all too often exercised crudely. Rather than study the complex and subtle ways in which democratic institutions shape incentives and sustain themselves over the long haul, Russian leaders have preferred to indulge in superficial manipulations aimed at securing immediate advantages for themselves and their factions.

Thus national party-list proportional representation (PR) is used to fill half of the seats in the 450-member State Duma not because of any view of how election laws influence the size, character, and behavior of political groupings, but because members of President Boris Yeltsin's entourage want the opportunity to sit in parliament at the head of some 'party' or other. 'Federal treaties' are negotiated between Moscow and the provinces not because they are a solution to the fragmentation of the Federation, but because they allow the negotiators to make bold claims about how much they are doing to aid the cause of stability. And the president predominates constitutionally over parliament not because of some coherent idea of the proper role of a chief executive, but because it was the Supreme Soviet (the State Duma's predecessor) and not the presidency that lost the great institutional power struggle of 1993.

If politics in Russia has sunk to the level of a mere war of personalities, as many lament, this debasement is but a symptom of the failure to realize that democratic political reform and market-based economic reform share the same underlying dependence on well-structured incentives. Hence the futility of any hope that new, more enlightened leaders or political parties can by themselves rescue the situation. The actions of any new elites will respond to the same incentives that guide the actions of current elites; if the incentives remain defective, so will the actions. Comprehensive market failure cannot be corrected by replacing one set of CEOs with another set, and the case of failed (or missing) political institutions is no different.

Meaningful political reform, then, requires an appropriate ordering of incentives; it is preeminently the lack of such an ordering that now bedevils Russia's transition to democracy. Three problems in particular call for an adept touch:

1. the way in which the Russian constitution shapes presidential-legislative relations;
2. the general approach to federalism and the way that Moscow tries to meet demands for regional autonomy; and
3. the failure to understand either the determinants of party systems or the role of parties in facilitating the resolution of political conflict.

Although some might hold that each of these problems can be treated separately by a particular reform or constitutional amendment, the truth is that piecemeal reform will not solve the grave problems besetting Russian democracy. What is needed first of all is a careful look at the *institutional determinants* of incentives—especially the methods and timing of elections and the basis of representation in parliament—before we can see how other reforms might promote stability and a coherent democratic process. Unless these decisive institutional issues are properly settled, we can expect that:

- Both the president and various factions within parliament will claim national mandates, and although the absence of a coherent party system may preclude effective action in the Duma, all points of constitutional conflict between the president and parliament will be active ones;

- Political parties will not do much to protect regional autonomy, so power struggles between national and regional leaders will continue unabated; and
- Even though presidential candidates may emerge who are currently unassociated with any particular party in the Duma, parliamentary elections will serve largely as primaries in the quest for the main prize, the presidency. Parties will remain highly fragmented; the most successful will be those that are best able to frame emotional appeals to nationalism.

Executive-legislative relations

The provisions of Russia's new constitution, which was ratified by popular vote during the same 1993 balloting that produced the new bicameral parliament, promise to extend the executive-legislative conflict that precipitated Yeltsin's coup against the old Supreme Soviet. Parliament legislates, but the president can rule by decree in areas where the law is silent. The president can veto acts of parliament; parliament can stymie presidential decrees by passing contrary laws, and if the president vetoes such a law, a two-thirds majority of both legislative chambers can override his veto. The president can hire and fire ministers, but parliament can pass a vote of no confidence in the government, in which case the president must either replace the cabinet or call new parliamentary elections. And although the 178-member Federation Council (parliament's upper house) expressly represents regional interests, the president can unilaterally overturn regional acts and laws in his role as 'protector of the constitution.'

These provisions reflect an extremely shallow understanding of the separation of powers, and place the president and parliament in direct opposition. (The former has the upper hand by virtue of his powers to dismiss parliament, call referenda, and act as constitutional guardian.) In a state with a smoothly functioning judicial system, the courts can sometimes resolve disputes between the other branches of government; in states with a well-developed civic culture, voters can do so as well. Russia enjoys neither of these advantages, and lacks the built-in incentives for compromise that characterize stable democracies. Thus the relative prospects of compromise and conflict depend largely on whether political leaders at a given moment believe that their individual purposes are best served by the one or the other.

To trace briefly the incentives affecting these leaders, it is reasonable to assume that, whatever their other aims, they all want to gain power and control government policy. Insofar as they abide by the rules outlined in the Russian constitution, they can achieve these goals only by securing the support of the electorate. Unfortunately for Russia, the details of the formal relationship between these aspiring or actual leaders and the voters militate against compromise and democratic stability.

The problem is not direct election of the president (with a runoff provision in case no candidate wins over 50 percent), but the electoral system used to fill the Duma. It is likely that the next elections to the Duma, scheduled for December 1995, will use the same procedures employed in 1993, with half (or two-thirds) of the deputies chosen in single-member constituencies and the rest by national party-list PR. Implemented ostensibly to facilitate the formation of national parties, to disadvantage opponents of reform with strong local support, and to help individual 'democratic' candidates, this system evinces a poor appreciation of the incentives that national party-list PR sets up for deputies, and of how those incentives might engender conflict with any president. With one-third or half of all candidates for the Duma competing through national party-list PR, and with parliamentary elections slated to take place in December 1995, six months before the presidential contest, successful parties in the Duma can assert the same mandate claimed by the president—a mandate that Vladimir Zhirinovsky sought to appropriate with 23 percent of the December 1993 list-PR vote, and which anyone who heads a party with any larger percentage is certain to assert as his own. Thus the stage will be set for more conflicts and crises.

Stable democracies avoid conflict in one of two ways. In presidential systems like that of the United States, legislators are elected from geographically defined constituencies, a structure of representation that dilutes the legislature's claim to a national mandate and gives individual legislators a primary interest in satisfying the voters back home. Even if the legislature is controlled by a party other than the president's, a president who claims a national mandate need not find himself locked in irreconcilable conflict with the legislature. Compromises can be reached via side bargains that link the president's national policy objectives to the specific interests of local constituencies.

Parliamentary systems represent a different approach to fostering compromise. Regardless of the way in which parliament is elected, and regardless of what mandate parties may or may not claim, the powers of the chief of state (whether a president or a constitutional monarch) are weak and the executive branch is, by definition, a creature of parliament. Real executive power rests with a government headed by a prime minister and cabinet sanctioned by parliament. Typically, a parliamentary vote of no confidence can bring the government down and necessitate the formation of a new cabinet or the holding of new elections. Although a directly elected chief of state may also claim a mandate if, say, an emergency arises, conflict is normally avoided by the chief of state's extremely limited involvement in general executive and legislative functions.

Whichever of these two forms of government may in principle be best for Russia—and respectable cases have been made for each—the sad truth is that the country has made the severe mistake of trying, in effect, to have both at the same time. The powers of the Russian presidency are indeed exceptional, but that presidency coexists uneasily with a parliament that, in addition to its normal lawmaking function, can decide whether the existing constitution is to be permanent or merely transitional, can lay down the rules that govern the president's emergency powers, can limit his authority to call referenda, and has some nominal control over the government itself (via the threat of a no-confidence vote).[3] This is a political structure that closely parallels the one employed in Weimar Germany, with all the dangers that portends.

Federalism

In the final analysis, the Duma is still in a fairly weak constitutional position vis-à-vis the president, which might serve to moderate conflict between them. Moreover, out of the 622

---

[3] The potential for treating the new constitution as a transitional document is provided for in Articles 135 and 136. Article 136 describes a difficult process for amending the main body of the document that parallels the American procedure (approval of two-thirds of the lower chamber, three-fourths of the upper one, and two-thirds of all federal subjects). Article 135, though, allows parliament, by a three-fifths vote in each chamber, to convene a new constituent assembly that can either approve its own creation with a two-thirds vote or secure approval in a direct referendum.

legislators in the two chambers, 397 have been elected from geographically distinct constituencies consistent with Russia's preexisting federal structure. Thus the motivations of a majority of deputies will derive ultimately from local constituency concerns. This raises the question of federalism, or more specifically, of whether federal institutions are consistent with representative structures.

With the possible exception of legislative-executive conflict, no issue in these early and uncertain days of Russian democracy has been more prominent than that of federalism, especially as it touches on the status of Russia's ethnic republics. Who is to control Russia's vast resources, and who is to oversee privatization of state property? Are the republics sovereign, able to conduct their own foreign policies or even secede from the Federation? What power does Moscow have over the existence of regional soviets? Whose laws are supreme, and in what domains? Should Russia's federalism be symmetric, or should the ethnic republics, which historically have enjoyed greater autonomy than the other parts of the Federation, be treated differently?

Without trying to specify the form of federalism that Russia should choose, three observations may be offered concerning the constitutional bargain that was ultimately struck and the negotiations that preceded it. The first is that formal talks with Russia's ethnic republics focused on a federal treaty that mainly just listed jurisdictions that belonged exclusively to Moscow and jurisdictions to be shared by Moscow and the republic governments (a residual-powers clause, now part of the constitution, is largely meaningless owing to the comprehensiveness of the other jurisdictional clauses). Second, all the republics demanded that they be identified as 'sovereign states,' with the presumption that this label, combined with the terms of the federal treaty, would protect their autonomy. Finally, all of the republics demanded that they retain the authority to renegotiate bilaterally the particulars of their relationship with Moscow, so that separate deals could be struck between regional and national governments over the disposition of joint jurisdictions.

These facts suggest several questions about what role, if any, an understanding of incentives played in negotiations over Russia's federal form. First, was any mechanism envisioned for enforcing the agreements set forth in the federal treaties? Second, was any process identified for resolving the ambiguities inherent in a treaty that encompassed virtually all activities and responsibilities of the state? Finally, what consequences were foreseen as likely to flow from the creation of an asymmetric federation that treated the heavily ethnic republics differently from the predominantly Russian jurisdictions?

Little attention was paid to any but the last of these questions. Instead, Yeltsin's first draft constitution, offered in April 1993 when the resolution of his conflict with the Supreme Soviet remained in doubt, bowed to political expediency. It called the republics sovereign, accorded each the right to negotiate its relationship with Moscow bilaterally, and, in a provision that could hardly be taken seriously by anyone interested in a system of balanced powers (keep in mind that the republics together account for only 15 percent of the Russian Federation's population), required that the representation of the republics be increased to whatever extent necessary to ensure their control of the Federation Council. Not surprisingly, Yeltsin dropped all these provisions in the constitution's final version, when he no longer needed the republics' support in his battle with the Supreme Soviet.

Yeltsin's final version adhered to the idea of enumerated powers, and incorporated the long lists of exclusive and joint jurisdictions that were the core of the federal treaty (Articles

71 and 72). Whatever protection the constitution provides for federal subjects rests on the powers of the Federation Council, a body much like the United States Senate in both form and function. With two deputies from each of Russia's 89 constitutionally recognized territories (republics, oblasts, krais, and so on), the Council has the power to approve any changes in the Federation's internal borders, to regulate the president's emergency powers, to approve the use of troops abroad and declarations of war, to try the president in the event of impeachment by the Duma, and to approve presidential nominations to the Constitutional Court. There are, though, two exceptions to the parallels between the Council and the U.S. Senate: The Duma can by a two-thirds vote override the Council's refusal to pass an ordinary statute (Article 105). Second, there is the vaguely worded requirement, found in Articles 95 and 96, that the Federation Council be 'formed' from the executive and legislative branches of the various jurisdictions represented. Although this provision is compatible with the idea that the chief executive and chief legislative officer of each region should be deputies to the Council, its exact meaning will remain murky until parliament specifies the method of selection. Until then, the president can decree any method of selection he likes.

The undifferentiated inclusion of republics with all other jurisdictions of the Federation suggests that Russia has opted for a symmetric federalism in which the autonomy and prerogatives of all federal subjects are safeguarded by their representation in an upper legislative chamber. But closer inspection reveals that this apparent guarantee is not really present. To see this, consider the indirect as well as the direct mechanisms whereby states in the United States ensure their autonomy against the national government.[4] Although that autonomy has eroded considerably over the last two centuries because of increasingly broad interpretations of constitutional provisions involving the equal protection of laws and the regulation of interstate commerce, states continue to enjoy a good deal more autonomy than is possessed by federal subjects of most other federalisms. Indeed, the uses to which the commerce and equal-protection clauses of the U.S. Constitution have been put demonstrate the ability of American officials (especially judges) to construe constitutional language in ways that justify nearly any allocation of jurisdictions and responsibilities.

Thus we must look beyond parchment enumerations of jurisdictions and guarantees of autonomy and consider the incentives of those who have the authority to change or reinterpret a constitution, or who can even override its provisions through force. In the United States, the key to the dynamic equilibrium of the federal system is the provision that the states control the election of the members of both branches of Congress that represent them and their residents (Article II, Section 4). This requirement does a simple thing: it ensures that political parties, although operating under only the two labels Democrat and Republican, are primarily state and local organizations. The U.S. does not have two parties: it has at least a hundred of them—fifty Democratic and fifty Republican ones. One can even argue that it has thousands, to the extent that state parties are merely collections of local ones that cooperate to compete in state or local elections, and that national parties emerge only every four years to nominate and support a presidential contender.

Thus while the competition for the U.S. presidency may call forth two national coalitions and party labels, a decentralized party system oversees the reelection prospects of individual

---

[4] This account of the American case largely follows William H. Riker, *Federalism* (Boston: Little, Brown, 1964).

members of the Senate and House of Representatives (if not presidents themselves). A president may influence events at the margin by influencing the public's apportionment of credit or blame for the state of the nation's economy or foreign relations, but as a veteran congressman once famously put it, in the United States at least, 'all politics is local.'

With their political fortunes tied to state or local constituencies and party organizations, U.S. senators and representatives have an incentive to resist the encroachments of national power if local interests so dictate. Moreover, with election to local and statewide office serving as the main route to national office, and with national legislators dependent on the same party structure for their survival as are local and state officials, the national government is seen less as a purely alien political force and more as a mere extension of local and regional governmental structures.

Two things keep this structure in balance. First, incumbent legislators have no incentive to change the rules except in ways that benefit themselves. Second, with competitive elections and, correspondingly, national political parties permeating all levels of government (or, to put it more correctly, with local parties permeating national ones), neither national nor regional elites want to change a system that supports their current positions and provides a path to future advancement.

No such equilibrium can be guaranteed for Russia. First, continuing uncertainty about key details of the rules under which the next president will be elected means that no one can know what role competition for that office will play in determining party structures. What advantages will accrue to candidates of parliamentary parties versus those who might emerge on the basis of purely populist appeals to Russian nationalism? Second, although the delegates to the first session of the Federation Council were chosen by direct plurality voting, that procedure was a temporary measure made necessary by Yeltsin's dissolution of regional soviets. Will popular elections again be used, or will a Moscow-directed appointment process be substituted in the name of stability? Although the regional leaders in the Council may prefer to win their mandates through direct election and begin developing local political organizations, will this trend continue as those elections become more honest and competitive? Third, Yeltsin's election decree and his newly proposed election laws give the central government in Moscow broad authority to regulate election rules and procedures. There is no guarantee that Russia's regions will play any significant role (aside from opportunities to manipulate vote tabulations) in determining the structural details of regional and local elections. Will the ad hoc decentralization of economic relations taking place throughout Russia today compel Moscow to try to further its control over the administration of elections to national office? Finally, it is a safe bet that Russia will continue to fill a significant number of Duma seats through national party-list PR, thereby undermining the forces favoring party decentralization and leaving deputies elected by PR with no incentive to defend local and regional autonomy.

Given the general weakness of the national government, especially its barely functioning judicial system, and considering the ability of regional governments to withhold the federal tax revenues that they collect and ignore the notional supremacy of federal law, more conflicts between the center and the regions are in store. The signing of the Moscow–Tatar 'treaty' in February 1994 may indicate a willingness to step back from the brink of wholesale instability, but ambiguously worded agreements that read much like Cold War-era accords between the United States and the USSR are no substitute for political structures that would give leaders at all levels and in all branches of government incentives to protect regional autonomy and to avoid approaching center–periphery relations as a game of all against one.

The political party system

A common lament about Russia's transition to democracy is summarized by Yegor Gaidar's political advisor, Vladimir Mau: 'Economic interest groups are now the key players in Russian politics; political parties, by contrast, have been and remain weak and unstable. In the corridors of power, they wield much less influence than associations of managers and entrepreneurs.'[5] True enough, but hardly surprising. There is nothing special about Russia that dictates political parties of a particular number or type. It is true that in an unsettled social and economic climate, the usual political divides—between left and right or between a preference for activist government versus *laissez-faire* policies—that underlie party systems elsewhere are complicated by other issues, such as imperial nostalgia or combative regionalisms fed by decades or centuries of living under the indifferent dominance of Moscow. On the other hand, if election laws encourage party fragmentation, then they will operate with added force in a society, like Russia's, that is already a riot of conflicting interests.[6]

Three features of Russia's political institutions contribute to the fragmentation and incoherence that characterize its party system:

1. nonsimultaneous presidential and parliamentary elections;
2. the likely presence of a majority-runoff feature in the next presidential election; and
3. the election of a significant part of the Duma by national party-list PR.

The failure to hold simultaneous presidential and parliamentary elections stems, at least in part, from Yeltsin's apparent desire to occupy an office that is somehow 'above politics' and that can avoid blame for administrative errors. But while this attitude may match the aspirations of a czar, staggered elections deny a president 'coattails' on which to carry a workable legislative majority into office with him as a product of his personal appeal and campaign strategy. When accompanied by a presidential unwillingness to associate with any specific party, nonsimultaneous elections undermine the ability of presidential elections to become a focus for the formation of parties.

The majority runoff derives partly from precedent and partly from the arrogant belief, common in Moscow political circles, that alternative procedures such as preferential voting are beyond the comprehension of Russia's citizens. Yet a runoff will discourage uncompetitive parties and candidates from folding, especially if they believe that they can use their first-round support as a bargaining chip. Thus if the incentive is not to win outright, but rather to block others and cut a deal for, say, cabinet posts, then a runoff can only exacerbate the party weakness that Mau deplores. Parties must find a constituency, and this procedure

---

[5] Vladimir Mau, 'The Ascent of the Inflationists,' *Journal of Democracy*, 5 (Apr. 1994): 32–35.

[6] There is a large literature on this subject, much of which is summarized in Rein Taagepera and Matthew S. Shugart, *Seats and Votes* (New Haven: Yale University Press, 1989). An update, with particular attention paid to the interaction between election laws and social cleavages, is provided by Peter C. Ordeshook and Olga Shvetsova in 'Ethnic Heterogeneity, District Magnitude, and the Number of Parties,' *American Journal of Political Science*, 38 (Feb. 1994): 100–23.

merely encourages small parties to act like economic interest groups and economic interests to act like parties.

Finally, the provision for electing half of the Duma by party-list PR in 1993 was intended, as we noted earlier, to stimulate the formation of transregional, transethnic parties. Coupled with registration requirements that compelled parties to secure signatures beyond Moscow and its environs, the provision appears at first glance to have been a success. Yet the sharp regional differences apparent in the support of the 13 parties that competed in December 1993 raise doubts on this score. Moreover, one must admit that the party loyalty of many of the list-PR deputies is questionable The attachments of those elected from single-member constituencies also remain unclear; some estimates call as many as a fifth of all deputies 'independents.'

The basic problem here is that the desire to see parties consolidate into coherent and nonradical alternatives is stymied by the incentives that national party-list PR creates. To be sure, the 5 percent threshold is a disincentive to the formation of wholly uncompetitive parties. Yet in combination with the failure to use the election of the president as a way to encourage the coordination of factions and future aspirants to that office, national PR offers ample incentives for ambitious politicians to use parliamentary elections as a soapbox for furthering their careers and presidential aspirations.

The parliamentary elections scheduled for December 1995 will probably play a role roughly comparable to that filled by U.S. presidential primaries. Various aspirants to the presidency will use the legislative campaign as an arena for displaying and enhancing the attractiveness of their respective platforms prior to the presidential vote slated for June 1996. In addition to rewarding even relatively small parties with seats, the parliamentary voting will encourage fragmentation among parties not in control of the presidency—a phenomenon often seen in U.S. presidential primaries. Unlike the American process however, there is no stage in Russia, except at the very last ballot, wherein presidential aspirants must coalesce and coordinate their ambitions. On the contrary, Russia's majority-runoff system merely encourages more of the party fragmentation that follows from national party-list PR.

Recommendations for reform

Nothing that we have said points to a quick fix for Russia's political ailments. Indeed, there is scant historical evidence that democratic processes can be sustained in a society experiencing massive deindustrialization and declines in population, living standards and life expectancy. Nevertheless, Russian politics has not been totally bereft of positive developments. Chechnya aside most leaders appear willing, albeit for different reasons, to abide for a time by the restrictions in the new constitution. Separatist sentiment on the part of key federal subjects like Tatarstan has muted. Of course, none of this implies the inevitability of democratic stability. Opponents of reform, believing Yeltsin irreparably weakened in the wake of his power struggle with the old parliament and the Chechen debacle, are biding their time until the next round of elections, when they can mount fresh attacks. Authorities in the Kremlin are undermining regional democratic development by insisting on continued control over regional executive authorities. Yeltsin himself, meanwhile, continues to try to fashion a stable order by signing hortatory 'Civic Accords' that have no means of enforcement and that fail to address the institutional deficiencies of Russian democracy.

Despite all the bad news, the case for institutional reform still deserves to be pressed. To that end, here are three suggestions. Each pertains to Russia's electoral processes, and none requires any change in the constitution.

The first is to abandon the majority runoff provision in presidential elections. Following the example of Costa Rica (a country whose stability makes it a Latin American standout), Russia should hold a presidential runoff only if no candidate tops 40 percent of the vote. Although some might object that a 40 percent threshold will make a mandate more elusive, the use of a 50 percent threshold in Russia today almost guarantees that no one will win on the first ballot, and that consequently the cobbled-together majority secured by the second-ballot winner will smack of 'corrupt bargains.' With the threshold down at 40 percent, however, weak candidates and parties have a stronger incentive to refrain from running or even forming, and the likelihood increases that one of the candidates will get the needed majority on the first ballot. By tracing out incentives, then, one sees that a mandate to lead is more likely to emerge if the system does not attempt to force it.

The second suggestion, concerning the method of electing deputies to the Duma, is twofold. First, one might allow each federal subject to determine and oversee the method of election of its own representatives. Such an abandonment of proscription and regulation by Moscow would strengthen the federal structure, decrease incentives for party factionalism, and reduce the ability of parliamentary parties to claim a mandate rivaling the president's. True, such a policy may initially boost opportunities for regional vote fraud—although such fraud is already so rampant that it may defy augmentation. At any rate, competition (with modest judicial oversight) should operate here as in markets to yield more efficient regional political competition. As we saw in the case of presidential majorities, the shortest road to free and fair elections and a party system that integrates rather than divides lies not in bureaucratic decrees from Moscow, but rather in intelligent use of the incentives that face would-be challengers for power in the regions and localities.

The drawback of this idea, at least in the minds of the power brokers in Moscow, is that it may give provincial 'reactionary forces'—those opposed to meaningful market reforms and more susceptible to *mafiya* influence—more strength in parliament. There is something of a risk here, to be sure, but it is a noble and necessary one. The will of the voters cannot be thwarted indefinitely by blatant manipulations, nor can a state be federal without a meaningful decentralization of political authority. A critical problem with democratic reform thus far is that it has been mostly 'top-down,' with little opportunity or incentive for democratic processes to take root regionally and locally. Decentralization of representation and the election laws gives local political elites an incentive to learn the rules of democracy and should help quell any urge to maintain a 'guerilla-war' relationship with Moscow.

An alternative suggestion would be to move closer to the German model by dividing Russia into, say, ten electoral districts, with a requirement that parties submit regional candidate lists. A party's seat allocation in the Duma would continue to depend on its share of the national vote, but it would be required to allocate its seats among its lists in accordance with how its vote is distributed across regions. This procedure encourages national parties (since it is a party's national vote that determines its overall seat allocation), as well as decentralization within those parties (since parties would seek to field locally strong candidates in each region). The drawbacks of this suggestion, aside from the disputes that might arise over the identities of regions, are that it leaves in place both incentives for party factionalization and the source of executive-versus-legislative 'mandate' disputes. Moreover, this alternative will do little to enhance Russia's federal structure unless it is accompanied by decentralization in the administration of elections.

Lest one be tempted to weigh the specifics of various proposals in too fine a balance, it should be emphasized that nearly anything would be an improvement on the current arrangement, which is the world's largest experiment with national party-list PR. As long as the current system stays in place, Russia will remain doomed to a muddled party system, with all the incoherence of parliamentary process thereby implied. One or several parliamentary parties will continue to claim a mandate in opposition to the president, even as the Duma itself remains too divided to offset the president's dangerous constitutional powers.

The Duma's failure to offer any clear response to Yeltsin's actions in Chechnya reflects not only nationalist sentiment and the strategic calculations of various deputies, but also the Duma's internal incoherence. Nor should we forget that Zhirinovsky would have remained a politically marginal buffoon had not national party-list PR afforded him the opportunity to translate his mastery of media manipulation into about 60 parliamentary seats.

The third suggestion is to reduce party factionalism by holding presidential and parliamentary elections simultaneously. Simultaneity affords the president a better opportunity to exert leadership, which is *not* the same as crude political control. Throughout Russian history, those directing the state have relied on the most obvious and extraordinary instruments of power rather than on persuasion, compromise, and the authority that comes from being seen as the people's spokesman. The lament that Russia is at the mercy of powerful personalities contesting for the reins of power may be accurate—such contests are certainly in line with Russian tradition. But rather than perpetuate this tradition by making the election of the president a singular event, reformers should strive to engender a different set of incentives among leaders. Simultaneous elections will encourage presidential candidates to link their election organizations to parliamentary parties, will compel politicians to choose between exerting parliamentary and executive leadership, and will allow a president to bargain away some of his formal authority and to look instead to an even more secure basis of power—the people's mandate.

Of course, these reforms cannot cure the many and complex ills of Russian democracy—no simple corrective can. Nor is there any reform that provides short-term insurance against the rise to power of some extremist. But the changes suggested here would represent a step in the right direction—namely, away from the naive populist democracy that Russia's democrats, inattentive to the intricate webbing of incentives that undergirds stable democracy, have wittingly or unwittingly implemented. Whatever steps are ultimately taken, it is imperative that political reform proceed in full recognition of the principle of self-interest and with an acute awareness that reform's implications cannot be reckoned until one traces the incentives that it creates or fails to create.

3 Democracy and Institutional Design in Russia

Eugene Huskey

The stunning political comeback of Boris Yeltsin serves as a reminder of the vital role of the individual in politics. A disengaged and irresolute president through much of his first term, Yeltsin revived himself in time to capture the support of the nation in the 1996 presidential elections. These elections also highlighted the many informal sources of power in Russia that lie beyond the constitution. One of the most influential of these was the media. Through a careful manipulation of the tone and content of campaign coverage, Yeltsin's backers managed to portray the contest between candidates as a referendum on good versus evil.

Personality, informal politics, and circumstance—these arc the forces that come to mind during periods of political transition. But a country's institutional arrangements also shape its development, often in profound though less obvious ways. Put simply, Russia's particular pattern of institutions and rules has favored certain political outcomes over others.[1] The decision to adopt an unusual variant of semi-presidentialism, for example, has had fateful consequences for the stability and efficacy of the new regime.[2] This chapter examines the impact of semi-presidentialism on Russia's post-communist transition as well as the ways in which the logic of semi-presidentialism has adapted to the distinct circumstances and culture of Russian politics.

The origins of semi-presidentialism in Russia, 1989–1991

At the end of the 1980s, faced with broad-based resistance to reform within the Communist Party apparatus, Mikhail Gorbachev sought alternative institutional arrangements that would at once enhance regime legitimacy and offer the leader an additional base outside of the party.[3] Invoking a variant of the Leninist slogan 'All Power to the Soviets,'[4] Gorbachev

Originally published as an article with the same title in *Demokratizatsiya: The Journal of Post-Soviet Democratization*, 4/4 (Fall 1996), 453–73. Reproduced (with minor abbreviations) by kind permission of the author and the Helen Dwight Reid Educational Foundation. © Heldref Publications.

[1] For an introduction to the role of institutions in politics, see S. Steinmo, K. Thelen, and Frank Longstreth, eds., *Structuring Politics. Historical Institutionalism in Comparative Analysis* (Cambridge: Cambridge University Press, 1992).

[2] The most comprehensive assessment of the variants of presidentialism and parliamentarism is found in Matthew Soberg Shugart and John M. Carey, *Presidents and Assemblies. Constitutional Design and Electoral Dynamics* (Cambridge: Cambridge University Press, 1992).

[3] After a difficult Politburo meeting in early 1988, when the Nina Andreeva affair was on the agenda, Gorbachev commented to an aide: 'Well, I understand finally with whom I'm working. One won't make perestroika with these people.' V. I. Boldin, *Krushenie pedestala* (Moscow: Respublika, 1995), 219.

[4] Whereas the Bolsheviks in 1917 employed the slogan *vsya vlast sovetam* [all power to the soviets], Gorbachev used a more ambiguous formulation: *polnevlastie sovetam* [full power to the soviets].

settled upon a reinvigoration of the moribund legislature. Following constitutional changes in December 1988 and competitive elections in February 1989, an extraordinary, if short-lived, experiment in 'speaker's parliamentarism' began.

From his post as chairman of the new Congress of People's Deputies, Gorbachev sought to formulate policy, manage a growing parliamentary bureaucracy, and direct floor debate, all the while maintaining his Communist Party office. It was an unworkable amalgam. Furthermore, parliament itself proved to be an unwieldy and unreliable vehicle of rule. In a period of mounting social and economic crises, the length and contentiousness of debates and committee hearings constrained executive action. Prime Minister Nikolai Ryzhkov estimated that parliamentary duties occupied a third of his ministers' time.[5] Parliament also began to insist on direct involvement in the implementation of policy.[6] Moreover, an essential component of efficient parliamentarism, a loyal and stable legislative majority, was missing. It was often unclear which faction presented the greater liability to Gorbachev: the conservative Communist majority, procedurally sycophantic but hostile to substantive change, or the vocal and independent-minded minority, which continually criticized the pace and depth of reforms.

Frustrated in his role as speaker, Gorbachev authorized the design of a new political architecture barely six months into the life of the parliament.[7] The goal was to create for the leader a more dignified and powerful constitutional office distinct from the legislature, and in so doing to disarm the democratic opposition, which itself had proposed the establishment of a presidency in the spring of 1989.[8] How this goal was to be accomplished became the subject of intense debate among Gorbachev's advisors in the first weeks of 1990. While some favored the establishment of an American-style presidential system, others, most notably Anatoly Lukyanov, rejected the separation of powers inherent in presidentialism as alien to Soviet and Russian traditions.[9] At the end of this brief in-house debate, Gorbachev opted for semi-presidential arrangements modeled largely on those of the Fifth French Republic, whose constitution combined elements of presidential and parliamentary rule.[10]

Semi-presidentialism had numerous advantages for Gorbachev personally and for a regime in transition from one-party rule.[11] Separating the posts of head of state (president) and head of government (prime minister) elevated the president above the unpleasant business of managing a vast and inefficient bureaucracy. Removed from daily politics, the

---

[5] M. Nenashev, *Poslednee Pravitelstvo SSSR* (Moscow: AO 'Krym,' 1993), 18.

[6] 'From the Archives,' *Demokratizatsiya*, 2 (Spring 1994): 316–31.

[7] According to Gorbachev, 'We are initiating new things in the economy and in politics. But without an executive mechanism we cannot achieve these initiatives. If there is no balance, we'll remain at the initial stage of meetings . . . I think the main source of this acceleration is a strong executive mechanism:' 'From the Archives,' *Demokratizatsiya*, 2 (Spring 1994): 330–1. See also Georgy Shakhnazarov, *Tsena svobody: reformatsiya Gorbacheva glazami ego pomoshchnika* (Moscow: Rossika, 1993), 136.

[8] Yegor Kuznetsov, 'The Making of a President. A Glimpse of the History of the Top Executive Post in the USSR,' *Demokratizatsiya*, 2 (Spring 1994): 222–7.

[9] 'We've Got a Special Way of Thinking. On the Establishment of the Soviet Presidency,' *Demokratizatsiya*, 2 (Spring 1994): 228–33 (interview with Georgy Shakhnazarov).

[10] Shakhnazarov claims that he was the prime mover behind the adoption of the French model. Shakhnazarov, *Tsena svobody*, 138. On the selection of the semi-presidential model, and on politics generally in the late Gorbachev era, see Archie Brown, *The Gorbachev Factor* (Oxford: Oxford University Press, 1996) 198 and *passim*.

[11] For an introduction to semi-presidentialism, see Maurice Duverger 'A New Political System Model Semi-Presidential Government,' *European Journal of Political Research*, 8 (1980) 165–87.

president could aspire to the majesty of a republican monarch. A dignified presidency seemed to promise a new source of legitimacy for a regime with failing ideology and institutions. If under semi-presidentialism the prime minister assumed direct responsibility for social and economic policy, the president played the leading role in matters of national security. This division of labor, which mirrored that in France, rewarded Gorbachev's passion for foreign affairs and his aversion to budgets. Under the new institutional arrangements Gorbachev was free to reach strategic compromises, whether with foreign dignitaries or with the miners and other groups within Russia. It then fell to the government to make good on his often exaggerated promises.

Semi-presidentialism was also the least disruptive alternative to the existing arrangements, requiring only the addition of a small presidential bureaucracy, initially staffed by some three hundred persons.[12] In this era of institutional transition, the presidency appeared to be the logical successor to the beleaguered Communist Party. At the end of the Soviet era, according to Georgy Shakhnazarov, the presidency 'gradually began to take over the Central Committee apparatus.'[13] A less charitable observer, Prime Minister Valentin Pavlov, called the apparatuses of the presidency and the Central Committee 'Siamese twins.'[14]

In the first weeks of 1990, Gorbachev, his advisors, and select parliamentary and republican leaders negotiated institutional choices that gave Soviet semi-presidentialism its distinctive shape. Four issues dominated their discussions: the powers of the presidency vis-à-vis the legislature; the relations between president and prime minister; the method of electing the president; and the role of the presidency in center-periphery relations. The debate over executive-legislative relations centered on the future of the Congress of People's Deputies. The Congress functioned in some respects like a constituent assembly, which assumes state sovereignty temporarily in order to lay the constitutional foundations of a new political order. But in the Soviet Union, this outsized institution—both in terms of its membership and authority—possessed a permanent mandate. It was at once an arbiter of constitutional issues, an electoral college for the other parliamentary chamber, the Supreme Soviet, and the highest legislative assembly, whose laws could not be challenged. Sharing the political stage with the Congress of People's Deputies would limit severely the authority of a Soviet president. But Gorbachev refused to heed the advice of aides who sought to restrict the powers of the Congress or to abolish the institution altogether. In most semi-presidential systems, for example, the president has the power to dissolve the parliament. The deputies' fear of dissolution can, at crucial moments, afford the executive important leverage over a recalcitrant parliament. In Soviet semi-presidentialism, however, the fate of the Supreme Soviet remained in the hands of the Congress. The president could only propose to the Congress that it dissolve the Supreme Soviet, a policy that Gorbachev believed would discourage the rise of an authoritarian executive.[15] The legislation on the presidency also kept

---

[12] This number would grow to four hundred by August 1991. V. I. Boldin *Krushenie pedestala* (Moscow: Respublika, 1995), 372.

[13] 'We've Got a Special Way of Thinking,' 230.

[14] Valentin Pavlov, *Upushchen li shans?* (Moscow: Terra, 1995), 166–8. Shakhnazarov notes that initially the meetings of the new Presidential Council bore a remarkable resemblance to those of the Politburo. They were held in the same room, with many of the same people, and with the same rituals. Georgy Shakhnazarov, *Tsena svobody*, 139–40.

[15] Yegor Leonodovich Kuznetsov, 'Sozdanie instituta Prezidenta SSSR. Politologicheskie aspekty' (Kandidat diss., Institute of State and Law, Moscow, 1994), 74. Kudryavtsev, among others, sought in vain to convince Gorbachev to accept the power of dissolution. Ibid.

in place the potentially powerful chairmanship of the Congress, a post assumed by the champion of Soviet parliamentarism, Anatoly Lukyanov. By retaining a Congress of People's Deputies with its full array of powers, Gorbachev and the Soviet elite created an institutional regime that invited executive-legislative stalemate in the USSR and, through inheritance, in post-communist Russia.

Perhaps the greatest danger posed by semi-presidentialism in any country is a divided executive.[16] Although the president enjoys a fixed term of office, the prime minister serves at the pleasure of the parliament. The potential arises, therefore, for the parliament to insist on a prime minister with political views unlike those of the president. When this occurs, the president and prime minister are forced to 'cohabit,' to use the French term, an awkward arrangement that leads inevitably to tensions over the distribution of power between the two executive leaders. Although working papers prepared for Gorbachev and his staff alerted them to the problems of cohabitation under French semi-presidentialism, the Soviet leader appears to have given little thought to the polities of a dual executive, apparently assuming that the president would retain indefinitely the support of the parliament, and hence the prime minister. On the question of intra-executive relations generally, Gorbachev seemed content with legislative provisions that assured his right to propose the appointment and resignation of the prime minister to the parliament, to consult with the prime minister on the appointment of members of the government, and to annul government directives. From discussions with deputies in the weeks before the creation of the presidency, it is clear that Gorbachev expected the prime minister to function much as he had throughout the Soviet era, that is, to oversee the economy and, in Gorbachev's own words, to stay out of 'politics.'[17] This view failed to recognize, however, that the invigoration of parliament had raised the profile and the potential power of the prime minister. Moreover, it betrayed a naive belief that economic management and public administration generally could be reduced to a technical task.

The lack of precision and coherence in the new institutional arrangements reflected, in part, the political constraints within which Gorbachev and his aides operated. Redesigning institutions naturally prompted resistance from those forces in the party, the parliament, and the republics that felt threatened by a strong presidency. Constitutional ambiguity and compromise helped to allay these fears. But the Soviet Union's new and confusing political system was also a product of Gorbachev's leadership style.[18] For Gorbachev, governing was less about carefully-crafted organizations and rules than creating solutions through negotiation. He saw the president operating above the fray of daily politics and administration in a realm that transcended the traditional branches of government. He remarked to deputies in the weeks before becoming president that he would be a mediator between executive and legislature.[19] Traditional lines of authority meant little to him. Rather than disciplining the

[16] For an analysis of the tensions between executive leaders in post-communist Eastern Europe, see Thomas Baylis, 'Presidents vs. Prime Ministers: Shaping Executive Authority in Eastern Europe,' *World Politics*, 3 (1996): 297–333.

[17] 'From the Archives,' 327–8. For insider accounts of the prime minister's office at the end of the Soviet era, see the interview with Nikolai Ryzhkov in M. Nenashev, *Poslednee Pravitelstvo SSSR* (Moscow: AO 'Krom,' 1993), and Pavlov, *Upushchen li shans?*

[18] For a critical assessment of this style, see the memoirs of Gorbachev's foreign policy advisor, A. S. Chernayev, *Shest'let s Gorbachevym: po dnevnikovym zapisyam* (Moscow: Kultura, 1993).

[19] 'From the Archives,' 327–8.

prime minister and his government directly, Gorbachev proposed to do so through the Congress. His was the approach of an international statesman and not a chief executive officer.

On some institutional questions, of course, Gorbachev had clear preferences. One of these was electoral rules. Few subjects excited more intense debate, both within Gorbachev's entourage and among the country's elite, than the method of electing the Soviet president. The choice was between direct election by the population and indirect election by the Congress of People's Deputies. Each option presented obvious risks and rewards to Gorbachev. Indirect election assured Gorbachev's ascent to the presidency and a rapid, peaceful transition to the new institutional regime. But it also deprived the president of a popular mandate, and in so doing promised to solidify the authority of the Congress of People's Deputies, which would serve as electoral college for both parliament and president. Unwilling to risk personal defeat or the strains that a competitive election campaign would place on the nation, Gorbachev insisted that the Congress select the first Soviet president, with subsequent presidential elections to be decided by direct popular vote.[20] The Congress agreed.

To overcome the objections of some republican leaders to the establishment of a presidency, Gorbachev agreed to grant them membership in a new body, the Federation Council, which would review policies on inter-ethnic and inter-republican relations. But the more fateful concession was the extension of the semi-presidential model to republican governments. During 1990, in a 'demonstration effect' encouraged by Moscow, fourteen of the fifteen Soviet republics hurried to adopt the institutional arrangements crafted and introduced in the center.[21] Few understood at the time the dangers this concession posed to the integrity of the union.[22] Newly established republican presidencies quickly became important symbols of nascent political communities, especially in cases where the local leader was willing to challenge the center. And just as in the center, presidents in many republics began to decouple themselves from the Communist Party, which had served to integrate the diverse peoples and territories of the Soviet Union. If before 1990, republican leaders—the Communist Party first secretaries—made their careers by proving their loyalty to Moscow, after the introduction of semi-presidentialism they ensured their political future by appealing to republican interests. Unlike the Communist Party of old, the fledgling Soviet presidency had neither the administrative nor ideological authority to impose its will on the republics. There was no longer a vertical command structure capable of ensuring the discipline of local leaders.[23]

---

[20] In this decision as well, he was following the precedent of the Fifth Republic in France. In France, however, the V Republic Constitution envisioned the indirect election of the president as a permanent feature of the political system. In the Gaullist-inspired referendum of 1962, the French electorate approved the change to direct elections for the president.

[21] The odd man out was Belarus, which retained the 'speaker's parliamentarism' of the late Soviet era until the introduction of a presidential system in 1994. See Alexander Lukashuk, 'Survey of Presidential Power: Belarus,' *East European Constitutional Review* (Fall 1993–Winter 1994): 58–61.

[22] One of these was Sergei Stankevich, whose memo of 2 February 1990, warned of the consequences of introducing republican presidencies. Yegor Leonodovich Kuznetsov, 'Sozdanie instituta Prezidenta SSSR. Politologicheskie aspekty' (Kandidat diss., Institute of State and Law, Moscow, 1994), 60.

[23] According to one Russian observer the system collapsed when the CPSU, which had been the central nervous system, shut down without something to take its place. Anatoly Utkin, 'Pyat rokovykh shagov Gorbacheva' *Rossiiskaya federatsiya*, 7 (1995): 6–7. Thereafter, each economic leader in factories and farms felt himself 'master in his own domain' *(svoega roda monarkhami v svoei votchine)*. Ibid.

The introduction of direct elections for republican presidents in 1991 further undermined Moscow's authority. If the center still retained some ability to influence the actions of republican deputies who had voted for presidents in the indirect elections of 1990, it carried little weight with ordinary voters. Indeed, in many republics the successful candidates for president ran against the center. The most dramatic example of this was in Ukraine, where a week before the election of 9 December 1991 the republican leader and presidential candidate, Viktor Kravchuk, encouraged his Slavic neighbors, Russia and Belarus, to sign an agreement—the Belovezhky accords—that declared their independence from the Soviet Union.

To understand the collapse of the USSR, then, one must not stop at the traditional contextual explanations, such as a lagging economy, a crisis of identity and belief, and a more demanding population.[24] The institutional choices made at the end of the Soviet era recast the structure of incentives in ways that rewarded those favoring disintegration. Although there was much in Russian and Soviet history—and in the demands of the moment—to recommend semi-presidentialism, there were other options, including the maintenance of traditional party rule, that would have produced very different political outcomes, especially over the short term. It was the will of a small group of men to create a presidency constrained by a mammoth Congress and then to introduce presidencies in the republics, decisions that had momentous consequences for the Soviet Union and the world. Established in part to save the Union, the presidency contributed mightily to the Union's demise.

The crisis of semi-presidentialism in Russia, 1992–1993

In the first two years of post-Communist rule, semi-presidentialist systems throughout much of the former Soviet Union fell victim to a disorder latent in all varieties of presidentialism, a stalemate between legislative and executive institutions. Unlike parliamentary systems, where only the legislature can claim a direct popular mandate, presidentialist arrangements produce what Juan Linz has called 'dual democratic legitimacies' for president and assembly.[25] Because both institutions are directly elected, each is able to promote itself as the bearer of sovereign authority. When the assembly and president are at odds, the system provides no constitutional means to defuse the crisis. A denouement occurs, if at all, because elites themselves craft a means of cohabitation. Parliamentary systems, by contrast, can simply turn out a wayward executive through a vote of no confidence.

The origins of executive-legislative stalemate in Russia are to be found, however, in the particular rules and circumstances of politics in the First Russian Republic as well as in the logic of presidentialism. The sequencing of elections was one source of the conflict. Almost a year and a half separated the Russian parliamentary elections of February 1990 from the presidential election of June 1991. Although it may be an exaggeration to claim that two different Russias went to the polls on these dates, popular perceptions—and arguably some

---

[24] For a lucid and compelling survey of the reasons for the collapse of the USSR, see Alexander Dallin, 'The Causes of the Collapse of the USSR,' *Post-Soviet Affairs*, 4 (1992): 279–302.

[25] See Juan Linz, 'Presidential or Parliamentary Democracy: Does It Make a Difference?' in *The Failure of Presidential Democracy*, vol. 1 of *Comparative Perspectives*, ed. Juan J. Linz and Arturo Valenzuela (Baltimore: Johns Hopkins University Press 1994).

values—had changed between the elections. The result was a state divided between a reform-oriented president and a conservative parliament. Whether February 1990 or June 1991 was the more representative moment for Russia in the competition between the dual democratic legitimacies, Yeltsin was able to claim a more recent mandate.

Initially, the timing of elections seemed to pose little threat to executive-legislative relations. In the first months after the Russian presidential election, the August coup and a program of national self-assertion united Russian institutions against their Soviet counterparts. But once the Soviet Union collapsed and the focus of political debate shifted from questions of statehood to those of economic reform, cracks began to appear in parliamentary support for the president. By the middle of 1992, the market-oriented initiatives of Yeltsin's acting prime minister, Yegor Gaidar, had provoked a large and aggressive opposition to the course of the president.[26] A changing agenda had combined with the sequencing of elections to produce a standoff between the president and parliament.

It would be naive, of course, to portray executive-legislative conflict in policy terms alone. Policy debates in the First Russian Republic were also extensions of struggles for personal and institutional power similar to those that had animated succession crises in Soviet history. Emboldened by a growing popular and elite opposition to the president's policies, the parliament and its leadership laid claim to a larger and more direct role in governing the country. Standing at the head of the anti-Yeltsin majority in parliament, the speaker, Ruslan Khasbulatov, sought to curtail presidential authority and revive elements of the radical parliamentarism associated with Soviet democracy. In the words of Nikolai Fyodorov, Yeltsin's justice minister, Khasbulatov sought to create 'a parallel center of executive power in the parliament.'[27]

In an immediate sense, the struggle between Yeltsin and Khasbulatov and between presidency and parliament was for control of the bureaucracy, especially the ministries that controlled guns, money, and property. To attract the loyalty of the officers of the state, each side used laws, patronage, and funding, the traditional weapons in the institutional confrontation endemic to presidentialism. It was a standoff that recalled the conflict between president and Congress in the United States in the wake of the Civil War. In the American case, a battle between legislature and executive on the right to make bureaucratic appointments led to the impeachment, though not the conviction, of President Andrew Johnson.

If presidentialism predisposes political systems to legislative-executive confrontation, it does not dictate the use of violence or other extreme measures as weapons in the political struggle. There are other means out of an impasse. In France, for example, staggered elections have returned parliamentary majorities opposed to the president. Rather than attempt to rule around the parliament through reserved powers or the plebiscite, the French president has, during periods of cohabitation, deferred to the parliamentary majority and retreated into a largely ceremonial role.[28] Thus, semi-presidentialism in France developed 'a

---

[26] Alexander Sobyanin analyzes the shift of parliamentary support away from the president and his policies in 'Political Cleavages among the Russian Deputies: The Current Crisis,' in *Parliaments in Transition*, ed. Thomas Remington (Boulder, Colo: Westview Press, 1994), 181–216.

[27] 'Nikolai Fyodorov: Parliament dopuskaet antikonstitutsionnye deistviya,' *Rossiiskie vesti*, 13 (Mar. 1993): 2.

[28] We would do well, however, to recall the anxiety that seized the French political elite in the months before the fateful parliamentary elections in 1986. The French press was filled with widely divergent articles about how to manage cohabitation. Thus, a consensus had to be forged; it did not exist before the fact.

safety valve that avoids the clash and crises of two popularly elected legitimacies by permitting the political system to function now as a presidential system, now as a parliamentary system.'[29] The French case serves as a reminder that institutional arrangements succeed or fail in large measure because of the willingness of elites to forge compromises in the available constitutional space. As Forrest McDonald remarked with regard to American politics, 'The lesson for the American framers,' which they took from seventeenth century English politics, 'was that the formal distribution of powers between legislatures and executive is not so important as institutionalized means of cooperation.'[30]

Why did Russian political elites fail where their American and French counterparts succeeded? More specifically, why did Yeltsin refuse to follow the lead of Mitterrand? One reason is that the circumstances differed. Not only was the election sequencing reversed—in France the parliament was elected *after* the president—but the stakes of Russian politics were far higher. The victors, it seemed, would define Russia's new economic model, its replacement ideology, and, perhaps, even its borders. They would also insure for themselves the accoutrements of modern life, such as desirable apartments, country homes, and automobiles. In Russia, there was as yet no revolving door to offer sustenance to the politically dispossessed. And because Russia lacked an institution common to Western democracies—a permanent civil service—all state officials felt threatened by the struggle between president and parliament.[31] Taken together, these circumstances raised the stakes of Russian politics in 1992–93 to a level with few historical precedents.[32]

Added to this unfavorable mix of institutional design and circumstance was an elite unschooled in the tactics of democratic accommodation. Most of the leaders in the presidency, parliament, and the Constitutional Court were neophytes in national politics, if not in public life generally.[33] Most retained the values learned in an authoritarian political culture, with its aversion to compromise and its emphasis on personal rather than legal authority. Few had yet developed a civic consciousness, which could elevate *raison d'état* above departmental or personal interests.[34] The elite itself, then, was ill-suited to the task of nurturing fledgling democratic institutions.

The impediments to democracy outlined here should not obscure elite maneuvers

[29] Ezra N. Suleiman, 'Presidentialism and Political Stability in France' in *The Failure of Presidential Democracy*, 151.

[30] Forrest McDonald, *The American Presidency: An Intellectual History* (Lawrence: The University of Kansas Press, 1994), 94.

[31] See, for example, Samuel Huntington 'Will More Countries Become Democratic?' *Political Science Quarterly*, 2 (1984): 193–218. In some sectors, such as justice, finance, and economics, state officials are now finding attractive jobs in the private sector. In fact, for some ministries and divisions of the presidential administration, it is becoming increasingly difficult to keep competent specialists who can make a better living outside of government. Sergei Filatov, 'Kto pridet zavtra v organy vlasti,' *Rossiiskie vesti*, 13 Sep. 1994, 1–2.

[32] As a precondition to democracy the economic security of officials may be more important than the oft-noted minimum living standard of the population at large.

[33] One of the most conspicuous examples of this was Valery Zorkin, the chairman of the Constitutional Court, whose frantic behavior in moments of crisis exacerbated tensions and undermined the authority of his institution.

[34] On the development of a civic consciousness in early modern Europe, see Donald W. Hanson, *From Kingdom to Commonwealth: The Development of a Civic Consciousness in English Political Thought* (Cambridge, Mass: Harvard University Press, 1970), especially the conclusion, 336–72. In *Making Democracy Work: Civic Traditions in Modern Italy* (Princeton: Princeton University Press 1993), Robert D. Putnam explores the elements of 'social capital' that have facilitated democratic accommodation in the West.

intended to make Russia's institutions work. President Yeltsin, for example, sought to deflect criticism of his policies and enhance his parliamentary support through periodic reshuffling of the government. His most dramatic concession came in December 1992, when he sacrificed his acting prime minister, Yegor Gaidar. Gaidar's replacement, Viktor Chernomyrdin, was a manager *(upravlenets)* whose background and beliefs struck a responsive chord for a time among the deputies. But these and other moments of elite accommodation brought only fleeting respite from executive-legislative conflict. When the new 'political year' began in September 1993, politics had reached a juncture through which only one elite group could pass. As Robert Sharlet has argued, each side insisted on a new constitutional framework favorable to it: 'one promoting the model of a parliamentary republic with a restricted executive, the other (Yeltsin's), a presidential model with a dependent legislature and a weak constitutional court.'[35] The First Russian Republic was unable to sustain dual democratic legitimacies.

The Second Russian Republic: Toward a delegative democracy?

Rather than face almost certain impeachment, Yeltsin disbanded the parliament in the fall of 1993, first by decree and then by force.[36] These extraconstitutional measures enabled the president to advance two ballot initiatives for 12 December 1993, both designed to enhance the sources of presidential authority. The first, elections to a new parliament, was expected to produce a workable legislative majority for the president. Pollsters close to the presidency believed that the mood of the country, together with the electoral rules that the president himself had dictated, would permit the party of reform, Russia's Choice, to form the core, if not an outright majority, in the successor parliament.[37] On 12 December, voters also cast ballots on a constitutional referendum. Last-minute changes to the draft constitution dramatically strengthened presidential power at the expense of the parliament. If denied a legislative majority, the president could use reserve powers to rule around the parliament. Thus, instead of the politics of alternation, as in semi-presidential France, Yeltsin advanced the politics of redundancy.[38]

Under the new constitution, which passed by a slim and still disputed majority, the formal structure of Russian government remained semi-presidential. A directly elected president shared executive responsibility with a prime minister, who needed the support, or more accurately the forbearance, of the parliament. But the rules governing the generation and accountability of the government reduced to a minimum the parliament's ability to limit executive authority. According to the prime minister's chief of staff, the government exercised executive power 'independently [*samostoyatel'no*], subordinate to the President but

[35] Robert Sharlet, 'Russian Constitutional Crisis: Law and Politics under Yeltsin,' *Post-Soviet Affairs*, 4 (Oct.–Dec. 1993): 320.

[36] In his autobiography, Yeltsin notes that after the Eighth Congress, he had no choice but to dismantle parliament or become a figurehead president. He was obviously not prepared to assume the latter role. Boris Yeltsin, *The Struggle for Russia* (New York: Random House, 1994), 205.

[37] See, for example, the analyses of Aleksandr Sobyanin, E. Gelman and O. Kayunov, 'The Political Climate of Russia's Regions: Voters and Deputies, 1991–1993,' *The Soviet and Post-Soviet Review*, 1(1994): 63–84.

[38] See Eugene Huskey, 'The State-Legal Administration and the Politics of Redundancy,' *Post-Soviet Affairs*, 2 (1995): 115–43.

not to the parliament, with whom it works in parallel.'[39] Individual ministers were not subject to confirmation, recall, or sanction by the legislature, though they were in theory subject to weekly parliamentary question time. Although parliament retained the formal right to reject a president's appointment to the office of prime minister, or to express no confidence in a sitting government, it could do so only under the most unappealing conditions. According to Article 111.4, a president could insist on his candidate for prime minister through three successive rejections by the lower chamber, the State Duma, after which the president installed an interim prime minister, dissolved the parliament, and called new elections. Moreover, Article 117.3 granted the president the option of ignoring the Duma's first vote of no confidence in the government. In the event a second no confidence motion passed within three months, the president could opt to dissolve the Duma rather than sacrifice his prime minister. The new institutional arrangements placed the president as well as the prime minister beyond the reach of all but the most united parliaments. To impeach the president, the State Duma first had to bring charges of high treason or other grave crimes against the president. These charges had to be supported by two-thirds of the deputies on the basis of a written opinion of a special Duma commission. As Vladimir Lysenko has noted, the president's power to dissolve the lower chamber—and keep in place the more malleable upper house, the Federation Council—'forestalls any attempt by the State Duma to raise first the question of impeaching the president.'[40] Should the Duma bring charges, the Supreme Court had to issue a finding that the elements of a crime were present, and the Constitutional Court had to confirm that the Duma had respected the appropriate procedures in the bringing of the charges. It then fell to the Federation Council to convict the president by majority vote. In the event impeachment proceedings reached this final stage, the Federation Council would be most unlikely to remove the president. Half of its members were local executive officials, most of whom served at the pleasure of Yeltsin.[41] Even after the parliamentary elections of December 1995, which returned a Duma that was even more hostile to the president than its predecessor, the new Federation Council retained a slim pro-Yeltsin majority.[42]

The design and operation of the Second Russian Republic exhibited many of the features of 'delegative democracy' found in Latin America. In the words of Guillermo O'Donnell:

Delegative democracies rest on the premiss that whoever wins election to the presidency is thereby entitled to govern as he or she sees fit, constrained only by the hard facts of existing power relations and by a constitutionally limited term in office.[43]

The key difference between representative—or institutionalized—democracy and delegative democracy lies in the nature of executive accountability. Whereas in representative democracies the president is accountable both vertically to the voters and horizontally to 'a

[39] Vladimir Kvasov, 'Konflikta mezhdu pravitelstvom i Prezidentom ne budet,' *Rossiiskaya federatsiya,* 6 (1994): 7–8.

[40] Vladimir M. Lysenko, 'Toward Presidential Rule,' *Journal of Democracy,* 5 (1994): 11.

[41] There remains, of course, the question of whether Yeltsin, or any other Russian president, would stand down if impeached. In his autobiography, Yeltsin seemed unwilling to accept the idea of impeachment of a directly-elected president. Yeltsin, *The Struggle for Russia,* 210.

[42] Laura Belin, 'Speakers of Federation Council, Duma Agree to Cooperate,' *OMRI Daily Report,* 2 Feb. 1996.

[43] Guillermo O'Donnell, 'Delegative Democracy,' *Journal of Democracy,* 5 (1994): 59.

network of relatively autonomous . . . institutions,'[44] in delegative democracies the president is accountable to the nation alone. Delegative presidents regard parliaments and constitutional courts 'as unnecessary encumbrances to their "mission" [and] they make strenuous efforts to hamper the development of such institutions.'[45]

How strenuously Yeltsin has hampered the development of these institutions in the Second Russian Republic is a subject on which reasonable observers may differ. But he has clearly been reluctant to respect democratic rules and structures designed to limit presidential power. That reluctance has been grounded not only in his political temperament but also in his desire to advance the cause of reform in Russia. Yet reform has both a procedural and a substantive dimension. It is not enough to decree change; one must be able to implement it. Again, Guillermo O'Donnell:

institutionalized democracies are slow at making decisions. But once those decisions are made, they are relatively more likely to be implemented. In delegative democracies, in contrast, we witness a decision-making frenzy, what in Latin America we call *decretismo*. Because such hasty, unilateral executive orders are likely to offend important and politically mobilized interests, they are unlikely to be implemented.[46]

When Yeltsin broke new ground on economic and law enforcement policies in the late spring of 1994, he did so by issuing his own decrees instead of submitting laws to parliament. Rather than 'build[ing] new legislative coalitions with every issue,'[47] the task confronting all leaders in multiparty presidentialist systems, the Russian president has often chosen the decidedly less troublesome option of initiating new policies by decree. Like party directives under the old regime, presidential decrees have been designed to serve as guidelines for subsequent parliamentary legislation. In the interim, they enjoyed the force of law as long as they did not contravene the constitution or existing legislation. Or so the constitution stipulates. In fact, some decrees have altered parliamentary laws.[48]

Although Yeltsin has been reluctant to accept parliamentary institutions and their leaders as full partners in governing, he has been willing to grant them a measure of dignity and influence. Among other things, he has cultivated parliamentary support at strategic junctures. Shortly after the disappointing results of the December 1993 and 1995 parliamentary elections, the president removed several visible reformers from their government posts as a concession to the new parliament. Indeed, with the ouster of Anatoly Chubais at the beginning of 1996, no vigorous advocate for economic reform remained in the Cabinet. Moreover,

---

[44] Ibid. 61.   [45] Ibid. 62.   [46] Ibid. 66.

[47] Scott Mainwaring, 'Presidentialism, Multipartism and Democracy. The Difficult Combination,' *Comparative Political Studies*, 26 (1993): 200. Mainwaring offers here a penetrating analysis of the importance of party system for presidentialism. He argues that two-party systems enhance the prospects for survival of transition regimes with presidentialist arrangements. Under presidentialism, multipartism exacerbates executive/legislative conflict, increases the likelihood of ideological polarization, and complicates interparty coalition building.

[48] See Nikolai Gorlov, 'Kak gotovyatsya Ukazy Prezidenta,' *Rossiiskie vesti*, 27 May 1994, 1, which provides an example of a decree that violates the existing law on state enterprises. Besides broad lawmaking authority of its own, the Constitution also grants the executive control over economic legislation considered by parliament. Article 104.3 states that revenue or expenditure bills may be introduced in the Duma only with the permission of the government, a provision common to many modern constitutions.

the president chose not to provoke a constitutional crisis over the parliamentary amnesty of February 1994, which freed the instigators of political violence in August 1991 and October 1993. In this episode, at least, he exhibited an essential trait of a democratic politician, the willingness to accept defeat.[49]

Yeltsin has also attempted to anticipate and defuse potential conflict with the parliament by creating agencies in the presidency for liaison with the legislature. Rather than establish a presidential party or even a presidential coalition in parliament, the president introduced a kind of *entente cordiale* with virtually all forces in the legislature.[50] As part of this strategy, he sought to co-opt the heads of the two chambers of parliament—the Duma and the Federation Council—by appointing them in 1994 to several key presidential structures, including the Security Council and the Council on Cadres Policy (*Sovet po kadrovoi politike*).[51] The politics of inclusion did not survive the December 1995 parliamentary elections unscathed, however. With a more confrontational parliamentary leadership, an imminent presidential election and growing concern about the political consequences of the war in Chechnya Yeltsin refused to extend membership in the Security Council to the new heads of the Duma and Federation Council in early 1996.

For its part, the parliamentary leadership has in general sought to minimize executive-legislative tensions. Contrary to the expectations of many, the speaker of the Duma in 1994 and 1995, the Communist-turned-Agrarian Ivan Rybkin studiously avoided direct public confrontations with the presidency.[52] Known in some circles as 'Mister Social Accord,'[53] Rybkin proved at least as cooperative as Vladimir Shumeiko, the chair of the Federation Council, who had been a close protégé of Yeltsin before his move from the presidency to parliament in December 1993. Because of a still fragmented party system and the remnants of apparatus dominance in the legislature, the parliamentary leaders have been able to resolve many conflicts with the executive through private negotiations.[54] Unlike their predecessor, Ruslan Khasbulatov, Rybkin and Shumeiko were steady and discrete, if not always agreeable, in their dealings with the president. And although the new speaker of the Duma, Gennady Seleznev, is less conciliatory than his predecessor, he too seems intent on avoiding a constitutional crisis. By presenting himself and fellow Communists as relatively benign politicians in the months leading up to the summer 1996 presidential election, Seleznev was preparing the ground for the campaign of the Communists' presidential candidate, Gennady Zyuganov.

[49] 'Democracy,' Mainwaring notes, 'presupposes the willingness of political actors to accept electoral and policy defeats. This willingness is enhanced when actors believe that defeats are reversible through the democratic struggle and that they are not catastrophic.' Scott Mainwaring, 'Presidentialism Multipartism and Democracy. The Difficult Combination,' *Comparative Political Studies*, 26 (1993): 219.

[50] The phrase is that of Mikhail Shchipanov in 'Osoboi prezidentskoi partii ne budet,' *Kuranty*, 7 Apr. 1994, 4.

[51] 'Novaya nomenklatura ili novaya kadrovaya politika?' *Rossiiskie vesti*, 23 Sept. 1994, 1.

[52] Rybkin and Yeltsin noted the 'constructive dialogue' between president and speaker that characterized the first session of the Duma. Aleksei Kirpichnikov, 'Duma: The President approves of the Duma, and its Chairman approves of the President,' *Segodnya*, 6 Oct. 1994, 1, as trans. in *The Current Digest of the Post-Soviet Press*, 40 (1994): 1.

[53] Mikhail Leontev, 'Premer Skokovets [*sic*] kak produkt "obshchestvennogo soglasiya",' *Segodnya*, 25 Oct. 1994, 1. For a revealing self-portrait, see I. P. Rybkin, *Gosudarstvennaya Duma: pyataya popytka* (Moscow: International Humanitarian Fund 'Znanie,' 1994), esp. 116–25.

[54] Thomas F. Remington and Steven S. Smith conclude that Shumeiko's position in the Federation Council is more dominant than that of Rybkin in the Duma, where parties are more developed and deputies more active. 'The Early Legislative Process in the Russian Federal Assembly,' *Journal of Legislative Studies*, 1 (1996).

Besides personal relations and pre-election posturing, the tactics of accommodation just described grow out of the prevailing balance of institutional power between the presidency and parliament. Although politically dominant, a president ignores or angers a parliament at his peril, especially at moments of political weakness. The 1993 Constitution elevated the presidency above parliament, but it also reserved sufficient powers for the legislature to complicate presidential rule. Three times in 1994, the Federation Council rejected the president's nominee for the post of procurator-general, Aleksei Ilyushenko, a candidate eventually abandoned by Yeltsin.[55] The Federation Council also turned down several presidential nominees to the Constitutional Court. Furthermore, to avoid confrontation with the legislature, in May 1994 Yeltsin reluctantly signed the Law on the Status of Deputies, which gave members of parliament broader personal immunity and more expansive rights to information from executive agencies.[56] The 'power ministries' and the head of Yeltsin's own presidential administration, Sergei Filatov, had vigorously opposed this bill. The debates over the 1995 budget also illustrated that the parliament and its leadership retained some capacity to limit executive action. In late 1994, the Duma and Federation Council overrode a presidential veto of legislation that required stringent executive reporting requirements in future budgets—the first veto override under the new Constitution.[57] It remains to be seen, of course, whether a parliament capable of amassing such super-majorities can serve as an effective brake on presidential rule. Much depends on the willingness of the president to accept legislative defeat.

Mitigating the effects of the anti-presidential majority in parliament have been the tactics of the legislative leadership and the institutional arrangements, which require a higher threshold of consensus before collective action is attractive. But two 'para-constitutional' factors are also at work.[58] Because Yeltsin's administrator of affairs (*upravliayushchy delami*) distributes housing, telephones, and vacation packages to legislative as well as executive personnel, the presidency has been able to use 'dacha politics' to influence individual deputies.[59] At the beginning of 1996, the new Duma speaker, Seleznev, insisted that responsibility for the maintenance of parliament and its deputies be transferred from the administrator of

[55] One should note, however, that Yeltsin kept Ilyushenko in the post as acting Procurator-General for a year. 'Sovet Federatsii otklonil ukaz Prezidenta,' *Izvestiya*, 7 Oct. 1994, 1, and *Izvestiya*, 26 Oct. 1994, 1. The procurator-general is one of several appointments that must receive the consent of the Federation Council. The others are the members of the Supreme Court, the Supreme Arbitration Court, and the Constitutional Court, and the deputy chair of the Accounting Chamber. For its part, the State Duma must give its consent to the appointment and dismissal of the chairs of the State Bank, the Accounting Chamber, and the Human Rights Agency. Articles 102–103.

[56] Sergei Chugayev, 'Kto vozmyot na sebya grekh narushit konstitutsiyu: prezident ili zakonodateli?' *Izvestiya*, 12 May 1994, 1.

[57] *RFE/RL Daily Report*, 26 Oct. 1994.

[58] For a discussion of the culture and informal rules—the para-constitutional elements—that explain the success of America's formal constitutional design, see Fred W. Riggs, 'The Survival of Presidentialism in America: Para-constitutional Practices,' *International Political Science Review*, 9 (1988) 247–78.

[59] Andrei Uglanov, 'Ministry prikhodyat i ukhodyat apparat ostayotsya,' *Argumenty i fakty*, 20 (1994): 3. The Administration of Affairs is a powerful, but little studied, arm of the Russian presidency, which now houses under one roof the remnants of the administrations of affairs of the Communist Party Central Committee and the Council of Ministers. For a revealing interview with the current head of the office, Pavel Borodin, see 'Kto vy, "tainyi" i "samyi glavnyi" ministr?' *Rossiiskaya federatsiya*, 25 (1995): 17–19. Where the budget of the apparatus of the Russian government (excluding the individual ministries) was 15 billion rubles in 1994, the Administration of Affairs received 82 billion rubles. 'O finansirovanii raskhodov iz federalnogo byudzheta vo II kvartale 1994 goda,' *Sobranie zakonodatelstva*, I (1994): 1.

affairs to the finance ministry. When deputies and their staffs failed to receive their pay for the preceding month, many had assumed that the delay reflected presidential displeasure with the new, more conservative parliament.[60]

Furthermore, the opposition has at times denied itself minor parliamentary victories in order to position itself for an assumption of executive power in the future. With the country in crisis and a presidential election scheduled for the summer of 1996, the anti-Yeltsin majority in parliament preferred to remain in opposition during the presidential campaign. The strategy of the conservative parliamentary majority was to restrict Yeltsin's freedom of maneuver without assuming governing responsibility. Thus, when a vote of no confidence was held in October 1994, the result was what might be termed a 'maximum losing coalition'—enough votes to distance the legislature from the executive and destabilize politics but not enough to force an early parliamentary election or to provoke a constitutional crisis.[61] This strategy was also apparent in the wake of the no confidence vote, when the Communist Party expelled one of its deputies, Valentin Kovalev, for assuming the Justice portfolio in the Chernomyrdin government. For the conservatives, there is nothing better than 'a discredited government hanging around the neck of the president.'[62]

The president's occasional defeats in parliament—or the more frequent concessions to the deputies—reveal as much about the vulnerabilities of a divided executive as the potential for a united legislature to frustrate executive action. Had executive agencies adhered to what the British call collective responsibility, the president's position vis-à-vis the legislature would have been virtually impregnable. But individual departments within the executive, most notably those responsible for defense, agriculture, and social spending, have publicized intraexecutive conflict as a means of mobilizing support for their positions in parliament, the executive, and the nation. And cutting across the major institutional divisions of Russian politics are sectoral cleavages that often set the executive against itself, thereby diluting the formal powers of the presidency vis-à-vis the assembly. Although such interest groups exist in all political systems, their effect is magnified in Russia because of the absence of rules and conventions to discipline executive officials. What Seweryn Bialer called the 'shapelessness' of the Stalinist political system has been replicated in post-Soviet Russia.[63]

One may argue that the most effective set of checks and balances in Russia is in the tension between sectoral elites rather than between state institutions.[64] Those wishing to

[60]   Robert Orttung, 'Duma Seeks Financial Independence from Presidential Administration,' *OMRI Daily Digest*, 13 Feb. 1996.

[61]   As is so often the case in Russian parliamentary votes, the motion failed because of high levels of tactical non-voting by deputies. Non-votes are counted as nay votes in the Duma. As Thomas F. Remington and Steven S. Smith point out, 'for the January–July 1994 period, the mean number of "yea" votes was 211 and the mean number of "nay" votes was 49, so the typical motion was defeated (211 is less than a majority) because of non-voting.' 'The Development of Parliamentary Parties in Russia,' *Legislative Studies Quarterly*, 4 (1995).

[62]   Andranik Migranian. 'Prezident dolzhen prinyat reshenie i naznachit premerom cheloveka, kotoryi sposoben sozdat pravitelstvo natsionalnogo spaseniya,' *Nezavisimaya gazeta*, 4 Nov. 1994, 1, 3. This argument was first made by Sergei Chugayev, 'Bolshinstvo politikov zainteresovano v krakhe pravitelstva,' *Izvestiya*, 27 Jan. 1994, 2.

[63]   Seweryn Bialer, *Stalin's Successors. Leadership, Change, and Stability in the Soviet Union* (Cambridge: Cambridge University Press, 1980), 16–17.

[64]   According to Alexander N. Yakovlev, even the late Soviet regime had a system of checks and balances of sorts. It was not legislative, executive, and judicial branches but rather the party apparat, the economic apparat, and the apparatus of coercion. Alexander Yakovlev, *The Fate of Marxism in Russia* (New Haven: Yale University Press, 1993), 108–9.

rationalize Russian government would reduce the power of these informal sectors. But to do so would eliminate the only potent source of horizontal accountability in the system and open the way for a new period of transition, from inefficient to efficient authoritarianism. Such is the dilemma of Russian politics in the post-communist era.

The perils of Russian presidentialism

The institutional design of the Second Russian Republic poses several perils for Russia's future. The first is that the winner-take-all consequences of presidential elections, taken together with a weak parliament, will discredit the fledgling regime in the eyes of the opposition. As Arend Lijphart has argued,

in democratizing and redemocratizing countries, undemocratic forces must be reassured and reconciled, and they must be persuaded not only to give up power but also not to insist on 'reserved domains' of undemocratic power within the new regime.

In Russia, this means providing incentives to Communists, Agrarians, and Liberal Democrats to stay in the political game. To his credit, Yeltsin seems to have understood that, whatever the formal powers of his office, Russia cannot be governed with a minimum winning coalition. Indeed, even before the appointment of a Communist minister in December 1994, Russia had in place a de facto coalition government, with ministers representing various political perspectives and sectoral interests. One may reasonably ask whether the Communist or Nationalist opposition would be as inclusive if they gained control of the presidency.

The increasing importance of regional and local government in Russia has also mitigated the winner-take-all consequences of presidential elections. As the central state has grown weaker, the governments of subject territories have assumed greater political authority. Through patronage powers and the postponement of local elections, Yeltsin has sought to rein in opposition elites in the provinces. But many local authorities continue to pursue policies that are directly at odds with the president's reform course.[65] If radical reformers can look to the experiments in Nizhny Novgorod for encouragement, Communists and Agrarians find comfort in the old regime politics characteristic of the 'red belt' regions south of Moscow.[66] The danger, of course, is that such regions will develop into 'reserved domains of undemocratic power'.

A second potential weakness of presidentialism arises from the rigidity of the fixed term of office for the president. Electing presidents at regular intervals—every four years in Russia, beginning in 1996—denies the voters an opportunity to remove executives who have lost the confidence of the nation, a not unlikely occurrence in a period of transition. As recent Russian history has already vividly demonstrated, resorting to impeachment to remove a president is likely to provoke a regime crisis. The death in office of the president would also destabilize the regime, quite unlike the loss of a prime minister in a

---

[65] See, for example, Michael Specter, 'Red Flag Aloft, a Russian City Defiantly Upholds Soviet Ways,' *New York Times*, 3 Feb. 1996, 1, 4.

[66] See Elizabeth Teague, 'Russia's Local Elections Begin,' *RFE/RL Research Report*, Feb. 1994, 1–4.

parliamentary system. In the event of the president's resignation, incapacity, or death, the Constitution of the Second Russian Republic transfers power to the prime minister and prescribes that a presidential election be held within three months. With a new state machinery traumatized by the loss of the leader, the nation would immediately be plunged into a divisive electoral campaign, or perhaps a Soviet-style succession crisis. One can only imagine the chaos that would ensue if Yeltsin died at the beginning of his second term, leaving Prime Minister Chernomyrdin to battle for executive supremacy with General Alexander Lebed, the recently appointed chief of the presidential Security Council.

Even during leadership successions determined by regularly-scheduled elections, presidentialism poses a threat by granting 'outsiders' immediate access to the country's most powerful institution.[67] Absent are the many filters built into recruitment of a prime minister in parliamentary regimes. To be sure, the election of an outsider may accelerate the dismantling of undemocratic rules and structures, especially in a country in transition from communism. It was Boris Yeltsin who campaigned successfully as an outsider against the party establishment in the Russian presidential election of June 1991. But the strong showing of Vladimir Zhirinovsky in December 1993 and 1995 reminds us that, in an era of crisis and video politics, extremist politicians may rise to power on a wave of popular frustration. A candidate able to win the votes of an alienated and uncertain electorate often lacks the skills to shape and sustain a governing consensus. In short, direct presidential elections in a weak party system are likely to bring to office unaccommodating elites.

Whence will come the new elites in government and parliament? In a parliamentary system, they would rise within the legislature itself on the basis of longevity, party loyalty, and competence. Presidentialism advances a more diverse elite more rapidly. In Russia, the new elite is emerging from the ranks of regional governors, army officers, academics, deputies, entrepreneurs, and industrialists.[68] Instead of party loyalty, personal loyalty promotes these careers. This combination of diverse personal loyalties and diverse *formations professionelles* will almost certainly complicate efforts at elite accommodation in Russian politics.

To this point we have focused on the challenges associated with all varieties of presidentialism. But semi-presidentialism contains an added danger that is often overlooked in the comparative literature: the politics of the dual executive. The logic of semi-presidentialism in the Second Russian Republic suggests that the president's ability to hire and fire the prime minister will ensure the cooperation of presidency and government. Such is not the case. Yeltsin has frequently chosen to rule around rather than through the government.[69]

The presence of presidential and prime ministerial management teams above the ministries has confused lines of authority within the executive and encouraged ministries to play

---

[67] This argument is developed in Juan Linz, 'Presidential or Parliamentary Democracy: Does It Make a Difference?' in *The Failure of Presidential Democracy*, 26–7.

[68] On the new Russian elite, see the research of the Russian sociologist, O.V. Kryshtanovskaya, discussed in Oleg Dmitriev, 'Staraya nomenklatura i novaya elita,' *Rossliskie vesti*, 3 June 1994, 2; see also, Irina Savvateeva, 'O tekh, kto nami pravit,' *Izvestiya*, 18 May 1994, 2.

[69] See Eugene Huskey, 'The State-Legal Administration and the Politics of Redundancy,' *Post-Soviet Affairs*, 2 (1995): 115–43.

the head of state and head of government against each other.[70] All too often, the result has been confusion and self-destructive competition, which is especially dangerous in Russia, where the ministries have a legitimacy that predates the democratic legitimacies of president and assembly. According to Yegor Gaidar, 'our ministries consider themselves first representatives of their own sphere of activity in the highest leadership of the country, and the interests of these spheres is very sharply divided.'[71] Because of this, the greatest peril facing Russia is not authoritarianism but warlordism, whether regional or departmental.[72] The transition regime in Russia is therefore struggling to modernize—or rationalize—executive authority as well as to democratize.[73] In this vital project of modernization, the dual executive implicit in semi-presidentialism retards efforts to impose discipline and a sense of collective responsibility on the ministries, which are the building blocks of state power.

In the 1996 elections, Russia retained a leader possessing super-presidential powers in a semi-presidential system of government. But the president's staggering institutional resources and formal powers offered the mere illusion of political strength. Although Yeltsin has exhibited occasional bursts of energy as leader, most notably during the election campaign itself, daily politics has remained the province of 'an oligarchy . . . of rival chief administrators, who [are] united by no common political opinion and therefore [are] in continual opposition to one another.'[74] The words are those of V. I. Gurko, an official in the Ministry of the Interior during the reign of Tsar Nicholas II. His subject: the collapse of the autocracy at the end of Imperial Russia. Post-Soviet Russia falls short of classic delegative democracy, where a vigorous central figure imposes his will on the state and society. Yeltsin is no Fujimori.

[70] Former Minister of Justice Yury Kalmykov complained that 'the presidential administration is a kind of Politburo, which supervises the government and interferes in government affairs.' 'Kalmykov Explains Decision to Resign,' Russian Television News, 1100 GMT, 9 Dec. 1994, as translated in *Foreign Broadcast Information Service*, 9 Dec. 1994, 12. The difference is that the Politburo imposed a measure of discipline on the government that is not matched by the Russian presidency.

[71] 'U nas net bolee vazhnoi problemy nezheli dogovoritsya o pravlilakh igry,' *Posev*, 5 (1995): 7–17. This is in interview with Gaidar.

[72] See Vera Tolz, 'Problems in Building Democratic Institutions in Russia,' *RFE/RL Research Report*, 4 Mar. 1994, 1–7, and Peter J. Stavrakis, 'State Building in Post-Soviet Russia: The Chicago Boys and the Decline of Administrative Capacity,' *Occasional Paper #254*, Kennan Institute for Advanced Russian Studies, especially 18–22 on 'ministerial feudalism.'

[73] I use the term modernization in the sense outlined by Samuel Huntington in his seminal article on the rise of modern politics in the West, 'Political Modernization: American vs. Europe,' *World Politics*, 3 (1966): 378–414.

[74] Quoted in Tim McDaniel, *Autocracy, Modernization, and Revolution in Russia and Iran* (Princeton: Princeton University Press, 1991), 54.

The Presidency and Political Leadership

Introduction

Archie Brown

Leaders in Russia have long done much to set the tone of political life and, historically, they have enjoyed enormous power. Compared with the powers of a Tsar or a Stalin, Boris Yeltsin's powers were relatively modest. Yet the Constitution which was hurriedly written in 1993 put the president in a strong position on paper and made it very difficult to remove him. Thus, even though by late 1999 the percentage of the population expressing confidence in Yeltsin had dropped to single digits, his resignation from the presidency on the last day of that year was not forced on him. He could have continued to occupy the Kremlin until the scheduled June 2000 date of the election. His decision to go early and to maximize the advantage of his chosen successor, Vladimir Putin, in a presidential election brought forward to March 2000 was essentially of his own volition. More precisely, there may have been influence on Yeltsin from within his trusted inner circle—or 'the Family', as it became known—to depart at this advantageous moment and catch his opponents off-balance, but neither public nor parliamentary opinion forced him to do it.

Yeltsin's particular style of rule, in combination with his declining health, meant that the powers he exercised on a day-to-day basis were less extensive than they might have appeared constitutionally. Which decrees were signed depended on the changing fortunes of a large body of courtiers. When Yeltsin chose to take an interest in a question (as he tended to do where personnel decisions or matters affecting the power ministries were concerned), he could unquestionably impose his will. Yet the notion of a 'super-presidential' system hardly tallies with the power struggles in the Kremlin in which groups and factions within the administration fought for supremacy while Yeltsin played a relatively passive role in most areas of policy-making. The extent to which Vladimir Putin, in his first year, was to succeed in imposing his will—in a number of areas, especially in relations with regional governors, where Yeltsin had preferred to do deals—indicated the extent to which there was a gap between the image of a 'strong President' which Yeltsin projected (and *headstrong* he certainly *was*) and the reality.

Russia has a dual executive—with a prime minister at the head of the government as well as a president and large presidential administrative apparatus. While the prime minister is in day-to-day charge of much policy-making, especially in the economic sphere, both constitutionally and in practice the president enjoys a higher authority. It is he who appoints the prime minister and who can dismiss him (or her, though no woman has, in fact, come close to being nominated). Although the appointment of a new prime minister requires the endorsement of the State Duma, the fact that the president also has the power to dissolve the Duma and call fresh elections, makes the lower house of the legislature reluctant to defy the president too often—even in Yeltsin's case where his relations with the Duma were often fractious—since, potentially, they have much to lose. Putin has so far enjoyed greater support within the Duma than Yeltsin had at any time since the formation of that legislative organ with the adoption of a new Constitution in December 1993.

The longest-serving of Yeltsin's prime ministers was Viktor Chernomyrdin who, like Yeltsin, emerged from the heart of the Soviet establishment. Yeltsin had been a regional party secretary and later a Secretary of the Central Committee of the Communist Party before becoming First Secretary of the Moscow Party organization. Chernomyrdin had a technocratic-party career, moving between the apparatus of the Central Committee of the party and ministerial posts. From 1985 until 1989 he was minister of the oil and gas industry of the USSR. In post-Soviet Russia he became the patron and, on his removal from office, the president of the world's largest gas company, Gazprom. Chernomyrdin was, however, a compromise choice of prime minister for Yeltsin, being appointed at the end of 1992 when the more radically reformist Yegor Gaidar was unacceptable to the Russian legislature. Although Chernomyrdin went on to serve Yeltsin loyally until his sudden dismissal in March 1998, Yeltsin was suspicious of what he believed to be Chernomyrdin's ambitions to succeed to the presidency. Following Chernomyrdin's abrupt removal, Yeltsin appointed and dismissed prime ministers with almost bewildering speed, making them scapegoats for economic failure. More paradoxically, they could also be punished for success. When Yevgeny Primakov, another compromise choice as prime minister in September 1998, in succession to Sergei Kirienko, succeeded in restoring a measure of economic stabilization and political calm, following an acute financial crisis in August of that year, he, too, was dismissed—at a time when, according to the opinion polls, he was Russia's most popular politician. Since, however, he was far from being Yeltsin's choice to succeed him, that, too, turned out to constitute grounds for dismissal.

The first two contributions in this section were written at the end of the Yeltsin era, but while the first elected Russian president was still in office. John Dunlop provides a broad-ranging survey of the Yeltsin years, emphasizing the low priority he gave to establishment of a rule of law and documenting declining public support for him. He notes also, however, the preservation of glasnost and political pluralism throughout the 1990s. George Breslauer analyses Yeltsin's style of rule which he sees as having been highly personalistic and patriarchal. He draws attention also to how his style evolved over time, as he relied increasingly on a small group of advisers, prizing loyalty to him above all other political virtues. Some of the most prominent of those who served in the presidential administration in the 1990s used the figures of speech of 'tsar' and 'court' to describe its ambience. Yeltsin himself was by no means averse to the former analogy.

Eugene Huskey, in a contribution first published here, examines the career of Vladimir Putin and the institutions which moulded him. He analyses both Putin's political inheritance and the institutional reforms and other political initiatives he has undertaken during his first year in the Russian presidency. There can be little doubt about Putin's determination to re-establish strong central state power and Huskey explains how he has asserted himself vis-à-vis both regional elites and sections of the financial elite. The new Russian president has already shown himself to be a coalition-builder, establishing working relationships with people from very different parts of the political spectrum. Whether, however, his professed commitment to 'reform' embraces also an appreciation of the necessary role to be played by a legitimate opposition remains, as Huskey suggests, an open question.

4   Sifting through the Rubble of the Yeltsin Years

John B. Dunlop

....

The question of what has gone wrong during the Yeltsin years, and why, is an almost bottomless topic. So many things have gone wrong since August 1991, the date of the failed coup against Gorbachev, and late 1999 that a full accounting would require a windy, thousand-page opus. It is obviously much easier to describe the few things that have gone right, or somewhat right, during the Yeltsin years. But first, this article examines what went wrong between August 1991 and December 1994, when the Yeltsin leadership made a foolhardy decision to invade Chechnya.

From Gorbachev to Grozny

THE AUGUST PUTSCH

There is a direct connection between the failed August 1991 coup and the Belovezh Forest agreements of early December 1991, which effected the formal breakup of the Soviet Union. Yeltsin was exaggerating, but not all that much, when he wrote, in his second volume of memoirs, that 'after August 19 [1991], the Union disappeared all by itself; it was gone in a day.'[1] The defeat of the putsch served to handcuff the KGB, the military, the Communist Party of the Soviet Union (CPSU), and the ruling institutions of the state, thus making it possible for the Soviet Union to fragment into fifteen separate states in less than four months.[2]

After the arrest of the leading plotters and several investigations into the putsch, five KGB generals (including General Vladimir Kriuchkov) found themselves in prison, while twenty-nine top-ranking officers were summarily sacked and thirteen others were officially admonished. The KGB had been 'decapitated.' In similar fashion, Defense Minister Dmitrii Yazov and another top general, Valentin Varennikov, found themselves in prison, while eight deputy defense ministers, nine chiefs of main or central administrations, and seven commanders of military districts of the army and navy were sacked. The Defense Ministry, too, had been 'beheaded.'

This chapter was first published in *Problems of Post-Communism*, 47/1 (2000), 3–15. Reproduced (with minor abbreviations) by kind permission of the author and M. E. Sharpe, Inc., NY.

[1] Boris Yeltsin, *The Struggle for Russia* (New York: Random House, 1994), 38. It was announced that three new volumes of Yeltsin memoirs—one of them to be devoted entirely to the Russo-Chechen crisis and war—were to have been published during 1999.

[2] For a detailed analysis of this process, see my essay 'The August coup and Its Impact on Soviet Politics,' in *The Collapse of the Soviet Union*, ed. Mark Kramer (Boulder, Colo: Westview Press, forthcoming).

The CPSU likewise found itself deeply compromised by the attempted putsch. A majority of the Secretariat of the Central Committee and most local Party organs had supported the coup, as had the Central Committee itself, as well as two-thirds of the regional Party organizations. Support for the coup among Soviet state structures was nearly as clear-cut as in the CPSU. Only one member of the cabinet, Environment Minister Nikolai Vorontsov, a non-communist, had declined to support the putsch, and only one Soviet ambassador, Boris Pankin, had come out in opposition to it. The USSR Supreme Soviet neglected to take any action during the coup attempt, while more than 70 percent of local soviets actively supported it. To sum up, the Communist Party, the institutions of the Soviet state, the KGB, and the Defense Ministry found themselves fully compromised by their support for and collaboration with the State Committee for the State of Emergency (GKChP), while the USSR found itself in a vastly weakened position vis-à-vis the union republics. The Soviet Union broke apart in a mere four months, and Russia found itself an independent state.

A REVOLUTION?

In October 1991, Professor V. Danilenko asserted in *Izvestiia* that the aftermath of the August putsch constituted what could with terminological precision be called a revolution. 'When people speak of the August events,' he wrote, 'the emphasis is most often placed on the blitz-coup [of August 19–21] and its collapse. . . . But there is another event—a blitz-revolution—for which the coup served as a detonator. . . . It is precisely this revolution that will, with time, become the main object of researchers' attention.'[3] This revolution, Danilenko noted, occurred after a direct clash between two powerful political forces striving for complete dominance. One of these forces he identified as 'the *nomenklatura*-bureaucratic *apparat* of the CPSU.' The other was the 'democrats,' whose political program he summarized thus: 'in politics—ideological pluralism, a multiparty system, and real freedom of the individual, in economics—market relations, a multi-tiered economy, private property, and freedom of enterprise.' The triumph of the 'democrats' over the Party *nomenklatura* had produced, as Danilenko saw it, a tidal wave, of change that might accurately be termed a revolution. During the period of post-putsch euphoria, it looked to many Russians and Westerners alike as if Russia had a realistic chance to transform itself into a 'normal, civilized country.' But that expectation turned out to be unrealistic.

In the months after the putsch, Yeltsin and his allies committed serious political and tactical errors that put their new 'revolution' at risk. In his second volume of memoirs, *The Struggle for Russia*, Yeltsin confides: '*I believe the most important opportunity missed after the coup was the radical restructuring of the parliamentary system*. . . . *The idea of dissolving the Congress and scheduling new elections was in the air (as well as a constitution for the new country)*, although we did not take advantage of it' [emphasis added]. And Yeltsin concludes: 'Maybe I was in fact mistaken in choosing an attack on the economic front as the chief direction, leaving government reorganization to perpetual compromises and political games. I did not disperse the Congress and left the soviets intact. Out of inertia, I continued to perceive the Supreme Soviet as a legislative body that was developing the legal basis for reform.'[4]

---

[3] *Izvestiia* (9 Oct. 1991): 3.   [4] Yeltsin, *Struggle for Russia*, 126–7.

NEAR-FATAL MISTAKES

Yeltsin's terse and somewhat grudging comments point to what in hindsight seem critical, indeed almost fatal, mistakes committed by him and his team. Gorbachev had earlier grafted a strong executive presidency onto a two-tier standing parliament consisting of the USSR Supreme Soviet and the 1,033-member Congress of People's Deputies. The Russian Soviet Federated Socialist Republic (RSFSR) had adopted the same cumbersome model. The jerry-built Russian state structure of December 1991 was anchored in an outmoded and self-contradictory Fundamental Law. As Richard Sakwa has commented:

There remained a fundamental 'constitutional' crisis because the 1978 Russian Constitution, a slightly modified version of the Soviet Constitution of 1977, was heavily amended but *in the absence of a new Constitution the balance between executive and legislative remained a matter of political struggle rather than constitutional law.* . . . Parliament itself enjoyed extensive powers under the existing [Soviet-era] Constitution and, dominated by conservative groups, was able to block the executive's ideas about constitutional reform and to undermine the government's [economic] reform program [emphasis added].[5]

As Sakwa rightly emphasizes, a sharp political struggle between the Russian presidency and parliament was highly likely given the self-contradictory 1978 RSFSR constitution. The conflict burst into the open during the Sixth Congress of People's Deputies, held from April 6 to 21, 1992. The Congress thwarted Yeltsin's aim of obtaining a new constitution, placed onerous controls on economic reform, and severely restricted the purchase and sale of land. Moreover, in July 1992, the Supreme Soviet effectively took control of the Russian Central Bank.

By March 1993, the Congress of People's Deputies, using its power to amend the constitution, had introduced 320 changes in the country's Basic Law, aimed at strengthening the Congress and weakening the presidency. Had the presidency and the parliament been controlled by persons of roughly compatible viewpoints, a political compromise might have been possible, and a new, internally consistent constitution crafted. But such was not the case.

Referring to the tactical mistakes made by Yeltsin during this period, Marshall Goldman has observed:

In the aftermath of his resistance to the August coup attempt, [Yeltsin] could have done almost anything he wanted to. Instead, he allowed the enthusiasm of the moment to dissipate. . . . In retrospect it appears he also lost the chance to promulgate a Constitution that in August 1991 could have provided him with the power he needed to carry out reforms. . . . [The August putsch] did serve to discredit those in the Party and leadership who opposed the reforms. However, taking advantage of Yeltsin's inaction, the Russian bureaucracy rallied and, under the crafty leadership of Ruslan Khasbulatov, began to thwart most of Yeltsin's subsequent reform issues.[6]

Realizing that the slipshod 1978 RSFSR constitution offered him zero chance of a political

---

[5] Richard Sakwa, *Russian Politics and Society* (London: Routledge, 1993), 56.
[6] Marshall I. Goldman, *Lost Opportunity: Why Economic Reforms in Russia Have Not Worked* (New York: Norton, 1994), 201.

solution, Yeltsin ought to have reached out to the Russian public—who, the polls showed, supported him at that time by a large majority—and held elections to a new parliament followed by a referendum on a new constitution. If successful, these steps could have averted the bloody tragedy of October 1993, and perhaps even prevented the emergence of a resurrected Communist Party in December 1992. These developments, in turn, might have rendered Yeltsin's ominous 'shift to the right' in early 1994 less likely.

DVOEVLASTIE

Russia's political crisis from early December 1992 through early October 1993 is an almost textbook case of what Russians call *dvoevlastie* ('dyarchy,' or dual power). For Russians, the term hearkens back to two of the severest trials in their country's history: the excruciating 'Time of Troubles' (1598–1613), during which Russia's survival as a state was in question, and the great crisis of 1917, in which the post-imperial Provisional Government was confronted by the Petrograd and Moscow soviets. That crisis culminated in the Bolshevik seizure of power on October 25 (Old Style), but was resolved only by the civil war of 1918–22.

The *dvoevlastie* crisis, too, nearly ended in civil war.[7] The Seventh Congress of Russian People's Deputies, held from December 1 to 14, 1992, initiated the crisis. Just before the Congress began, the Russian Constitutional Court (which under its ambitious and unscrupulous chair, Valentin Zorkin, had openly begun to side with the Khasbulatov forces) ruled that Yeltsin's decrees of August and November 1991 had been neither fully consti-tutional nor fully unconstitutional. These edicts had first suspended and then banned the Communist Party of the Soviet Union and the Russian Communist Party and nationalized their buildings and bank accounts. The Communist Party, the court ruled, had a legal right to reestablish local branches, that is, to rebuild itself 'from the bottom up. ' Communist deputies entered the Seventh Congress with an understandable sense of political momentum and impending victory over the executive branch.

IMPEACHMENT REARS ITS HEAD

On the first day of the December 1992 Congress, a secret-police employee from Irkutsk Oblast, Ivan Fedoseev, offered a motion that the Constitutional Court be asked to rule on whether Yeltsin should be removed from office for numerous infringements of the constitu-tion. The motion failed, but the issue of impeaching the president would remain front and center for the next ten months (and, with intermittent gaps, for the next seven years). A motion demanding for the Congress the power to confirm and to remove the prime minis-ter, the deputy prime ministers, and the ministers of finance, economics, foreign affairs, defense, security, and internal affairs narrowly failed. In a secret ballot, 690 Congress deputies voted for the motion, four short of the number needed for passage.

A constitutional coup was thus narrowly averted. Yeltsin stormed out of the hall in disgust, taking approximately 120 deputies with him, but not, significantly, his own 'power ministers,' who remained behind to testify. Under an agreement brokered by Zorkin, Yeltsin was forced to replace Egor Gaidar, his acting prime minister, with a compromise 'centrist' candidate, Viktor Chernomyrdin.

---

[7] The account that follows is a condensed version of the narrative in the 'postscript' section of the expanded, paperback edition of my book, *The Rise of Russia and the Fall of the Soviet Empire* (Princeton: Princeton University Press, 1995), 303–26.

By the end of the Seventh Congress, it had become clear that Russia was fully mired in *dvoevlastie*. The four-day Extraordinary Congress of People's Deputies, held from March 10 to 13, 1993, deepened the crisis. This Congress annulled the compromise agreement that had been reached at the Seventh Congress and stripped Yeltsin of the emergency powers that the Fifth Congress had granted him in November 1991. Henceforth the president would not have the right to issue decrees having equal force with laws adopted by parliament. On March 13, the Congress cancelled Yeltsin's proposed referendum to ask voters whether they desired Russia to become a presidential republic and whether they favored private ownership of land. (The 'Democratic Russia' organization had collected 2.5 million signatures in support of holding a referendum on the second question. Obviously, if the voters had backed the question, it would have accelerated agricultural reform.)

ON THE BRINK

The Ninth Extraordinary Congress of People's Deputies, held from March 26 to 29, 1993, saw the country perched on the brink of civil war. The crisis had been precipitated on March 20, when Yeltsin announced on national television that he had signed a decree enacting 'special rule.' The Supreme Soviet convened immediately to discuss impeachment, and two days later the Constitutional Court ruled that Yeltsin's decree violated the constitution. Yeltsin was then flagrantly betrayed by two key figures, Vice President Aleksandr Rutskoi and Security Council secretary Iurii Skokov, who, after verbally indicating that they favored special rule, refused to initial a document instituting it. Defense Minister Pavel Grachev warned that the military might be drawn into the crisis. The key moment occurred when, in a secret ballot, 617 deputies voted for Yeltsin's impeachment, seventy-two short of the 689 votes required for the initiative to pass.

As this dreadful spasm of *dvoevlastie* showed, the Russian president and his supporters were desperately seeking a way to reach over the heads of a retrograde parliament to the electorate, which, as numerous surveys of public opinion showed, strongly backed Yeltsin over parliament. After narrowly avoiding impeachment at the Ninth Congress, Yeltsin managed to schedule a referendum for April 25, 1993. In the referendum, 58 percent of those casting ballots expressed confidence in Yeltsin, and 53 percent expressed confidence in his government's socio-economic policies. More than two-thirds were in favor of holding early elections for a new parliament, while slightly less than half supported early presidential elections.[8] Had the members of parliament been interested in the views of the electorate they claimed to represent, they would have altered their course and begun to work constructively with the president.

The entire *dvoevlastie* conflict points to the severe deficiencies in the Russian political culture of the immediate post-communist period. The parliament (and especially its chair), the vice-president, and the chair of the Constitutional Court appeared to have had no concept of their appropriate roles under a democracy. For each of them a naked struggle for political power became paramount and all-consuming.

---

[8] According to election specialists A. A. Sobianin and V. G. Sukhopolskii, virtually all of the falsification of ballots during the April 1993 referendum was directed against Yeltsin. See their study *Demokratiia, orgrachinennaia falsifikatsiiami* (Democracy Limited by Falsification) (Moscow: Proektnaia gruppa po pravam cheloveka, 1995), 111–12.

'CIVIL WAR'

The fourteen-day political crisis of September–October 1993 culminated in the bloody 'October events,' as they have come to be known in Russia. During the armed coup attempt on the night of October 3–4, 145 persons were killed and 733 were wounded. The clash was triggered on the evening of September 21, when Yeltsin issued Presidential Decree No. 1400, which dissolved both the Congress of People's Deputies and the Supreme Soviet and called new parliamentary elections for December 12. This action was a direct analogue to his attempt of March 20, which had come perilously close to pitching the country into civil war. The president apparently believed that he had no choice other than to launch a preemptive strike. The Supreme Soviet, led by Ruslan Khasbulatov, had drafted amendments to the constitution and the Criminal Code that were to be brought before the Tenth Congress, scheduled for November 1993. These amendments were designed to reduce Yeltsin's power radically, transforming him into a ceremonial head of state. The amendments to the Criminal Code would, in addition, have imposed criminal penalties for refusal to comply with parliamentary decisions.

On September 22, the Supreme Soviet made Vice President Rutskoi acting president of Russia. A motion offered by hard-line deputy Sergei Baburin instituted the death penalty for persons attempting to change Russia's political system by force. This action threatened Yeltsin and his entourage with possible execution. The Constitutional Court, predictably, announced that it had ruled Yeltsin's decree to be not in accord with the constitution, thereby offering grounds for removing him from office. 'Acting President' Rutskoi then named an acting defense minister and an acting security minister.

Rutskoi assembled a force consisting of three battalions of Moscow reservists, mainly officers, about one hundred *spetsnaz* (special forces) soldiers from the Dniester battalion in the breakaway Trans-Dniester Republic, former police operatives of the Riga OMON, a volunteer detachment of Cossacks, representatives of ultra-left communist youth groups from Ukraine, and a unit of well-trained neo-Nazi 'storm troopers' headed by their führer, Aleksandr Barkashov.

In the early afternoon of October 3, mass rallies were organized by two skillful demagogues backing Rutskoi. Shortly after 3:00 p.m., the combined crowd, estimated at between 5,000 and 10,000, broke through a heavy police cordon and swarmed up to the Russian White House.

'WE HAVE WON!'

At about 3:30 p.m. Rutskoi, apparently convinced that the crowd represented the first fruits of a long-awaited popular uprising against Yeltsin and the government, came out on a balcony of the parliament building and shouted: 'We have won!. Thank you dear Muscovites! ... Now form up detachments and take the mayor's office, then on to Ostankino [the large television complex]!'[9] Also standing on a balcony of the Russian White House, Khasbulatov exhorted the crowd: 'I call on our glorious soldiers to seize tanks and take the Kremlin by storm.'[10] At 5:00 p.m. on October 3, the military and the Security

---

[9] Cited in Veronika Kutsyllo, *Zapiski iz Belogo Doma, 21 sentiabria–4 oktiabria 1993* (Notes from the White House: 21 Sept.–4 Oct. 1993) (Moscow: Kommersant, 1993), 114.

[10] Cited in 'Mass Misjudgment,' *Economist* (9 Oct. 1993): 57.

Ministry were openly pursuing a policy of 'neutrality' in the conflict, while the Ministry of Internal Affairs (MVD) had fallen back in confusion and disarray.

On the night of October 3–4, the rebels took or attempted to take some key installations in Moscow. But the momentum soon shifted. The Russian White House was successfully assaulted on October 4 by forces loyal to Yeltsin, and the rebellion was crushed. Although his victory had been of the narrowest possible kind, Yeltsin found himself suddenly catapulted, as he had been on August 21, into a uniquely advantageous position.

Having achieved a harrowing victory over the 'rebels,' Yeltsin felt vulnerable and distrustful of the military and the secret police, both of which had seemingly been looking out for their own interests rather than his. It is clear, in retrospect, that Yeltsin was deeply traumatized by the rebellion. In fact, he appears never to have recovered psychologically or spiritually from the shock caused by the October events. They served, unquestionably, to make him a harsher and more brutal ruler. Personal survival and the well-being of himself and his family became his overriding concern. According to General Korzhakov, Yeltsin confided to him at the time: 'I don't trust anyone but you, Aleksandr Vasilevich. I want you to create a small KGB. My own personal mini-KGB.'[11] On November 11, 1993, Korzhakov did just that, and this 'mini-KGB' played a major role in preparing the way for the invasion of Chechnya one year later.

THE DECEMBER 1993 REFERENDUM AND ELECTIONS

For Yeltsin and his entourage, the crisis of October was almost immediately followed by another crisis in December. On December 12, Russian voters were asked to go to the polls to ratify the draft of a new constitution embodying a 'Gaullist' strong presidency and elect deputies to a new parliament. The officially reported results of this vote have come to be viewed as a setback for the president and for moderates. True, Yeltsin did coax the required 50 percent of eligible voters to come to the polls, and a majority cast ballots for the new constitution. But the announced composition of the new State Duma was disappointing.

In the voting for the 225 Duma seats reserved for party-list candidates, the four democratic parties running had managed to accumulate only 34 percent of the vote, while the Communists and Agrarians had received 20 percent combined. Even more shocking, 23 percent of the party-list vote had gone to the neo-fascist demagogue Vladimir Zhirinovskii. (When party-preference and single-mandate votes were combined, Egor Gaidar's 'Russia's Choice' emerged as the largest Duma faction with 103 seats, but Zhirinovskii's came in second with sixty-six, followed by the Communists with sixty-two, and the Agrarians with forty-nine. The other two democratic factions that cleared the 5 percent barrier held a total of fifty-seven seats.)[12] Clearly this would not be an easy parliament for any reform-minded government to work with.

[11] In Aleksandr Korzhakov, *Boris Yeltsin: ot rassveta do zakata* (Boris Yeltsin: From Sunrise to Sunset) (Moscow: Interbuk, 1997), 404.

[12] On the elections, see Michael McFaul, *Understanding Russia's 1993 Parliamentary Elections* (Stanford, Calif: Hoover Institution Essays in Public Policy, 1994); A. B. Zubov and V. A. Kolosov, 'Chto ishchet Rossiia?' (What Is Russia Searching For?), *POLIS*, 1 (1994): 93–112.

FALSIFICATION?

On the face of it, the voters had expressed skepticism about the course of economic and political reform being advocated by the moderates and 'democrats.' But were the reported results accurate? A Russian specialist on elections, A. A. Sobianin, and a leading journalist, Kronid Liubarskii, have argued that massive falsification took place in the reporting of the results of both the December constitutional referendum and the Duma vote. While much of the evidence to support their claim was apparently destroyed by local election officials, strong circumstantial evidence remains to support their charges. They argue:

The president and the government were very interested in the rapid adoption of a new constitution and the formation of a new parliament. . . . However, the organization and conducting, in a compressed period of time, with the ensuring of the necessary turnout of voters, was—as was completely clear at the time—absolutely impossible without the help of the organs of power of the 'subjects' of the federation, and, first of all, of their executives, that is, of the local heads of administration. It was very important to interest them *personally* in a successful conducting of the elections.

'Such interest,' Sobianin and Liubarskii concluded, 'was found in the announcement of the election of the first membership of the Council of the Federation.'[13] In other words, Yeltsin and his entourage entered into a Faustian bargain with the regional heads of administration. Those officials would guarantee the required 50 percent turnout for the vote on the new constitution so that it would be adopted (this turned out to be no problem). In return, the heads of administration would be given a free hand to rig the election results not only in favor of their own election to the new Council of the Federation, but also in favor of the Duma party lists that they personally supported. The composition of the State Duma by Sobianin and Liubarskii's count is shown in Table 4.1.

Table 4.1 **Composition of the State Duma according to Sobianin and Liubarskii**

Party	Seats		
	Earned	Awarded	Difference
Russia's Choice	58	40	−18
Liberal Democrats	36	59	+23
Communists	28	32	+4
Agrarians	14	21	+7

Source: Kronid Liubarskii and Aleksandr Sobianin, 'Fal'sifikatsiia-3' (Falsification-3), *Novoe vremia*, 15 (1995): 10.

[13] Kronid Liubarskii and Aleksandr Sobianin, 'Fal'sifikatsiia-3' (Falsification-3), *Novae vremia*, 15 (1995): 10. Sobianin's findings concerning the 1993 elections and referendum are strongly supported in *Politicheskii almanakh Rossii, 1989–1997* (Political Almanac of Russia, 1989–1997), vol. 1, ed. Michael McFaul and Nikolai Petrov (Moscow: Carnegie Center, 1998), 178–9, 320–4.

'In all,' they believe, 'the "reformers" would then have received ninety-three mandates on the party lists against seventy-eight for the Liberal Democrats, Communists, and Agrarians (not the reported sixty versus 112), and the whole history of the Fifth State Duma would have been completely different.' As a result of the falsified official results, they conclude, '"*political" if not electoral Russia began indeed to move to the right, a process culminating at the end of 1994 in the Chechen catastrophe*' [emphasis added].[14] Interestingly, Viacheslav Kostikov, Yeltsin's press secretary until early 1995, believes that as many as 8 million votes for the State Duma in December 1993 may have been 'falsified.'[15] Sobianin and Liubarskii, for their part, think that the figure is nearer 9–11 million.

And what about the December 1993 referendum on the 'Yeltsin constitution'? In the opinion of Sobianin and another specialist on elections, V. G. Sukhopolskii, Yeltsin did not actually attract the necessary 50 percent of eligible voters. 'According to our calculations,' they write, 'in all there took part in the elections of December 12, 49 million out of 106.2 [million] registered voters, or 46.1 percent [of the total].'[16] 'These figures,' analyst Valerii Vyzhutovich commented on the pages of *Izvestiia*, 'are political dynamite. Because if only 46.1 percent of the electorate participated in the vote, then *the Constitution was not adopted*.'[17] However, the Russian public appears to have soon adjusted to the presence of this smoking gun and then forgotten about it.

If the December 1993 voting results had been accurately tabulated and correctly reported, then a new parliament with a strong democratic representation could have been put in place. Such a parliament could have worked with President Yeltsin and his administration to draft a new constitution that would, predictably, have granted less-sweeping powers to the president and more real power to the parliament. That, in turn, might have helped to prevent the Chechen debacle of 1994–96, inasmuch as Yeltsin largely ignored the views of a constitutionally weak parliament in launching and prosecuting the war.[18]

Over the course of 1994, according to Kostikov, Yeltsin became increasingly isolated from the moderates in his entourage and from Russian 'democrats' in general. During this period, 'Yeltsin manifestly distanced himself from the democratic parties' and thus had 'no one to lean upon for support.'[19] One of the chief priorities of the emerging 'party of war,' whose central figure was Korzhakov, was to isolate the president from political moderates. As Sergei Yushenkov, a retired military officer and the chair of the 1993–95 Duma defense committee, has put it: 'The closest aides to Yeltsin succeeded in isolating their patron first from meetings with democratic society and then from meetings with its representatives, and finally from those leaders of the democratic movement with whom he had previously maintained constant contact. There took place the *isolation* of Yeltsin from sources of objective information.

[14] Liubatskii and Sobianin, 'Fal'sifikatsiia-3,' 11–12.

[15] Viacheslav Kostikov, *Roman s presidentom: Zapiski press-sekretaria* (Romance with the President: Notes from the Press Secretary) (Moscow: Vagrius, 1997), 268.

[16] Sobianin and Sukhopolskii, *Demokratiia, orgrachinennaia fal'sifikatsiiami*, p. 98.

[17] *Izvestiia* (4 May 1994).

[18] On this, see V. Kurochkin, *Missiia v Chechne* (Mission to Chechnya) (Moscow: Pomatur, 1997); and S. N. Yushenkov, *Voina v Chechne i problemy rossiiskoi gosudarstvennosti i demokratii* (The War in Chechnya and Problems of Russian Statehood and Democracy) (Moscow, 1995).

[19] Kostikov, *Roman s prezidentom*, 299–300.

He became a captive of illusions.'[20] Sergei Filatov, a political moderate serving as Yeltsin's chief of staff, and like-minded colleagues 'learned of important decisions or of cadre assignments from press agency reports.' The Presidential Council, an organization of leading intellectuals that had been advising Yeltsin, '*de facto* ceased to act.'[21]

The bacillus of imperialism

The benighted decision on December 11, 1994, to invade Chechnya—and the even more catastrophic New Year's Eve decision to assault its capital, Grozny—capped a growth in neo-imperialist sentiment that had been spreading among Russian elites since early 1993. Under acting Prime Minister Gaidar and Foreign Minister Andrei Kozyrev, the country had been relatively immune to the bacillus of imperialism, but Gaidar's firing in December 1992 set the stage for a return of traditional imperialist sentiment.

By the spring of 1993, as Shireen Hunter has noted, a 'Russian Monroe Doctrine was already emerging.'[22] The corollaries to this doctrine included the primacy of the 'near abroad' in Russian foreign policy, the necessity for Russian predominance in this region, a belief that it should remain an economic sphere of influence and a captive market for Russia's goods, and a conviction that the West should be firmly excluded from the Caspian region. Azerbaijan's signing of three landmark offshore oilfield deals, worth $8 billion, in September 1994 alarmed the neo-imperialists among Russian elites. The invasion of Chechnya was meant to intimidate the former Soviet republics of the Caspian region and to warn off the West and its oil companies.

Neo-imperial yearnings and moods persist in the Russian public, and in the spring of 1999 were aggravated by resentment against NATO for its relentless bombing of Yugoslavia over Kosovo. A 1999 survey reported that 85 percent of Russians regretted the dissolution of the Soviet Union, compared with 69 percent in 1992. In addition, 69 percent of those contacted by the poll said they were '*very* upset' about the dissolution of the Soviet Union, compared with 36 percent in 1992.[23] The foreign leader best liked by present-day Russians, another poll showed, was the authoritarian president of Belarus, Aliaksandr Lukashenka, with a 69 percent approval rating. Nursultan Nazarbaev of Kazakstan came in second with 55 percent.[24]

The rule of law and the soft state

Yeltsin's sinking popularity during the war with Chechnya made him vulnerable to manipulation by tycoon Boris Berezovskii and other oligarchs, who used the president's daughter, Tatiana Diachenko, as a helpful go-between. Their immense influence, in turn, exacerbated the already severe lack of a rule of law in Russia. A corrupt 'soft state' made its appearance during the first Yeltsin term. It plumbed new depths during his second term.

[20]   Yushenkov, *Voina v Chechne*, 13–14.
[21]   Kostikov, *Roman s prezidentom*, 323–5.
[22]   Shireen Hunter, *The Transcaucasus in Transition: Nation-Building and Conflict* (Washington: Center for Strategic and International Studies, 1994), 154.
[23]   Interfax (28 Jan. 1999). The poll was conducted by *Obshshestvennoe mnenie*.
[24]   USIA Opinion Analysis M-31–99 (23 Feb. 1999).

RUSSIA WITHOUT LIMITS

Russian commentators often use the term *bespredel* ('anarchy,' or a condition 'without limits') to describe the Yeltsin years. The unwillingness or inability to institute the basic rule of law represents, arguably, the single greatest failure of the Yeltsin presidency. (In fairness, this problem has beset all the republics of the former Soviet Union.) Despite boasting the formal trappings of a law-based state (a constitution, courts, and so on), the Soviet Union was a lawless state that kept its citizenry in check through a variety of 'sticks' (an intrusive official ideology manipulated by the Party apparatus, the KGB, a far-flung network of informers, etc.) but also with some 'carrots' (a poor but nonetheless real system of health care, paid vacations, etc.). As the late Leonard Schapiro once observed, in the Soviet Union 'there [was] no legal structure, because the law [was] purely an instrument in the hands of the ruling elite.'[25] Peter Solomon recently argued the same point: 'The legacy left by Soviet power to its successor states,' he writes, 'did not include legal order. . . . the standards required for a market economy were absent. A hierarchy of legal rules, open to scrutiny and enforceable, did not exist. . . . Courts were dependent upon the good graces of politicians.'[26]

Despite much talk about a law-based state in the post-communist period, the situation described by Schapiro and Solomon has continued, indeed perhaps worsened, in the Yeltsin years. One striking example should suffice: According to the memoirs of General Korzhakov, on December 1, 1994, ten days before the Russian invasion of Chechnya, Boris Yeltsin complained bitterly about media mogul and banking magnate Vladimir Gusinskii during a meal with Korzhakov and General Mikhail Barsukov, head of the Kremlin Guards: 'Why can't you take care of this Gusinskii person?! What is he up to? Everyone is complaining about him, including my family. How many times has it happened that Tatiana or Naina [Yeltsin's daughter and wife] is riding in a car and the road is closed off because of that Gusinskii? His NTV has cast aside all restraint and is behaving insolently. I order you: take care of him!'[27]

YELTSIN'S OPRICHNIKI

Statements by Korzhakov must be treated with caution, but in this instance Yeltsin's chief bodyguard may be reliable. Furthermore, Yeltsin has never disputed Korzhakov's version of these events. The following morning, December 2, armed men dressed in paramilitary gear but wearing no distinguishing badges arrived at Gusinskii's dacha outside Moscow. They belonged to a *spetsnaz* unit attached to the Presidential Security Service and headed by Korzhakov's assistant, Rear Admiral Gennadii Zakharov, who had earlier served abroad as a Soviet saboteur *(diversant)*.

The seven cars carrying Zakharov's heavily armed *spetsnaz* followed Gusinskii and his personal bodyguards as they drove from the dacha to the building in central Moscow that housed Gusinskii's MOST Bank and offices of the mayor, Iurii Luzhkov. As they drove into the city, Zakharov's men tried to get Gusinskii's guards to open fire, but the latter 'did not give in to the provocation.'[28] If they had, Gusinskii might have been killed in the shootout.

At around 5 p.m. that afternoon, Zakharov's heavily armed men, wearing ski masks,

---

[25] Ellen Dahrendorf, ed., *Russian Studies/Leonard Schapiro* (New York: Viking, 1986), 23.
[26] Peter H. Solomon, 'The Limits of Legal Order in Post-Soviet Russia,' *Post-Soviet Affairs*, 2 (1995): 89.
[27] Korzhakov, *Boris Yeltsin*, 285.
[28] *Segodnia* (6 Dec. 1994): 3.

seized several of Gusinskii's bodyguards and drivers and forced them to lie down on the snow-covered ground for two hours. Watching this scene from his office, an alarmed Gusinskii telephoned Evgenii Savostianov, deputy chair of the Federal Counterintelligence Service (FSK) and director of that organization's operations in Moscow, and he sent some men to check out the situation. These operatives reported back that the Presidential Security Service was behind the incident. This identification immediately cost Savostianov his job. The FSK group arrived at the MOST building at 2:00 p.m., and by 4:00 p.m. Yeltsin had signed papers relieving Savostianov of his duties.[29] Shortly thereafter, despite severe harassment at the airport, Gusinskii fled abroad until such time as his political prospects improved.

This incident typifies and encapsulates Boris Yeltsin's notion of the rule of law. It coincides precisely with Schapiro's description of the Soviet conception of the rule of law. For Yeltsin, such issues as freedom of the press, freedom of speech, and freedom of movement pale before what he sees as the necessity to deal brutally with political opponents and enemies.

'The rule of law concept,' John Whyte has written in describing the Western view of a *Rechtsstaat*, 'is based on the praise of rules. Rules, rather than being seen as prisons, or impediments to developing rich and supportive social communities, are seen as the condition for freedom and diversity because they limit, with the force of law, those that seek to limit others. The rule of law rests on the moral satisfaction of observing promises, honoring commitments, and enforcing legitimate rules.' He concludes: 'These outcomes are morally satisfying because they give purpose to one's autonomy. . . . The rule of law is hostile to arbitrary force, especially when it takes the form of state action, because that force leaves individuals with no control over their own futures.'[30]

Russia under Boris Yeltsin exhibits the obverse of Whyte's definition of the rule of law. That it has become an enormously lawless and corrupt state is well known, but the extent of the corruption is difficult for many Westerners, and even specialists in Russian politics, to grasp.[31] Nowhere has the level of corruption been more scandalous than in the 'restoration project' allegedly conducted in Chechnya in 1994–96. This 'work' was principally overseen by First Deputy Prime Minister Oleg Soskovets, a close associate of Korzhakov, who served as the head of the State Commission for the Restoration of the Chechen Economy. To summarize the issue, the vast sums supposedly sent to Chechnya were in fact plundered by Soskovets and his allies, and by favored banks, such as Menatep, that were authorized by his committee to 'disburse' the funds in Chechnya. The funds were also looted, though in smaller amounts, by leaders of the pro-Russian or quisling Chechen government during the war. Among them was the mayor of Grozny, Bislan Gantamirov (Gantemirov), who in 1999 was sentenced to six years' imprisonment by a Russian court for having embezzled the equivalent of $1.7 million earmarked by Moscow for the reconstruction of Chechnya.

---

[29] Korzhakov, *Boris Yeltsin*, 286, and *Segodnia* (6 Dec. 1994). Yeltsin and Savostianov were later reconciled, and Savostianov became deputy head of the presidential administration.

[30] John D. Whyte, 'The OSCE Role in the Constitutional Development of CIS States,' in *Balancing Hegemony: The OSCE in the CIS*, ed. S. Neil MacFarlane and Oliver Thranert (Kingston, ON: Centre for International Relations, Queen's University, 1997), p. 177.

[31] On the issue of corruption in Russia, see Matt Bivens and Jonah Bernstein, 'The Russia You Never Met,' *Demokratizatsiya* 6, no.4 (fall 1998): 613–47; Peter Reddaway, 'Questions About Russia's "DreamTeam,"' *Post-Soviet Prospects* 5/5 (Sept. 1997).

THE 'BLACK HOLE' OF CHECHNYA

The extraordinary scam connected with 'restoring' Chechnya was openly covered in the pages of the Russian press. In September 1995, for example, there were reports of a heated exchange between Vladimir Petrov, first deputy finance minister, and Oleg Lobov, secretary of the Russian Security Council, during a session of the State Commission for the Restoration of the Chechen Economy. The aforementioned Soskovets backed Lobov when Petrov attempted to show that far too much money from the state budget was already being allocated for Chechnya. 'The capital expenditures for [the restoration of] Chechnya already comprise one-quarter of all investment allocations of the state,' Petrov complained. And he continued: 'The budget is not made of elastic; the ministry also owes 2 trillion rubles to the Pension Fund.' And a final pointed protest: 'The expenditures on Chechnya are not legally sanctioned—they do not exist in the budget.'[32] However, Lobov and Soskovets, two of Russia's most powerful officials at the time, easily steamrollered Petrov's timid protests. The trillions of rubles earmarked for the restoration of Chechnya (that is, for their own pockets, and for those of their allies and associates) were more important to Lobov and Soskovets than any whining pensioners, who, in any case, were likely to vote for the communists in the next election.

Around the same time, reports surfaced that the Russian Security Council, administered by Lobov, was demanding that a Grozny branch of the Russian Central Bank be organized. Apparently there had been 'complaints' against Menatep and other authorized banks with offices in Grozny.[33] This demand seems, at least in part, to have stemmed from a developing rivalry between Lobov and Soskovets over control of the flow of cash 'to Chechnya.' The Security Council noted with anger that toward the end of August, armed men had 'assaulted' the Grozny branch of the Menatep Bank (no one had been hurt in the incident) and had made off with 'the equivalent of half a billion dollars'!

In September 1995, the leader of the Agrarian Party of Russia, Mikhail Lapshin, held a press conference in Moscow after returning from a visit to the North Caucasus region. Russian builders, he said, had reported 'the restoration of 7,000 homes destroyed in Chechnya during the course of military actions,' but he had not seen 'a single such [restored] house' during his visit.[34]

In December 1995, Mikhail Zadornov, chair of the Budget Committee of the State Duma (and very briefly a first deputy prime minister in May 1999) stated publicly that his committee had decided not to authorize the 5.1 trillion rubles earmarked by the Russian government for the restoration of Chechnya. The government, he complained, had still 'not gotten around to acquainting the deputies with the program for the restoration of Chechnya, and it is difficult to explain to representatives of other regions why such enormous sums are being sent to one subject of the Federation, while in others wages have not been paid for half a year.'[35]

Similarly, an article appearing in *Segodnia*, entitled 'The Caucasian Klondike,' observed:

The financial interest toward Chechnya of the Russian government and of other persons involved in the war is growing in geometric progression. Hardly could one find another explanation for the

---

[32] *Segodnia* (15 Sept. 1995).   [33] *Segodnia* (31 Aug. 1995).
[34] *Segodnia* (13 Sept. 1995).   [35] *Segodnia* (7 Dec. 1995).

colossal funds which the Ministry of Finance plans to invest [in Chechnya]. . . . In a region where not more than one percent of the population [of the Russian Federation] live, it is planned to invest $6.6 billion, which is comparable, say, to the total amount of IMF credits allocated for stabilization in Russia.[36]

Finally, in February 1996, *Izvestiia* reported that the Budget Committee of the State Duma was sharply questioning the legality of the expenditures for Chechnya contained in Yeltsin's Decree No. 86 (January l996).[37] The Duma committee noted that the decree had not been published and was therefore unconstitutional according to the 1993 Yeltsin constitution. If the decree had been published, as was legally required, the committee would have been in a position to appeal it to the Russian Constitutional Court.

Zadornov underscored the extraordinary size of the allocations for the restoration of Chechnya foreseen in Yeltsin's secret decree (which Zadornov had managed to get a copy of): a total of 16.2 trillion rubles, plus $1 billion in foreign loans. That sum, Zadornov noted, 'was more than for any socially significant program contained in the 1996 budget,' which, he said, planned to spend 11 trillion rubles for science and 7.5 trillion for health, whereas 'the entire social policy' of the country would cost the Russian treasury 12.6 trillion rubles. 'Against the background of these figures,' he complained, 'the Chechen expenditures look simply monstrous.' The projected Chechen restoration expenditures, Zadornov continued, would serve to weaken the country's investment program. Important construction work would be deferred on the Moscow and St Petersburg subways, while military personnel who had been thrown into retirement would not receive 5 trillion rubles in housing subsidies, and those leaving the Russian North would not receive 1.2 trillion in subsidies.

These accounts, taken from the Russian press, reveal the lawlessness and staggering greed of Yeltsin and his entourage. The most vital social services, including pensions and public health, were to be postponed indefinitely, if necessary, so that high-ranking state officials could line their pockets with scores of trillions of rubles. The strictures and objections of the Duma, whose deputies were the elected representatives of the people, were contemptuously ignored, as were published reports in the Russian press. The provisions of the 1993 constitution were also flatly ignored. Yeltsin, Soskovets, Lobov, and the others were quite obviously above the law. They could justifiably say: 'L'état c'est moi.'

Of course, the so-called restoration of Chechnya represented only one of many scams run with the backing and collusion of high-ranking government officials during the Yeltsin years. In May 1999, for instance, it was reported that the just-confirmed prime minister, Sergei Stepashin, had asked his first deputy prime minister to investigate the disappearance of 'a $100 million external credit that did not reach Kemerovo Oblast.' The governor of Kemerovo Oblast, Aman Tuleev, for his part, was quoted in the same article as stating that he had informed Stepashin about the need to investigate how 'millions of rubles [for the coal sector] . . . simply evaporated in commercial banks.'[38]

RESTRICTIONS ON RELIGIOUS LIBERTY

Not only has lawlessness been the rule under Yeltsin's leadership, but in certain spheres it has worsened during his second term. On September 26, 1997, Yeltsin signed into law new

---

[36] *Segodnia* (6 Dec. 1995).   [37] *Izvestiia* (10 Feb. 1996).   [38] *RFE/RL Newsline* (21 May 1999).

restrictive legislation on religion that took the country away from the legal reforms of the early 1990s and back to the draconian 1975 Brezhnev-era law on religion.[39] The 1997 law cancelled virtually all the improvements introduced by the 1990 USSR and RSFSR laws on religion. Support for the new restrictive law, it should be noted, was overwhelming in both houses of parliament, so in this instance the parliament was as responsible as the president for a travesty of legal order. In the State Duma, 358 deputies voted in favor of the law, six against, and there were four abstentions. (Five of the six votes against the law came from members of the Yabloko faction in the Duma, while the late Galina Starovoitova was one of the four who abstained.) The bill passed the Federation Council unanimously.

The new bill Yeltsin signed into law in September 1997 represented a juridically illiterate hodgepodge riddled with internal contradictions and directly violating eight articles of the 1993 constitution, as well as many international treaties signed by the Russian Federation, as the self-proclaimed successor of the Soviet Union. It violated, for example, four articles of the Universal Declaration of Human Rights and seven articles of the UN Declaration on the Elimination of All Forms of Discrimination on the Basis of Religion and Beliefs.

Under what was undoubtedly the most controversial section of the new law, Article 27, members of unregistered religious bodies—that is, bodies not granted or not wanting registration by local and state authorities—were explicitly declared *not* to be 'equal before the law' with other Russian citizens. Unregistered religious groups were likewise declared not free to own churches or other houses of worship, not free to disseminate their faith in public meetings or through the printed word, and not free even to hold church school picnics. Article 27 likewise resurrected one of the most restrictive practices sanctioned by the Brezhnev law of 1975, for it directly prohibited adherents of unregistered religious bodies from visiting sick or dying co-religionists in prisons and hospitals, and even from providing them with the last rites.

Why was an overtly discriminatory bill in clear violation of the constitution, not to mention numerous articles of international law, able to garner overwhelming support in both houses of parliament and in the presidential administration? In an article appearing in *Nezavisimaia gazeta*, Aleksandr Morozov observed:

In Russia, there is no civil society; there is only the populace and the regime, while the regime does not enjoy the support of the populace. . . . Under such conditions, the role of the Russian Orthodox Church as the sole state institute which conjoins all Russians [*russkikh*] is naturally growing. . . . The vote on the new law 'On Freedom of Conscience' should be seen in this light.[40]

A 1999 poll conducted by the All-Russian Center for the Study of Public Opinion (VTsIOM), it should be noted, showed that the Orthodox Church and the armed forces were the two institutions that present-day Russian citizens most respected (63 percent approval and 53 percent approval, respectively).[41] The fact that the leadership of the official Orthodox Church—many of them, including the patriarch, still holdovers from the Brezhnevite ecclesiastical *nomenklatura*—badly wanted the bill passed was sufficient for most deputies

---

[39] On the 1997 law on religion, see my article 'Russia's 1997 Law Renews Religious Persecution,' *Demokratizatsiya* 7, 1 (winter 1999): 28–41. For the text of the new law, see *Rossiiskaia gazeta* (16 Sept. 1997): 5–6.

[40] *Nezavisimaia gazeta* (25 Dec. 1997): 1, 3.

[41] USIA Opinion Analysis M-27–99 (11 Feb. 1999).

and for the presidential administration. The communists under Gennadii Ziuganov and the Zhirinovskiites supported the bill quite vigorously. A vote in favor of the bill was viewed as a duty by Russian nationalists and by National Bolsheviks like Ziuganov.

THE SOFT STATE

Absence of the rule of law and absence of legal culture are subsets of a larger problem that political scientists are wont to term a 'soft state.' According to political scientist Thomas Remington:

Yeltsin's Russia today displays all the pathologies of a soft state: government cannot ensure policy is carried out, or even guarantee the timely payment of wages to employees; announcements about new state agencies and progress are made and soon forgotten, and a crisis in law enforcement is manifested by the enormous rise in organized crime, deep government corruption, and lax fiscal control.

And Remington concluded:

Elites and the public alike tend to assume that the answer to a breakdown of the legal order is more state power: *stateness* is confused with *law*. Frequently, as a result, the authorities grant law enforcement bodies wide extra-legal powers while restricting the civic rights of citizens. This in turn undermines respect for the law still further. Legal anarchy and uncertainty encourage the varieties of anti-social, beggar-thy-neighbor behavior in society that prevent the consolidation of democratic and capitalist institutions.[42]

That Russia's corrupt and inefficient soft state is seen by its citizens as failing to provide basic protections was shown convincingly in a poll conducted in early 1999 by a prestigious polling organization, VTsIOM (*see Table 4.2*). These are troubling figures. The Russian masses see themselves as having been cast into a Darwinian world in which the state is uninterested in or incapable of protecting their lives and basic freedoms.

Eighty-four percent of the respondents in the same poll cited corruption in the police as a key problem, 74 percent singled out corruption in the courts and judicial system, 69 percent cited corruption in the State Duma, and 68 percent mentioned corruption in the federal government.[43] Similarly, in a poll taken by VTsIOM in early 1999, 37 percent of the respondents believed that the well-publicized investigations into corruption then being carried out by the General Procuracy represented an 'ostentatious ballyhoo covering up the inactivity of the law enforcement organs,' while 30 percent thought that the General Procuracy's actions were 'connected to the struggle for power and due to material considerations.' Only 15 percent felt that a 'real struggle against the plundering of state property' was taking place.[44]

The demographic and public health consequences resulting from the emergence of a soft state are striking. A total of 1.7 million children were born in the Russian Federation in 1991, but by 1997, the number had dropped to 1.2 million. In contrast, there were 1.6 million

---

[42] Thomas F. Remington, 'Democratization and the New Political Order in Russia,' in *Democratic Changes and Authoritarian Reactions in Russia, Ukraine, Belarus, and Moldova*, ed. Karen Dawisha and Bruce Parrott (New York: Cambridge University Press, 1997), 110.

[43] USIA Opinion Analysis, M-27–99 (11 Feb. 1999). The polling was conducted by VTsIOM.

[44] *Segodnia* (3 Mar. 1999).

Table 4.2 **How good a job has the federal government been doing at. . . (percent)**

	Good, very good	Bad, very bad
Guaranteeing timely payment of wages, salaries, and pensions	3	94
Social protection of the unemployed, homeless, and needy	3	93
Fighting organized crime	4	92
Maintaining law and order	8	87

Source: USIA Opinion Analysis, M-27-99 (11 Feb. 1999). The poll was conducted by the All-Russian center for the Study of Public Opinion (VTsIOM).

deaths registered in 1991, whereas 2 million were recorded in 1997. Between 1990 and 1997, there was a 35 percent decline in Russian consumption of meat, a 41 percent drop in the consumption of milk, and a 31 percent decline in the consumption of eggs, while the consumption of potatoes rose 19 percent. The incidence of tuberculosis per 100,000 population rose from 35.8 to 73.9, of syphilis, from 13.4 to 277.3, and of psychic disorders, from 274.3 to 348.2.[45]

Not surprisingly, given the abysmal performance of their soft state, Russians are in an angry and pessimistic mood. Pollsters traditionally regard the question of whether or not a country is heading in the 'right' direction as *the* key question to be put to respondents. Only 6 percent of those surveyed in a 1999 nationwide poll thought that the country was heading in the right direction, while 71 percent believed that it was heading in the wrong direction, and 13 percent did not think that it was moving at all.[46]

Things are so bad that many Russians are in an escapist mood. One recent poll showed that 54.3 percent of the respondents would have liked to have been born during the reign of Peter the Great, while another 15 percent wanted to emigrate abroad.[47] Another poll showed that more than half the respondents believed that the era of Leonid Brezhnev had represented a 'golden age' for the country.[48]

Has anything gone right during the Yeltsin years?

In light of the manifold pathologies characterizing the soft Russian state, Russia may seem to be a wasteland, but such a perception would be inaccurate. First, there has been the continued miracle of *glasnost*, first launched in 1986–87 by Gorbachev and Aleksandr Yakovlev.

Despite the many threats emanating from government and regional leaders, from oligarchs, criminals, and so on, *glasnost* has shown itself to be a resilient instrument of Russian proto-democracy. Even television and radio—despite enormous pressure—have retained a

[45] 'Genotsid rossiiskogo naroda' (Genocide of the Russian People), *Kommersant daily* (13 May 1999).

[46] USIA Opinion Analysis M-4-99 (12 Jan. 1999). The polling was done by the Institute for Comparative Social Research (CESSI).

[47] *Moskovskii komsomolets* (9 Feb. 1999). The polling was done by VTsIOM.

[48] Agence France-Presse (29 Jan. 1999), citing a poll by *Obshchestvennoe mnenie*.

degree of trust on the part of viewers and listeners. Thus an early 1999 poll found that 53 percent of respondents had 'a fair degree of trust' in Russian radio, while 55 percent had a comparable degree of trust in Russian television.[49]

As political theorists like Larry Diamond of the Hoover Institution have emphasized, Russia should be viewed as an electoral democracy, roughly of the same genus as, say, Guatemala, Mozambique, or Paraguay. While electoral democracies do not rise to the level of liberal democracies, they are clearly preferable to what Diamond terms pseudo-democracies (Azerbaijan, Kazakstan) and authoritarian regimes (Turkmenistan). An electoral democracy, a definite achievement for post-communist Russia, 'is a civilian, constitutional system in which the legislative and chief executive offices are filled through regular, competitive, multiparty elections with universal suffrage.'[50]

Obviously, vote-rigging and electoral fraud remain major problems, but the achievement of electoral democracy in Russia has to date been a real if limited achievement. Having served as an election monitor in Russia in 1995 and 1996 and in Azerbaijan in 1998, I have concluded that flawed and partially rigged elections can, at least in certain instances, be preferable to no elections at all.

A nationwide poll taken early in 1999 by VTsIOM demonstrates that there is still note-worthy, if eroding, support for political democracy among the Russian populace. Of course, in light of the passivity and anomie characteristic of most Russian voters, it is not clear that they would be prepared to take action to preserve the freedoms they continue to value. The results of the poll are shown in Table 4.3.

Linked to the emergence of electoral democracy is the practice of electing governors and the members of the regional assemblies. This reform has brought about a healthy decentral-ization, necessary in so vast and sprawling country as Russia. To be sure, many of the elected governors and regional assemblies have turned out to be corrupt or not up to the job, and authoritarian enclaves have emerged, but the regional elections have nonetheless been a good thing. Former prime minister Evgenii Primakov's expressed wish to do away with the practice of electing governors would have constituted a serious political setback.

Lastly, there is what might be called the miracle of Yabloko, a major political faction in the State Duma that is committed to democracy and to a real, rather than 'virtual,' market

Table 4.3 **In your opinion, would it be permissible to do the following to restore order? (percent)**

	Yes	No	Don't know
Cancel scheduled elections	26	63	11
Ban meetings and demonstrations	21	68	12
Establish censorship of the mass media	26	60	15

Source: USIA Opinion Analysis, M-27-99 (11 Feb. 1999)

[49] USIA Opinion Analysis M-27–99 (11 Feb. 1999). Poll by VTsIOM.
[50] Larry Diamond, *Developing Democracy: Toward Consolidation* (Baltimore: Johns Hopkins University Press, 1999), 10, 279–80.

economy, but that has also been an unsparing critic of corruption and the abuse of state power. The Russian public has taken note of this unique party, headed by economist Grigorii Yavlinskii, and has rewarded it in election after election. Yabloko is the only unquestionably pro-democracy party certain to clear the 5 percent barrier in the December 1999 Duma elections (it could gain 15 percent of the party-list vote, coming in third behind the communists and the Fatherland–All Russia Coalition).

The example of Yabloko suggests that a path different from that taken by Yeltsin and his corrupt regime was open to non-communists and non-nationalists in the period following the August 1991 putsch. Reviled both in Russia and the West as naive and hopeless Don Quixotes, the deputies affiliated with Yabloko have earned the trust and support of a significant segment of the Russian electorate.

This small list of successes or partial successes—to which others, such as the striking productivity of the country's private plots and small farms, might be added—obviously fails to mitigate the overall dismal picture of a largely failed Russian state. The exhortation that should be addressed to aspiring Russian leaders and politicians is not 'It's the economy, stupid' but, rather, 'It's the rule of law, stupid.' Unfortunately, as Yeltsin wrote in his memoirs, 'Everyone knows that we Russians do not like to obey all sorts of rules, laws, instructions and directives. . . . We are a casual sort of people and rules cut us like a knife.'[51] Until the fundamental elements of the rule of law are introduced into Russia—and there appears little realistic prospect of this happening over, say, the next five years—that unhappy country will remain a land of chaotic *bespredel*, and more unpleasant surprises will likely follow.

[51] Yeltsin, *Struggle for Russia*, 139–40.

5   Boris Yeltsin as Patriarch

George W. Breslauer

....

Boris Yeltsin's tumultuous years in Moscow politics, first as challenger of communist rule in the USSR, then as president of post-communist Russia, are presumably drawing to a close. While the scholarly literature on Gorbachev's leadership is extensive, books that take a comprehensive and long view of Yeltsin's leadership are relatively few in number,[1] while others deal largely with his career before 1992.[2] This will soon change. A large number of volumes are in the pipeline, including comprehensive studies by Leon Aron, George Breslauer, Jerry Hough, Eugene Huskey, Peter Reddaway and Dimitri Glinski, Georgiy Satarov, and Liliya Shevtsova.

When we undertake a holistic depiction or evaluation of a leader's performance in office, we typically focus on many things: his style of leadership; his self-image and identity as leader; his goals, beliefs, and perspectives on power and policy; and his ability to combine political skills with visionary qualities and programmatic rationality. We also focus on the context and constraints within which he operates and his effectiveness in 'stretching constraints'[3] through acts of leadership. The present article, however, focuses only on Yeltsin's leadership *style*, and specifically on one dimension of that style—his patriarchalism—and the evolution of its expression over time.

Yeltsin's personalistic urge

Patriarchalism is a subtype of a much broader type of leadership: personalism. Yeltsin always had a preference for being a personalistic leader. He had a life-long urge to be in charge. As he put it in his autobiography: 'For more than thirty years now, I've been a boss. . . . Not a bureaucrat, not an official, not a director, but a boss. I can't stand the word—there's something about it that smacks of the chain gang. But what can you do? Perhaps being first was always a part of my nature.'[4] An earlier autobiography records many stories of the leadership role he played among his friends and of his penchant for assuming the preponderance of

This chapter was first published in *Post-Soviet Affairs*, 15/2 (1999), 186–200. Reproduced by kind permission of the author and V. H. Winston (Bellwether Publishing).

  [1] Dimitri Mikheyev, *Russia Transformed* (Indianapolis: The Hudson Institute, 1996).

  [2] John Morrison, *Boris Yeltsin: From Bolshevik to Democrat* (New York: Dutton, 1991); Vladimir Solovyov and Elena Klepikova, *Boris Yeltsin* (New York: Putnam, 1992); Pilar Bonet, *Nevozmozhnaya Rossiya. Boris Yel'tsin, provintsial v Kremlye*, published in *Ural* (Yekaterinburg), 4 Apr. 1994.

  [3] Warren F. Ilchman and Norman T. Uphoff, *The Political Economy of Change* (Berkeley, CA: University of California Press, 1969).

  [4] Boris Yeltsin, *The Struggle for Russia*, (New York: Random House, 1994), 179.

risk—as, for example, when he insisted on being the one among his friends to disarm a grenade, losing two fingers in the process.[5] People who knew him early in his career in Sverdlovsk report that he was an assertive, demanding, and harsh boss.[6]

When he was promoted to the position of first secretary of the Moscow city party organization, Yeltsin's personalistic leadership style became widely known. His purges of the party apparatus and his surprise appearances at local shops to lambaste managers for corruption reflected his belief that the job could only be accomplished by someone with a take-charge mentality who was unconstrained in restructuring his domain. He fashioned himself a turnaround artist, undertaking wholesale clean-up operations that would break most men.[7] One admiring associate refers to Yeltsin's treatment of officialdom as 'harsh';[8] a contemptuous former associate writes that Yeltsin was frequently 'rude' and treated those who worked for him like a 'totalitarian boss' and a 'true party despot.'[9] An interviewee referred to Yeltsin's leadership style in Moscow as 'strict and tough' (*zhostkiy*).

We see other glimpses of Yeltsin's urge to be 'on top' in his attitudes toward his own superiors within the CPSU. He was jealous of the leaders of *perestroyka*—men like Gorbachev and Ligachev—who had been his peers as heads of regional party organizations but had made it to the top in Moscow before he had.[10] He found it galling to be treated as a subordinate. His resentful descriptions of Gorbachev's Politburo meetings[11] read as if written by an ambitious new member of a board of directors who has become emboldened by membership, but who does not yet understand that the most important decisions are usually made in closed session by an executive committee of the board!

Pilar Bonet records a vivid incident from Yeltsin's years as head of the Sverdlovsk party organization.[12] When Central Committee secretary Yegor Ligachev came to visit the province, Yeltsin had to exit the car in which they were riding together to contain his rage at Ligachev's demeaning questions about why things allegedly were not going well in Sverdlovsk.[13] The same impulses must have contributed to the recklessness with which he challenged the leadership—and Yegor Ligachev by name—in 1987, and was purged from his lofty positions for his efforts.

[5] Boris Yeltsin, *Against the Grain*, (New York: Summit Books, 1990), 29.

[6] See Bonet, *Nevozmozhnaya Rossiya* 24, 141; Pilar Bonet, 'Lord of the Manor: Boris Yel'tsin in Sverdlovsk *Oblast*,' *Occasional Paper #260*, Washington, DC: The Kennan Institute for Advanced Russian Studies, 1995, p. 1; see also Yeltsin's self-depiction: 'a provincial first secretary was a god, a czar-master of his province', Yeltsin, *Against the Grain 70*.

[7] See ibid. 29.

[8] Lev Sukhanov, *Tri goda s Yel'tsinym* (Riga: Vaga, 1992), 20.

[9] Aleksandr Korzhakov, *Boris Yel'tsin: Ot rassveta do zakata* (Moscow: Interbuk, 1997), 49, 51.

[10] Boris Yeltsin, *Izpoved' na zadannuyu temu* (Sverdlovsk: Srednye-Ural'skoye knizhnoye izdatel'stvo, 1990), 85–9. See also Fyodor Burlatskiy, *Glotok svobody*, vol. ii. (Moscow: Kultura, 1997), 127–31, which is based on interviews with Yeltsin's associates. This sentiment coexisted, however, with genuine admiration for Gorbachev for having launched *perestroyka*. Disillusionment with Gorbachev only began in 1987, when the party leader failed to respond to a letter from Yeltsin detailing top-level obstacles to reform, including obstruction by Yegor Ligachev (see Korzhakov, *Boris Yel'tsin* 52, 64–5).

[11] See Yeltsin, *Against the Grain* 91, 142–6.

[12] See Bonet, *Nevozmozhnaya Rossiya* 105–6.

[13] I was told a strikingly similar story about Yeltsin's first trip to the United States from an American who accompanied him to Texas. Yeltsin was angered by something his American host, who was riding with him, had said, and proceeded to stop the car, exit it, and run down the street to contain his anger (personal communication, not for attribution).

Six Yeltsins

But the reality of Yeltsin's personalistic urge, and the memory of his titanic struggles against opponents, should not blind us to the fact that he was capable of striking many leadership postures, depending on the context in which he was operating and the political strength of his opponent or interlocutor. Although others may recall or discover still more postures, or may suggest better labels for the six than I have come up with, I count 'six Yeltsins' in evidence since 1987. Three of them are egocentric and inflexible; three, to varying degrees, are accommodative and interactive.

In the first grouping, there is Yeltsin the *awesome antagonist* who unleashed thunder on Ligachev, Gorbachev, the coup plotters, the Supreme Soviet, and Chechnya when his patience with them had run out or their relationship had reached the point of no return. There is also Yeltsin the *heroic mobilizer of the people* who won almost 90 percent of the vote in the 1989 elections and who stood on the tank during the August 1991 coup. Then there is Yeltsin the *patriarch* who treats his political dependents as his extended family, within which he demands obedience and dispenses absolution to those who have 'sinned,' and who treats Russia as his patrimony, within which he dispenses both challenges and rewards.

In the second grouping of postures, within which Yeltsin's autocratic tendencies are restrained or repressed, there is Yeltsin the *hard but flexible bargainer* (or, at times, the *stern arbitrator*), who alternately implores, cajoles, threatens, and accommodates in order to strike deals, as in his efforts to secure the Duma's ratification of Sergey Kiriyenko as Prime Minister in April 1998 or in his annual struggles with the Duma over the budget. Then there is Yeltsin the *respectful, businesslike interlocutor*, a posture he has adopted, when healthy and sober, in his dealings with heads of state of lesser powers over which Russia has little control: China, Eastern Europe, and small or middle-sized powers elsewhere.[14] Finally, there is Yeltsin the *chummy pal*, the posture he adopts when dealing with heads of state of the G-7 ('my friend' Bill, Helmut, or even Ryu).

This chapter focuses on the third category within the first grouping of postures: Yeltsin as patriarch. It is a posture that has been less visible to the observer than have many of the others. And it is one that, felicitously, has been revealed quite vividly in the spate of memoirs by Yeltsin's political associates that has appeared in recent years.

Yeltsin as patriarch

Personalism is not necessarily the same as despotism—though all despots are, by definition, personalistic. Personalism is a form of rule in which the leader is not held accountable—formally, regularly, and frequently—to institutions that can substantially constrain his discretion. Beyond that, personalistic rulers *can* be generous, proper, and temperate; they are not necessarily tyrannical, capricious, or corrupt. Patriarchalism is a form of personalism that treats the political community as a household within which the leader is the *paterfamilias*; patriarchs typically rely on tradition, rather than charisma or rational-legal norms,

---

[14] A subcategory of this would be *awed interlocutor*, evident in his earlier behavior when meeting with Patriarch Aleksiy. See Vyacheslav Kostikov, *Roman s prezidentom* (Moscow: Vagrius, 1997), 134, 240.

to validate their right to rule as they please.[15] But the concept does not prejudge how the ruler distributes benefits, be these material or honorific, and whether he is generous or stingy, responsive or unresponsive to his staff's personal feelings.

Examination of the memoir literature, bolstered by the author's personal interviews with some men who have worked under Yeltsin, offers insight into the nature of Yeltsin's self-conception as a leader. Within his inner circle, he viewed himself as head of the household, as a leader who demanded total loyalty to himself and his commands, and who exercised maximal discretion over the public and, at times, private lives of his subordinates. There was nothing impersonal about these relationships, nothing based on procedural propriety or the prerogatives of office—except his own. The staff and officials of the presidential administration were his retainers, not his lieutenants. He treated his entourage as a family with himself as its head, rather than treating it as a corpus of professionals of which he was chief executive. This is not a formal distinction; it had striking behavioral consequences.

Yeltsin compelled his subordinates to try to improve themselves along lines dictated by him. According to Bonet's research on Yeltsin's tenure in Sverdlovsk,[16] he insisted that all his assistants wear formal clothes. When they were not dressed formally enough for him, he made them return home to change their clothes. He also 'turned the obkom [the regional party committee—GB] into a volleyball league,' dividing it into five teams in which members of the provincial party committee (obkom) were required to participate, both to foster bonhomie and to improve the physical fitness of his political elite.[17] As president of Russia, Yeltsin continued the pattern. After the August 1991 coup, he ordered a house to be built where he, his wife, and his daughters' families, as well as all the top officials in his administration and their families, would reside. He insisted that one apartment be held in common by residents of the apartment building, so that joint celebrations could be held there. Similarly, Yeltsin insisted that members of his entourage share his passion for playing tennis, and that they display proper deference by losing to him on the court. He further organized a 'Presidential Club,' into which members of his staff and cabinet were selectively initiated. He demanded that, in his presence, or at the Presidential Club, associates not use swear-words.[18]

Former press secretary, Vyacheslav Kostikov, notes in his memoirs that Yeltsin considered himself 'something like the father of an extended family [semeystvo].' He enjoyed flaunting his patriarchal authority, and liked it when he had the opportunity to demand that somebody apologize for a bureaucratic inadvertence: 'ask papa for forgiveness.' He liked a good

[15] See Max Weber, *The Theory of Social and Economic Organisation* (New York: Free Press 1947), 346; Reinhard Bendix, *Max Weber: An Intellectual Portrait* (Garden City, NY: Doubleday, 1960), 330–60; H. E. Chehabi and Juan J. Linz, eds., *Sultanistic Regimes* (Baltimore: Johns Hopkins University Press, 1998), ch. 1. Note that, as used by Weber and his followers, patriarchs are male; however, their usage does not correspond to the usage in current feminist literature, which treats male domination of women as a product or distinguishing characteristic of patriarchy. In the usage employed in this article, a patriarch is a leader who dominates subordinates of both genders. Moreover, as I will discuss below, Yeltsin's patriarchalism deepened over time. It was more frequently manifested after 1993.

[16] See Bonet, 'Lord of the Manor' 8.

[17] See Bonet, *Nevozmozhnaya Rossiya* 80–83.

[18] On the communal apartment building, see ibid. 138–46; on tennis, see Yeltsin, *The Struggle for Russia* 234–6; on Yeltsin's need to win on the court, see Korzhakov, *Boris Yel'tsin* 61; on the Presidential Club, see Kostikov, *Roman s prezidentom* 319, Korzhakov, *Boris Yel'tsin* 24–25, and Yeltsin, *Struggle for Russia* 236–7; on swear-words, see ibid. 237 and Korzhakov, *Boris Yel'tsin* 309.

spread with vodka, during which he would offer long toasts and enjoy his role as head of the family.[19]

Memoirs by associates—including those by Yeltsin himself—are laced with additional examples of this attitude. Vyacheslav Kostikov[20] affirms that Yeltsin harbored a great deal of sentimentality, almost love, for Gaydar and says that, for Yeltsin, Gaydar was his 'alter ego' (*vtorym ya*). Yeltsin is reported to have referred to Chubais and Nemtsov as 'like sons to me.'[21] Yelsin's ghostwriter and eventual chief-of-staff, Valentin Yumashev, appears in a photograph with Yeltsin in one memoir, with a caption that reads: 'For the President, V. Yumashev is almost like a son. It is not for nothing that his patronymic is Borisovich.'[22] Kostikov's memoir (1997) is entitled *Love Affair with a President*. An interviewee and former Yeltsin aide avers that, in the early 1990s, Yeltsin 'loved' his young advisors and they 'loved' him in return.[23]

During the 1980s, Yeltsin's relationship with his bodyguard, Aleksandr Korzhakov, was intimate to the point that the two exchanged blood from their fingers on two occasions to affirm their eternal loyalty to each other as 'blood brothers'[24] (Yeltsin was in his mid-50s at this time). Korzhakov refers to a vacation he and Yeltsin took in 1986 as our 'honeymoon.'[25] Yeltsin was the designated 'wedding patriarch' at the marriage of Korzhakov's daughter.[26] Streletskiy writes of the psychology of those responsible for guarding party and governmental officials under Yeltsin: 'bit by bit they are turned into "members of the families" of those they are guarding.'[27] Tellingly, when Yeltsin rebuked Korzhakov in May 1996 for getting involved in politics, the blood brother proclaimed to Yeltsin's daughter that 'it would be mild to say that I do not love Boris Nikolaevich.' Tatyana flew into a rage at this statement.[28]

In such an administrative context, the key to both political longevity and political influence was to capture the attention and the ear of the patriarch. But this had to be done with all proper deference. Indeed, when seven members of Yeltsin's staff wrote a joint letter to their boss in 1994, urging him not to repeat his embarrassing, apparently drunken, performance in Berlin, Boris Nikolaevich was livid. His reaction, however, was that of a patriarch, not an executive: he demanded that each of them, individually, admit to him their 'guilt' and express 'repentance.'[29]

Yeltsin's patriarchal self-conception extended beyond his immediate entourage and economic ministers. It also encompassed members of the military leadership. On this score, the recent, detailed study—part memoir, part research project—by Viktor Baranets[30] is useful and has an air of credibility, though of course it is only a single source, written by a man who

[19]   See Kostikov, *Roman s prezidentom* 8, 25.

[20]   See Kostikov, *Roman s prezidentom* 278, 157.

[21]   *Financial Times*, 16 Sept. 1997.

[22]   Valeriy Streletskiy, *Mrakobesiye* (Moscow: Detektiv-Press, 1998), last page of book, unnumbered. Note also the following observation by a Russian journalist: 'Presidential policy has long been a family business, in which Yumashev is admitted with the rights of a relative,' Aleksandr Gamov, in *Komsomol'skaya pravda*, 8 July 1998.

[23]   Oleg D. Poptsov, *Khronika vremyon tsarya Borisa* (Berlin: Sovershenno sekretno, 1995), 269.

[24]   See Korzhakov, *Boris Yel'tsin* 223.

[25]   See ibid. 63.

[26]   See ibid. 243.

[27]   See Streletskiy, *Mrakobesiye* 24.

[28]   See Korzhakov, *Boris Yel'tsin* 358.

[29]   See ibid. 220–3; Kostikov, *Roman s prezidentom* 328–31.

[30]   Viktor Baranets, *Yel'tsin i ego generaly* (Moscow: Sovershenno sekretno, 1998).

was quite alienated by Yeltsin's treatment of the Russian military. Here, too, we encounter the use of intimate, familial metaphors. Defense Minister Grachev 'loved' Yeltsin,[31] and the two men once declared their 'eternal friendship and love' for each other.[32] When he awarded Grachev a special presidential gold medal in a public ceremony, Yeltsin declared that this 'is my personal gift to you.'[33]

THE PATRIARCH AS ABUSIVE PARENT

The language of familial intimacy and love is one discursive indicator of a patriarchal self-conception. But Yeltsin also reserved to himself the right verbally to abuse members of the executive branch. As Baranets[34] documents, in October 1993, when Yeltsin sought military support against the Supreme Soviet, one of the participants at the meeting told Baranets that 'we were sitting there and feeling as if our strict and enraged father had come to our school in order to listen to the principal's complaining about our bad behavior.' Several years later, after having decided to fire Defense Minister Rodionov and Chief of the General Staff Viktor Samsonov, Yeltsin first harassed them verbally in front of their subordinates.[35]

Nor were the military the only victims. Other members of Yeltsin's cabinet were subjected to open, verbal abuse: Foreign Minister Kozyrev, Interior Minister Yerin, and Nationalities Minister Yegorov are specifically mentioned in memoirs as having gotten the treatment,[36] while Kostikov implies that Prime Minister Viktor Chernomyrdin was so victimized as well.[37]

Yeltsin also felt at liberty to be *physically* abusive. He could be very cruel to the most loyal of his aides, especially when he had been drinking. Whatever the foibles of presidents and prime ministers elsewhere, it is difficult to imagine them 'playing the spoons' on the heads of their ranking assistants and, when the others in the room responded with laughter, augmenting the speed and force of the spoon-pounding, as well as the number of heads being pounded.[38] It is also difficult to imagine them emulating Yeltsin's behavior on a boat on the Yenisey River, when he lost patience with the interruptions by his press secretary and ordered his bodyguards to toss the man overboard. When his bodyguards hesitated, on the assumption that he was kidding, he reiterated that he was serious and saw that the hapless press secretary went over the side.[39]

Nor did Yeltsin's abuse of his most dependent and servile subordinates cease at the boundary of the Russian executive and presidential branches. We also learn that he played the spoons on the head of the president of Kyrgyzstan, Akayev![40] Unless this was mutual, good-natured play (not clear from the memoir account), it is a stunning indicator of the extent to which Yeltsin may have considered portions of the Commonwealth of Independent States (CIS) to be part of his political household.

---

[31] See ibid. 230.

[32] See ibid. 170.

[33] See ibid. 248–9.

[34] See ibid. 26.

[35] See ibid. 77, 122.

[36] Yegor Gaydar, *Dni porazheniy i pobed* (Moscow: Vagrius, 1997), 107–8, 333–4; Korzhakov, *Boris Yel'tsin* 52–3.

[37] See Kostikov, *Roman s prezidentom* 347.

[38] See Korzhakov, *Boris Yel'tsin* 81–2.

[39] See Korzhakov, ibid. 253–4.

[40] See Korzhakov, ibid. 82. This was corroborated by others, none of them admirers of Korzhakov, interviewed by me in Moscow in June 1998.

THE PATRIARCH AS GENEROUS BENEFACTOR

While Yeltsin would frequently abuse his subordinates and those most dependent upon him, he could also be generous toward members of the political family. He enjoyed giving gifts (usually expensive watches) to his staff.[41] The gestures reached beyond the inner circle as well. He became the focus of innumerable requests for special favors—tax exemptions, in particular—from representatives of regional and sectoral interests. Reportedly, he found it difficult to say 'no' in the face of opportunities to assist friends, maddening his budget-conscious finance minister in the process.[42] Moreover, such tendencies extended beyond the borders of the Russian Federation. Yegor Gaydar reports in his memoir his fear that Yeltsin, if left alone with the leaders of Belarus, would concede more than Russia could afford in economic policy.[43] An interviewee added that such fears were well-founded, but not because of Yeltsin's (very real) ignorance of economics or ideological commitment to CIS Integration. Rather, what drove Yeltsin in such conversations was paternalism and a sense of communalism. As this interviewee put it, Yeltsin's expressed sentiment was: 'We're a family here. Let's dispense with the formalities! Why should we wrangle? Here, I'll give you this!' This extended beyond the Russia–Belarus relationship, according to this insider, and helps to explain Russia's flexibility in relations with Ukraine and Kazakhstan (the latter, regarding Caspian Sea oil). The same interviewee averred that, in CIS relations, Yeltsin 'could be generous to a fault.'[44]

Yeltsin also thought in generous-patriarchal terms about his relationship with the Russian population. He thought of himself as 'Director of all of Russia,'[45] whose election as president had validated his right to interpret the will of the people. Because of his overwhelming victories in confrontations with the old system and in free elections, he didn't believe he had to account, or explain himself, to anyone.[46] But he also thought of himself as a 'people's tsar,'[47] benevolent and caring, though strict when necessary. When he would offer reassurances to the populace that their pain would shortly ease, he felt like a Russian priest, lifting the spirits of his flock.[48] On a tour of Russia in 1992, he brought along hundreds of millions of rubles for 'gifts to the working people.' He knew that this violated the prevailing economic policy, 'but he considered it possible for himself to make tsarist gestures.'[49]

[41] See Korzhakov, *Boris Yel'tsin* 54. As Korzhakov notes, this notion that the '*shef darit*' (the chief or patron gives a gift) was one that Yeltsin enjoyed practicing in his Sverdlovsk days as well.

[42] See Kostikov, *Roman s prezidentom* 216–17. See also Eugene Huskey, *Presidential Power in Russia* (Armonk, NY: M. E. Sharpe, forthcoming); Anatol Lieven, *Chechnya: Tombstone of Russian Power* (New Haven, CT: Yale University Press, 1997), 171; Victor Sergeyev, *The Wild East: Crime and Lawlessness in Post-Communist Russia* (Armonk, NY: M. E. Sharpe, 1998), 117–18. Huskey reports that Finance Minister Lifshits lamented that Yeltsin does not understand the economy 'and tries to help everyone . . . but some people need to be imprisoned rather than helped,' and that Economics Minister Yasin complained that Yeltsin had 'his favorite directors who can open any doors.'

[43] See Gaydar, *Dni porazheniy* 183–84.

[44] While I have no evidence on the matter, such an attitude may have informed Yeltsin's relations with Tatarstan's President Shaymiyev and the generous terms Yeltsin offered to secure the treaty of February 1994 that afforded that republic substantial autonomy within the Russian Federation.

[45] See Kostikov, *Roman s prezidentom* 306–7; Poptsov, *Khronika* 283.

[46] See Kostikov, *Roman s prezidentom* 304.

[47] See Burlatskiy, *Glotok svobody* 315.

[48] See Kostikov, *Roman s prezidentom* 21–2.

[49] See ibid. 42–3. Huskey argues that Yeltsin conceived of the presidency as 'the country's primary institutional patron,' and of the president as standing above all branches of government and sending 'emissaries' to them. The evidence displayed in the present article supports Huskey's characterizations.

POLICING THE BOUNDARIES OF THE FAMILY

As patriarch, Yeltsin demanded the right to define the boundaries and membership of 'the family.' This meant that he could banish 'wayward sons' or forgive them and return them to the fold. The choice was his, and the criterion he employed seems to have been whether or not they joined the formal political opposition to him after losing their job. Joining an anti-Yeltsin bloc amounted to turning against the family and could not be forgiven easily. But Ye. Gaydar, A. Chubais, B. Fyodorov, S. Filatov, S. Stepashin and others managed to secure reappointment when Yeltsin found it useful to tap their talents once again. They had never gone into formal opposition against him after being fired, though they did criticize individual policies—such as, in the case of Gaydar, retreats on economic policy or the decision to invade Chechnya. But others who wrote unabashedly anti-Yeltsin memoirs, or who joined oppositional groupings, were usually treated as beyond redemption.[50]

How far did Yeltsin's conception of his patriarchal reach extend? Clearly, it extended beyond his personal staff to include members of the government and their subordinates within the executive branch, even those who were subject to confirmation by the parliament. But did he also treat officials with independent power bases like children? Did he conceive of 'the family' as encompassing more than just his entourage, his cabinet, and the executive branch of government—that is, did his conception extend to regional governors, republican presidents, and heads-of-state within the CIS? On this score, much research remains to be done. The published sources used for this article provide little insight. Interviewees generally agreed that Yeltsin conceived of regional governors as his dependents, sought to maximize their dependence upon him, and had 'favorite sons' among them. A recent example of this might be Governor Dmitriy Ayatskov of Saratov *oblast'*, who accompanied Yeltsin to the G-8 meetings in England in May 1998, and whom Yeltsin introduced to Bill Clinton as 'the best governor' and the future president of Russia.[51] One interviewee reports that in the early 1990s, before the local election of governors, Yeltsin, in his travels to regions, could adopt the posture of a stern father, which sometimes caused those leaders to switch abruptly from a posture of demanding to one of begging. He tended to speak down to regional governors. For similar reasons, another interviewee claimed, Yeltsin came to dislike the Federation Council (the upper house of parliament), because the governors who dominated that body, after they were no longer appointed but elected in 1996–1998, were evolving into a political bloc of sorts, led by Speaker Yegor Stroyev. Yeltsin preferred to deal individually with the governors, buying off those whose support he needed, inviting individual governors for drinks, to the sauna, and the like.[52]

---

[50] Although Korzhakov argues that no rhyme or reason can explain Yeltsin's cadre policies, subject as these allegedly were to the whims of accident and alcohol, he subsequently undermines the claim by noting that Yeltsin was prepared to allow Gorbachev to retain all kinds of privileges after his resignation, but that once Gorbachev began to criticize Yeltsin publicly, Yeltsin sharply reduced the privileges. Similarly, Korzhakov advised Grigoriy Yavlinskiy to rein in his ambition and support Yeltsin, for by openly challenging the President, Yavlinskiy was destroying his chances of being incorporated back into the establishment; see Korzhakov, *Boris Yel'sin* 123, 130, 249. To be sure, Yeltsin has tried to bribe and implicate former oppositionists—such as General Aleksandr Rutskoy—to secure their cooperation, though this is not the same as inviting them into his government or confidence.

[51] *Russian Regional Executives Handbook* (New York: East-West Institute, 1999).

[52] In this respect, Yeltsin's leadership strategy resembles that of so-called 'sultanistic' leaders elsewhere. See Chehabi and Linz, *Sultanistic Regimes*.

Did Yeltsin's conception of the family extend beyond regional governors to include republican presidents and leaders of the post-Soviet states as well? I have even less evidence on this score, and would appreciate feedback from readers who have come across such information. We have seen, however, that Yeltsin felt at liberty physically to abuse President Akayev of Kyrgyzstan, and that he 'could be generous to a fault' in formal negotiations with some CIS leaders. Several interviewees expressed their belief that Yeltsin conceives of the 'Near Abroad' as falling within his patrimony. An indirect indicator of the extent to which Yeltsin may consider the CIS to be his patrimony appeared most recently, in March 1999. In line with an anti-corruption campaign being waged by Prime Minister Yevgeniy Primakov, which has targeted financial tycoon Boris Berezovsky, Yeltsin suddenly fired Berezovsky as Executive Secretary of the Commonwealth of Independent States. If these newspaper reports are accurate, the Russian leader began a process of building consensus among leaders of those states—who had collectively appointed Berezovsky to the post—only when informed that he did not have the right unilaterally to dismiss the Executive Secretary.[53]

Yeltsin's self-conception as patriarch of an extended family, defining the boundaries and membership of that unit and jealously guarding his decisionmaking prerogatives, did NOT extend beyond the limits of the CIS—to Eastern Europe, for example. And of course it did not extend to relations with leaders of the great powers, where he could hope to be treated at best like an equal, at worst as a supplicant. But there was an affinity between Yeltsin's conception of politics as *personalistic* and *intimate* and the kinds of relationships he tried to build with leaders of the G-7. His personal rapport with German Chancellor Helmut Kohl is well known. His relations with President Clinton are based on a degree of informality ('my friend Bill') that did not mark, say, Brezhnev's relations with Nixon, or even Gorbachev's relations with Reagan.[54] Even on his visit to Japan, where formality is the norm, Yeltsin publicized his relationship with the new Japanese Prime Minister, whom he was meeting for the first time, in the same terms: 'my friend Ryu.'[55] Yeltsin did not treat these as relationships solely between chief executives, so much as relations between chief executives who shared a personal attraction. And he did not conceive of the G-7 as an organization so much as a *club*, into which he was eager and determined to be drawn.

The evolution of Yeltsin's style

Yeltsin entertained a personalistic self-conception throughout his political career; he always wanted to be 'in charge.' But his operating style evolved over time, with *patriarchalism* becoming a *dominant* orientation only after 1993. Memoirs by close aides of the late 1980s make no mention of the traits we have been emphasizing to this point, stressing instead his charismatic personalism.[56] Several memoirs by people who worked with Yeltsin both before

[53] *International Herald Tribune*, 6–7 Mar. 1999, p. 2.

[54] Indeed, Korzhakov, *Boris Yel'tsin* 235, suggests that, during his visits, Yeltsin behaved like Clinton's 'older brother.'

[55] '"We became friends," Yeltsin said at a press briefing with Hashimoto, before the two wrapped up their two-day meeting with hugs and kisses "We'll address each other by name—Boris and Ryu."' (quoted in *The Boston Globe*, 3 Nov. 1997, p. A2).

[56] See Sukhanov, *Tri goda*; Viktor Yaroshenko, *Yel'tsin: Ya otvechu za vsyo* (Moscow: Redaktsiya zhurnala 'Vokrug sveta', 1997).

and after 1993 distinguish between the early President Yeltsin and the late President Yeltsin, with the breakpoint coming sometime in 1993. Before then, Yeltsin was a populist who was confident of his ability to mobilize the masses against his political adversaries. He also enjoyed enormous charismatic authority within his entourage and rational-legal authority derived from his public election as president in June 1991. In addition, within his inner circle, while demanding the deference due a patriarch, he was also accessible, consultative, and receptive to a range of policy advice. By late 1993, however, Yeltsin had lost confidence in his ability to rally the masses, a conclusion reinforced mightily by the results of the December 1993 parliamentary elections.[57] The memoir he published in 1994 ends with the prosaic promise to give the Russian people 'stability and consistency in politics and the economy' and with the declaration that 'the only definite guarantor of calm is the president himself,'[58] both of which are features of a patriarchal orientation.[59] The system-builder had evolved into an authoritarian system-manager. Thereafter, we are told, Yeltsin's presidential administration took on still more of the attributes of a 'court' and still fewer of the attributes of a 'cabinet.'

Yegor Gaydar writes that around this time, Yeltsin began to present himself as a benevolent tsar surrounded by a huge court.[60] Increasingly over time, Kostikov reports, Yeltsin referred to himself in the third person.[61] According to Korzhakov, Yeltsin began to be heavily preoccupied with his personal security.[62] He also narrowed the circle of those to whom he would turn for advice, and allowed the security personnel in his entourage to have a major influence on policy.[63] As Kostikov lamented, 'we ["democrats"—GB] were pained that, in relations with Boris Nikolaevich, a steady disappearance of democratism, accessibility, and relations of trust was occurring.'[64] One former associate explains this trend as a joint product of the physical pain and exhaustion Yeltsin experienced at this time and the emotional anguish of having 'lost' the December 1993 parliamentary elections after having expended so very much energy to prevail over the Supreme Soviet in 1993. He had been expending so much 'negative energy' for so many years that, by 1994, his entourage could bring him 'bad news' only when it was packaged with three times as much 'good news.'[65] Whatever the exact cause of the change, it was unmistakable. It led Gaydar to remark to Kostikov in January 1994 that 'we must return Yel'tsin to Yel'tsin,'[66] which meant that they must find a way to curb Yeltsin's authoritarian impulse, reinforce his consultative strain, and prevent him from relying excessively on alcohol as an escape. Yeltsin had evolved from a

[57] See Kostikov, *Roman s prezidentom* 151–2; Gaydar, *Dni porazheniy* 230–1, 313–314; Korzhakov, *Boris Yel'tsin* 330.
[58] Yeltsin, *The Struggle for Russia* 292.
[59] Jowitt argues that 'As a mode of leadership, patriarchalism has historically had several distinguishing features including a stress on orderly rather than charismatic (i.e., highly random and arbitrary) management, direct concern with the economic welfare of the social unit involved, personalized attention to solidarity issues, and emphasis on authoritarian and disciplinary behavior.' Kenneth Jowitt, 'An Organisational Approach to the Study of Political Culture in Marxist-Leninist Systems,' *American Political Science Review*, 68/3 (1974), 1190.
[60] Gaydar, *Dni porazheniy* 295.
[61] Kostikov, *Roman s prezidentom* 308.
[62] Korzhakov, *Boris Yel'tsin* 133.
[63] Gaydar, *Dni porazheniy* 300.
[64] Kostikov, *Roman s prezidentom* 322)
[65] Interview, Moscow, June 1998; see also Korzhakov, *Boris Yel'tsin* 251.
[66] See Kostikov, *Roman s prezidentom* 296.

'people's tsar'[67] into an embattled, increasingly reclusive monarch. His personalism, while a constant throughout his years as president, had evolved from a populist and consultative variant into a more patriarchal and exclusionary variant.

Sources of Yeltsin's patriarchal style

Most of this article has been descriptive, highlighting a feature of Yeltsin's leadership style that has largely been hidden from view until now. Now let us turn briefly to explanatory concerns: to what should we attribute Yeltsin's affinity for a patriarchal leadership style? Of course, *opportunity* is one part of the explanation: he could get away with it. But what factors might have driven him to seize that opportunity and to extend it to the reaches that he did? Five such factors occur to me, some of which complement each other, others of which may be mutually exclusive.

First, this may have been a product of Yeltsin's distinctive personality. Certainly, both his memoirs and his behavior toward the Politburo in 1987 suggest that he was unusually resistant to being socialized into conformist norms. Throughout his life, he was a *risk-seeker*, perhaps even addicted to risk; I count 19 incidents mentioned in his two memoirs that entail close brushes with death or political ruin. His success as a survivor, and in resurrecting himself politically after 1987, led him to develop a sense of his own *predestination*,[68] a conclusion that is confirmed by the memoirs of his aides,[69] and the observations or research by a fellow politician.[70]

A second possible explanation for Yeltsin's patriarchalism is to view it not as a product of his unique personality, but as a manifestation of a more widespread political type within Soviet elite political culture. From this perspective, many former heads of regional party organizations likely embraced a patriarchal leadership style—though Soviet regions were marked, during the post-Stalin era, by a diversity of types of leaders, all of them committed to the leading role of the party, but only some of them inclined toward this way of ruling. At the all-Union level, moreover, patriarchalism was one component of the leadership style of most CPSU general secretaries, though to varying degrees.[71] Hence, Yeltsin's incorporation of patriarchal elements into his earlier leadership style would be viewed as a product of his exposure to, and socialization into, one variant of Soviet elite political culture. This conclusion would not be incompatible with the further observation that his personality made him comfortable with the role into which he was being socialized.[72]

A third explanation is more a corollary of the second. The patriarchal political type is familiar to students of Third World countries and world history more generally. It is a characteristic of many traditional monarchies, including, notably, the Russian tsarist

[67] See Burlatskiy, *Glotok svobody* 315.

[68] See Yeltsin, *Against the Grain* 19; and Yeltsin, *The Struggle for Russia* 84, 197.

[69] See Sukhanov, *Tri goda* 225; Kostikov, *Roman s prezidentom* 308.

[70] Valentin Fyodorov, *Bez tsenzury: Yel'tsin* (Moscow: Golos, 1995), 58.

[71] Jowitt, 'An Organizational Approach' 1190, coins the suggestive term 'patriarchal-executive' to characterize the leadership style of Rumania's Ceausescu during 1965–1972.

[72] For a seminal analysis of Yeltsin's socialization into a particular subtype of Soviet political culture, see Mikheyev, *Russia Transformed* chs. 1–3; Mikheyev, however, does not emphasize Yeltsin's patriarchalism.

tradition.[73] It has much in common with the 'Big Man' phenomenon in African societies. National-liberation leaders in non-Leninist Third World countries often become patriarchal once they are governing an independent country. Thus, this particular feature of Soviet elite political culture is reflective of a broader, analogous phenomenon in certain types of societies and situations. And it is a feature of Stalinist political culture that reinforced the legacy of pre-Soviet approaches to leadership, from which Yeltsin even derived one of his role models.

A fourth explanation focuses not on leadership style as an end in itself, but rather on the ends to which the style was to be devoted. Here we focus on the rational, purposive, and calculative side of things, one dimension of which concerns Yeltsin's *beliefs* about the kind of leadership Russia needed to make historical progress after communism. He wrote in his memoirs that both the Russian bureaucracy and the Russian people required a 'strong hand' to budge them from their inertial and nihilistic behavioral patterns: 'somebody had to be the boss.'[74] He ended the same memoir with the promise to bring 'stability and consistency' to Russian society, and declared that only the president was capable of guaranteeing this.[75] If Yeltsin had a psychodynamic urge to be treated as a patriarch, it is possible that these beliefs were mere rationalizations for the realization of his psychological urges; this is an unresolved issue in psychological theory. But, at minimum, advocates of this explanation could argue that the psychodynamic and the cognitive were mutually reinforcing.

If Yeltsin's beliefs about 'what Russia needed' constitute his substantive (i.e., programmatic) rationality, a fifth explanation looks at beliefs about 'what Yeltsin needed'—his personal-political rationality. From this perspective, while the inclusion of a patriarchal element in Yeltsin's political style may have been a product of personality, socialization, and/ or beliefs, the eventual *ascendancy* of the patriarchal was a product of political insecurity. While he had been freely elected president of Russia, and enjoyed enormous charismatic authority after August 1991, these sources of political popularity can be wasting assets. During his struggle with the Supreme Soviet in 1992–1993, he could never be certain that he would not be removed from office by force. Nor, in October 1993, did he find it easy to gain military support for assaulting the parliament. And he could never be confident that his administrative staff was devoted to implementing his declared policies. Hence, even if he were not already so inclined (which he was), circumstances would have nudged Yeltsin toward suspicion—an insistence on personal loyalty, a tendency to test the loyalties of his associates and appointees, an urge to show them who was boss, and a simultaneous urge to insure his personal security by developing intimate personal relationships with his defense minister (Pavel Grachev) and his bodyguards. Thus, while political uncertainty was a constant throughout his years as Russian president, political self-confidence, authority, and credibility were variables. As Yeltsin's confidence declined in his ability to solve the country's problems, to mobilize the masses, to control the 'force ministries,' and to maintain his authority and credibility as an effective leader, so too did his level of patriarchalism increase.

The *causes* of Yeltsin's political behavior are one thing; the *consequences* are another. The latter will be the focus of a subsequent study.

---

[73] Ibid. 68, quotes a televised interview of November 1993 in which Yeltsin said that his role models were Andrey Sakharov, Margaret Thatcher, and Peter the Great.

[74] See Yeltsin, *The Struggle for Russia* 6; also, pp. 7, 17, 18–19, 109.

[75] See Yeltsin, ibid. 292–3.

6 Overcoming the Yeltsin legacy: Vladimir Putin and Russian political reform

Eugene Huskey

Few leaders in modern times have risen to power more quickly or improbably than Vladimir Putin. Thanks to Boris Yeltsin's patronage, including his dramatic and shrewdly timed exit from the historical stage on millennium's eve, Putin moved from political obscurity to the presidency of a great nation in a little over a year.[1] Not since the selection of Brezhnev's Man Friday, Konstantin Chernenko, as general secretary has a more unlikely and untested leader ruled Russia. If Boris Yeltsin claimed the Russian presidency at the beginning of the 1990s as a self-made man, Vladimir Putin came to office as a reluctant *dauphin* manoeuvred into power by Yeltsin and his associates.

In spite of his indebtedness to his patron, Putin has refused to play the role of the deferential heir. To be sure, he signed a decree offering Yeltsin and his immediate family a measure of legal and personal security,[2] and he showed every indication of continuing, and even deepening, the commitment to market-oriented reforms that Yeltsin had begun. However, on vital questions relating to the use and distribution of political power in Russia, Putin openly challenged the Yeltsin legacy. Within days of taking office, the new president introduced bills that promised to return Russia to a more traditional Moscow-centred—and one-man centred—style of rule. These proposals represented a call to regather power that had become broadly dispersed across the Russian political landscape in the 1990s. The role of the centre was to rise at the expense of the periphery, the executive at the expense of the legislature, and the state at the expense of society, especially its most financially prominent representatives, the so-called oligarchs.

After noting the new Russian president's peculiar rise to power, this chapter interprets the radical institutional reform of Putin's first months in office as a logical, and in some respects necessary, response to the institutional inheritance of the Yeltsin era. Although it has become a commonplace in the literature on Russian and comparative politics to refer to the Yeltsin regime as superpresidential, with inordinate authority concentrated in the hands of the country's leader, the reality is that power became highly fragmented under Yeltsin,

---

Chapter specially commissioned for this volume.

[1] A search for articles on Putin in Lexis-Nexis Academic Universe, which covers a large number of publications on Russia in English and in translation, revealed the following number of 'hits' on Putin: 1994–1; 1995–2; 1996–7; 1997–21; 1998–365. By comparison, in 1998 Grigory Yavlinsky appeared in 720 articles. Only in 1999 does Putin become a very visible figure in the Russian and foreign press.

[2] 'O garantiiakh Prezidentu Rossiiskoy Federatsii, prekrativshemu ispolnenie svoikh polnomochii, i chlenam ego sem'i', *Sobranie zakonodatel'stva*, no. 1 (2000), st. 111.

whether between central and provincial elites or within and between executive and legislative institutions in Moscow. Indeed, the governing crisis that afflicted Russia in the 1990s had its roots in part in the failure of presidential leadership to assure institutional cooperation and cohesion in the face of the enormous strains imposed by the transition from Communism. By the end of the 1990s, the absence of institutions, ideas, or leaders that could integrate the interests of diverse elites was rendering Russia ungovernable. It was this legacy that Putin inherited, and sought to overcome, not by relying on the institutions associated with integrative politics in democratic countries, such as political parties or social movements, but by reviving a disciplined and centralized state machinery.

Putin's short march

During the summer of 1996, as the country went to the polls to elect Boris Yeltsin to a second term, Vladimir Putin was an unemployed city official from St Petersburg in search of a job. Like many Russians in the wake of Communism's collapse, Putin was struggling to find his niche in the new order. A lawyer by training, he had realized his boyhood ambition by joining the KGB after graduating from Leningrad State University in 1975. But after fifteen years in the security services, including five as an intelligence officer in East Germany, Putin began to 'reprofile' himself, apparently disillusioned by the collapsing Soviet state. For a short time he pursued graduate studies in law at his Alma Mater while working as assistant to the university rector for foreign relations—an office traditionally filled by KGB personnel in Soviet universities. However, only a few months into the graduate programme, he abandoned his studies and his university post to work for his former professor, the newly elected mayor of St Petersburg, Anatoly Sobchak.

Sobchak's democratic credentials, which were earned as a legislator on the national stage, began to fade when he returned to St Petersburg to confront an opposition-minded city council and a myriad of intractable social and economic problems. In Sobchak's five controversial years as mayor, Putin remained throughout a fierce loyalist, rising from the position of assistant for foreign economic relations to become one of the city's deputy mayors. Putin at times assumed an overtly political role by lobbying council deputies as well as the administrative heads of St Petersburg's boroughs. In the fiercely contested mayoral election campaign in 1996, Putin adopted an uncharacteristically visible and aggressive profile, at one point labelling Sobchak's opponent, Vladimir Yakovlev, a 'Judas' during a television interview. Moreover, he encouraged all members of the mayor's staff to pledge to resign from office *en masse* if Sobchak should lose. Not surprisingly, the victory of Yakovlev over Sobchak in early June 1996 led to Putin's resignation from city government.[3]

With a career in public service in St Petersburg foreclosed for the foreseeable future, Putin considered two options: private legal practice in St Petersburg and government service in Moscow. Through his work for the Yeltsin campaign in St Petersburg and his contacts with former colleagues from St Petersburg who now occupied key positions in the capital, including Aleksei Bolshakov and Aleksei Kudrin, the latter a fellow deputy mayor for Sobchak in the early 1990s, Putin received an offer of employment in Moscow as head of the presidency's Department for Relations with Society. But in a telling phrase from his memoirs, Putin

---

[3] *Ot pervogo litsa: razgovory s Vladimirom Putinym* (Moscow: Vagrius, 2000), 104–10.

revealed that such work, which dealt with the building blocks of democratic politics, political parties, and civic organizations, 'did not suit' him.[4] Through the last-minute intervention of Bolshakov, a deputy prime minister, Putin found more agreeable work in the presidential administration as deputy to Pavel Borodin, who oversaw a vast empire of presidential property that ranged from Moscow apartments to provincial factories and resort hotels.

From here, Putin's career advanced at breakneck speed. During the next eighteen months, he received two promotions within the presidential bureaucracy, the first to head the Monitoring Administration, a corps of presidential auditors who primarily review compliance of provincial governments with federal laws and decrees, and the second to serve as deputy leader of the presidential administration with special responsibility for relations with the provinces. It was in these posts that Putin first came into close contact with provincial leaders and first became familiar with the scale of embezzlement and corruption in the regions as well as the problems posed by the lack of an efficient executive hierarchy—or *vertikal*—to link Moscow with the provinces. As the analysis below makes clear, the attempt to construct a *vertikal* would become one of the central themes of the Putin presidency.[5]

In Russia's semi-presidential arrangements, elites circulated regularly between presidential offices and the government and its ministries, just as they had between the Communist Party Central Committee and the Council of Ministers in the Communist era. Thus, the transfer of Vladimir Putin in July 1998 from the presidential administration to the directorship of the FSB, a successor to the KGB, represented a logical progression for an official of Putin's rank and background—though if Putin is to be believed, neither he nor the leadership of the FSB was enthusiastic about the posting.[6] Within a few months, Putin added to his responsibilities the chairmanship of the presidency's Security Council, a cabinet uniting leading officials in the field of national security and foreign affairs.

The advancement of Putin was part of a broader initiative by Boris Yeltsin at the end of the 1990s to fill key executive posts with what the Russians call *siloviki*, officials with experience in 'power ministries' such as the army, police, and security services. Yeltsin had always had a favourite group in ascendance in his administration—whether leaders of the late Soviet-era 'democratic' movements, young economists, experienced industrial managers, or image-makers—and it was now the turn of the law-and-order types to give the Russian executive a distinct face. This militarization of cadres coincided with the financial crisis of August 1998, with war clouds gathering again in the Caucasus, and with talk of emergency measures to restore political and economic stability.[7] During this period a former head of the Border Guards, Nikolai Bordiuzha, became presidential chief of staff and three prime ministers in succession were drawn from among *siloviki*: Yevgeny Primakov, a leader of the intelligence services under Gorbachev and Yeltsin; Sergei Stepashin, a former head of the ministries of justice and internal affairs, and, in August 1999, Vladimir Putin.

---

[4] Ibid. 120. After uttering the phrase, '*eto mne bylo sovsem ne po dushe*', Putin goes on to comment: 'But what was I to do? If it was to be working with society, then so be it' (*Kuda mne devat'sia? S obshchestvennost'iu tak s obshchestvennost'iu*). Ibid.

[5] Putin would also have encountered numerous examples of corruption as head of legal affairs for Borodin, who has been implicated in—but not convicted of—large kickback schemes. If there were illegalities in the operation of Borodin's office, it is difficult to believe that Putin was not at least aware of them.

[6] *Ot pervogo litsa*, 125–7.

[7] Recall that at the end of 1998, Yeltsin had launched a campaign against 'extremist' forces that seemed to invite extraordinary measures to combat this threat to the state.

Although Putin's transfer from the FSB to the chairmanship of the Russian government fitted into a pattern of personnel appointments, it nonetheless caught the Russian establishment and public by surprise. Only three months earlier, Yeltsin had unexpectedly removed the highly popular Primakov in favour of Stepashin, whom the president hinted could become his heir apparent. Now Stepashin was asked to step aside to make room for another young, and far less experienced, *silovik*.[8] If Yeltsin had been somewhat coy in his designs for Stepashin, he was open and effusive in his promotion of Putin as his successor. But far from assuring Putin's election as president, Yeltsin's public designation of the new prime minister as his political heir in some ways complicated Putin's campaign for the presidency. That Yeltsin's recommendation counted for little was evident in opinion polls taken in September 1999, when Putin lagged the field of presidential candidates by a staggering margin.[9]

How did Putin manage to overcome his relative obscurity and his association with a discredited leadership to win a first-round victory in the March 2000 presidential election? Three factors seem to explain Putin's electoral success. The first relates to what Russian political scientists might call the 'technology' of the transfer of power. Yeltsin's decision to resign on 31 December 1999, six months before the end of his term, altered fundamentally the electoral calculus by shortening the presidential campaign, by allowing Putin to serve as acting president, and by casting Yeltsin and his era in a more favourable light. The resignation triggered constitutional provisions that called for elections to be held within three months, that is by the end of March. Truncating the campaign put Putin's opponent at a decided disadvantage because they had planned to begin their campaigns in earnest in the early spring. Given the suddenness and timing of the announcement—it came at the beginning of an almost two-week national holiday—campaign staffs had little more than two months to present their candidate to voters in the world's largest country. Furthermore, an early election reduced the likelihood that a protracted conflict in Chechnya would diminish support for Putin, who had assumed personal responsibility for the prosecution of the war.

Had the presidential campaign been conducted on a level playing field, of course, the timing of the election may not have mattered. But the institutional advantages enjoyed by incumbents in all countries were even more pronounced in Russia, where Putin received far more frequent and favourable coverage by the broadcast media than his opponents. Moreover, he used presidential decree-making authority to distribute financial benefits to key voting blocs during the campaign. And while his opponents criss-crossed the country in search of votes, Putin spent most of his time in Moscow tending to the nation's business and projecting an image that he was above politics.

Elections are rarely won, however, on institutional advantage alone. Putin's success derived in no small measure from the very contrast in leadership style between the young, energetic, and decisive acting president and his old, infirm, and disengaged patron. Whether in his compulsively overbooked daily schedule or in his occasional bursts of bravado, such as a judo session or a flight to Chechnya in a fighter jet, Putin was inviting the nation to compare him to his predecessor. Nowhere was the contrast in leadership more stark than on

---

[8] Putin's confirmation by the Duma came swiftly and with little resistance owing to the deputies' desire not to complicate the schedule for the forthcoming parliamentary elections and to the similarities between Putin and his predecessor. Aleksandr Sadchikov, 'Duma mozhet podderzhat' Putina', *Izvestiya*, 10 Aug. 1999, p. 3; Sadchikov, 'Torg neumesten', *Izvestiya*, 17 Aug. 1999, p. 3.

[9] See the revealing graph at http://www.russiavotes.org/.

the Chechen conflict, where Yeltsin's approach had been to allow others to prosecute the war and make the peace. Although the president was formally responsible for operational control of the armed forces, Putin quickly emerged as the effective commander-in-chief, reporting to Yeltsin only after 'missions had already been concluded'.[10] It was Putin, not Yeltsin, who met daily with the heads of the uniformed services to co-ordinate action on the ground. Putin was in every sense Russia's war leader in a conflict that generated broad popular support. This support rested on the public's outrage over the invasion of Chechen rebels into Dagestan and the bombing of civilian apartment buildings—allegedly by Chechen terrorists—as well as its long-standing prejudice against the Chechens as a people and its desire to expiate the humiliation associated with the country's rapid descent from power, most vividly illustrated in the military debacle that was the first Chechen war. As the Russian army advanced further into Chechnya, Putin advanced further in the polls. Through his aggressive policies and rhetoric towards Chechnya, Putin managed by the end of 1999 to distance himself from the Yeltsin legacy while remaining the loyal heir. In the eyes of the public, he had become his own, and not just Yeltsin's, man.

But this was not simply a populist campaign. Putin's electoral victory would not have been possible without the vigorous support of key members of the Russian political establishment who viewed the acting president as the candidate best able to protect their person, property, or power. In presidential or semi-presidential regimes that lack a mature private sector and legal system, an electoral defeat can have devastating consequences, including criminal prosecution or financial ruin, for elites associated with the losing candidate. For Yeltsin's relatives and close associates—members of the so-called 'Family'—as well as for many oligarchs and provincial leaders, Putin appeared to offer a reliable shelter, or *krysha*, for the future. In return, these elites offered access to campaign funds, favourable and frequent media coverage, and political machines that could deliver the votes.

As late as December 1999, however, there was no single establishment candidate for the presidency. Russian elites were deeply divided between the Yeltsin camp and economic and political leaders associated with the mayor of Moscow, Yury Luzhkov, and the president of Tatarstan, Mintimer Shaimiev. That this second axis within the establishment virtually evaporated in the run-up to the March 2000 presidential election was due to Yeltsin's unexpected resignation and to the poor results of the Luzhkov-Shaimiev electoral alliance, Fatherland–All Russia, in the December 1999 parliamentary elections, in which a newly created party linked to Putin, Unity, made a surprisingly strong showing. Once popular sentiment had tipped in favour of Putin, previously wavering elites, including most of Russia's governors, scurried to ally themselves with Yeltsin's heir. Only the ideologically committed at both extremes of the political spectrum were willing to stay off the bandwagon. Within weeks, many in the establishment would have reason to regret their role in the election of Vladimir Putin as Russia's second president.

Putin in power

Cautious in personnel and policy decisions during his months as acting president, Putin wasted no time after his inauguration in launching a vigorous campaign to reassert

---

[10]   *Ot pervogo litsa*, 134.

presidential power. Shortly after assuming the presidency on 7 May 2000, he delivered a television address to the nation that called for a dictatorship of law to restore strong and centralized government. The tenor of these remarks, and the radical institutional reforms that followed, reflected Putin's aggressive style of leadership as well as disquiet about his political inheritance. If Yeltsin had learned to live with Russia's untidy and confused political arrangements, which forced the president into permanent negotiations with governors, deputies, and oligarchs, Putin insisted on the establishment of a regime that favoured command over compromise, or to put it more generously, law and administration over politics.

Ever respectful towards Yeltsin the individual, Putin adopted rhetoric and policies that implicitly rebuked Yeltsin's legacy, at least as it related to Russia's condition and to the vitality and effectiveness of the state. In the State of the Union address delivered in July 2000, he stated that Russia faced an economic and demographic catastrophe. 'The very survival of the nation' is at stake, he warned.[11] Taken together with the crisis in Chechnya, this alarmist language helped to create an atmosphere of emergency that could justify radical institutional reforms.

Unfortunately, much of the Western literature on Russian politics failed to prepare us for Putin's campaign to remake Russian institutions. If one accepts, as many Western scholars did, that Russia's political arrangements were superpresidential under Yeltsin, then Putin's attempt to concentrate still more power in the presidency appears unnecessary and dangerous.[12] To be sure, with the dissolution of parliament and the introduction of a self-serving constitution in late 1993, Yeltsin had hoped to create a superpresidential order. But the very design of the country's institutions, the resistance of regional and financial elites, widespread corruption, and Yeltsin's own tactics, especially in the field of personnel policy, ensured that political power would remain broadly distributed across the political landscape. As Lilia Shevtsova has argued,

Yeltsin meant to create a pure pyramid of power that needed no other institutions, but the emergence of pluralism in society and among the political elite and a devolution of power from the centre to the regions precluded this design. The 'presidential pyramid' is in fact a false front for a ramshackle regime built of ill-fitting parts.[13]

In the absence of integrative state and social institutions and a national consensus on basic political values, the proliferation of power centres contributed to the creation of what the French call a *société bloquée*, or stalemated society. Thus, Putin did not inherit a superpresidential order, he sought to build one.

---

[11] Russian President's Address to Federal Assembly, Russia TV, Moscow, in Russian 0800 GMT 8 July 2000, BBC Monitoring.

[12] See e.g. M. Steven Fish, 'The Executive Deception: Superpresidentialism and the Degradation of Russian Politics', in Valerie Sperling, ed., *Building the Russian State: Institutional Crisis and the Quest for Democratic Governance* (Boulder, Colo: Westview, 2000), 177–92.

[13] Lilia Shevtsova, *Yeltsin's Russia: Myths and Reality* (Washington: Carnegie Endowment for International Peace, 1999), 277.

THE ASSAULT ON PROVINCIAL ELITES

Putin's primary challenge to the Yeltsin institutional inheritance came in presidential decrees and legislative proposals issued in the weeks after the inauguration. These measures were designed to accomplish what Yeltsin had been unable to achieve during his two terms in office: the establishment of an effective mechanism of central control—a ruling *vertikal'* —over the unruly provinces. In a decree with wide-ranging implications for Russian federalism, Putin fundamentally restructured the institution of presidential representatives to the provinces.[14] Introduced in 1991 to serve as the eyes and ears of the president in the country's republics and regions, most of these representatives had by the mid-1990s become the pawns of provincial authorities. In order to reduce the representatives' physical proximity to, and political dependence on, the leaders of individual provinces, Putin carved Russia into seven federal administrative districts and appointed a presidential representatives of formidable stature and authority to each. In keeping with the militarization of cadres policy begun in the late Yeltsin era, five of the seven representatives were generals from the armed forces or security services.[15] Instead of an easily manipulable presidential emissary with a skeletal staff, provincial élites now faced scrutiny from an imposing zonal branch of the presidential bureaucracy, whose inspectors continued to operate in the individual republics and regions.

The presidential representatives became the leaders of what amounted to seven new federal capitals, or mini-Moscows, which existed in territorial configurations that roughly paralleled Russia's military districts and ignored the ethnic dimension in Russian federalism. Each presidential representative directed a staff of approximately 100 persons and assumed co-ordinating authority over officials from the many other federal agencies that quickly set up branches in these federal capitals.[16] The ministries of justice and internal affairs, the Procuracy, the tax police, and the FSB opened their own bureaux at the new administrative level within weeks of the establishment of the seven federal administrative districts.[17] It was a measure of the growing importance of the seven federal capitals that even private institutions, such as *Sviaz' invest*, the telecommunications company, reconfigured their own internal territorial divisions to accord with the new divisions of the Russian state.

In forming the new federal superdistricts, Putin sought to introduce into the provinces

---

[14] 'O polnomochnom predstavitele Prezidenta RF v federal'nom okruge', *Sobranie zakonodatel'stva*, no. 20 (2000), st. 2112. For a sound early analysis of the reform, see Pavel Felgenhauer, 'Russia's Seven Fiefdoms', *Transitions*, 12 June 2000.

[15] The appointees with their respective postings were: General Viktor Kazantsev (Northern Caucasus District—Rostov-on-the-Don); Sergei Kirienko (Volga District—Nizhny Novgorod); General Viktor Cherkesov (North-Western District—St Petersburg); General Petr Latyshev (Urals District—Ekaterinburg); General Georgii Poltavchenko (Central District—Moscow); General Konstantin Pulikovsky (Far Eastern District—Khabarovsk); Leonid Drachevsky (Siberian District—Novosibirsk). For a brief discussion of Putin's reasons for selecting these individuals, see Natal'ia Kalashnikova, Aleksei Makarov, 'Semigeneral'shchina v deistvii', *Segodnya* Online, 19 May 2000.

[16] On the early organization of offices of the new presidential representatives, see 'Aleksandr Abramov: Gubernatorov ne budut goniat' kak zaitsev', *Izvestiya*, 26 May 2000, pp. 1, 3. The decree notes, in article 10, that the zonal officers of the presidency's Main Monitoring Administration (*Glavnoe kontrol'noe upravlenie*) will be integrated into the offices of the presidential representatives.

[17] The law-related ministries clearly welcomed this centralizing move by Putin. In the words of the Justice Minister, Yury Chaika, 'the federal authorities had been turning a blind eye to the arbitrariness of provincial elites, especially those in the national republics, for fear of offending them.' Andrei Kamakin, 'Miniust prismotritsia k gubernatoram poluchshe', *Segodnya* Online, 27 May 2000.

agents of the central state who would remain unswervingly loyal to directives emanating from Moscow, and in the first instance from the presidency. Such federal personnel were becoming ever rarer in the republics and regions because of the levers of influence available to provincial leaders. The latter offered needed goods and services to poorly paid and poorly provisioned federal personnel and vetted federal nominees serving in their territories. Taking the Procuracy as an example, procurators in the regions were selected by the procurator-general in Moscow but always with 'the agreement of the government of the subject territories', which meant the presidents and governors. Although there were a few provinces where the regional procurators and governors were at odds, notably Cheliabinsk, Tver, and Kursk, in most cases they worked 'hand in glove'.[18]

The threat that more authoritative and independent presidential representatives would monitor more carefully the behaviour of provincial leaders could not by itself guarantee the periphery's compliance with Moscow's wishes. What gave this administrative reform its bite was a corollary bill that granted the president the right to remove elected provincial leaders from office if they failed to bring provincial legislation in line with federal laws after they were warned to do so on the basis of a court finding. This law invited presidential representatives as well as procurators and other law-enforcement personnel to uncover discrepancies between federal and provincial legislation that could serve as a pretext for removing heads of administration from office and/or shutting down provincial parliaments.[19] Because a significant proportion of all provincial laws and regulations did not correspond to the principles of federal legislation, provincial elites had good reason to feel insecure in their jobs, and therefore more likely to follow the lead of Moscow. Putin's statements on the subject only deepened the growing sense of vulnerability among provincial leaders. 'It is simply essential . . . to restore an effective vertical chain of command in the country . . . It's a scandalous thing when—just think about the figures—a fifth of the legal acts adopted in the regions contradict the country's basic law . . .'[20] In several particularly egregious cases of a conflict of laws, Putin acted immediately to annul regional legislation or send warning letters to governors.[21]

Equally disturbing for the defenders of devolution in Russia was the provision in the draft that allowed Putin to remove from office temporarily any head of provincial government against whom a criminal investigation had been launched. In a country where criminal investigations can easily drag on for months or even years, where criminal prosecution has been a central feature of the political struggle, and where most people are guilty of something anyway—'show me a man and I'll find you an article in the criminal code to match'—the ability to remove an elected official on the strength of suspicion of a crime presented the president with a powerful means of neutralizing opposition to his policies. Moreover, the proposed removal of provincial leaders from the Federation Council, to be discussed below,

---

[18] The expression in Russian is 'dusha v dushu'. Andrei Kamakin, 'Gubernatory okruzhaiut', *Segodnya* Online, 25 May 2000.

[19] On 1 June 2000, the procurator-general ordered his organization to identify expeditiously all the laws of the provinces that were not in line with federal legislation. Petr Akopov, 'Ul'timatum Ustinova', *Izvestiya*, 2 June 2000, p. 3.

[20] 'Putin Announces Major Revamping of Senate', *Rossiyskaya gazeta*, 19 May 2000, p. 3, as trans. in *Current Digest of the Post-Soviet Press*, 52 (1999), 5.

[21] Svetlana Babaeva, 'Moskva vzialas' za regiony', *Izvestiya*, 12 May 2000, p. 4

promised to strip the republican presidents and regional governors of their parliamentary immunity. Such measures placed enormous power in the hands of procurators and criminal investigators and threatened to politicize a court system that was struggling to assert its independence. These changes laid the groundwork for presidential leadership based on intimidation and *diktat* rather than persuasion and compromise.[22]

A further source of tension between the Russian president and provincial elites was the proposed reform of local administration—that is, the governments of cities and rural districts that lay within the country's eighty-nine republics and regions.[23] Where presidents and governors through the 1990s sought to subordinate the mayors and heads of district governments to their rule—going so far as to eliminate local government altogether in one republic—the Russian president had presented himself as a protector of local interests against overbearing provincial leadership. Recognizing the desire of republican presidents and regional governors to dominate their respective territories, Putin appeared to offer them heightened power vis-à-vis their own peripheries in new draft legislation on local administration.[24] Just as the bill on provincial government allowed the president to remove presidents and governors who violated federal law, the proposed law on local administration gave these same presidents and governors the authority to dismiss mayors and heads of district government who did not adhere to principles set out in provincial or federal legislation. But this apparent sop to the embattled provincial leaders came at a price: the president of the Russian Federation also acquired the right to dismiss miscreant local leaders, and the centre for the first time received the authority to reach over the provincial elites to regulate the 'details of the structures of local government' in any city with more than 50,000 persons.[25]

Among the measures advanced by Putin to diminish the prominence and authority of provincial elites, none was more controversial or vigorously opposed than the bill designed to strip presidents and governors of their membership in the upper house of parliament, the Federation Council.[26] As part of the peculiar institutional design inherited from the Yeltsin era, Russia's eighty-nine presidents and governors—along with the speakers of provincial parliaments and the mayors and city council leaders in Moscow and St Petersburg—

---

[22] It also placed extraordinary powers in the hands of procurators and other law-enforcement personnel.

[23] On this layer of Russian government, see Peter Kirkow, 'Local Self-Government in Russia: Awakening from Slumber?' *Europe-Asia Studies*, 1 (1997), 43–58.

[24] For an excellent analysis of the provincial elite's position between federal and local power, see Jean-Charles Lallemand, 'Politics for the Few: Elites in Bryansk and Smolensk', *Post-Soviet Affairs*, 4 (1999), 312–35.

[25] Previously, Moscow had asserted the authority to intervene directly in local government only in cases where national security was at issue, such as border zones or closed cities with secret defence plants. Zakonoproekt 'O vnesenii izmenenii i dopolnenii v Federal'nyi zakon "Ob obshchikh printsipakh organizatsii mestnogo samoupravleniya v Rossiyskoy Federatsii"', *Gazeta.ru*, 9 June 2000. See also the *poiasnitel'naya zapiska k proektu* in the same issue of *Gazeta.ru*. For a critique of the proposed law, see Vsevolod Vasil'ev, 'Mestnoe samoupravlenie i federal'naya vlast'', *Nezavisimaya gazeta* Online, 14 June 2000. For an attempt by Putin's allies to undermine the authority of the president's nemesis, the elected mayor of St Petersburg, Vladimir Yakovlev, by establishing a new post of chair of city government, see Vadim Nesvizhskii, 'Gubernatora Yakovleva lishat vlasti', *Segodnya* Online, 19 May 2000. Aleksei Makarin, 'Strashnaya mest'', *Segodnya* Online, 31 May 2000.

[26] For the draft, see 'O poriadke formirovaniia Soveta Federatsii Federal'nogo Sobraniya', *Gazeta.ru*, 9 June 2000 and the *poiasnitel'naya zapiska* that follows. The extent of provincial opposition to the bill revising Federation Council membership was evident in the pressure many presidents and governors brought to bear on Duma deputies from their regions. In Cheliabinsk, for example, when a deputy refused to bend to pressure from Governor Petr Sumin to vote against the bill, tax inspectors showed up at the factory where the deputy had been director. Aleksei Makarkin, 'Strashnaya mest'', *Segodnya* Online, 31 May 2000.

occupied the 182 seats in the Senate by virtue of their offices. It was not only an awkward arrangement—the workload of the chief executives forced the upper house into truncated and zonal sessions—it also accorded provincial leaders an unusually prominent and direct role in national politics. Able to deliver their own votes on important federal legislative or personnel matters as well as the votes of constituents within their territories during a presidential election, republican presidents and regional governors were exceptionally well positioned to extract concessions from the Russian president and other officials in the central executive. Thus, the devolution of power in the 1990s followed in part from the ability of provincial elites to operate as both federal and republican/regional politicians.[27] One need only imagine the consequences for American federalism if the framers had made the governors of the states members of the US Senate.

To placate hostile provincial leaders who were alarmed by the attempt to remove them from the Federation Council, Putin offered two palliatives. First, he proposed granting the presidents and governors an important role in the selection of their replacements in the upper house.[28] Second, Putin entertained the idea of creating a consultative council that would bring the president together periodically with provincial leaders to discuss matters of common interest. But the difficulty of holding frequent or even regular meetings virtually assured that, even if introduced, such a body would share the fate of other 'state councils' that had come and gone over the preceding decade. It seemed unlikely in any event to rival in importance an existing presidential body, the Security Council, whose visibility and membership had just been enhanced with the addition of the seven presidential representatives from the newly created federal superdistricts.[29] This membership change was further evidence that in elevating the status of presidential representatives, Putin diminished the role of provincial elites.

THE ASSAULT ON FINANCIAL AND LEGISLATIVE POWER

Institutional reforms curtailing provincial power represented only one of several initiatives aimed at strengthening the presidency and the state—two concepts that appeared to blur together in Putin's mind. If the most potent constraint on presidential power in the late Yeltsin era had been provincial elites, the winners in the partition of Russian wealth in the 1990s—the oligarchs—were another formidable group limiting presidential and state authority. Through their control of key media outlets, their development of client networks in federal and provincial governments, and their evasion of taxes, the oligarchs helped to define the informal rules of the political game and weaken the state. Although great economic wealth offers the potential for political influence everywhere, in Russia the absence of a rule of law, a well-developed and competitive private sector, and a tradition of public service among state officials enabled the oligarchs to corrupt the operation of the state.

[27] See Kathryn Stoner-Weiss, 'Central Weakness and Provincial Autonomy: Observations on the Devolution Process in Russia', *Post-Soviet Affairs*, 1 (1999), 100.

[28] After a conciliation commission meeting in July, the Duma version of the bill granted the members of the Federation Council the right to hire and fire their replacements and postponed the introduction of the measure until January 2002. Yevgeny Yur'iev, 'Voyna do pol'noy rotatsii', *Segodnya* Online, 20 July 2000.

[29] The seven presidential representatives made up almost a third of the twenty-four-member body. For the membership, see 'Ob utverzhdenii sostava Soveta Bezopasnosti RF', *Sobranie zakonodatel'stva*, no. 22 (2000), st. 2290.

Socialized professionally in an institution—the KGB—that elevated state interests above all others, Putin appeared to have a particular aversion to the high profile that the oligarchs had assumed in Russian political life. Putin quickly moved beyond his stated policy of 'equidistancing the oligarchs from the authorities' to a frontal assault on oligarchical power, which began in late May 2000 with the arrest of a leading oligarch, Vladimir Gusinsky, on charges of embezzlement. It remains unclear whether Putin personally approved the detention of the head of the Media-Most business empire, which includes prominent media such as the newspaper *Segodnya* and the television network NTV, but at a minimum the president's confrontational approach to the oligarchs signalled to the law enforcement community that financial elites were no longer untouchable. Within weeks of Gusinsky's arrest, procurators raided several other high-profile companies to issue arrest warrants, among them the country's largest commercial concern, Gazprom. Also under criminal investigation or arraignment by late July 2000 were Vagit Alikperov of LUKoil (tax evasion), Vladimir Potanin of Norilsk Nickel (illegal privatization of shares), and Boris Berezovsky of Avtovaz (underground production).[30]

Did the flurry of very visible criminal investigations launched in the wake of Putin's inauguration represent merely a settling of scores with uncooperative oligarchs or the beginning of a broad-based campaign against criminality and corruption in Russia? Was Putin's much-criticized campaign for a dictatorship of law simply an instrument in an escalating intra-elite struggle or an attempt to restore the authority and efficacy of the state? Although the evidence available in the mid-summer of 2000 does not allow one to reach definitive conclusions to these questions, it does suggest that Putin himself was committed to ending widespread law-breaking at all levels of society, whether through more vigorous law enforcement or the revision of laws such as the tax code, which in its confused and confiscatory form encouraged citizens and businesses to violate the law. If the Yeltsin legacy drove many Russians to seek protection for legitimate pursuits from illegitimate sources, such as private racketeers or corrupt public officials, Putin seemed intent on reclaiming for the state writ large the role of public patron. The president had every reason to prefer an honest and efficient bureaucracy, which would enhance presidential power while encouraging foreign investment and reducing the costs of doing business, advantages that would not be lost on a former economic development officer for the city of St Petersburg. Unless, however, civil servants become more scrupulous, competent, and public-spirited, they will continue quietly to erode and distort presidential power, no matter how successful Putin is in the visible struggle with the country's elites.

Besides the governors and oligarchs, the other elite group restraining presidential power has been Duma deputies. Yeltsin bequeathed Putin executive-legislative relations that forced the president to compromise continually with the parliament on matters of personnel and policy, an arrangement that most would regard as reasonable in light of Russia's semi-presidentialism and the successive electoral verdicts that pitted a reform-minded president against more conservative legislators. Putin has sought to overcome parliamentary opposition to reform by using two party-building strategies shunned by Yeltsin. First, whereas Yeltsin had always avoided direct association with a political party, Putin has identified

---

[30] Olga Proscourina, 'Oligarchs' Summer Plans Spoiled', *Transitions*, 10 July 2000; Michael Wines, 'Russian Puzzle: What does the War on Tycoons Mean?' *New York Times*, 15 July 2000, p. A3.

himself openly with a new party of power, Unity, created in the autumn of 1999. Second, Unity has insisted on a high level of internal party discipline in parliamentary voting, which many in Russia mistakenly associate only with Communist Parties. When a prominent member of Unity, Vladimir Ryzhkov, voted against Putin's proposals to remove governors from the Federation Council and to revise the law on local administration, he was excluded from the party. In his words, an official in the presidential apparatus, Vladislav Surkov, exercises 'very tough' and 'total' oversight of Unity and another pro-presidential fraction, People's Deputy. 'Each vote is reviewed, and any incorrect vote will prompt an investigation.'[31] Moreover, according to Ryzhkov, the Kremlin uses informants in almost all the party fractions in parliament to influence their behaviour. Because of the success of this party strategy, because of Putin's continuing popularity, and because of the revival of a psychology of compliance that had been largely dormant in the Yeltsin years, the president has seen his legislative initiatives pass through parliament with unusual speed and integrity.[32]

A rationalization of authority or a prelude to dictatorship?

The dramatic first months of the Putin presidency raise difficult analytical and interpretive questions to which responses must, at this juncture, remain provisional. Can Putin, the novice politician, overcome mounting resistance to his bold attempts to concentrate power in the presidency, whether from angry oligarchs like Boris Berezovsky, who feel betrayed by the president, or provincial elites like President Ruslan Aushev of Ingushetia, who treat Russia's new leader with contempt?[33] If radical institutional reform challenges the political authority and in some cases even the personal freedom of the governors, the oligarchs, and the deputies, why should these elites comply with Putin's leadership? Put another way, what are the weapons in Putin's arsenal whose use or mere existence encourages the cooperation of Russia's strategic elites?

The most obvious advantage enjoyed by Putin is his position as a single, committed actor facing groups that are fractured and bickering. Where Putin has been able to act thus far with dispatch and purpose, the elite response has been dilatory and divergent. But whether the advantages enjoyed by Putin in the summer of 2000 can be transformed into a more permanent regathering of power in Russian politics depends on the president's ability to bring governors, deputies, and business leaders into a new ruling coalition. Where some leaders would employ ideas or charisma to accomplish this, Putin appears content to rely on three sets of negative incentives to attract support for his pro-presidential front: one legal, one electoral, and one financial. First, those who challenge presidential policies may expose

[31] 'Takoy prokremlevskoy Dumy u nas eshche ne bylo', *Novaya gazeta* Online, 10 July 2000. On the question of party discipline in provincial branches of Unity, see Avtandil Tsuladze, 'Kolpak dlya regionov', *Segodnya* Online, 11 May 2000.

[32] During the Yeltsin era, nominees for the post of procurator-general were at times delayed for months, but when Putin proposed Vladimir Ustinov in mid-May 2000, the Senate approved him without even the requisite paperwork. The comment from the chair of the Federation Council, 'Ustinov's alive, what kind of materials could we need on him?' Viktoriya Sokolova, 'Ustinov proshel senat bez dokumentov', *Izvestiya*, 18 May 2000, p. 3.

[33] For the text of Berezovsky's impressive critique of Putin's reforms, see 'Polnyi tekst otkrytogo pis'ma deputata Gosudarstvennoy Dumy Borisa Berezovskogo prezidentyu Rossii Vladimiru Putinu', *Gazeta.ru*, 9 June 2000. Aushev, a general, was removed from the military ranks shortly after Putin came to power because of his hostility to the president. Oleg Odnokolenko, 'V spiskakh ne znachitsia', *Segodnya* Online, 1 June 2000.

themselves to criminal prosecution or disruptive and potentially costly civil suits and administrative reviews directed against their businesses. The presidential representative to the Duma, Aleksandr Kotenkov, warned that once parliamentary immunity was lifted, sixteen governors would 'serve time immediately'.[34] Second, politicians who refuse to support Putin may find a popular president unwilling to back their re-election, or indeed unwilling to accept that their post should be elected at all. Putin has considered proposing the appointment rather than the election of governors. Finally, provincial leaders and deputies who oppose Putin's initiatives may receive less generous allocations from the central budget for themselves and their constituencies. Concern about the use of federal budget disbursements as a political weapon by the centre has risen in recent months with proposed revisions to the 2001 budget. According to a Duma deputy:

The governors are afraid. In the draft budget for 2001, the distribution between the centre and regions is changing sharply. Now it's about 50/50, but they are proposing a 70/30 split in favour of the centre. A governor worries that tomorrow he'll go to the Ministry of Finance for money . . . and they'll ask him, 'And how did you vote?' Governors are scared to express their disapproval [of the president] openly, before the television cameras . . . They are in a trance.[35]

The success of this negative leadership strategy towards the elites depends on numerous factors, among the most important of which are the continued loyalty of the Procuracy and power ministries and the broad support of the nation. By squeezing recalcitrant elites between the representatives of state violence and the voters, Putin believes that he will be able to dismantle the petty fiefdoms that developed throughout Russia in the Yeltsin era. Leaving aside for the moment the reliability of the *siloviki* as a base of political support, Putin has been able thus far to attract public support because of the broad appeal of his policies. For Communists and nationalists, he offers the promise of a strong state with discipline and law and order at home and respect and engagement abroad. For the liberal professions and small and medium-sized businesses, Putin appears to be the champion of a market economy, lower taxes, and even government deregulation. For those in the political centre, that ideologically indeterminate space in Russia occupied by the parties of power during much of the last decade, Putin is the patron who runs the machinery of state, the traditional source of perquisites and privilege. Similarly, in the realm of foreign policy, the president advocates 'liberal patriotism', a slogan that appeals to several constituencies at once.[36] To put it crudely, there is something here for almost everyone, and at times one wonders if this approach derives from

---

[34] Aleksandr Sadchikov, 'Chernyy spisok', *Izvestiya*, 6 June 2000, p. 3. Kotenkov uses more explicit language than most in the presidency. On another occasion, he warned the deputies, 'isn't it better to make peace with the president than to be in serious conflict with him?' Svetlana Sukhova, 'Vsya vlast' Sovetu bezopasnosti', *Segodnya* Online, 26 May 2000. For a critique of Kotenkov, see Anatoly Kucherena, 'Gospodin Kotenkov kak zerkalo diktatura zakona', *Nezavisimaya gazeta* Online, 6 June 2000.

[35] 'Takoy prokremlevskoy Dumy u nas eshche ne bylo' *Novaya gazeta* Online, 10 July 2000.

[36] This slogan seemed to confirm Putin's own ideology as a 'statist liberal'. According to Marcia Weigle, 'the statist liberals assume that in the crisis conditions produced by the postcommunist transition, Russian society is incapable of self-rule and requires the guiding hand of the state to both guarantee social order and to introduce the structures of market economy.' Marcia A. Weigle, *Russia's Liberal Project: State-Society Relations in the Transition from Communism* (University Park, Pa.: The Pennsylvania State University Press, 2000), 400.

political naïveté or disingenuousness. Shortly after launching the assault on provincial power, Putin uttered a worryingly Orwellian phrase: 'under no circumstances can we weaken the powers of the regional authorities—they are a link on which federal authorities cannot but rely.'[37]

The question for the future is whether such 'dialectical' thinking can sustain broad public support as events require Putin to choose between liberty and authority, between freedom and the state. Already one has seen the defection of a segment of the liberal intelligentsia outraged by human rights violations in Chechnya and by growing restrictions on press freedom. Furthermore, a permanent negative leadership strategy towards Russia's elites is almost certainly doomed to failure. As Rousseau, and even the Soviet leadership, understood, 'the strongest man is never strong enough to remain forever the master, unless he transforms his might into right and obedience into duty'.[38]

If one accepts the controversial—but in my view defensible—argument that Yeltsin's legacy of hyperpluralism prevented the development of a modern state and a 'normal society' in Russia, then bold measures of some sort were needed to restrain the power of elites who were effectively privatizing or hijacking the state.[39] Gail Lapidus observed that at the end of the Yeltsin era, Russia was facing 'an uncontrolled and seemingly uncontrollable unraveling of central power'.[40] To invoke Samuel Huntington's analysis of the rise of modernity in continental Europe, unity and progress require centralized power and rationalized authority, by which he meant the replacement of religious, familial, aristocratic, regional, and local suzerains 'by a single, secular, national political authority'.[41] For all of their flaws, federal law and administration in Russia are to be preferred to the highly personalist and patrimonial regimes that have been taking root in many provinces, such as Kalmykia.[42] Thus, the benign interpretation of Putin's early months in office is that he was trying to restore a Russian state that could 'tax resources, conscript manpower, and innovate and execute policy',[43] basic functions that it was straining to carry out by the end of the Yeltsin era.

Any assessment of Putin's institutional reforms must recognize that all political leadership entails risks, which are only heightened in a transition era. Not to have acted against the deepening of the old Russian scourges of localism and departmentalism risked postponing indefinitely what Archie Brown has called—using Churchillian rhetoric—'the end of the

---

[37] Russian President's Address to Federal Assembly, Russia TV, Moscow, in Russian 0800 GMT 8 July 2000, BBC Monitoring.

[38] J.-J. Rousseau, 'On the Social Contract', in *Rousseau's Political Writings* (New York: Norton, 1988), 87.

[39] Kathryn Stoner-Weiss noted that '[t]he imposition of price controls, trade restrictions, and threats of tax withholding in many regions since August 17, 1998 have made some analysts and observers harken back to the Russia of the early 1990s, when the survival of the Russian state appeared to be at serious risk'. 'Central Weakness and Provincial Autonomy: Observations on the Devolution Process in Russia', *Post-Soviet Affairs*, 1 (1999), 87.

[40] Gail Lapidus, 'Asymmetrical Federalism and State Breakdown in Russia', *Post-Soviet Affairs*, 1 (1999), 76. (See also chapter 24 of this volume.) As Jeff Kahn argues, 'many provincial elites, especially those from the republics . . . rejected the principle that federalism entails a pooling and reduction of the individual sovereignties of constituent units into a new, fully sovereign entity'. Jeff Kahn, 'The Parade of Sovereignties: Establishing the Vocabulary of the New Russian Federation', *Post-Soviet Affairs*, 1 (2000), 82, 85.

[41] Samuel Huntington, 'Political Modernization: America vs. Europe', *World Politics*, 3 (1966), 378.

[42] George Breslauer's analysis of Yeltsin's personalist leadership style could be applied with even greater force to many provincial elites. See his 'Boris Yel'tsin as Patriarch', *Post-Soviet Affairs*, 2 (1999), 186–200.

[43] Samuel Huntington, *Political Order in Changing Societies* (New Haven: Yale University Press, 1969), 1.

beginning' in Russia's transition from Communism.[44] Of course, Putin's current course exposes Russia to other risks. These include the continuing 'lethargy of political society',[45] as change once again comes from above rather than below; the growth of legal nihilism, as the president himself raises the spectre of law's use as a political weapon and introduces what amount to constitutional changes without changing the constitution;[46] and the increasing dependence of the president on one group in Russian officialdom, the *siloviki*, who may expose Putin to a form of blackmail if his public popularity wanes.

Finally, and most ominously, should Putin succeed in the campaign to strengthen the presidency and the central state, there is a risk that an attempt to rationalize state authority may degenerate into a new authoritarianism. One cannot rule out the rise of a future leader—a statist with a world-view uncluttered by liberal values—who is willing to use the heightened powers of the Russian presidency to silence all opposition. For all of his faults, Yeltsin tolerated the development of political opposition as an idea and institution. This is one part of the Yeltsin legacy worth preserving. A major test of Putin's reforms is whether they will preserve space for an essential ingredient of a constitutional order—a legitimate opposition. To use the language of Steven Solnick, it is still too early to know whether Putin will be able to 'create a central government that is strong enough to keep the country whole, yet limited enough to prevent a return to tyranny'.[47]

[44] Archie Brown, 'The Russian Crisis: Beginning of the End or End of the Beginning?', *Post-Soviet Affairs*, 1 (1999), 56–73.

[45] M. Steven Fish, 'The Executive Deception: Superpresidentialism and the Degradation of Russian Politics', in Valerie Sperling, ed., *Building the Russian State: Institutional Crisis and the Quest for Democratic Governance* (Boulder, Colo: Westview, 2000), 190.

[46] Although Putin seemed open to the rewriting of the constitution, that would come only after the institutional reforms changing the country's basic political arrangements were *faits accomplis*. Petr Akopov, 'Pervaya popravka Vladimira Putina', *Izvestiya*, 5 June 2000, p. 1.

[47] Steven L. Solnick, 'Is the Center Too Weak or Too Strong in the Russian Federation?' in Valerie Sperling, ed., *Building the Russian State* 137.

Section 3

The Legislature and the Law

Introduction

Archie Brown

Historically, neither legislatures nor the law have occupied a prime place in Russian politics. This remained largely true even in the last decades of pre-revolutionary Russia when, however, something approaching a rule of law took firmer root and when, between 1906 and 1917, political pluralism was partly institutionalized through the creation of a new legislature—the State Duma. The relationship, however, between this quasi-parliament and the executive remained uneasy. The Emperor Nicholas II continued to believe that that such limitations on his autocratic power as he had conceded under revolutionary pressure in 1905 could, if he so wished, be reversed.

Yet the degree of political pluralism in late Imperial Russia contrasted sharply with what was to follow. The pre-revolutionary legislature was a much more significant institutional actor than the legislatures of the Soviet period. As noted in an earlier section, the Supreme Soviet met for only a few days in the year and passed much legislation retrospectively. Laws were, for the most part, deliberated upon and determined elsewhere and the Supreme Soviet's main function was to rubber-stamp whatever had been given the imprimatur of the Communist Party political hierarchy. Ministries as well as party organs were—until the late 1980s—not, in practice accountable to the legislature. Moreover, party discipline and the norms of the system were such that negative votes were not recorded in the Supreme Soviet until late in the Gorbachev era. One of the aims and achievements of the Gorbachev reforms was to turn a pseudo-parliament into a serious legislative assembly. The decision to create a new legislature, the Council of People's Deputies of the USSR, was taken in 1988 (as is discussed more fully in the introduction to Section 1). It was not to be in constant session throughout the year but was to occupy many more working days than the old unreformed Supreme Soviet. In an equally important reform, the Congress of People's Deputies was to elect an inner body, which retained the name, 'Supreme Soviet', while becoming a completely different institution in substance. The new Supreme Soviet was to meet for two-thirds of the year in two sessions lasting some four months at a time.

Elections for most of the seats in the Congress of People's Deputies were contested—unlike the single-candidate 'elections' for the old Supreme Soviet. These new institutional arrangements, which came into being at the federal level for the whole of the Soviet Union in 1989, were replicated in the Russian republic in 1990. After the Soviet Union was disbanded at the end of 1991, Russia had, accordingly, a Congress of People's Deputies and a smaller, more permanent working legislature, the Supreme Soviet of the Russian Federation. These, however, existed alongside a new Russian presidency, created in 1991. Boris Yeltsin, who in 1990 became the first chairman of the new-style Russian Supreme Soviet, was elected president of

Russia in June 1991, defeating all rival candidates in the first round. When Russia became the largest of the successor states to the USSR, there was real ambiguity about where the president's powers and those of the Congress of People's Deputies began and ended.

The first two years of post-Soviet Russia's existence were a time of struggle between the executive and legislature, personified in the rivalry between President Yeltsin and the chairman of the Supreme Soviet, Ruslan Khasbulatov, who had earlier been Yeltsin's ally and whom Yeltsin had, indeed, supported as his successor in the most powerful post within the legislature. This period of *dual power* ended with a bloody showdown when Yeltsin dissolved the increasingly intransigent legislature he had inherited from the late Soviet period in September 1993. Deputies who refused to accept the dissolution and who remained in their parliament building—the Moscow White House—were forced to leave it by 4 October when it was shelled by troops loyal to the Russian president.[1] Scores of people were killed in the process, and public disillusionment with the manner in which dual power had been brought to an end helped to account for the very low turn-out in the December 1993 elections for a new legislature.

The same month saw the adoption of a speedily written Constitution which strengthened the powers of the presidency and left the new legislature significantly weaker than its predecessor. The lower house was named the State Duma, thus emphasizing continuity with pre-revolutionary Russia rather than with the Soviet Union, and the upper house, which gave representation to the constituent parts of the federation, was called the Federation Council. The Duma roughly corresponded to the House of Representatives in the United States and the Federation Council to the Senate in terms of mode of representation, although the House in the United States and, still more clearly, the Senate are much more powerful than their Russian equivalents.

While not disputing the fact that the 1993 Constitution strengthened the presidency at the expense of the legislature, Paul Chaisty—in the chapter which opens this section—notes that over a third of all bills which passed into law emanated from deputies rather than from the government and that the State Duma has established itself as a political institution of some substance. Breaking with his predecessor's confrontational style in relations with the legislature, Vladimir Putin did something that was inconceivable for Yeltsin—namely, offering the Kremlin's backing to a member of the Communist Party, Gennady Seleznev, to continue in office as Speaker of the State Duma. Thereby, recognition was given both to the strong presence of the KPRF in the Duma and to the role of Seleznev as a power broker.

Eugene Huskey notes (in Chapter 8) that even in the Yeltsin era there was much behind-the-scenes negotiation between leading members of the legislature, on the one hand, and the presidential administration and the government, on the other. The virulence of the confrontational rhetoric in the Second Russian Republic was not always reflected in political behaviour unseen by the television cameras. Yet Huskey also points to the extent to which President Yeltsin could ignore the Duma or circumvent their law-making powers by substantial recourse to the issuing of decrees. He notes, additionally, that the weakness of party factions in the Federation Council, half of whose members were presidents of republics or regional governors,

---

[1] On this leadership struggle and, in particular, on the conflicting institutional jurisdictions which gave rise to it, see Archie Brown, 'Political Leadership in Post-Soviet Russia', in Amin Saikal and William Maley, eds. *Russia in Search of its Future* (Cambridge: Cambridge University Press, 1995), 28–47.

made the process of squaring them more laborious, inasmuch as deals had to be made with one member at a time.

Because the members of the Federation held crucially important posts in their own republics and regions, they spent far less time in Moscow than deputies of the State Duma. Yet, the fact that a number of important appointments by the Kremlin required the ratification of the Federation Council meant that they, too, could frustrate the executive—as they did when in 1999 they refused to accept the removal, which Yeltsin had insisted upon, of the procurator-general, Yury Skuratov. Demonstrating his superior authority (at least in the early stages of his presidency) Putin was able to get the upper house's endorsement of Skuratov's departure soon after assuming office. In the hope of ensuring that the Federation Council would remain pliable, he went on to propose sweeping reform of that body, whereby in future the republican and regional representatives would not include anyone from the presidential or gubernatorial ranks.

One of the aims of reformers in the second half of the 1980s was the creation of a law-governed state (*pravovoe gosudarstvo*). It was a goal to which Mikhail Gorbachev publicly subscribed and it came as a shock to veteran Communist Party *apparatchiki* when he made it clear that the party, too, must be bound by the law. A rule of law, in many respects, remains an aspiration in Russia at the beginning of the twenty-first century rather than a reality. In some respects, indeed, life has become more difficult for the legal profession than it was in the last years of the Soviet Union. As Peter Solomon and Todd Foglesong observe in a recent book: 'Not only did the Soviet period leave Russia with administration of justice characterized by a strong accusatorial bias and little leverage against state officials, but also post-Soviet experience has impoverished the courts and produced a surge of crime that makes it more difficult to improve the position of the accused.'[2] Those authors see the main hope for judicial reform as lying in the fact that the more efficient working of both the economy and government requires better implementation of the law.[3] Thus, even if the rule of law in the abstract is not necessarily a high priority for Russia's leaders, they should recognize that it would bring some practical advantages.

Yet, as Kathryn Hendley argues in Chapter 9, there remains a need to stimulate a demand for law. Hitherto, she observes, Russian managers have not found the law to be the most effective means of protecting the interests of their economic enterprise. Informal relationships with major political actors and patronage and security networks still play a key role in the running of the economy.[4] The supply of good law is much less of a problem, argues Hendley, than the disinclination of the political and economic elite to accept that the law applies also to them and to seek legal remedies when redress is required. She points to the wide gap between the ideals of legal reformers and everyday Russian reality and to the vicious circle whereby the 'courts will become legitimate only through widespread use, but using courts that lack legitimacy may not be in the short-term interests of the parties in conflict'.

The unwillingness of high officialdom to accept that they, as well as ordinary citizens, are

---

[2] Peter H. Solomon, Jr., and Todd S. Foglesong, *Courts and Transition in Russia: The Challenge of Judicial Reform* (Boulder, Colo.: Westview, 2000), 192.

[3] Ibid.

[4] The existence of that particular continuity between Soviet and post-Soviet Russia is persuasively argued by Alena Ledeneva in her book, *Russia's Economy of Favours: Blat, Networking and Informal Exchange* (Cambridge: Cambridge University Press, 1998).

subject to the law may, ultimately, be a more serious problem than the phenomenon that has become known as 'the Russian mafia'. While Russian businesses do feel the need to seek protection in one form or another, the problem is put into a comparative perspective in Chapter 10 by Peter Rutland and Natasha Kogan. They show that the Russian case, in respect both of disregard for the law and the presence of organized crime, is far from unique and that it tends to be discussed in unnecessarily fatalistic terms. Solutions to the problem will gradually be found, Rutland and Kogan suggest, in the course of the evolution of the political process and are unlikely to be resolved speedily by means of a quick fix, campaign, or crusade.

7   Legislative Politics in Russia

Paul Chaisty[1]

Parliamentary institutions did not play a major role under Communism. The 'rubber-stamp' assemblies of the Soviet type were portrayed, in the comparative literature of the time, as an extreme symptom of the wider malaise of legislatures in political systems.[2] However, the late 1980s and early 1990s saw the revival of legislative institutions across Eastern Europe. In the Soviet Union, Mikhail Gorbachev's constitutional reforms produced new representative and legislative assemblies that became a pivotal force for political change. This was especially true in Russia. The Russian parliament—a two-tier Congress of People's Deputies and Supreme Soviet—emerged as the focal point of opposition to the rule of both Mikhail Gorbachev and Boris Yeltsin in the late Communist and early post-Communist periods. These conflicts gave rise to contrasting views on the necessary direction of constitutional and parliamentary development in Russia, encapsulated by slogans such as 'Strong Parliament—Strong President', 'Super-Presidentialism', and 'All Power to the Soviets'.

Boris Yeltsin's victory over the Russian parliament, in the tragic events of October 1993, cleared the way for a new constitution that mirrored the preferences of presidential constitution-makers. For some, Russia's new constitution, approved by referendum on 12 December 1993, produced a 'pocket parliament'. Conversely, others have recognized the resilience and development of parliamentary power in Russia since 1993. This chapter will examine these differing accounts by concentrating on the defining power of the legislature: to legislate. The main focus of attention will be the principal law-making actor in the new Federal Assembly: the State Duma, the parliament's lower house. Of particular interest is how the internal organization of the lower house, the formation of majorities, and legislative bargaining between the Duma and the main veto players in the Russian constitution—the president, the government, and the parliament's upper house or Federation Council—shape legislative outcomes.

The constitutional framework

THE BICAMERAL STRUCTURE

The Russian Federal Assembly is a bicameral institution. In contrast to its legislative predecessor, the Supreme Soviet, the two houses of the Federal Assembly—the State Duma and

Chapter specially commissioned for this volume.

[1] This chapter incorporates research conducted during a post-doctoral fellowship funded by The British Academy.

[2] J. Blondel, *Comparative Legislatures* (New Jersey: Prentice-Hall, 1973), 6.

the Federation Council—are separate and self-governing bodies. This choice of design was made by the Constitutional Conference in July 1993, a body which represented, though not in its entirety, the interests of presidential rule-makers. In marked contrast to the Congress of People's Deputies' (CPD) preference for a nominal bicameral system, with limited differentiation between the organization and functions of the two houses, the Constitutional Conference set in place a legislative structure with two independent assemblies.

Each house performs distinct functions in relation to Russia's dual executive. The State Duma's authority centres on the composition and survival of the government. The lower house approves the president's nominee for the post of prime minister, and can propose a vote of no confidence in the government. By comparison, the Federation Council approves the president's use of emergency powers; schedules presidential elections, and rules on Duma-initiated charges to impeach the president. Both houses have significant powers of patronage. The Duma appoints and removes from office the head of the Audit Commission, the human rights commissioner, and the head of the Central Bank; the Federation Council appoints judges to the Federal Constitutional, Arbitration, and Supreme Courts, and appoints and dismisses from office the procurator-general, and the deputy chair of the Audit Chamber. The upper house is also authorized to confirm changes to the territorial components of the federal structure, while the declaration of amnesties falls within the Duma's jurisdiction. Finally, both houses share the power to pass federal and constitutional law.

The mode of selecting representatives to both houses differs significantly. While the 450 deputies of the State Duma are directly elected—half from party lists, and half from plurality single-mandate constituencies—the Federation Council is formed from representatives of each regional legislative and executive branch, a total of 178 members.[3] The decision to combine both party and regional elite representation in the new Federal Assembly was reached after the October 1993 crisis. Change to the rules on the composition of the Federation Council represents a rare occasion when President Yeltsin directly intervened to amend the otherwise mainly unaltered draft of the Constitutional Conference.[4] While the initial blueprint specified a directly elected upper chamber, the final constitutional outcome left open the procedure for 'forming' the Federation Council.

The exact formula for selecting the membership of the upper chamber was never satisfactorily resolved by presidential rule-makers. It was not until December 1995 that the law on the formation of the Federation Council was finally approved. Under this law, the upper house was formed from the elected heads of Russia's regional legislative and executive branches of power, but this method of selection was contested from the outset. While supporters maintained that the new composition would allow the upper house to play a stabilizing, even reconciling role in the aftermath of the October crisis,[5] critics argued that a membership of 'part-time'[6] legislators would be unable to exploit the assembly's significant constitutional powers.[7] In the event, this arrangement was short-lived; it was one of the first

---

[3] Two representatives from each of Russia's eighty-nine regions.

[4] V. Sheynis, 'Ternistyy put' Rossiyskoy Konstitutsii', *Gosudarstvo i Pravo*, 12 (1997), 69.

[5] I. Shablinskiy, 'Senatory po sovmestitel'stvu', *Konstitutsionnoe Pravo: Vostochnoevropeyskoe Obozrenie*, 4:13/1:14, 1995/6, 35.

[6] The upper house was composed of regional governors, presidents, and the chairs of regional parliaments. It usually convened once a month.

[7] V. Sheynis, 'Ternistyy put'', 72.

casualties of President Putin's efforts to rein in the power of Russia's regional leaders. The new composition of the upper house, to be in place by January 2002, will consist of full-time representatives appointed by the legislative and executive branches in each region.

Likewise, the 'party-list' component of the Duma's electoral system has come under question. The success enjoyed by opposition parties in the Duma's first two elections—1993 and 1995—has led to calls by presidential supporters for the abolition of the electoral system's proportional element.[8] Moreover, the resulting distinction in the Duma's internal rules between 'factions' (electoral associations that receive 5 per cent or more of the list vote) and 'deputy groups' (political organizations formed within the assembly from a minimum of thirty-five deputies—the overwhelming majority elected in single-mandate constituencies) is criticized by 'independent' and group deputies for producing a de facto hierarchy of deputies within the assembly.

ASSEMBLY–EXECUTIVE RELATIONS

The separation of powers between the Federal Assembly and the executive branch was also crafted by the Constitutional Conference. However, the CPD's input into the detail and design of the final constitutional arrangements was not insubstantial. The CPD's own Constitutional Commission (1990–3) set the standard for a hybrid presidential system in preference to a US-style presidential model. This innovation was partly a tactical concession made by the Constitutional Commission to win the support of parliamentary deputies for a new constitution after the August coup of 1991. The defining feature of this constitutional variant was the dual executive, with a popularly elected president as the head of state, and with executive power exercised by the government, in turn dependent on parliament for both its composition and survival. Initially presidential supporters, such as Sergei Shakhray, persisted with their proposals for a presidential system of rule, with unified executive power subordinate to the president.[9] But by the spring of 1993 presidential rule-makers had moved towards the parliament's position, albeit with a constitutional draft that conferred greater powers on the president.

The 1993 constitution expands the president's powers in three crucial respects.[10] First, the president is empowered to dissolve the State Duma on occasions when it rejects the president's candidate for prime minister on three consecutive votes; supports two votes of no confidence in the government within a three-month period; or fails to support a government-initiated vote of confidence. Thus, the Duma's control over the government is compromised by the president's powers of dissolution. Second, the 1993 constitution restricts the Federal Assembly's power to shape government composition, and limits its powers to oversee and censure government officials. In contrast to drafts submitted by the CPD's Constitutional Commission, only the post of prime minister is subject to confirmation by the State Duma, and the lower house cannot dismiss individual ministers. Finally, the president gained significant residual powers over the parliament as 'guarantor of the constitution'. This obscure feature of the 1993 constitution gives the president, as we shall see, an important additional veto power.

---

[8] V. Medvedev, 'Kakoy parlament nuzhen rossii ?', *Nezavisimaya gazeta*, 26 Nov. 1997.

[9] *Federatsiya*, 16 (1992).

[10] It is important to note that the veto and decree powers bestowed on the president by the 1993 constitution were also included in the CPD's final constitutional draft, published on 16 July 1993.

Paradoxically, in seeking to bolster the president's powers, the framers of the 1993 constitution added several parliamentary features: the Duma's prerogative to move motions of no confidence in the government as a whole; the president's conditional power to dissolve the lower house; and the government's right to introduce legislation independently of the president. All three elements had been absent from the later drafts of the CPD's Constitutional Commission. The key parliamentary feature—of a constitution that displays, in the words of Victor Sheynis,[11] 'under-parliamentary' characteristics (*nedoparlamenskoy*)[12]—is the president's power of dissolution. In crafting the 1993 Constitution, the framers seemed keenly aware that the checks and balances inherent in a pure presidential system would give the parliament too much independence. By adding the power of dissolution, the president gained the means to nullify government crisis caused by unstable parliamentary majorities or political deadlock and conflict resulting from parliaments with coherent anti-government majorities. According to one seasoned constitution-maker, Boris Strashun, this innovation was shaped by the experience of the 1992–93 political impasse:

And it is possible to raise the question: why did the Constitutional Conference, under the aegis of the president, prepare a project with prevailing parliamentary traits? The answer is simple: the conflict between the legislative and executive branches, that could not be resolved by constitutional means, induced the authors of the constitutional project to press for the mechanism of parliamentary dissolution as a means for resolving constitutional crisis. And once dissolution exists, all the other features inherent in a parliamentary republic, and essential to ensure the necessary balance of powers, fall into place.[13]

Moreover, the constitution gives legislators few of the levers to check and oversee executive power that are associated with presidential systems. The parliament's powers of interpellation are not defined by the constitution. Nonetheless, efforts have been made to redress this imbalance. The parliament's power to pass 'constitutional' legislation, elaborating the functions and duties of institutions and procedures outlined by the constitution, has enabled the legislature to formalize its executive-oversight powers. The Law 'On the Government', passed in December 1997, detailed the assembly's powers of scrutiny and investigation, and represented a significant achievement by the Duma during Yeltsin's second term.

The procedural dimension of Russian law-making

Within Russia's constitutional rules, the State Duma is the principal law-maker. Bills must be approved by the Duma before they can proceed, and although the Russian constitution confers on the president the power to legislate by decree, such decrees are subordinate to statute law in the Russian hierarchy of legislation. In the 1993 constitution, all deputies and members of the Federal Assembly have the right to initiate legislation; the minimum requirement of ten deputies, as stipulated by the CPD's constitutional draft, was dropped.

---

[11] Former Supreme Soviet and Duma deputy, and active participant in the constitution-making process.

[12] V. Sheynis, 'Ternistiy put'', 70.

[13] B. Strashun, 'O "smeshannoy" forme pravleniya v proekte Konstitutsii Rossiyskoy Federatsii', *Konstitutsionnoe soveshchanie: informatsionnyy byulleten*', 2 (1993), 56.

The power to initiate legislation is also conferred on the president, government and regional parliaments, as well as federal courts within a specified jurisdiction. As in earlier CPD's drafts, political parties do not possess the right of legislative initiative, and all legislation with financial or budgetary implications must receive government scrutiny.

One of the few areas where the 1993 constitution increases the power of the legislative branch is through the parliament's power to approve federal constitutional law. Although the Constitutional Court ruled that such laws cannot be used to amend the constitution, they flesh out constitutional rules in several key areas: on the use of referendums; on states of emergency and martial law; on the formation and activities of the Constitutional Assembly, the government, and all Federal Courts; and on the procedure for altering the federal structure. Unfettered by formal presidential veto this feature of the 1993 constitution gives the parliament important rule-making powers, powers that have been used to signifi-cant effect. For example, seven constitutional laws were passed over the first five years of the parliament.[14] Yet, the passage of such legislation is far from straightforward. To be approved by the assembly, constitutional laws require an absolute two-thirds majority in the Duma, and an absolute three-quarters majority in the upper house. Furthermore, as 'guarantor of the constitution', the president can always stymie such laws by referring them to the Consti-tutional Court. One example of this was President Yeltsin's initial refusal to sign the law 'On the Government' after the bill had received the approval of both houses of the Federal Assembly in 1997.

Similarly, the parliament's capacity to enact statutory legislation is constrained by a number of veto points. First, the Federal Assembly's bicameral structure presents two hur-dles. To receive approval by the Federal Assembly, bills must secure the support of an absolute majority in both chambers. If this support cannot be obtained in the upper house, then either a Conciliation Commission is formed from members of both houses to reach a compromise solution, or the Duma can override the upper chamber with the support of an absolute two-thirds majority. On overcoming these barriers, legislation then passes for presidential approval. If this is not forthcoming, and if subsequent negotiations between the Federal Assembly and the president fail to broker an agreement, then an absolute two-thirds majority of both houses is required to override the president's veto. However, the success of the Federal Assembly in overturning presidential vetoes does not necessarily guarantee the automatic ratification of legislation. The absence of constitutional rules outlining the par-liament's powers in the event that the president refuses to sign bills approved by both houses of the Federal Assembly, again permits the president to invoke his residual powers as 'guar-antor of the constitution' to block legislation. Given the advantages that this confers on the president, it is not surprising that Yeltsin resisted attempts by Duma law-makers to make veto overrides binding on the president.[15]

Although the majority requirements for the passage of constitutional and statutory laws differ, they pass through similar legislative processes in the Federal Assembly. As in other legislative assemblies, bills are passed following several stages of preparation and scrutiny. Legislation is first considered by the Duma. The Duma Council, the chief presiding organ of

[14] I. Grankin, *Parlament Rossii* (Moscow: Konsaltbankir, 1999), 159.
[15] Duma amendments on this question were proposed during the discussion of a president-initiated bill 'On the Order of Passing Federal Constitutional Laws and Federal Laws' in 1998.

the assembly, is the body that initially decides if, and when, bills are to be examined by the assembly. If a bill meets the requirements stipulated by the Duma's internal standing orders,[16] the Duma Council selects one or several standing committees to prepare the legislation for discussion in a plenary session of the assembly. In committee, 'working groups' are formed on an ad hoc basis to conduct the necessary preparatory work within a time scale set by the Duma Council. On completion of this work, the legislation is sent back to the Duma Council which, in turn, schedules the date for its 'first reading' in a plenary session of the Duma. The first reading involves the general discussion of the bill, and deputies vote on whether it should be sent for further preparation in committee. If the bill is passed, the committee responsible examines amendments in detail, and solicits the recommendations of expert bodies such as the Duma's Legal Department. During the crucial 'second reading', deputies vote on the proposed amendments, and the amended bill is passed or rejected in full. On the passage of the bill, the steering committee and Legal Department then address any outstanding legal inconsistencies, and the legislation is sent for its 'third reading'. At this stage deputies vote on the bill as a whole, and if successful the bill is sent to the upper house for scrutiny. Here legislation is subjected to a similar process, although the chair performs the functions exercised by the Duma Council in the lower house. If legislation is subsequently rejected by either the Federation Council or the president, compromise is reached through those procedures outlined by the constitution.

Agenda-setters in the State Duma: parties, committees and deputies

In the Duma's constitution, the formal power to set the legislative agenda rests with faction and group leaders in the Duma Council.[17] This feature of the assembly's organization contrasts with the Supreme Soviet, where the parliamentary speaker and committee chairmen in a steering organ, known as the praesidium, exercised legislative decision-making. The choice of a partisan governance structure was the outcome of proposals drafted by rule-makers in the Presidential Commission on Legislative Proposals, set up in the aftermath of the October crisis, and by party leaders elected under Russia's new electoral rules in December 1993. However, opinions differed between political forces on the method for sharing power.[18] After considerable debate during the inaugural sessions of the First Duma (1993–5), institutional arrangements emerged that incorporate a mixture of majoritarian and power-sharing rules and practices to divide agenda-setting between factions, committees, and deputies in plenary sessions of the house.

PARTISAN GOVERNANCE

According to the Duma's rules, factions and deputy groups have equal rights irrespective of their size. This principle extends to the composition of the assembly's Duma Council. In this

---

[16] For example, legislation that has financial implications for the state budget must be accompanied by a government resolution. See Article 105, *Reglament Gosudarstvennoy Dumy Federal'nogo Sobraniya* (Moscow: Izvestiya, 1998), 81–2.

[17] As explained above, factions are electoral associations that receive 5 per cent or more of the vote in a general election, while deputy groups are formed within the assembly from a minimum of 35 deputies.

[18] See Moshe Haspel, 'Should Party in Parliament be Weak or Strong? The Rules Debate in the Russian State Duma', *Journal of Communist Studies and Transition Politics*, 14/1 and 2 (1998), 178–200.

body, the leaders of each faction and deputy group, plus the chairman of the Duma, have voting powers of equal weight—a total of twelve members in the First Duma, eight in the Second Duma (1995–9), and ten in the Third Duma (1999–). In addition, committee and deputy chairs of the Duma may attend Council sessions, with the right of a consultative vote; and presidential, government, and regional representatives may also attend, together with rank-and-file deputies who possess the right to introduce proposals. Therefore, although the Duma Council is very much a 'political club', it is also a forum in which other Duma and state functionaries can participate. In fact, the attendance of committee chairs at Council sessions has increased markedly in recent years.

The partisan power-sharing basis, on which the Duma Council was formed at the First Duma, also shaped arrangements for dividing up the main leadership posts in the assembly. Under the tutelage of the Duma's first chairman, Ivan Rybkin, faction leaders bargained over a 'package' of leadership posts including five deputy chairs of the Duma, twenty-three committee chairs and their deputies, the human rights commissioner, and the chairman of the Mandate Commission. The agreement was then ratified during the Duma's inaugural session. This arrangement was shaped by the particular political configuration of the First Duma, when in the absence of a majority faction or coalition the Duma's political leaders were forced to coalesce and bargain over the assembly's leadership posts. In the context of the Duma's conflict-ridden predecessor, this development was a considerable achievement.

However, from the outset it was clear that despite the formal equality of factions and groups in the Duma's rules, faction leaders exerted most influence over the final package settlement. Moreover, those temporary alliances that were formed during the course of package negotiations started to come unstuck during the Second Duma. On three occasions, the Communist faction (KPRF), the largest in the Second Duma, challenged the unwritten prerogative of factions and groups to change or replace their original nominees for Duma posts.[19] Ultimately, the KPRF agreed to respect the original package agreement, but the power-sharing consensus for apportioning key positions in the Duma was already undermined.

Developments in the Third Duma appeared to confirm a move towards majoritarianism in the organization of Duma affairs. An ad hoc alliance between the KPRF and the Kremlin-backed faction 'Unity', plus a number of smaller factions and groups, agreed to support the Communist candidate, Gennady Seleznev, for the post of Duma chair. This was to be in return for a package deal that excluded several key liberal and centrist factions—Yabloko, the Union of Rightist Forces (SPS), Fatherland–All Russia (OVR)—but, yet again, the challenge was only partially successful. The decision to boycott the assembly by those factions ostracized from the deal precipitated a compromise that revitalised the package regime. The SPS, the seventh largest grouping in the assembly, secured control over the pivotal Legislation Committee, and committee posts were divided up between factions and groups in proportion to their overall support in the assembly. The main loser in this process, Yabloko, was also partly compensated by acquiring leadership of the Audit Chamber.[20] Therefore, for the moment, it may still be premature to write off package agreements as a mechanism for

[19] Attempts by the government faction, Our Home is Russia (NDR), to replace their chair of the Defence Committee, General Rokhlin, and to appoint a new first deputy chair following the resignations of Alexander Shokhin and Vladimir Ryzhkov, encountered resistance from the KPRF.

[20] However, the chair of the Audit Chamber is not a Duma post. In accepting this position, Sergei Stepashin gave up his seat in the Duma.

sharing power in the Duma. Without parliamentary majorities, or the governance structures that would support majority rule, inclusive methods of power-sharing are still required for the Duma's effective functioning. However, it is unlikely that such arrangements will survive the election of future parliamentary majorities.

This parliamentary 'crisis' clearly centred on the Kremlin's apparent duplicity in supporting the KPRF's candidate, Gennady Seleznev, for the post of Duma chair, at the expense of its reputed allies in the SPS. The reasoning behind the Kremlin's strategy merits a more detailed account elsewhere, but as far as Duma politics are concerned, such developments are an inevitable consequence of the majoritarian basis on which the chair is elected. While the chair is a less powerful post than the speaker of the old Supreme Soviet its incumbent can still wield significant influence, especially when attached to a political grouping that enjoys widespread support in the assembly, as was the case for Seleznev in the Second Duma. Despite the formal rules that constrain the chair's capacity to manipulate procedure in plenary debates or to intervene in the affairs of the Duma's standing apparatus, both Rybkin and Seleznev have been criticized for high-handed action on occasions. However, it is the chair's role as chief representative of the assembly in dealing with the executive branch that makes the position such a coveted office of state. The chair represents the lower house when conciliatory procedures are invoked to resolve disagreements on an inter-institutional level. In such situations, the chair's role in mediating conflicts on legislation or in defusing potential political crises can be crucial. For example, in October 1997 Seleznev was able to avert a Duma vote of no confidence in the Chernomyrdin government by extracting legislative concessions from the president. During Yeltsin's second term this aspect of the chair's role became more pronounced with the formation of consensus-seeking bodies, like the 'Council of Four': a forum for both chairmen of the Federal Assembly to meet with the president and prime minister on a regular basis.

COMMITTEES

The Duma's partisan arrangements also shape the size and jurisdictions of the assembly's committees. Despite attempts to rationalize and institutionalize the network of Duma committees, their number is ultimately determined by the package negotiations at the start of each newly elected Duma. To balance the competing demands of individual factions and groups for leadership posts, the number of legislative committees has grown over the first three Dumas: twenty-three in the First Duma, twenty-eight in the Second, and twenty-eight committees, plus seven newly created commissions, in the Third Duma. The jurisdiction of Duma committees, and the political affiliation of committee heads, reflect the interests and expertise of political groupings. In some cases, committee portfolios are sought for their distributional benefits. For example, members of the Agrarian Party are consistently over-represented in the Committee for Agriculture; and the deputy membership of the Budget Committee generally exceeds the formal limit on committee members. In other cases, factions and groups put forward candidates who have the requisite policy expertise. For instance, Yabloko retained the chairmanship of the Budget Committee at the Second Duma mainly because they had, in Mikhail Zadornov, the previous incumbent of the committee who enjoyed widespread support.[21] Therefore, as in other parliaments,

---

[21] In fact, when Zadornov left the Duma in 1997 to take up the post of finance minister, Yabloko could not find a suitable replacement and lost the chair to the deputy group Russia's Regions.

committee specialization provides an important source of information and expertise for the Duma as a whole.

However, while party leaders play a key role in forming the committee system, and are formally responsible for setting the legislative agenda in the Duma Council, committees retain a high degree of autonomy in the legislative sphere. Factions and groups exercise limited influence over committee agendas, and there is little evidence to show that they co-ordinate policy and legislative strategy across committees. Although the participation of factions and groups varies according to the legislation under discussion, in most cases deputies enjoy a high level of personal control over legislative activity in Duma committees. This is caused by several factors. First, there is a constitutional dimension. The right to initiate legislation, as we have seen, rests with individual deputies rather than with political groupings or leaders. Second, in exercising this constitutional right, committees offer deputies far greater resources and expertise than either factions or groups. Most active legislative committees possess permanent staff, or experts co-opted by legislative working groups, that command a far higher level of legislative expertise than any faction or group could possibly muster. Hence, while it is not unusual for deputies and committee apparatchiks to write legislation themselves, it is extremely rare for factions and groups. Third, the powers and resources that deputies enjoy make committees the focus for lobby activity in the Duma. Lobbies representing state and private interests—operating through both 'open' and 'secret' channels—constitute a major source of legislative initiative, and further exacerbate the diffuse character of Duma law-making.[22] The result is a legislative process that furthers particularistic interests.

The activities of committees are not just confined to the initiation and preparation of laws. Committee chairs also exert considerable influence over the legislative agenda of the Duma as a whole. Although committee chairs are denied voting rights in the Duma Council, their right to propose bills for 'reading' in plenary session is used effectively. This feature of legislative affairs further illustrates the weak control that parties exert over the early stages of law-making. Moreover, the Duma Council appears unable to enforce deadlines on committees chosen to prepare and scrutinize legislation. For example, the Foreign Affairs Committee was criticized at the Second Duma for its failure to complete work on a batch of international treaties and conventions, some going as far back as 1995.[23] The Council has also been seen to lack the expertise, time, and collective will to filter out defective committee projects before they are discussed in the chamber. As a consequence, deputies on the floor of the Duma are left to deal with problems, both political and technical, that are resolved at the early stages of the legislative process in other parliaments.

Thus, arguably the Duma in plenary session performs a key agenda-setting and decision-making role. In part, this is an inevitable consequence of disorganization and weak party control at lower levels of the legislative process; but it is also a result of the Duma's rules and the power they give rank-and-file deputies to override the legislative gate-keeping functions of parties and committees. The Duma, as a whole, reserves the right to overturn decisions made by the Duma Council, and in practice the Duma's agenda is frequently amended on

[22] See A. L. Lyubimov, *Lobbizm kak konstitutsionno-pravovoy institut* (Moscow: Institut Gosudarstva i Prava, 1998).

[23] Vladimir Ryzhkov identified a total of forty bills at the start of the winter 1998 session. *Gosudarstvennaya Duma: stenogramma zasedaniy.* Byulleten' 146 (288).

the floor. Deputies can also challenge the jurisdiction of committees to legislate in specific policy areas through the introduction of 'alternative' projects. According to Vladimir Ryzhkov,[24] the result is a highly democratic law-making process:

the democratization of our parliament is greater than the democratization of a number of Western parliaments where laws over which there is some legal doubt are simply excluded from the agenda. We have a different approach. Anyone who has the right to initiate legislation can bring up a question and insist that the house vote on it.[25]

But this process can also be the source of instability and conflict. In the heated atmosphere of Duma debates, deputies can find their loyalties divided between committee and faction or group. Members from different committees will seek the backing of their party colleagues for particular initiatives in faction and group meetings where voting strategies are decided, but this is still no guarantee of success when bills are debated in the chamber.

VOTING AND MAJORITY FORMATION

In the absence of constitutional rules binding governments to parliamentary majorities, and of the discipline that governments impose on supporting majorities in parliaments, the voting strategies of Duma factions and groups bear some resemblance to those of parties in presidential systems, with legislative coalitions forming for individual votes. However, it must be stressed that this feature of Duma politics is also the product of electoral and party systems that have so far failed to deliver majority coalitions. Given Russia's mixed system of presidentialism—with governments possessing significant legislative powers while remaining partially dependent on the Duma for their composition and survival—large pro- or anti-presidential majorities could seriously test current practices in the future.

The rules regulating the size of majorities needed on substantive questions are set by the Constitution. When voting on legislation, or on resolutions concerning questions that fall within the Duma's constitutional jurisdiction—such as resolutions confirming prime-ministerial appointments, or expressing no confidence in the Russian government—an 'absolute' majority of all Duma deputies (226 votes in total) is required. Larger majorities, comprising two-thirds of all deputies, are needed to pass federal constitutional laws, to impeach the president, and to overturn legislative vetoes by the president or Federation Council. Moreover, the Duma can, within its own rules, decide procedural questions by a 'simple' majority of those deputies present. This arrangement is not insignificant; procedural votes can have an important bearing on substantive questions. For example, two defining moments during the Second Duma—the third vote on Sergei Kirienko's appointment to the post of prime minister in April 1998, and the vote to impeach President Yeltsin in May 1999—centred on the form voting should take: by 'open' or 'secret' ballot.[26]

The success of factions and groups in building winning coalitions hinges on their internal

---

[24] Former first deputy chair and NDR faction leader in the Second Duma following Shokhin's resignation.

[25] *Gosudarstvennaya Duma: stenogramma zasedaniy.* Byulleten' 146 (288), 22.

[26] See P. Chaisty, 'Defending the Institutional Status Quo: Communist Leadership of the Second State Duma', 2001 (forthcoming).

cohesion. In this respect, political groupings in the Duma have made major advances on their predecessors in the Supreme Soviet. The movement of deputies between political groupings fell significantly across the first two Dumas. In the First Duma, three deputy groups were formed after the initial registration, while just one group, 'People's Deputy', was created towards the end of the Second Duma, and was never officially registered. The main upheaval in the composition of factions and groups occurred towards the end of both parliaments when the realignment of political forces in preparation for new elections took its toll. Levels of internal party voting discipline also increased in the Second Duma, with the KPRF and Zhirinovsky's LDPR (Liberal Democratic Party of Russia) factions consistently the most disciplined. Yet, the formation of absolute majorities in the assembly continues to be jeopardized by the large numbers of deputies who regularly fail to participate in voting. In the Second Duma, on average one-third of deputies did not vote in Duma debates.[27] However, this is not necessarily inconsistent with more cohesive Duma parties; factions and groups will often take the decision not to vote, rather than vote against or abstain, for tactical reasons.[28]

As Table 7.1 shows, the name, number, and size of factions and groups have varied substantially from election to election. To date, only three factions have remained permanent fixtures in the Duma: KPRF, Yabloko, and LDPR.[29] Nonetheless, the fluidity of party labels belies a political spectrum that has points of comparison across all three Dumas. Government interests have been served by three factions since 1993: the 'Party of Russian Unity and Accord' (PRES), 'Our Home is Russia' (NDR), and Unity. Russia's regional elite has maintained its voice in the Duma through the 'New Regional Policy Group' in the First Duma and 'Russia's Regions' in the Second and Third Dumas. Finally, the liberal faction Russia's Choice resurfaced as SPS (The Union of Rightist Forces) in the Third Duma; and there are elements of continuity running through the groupings Women of Russia and Popular Power, the Agrarian Party and the Agrarian Party Group, and the Agro-Industrial group. Arguably, only one new political force has emerged since 1993: 'Fatherland–All Russia'.

However, the erratic fluctuation in the number and size of political groupings complicates the identification of those party alliances capable of forming winning majorities. In the absence of stable voting coalitions with clearly defined policy agendas, those factions and groups that are most effective at bargaining and attracting votes prove to be pivotal. During the First Duma, three 'core' factions—Russia's Choice, PRES, KPRF—each enjoyed varied degrees of success in forging voting coalitions. According to Gelman, the KPRF was most successful building alliances in support of legislation, but failed to mobilize majorities opposed to executive-initiated measures.[30] At the Second Duma, a de facto alliance of the KPRF, Agrarian, and Popular Power groupings, whose combined number fell only a handful short of an absolute majority, was pivotal. Together with other groupings, most notably

---

[27] 'Gosudarstvennaya Duma: Analiticheskoe upravlenie', *Gosudarstvennaya Duma vtorogo sozyva (1996–1999)* (Moscow: 1999), 80.

[28] Even after a special hour was set aside for voting towards the end of the Second Duma, several factions and groups continued to show high levels of absenteeism.

[29] LDPR was renamed the Zhirinovsky Bloc during the 1999 parliamentary elections, but it has retained the faction name LDPR.

[30] V. Gelman, 'Kommunisty v strukturakh vlasti: analiz deyatel'nosti', *Vlast'*, 6 (1996), 22.

Table 7.1 **Political complexion of the First, Second and Third State Dumas**

Political grouping	Membership	
First Duma (1994–5)	1994	1995
Factions		
Russia's Choice	73	49
Liberal Democratic Party of Russia (LDPR)	59	55
Agrarian Party of Russia	55	50
Communist Party of the Russian Federation (KPRF)	45	47
Party of Russian Unity and Accord (PRES)	30	13
Yabloko	28	27
Women of Russia	23	20
Democratic Party of Russia	15	11
Groups		
New Regional Policy	66	36
Liberal Democratic Union of 12 December	35	–
Russia	–	58
Stability	–	37
Second Duma (1996–9)	1996	1999
Factions		
Communist Party of the Russian Federation (KPRF)	147	119
Our Home is Russia (NDR)	66	52
Liberal Democratic Party of Russia (LDPR)	51	40
Yabloko	46	44
Groups		
Russia's Regions	42	36
Popular Power	38	43
Agrarian Deputy Group	37	34
Third Duma (2000–)	2000	
Factions		
Communist Party of the Russian Federation (KPRF)	89	
Unity	83	
Fatherland-All Russia (OVR)	46	
Union of Rightist Forces (SPS)	31	

Table 7.1 **continued**

Political grouping	Membership
Yabloko	21
Liberal Democratic Party of Russia (LDPR)	16
Groups	
People's Deputy	57
Agro-Industrial Deputy Group	42
Russia's Regions (Union of Independent Deputies)	40

Sources: Material published by the apparatus of the State Duma.

LDPR, this alliance determined the success of legislative initiatives in a number of policy areas, including social, economic, defence, and foreign policy. However, the fragility of these arrangements was exposed on several critical votes, in particular on the appointment of successive prime ministers following Victor Chernomyrdin's dismissal; and in voting on the annual budget, the leftist alliance was placed under strain.

Legislative output

In terms of the quantity of laws generated, the Duma is a highly productive legislative institution. As Figure 7.1 shows, over the first two Dumas more than one thousand legislative projects passed by the assembly were eventually signed into law by the president. Also, this number does not include the large proportion of bills that were either rejected along the way, or never reached the floor of the assembly. For example, in the Second Duma, of 3,134 bills recommended for scrutiny by the Duma Council, only half (1,662) received their first reading.[31] The Duma's legislative activity is spread across a number of policy areas. Foreign treaties comprise a significant proportion of laws passed by assembly, but a large volume of legislation is also produced in the fields of social, economic, financial, and legal policy. Within these policy areas, a number of important constitutional and federal laws have been enacted: laws 'On the Government', 'On Production Sharing', and on the 'Civil' and 'Criminal' Codes to name just a small selection. Nevertheless, as Chairman Seleznev openly admits, efforts to target and structure the assembly's activities have been less effective.[32]

PRIORITIZING LEGISLATIVE ACTIVITY

In the absence of government or opposition majorities with clearly defined legislative programmes, the Duma agrees on a 'model' calendar of laws for each legislative session.[33] The

[31] 'Gosudarstvennaya Duma: Analiticheskoe upravlenie', 5.

[32] 'Rabochaya vstrecha Predsedatelya Gosudarstvennoy Dumy G.N. Selezneva s predstavitelyami federal'nykh organov gosudarstvennoy vlasti po voprosam obespecheniya zakonodatel'noy deyatel'nosti', (Moscow, 29 March 1999), 4.

[33] The Duma convenes for two sessions each year: spring and autumn.

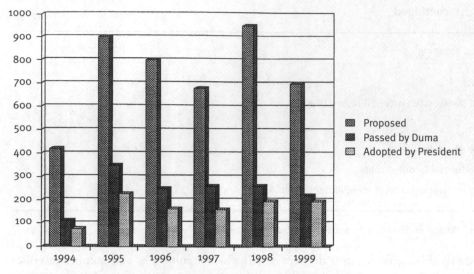

Figure 7.1 **Volume of Russian legislation proposed and adopted** [a]
Source: Material published by the apparatus of the State Duma.
[a] Includes both statutory and federal constitutional laws

preparation of this calendar provides the opportunity for all branches of government to recommend legislative projects; and through a cross-branch co-ordinating commission a list of bills deemed to be of 'priority' importance is agreed. The emergence of mechanisms to facilitate the planning and co-ordination of legislative initiatives is an important development, and gained extra momentum in the Second Duma under the direction of its first deputy chair, Alexander Shokhin. During this Duma, the assembly passed approximately one-third of bills designated 'priority' status, and almost half were scrutinized in plenary session. However, in terms of overall legislative output, priority and planned legislation continues to constitute a small number of the bills considered. The majority of bills that are scrutinized and approved by the assembly consistently fall outside the Duma's official plan. For example, in the first year of the Second Duma, work on priority legislation in plenary sessions comprised just one-third of all legislative activity.[34] The apparent failure of Duma leaders to fulfil their legislative objectives in turn raises questions about the capacity of the assembly's governance structures to regulate and co-ordinate Duma law-making.

According to some critics of the Duma's legislative process, this problem is partly the result of the Duma Council's weak legislative function. Deputies aligned to both government and opposition forces have questioned the virtues of the Council's leadership on legislative affairs. Former head of the government faction (NDR), Alexander Shokhin, has criticized faction leaders for failing to impose order on the Duma's work. Too often, he argues, bills proposed by committees are approved by the Council 'on the nod' without reference to the official programme.[35] This observation appears to have some basis in fact. Of the vast number of bills that pass through the Council—over three thousand during the

---

[34] A. Shokhin, 'Prioritety zakonodatel'noy deyatel'nosti', *Vlast'*, 4 (1997), 6.
[35] Ibid., 6.

Second Duma—only a small proportion were rejected. The Council's weak legislative role is explained by Vladimir Isakov[36] in terms of its partisan composition:

Discussions in the Duma Council display a very definite political character. Slogans and posturing predominate. We pass decisions about the inclusion or exclusion of bills, but we don't discuss those bills . . . and when an author attempts to develop argument about why his proposal is better than another, the typical reaction from the chair is 'We will discuss this in the plenary session, everything will be discussed in the session . . . we don't have such discussions in the Council !'[37]

Thus, the Duma Council provides little resistance to the centrifugal forces that drive law-making in the Duma. While parties can play an important role in shaping the outcome of legislative decision-making on the floor of the assembly, they provide few incentives for deputies to aggregate and channel their interests through the initiation and preparation of laws. Proposals on practical ways to address these problems have been a topic for debate in Duma circles. For some, the problem centres on integrating committees into the organization of Duma governance.[38] Others have sought proposals to strengthen the Duma Council and to streamline the work of the Duma in plenary session,[39] while more radical proposals have focused on ways to curtail the freedom of deputies to initiate legislation.[40]

However, despite its limitations the existing system continues to offer an important degree of flexibility in legislative affairs. The informal relationships that underpin Duma law-making facilitate widespread bargaining on legislative initiatives. The log-rolling that accompanies much of the Duma's legislative activity helps to accommodate the shifting preferences of Russian legislators in times of political and economic crisis, and contributes towards the construction of winning coalitions. While these arrangements are far from ideal, conflicts have been mediated on a wide range of policy issues, most notably budgetary policy.

VETO PLAYERS IN THE LAW-MAKING PROCESS

For critics of the Russian Constitution, the internal processes of Duma law-making cannot be treated in isolation from the constraints of higher-order constitutional rules. As we have already seen, the 1993 Constitution imposes several checks on the Duma's power to legislate; the veto powers of the Federation Council, the government, and the president present the Duma with a formidable range of obstacles. It has been suggested that the policy bargaining and log-rolls we observe in Russian law-making are a necessary consequence of the constitutional constraints placed on legislators.

Although members of the Federation Council have the power to initiate legislation, this work takes up only a small segment of the assembly's time. Between 1995 and 1999, for example, the Federation Council initiated just 3 per cent of all laws eventually approved by the president.[41] For the most part, the upper house is concerned with the scrutiny and

---

[36] A parliamentary veteran of both the Supreme Soviet and the State Duma, and a vehement critic of President Yeltsin. Chair of the Legislation Committee in the First Duma.

[37] Interview, 25 Mar. 1999.

[38] Vladimir Isakov has consistently argued for the dual leadership of parties and committees over Duma affairs. See V. Isakov, *Amnistiya: parlamentskie dnevniki, 1994–1995* (Moscow: Paleiya, 1996), 184.

[39] A. Shokhin, *Vzaimodeystvie vlastey v zakonodatel'nom protsess* (Moscow: Nash dom/L'Age d'Homme, 1997).

[40] Medvedev, 'Kakoy parlament nuzhen rossii?'.

[41] 'Gosudarstvennaya Duma: Analiticheskoe upravlenie', p. 6.

approval of bills prepared and passed by the Duma. In this capacity, the Federation Council has become a more active veto player, despite the intermittent nature of its work. For example, during the Duma's second term, the upper house vetoed 23 per cent of all laws passed by the Duma.[42]

Similarly, the president's role has, to date, been reactive rather than proactive in shaping the passage of bills. This was especially marked during President Yeltsin's second term when the president was responsible for only 10 per cent of all bills passed by the Duma.[43] By contrast, over the same period Yeltsin invoked the presidential veto to reject one-fifth of all bills approved by the Federal Assembly.[44] Also, using his residual powers as 'guarantor of the constitution', Yeltsin refused to sign thirty-seven bills between 1994 and 1997 on rather vague 'constitutional' grounds.[45] Conversely, the government has increasingly played a more active legislative role. During Yeltsin's second term, the volume of legislation initiated by the government increased significantly.[46] But, the government has also emerged as an important veto player. Its constitutional prerogative to scrutinize all bills with fiscal and budgetary implications has developed as a notable veto power. The absence of constitutional rules defining the time period within which the government must complete its scrutiny of such bills gives government bureaucrats the added opportunity to thwart the passage of legislation. Roman Popkovich, Defence Committee chair and NDR member in the Second Duma, summed up the frustration of many deputies when he proclaimed: 'I think that if we sent bills [*to Finland*] they would be returned four time faster than from the government . . . not one bill which we [*the Defence Committee*] have sent to the government was returned on time.'[47]

Figures for the period between 1996 and 1999 would suggest that the veto powers of the executive branch are effective. While deputies in the Second Duma were the initiators of the largest number of bills passed by the assembly (48 per cent), they were formally responsible for only 38 per cent of those bills eventually signed into law by the president. By comparison government-backed bills fared significantly better. Although government initiatives comprised just 35 per cent of bills approved by the Duma, they constituted the largest number of bills passed by the president (42 per cent).[48]

However, these aggregate figures also reveal that deputies remain the authors of well over one-third of all federal laws enacted in Russia. To a degree, this reflects the Duma's relative success in overcoming the veto constraints described. As can be seen from Table 7.2, of those bills vetoed by the president or the Federation Council during the 1996–9 period, the president eventually approved almost half of them. In most cases, as we can also see, these bills were approved after a compromise was reached between the Duma, the Federation Council, and the president.

---

[42] Ibid. 7.

[43] Ibid. 6. During the First Duma the president initiated 19 per cent of bills passed by the Duma, see T. Remington, S. Smith, and M. Haspel, 'Decrees, Laws, and Inter-Branch Relations in the Russian Federation', *Post-Soviet Affairs*, 14/4 (1998), 299.

[44] 'Gosudarstvennaya Duma: Analiticheskoe upravlenie', p. 7.

[45] Remington *et al*, 'Decrees, Laws, and Inter-Branch Relations', 301.

[46] The government initiated 35 per cent of bills passed by the Second Duma. 'Gosudarstvennaya Duma: Analiticheskoe upravlenie', p. 6. In the First Duma, the government was the initiator of just 19 per cent of bills passed by the assembly. Remington *et al*, 'Decrees, Laws, and Inter-Branch Relations', 299.

[47] 'Rabochaya vstrecha', 19. Words in parentheses added.

[48] 'Gosudarstvennaya Duma: Analiticheskoe upravlenie', 6.

Table 7.2 **Results of federal legislative proceedings, 1996–1999** [a]

Of 971 Bills passed by the State Duma [b]	Federation Council (%)	President (%)
Vetoed	23	20
Approved after intra- and inter-branch agreement	10.5	5.7
Approved after Duma override	4.1	3.6
Rejected after intra- and inter-branch agreement	0.1	2.6
Rejected after Duma override	0.8	1.6
Failed to overcome veto	8.4	10
Signed into law after initial veto	10.4	8.4

Sources: 'Analiticheskoe upravlenie', *Gosudarstvennaya Duma vtorogo sozyva (1996–1999): Informatsionno-analiticheskiy byulleten'* (Moscow: 1999), 7.

Notes: [a] 57 per cent of bills passed by Duma were signed into law without any changes.
 [b] This figure covers the period up to 26 Nov. 1999.

The use of procedures to resolve conflicts on legislation is an important development. As Grankin shows, the number of 'conciliation' and 'special' commissions convened to broker deals between both houses, and between the Federal Assembly and the president, has increased significantly since 1993.[49] This reflects a general rise in the volume of legislative traffic, but this in itself is not inconsequential. The large number of laws passed by the president, and the willingness of both the legislative and executive branches to bargain on legislation, would suggest that the president's power to enact decrees has not usurped the parliament's legislative function. In an important study by Remington *et al.*, some evidence is found for a correlation between 'issue salience' and the president's use of decrees, but in most cases the authors find that policy is made by the enactment of laws rather than decrees.[50]

Conclusion

The emergence of consensus-seeking procedures to resolve conflicts on legislation between the legislative and executive branches is a positive development. It may even assuage the fears of those who predicted that the separation of powers in the 1993 constitution would generate conflict and deadlock over legislation. However, it would be premature to talk about the consolidation of legislative relations on this basis. The president's substantial powers may still be the source of more serious conflicts in the future, if the policy preferences of actors in both branches diverge significantly. Nonetheless, in light of the political impasse that stifled such institutional developments in the early post-Communist period, the advent of mechanisms to mediate conflicts on both an intra- and inter-institutional level is a major achievement.

[49] 10 (1994), 69 (1996), 78 (1997), and 117 for the first ten months of 1998. Grankin, *Parlament Rossii*, 203.
[50] Remington *et al.*, 'Decrees, Laws, and Inter-Branch Relations'.

However, while procedures used to facilitate compromise and consensus are a response to Russia's institutional and policy disorder, they are only a partial remedy. The fragmentation of legislative agenda-setting in the Duma, caused in part by the weak centripetal forces of party and government, gives rise to a de-centred process of law-making that undermines countervailing efforts to prioritize and regulate legislative activity 'from above'. Thus, the question of how to integrate parties and the executive into the legislative process is an ongoing subject for discussion in political circles. If this debate is to translate into serious attempts at reform, a concerted effort on all sides is required. Yet important divisions still remain over both the scale and direction of such change.

8 Legislative-Executive Relations in the Yeltsin Era

Eugene Huskey

....

Ruling with the parliament

To overcome parliamentary resistance to presidential leadership, Boris Yeltsin employed diverse levers of influence, some grounded in formal powers, others in paraconstitutional practice. Perhaps most surprising is the frequency with which the Russian president conceded to the will of parliament on some issues in order to avoid debilitating confrontations. In the spring of 1994, for example, the Russian president agreed to sign the Law on the Status of Deputies, which granted the deputies unfettered access to Government officials and agencies and expanded their immunity from prosecution. In accepting this controversial bill, the president overruled most of his senior advisors in the presidency, including Sergei Filatov and the head of the State-Legal Administration.[1]

It was in the field of personnel policy, however, that the president made his most visible and significant concessions. Put simply, Yeltsin periodically defused the rising hostility of parliament and the nation by sacrificing unpopular ministers. Like a sated beast, following each sacrifice the parliament lost for a time the will to stalk the executive. Whereas noteworthy Government reshuffles occurred every few months through most of the Yeltsin presidency, the replacement of a prime minister took place only once in Yeltsin's first term, in December 1992, when Viktor Chernomyrdin replaced Yegor Gaidar. For Yeltsin, as for all leaders in semipresidential systems, the prime minister is usually held in reserve, to be sacrificed when all other means of fending off the parliament and the nation have been exhausted. An indication of the rapid erosion of presidential authority in 1998 was Yeltsin's dismissal of two prime ministers in less than six months, Chernomyrdin in March and Kirienko in August. When Yeltsin attempted to return Chernomyrdin to the prime ministership in late August, he was rebuffed twice by the parliament. Rather than risk a constitutional crisis or a new election by subjecting Chernomyrdin to a third and final confirmation vote, Yeltsin selected another candidate, Yevgenii Primakov, who enjoyed broad support in the Duma.

The president's concessions on personnel represented one strand in a complex web of

---

This is an abbreviated version of chapter 6 of Eugene Huskey, *Presidential Power in Russia* (Armonk, NY: M. E. Sharpe, 1999). Reproduced by kind permission of the author and M. E. Sharpe Inc., NY.

[1] Sergei Chugaev, 'Kto voz'met na sebia grekh narushit' konstitutsiiu: prezident ili zakonodateli?' *Izvestia*, 12 May 1994, p. 1

relationships between the executive and legislature. In return for the support or forbearance of the parliament, deputies extracted—or the president proffered—a variety of 'goods,' some benefiting the parliament as a whole, others targeting individual leaders. Such exchanges included apartments, transportation, and vacation packages allocated to deputies by the president's Administration of Affairs, and posts on the presidency's Security Council, granted to the leaders of the Duma and Federation Council. Whether designed to co-opt deputies more broadly or to enlist their temporary support for a bill before parliament, such measures have been instrumental in taming a legislature whose political instincts are decidedly antipresidential.[2]

Corruption in parliament has also weakened the resolve of deputies. Of course, private gain, or at least private sustenance, is a concern of politicians in all but the most revolutionary environments. But in Russia, as in many developing societies, corruption has assumed a particularly insidious and blatant form in the legislature. Among the 450 members of the Duma elected in December 1995, more than 30 were under criminal investigation by the prosecutor's office. Because criminals fearing prosecution could hide behind Russia's generous parliamentary immunity, which could only be revoked by a majority vote of the assembly, some outlaws sought refuge in a parliamentary seat. Criminal elements were especially numerous among the more than fifteen thousand persons registered as 'aides' to parliamentarians. When a police investigator went to the Duma for a committee hearing on a draft of the Criminal Procedure Code, he 'found [himself] at something resembling a gathering of crime kingpins. [He] probably saw more old acquaintances in the Duma than . . . in the prisons cells at Butyrki!'[3] In 1996 alone, twelve parliamentary aides were murdered—presumably because of their ties to the criminal world.[4]

The Duma attracted criminal elements in part because of the illicit trade in votes. According to a report in *Izvestia* in 1997, 'making laws "to order" has become a very stable and perhaps the most dependable way for deputies to augment their personal and party budgets.' In passing the law on mineral rights, for example, several leading energy companies were reportedly among the businesses that 'placed the order.'[5] One could argue, of course, that business interests in the United States exercise similar power over individual members of the legislature through campaign donations and other forms of financial and political support. But not only is this activity less regulated and visible in Russia, it also enables the executive itself to use monetary rewards to generate a legislative majority. According to one source, in order to push through the 1997 budget, 'circles close to the Government' channeled $27 million to the Communist and Liberal Democratic parties, two of the parliament's largest and most opposition-minded factions.[6] While functionally valuable as an antidote to executive-legislative gridlock, such criminality undermines the very

---

[2] On the use of goods to encourage parliament to confirm Sergei Kirienko as prime minister, see Evgenii Iur'ev, 'S tiazhelym serdtsem i ushchemlennym statusom,' *Segodnia* online, 30 July 1998, and Celestine Bohlen, 'Communists Risking Perks and Power in Yeltsin Battle,' *New York Times*, 24 Apr. 1998, pp. Al, A6.

[3] Anatolii Stepovoi, 'Access to Okhotnyi Row,' *Izvestia*, 27 Feb. 1997, pp. 1–2, as translated in *Current Digest of the Post-Soviet Press*, 9 (1997), 12. Vladimir Zhirinovskii was reported to have had over two hundred aides himself. Ibid.

[4] Ibid.

[5] Igor Vandenko, 'We Say "Deputy" but Mean Broker' *Izvestia*, 30 May 1997, pp. 1–2, as trans. in *Current Digest of the Post-Soviet Press*, 22 (1997), 16.

[6] Ibid.

foundations of representative and responsible government. It is no wonder that parliament is unable to halt the 'bloating and corruption' in the executive.

The ability of the president to generate temporary majorities in a hostile parliament also rests on the deputies' lack of a will to power and their peculiar sense of functional dualism. Deputies often view themselves as lawmaking professionals as well as partisan politicians. In the first role, deputies want to pass legislation, and the threat of a presidential veto encourages them to reach compromises with the executive in order to avoid stalemate. Recognizing the space for political accommodation that this incentive structure provides, the presidency has regularly employed three institutions to advance its legislative agenda. The first is the Domestic Policy Administration, which informs the president of the correlation of political forces in parliament while at the same time trying 'to convince deputies of the advantages [*tselesoobraznost'*] of the legislative initiatives of the president.'[7] The second institution is the presidential representatives to the Duma and Federation Council, who represent somewhat tepid versions of a Government whip in a parliamentary system. In the Russian case, this figure is part political operative, part legal official, someone who oversees the movement of a bill from its drafting in the executive—at which stage he advises the president on the parliament's likely reaction to the legislation—through its various committee hearings and the requisite three readings before the chambers.[8] In addition, for important bills, the leader of the Executive Office of the President also assigns a high-ranking Government official to 'bulldog' the bill through the two houses. Whether presidential representative or minister designated ad hoc, these officials serve as important conduits of information between executive and legislative leaders. In cases where the legislation originates in the parliament rather than the executive, after a bill's first reading the presidential representative communicates to the legislature any changes in the law desired by the president. Suggestions for legislative revisions usually emanate from the president's State-Legal Administration, which carefully reviews all draft legislation.[9]

In the summer of 1996, Boris Yeltsin created a Political Consultative Council that included leading officials from executive and legislative institutions. Where conciliatory commissions reviewed specific bills, the Consultative Council discussed the broader course of Russian political and economic development. It offered another venue through which the president and his prime minister could work to co-opt key members of parliament and thereby transform the tenor of executive-legislative relations from confrontation to cooperation.[10] By early 1998, the Consultative Council had transmogrified into the Big Four, an informal committee uniting the president, prime minister, speaker of the Duma, and chairman of the Federation Council.

---

[7] V. A. Vinogradov, *Koordinatsiia pravotvorchestva v Rossiiskoi federatsii* (Moscow, 1996), 31. My thanks to Peter Reddaway for bringing this source to my attention.

[8] For the statute governing this institution, see 'O polnomochnykh predstaviteliakh Prezidenta RF v palatakh Federal'nogo Sobraniia RF,' *Sobranie zakonodatel'stva*, no. 11 (1996), st. 1034. Presidential representatives insist that they are merely lawyers who ensure adherence to legal and constitutional norms. The reality is far more complex and more political.

[9] A detailed description of the role and authority of presidential institutions in the legislative process may be found in 'Polozhenie o poriadke vzaimodeistviia Prezidenta RF s palatami Federal'nogo Sobraniia RF v zakonotvorcheskorn protsesse,' *Sobranie zakonodatel'stva*, no. 16 (1996), st. 1842.

[10] See Robert W. Orttung and Scott Parrish, 'From Confrontation to Cooperation in Russia,' *Transition*, 13 Dec. 1996, pp. 19–20.

The idea of establishing alternatives to a recalcitrant parliament first surfaced in the early 1990s, when President Yeltsin created a Social Chamber (*obshchestvennaia palata*) comprised of representatives from the country's leading religious, ethnic, and civic associations. Although the Social Chamber never assumed an especially active or visible role in public affairs, its very existence threatened for a time the parliament's monopoly as the nation's assembly. It also provided the president with a ready-made alternative leg of legitimacy on which to stand in the event of a dissolution of parliament.[11] But when Yeltsin shut down the parliament in September 1993, he looked not to the Social Chamber but to regional elites for political support. In the first few days after the closing of parliament, Yeltsin considered creating a Council of the Federation, made up of leading provincial officials, to legitimate his rule during the interregnum. However, the relative popular quiescence that followed the military defeat of the parliamentary opposition apparently convinced the Russian president that he could rule alone until the introduction of a new constitution.

The concept of a pro-presidential assembly of regional elites found its way, however, into the 1993 constitution in the form of the upper house of the Federal Assembly, the Federation Council, sometimes referred to informally as the Senate. Believing the indirectly elected Federation Council to be a desirable counterweight to a directly elected Duma, the framers of the 1993 constitution made the upper house a permanent body, not subject to dissolution. Thus, Russia's institutional arrangements reduced the stakes of a Duma dissolution. Any future closure of the Duma would leave one-half of the assembly still in place.

Unlike in some parliamentary and semipresidential systems, Russia does not permit the president to dissolve a parliament on his own, even after a certain time period has elapsed following parliamentary elections. A constitutional dissolution of parliament may occur only as a result of the deputies' own actions. If the Duma rejects the president's nominee for prime minister thrice, the parliament is dissolved and new elections held.[12] The president may also dissolve the Duma if it expresses no confidence in the Government. If the Duma initiates the no-confidence motion, the president is empowered to dissolve parliament if a majority of the deputies vote against the Government twice within a three-month period. When the Government itself raises the question of parliamentary confidence in its work, the president may dissolve the Duma within a mere seven days after the motion of confidence fails.[13] In order to pressure the Duma into passing the 1998 budget, Prime Minister Chernomyrdin considered calling for a vote of no confidence in late 1997.[14]

[11] Yeltsin had also sought unsuccessfully at the end of 1994 to create a commission for the coordination of legislation that would serve as a multibranch supercommittee for legislative drafting. According to Georgii Satarov, this commission would have included ten members each from the presidency, Government, Duma, Federation Council, Election Commission, and Social Chamber. Such a commission would have limited its work to major policy issues, such as the electoral law, the budget, tax and privatization policy, and 'state construction.' Andrei Kolesnikov, 'Smozhet li "trekhgolovyi Gaidar" spasti ekonomiku Rossii?' *Rossiiskie vesti*, 18 Nov. 1994, p. 1. Rather than develop a strong presidential party, Satarov sought to create a consociational institution where members of the executive, legislative, and society would develop laws before they were presented to parliament. See 'Effektivnost': "te resheniia, kotorye liudi gotovy vypolnit,"' *Rossiiskie vesti*, 5 Aug. 1994, p. 1; and Dmitrii Orlov, 'Prezident prodolzhaet poisk mekhanizmov vzaimodeistviia s Federal'nym Sobraniem,' *Rossiiskie vesti*, 18 Nov. 1994, p. 1.

[12] Presumably, these votes would occur within three weeks after the president first nominated the prime minister. Article 111 of the constitution states that the Duma must vote initially within a week of the submission of the prime minister's candidacy.

[13] *Konstitutsiia Rossiiskoi Federatsii* (Moscow: Iuridicheskaia literatura, 1994), Article 117.

[14] 'Yeltsin May Dissolve Duma if it Fails to Vote for Budget,' *Interfax*, 1459 GMT, 21 Nov. 1997.

Despite the fact that the deputies retain the ultimate decision regarding their fate, it would be a mistake to view dissolution politics as a one-sided parliamentary game. By appointing a prime minister who is unacceptable to deputies, the president can in effect force the Duma to seize the poison pen. Likewise, the prime minister at a moment of enormous unpopularity could provoke the Duma into dissolution by calling for a no-confidence vote. In this sense, the president is as much the master of the parliament's fate as the deputies. Indeed, the mere circulation of rumors that the executive plans to encourage a Duma dissolution— such as occurred in the summer of 1997—may serve to intimidate the deputies into a less confrontational posture.

Given their fear of the unknown in electoral politics, many Duma deputies have been reluctant to move beyond opposition to specific policies of the executive to a complete withdrawal of confidence in the prime minister and his Government. According to one observer: '[W]hile [the Duma] periodically threatens the Government with a vote of no confidence, it is simultaneously afraid of its own radicalism. It doesn't want to end up being dissolved.'[15] Only twice in the Chernomyrdin era, in October 1994 and July 1995, did deputies advance a no-confidence motion in the Government, and only in the latter instance did the motion pass. That the Duma failed to follow this up with a second and decisive vote of no confidence reflected the unwillinguess of deputies to risk their seats, and in many cases their livelihood, to contest elections whose outcome would not alter fundamentally the distribution of power between president and parliament.[16] Regardless of the results, the Duma would not be able to force a prime minister on the president, as in France. Indeed, a dramatically increased majority of opposition forces in parliament might encourage the president to reduce his cooperation with the assembly, or to close it altogether by unconstitutional means. Furthermore, because the constitution allows the president to rule for up to four months after a parliamentary dissolution, by forcing new elections the deputies would remove legislative oversight of the executive for a lengthy, and potentially crisis-ridden, period. Here again, the institutional design of Russian politics favors the president at the expense of parliament.

Ruling around the parliament

Through the use of institutions such as the presidential representative and the conciliation commissions, Yeltsin showed willingness to adhere to the logic of semipresidential rule on some issues. But impatience with parliamentary obstruction and delays led the Russian president at times to invoke the rhetoric and methods of rule associated with authoritarian regimes. Frustrated with the parliament's refusal to accede to desperately needed budget cuts, Yeltsin rashly announced in July 1997 that he would no longer allow the Federal Assembly to make any important decisions: 'The Government should tackle 80 percent of issues on its own, without referring them to parliament . . . In future only 20 percent of

---

[15] Valery Vyzhutovich, 'Bicameral Cabinet: The Government Is Split,' *Izvestia*, 22 Apr. 1997, p. 2, as trans. in *Current Digest of the Post-Soviet Press*, 16 (1997), 5.

[16] According to Sergei Chugaev, the Duma sought to use the threat of a no-confidence vote as a chip 'in its trading with the president over changes in ministerial portfolios.' 'Duma predpochitaet otstavke pravitel'stva torgolviu s prezidentom,' *Izvestia*, 19 Oct. 1994, p. 4.

measures should be referred to parliament for approval.'[17] In the event, the president did not carry through on this threat. But he continued to remind the parliament of the lawmaking powers that he held in reserve. In the summer of 1998, amid a severe financial crisis, Yeltsin promised to enact a packet of anticrisis measures demanded by the IMF if the parliament failed to approve it. The politics of presidential engagement and cooperation with parliament represented, therefore, only one face of governing in Russia. The other, darker, side of Russian politics exhibited features familiar to students of autocracy, including the refusal of the supreme leader to be checked by other state institutions.

At least through the middle of Yeltsin's second term, the president and his legislative assistants adopted a generally harsh public tone toward the Duma while exhibiting moderation toward the Federation Council. For years, Yeltsin refused to make an appearance in the Duma, upset by what he considered to be its lack of respect toward the presidency. In April 1998, rather than present his nominee for prime minister in person, as is customary in many semipresidential systems, he instructed his representative, Aleksandr Kotenkov, to introduce the nomination of Sergei Kirienko. This departure from protocol was all the more insulting because the majority of Duma members regarded Kotenkov with suspicion or disdain. Unlike his predecessor in the Duma, Aleksandr M. Yakovlev, or his counterpart in the Federation Council, Anatolii Sliva, Kotenkov was a brusque and undiplomatic lawyer whose attitude toward Duma deputies bordered at times on contempt. As Kirienko was forming his cabinet in the spring of 1998, party factions in the Duma were exerting pressure on the president and prime minister designate to include some of their leaders in the new Government. During these negotiations, Kotenkov damned the Duma with faint praise when he said that he knew 'virtually all the deputies, and there are [some] really outstanding characters among them deserving to hold a ministerial post. But there are no more than ten such people.'[18] In other words, from among the 450 members of the Duma, an organization that in most semipresidential systems would serve as the prime recruiting pool for the Government, Kotenkov regarded only 2 percent as qualified to become ministers. Kotenkov's careful scrutiny of Duma voting procedures also angered many deputies. On several occasions, he accused the Duma of counting the votes of deputies who were absent from the chamber—and even the country—during roll call. Such a challenge to the validity of the Duma's voting results led the president to reject the override of his veto on a conservative Land Code in 1997.[19]

To avoid parliamentary constraints, Yeltsin has relied heavily on presidential decrees as an instrument of direct rule. In so doing, he has employed the authority of a constitution that his team of advisors tailored to his needs. Article 90 empowers the Russian president to issue decrees (*ukazy*) and directives (*rasporiazheniia*) as long as they do not contradict other provisions of the constitution or parliamentary statutes (*zakony*). Given the paucity of new Russian laws, and the illegitimacy of much of the Soviet legal inheritance, Yeltsin enjoyed

---

[17] Fred Weir, *Hindustan Times*, 30 July 1997, as printed in Johnson's Russia List, 30 July 1997.

[18] 'Kotenkov Says Only 10 Deputies Deserve Ministerial Posts,' ITAR-TASS in English, 1442 GMT, 27 Apr. 1998, as printed in *BBC Summary of World Broadcasts*, 29 Apr. 1998.

[19] 'Press Conference with Presidential Representative at the State Duma,' Official Kremlin International News Broadcast, 29 Sept. 1997; 'Lower House Protests over Remarks by Yeltsin Representative,' *Interfax*, 0725 GMT, 25 Sept. 1997, as trans. in *BBC Summary of World Broadcasts*, 26 Sept. 1997.

sweeping lawmaking authority, especially during his first term.[20] Thus, ruling around parliament by decree assumed a patina of respectability and legitimacy, even if some decrees appeared to encroach on existing parliamentary laws. Like numerous presidentialist regimes in Latin America, Russia sanctioned *decretismo* as a means of overcoming the legislative stalemate that plagues presidential and semipresidential regimes in transition.[21] In the view of Robert Orttung and Scott Parrish, the Russian presidency enjoys 'what are probably the strongest legislative powers of any elected president in the world'[22]

The scale of Yeltsin's decree-making activity was staggering. Recall that the order to dissolve the parliament in September 1993 was the fourteen hundredth decree issued that year. The number of decrees signed annually continues to approach one thousand. To be sure, a relatively small percentage of these decrees possess what lawyers would call normative authority; that is, they rarely set down a permanent or general rule that binds the bureaucracy and society. Most affect a single institution, a single region, or even a single individual. Indeed, fully a third of the decrees issued by Yeltsin in 1996 merely announced the appointment—or in some cases, dismissal—of judges and high-ranking executive officials, such as ambassadors, ministers, and regional representatives. The president uses the more humble 'directives' to hire and fire less exalted officials, those occupying posts at department head level and below in the presidency and at deputy minister level and below in the Government. Another sizable minority of the decrees issued in 1996, approximately one-quarter of the total, concerned the management of executive agencies or the supervision of national security affairs, two areas over which the Russian president has traditionally exercised hegemony. Presidential decrees, for example, launched the reorganization of the Ministry of Internal Affairs in the spring of 1996 and established a new passport regime later that same year.[23]

A recognition of the diverse uses to which presidential decrees are put in Russian administration should not obscure, however, their lawmaking role in matters that lie within the provenance of parliaments in most democratic regimes. A quarter of the decrees issued in 1996 addressed policy questions in areas as diverse as economics and finance, education, culture and science, and social security. One of the centerpieces of economic reform in Russia, the privatization of state property, was introduced almost exclusively through presidential decrees. Likewise, the decision to move to a convertible currency was made by decrees and not laws. Because parliamentary statutes were silent on these subjects, the president and his economic advisors could claim constitutional authority for these initiatives. Presidential decrees were filling in empty normative space.

[20] The pace of parliamentary lawmaking slowed down markedly after the collapse of the First Russian Republic, only to pick up again by the end of Yeltsin's first term. During its first four months, the Duma elected in December 1993 did not pass a single law, save a technical statute on how laws should be published (a *zakon o zakonakh*). And before that bill was rejected by the upper house, Yeltsin published his own decree regulating the publication of laws. Leonid Nikitinskii, 'Sud'ba zakona o zakonakh,' *Izvestia*, 26 Apr. 1994, p. 2.

[21] On the Latin American cases, see Guillermo O'Donnell, 'Delegative Democracy,' *Journal of Democracy*, 1 (1994), 66.

[22] Robert W. Orttung and Scott Parrish, 'From Confrontation to Cooperation in Russia,' *Transition*, 13 Dec. 1996, p. 17. Matthew Soberg Shugart makes a similar point in his 'Executive-Legislative Relations in Post-Communist Europe,' *Transition*, 13 Dec. 1996, p. 9.

[23] Data based on analysis of decrees published in *Sobranie zakonodatel'stva* for 1996. Thomas F. Remington, Steven S. Smith, and Moshe Haspel offer a detailed examination of decree-making in 'Decrees, Laws, and Inter-Branch Relations in the Russian Federation,' *Post-Soviet Affairs*, 4 (1998), 287–322.

In most cases where presidential decrees appeared to be at variance with existing statutes, the laws in question were legacies from the Soviet era. That did not mean, however, that the laws necessarily lacked legal force. Just as Soviet Russia accepted for a time part of the legal inheritance from the tsarist regime, numerous laws that had been adopted in the Soviet era were adapted to the changing political and economic environment through statutory revision. When Yeltsin issued his controversial decree to combat organized crime in May 1994, it violated provisions of the long-standing, and much-amended, Criminal Procedure Code.[24] Similarly, the president's decree privatizing peasant land in June 1996 not only contradicted existing statutes on real property, it directly flouted the will of a majority of the sitting parliament, which had pointedly refused to pass a new law on land with similar provisions. Thus, although Yeltsin may have preferred to rule with the parliament, he was prepared to rule around it if it repeatedly refused to accommodate his interests.

Once enacted and signed into law, parliamentary statues also faced neglect or distortion at the hands of executive officials responsible for implementing the law. In this regard, little had changed from the Soviet era: laws remained without effect until they had been 'concretized' through the issuance of enabling acts by the Government and relevant ministries. It was therefore these substatutory acts, and not the laws themselves, that moved officialdom to action. How faithfully and quickly bureaucrats executed the law depended on the directives, orders, and instructional letters that they received from ministers and other executive leaders. Without a well-developed system of administrative courts, a culture of legality and bureaucratic discipline, or a tradition of individual ministerial responsibility to parliament through interpellation or votes of confidence, the assembly has not been able to ensure the faithful execution of the laws by the presidency and the Government.[25]

Conclusion

The widely divergent assessments of Boris Yeltsin's political leadership—a democrat to some, a dictator to others—follow as much from the two faces of presidential power as from the polarization of Russian society. Those sympathetic to Yeltsin point to the constant give-and-take between president and parliament over legislation and patronage, a pattern of political exchange that is certainly familiar to students of American politics.[26] Each institution has formal and informal levers of influence that it uses to advance its interests. To be sure, the balance of constitutional power is tilted heavily in favor of the president, a result of his clan's dominance among the document's framers. But the parliamentary opposition has its own heavy weapons, including the ability to mobilize popular protests against executive action. Signaling its dissatisfaction with the policies of the president, the Communist Party began to organize massive strikes throughout the country in the summer of 1997, and in so doing sought to put pressure on the executive to moderate the second round of radical

---

[24] This act was revoked by a subsequent presidential decree in June 1997.

[25] On interpellation of Government ministers, see Liubov' Vladimirova, 'Deputaty prevrashchaiut "Chas Pravitel'stva" v vecher voprosov i otvetov,' *Rossiiskie vesti*, 21 June 1994, p. 1.

[26] For a detailed study of the methods and institutions—including the White House's Office of Congressional Relation—used by American presidents to influence Congress, see Nigel Bowles, *The White House and Capitol Hill* (Oxford: Oxford University Press, 1987).

economic reform directed by Chubais and Nemtsov. Yeltsin's decision to abandon his young prime minister, Sergei Kirienko, after only five months in office must also be seen as a reaction to rising discontent among members of parliament as well as Russian oligarchs and foreign investors.

Those who view Yeltsin's presidency as a continuation of the autocratic tradition will emphasize instead the willingness of the president to rule around parliament at moments of crisis or frustration. Given the institutional design of the Second Russian Republic, Yeltsin doesn't have to suspend parliament; he may simply ignore it. Like the Dumas that sat under the last Russian tsar, Nicholas II, the current State Duma in Russia exerts influence but does not in any real sense share sovereignty with the chief executive. Despite its antipresidential majority, the parliament cannot force the hand of the executive.

The political opposition has chosen, therefore, to play two parallel games. On the field of rhetoric—in speeches, newspaper articles, and party programs—the Communists and nationalists portrayed Yeltsin and his advisors as the enemies of Russia. But behind the scenes, they continually negotiated with the presidency and Government over the allocation of jobs, funds, and the other 'goods' of state. Without this kind of engagement, the opposition would have enjoyed few spoils of office.

Cooperation has had its limits, however. At least until the Primakov Government, the Communists and nationalists refused to be drawn into public actions that would blur the lines between Government and opposition. When Yeltsin included a Communist, Valentin Kovalev, in the cabinet in the fall of 1994, the Communist Party expelled him and thereby avoided the perception that it had joined the Government. It sought to avoid even partial responsibility for the actions of the executive.

In periods of crisis, such as Russia experienced in the 1990s, opposition to the ruling elite has been a politically comfortable and electorally advantageous position. For this reason, deputies were alarmed in the summer of 1996 when a little-understood provision of the budget law forced the parliament to approve the specific cuts to be made in the annual sequestration of funds. Previously, reducing expenditure had been the sole responsibility of the executive. Where parliament offered generous funding to institutions and programs at the beginning of the budget year, the executive was forced in the middle of the year to scale it back. Most deputies preferred to keep it that way.[27] Indeed, some analysts argue that the Duma intentionally passed deficit-ridden budgets to satisfy not only the struggling pensioners, soldiers, and students but prominent banking interests who stand to make handsome profits on the financing of the state deficit. In general, the higher the deficit, the higher the yield on state bonds held by the banks and by

---

[27] The involvement of the Duma in the sequestration of funds followed from a provision, article 69, in the 1997 Law on the Budget, which stated that the legislature should participate equally with the Government in decisions to reduce budgetary expenditures if the treasury received less than 90 percent of planned revenues. This provision directly contradicted, however, the law on the budget process, which holds that the executive is solely responsible for such midyear budgetary cutbacks. See Aleksandr Bekker, Nikolai Ivanov, and Igor' Moiseev, 'Gosduma priachet golovu v pesok,' *Segodnia* online, 22 May 1997, and 'Chut'-chut' politicheskogo teatra, nemnozhko kompromissa i maksimum dokhodnykh,' *Segodnia* online, 21 May 1997. As an article in the newspaper of the presidency indicated, the executive did not believe parliament could deal responsibly with a budget shortfall. Their instinct was either to 'introduce emergency measures to resolve the crisis or to print 300 trillion rubles.' Elena Ishkova, 'Srazhenie za chestnyi biudzhet,' *Rossiiskie vesti*, 22 May 1997, p. 1.

bureaucrats and enterprise directors with access to funds that can be invested, even if for a short term.[28]

The primary focus of this account—and of most Western analyses of parliamentary politics in Russia—has been on the lower house, the Duma. Under the constitution of the Second Russian Republic, the Duma appears the more politically weighty of the two chambers by virtue of its ability to express no confidence in the Government and to override Federation Council decisions with a two-thirds majority vote. Furthermore, unlike the Federation Council, the Duma is a directly elected chamber; as a result, it is here that one finds the seeds of party development in Russia. It is also in the Duma that one sees most clearly the economic or class cleavages that have been the staple of politics in the West in the last two centuries. In short, the Duma exhibits features that Western political scientists regard as familiar and important in democratic assemblies. However, the Federation Council's power of confirmation over key judicial and executive appointments has constrained presidential appointment policy. Still more important than the powers of the chamber is the political prominence of its members and the centrality of center–periphery issues to its debates. Most Duma deputies are what the British might call 'lobby fodder,' political followers who lack visibility and an institutional base. Half of the members of the Federation Council, though, have been governors of regions or presidents of republics, with their own bureaucratic bases outside parliament; the other half are speakers of the provincial legislatures.[29] Generating support for the president in the Federation Council requires, therefore, different skills and a different currency of exchange than in the Duma. Because of the weakness of party factions in the Federation Council, it is not enough to win over the leaders of the chamber. Support must be built one member at a time.

Beginning in 1996, under pressure from provincial elites, the president permitted the direct election of regional governors, most of whom had previously been the appointees of the president. This change in the country's institutional design promises to alter the relations between executive and legislature, between Duma and Federation Council, and between center and periphery in Russia.[30] Although the appointed governors were never really the prefects of the president—to be effective, they also needed the support of local elites—in the new incentive structure they must work to secure their electoral base as well. This reorientation of political loyalties began to present the greatest challenge yet to presidential rule. As members of the parliament in Moscow and as chief executives and legislative speakers in the country's eighty-nine subject territories, these regional elites were emerging as the brokers of Russia's political future.

---

[28] See the important article by Irma Savvateeva, 'The Budget Debate Might End with New Elections to the Duma,' *Izvestia*, 21 Nov. 1996, pp. 1–2, as trans. in *Current Digest of the Post-Soviet Press*, 47 (1996), 9.

[29] In one of the many wrinkles in Russia's political transition, the initial elections for Federation Council seats, in December 1993, were direct contests in which voters cast ballots for two candidates in each region or republic. Beginning with the December 1995 elections, however, the constitutional provisions applied, and Federation Council members now hold their seats by virtue of their being the chief executive or legislative speaker of a region or republic.

[30] It is in the interest of the Federation Council to change the electoral law to eliminate the 225 proportional representation seats in the Duma. If at the next election all seats were in single-member districts, where provincial elites have greater influence in the nomination of candidates, the regional governors and republican presidents— and the chamber in which they sit—could dominate the lower house. See Aleksandr Trifonov, 'Molchanie Kremlia', *Vlast'*, 16 June 1998, p. 23.

9   Rewriting the Rules of the Game in Russia: The Neglected Issue of the Demand for Law

Kathryn Hendley

....

As a Hollywood movie put it, 'if you build it, they will come.' This catchphrase captures the flavor of the assumptions underlying legal reform in Russia over the past decade. Recognizing that, to a great extent, law had been marginalized during the Soviet period, domestic policymakers and their foreign advisers identified two key reasons why Russians shied away from using the law to protect and advance their interests. The first centered on the well-chronicled shortcomings of Soviet law, apparent in both its generally poor quality (for example, rampant internal inconsistencies, its declaratory character, lack of transparency) and the politicization of legal institutions by the Communist Party. The second reason lay in the absence of key incentives, primarily private property; the existence of which—it was reasoned—would lead individuals and firms to desire and use law to protect their newfound property interests. From this line of thinking, it presumably followed that if these problems were fixed and the 'correct' laws and legal institutions were put into place, then Russian citizens would begin to make use of them. Although this connection between supply of and demand for law may have seemed self-evident, it has proven elusive in practice.

To be sure, Soviet-era reluctance to mobilize law was, in part, a product of dissatisfaction with laws that often contradicted one another and with the administrative acts, or *podzakonnye akty*, that complicated their implementation, not to mention abiding doubts about the courts' independence. Certainly, reforms aimed at remedying these legacies of the Soviet legal system represent a step forward. Moreover, private property has elsewhere proven to be a powerful engine for legal development. But merely rewriting the 'rules of the game,' while undoubtedly a necessary prerequisite to stimulating a demand for law, has not sufficed— given the absence of efforts to address the more deeply rooted causes of Russians' antipathy toward law. Decades of watching law being used in a crudely instrumental fashion in order to serve the various ends of the Communist Party have taken their toll. Similarly, the obvious ability of the party elite to manipulate the outcome of court procedures led many to conclude that power trumps law, that 'telephone law' is more potent than written legislation.

Not surprisingly, then, Moscow's embrace of the rule-of-law state (*pravovoe gosudarstvo*), beginning with Gorbachev and continuing with Yeltsin, has been greeted with considerable skepticism by ordinary citizens. The idea that law could be used by ordinary citizens to protect themselves from arbitrary or illegal actions by the state or to advance their own

This chapter was first published as an article in *East European Constitutional Review*, 8/4 (1999), 89–95. Reproduced by kind permission of the author and the *East European Constitutional Review*.

interests in private transactions was viewed as unrealistic in the post-Soviet context. Such attitudes are unlikely to change quickly. Even though the Communist Party has been stripped of its monopoly on power, most feel that overweening political power has been exchanged for a comparable economic power. From the outside, the system may look different, but to citizens, the bottom line is the same. The powerful are able to manipulate both the substance of law and the outcome of specific cases. Whether these perceptions are borne out by contemporary reality is still open to question. But they have to be recognized as a powerful constraint not just on meaningful legal reform but on the demand for law itself regardless of how good the 'supply' may be. As things stand now, citizens are unlikely to respond immediately to overblown rhetoric about the importance of establishing a *pravovoe gosudarstvo*, or even to changes in the letter of the law, whether legislative or institutional. The Soviet legacy of campaigns in which such changes were announced with great fanfare only to be forgotten when the noise died down created a situation where Russians judge by deeds not words. They will adapt their behavior to the legal system only when they are convinced that the law is potentially useful to them.

Building a new legal system

Comparing snapshots of the legal landscape in 1985 and in 1998 would make immediately apparent the fundamental and far-reaching nature of recent reforms. A full catalogue of the changes is beyond the scope of this article, but a few deserve singling out. Even before the Communist Party was divested of its power, its influence (at least on a formal level) over the courts of general jurisdiction had deteriorated. Indeed, the judicial branch is finally out from under the thumb of the Ministry of Justice and has become self-governing. A constitutional court has been created and, after a bit of a false start, has begun to find its own voice; for example, the court has shown a willingness to take on thorny political issues affecting both Moscow and the regions. Economic (or *arbitrazh*) courts, which deal with commercial disputes, have been established on the institutional foundation of the Soviet-era *gosarbitrazh* (which lacked the accoutrements of a court and functioned more like an administrative agency). In addition, the number of new law-related institutions that have been created rivals Roosevelt's record during the early New Deal years. Agencies have been founded to assist in the implementation of antimonopoly, bankruptcy, securities, privatization, and other laws. Judged in quantitative terms, the legislative output during this period has also been extraordinary. Laws have been passed that institutionalize various features of the market economy and the democratic political order. Principal among these are the Constitution, and the criminal and civil codes.

Returning to the basic premise of the reformers, can we say that the supply of law has been, or should have been, adequate to stimulate demand? In pondering this question, we need to be realistic in our expectations. No legal system is ever fully realized. Inevitably, progress is piecemeal and relative. The goal is not perfection—not a flawless *pravovoe gosudarstvo*—but adequacy. Are enough of the necessary laws and institutions in place such that Russian citizens are able in principle, to mobilize their rights in relation to both private and state actors? The answer to this question is a resounding *yes*. On paper, Russians enjoy a relatively full panoply of rights (both civil and economic), and the procedural mechanisms exist to permit their exercise. (The laws are neither ideal nor enforced in full measure; but they are on the books.) The reformers' position has been that the 'building' of this new and improved legal system, replete with enforceable property rights, is a sine qua non for stimulating an increased use of the law.

Mobilizing law in post-Soviet Russia

But what is the reality? To what extent have the reforms of key laws and legal institutions given rise to increased use and thus stimulated demand for yet more law? Assessing levels of the use of law and the demand for more law is hazardous at best. Statistics document, over the past few years, increased caseloads of both the courts of general jurisdiction and the *arbitrazh* courts. But these cases undoubtedly represent the tip of the iceberg of potential disputes, and so drawing general conclusions from these data is not prudent. They indicate only that some individuals and firms are using legal institutions to resolve their disputes. But the same could be said of the Soviet period.

Demand might also be judged by the participation of society in the lawmaking process and the level of agitation for new laws and legal institutions coming from citizens and grassroots organizations. But with certain notable exceptions, legal reform has been top-down. Many of the reforms draw heavily on examples from abroad, with foreign advisers often participating actively in the drafting process. All too often the drafters' preoccupations were more with technical perfection than with how concepts borrowed from elsewhere would interact with Russia's own preexisting law and legal culture. This was most evident in the realm of economic law but was a persistent feature apparent in the overall legal reform effort. To be fair to the reformers, there was no hue and cry from ordinary citizens to be included in the process, while there was enormous pressure, generated both internally and by foreign donors, to move swiftly. As might be expected based on their historical experience, ordinary Russians took little interest in new laws and institutions.

This apathy toward law is not surprising. Indeed, rather than materializing spontaneously within Russian society at large, the demand for law is likely to emerge first among economic actors. Their payoff for using law is more readily apparent than benefits to other groups. Remedies for contractual breaches are more tangible than the merely moral satisfaction that results from prevailing in a criminal or human-rights claim. Outside the realm of litigation, a properly functioning legal system, based on clear, evenhanded norms, can greatly reduce transaction costs for businessmen. Russia's reformers actually agree with this point, though for different reasons. They contend that the impetus for further legal change will come from those groups within society that have obtained significant amounts of property through the privatization process. Prominent among such groups are enterprise managers. Examining their attitudes and behavior may provide some insight into the broader question of the demand for law.

Given the heavy weight of the past on the present in Russia, it is important to acknowledge our starting point. During the Soviet period, enterprise managers did not rely primarily on law to protect their interests. This is not to say that law did not exist. On a superficial level, law was used extensively. Enterprises memorialized their trading relationships in the form of contracts and brought claims against one another with considerable regularity in *gosarbitrazh* (though this served more as a signaling device to ministries than as a mechanism for resolving bilateral disputes). But the contractual form was largely empty of substance. Legal niceties mattered less than plan fulfillment. Enterprise managers understood that their protection depended not on the force of law but on their political connections and their ability to bring pressure to bear on their trading partners. Within the realm of the economy (as in much of the rest of Soviet society), law was not a freestanding bulwark but a malleable instrument available exclusively to the state and the Communist Party elite that stood behind it.

Believing that this way of proceeding was motivated by the political corrosion of the Soviet legal system, reformers anticipated that changing the rules of the game would provoke behavioral changes. These expectations were grounded both in the ongoing qualitative improvements to the legislative base and in the introduction of private property, which gave these managers something tangible to protect. The underlying assumption is that reliance on law is inherently more efficient than the use of political power because the associated transaction costs (in terms of both time and money) are, in theory, so much lower. As a result, the reformers anticipated that enterprise managers, as rational actors, would shift from a reliance on personal connections and patron–client networks to a reliance on the impersonal rules and institutions at the core of the new Russian legal system.

But what is rational may differ in different settings. The experience of Russian managers has not taught them to count on law as a mechanism for maximizing an enterprise's interests. For them, believing in the usefulness of law would require an enormous leap of faith. It is not that these managers do not grasp the Western argument about the efficiency of law. They do. They just do not see the pertinence of this argument and, perhaps, of law itself to their circumstances. The concept of law as a relatively neutral and stable set of norms by which they can organize transactions is foreign to them. On the other hand, the role of law, during the Soviet era, as a handmaiden to politics is well-documented and deeply etched in the Russian psyche. Why should they place their faith in law—and alter their behavior accordingly—when they have so little experience with law as a means of protecting and advancing their interests and so much experience with law as an instrument of the state? If we put ourselves in their shoes, we begin to understand their hesitancy and resistance to embracing law. When asked why they avoid the courts, managers often reveal their suspicion that extralegal powers will inevitably override a legally correct position. For example, a Moscow auto-parts-factory manager told me that, notwithstanding their huge debts, it was pointless to sue the giant auto assembly plants on their home turf (for example, to sue AvtoVAZ in Toliatti or GAZ in Nizhniy Novgorod). He had no particular evidence for his belief, but his misgivings sufficed to keep him away from the courts. (His reluctance to sue was no doubt also influenced by his unwillingness to risk losing future orders by angering these large auto plants.)

Rather than turning to law, Russian managers prefer to stick to tried-and-true methods of conducting business. When problems arise and negotiation proves fruitless, their recourse is typically not to the courts but to informal mechanisms. Sometimes, this involves protracted negotiations between long-term trading partners. The cash-poor status of many industrial enterprises has given so-called intermediaries, who can dispose of goods acquired in barter exchanges, a more central role. Still another option is turning to political patrons for assistance. In all cases, the goal, as during the Soviet era, is to exert pressure on trading partners in order to force payment of amounts owed. One key difference between the processes now and during the Soviet period is that they have grown even more onerous and time-consuming. This increased difficulty is the result of the rise in barter and the almost constant turnover of personnel within a governmental apparatus buffeted by the shifting winds of power. Patronage networks have become more fragile and tenuous. Moreover, often enough, these networks now extend into the shadowy world of organized crime. Few Russian enterprises are strong enough to survive without some sort of security service, or *krysha* (though some have brought this function in-house). For most, these methods of resolving disputes are preferable to relying on law. Indeed, they may be more efficient, in a real-world sense, because they are more familiar.

The low demand for law that is otherwise in reasonable supply

Let us consider, somewhat more closely, why law should be in such meager demand. A number of reasons come to mind, many of which are suggested by, but resonate beyond, the specific circumstances in which enterprise managers find themselves.

THE POTENT LEGACY OF SOVIET LEGAL CULTURE

Changing established patterns of behavior is never easy. Inertia sets in; people fall into ruts. This is certainly true of Russian managers. General directors, in particular, know how to manipulate the patron–client system inherited from the Soviet period. They sit at the center of a highly complex web of connections that is largely personal. Ultimate power rests with these directors. Only they can tug on one or another string and expect results. Such a system represents (at least in theory) the antithesis of a reliance on impersonal laws and institutions to resolve disputes without regard to the status of the litigants. But while recourse to law may appear more efficient—since problems can be resolved more quickly—what is less apparent is a collateral loss of power by managers. Accustomed to unquestioned power within the enterprise and in their interenterprise relations, activist general directors are loathe to give up any piece of it. Once a dispute is handed over to the courts, a director can do little but sit and wait for the decision. Before shifting to a reliance on law, directors have to believe that judges and laws are relatively impartial; in other words, that their enterprise has an equal chance to prevail. In the face of such a belief flies both historical experience and the long-standing skepticism of law among Russian citizens.

The shift to a reliance on law makes sense only if it is made almost simultaneously by a substantial majority of potential litigants. Managers are understandably reluctant to be the first to make the move, thereby ceding an advantage to law-adverse trading partners who could still appeal to political or other patrons. The safer option is to stay the course. In this, we find a classic dilemma of collective action. Inured to high-flown if empty rhetoric about 'reform,' managers (and others) thus may be waiting for concrete evidence of law's usefulness. If so, we may find ourselves trapped in a vicious circle. In economic transactions, the value of law lies in its ability to provide a common language (basic rules and a preapproved forum for resolving disputes) that need not be contested in every new transaction. If, however, significant numbers of potential users persist in bypassing it, then the law loses this critical virtue. Proof of utility will appear only if and when a specific law or legal institution is, in fact, widely used.

METHOD OF CARRYING OUT REFORMS

Also important is the way legal reform has been carried out. The reformers had a vision of what was required to make the Russian legal system 'normal' and believed they knew best what Russian society needed. This experts-know-best attitude, needless to say, contains troubling echoes of the Soviet past. There is a long tradition, dating back to czarist days, of reform descending from above. This tradition, unfortunately, lives on in post-Soviet Russia. Thus, when designing the legal building blocks of the market economy, such as a civil code or the joint-stock-company law, little effort was made to fathom how existing enterprises were actually doing business. Instead, attention was focused on adapting laws that had worked in other contexts to Russian circumstances (sometimes this may have meant no more than translating other countries' laws). Such an approach ignored the negative experiences of Latin America and Africa, where this path had been followed decades earlier. Simply put 'transplanting' laws has all too often been a dismal failure.

Russia's lack of market experience since 1917 has opened up a particularly wide gulf between laws on the books and actual practice. Consequently, the import of sophisticated legal tools has often had disparate effects on various economic actors. Those well trained in market principles have been able to use these new tools to their advantage, while most were merely puzzled. A good example of this disparate impact is the requirement that large companies (those with more than 1,000 shareholders) use cumulative voting to elect members of the board of directors. Institutional investors have used this rule to elect their representatives to the board while worker-shareholders never fully mastered this mechanism, never understood how to use it to their advantage.

For ordinary Russians, the most recent round of legal reform came across as more of the same—as just another campaign. During the Soviet period, people learned to turn a deaf ear to proclamations of legal innovation, secure in the knowledge that everything would revert to normal in a matter of weeks or months. The persistent inability or unwillingness of the Gorbachev and Yeltsin governments to follow through on reforms and work on the tough questions of implementation has convinced the public that nothing has changed. Enterprise managers and others need to be convinced, in a positive fashion, that law has assumed a new significance. They will not take it on faith.

SHORTCOMINGS IN THE RUSSIAN LEGAL SYSTEM

The most often-heard explanation for lack of demand is that Russians shy away from law because the legal system is so flawed. (Delays in the judicial process are routinely cited.) The popular press in Russia fuels this wariness of law with Dickensian tales of simple cases that drag on for years, even decades. Abuses certainly occur. But again, they are an unfortunate fact of life plaguing judicial systems throughout the world. In Russia, the delays are much worse (both in fact and in perception) in the courts of general jurisdiction than in the *arbitrazh* courts. Even so, the official statistics for 1996, indicating that the statutory deadlines for resolving cases were exceeded in 14 percent of cases heard in courts of general jurisdiction and in less than 5 percent of the *arbitrazh* courts, suggest that the problem is less pervasive than critics would have us believe. At the same time, delays cannot be dismissed as unimportant, particularly to a legal system struggling to establish its viability. All too often, justice delayed does indeed amount to justice denied.

Another shortcoming frequently pointed to is the persistent difficulty in getting judicial decisions enforced, particularly in the *arbitrazh* setting. V. F. Yakovlev, the chairman of the higher *arbitrazh* court, has described this as the Achilles' heel of the *arbitrazh* system. After years of delay, legislation has been passed creating the *sudebnye pristavy* (bailiffs), who are to replace and improve upon the service provided by the *sudebnye ispolniteli*. Yet this institutional reform is unlikely to solve the problem permanently, for non-enforcement of judgements has to do less with the competence or resources of those charged with enforcing judicial decisions and more with the evermounting debts of enterprises (both to tax authorities and trading partners). These overwhelming obligations have left companies illiquid and patently unable to satisfy judgements against them (when the insolvency is not a façade, concealing resources diverted elsewhere). If the bank accounts are empty, then the only option is to seize an enterprise's equipment or fixed assets and sell them at auction. No judicial system in the world, however, could take such a broad hands-on approach to enforcing decisions, except under rare and unusual circumstances. High levels of voluntary compliance are the norm elsewhere, but they are the exception in Russia. Once again, we confront a vicious circle. The courts will become legitimate only through widespread use, but using courts that lack legitimacy may not be in the best short-term interests of the parties in conflict.

Flaws in the Russian legal system undoubtedly contribute to the lack of demand for law But this does not mean that, if the flaws were eliminated, demand would automatically materialize. As I noted above, many shortcomings already have been remedied, and yet demand remains elusive. The reality is that all legal systems are riddled with flaws, either more or less serious than those in Russia, and yet they are not plagued by the level of apathy and doubt regarding law that is all too commonplace in Russia. It has become increasingly apparent that there is a fundamental misalignment between the new 'rules of the game' and the game itself. What works in Western Europe or in the United States may be inappropriate for Russia, where market relations are still in a formative period. Yet reformers seem to have deliberately put into place laws that did not reflect how business was actually being done but rather how the reformers would like to have seen business being done. Presumably their motive was to bring Russian law into line with that of the advanced industrialized world and thereby to pull the country into the global market. But the gap between the ideal of the reformers and the reality of Russian enterprises was and still remains too wide. This disconnect between legality and reality can only confirm average Russians in their ingrained, lifelong habit of skepticism toward law

LACK OF LEGITIMACY OF THE RUSSIAN STATE

If law is to become a societal touchstone, then it has to be applied in equal measure to all, regardless of power or status. Because law was so openly manipulated by the Communist Party during the Soviet period, to achieve policy goals, it is even more important that the post-Soviet Russian state adhere to the basic principle of equality before the law. While the situation has certainly improved, examples of insiders (both individuals and enterprises) being granted special exemptions remain commonplace. The sense that there are two standards—one for the ordinary citizen and another for the privileged elite—persists (though the composition of the elite has changed). Under such circumstances building respect for law is dauntingly difficult.

Stimulating demand

What might be done at this point in Russia's history to improve the image of law, and to make its use more palatable to its citizens? Is the answer more but better-drafted laws? Alternatively, is the answer better implementation of existing laws? Of course, both are important and need to be incorporated in any strategy. But the harsh reality is that there are no simple solutions. Still, a few guiding principles are worth stressing.

First, policymakers should shift their attention from supply to demand, in other words, from state to society. The laws and legal institutions should be reexamined from a bottom-up perspective. Providing remedies on paper is of little value if they are framed in obtuse legalese that is incomprehensible to nonlegal specialists or if they are ineffective. Policymakers need to think creatively about how to fashion remedies that are both appealing and realistic. For example, unpaid workers who sue their employers for back wages often discover, after 'winning,' that the sued enterprise has no liquid assets. The futility of their suit gives them little reason to view the law positively. Touting the existence of a remedy for wage arrears only makes state officials look out of touch and insensitive. Perhaps they need to be less ambitious. Perhaps the 'rules of the game' for Russia in this time of transition need to be simpler and less sophisticated than those used elsewhere. After all, people will certainly not obey rules they cannot even understand or, if complied with, prove ineffectual.

This shift away from supply to demand will necessarily require a greater commitment on the part of the state to enforcement. But enforcement alone is not the answer. The resources required to run the courts and other legal institutions in a way that makes them usable are also essential. Moreover, rigorous-seeming implementation of laws that do not 'fit' into the existing legal culture are ultimately futile. All-important, on the other hand, is a commitment on the part of the state to obey the rules it imposes on others. Although professing publicly the ideals of the *pravovoe gosudarstvo*, the Russian government habitually exempts itself and its officials from the law. Self-exemption is most obvious in the arena of tax policy, where the state's failure to pay its own debts has provided a convenient excuse for Russian enterprises not to pay their taxes. As one company official put it, 'the government lies to us, so we lie to the government.' Whether this downward spiral can be halted—in the area of taxes or elsewhere—remains unclear.

Finally and most importantly, the appeal of law by itself cannot be assumed, either on an individual or societal level. Law's potential to serve as a common language, facilitating market transactions and easing democratization, has to be demonstrated, not assumed. This may require outreach efforts on the part of the Russian government, on both the national and regional levels, and a willingness to allow greater involvement of citizens and nongovernmental groups in the lawmaking process, in order to give them some sense of ownership—a stake—in the resulting legislation. Perhaps the motto of Russian legal reform should be changed to 'seeing is believing.' Or perhaps the concept of private property, which ostensibly is the ultimate material incentive, should be applied to both the state and the law per se—it is 'our' state, and the law belongs to us, too.

10 The Russian Mafia: Between Hype and Reality

Peter Rutland and Natasha Kogan

Pick up any newspaper or even academic journal about Russia these days and the chances are that it will feature lurid tales of extravagant crime and corruption. If you ask the average American what they associate with Russia, they will probably say 'mafia.' Organized crime has joined Siberia, snow, caviar, and communism in the popular imagery of things quintessentially 'Russian.'

For the past several years, journalists and commentators have had a hard time framing their stories about Russia. During the perestroika era, the dominant paradigm was that of a struggle between Good and Evil, between Reform and Reaction, with first Mikhail Gorbachev and then Boris Yeltsin carrying the banner of the righteous. After 1991, the story became that of a heroic band of liberal reformers, battling the sinister nomenklatura in the name of 'market democracy'. That story began to tire after a while. Yeltsin's image as democratic hero was tarnished by the shelling of the parliament in October 1993 and the invasion of Chechnya in December 1994. It became less and less easy to describe Russian politics in terms of a battle between right and wrong. And if indeed the reforms have succeeded, then Russia can be treated like Brazil or India, whose domestic politics are largely ignored by the American media. Russia remains different in that it is the world's second largest nuclear power and thus will be guaranteed coverage of its military and diplomatic affairs. But the transition to democracy has made it more and more difficult for Moscow-based American correspondents to get their copy into the pages of their newspapers back home.

Hence, right on cue, the appearance of a new paradigm: Russia as mafia stronghold. Exit the dour, sinister nomenklatura: enter the gun-toting, Gucci-shod New Russians. The image of Moscow as the center of a global communist conspiracy has been replaced, almost overnight, by the myth of the Russian mafia. A pivotal role was played by the 1995 appearance of Stephen Handelman's well-written book, *Comrade Criminal*. A symbolic turning point was the tragic shooting death in November 1996 of American businessman Paul Tatum, who was embroiled in feuding over the ownership of Moscow's Radisson-Slavyanskaya hotel. (No matter that more Americans have died while covering Yeltsin's military actions in 1993 and 1995 than at the hands of the Russian mob.)

This return to a demonic image of Russia fits a centuries-old pattern of Westerners treating Russia as the great 'other': a tradition exemplified by the Marquis de Custine's *Empire of the Czar*, written in 1839 (on the basis of a three-week visit). Russia's size and backwardness make it sinister and threatening, all the more so because it is adjacent to

This chapter was first published as an article in *Transition*, March 1998. Reproduced by kind permission of the authors and *Transition* (www.tol.cz).

Europe. In Russia, like in Texas, everything has to be bigger and better, or worse. This proclivity for exaggeration is displayed not only by Western outsiders, but also by Russians themselves. The tendency toward apocalyptic imagery is vividly illustrated by the popular image of the Russian mafia, portrayed by news reports and by Hollywood as more clever, devious, ruthless, erratic, and free-spending than any other nation's criminals. While the Colombian mafia deal in cocaine, their Moscow brethren trade in nuclear weapons, submarines, and the like. Russians are recognized to be clever (a nation of chess players and cosmonauts), so the evil genius of the KGB is now being recycled in mafia guise. Nine times out of ten, in Hollywood action movies the villains speak with Slavic accents. While Latino drug lords are rarely seen wielding anything more complicated than a cellular phone, Russian hoodlums typically have at their beck and call computer wizards who can tap into the CIA's lunch menu.

How big a problem?

Polls suggest that the Russian public believes the mafia has replaced the nomenklatura as the shadowy power ruling the country. An August 1997 poll asked respondents, 'who do you believe runs Russia?' A remarkable 52 percent selected as their first choice 'the mafia, organized crime,' followed by the state apparatus, 21 percent; the president, 14 percent; regional authorities, 11 percent; and the government, 10 percent.[1]

Separating myth from reality is difficult. It is important to differentiate between the various types of criminal activity, rather than lump them together into the seamless web of 'Russian mafia.' One can distinguish between street-level organized crime, which revolves around the use of violence (extortion, killings, etc.) and elite-level crony capitalism, using political connections to win government contracts, for example. The two can overlap—losers in a political battle may resort to violence to intimidate their opponents—but on balance the distinction is worth preserving. The situation is analogous with that of democratic governments that occasionally resorted to assassination (from Spain to the United Kingdom) but in general based their rule on a popular mandate and not on fear.

Reliable statistics about the extent of organized crime and crony capitalism in Russia are hard to come by, and the categories they are based on are rather opaque. It seems to be in everybody's interests to talk up the role of the mafia. The police have a vested interest in exaggerating the strength of the mafia as a way of boosting their own budget. Yeltsin periodically rails against the mafia because it provides another rationale for his authoritarian rule. Reformers use it as an excuse to explain the slow pace of economic recovery. Opposition politicians use it as another club with which to beat Yeltsin reformers. Journalists find that the mafia makes great copy. International advisers have nothing to lose by stressing the threat posed by the mafia, it is another reason for Western governments to spend money on their services, to protect us from the latest Russian threat. And the mafia itself benefits from the image of organized crime as an all-conquering force, because fear is their stock in trade.

In fact, very few have an interest in downplaying the mafia's influence. Almost the only people with an incentive to understate its power are successful mafia leaders, especially if

---

[1] *Moskovskii komsomolets*, 5 Sept. 1997.

they are trying to legitimize their business dealings. From their lips, however, the message—even if true—is likely to be discounted. For example, few in an audience of U.S. executives at a Harvard University investment forum seemed convinced by the assurances of Boris Berezovsky, auto dealer turned oil magnate, that crime is not a barrier to doing business in Russia.

The Carnegie Endowment's Anders Aslund is one of the few Western voices questioning the mafia orthodoxy. Western business executives have a direct interest in an accurate assessment of the situation: their projects, and perhaps their lives, are on the line. But for the most part they are not inclined to broadcast their findings. If they conclude that organized crime is a real problem in Russia, it makes more sense for them to walk quietly away rather than possibly antagonize the Russian with a hue and cry. Similarly, if a Western corporation decides that organized crime is a manageable problem, it is better to get on with the deal-making and let competitors worry about the latest Russian 'menace.'

What can one learn from statistics about the real situation? Hard numbers are few and far between. Russia has an extremely high homicide rate: twice that of the United States, and on a par with South Africa. More worrying still, the rate doubled between 1991 and 1994. But it is not clear how many of these 30,000-plus annual killings are mafia-related. Contract killings, identified as such by the police, are running at about 500 per year, and the largest single group among the victims are other criminals. Random violence is the main threat, both for ordinary Russians and for Western businessmen. The Interior Ministry releases scary-sounding figures every month or so enumerating how many tens of thousands of economic crimes have been committed, and estimating that 'organized crime' controls 30 percent to 50 percent of the Russian economy. The official agency Goskomstat estimates that unreported economic activity amounts to 23 percent of gross domestic product. The latter category is not coterminous with 'organized crime.' Some criminal-controlled business is reported to the authorities and falls into the 'official' economy; and some of the shadow economy is not under the mafia's thumb.

That said, it is clear that the contemporary Russian economy, from the corner store up to the national budget, is far removed from the 'perfect competition' models of economics textbooks. Most owners of stores and service outlets have to pay protection money (either to the mob or to the police) to stay in business. The payments may range from 10 percent to 50 percent of overall turnover, which helps explain why everything from beer to tooth-paste tends to be more expensive in Russia than in, say, Poland. At the company level, the success of many transactions depends on the manager's position in local elite networks, whether it be renting of premises, shipping goods on the railway, or avoiding payment of wages and taxes. Crony capitalism has dominated the privatization process, under which 70 percent of Russia's state-owned industry has been transformed into privately owned joint-stock companies. While reformers promised that voucher privatization would create a new middle class, in fact it delivered assets into the hands of insiders: either Soviet-era industrialists or new-era bankers.

Organized crime and clan politics are serious problems for Russian society. But it is not clear that they are disabling problems, nor that Russia is unique in confronting them, nor that Russia must follow Western models in trying to get them under control.

How unique is Russia?

Apart from ritual references to American robber barons, discussions of organized crime and crony capitalism in Russia rarely acknowledge that these problems are present elsewhere in the world. In fact, a glance at any day's newspaper will confirm that capitalism is flawed everywhere. It is simply not true that 'market imperfections' are confined to an early, transitional phase of a country's development, after which clean and transparent government prevails. Capitalist democracies must wage a constant struggle to prevent corruption from taking root. In the United States, for example, mob control has extended not just to drugs, gambling, and prostitution, but also in many cities to such mundane activities as garbage collection, construction, trucking, laundries, and meat deliveries. The mafia markup on these activities added probably 25 percent to the cost of doing business in New York, and it was only after the Racketeer Influenced and Corrupt Organizations Act (RICO) in 1970 that federal prosecutors started to make inroads into the mob's operations. At a higher level, the Clinton administration's second term has been dogged by repeated accusations of campaign-finance abuse and influence peddling, involving sums roughly akin to those in Russian financial scandals.

Europe is hardly immune to such problems. Almost the entire Italian political establishment has collapsed in the last decade in the wake of 'tangentopoli' scandals linking politicians, banks, media, and mafia. Sicily is a special case, but not unique. Early February saw the assassination of the prefect in the French province of Corsica. No Russian official of that rank has yet been slain. In Turkey two years ago a car crash led to the exposure of ties between drug smugglers, the police, and the True Path ruling party, revealing that mob hitmen were used to take out Kurdish nationalist leaders. Even in staid Belgium, a scandal over kickbacks in a helicopter purchasing deal led to the resignations of Socialist Party leaders. In France and Germany, subsidies are shoveled into loss-making, state-owned banks and enterprises, in violation of national and European Union legislation; Volkswagen has been fined for stealing secrets from General Motors.

Moving on to the Pacific Rim, we find countries where crony capitalism has been a way of life for decades and until recently was even seen as the key to economic growth and prosperity. The family networks of Benazir Bhutto in Pakistan or President Suharto of Indonesia make the nepotism of Boris Yeltsin (appointing his son-in-law director of Aeroflot) seem trifling. Take the comparison between Russia and China. Which country is more corrupt? True, China is growing while Russia is stagnating, but does this fact alone prove that China's economic structure is more healthy? One could argue that part of the problem was that the Russian elite did not go about their corruption in an organized way. While Russian army officers were siphoning off gasoline and selling ships for scrap, the Chinese People's Liberation Army was opening television assembly plants and buying Hong Kong hotels.

Latin America provides plenty more examples of less-than-ideal capitalist processes at work. While contract killings and kidnappings number in the hundreds in Russia, they number in the thousands in Colombia. Corruption scandals in Mexico have seen the assassination of presidential candidates (something not witnessed in Russia) and led to the flight of former President Salinas to Ireland. In Latin America, not only is the level of violence higher than in Russia, but it is overlaid by the prospect of armed insurrection by the impoverished peasantry. The possibility of a social revolution is totally absent in Russia. The comparison with Latin America is all the more telling because that region is America's backyard. Migration and *narcotraficantes* carry the problems of Latin America right into American cities, on a scale that dwarfs the exploits of Russian mobsters in Brighton Beach in New York City. If there are relatively few states in the world in a position to lecture Russia about the threat of crime and corruption, the same is true of business corporations. Many companies have episodes in their recent history they would prefer to forget, such as British Petroleum's role in the coup that installed the Shah of Iran. It is rather hypocritical for Western commentators to castigate Russian firms for capital flight and tax avoidance. The whole network of offshore banking facilities was set up by Western financial interests precisely to enable businesses to avoid taxes and other forms of government regulation, yet it is perfectly legal. Similarly, transfer pricing was invented by multinational corporations to move profits out of the reach of national tax authorities by manipulating reported production costs. Perhaps one-third or more of the output of leading multinationals escapes taxation in this and other ways. The same issue of *The Economist* that condemns Russia for slack tax collection includes advertisements from Big Four accountancy firms seeking transfer-pricing specialists. Less important, but equally telling, is the fact that most of the Western advisers in Moscow working for organizations such as the World Bank and the European Bank for Reconstruction and Development and lecturing the Russians about the need to improve tax collection are themselves drawing tax-free salaries.

Two wrongs do not make a right. Organized crime and crony capitalism are bad for business, and Russia does need more open, competitive markets if its economy is to revive. However, Western observers should not adopt a holier-than-thou position when confronting Russia's problems. Above all, one should maintain a sense of historical perspective. Russia has been experimenting with capitalism for less than a decade, while other countries' experience is measured in centuries. Even the Chinese reforms started back in 1978, and Beijing has moved slower than Moscow in some areas (most notably, in the liberalization of capital markets and foreign trade).

The liberal solution

Thus, a major flaw of the debate about the Russian mafia is the tendency to treat Russia as unique. A further peculiarity is its fatalistic tone. The mafia is presented as a relentless evil that the forces of good are powerless to resist. It is pointless turning to the Russian state to clean up organized crime, because politicians and policemen already are in bed with the mob. The Russian state is part of the problem, not part of the solution. Faced with such an apparently closed circle, the onlooker can only shrug with despair.

What do proponents of that thesis suggest should be done to reverse this sorry state of affairs? Their solutions boil down to the admonition 'be like us.' If only Russia were to adopt the mores and practices of developed capitalist countries, such as Britain or the United States, it would be able to slay the Hydra of corruption. Over the past couple of years Moscow has played host to a stream of delegations urging the Russian government to tackle the corruption problem, from constitution lawyers to World Bank teams preaching the importance of 'good governance.' It is now generally agreed that it was a mistake to privatize state assets without first establishing a framework of property rights, effective laws, and enforceable contracts, although this was not what most American advisers were telling the

Russians in 1992. Previously, it was assumed that the rule of law was a luxury that Russia for cultural and historical reasons would not adopt until later. Now the rule of law is considered essential to ensure Russia's progress toward a market economy. President Yeltsin's decree power may have been necessary to stem communist revanchism and to ensure that Russia's shift to a market economy was irreversible.

But presidentialism turns out to be a slender reed upon which to construct a civil society. Most advice proffered to Russia on how to tackle crime and corruption consists of wish lists of liberal institutions. The bill of liberal fare typically includes the following elements: laws that clearly define property rights and lay down procedures for adjudicating disputes and enforcing contracts; an independent judicial system with well-paid judges and investigators; better pay for civil servants and police to help reduce the temptation to take bribes; media independent of the ruling political and economic elite, committed to exposing malfeasance; free and fair elections to ensure the appointment of political leaders responsive to the public interest; and the introduction of international norms for arbitration of commercial disputes and full cooperation with international police agencies.

Few would disagree with the desirability of such institutions. Francis Fukuyama was basically right—liberal values have triumphed across the industrialized world. The problem comes in moving from ideals to reality. The Russian government is urged to introduce such measures, without delay, because this is the only sure way to stamp out the mafia. It is true that if Russia possessed sound laws and an independent judiciary, corruption could be effectively combated. But this liberal solution fails to explain just how these stalwart institutions are to be introduced. Can they be conjured up out of thin air by a well-meaning government? How much international aid would be sufficient to ensure that they take root? Advocates of the rule of law as the solution to Russia's problems often commit the error of moving from 'ought' to 'is', of assuming that what ought to happen will actually happen (a reversal of the 'naturalistic fallacy').

The net result of such urging is to leave the Russian government in a chicken-and-egg dilemma. Until Russia establishes rule of law, it will not be able to tackle corruption. But given the prevalence of entrenched corruption, the chance of such liberal institutions being established must be close to zero. The liberal blueprint of a law-governed society may prove to be as divorced from reality as Nikita Khrushchev's plan to overtake the United States by 1980.

Faced with such a fundamental dilemma, one retreats into metaphor. A favorite image of Russian intellectuals is that of an English lawn. A visitor to an Oxford college asks a groundsman: 'How do you get such perfect lawns?', to which the aged retainer replies: 'Easy. Sow the grass and then roll it twice a week for 200 years.' While it is reassuring to believe the adage that time heals all wounds, the response 'Come back in 200 years' is an excuse for doing nothing. It typifies the Russian intelligentsia's traditional fatalism, which is occasionally interrupted by still more damaging bouts of revolutionary vigor. It is no help at all in tackling contemporary problems. The English lawn metaphor of the Russians is not that far from a favorite analogy of American commentators, that of the robber barons. Relax, we are told. America too had its Wild West phase. Russia's problems will be cured with the passage of time. Contemporary Russian capitalism is merely experiencing growing pains, akin to the robber barons of late 19th century America. Once the giant corporations have enriched themselves and created a national market and a pool of capital, a Progressive movement will arise, break up the trusts, and establish fair rules of the game, thus ensuring that a broader section of the population shares in the fruits of progress.

The robber baron analogy is superficially more attractive than the English lawn but is equally flawed. The robber barons arose in a country that had already experienced 200 years of lawn-rolling, in the form of private property and the rule of law. It also had 100 years of experience as a pluralist democracy (albeit with restrictive franchise), without which it is unlikely that the Progressive movement could have arisen. Third, the robber barons garnered their wealth during a period of sustained economic expansion. The Russian mafia is reaping its harvest at a time of unprecedented economic contraction. The trajectories are quite different and offer little ground for optimism.

What is to be done?

What, then, should Russians of good will do to turn back the mafia tide? The first point to underline is that the solution, if there is one, will be home-grown. The appropriate mix of sticks and carrots that will goad Russian society onto the true and righteous path will be devised not in Harvard Yard or on Washington's H Street (home of the World Bank) but in Moscow and St Petersburg. There are indeed universal truths and universal values, but they are realized in specific places and in specific ways. In the case of Russia's transition to a market economy, Western observers assumed that things would go according to (their) plan and were shocked to discover that there was a worm inside the capitalist apple. Both the shock therapy and voucher privatization programs launched in 1992, which got Russia into this capitalist mess (but out of the communist mess), were forged in-country and deviated from the 'Washington consensus' on how the economic transition should be managed. They were flawed solutions to Russia's economic problems, but they were the ones that took root and moved Russia forward.

Thus, any solution that does not have an identifiable Russian component should be dismissed as infeasible. With regard to the transition to rule of law, Western advisers should try to get ahead of the curve. Rather than proceed on the assumption that Russian institutions will be generic reproductions of their Western exemplars, we should recognize that they must be customized to meet the extraordinary conditions of present-day Russia. And only Russians can come up with a formula for a 'capitalism with a Russian face' that stands a chance of working in their country. A first step in this direction is to move away from hypothetical legal frameworks to the realities of political power. Unless one specifies the political conditions conducive to the emergence of a coalition in favor of battling corruption, reforms promoting the rule of law will remain mere castles in the air.

Sometimes the political conditions that favor an assault on corruption may directly contradict the prescriptions of rule-of-law reformers. For example, it is often assumed that an independent judiciary is a sine qua non for battling corruption. However, Indian experience suggests the opposite. India has had the benefit of a formally independent judiciary for all its 50 years, yet its judges were too weak politically to stand up against entrenched oligarchic interests. Hence many anti-corruption cases dragged on in the courts for decades. Only in recent years, with growing media and public attention on corruption, has the judiciary begun to play a more effective role, using the Central Bureau of Investigation to go after corrupt politicians. Does this mean that democracy is the answer? If we open the floodgates of electoral politics, will the mighty tide of public opinion flush corruption out of the system? No, democracy is not the silver bullet that will slay the monster of corruption, any more than is the rule of law. Experience in just about every democracy in the modern world shows that democracy is highly compatible with corruption, particularly in this media age, when money buys votes through the prism of television advertising. Moreover, there are numerous disturbing examples of corrupt politicians using anti-corruption drives to remove their opponents (usually equally corrupt) and maximize their own ill-gotten gains. It is often forgotten that Belarusian President Alyaksandr Lukashenka rose from obscurity as a parliamentary deputy and former collective-farm chairman by accusing the former Belarusian leadership of corruption. Once in office he created a network of parastatal agencies to line his own pockets, and he still cynically used anti-corruption charges to jail officials who fell out with him (such as the head of the central bank). Similarly, Slovakia's Vladimir Meciar, who presides over one of the most corrupt regimes in Central Europe, is one of the few politicians in the region to have won twice in fair elections.

How then is one to devise a political strategy for a battle with the mafia? First, one should read the bumper-sticker adage: 'think globally, act locally.' A province-by-province approach is the best way to set about tackling the problem. It is unrealistic to expect a quick fix through a policy shift in Moscow that is then imposed on the rest of the nation. Russian politics today simply does not work that way (few countries do). Across Russia's vastly diverse political and economic landscape, some areas are more primed for a clean-hands campaign than others. The battle against corruption must be fought city by city, gang by gang. This is the approach adopted by the pioneering project, the 'United Research Centers for Organized Crime in Eurasia,' devised by Louise Shelley of Washington's American University. The project involves the funding of centers for training and support of anti-crime operations in several Russian and Ukrainian cities, including Moscow, St Petersburg, Yekaterinburg, Irkutsk, and Vladivostok. By working with and through local procurators and police officials the project should avoid the Moscow-centric and at times almost neo-colonialist philosophy of many other aid programs.

Power ministers

Of course, one should not underestimate the challenges such local initiatives will face. Not the least of them is the need to reform the structure, personnel, and mentality of the police apparatus. In contrast to the structures of economic administration, 'power ministries' have survived since the Soviet era. Even when not in bed with the mafia, their attitude toward the imposition of law and order may be more disruptive of public order and economic progress than the evil they are supposed to eradicate. One must be wary of fostering 'strongman' solutions, with their arbitrary arrests and violations of human rights. As the experience of Colombia and Turkey has shown, repressive actions by a 'strong' state may merely cause criminal organizations to sink even deeper roots into society. Turning to the political feasibility of a crackdown on corruption, one should recognize that whichever coalition for change emerges, it will have to include some insiders. It is naive to imagine that a popular movement will arise from outside the current ruling elite, which will throw up new leaders (Aleksandr Lebed? Boris Nemtsov?) willing and able to clean out the Augean stables of the

Kremlin. Such a process in a newly minted democracy is more likely to throw up a Meciar or Lukashenka than a Teddy Roosevelt.

One can see two sorts of insiders rallying around a clean-up campaign: the new rich who clawed their way to the top via criminal methods, and the old elite who shifted from the Soviet nomenklatura to private corporations without violence. As to the first group, it is reasonable to assume that once Russia's crime bosses have sated themselves, they will yearn for a quieter, calmer life. Having accumulated wealth through dubious means, their capital can then multiply through investment in legitimate businesses. Going straight would make daily life easier for the bosses: less need for bodyguards and armored cars, less fear that one's children may be kidnapped or caught in the crossfire of an assassination attempt. Few (god)fathers want their children to follow a life of crime. There are some moral conundrums raised by the phenomenon of the poacher-turned-gamekeeper, but it is still better than if he stayed a poacher.

Morality aside, there are still some practical problems with the idea that criminals may choose to turn legitimate. Lesser mafia figures and would-be crony capitalists will resent the efforts of the first wave to raise the drawbridge behind them and will try to fight back. An important consideration is that the internationalization of the Russian criminal elite gives them an exit option. They can take their money and leave the country. It is already common for them to buy real estate and place their families in Cyprus or the south of France, or in Prague, London, and Berlin. However, to the extent that they still try to do business in Russia, legal or illegal, it may be in their interest to see stability in that country.

What of the not-so-criminal insiders? Why have they been so slow to act and permitted the wave of legal chaos and criminality which has engulfed Russia? Why, if there is such a small, powerful oligarchy, largely a continuation of the Soviet-era nomenklatura, have they done such a lousy job of running their country? The answer lies in the incredibly short time frame of the analysis and the enormity of the challenges they faced. Seven years is a preciously short period in which to construct the institutional structure of a capitalist democracy.

The mafia was born in Soviet labor camps and had been up and running for decades when communism collapsed in 1991. Mafia figures were well placed to take advantage of the chaos of the early years of transition. In contrast, legitimate business leaders had to disentangle themselves from the chaos of the collapsing command economy and steer a path through the minefield of competing jurisdictions (Soviet versus Russian, then federal versus regional). Only now are they starting to organize themselves and lobby the Russian state for improved legislation. Political scientist Mancur Olson has noted that time and resources are needed to mobilize large groups for collective action, which will result in diffuse benefits such as the rule of law.

The Russian business elite fits this model quite well. It would have been unrealistic to expect a lobby for fair and open government to spring, fully formed, out of the wreckage of the Soviet economy. By 1998 the new and old economic elites have forged a rough-and-ready consensus around the basic principles of market economy: private property, price liberalization, and an end to hyperinflation. They even circled their wagons in support of Boris Yeltsin in the 1996 election. The next step is to eliminate violence from the economic system, to develop a workable body of law, and to introduce more competitiveness. This can—and must—be accomplished through the evolution of the political process. It cannot be achieved through the launching of a crusade.

Elections and the Electoral System

Section 4

Elections and the Electoral System

Introduction

Archie Brown

Competitive elections have now become a regular and recognized feature of Russian politics. That by the year 2000 contested elections would have come to be taken for granted in Russia was something it would have seemed hazardous to predict as comparatively recently as 1985. Yet, the elections in post-Soviet Russia have been relatively free, albeit less than entirely fair. Convincing evidence has been presented of vote-rigging, beginning with the struggle for control of the new legislature in 1993 and including the most recent presidential election of 2000.[1] However, it would be hard to find a serious political analyst who would argue that a radically different outcome would have ensued on either of these occasions, or on any in between, if all of the votes had been counted honestly. In the presidential election of March 2000, Vladimir Putin might have been forced to contest a second round, but, on the basis of the best survey research, it is sufficiently clear that he would have been successful in the run-off. The bias of television—which is by far the most important medium of communication in Russia—has been of greater electoral consequence. Linked to this, but going beyond it, a highly significant factor in determining electoral outcomes has been the vast discrepancy between the financial resources of rival parties and candidates. The need to accumulate exceedingly large sums of money in order successfully to fight a campaign is scarcely a peculiarity of Russia, although it is much more of a problem in the United States than in the European democracies where there are far more stringent controls over electoral spending.

In a chapter specially written for this volume, Yitzhak Brudny examines the electoral cycle which began with the election of the State Duma in December 1999 and was completed with the choice of Putin as president of Russia in succession to Yeltsin in March 2000. He notes how skilfully the state media were used to project the image of Vladimir Putin as a strong and competent leader and how the new political movement, Unity, benefited in the parliamentary election from its association with the increasingly popular Putin. Brudny examines the social composition of the electoral support for different parties and movements and finds that partisans of the Union of Right Forces (SPS) and Yabloko have a lot in common, being younger, well-educated city-dwellers who have accommodated themselves to the changes of the past decade and a half. In this respect, they differ from the average voter and, most strikingly, from the supporters of the Communist Party (KPRF). Supporters of the KPRF, however, have the clearest sense of ideological identity.

So far as the presidential election of 2000 is concerned, Brudny is able to show the extent to

---

[1] See Lilia Shevtsova, *Yeltsin's Russia: Myths and Reality* (Washington: Carnegie Endowment for International Peace, 1999), 96–7 and 191; and Yevgeniya Borisova, 'And the Winner Is?', in *Moscow Times*, 9 Sept. 2000.

which Putin garnered cross-party support—not only (as might be expected) gaining the votes of more than three-quarters of Unity voters, but also more than half of the supporters of the Union of Right Forces and about a third of those who normally would support Yavlinsky or Zhirinovsky. Among the threats to the development of democracy exposed by the electoral cycle of 1999–2000 were, as Brudny argues in Chapter 11, the extremes to which negative campaigning was taken, especially as it was conducted through the state-controlled media (a point elaborated also by Laura Belin in Chapter 23) and the extent to which one of the most successful participants in the parliamentary election, Sergei Shoigu, and the victorious presidential candidate, Vladimir Putin, purported to be above politics.

Another problem, touched upon already, is explored in detail in Chapter 12 by Vladimir Gelman—namely the role of money in Russian elections. The issue is not only the large sums required but, at least as important, the lack of transparency and accountability in the way they are spent. Gelman suggests that in the 1996 presidential election, the $3 million that was legally expended in support of Yeltsin's campaign was the merest tip of the iceberg, and that the 'under-water' portion was certainly many times as large and possibly even hundreds of times greater. Money alone, of course, is no guarantee of success, as Gelman notes. While some wealthy businessmen have been able to get themselves elected to the State Duma, others—despite their best efforts, supported by ample personal fortunes—have signally failed to do so. Substantial sources of political finance are a necessary, but not a sufficient condition for electoral success.

The focus of Chapter 13 by Robert G. Moser is on the institutional design of Russia's electoral systems rather than on the electoral process which is the main concern of the two earlier chapters in this section. Moser points to the fact that, ever since the pioneering work of Maurice Duverger, it has been assumed that plurality (or 'first-past-the-post') electoral systems tend to produce two large parties and that forms of proportional representation encourage support for, and therefore the flourishing of, a significantly larger number of parties. In Russia, Moser observes, the opposite appears to have happened in the two parallel electoral systems. Russia makes for an interesting case-study precisely because it elects half the members of the State Duma under a plurality system and half by proportional representation. Since elections for the Duma by these different means take place simultaneously, the influence on support for a variety of parties of one electoral system may be affected by the existence of the other. Yet, as Moser shows, in 1993 and 1995 very different results were produced by the plurality elections from those carried out by PR. Local notables and independent candidates did well in the 'first-past-the-post' elections and thereby helped to undermine the salience of political parties, whereas it was in the segment of the Duma elected by proportional representation that national figures and nationally recognized political parties were able to hold sway. Thus, Vladimir Zhirinovsky's Liberal Democratic Party was very successful in the PR part of the election while failing miserably to make much headway under the conditions of 'first-past-the-post'.

While the high 5 per cent threshold which parties had to cross in order to get representation in the Duma in the PR part of the electoral process ensured that a relatively small number of parties would actually take their seats in the legislature, this did not discourage a large number of parties or movements from making the effort to compete. And contrary to what has been predicted of electoral systems more generally, in Russia the plurality system encouraged localism. It resulted in the election of people who increasingly frequently were the nominees of the local governor or republican president or who, alternatively, owed their success to their independent standing. To an extent surprising in a first-past-the-post system, they were not the representatives of nationally organized parties who fared poorly under these electoral provisions in Russia. In what Moser has called 'a laboratory for study of the effects of proportional representation and plurality systems', the Russian experiment, in the electoral sphere as in other areas of political and economic life, has shown a capacity for producing the unexpected.

11 Continuity or Change in Russian Electoral Patterns? The December 1999–March 2000 Election Cycle

Yitzhak M. Brudny

On 18 December 1999, elections took place for the lower house of the Russian parliament, the Duma. On 26 March 2000, the parliamentary elections were followed by a pre-term presidential ballot, triggered by the resignation of President Boris Yeltsin on 31 December 1999. The two elections were inextricably linked. The strong showing of the Unity electoral alliance, supportive of Prime Minister Putin, in the December election gave Yeltsin the confirmation he needed to appoint Putin as acting president. This was designed to give Putin the significant advantage of incumbency over his potential rivals in the forthcoming presidential elections.

The 1999 Duma elections constituted the third consecutive parliamentary ballot since the present electoral system was introduced in 1993. The 2000 presidential ballot was the second since the collapse of Communism, and the third overall since the introduction of the executive presidency in 1991. That both the presidential and parliamentary elections were taking place for the third time in the ten-year period enables us to pose the following question: did those factors that played a crucial role in determining the results of previous parliamentary and presidential elections also determine the results of the 1999–2000 election cycle? The existing scholarly literature provides no unanimous answer regarding the question of what are the causal factors determining the outcome of Russian elections. Such factors as the electoral rules in place, the organizational and administrative resources of the competing parties, media manipulation, the intensity of campaign efforts, the social structure of the electorate, the economic conditions, and the political values of Russian voters are all mentioned as factors explaining the results of past Russian parliamentary and presidential elections.[1]

Chapter specially commissioned for this volume.

[1] On the Russian parliamentary and presidential elections that took place prior to the 1999–2000 election cycle see Stephen White, Richard Rose, and Ian McAllister, *How Russia Votes* (Chatham, NJ: Chatham House, 1997); Matthew Wyman, Stephen White, and Sarah Oates, eds., *Elections and Voters in Post-Communist Russia* (Aldershot: Edward Elgar, 1998); Timothy J. Colton, *Transitional Citizens* (Cambridge, Mass.: Harvard University Press, 2000); Timothy J. Colton and Jerry F. Hough, eds., *Growing Pains* (Washington: Brookings Institution Press, 1998); Peter Lentini, ed., *Elections and Political Order in Russia* (Budapest: Central European University Press, 1995); Laura Belin and Robert W. Orttung, *The Russian Parliamentary Elections of 1995* (Armonk, NY: M. E. Sharpe, 1997); Jerry F. Hough, Evelyn Davidheiser, and Susan Goodrich Lehmann, *The 1996 Russian Presidential Election* (Washington: Brookings Institution Press, 1996); Michael McFaul, *Russia's 1996 Presidential Election* (Stanford, Calif: Hoover Institution Press, 1997).

In my previous work on Russian elections, I emphasized the importance of certain political factors such as the campaign strategies of parties and candidates, their organizational, financial, and media resources, as well as their prior experience in running an electoral campaign, while downplaying such factors as economic voting. I have also argued that the ability of parties and candidates to exploit the existing social cleavages played an important role in their electoral fortunes.[2] In the 1999 elections, age, education, economic well-being, and size of the community continued to be major factors in determining the allegiance of the Russian electorate.

In addition to the political and social variables, I argue that the results of the 1999–2000 election cycle were affected by an important psychological factor. The voter optimism about the future that prevailed on the eve of both elections was a crucial factor in the popularity of Unity and of Putin. While emphasizing the importance of political and psychological factors, I maintain that such factors as the skilful manipulation of state media by the presidential administration and the patriotic fervour resulting from the Chechen war cannot be regarded, as some observers claim, as the two main variables that explain the outcome. Finally, I argue that the institutional design of the electoral system clearly mattered. The incentives built into the parliamentary and presidential electoral laws, as well as the more aggressive behaviour of the Central Electoral Commission (hereafter CEC) in interpreting and enforcing these laws, shaped the strategy of the actors, and had an impact on the results.

Part One: the 19 December 1999 parliamentary election

SIGNIFICANCE OF THE DUMA ELECTIONS

The striking feature of the Russian post-1993 constitutional design is the power imbalance between the executive and legislative branches of government. The executive branch, especially the institution of the presidency, is far stronger than the parliament. The latter has no influence on the composition of the government and the president can use his right to issue executive decrees to bypass the parliament.

If political reality were a faithful reflection of the constitutional architecture, the incentive to take an active part in the Duma elections would be very low. However, pro-government and opposition parties hotly contested the three Duma elections that took place between 1993 and 1999. In part, this was the consequence of the reality that the Duma 'far from being a "fig leaf," had become a counterweight to the presidency.'[3] Moreover, parliamentary elections, coming only months before the presidential ballot, serve both the function of a referendum on government policies and as a presidential primary. As we will see below, the poor performance of the Fatherland–All Russia alliance forced its leaders, Luzhkov and

---

[2] Yitzhak M. Brudny, 'St. Petersburg: The Election in the Democratic Metropolis,' in Colton and Hough, *Growing Pains*, 349–95; Yitzhak M. Brudny, 'In Pursuit of the Russian Presidency: Why and How Yeltsin Won the 1996 Presidential Election', *Communist and Post-Communist Studies*, 30/3 (Sept. 1997), 255–75.

[3] Thomas F. Remington, 'The Evolution of Executive-Legislative Relations in Russia since 1993,' *Slavic Review*, 59/3 (Fall 2000), 501. In the crucial area of economic policy international financial institutions require legislative approval for various reforms as condition for loans and grants. It was the failure to gain such an approval by the Kirienko government that played a major role in the financial crisis of August 1998.

Primakov, to withdraw from the presidential race in 2000, while the strong showing of Unity made its (unofficial) leader, Putin, the undisputed favourite in the presidential race.[4]

INSTITUTIONAL DESIGN AND ITS EFFECTS

Article 96 of the 1993 Russian Constitution explicitly states that elections are the subject of specific legislation rather than part of the Constitution itself. This provision had a fundamental impact on both the 1995 and 1999 elections. In both cases, specific laws stipulating rules for the forthcoming election had to be enacted. It introduced a certain element of uncertainty since the electoral laws were adopted relatively late—Yeltsin signed the 1995 parliamentary election law on 21 June 1995, while the 1999 election law was signed on 24 June 1999—and their constitutionality was challenged in court, sometimes on the very eve of the elections.

The designers of the Russian electoral system took the Federal Republic of Germany as their model in creating a relatively small number of strong electoral parties. The high 5 per cent threshold in the proportional representation portion of the ballot was designed to deter small parties from running, while the 'first past the post' system in the single-member district part of the ballot attempted to force parties with similar ideological profiles to run mutually agreed-upon candidates. The reality, however, hardly fulfilled the original expectations. In the December 1995 election, forty-three parties were on the ballot and only four passed the 5 per cent threshold, with 49.5 per cent of the vote cast for parties that failed to enter the Duma.

To avoid a repetition of this situation, a variety of amendments were introduced in 1999 to provide new rules of the game. The powers of the CEC were substantially enhanced with the tacit understanding that it would use its powers to reduce the number of participating parties. Thus, the CEC was required to verify 20 per cent of the 200,000 signatures needed for inclusion on the ballot, and disqualify those parties with 15 per cent or more invalid signatures. Moreover, the CEC acquired the right to disqualify candidates who did not submit an accurate statement of income and property holdings, the existence of a criminal record, or foreign citizenship. Disqualification of any of the three top candidates of the party list or 25 per cent of the candidates on the entire list automatically excluded the party from the ballot. This would also happen if one of the top three candidates, or 25 per cent of the entire list, withdrew voluntarily. LDPR fell victim to this rule since its whole list was disqualified by CEC on the grounds that candidates on the second and third slots on the party list provided incorrect personal information. Zhirinovsky was forced hastily to submit a new list of candidates and run under the aegis of Zhirinovsky's Bloc rather than of the LDPR.[5]

---

[4] The Duma is also an important source of wealth for parties and individual deputies since government and a variety of Russian corporations who have interest in legislative outcomes that favour their interests are actively lobbying members of important Duma committees. According to one source, in order to assure the passage of the 1997 budget the government transferred $27 million to the coffers of KPRF and LDPR; see Eugene Huskey, *Presidential Power in Russia* (Armonk, NY: M. E. Sharpe, 1999), 172.

[5] KPRF also felt the effect of this rule. Fearing that the Kemerovo oblast governor, Aman Tuleev, might withdraw from the list and thus eliminate the party from the ballot, KPRF moved him from the third slot on its list, which he held during the 1995 election, to the fourth slot in 1999. Tuleev did not forget this slight and virtually did not campaign for KPRF in his own region. Instead, he almost openly endorsed Unity. As a consequence, the support for KPRF fell from 48.1 per cent of the vote in 1995 to 28.9 per cent in 1999. Unity, on the other hand, won Kemerovo with 33.7 per cent of the vote.

A major innovation of the 1999 electoral law was the introduction of a 2,087,250 rouble ($77,000) deposit as an alternative (to signature-gathering) method of placing a party on the ballot. However, to deter small parties, the election law also stipulated that parties garnering less than 3 per cent of the vote would not have their deposit returned. Moreover, parties failing to clear the 2 per cent threshold would have to reimburse the CEC for free television and radio time allocated to them.[6]

Finally, the election law attempted to deter small parties by stipulating that candidates running both on a party list and in a single-member district would not be allowed to use free television and radio time allocated to the promotion of the party list. In the end, the combined effect of all these measures was significant: the number of parties on the ballot declined from forty-three in 1995 to twenty-six in 1999.

PARTIES AND THEIR CAPACITIES AND GOALS

The fundamental purpose of the electoral law—the election of 225 Duma members on the party list ballot with a 5 per cent threshold, and the election of additional 225 members in the single-member constituencies—did not change from 1995 to 1999. This meant that the success of a party was highly dependent upon the availability of substantial financial and organizational resources on both the national and regional level, as well as politicians with national and regional name recognition. In the 1995 election, KPRF proved that it had the resources to win the parliamentary election. It came first with 22.7 per cent of the party list vote and won fifty-eight single-member district seats. This enabled the party to take control of the crucial post of Duma speaker, as well as nine (out of twenty-eight) key Duma committees. In the following years, KPRF demonstrated its regional strength by helping to elect fifteen regional governors.

Unlike in 1995, the KPRF did not treat the parliamentary election as a presidential primary. The party knew that its leader, Zyuganov, had no chance of winning the 2000 presidential ballot against such contenders as Luzhkov, Primakov, or Putin. While strongly anti-systemic in its ideology and rhetoric, particularly since gaining control of the Duma and winning scores of governorships, KPRF clearly acquired a stake in the existing system and was very careful not to provoke a major systemic crisis that could lead to a crackdown. This made the KPRF of late 1990s somewhat similar to the German Social-Democratic Party (SDP) of the 1890s. Like the SDP in Wilhelminian Germany, KPRF competed in the elections in order to be a major force in the parliament and to consolidate its domination of the left-wing electorate.

Of the five nationalist parties on the ballot only Zhirinovsky's LDPR had any chance of passing the 5 per cent threshold. Since his stunning success in the 1993 parliamentary election (22.8 per cent of the vote), Zhirinovsky's electoral fortunes had been on a steady decline: in the 1995 elections LDPR was down to 11.2 per cent of the vote, and in the 1996 presidential election Zhirinovsky received 5.7 per cent of the vote. By 1999 Zhirinovsky had lost his credentials as the embodiment of the anti-systemic opposition by supporting the government in crucial ballots, including the impeachment or nomination of the prime minister. Moreover, some of his key issues, such as crushing the Chechen uprising, were

---

[6] In fact, with the exception of LDPR, none of the thirteen parties that posted a deposit to be on the ballot received even 1 per cent of the vote.

adopted by the Putin government and by the Unity electoral alliance. At the same time, his pro-government stand essentially guaranteed him easy access to the government-controlled television channels that were the key to his electoral successes in the past.

In a significant shift from the 1995 elections, in which eleven liberal parties were on the ballot, in 1999 the high threshold helped to reduce the number of liberal parties to three. In the aftermath of the 1995 parliamentary election, Yabloko emerged as the most important liberal party in Russia. However, in the 1995 elections Yabloko had received only 42 per cent of the total liberal vote (6.9 per cent out of 16.1 per cent) and viewed the 1999 election as an opportunity to capture the majority of the liberal vote. In order to expand its electoral base among liberal voters, the party had to shed its image of perennial opponent of Yeltsin's government. This explains why, in August 1999, Yabloko embraced former prime minister Stepashin and placed him in the second slot on the party list. As part of the same strategy Yabloko welcomed the minister for nationalities affairs, Vyacheslav Mikhailov, as well as the former finance minister, Mikhail Zadornov, who had left the party after he joined the government.

The most important barrier that stood between Yabloko and its electoral goal was the Union of Right Forces (*Soyuz pravykh sil*, hereafter SPS), an electoral alliance of pro-Yeltsin prominent liberal politicians, such as Sergei Kirienko, Boris Nemtsov, and Irina Khakamada, and Russia's Democratic Choice Party (*Demokraticheskiy Vybor Rossii*, hereafter DVR), led by Anatoly Chubais and Yegor Gaidar. In 1995 DVR received 3.9 per cent of the vote and failed to enter the Duma largely because of nine small liberal parties that garnered 5.5 per cent of the vote. In December 1998, mindful of the 1995 experience, the pro-Yeltsin liberals began organizing a broad alliance of all the major liberal movements and politicians not affiliated with Yabloko. In September 1999 this alliance finally took shape as the Union of Right Forces with Kirienko, Nemtsov, and Khakamada heading the list. Among regional leaders only the Samara oblast governor, Konstantin Titov, joined the alliance.[7]

If at the centre of the 1993 and 1995 elections was a confrontation between pro-government and Communist and nationalist opposition parties, at the centre of the 1999 election was a confrontation between two centrist electoral alliances, Fatherland–All Russia and Unity, each representing a different faction within Russia's ruling elite. For each of these alliances the 1999 election constituted an unofficial primary for the 2000 presidential election.

The emergence of Fatherland–All Russia (*Otechestvo–Vsya Rossiya*, hereafter OVR) was a direct consequence of the 1997–8 split within the ruling elite—with the mayor of Moscow, Yury Luzhkov, and his supporters breaking from Yeltsin and his entourage.[8] In the summer of 1998 Luzhkov created the Fatherland movement to promote his presidential ambitions. All Russia was formed in April 1999 with the specific purpose of influencing the outcome of the forthcoming parliamentary and presidential elections. It was essentially a club of regional leaders led by the presidents of Tatarstan and Bashkortostan, Mintimer Shaimiev and Murtaza Rakhimov respectively, and the mayor of St Petersburg, Vladimir Yakovlev. In

---

[7] On the evolution and politics of SPS, see also Aleksei Zudin, 'Soyuz pravykh sil', in Michael McFaul, Nikolai Petrov, and Andrei Ryabov, eds., *Rossiya v izbiratel'nom tsikle 1999–2000 godov* (Moscow: Carnegie Endowment for International Peace, 2000), 180–96.

[8] On the evolution and politics of OVR, see also Boris Makarenko, 'Otechestvo–Vsya Rossiya', in McFaul, *Rossiya v izbiratel'nom tsikle*, 155–66.

August 1999, despite frantic efforts of the Yeltsin administration to prevent it, All Russia formed an electoral alliance with Fatherland on the condition that former prime minister Yevgeny Primakov, the most trusted Russian politician at the time, be its leader.

OVR presented the Yeltsin administration with its most dangerous and well-matched political opponent since October 1993. The movement enjoyed the support of over twenty major regional leaders who could influence the choice of approximately 37 per cent of Russian registered voters.[9] OVR had deep financial pockets and a strong presence in the electronic media with the support of the Media Most Corporation and its flagship NTV national television channel, as well as the TV Centre national television channel.

As late as mid-September 1999, less than 100 days before the ballot, the government had no electoral alliance it could call its own. This prompted several leading figures in the presidential administration, including Putin, to begin urgently negotiating for the creation of a new pro-presidential electoral alliance with regional leaders who had not joined OVR.[10] By early October, Unity (*Yedinstvo*) came into existence, supported by thirteen regional leaders who could influence the choice of only 13 per cent of Russian registered voters.[11]

Contrary to OVR's list, which had many well-known Russian politicians and public figures, Unity's candidate list consisted almost completely of little-known candidates. At the top of the list were the minister for emergency situations, Sergei Shoigu, Olympic champion wrestler Alexander Karelin, and senior criminal investigator Alexander Gurov. While having name recognition, none could bring many votes to the ticket. In the 1995 election Gurov was the second candidate on a small liberal list that attracted only 1.6 per cent of the vote. 'Decorating' the list with popular athletes, like Karelin, had not proved to be an effective strategy for attracting votes in the past. Finally, Shoigu, while an important minister, was hardly a popular politician. In short, Unity could not expect to win votes on the strength of its electoral list. Nor was it likely to win on the basis of its platform—non-existent except for its claim of being centrist and supporting Putin. Created at the last possible moment, Unity had no meaningful organization and in order to campaign, it had to rely on the bureaucratic structures of the federal government and the administrations of the governors sympathetic to the movement. It could also rely on the support of three national television channels: RTR (owned and controlled by the government), ORT and TV-6 (both controlled by Boris Berezovsky, a tycoon with close ties to the presidential administration).

THE CAMPAIGN AND ITS EFFECTS

Recent research on elections in stable democracies suggests that campaign efforts in parliamentary elections do have a significant impact on electoral behaviour.[12] Given the fact that the levels of political identification with political parties in Russia is far lower than in the West, it is only reasonable to expect an increasingly important role for the campaign,

---

[9] In addition to the mayors of Moscow and St Petersburg and presidents of Tatarstan and Bashkortostan, the alliance enjoyed a support of the regional leaders of Karelia, Mordovia, Ingushetia, Udmurtia, Kabardino-Balkaria, Khanty-Mansi, Irkutsk Chelyabinsk, Kirov, Murmansk, Novosibirsk, Nizhny Novgorod, and Yaroslavl.

[10] On the evolution and politics of Unity, see also Aleksei Makarkin, 'Partii vlasti', in McFaul, *Rossiya v izbiratel'-nom tsikle*, 144–52.

[11] Among Unity's supporters were heads of regional governments of Kalmykia, Tuva, Chukotka, Tver, Rostov, Kursk, Kaliningrad, Primorye, Omsk, Khabarovsk, and Leningrad oblast.

[12] Shawn Bowler *et al.*, 'The Informed Electorate?' in Shawn Bowler and David M. Farrell, eds., *Electoral Strategies and Political Marketing* (New York: St Martin's Press, 1992), 204–22.

especially in the electronic media, in determining actual electoral outcomes. The 1999 elections fully confirmed this expectation. At the same time, the effectiveness of the campaign was more crucial to the new parties without an established electorate.

As we mentioned earlier, the KPRF set as its goal domination of the left and tailored its campaign to reiterate its credentials to this targeted electorate. Given that the core of this electorate consisted of pensioners and peasants, the KPRF promised to raise pensions, preserve free medicine, and keep energy prices low for agricultural consumers.[13] As one can see from Tables 11.1 and 11.2, 88 per cent of KPRF voters decided to support the party before the campaign even started and only 10 per cent made their decision after the campaign had begun. Moreover, from October to December, KPRF ratings in the polls fluctuated within 3 percentage points (26–9 per cent). All this suggests that the campaign had little or no effect on the party's overall popularity and it attracted fewer new voters in comparison to other parties.

Zhirinovsky's campaign goal was to retain as much of his old electorate as possible. Since his campaign relied on electronic media, access was crucial. Contrary to the 1995 election when Zhirinovsky was largely kept out of the national television studios, in 1999, because of his pro-government voting record in the Duma, Zhirinovsky was given virtually unrestricted assess to pro-government television channels. The two most watched television channels, ORT and RTR, devoted 15 and 10 per cent, respectively, of their election news coverage to LDPR. In the crucial last four weeks before the election, Zhirinovsky gave at least seven interviews to ORT and RTR, and six to TV-6. Moreover, even the anti-government NTV devoted 11 per cent of its election news coverage to Zhirinovsky, including a live debate

Table 11.1 **Time of decision of voters**

Time of decision	KPRF	Unity	OVR	SPS	Yabloko	LDPR
Before start of the campaign						
Over six months before elections	79	4	31	20	61	59
Three to six months before elections	4	5	18	7	8	10
Two to three months before elections	5	31	23	28	18	10
Total before start of the campaign	88	40	72	55	87	79
After start of the campaign						
Two to three weeks before elections	4	36	15	25	8	11
Last week before elections	4	15	8	12	5	7
On the election day	2	3	3	7	1	4
Total after start of the campaign	10	53	26	44	14	22
Refuse to answer	1	5	1	1	0	0

Source: Public Opinion Foundation at www.fom.ru.

[13] Gennady Zyuganov, 'Otvety narodu,' *Zavtra*, 7 Dec. 1999.

Table 11.2 **Ratings of parties, August–December 1999**

Party	August	September	October	12–15 Nov.	3–6 Dec.	11–14 Dec.	Actual Result
KPRF	31	32	26	29	26	24	24.3
Unity	–	–	5	8	17	21	23.3
OVR	16	22	21	11	10	12	13.3
Yabloko	10	12	11	9	10	8	5.9
SPS	2	4	4	6	5	7	8.5
LDPR	5	4	3	4	5	4	6.0
NDR	4	4	2	1	1	1	1.2
Difficult to answer	11	10	15	19	16	12	–

Source: VTsIOM at www.polit.ru/vciom.html.

with the SPS leader, Nemtsov, on 25 November.[14] While his ratings fluctuated only slightly in November and December, 22 per cent of his voters made the decision to vote for his party after the campaign had began. This suggests that the campaign, and particularly the media, was crucial to Zhirinovsky's passing the electoral threshold.

Yabloko and SPS had to conduct their electoral campaigns facing stiff competition with OVR in Moscow and St Petersburg, their traditional electoral strongholds. OVR's attempt to undermine electoral support for Yabloko and SPS in the two largest Russian cities made the competition between the two parties, which included live debates on NTV between Chubais and Yavlinsky (25 November) and Kirienko and Yavlinsky (9 December), even more fierce. In this contest, SPS consciously attempted to appeal to young urban voters by presenting itself as the party with a young leadership and by advocating the use of professional soldiers and not draftees in Chechnya and other locales where the Russian military was engaged in fighting.

At the same time, recognizing the popularity of the Chechen war, SPS came out clearly and aggressively in its support. SPS attempted to draw a clear distinction between itself and Yabloko by emphasizing the latter's rather ambivalent stand on the war. SPS also repeatedly accused Yabloko of being a 'do nothing party' that would not take responsibility for the economic reform. Finally, late in the campaign, SPS attempted to jump on the bandwagon of Putin's rising popularity. On 13 December the SPS campaign aired a clip showed Kirienko meeting Putin in the Kremlin and four days later Kirienko officially endorsed Putin as presidential candidate.

Yabloko was largely on the defensive in its confrontation with SPS. To rebuff its characterization as a 'do nothing party', Yabloko highlighted its legislative achievements in the Duma

---

[14] *Preliminary Report on Monitoring of Media Coverage during the Parliamentary Elections in the Russian Federation in December 1999* (Dusseldorf: The European Institute for the Media, 1999) at www.eim.org; *RFE/RL Russian Election Report*, no. 5 (3 Dec. 1999) at www.rferl.org.

as well as Stepashin's record as prime minister in reducing wage and pension arrears and fighting crime. At the same time, it reminded voters that SPS leaders were responsible for the highly unpopular 'shock therapy' reform of 1992 and that the financial crisis of August 1998 occurred when Kirienko was prime minister.

The campaign strategy adopted by SPS worked, while Yabloko's campaign can be considered a failure. Between September and December, SPS doubled its support in the polls. Moreover, 44 per cent of its voters made the decision to vote for the list after the campaign had begun. Yabloko's ratings, however, stagnated during the same period. Only 14 per cent of Yabloko voters decided to cast their vote for the party after the campaign had begun and this clearly indicates a failed campaign strategy.

While being the party of the ruling elite, OVR made a conscious effort to disassociate itself from the Yeltsin administration. OVR's campaign plan was to present itself as a centrist political movement critical of the neo-liberal economic reforms of the Yeltsin administration, and pledging greater state support for industry and agriculture. In a thinly veiled criticism of the presidential entourage, OVR pledged to fight corruption in the highest echelons of government.

OVR's campaign plans, however, failed to take into account the ability of the presidential administration and its allies to use negative campaign tactics to discredit its main political opponent. Starting in mid-October, the two most watched television networks, ORT and RTR, launched sharp personal attacks on Luzhkov, Primakov, and other OVR leaders. Luzhkov was accused of graft, nepotism, corruption, and even conspiracy to commit murder, while Primakov was blamed for failing to prevent the NATO bombing of Yugoslavia, ordering the assassination of Georgia's president, Eduard Shevardnadze, destroying the Russian defence industry, and being too old and too infirm to lead the country.[15] The Chechen factor also played a significant role in the OVR bashing. ORT repeatedly attacked the presidents of the republics of Ingushetia and Kabardino-Balkaria, both supporting OVR, as harbouring Chechen terrorists, thus branding Luzhkov and Primakov as guilty by association.

While some Russian and Western observers claimed that these broadcasts determined the results of the 1999 and, ultimately, the 2000 elections, in reality it was a far more complex situation. A November 1999 study found that only 46.6 per cent of Russians trusted the news and political programmes shown on ORT and 28.1 per cent trusted those on RTR. These figures are not sufficiently high to conclude that the attacks on OVR leaders appearing on ORT and RTR single-handedly determined the election results.[16]

A comparison of the popularity ratings of OVR and Putin in October and November 1999 (see Table 11.6) reveals that OVR's decline in ratings and the rise of Putin's take place simultaneously. Putin, however, owes his rising popularity largely to the popular Chechen war, with which he was closely identified, and to the optimism expressed by Russian citizens about the Russian economy and their personal future in late autumn 1999.[17] The rise in

---

[15] For the detailed list of accusations levelled against Luzhkov and Primakov, see *RFE/RL Russian Election Report*, no. 7 (17 Dec. 1999) at www.rferl.org.

[16] 'Otnoshenie rossiyan k populyarnym televizionnym programmam', at www.romir.ru.

[17] According to VTsIOM's post-election poll, 72 per cent of the population supported the government policies in Chechnya in December 1999; see www.polit.ru/documents/16134.html. In a study conducted by ROMIR in November 1999, 46.5 per cent of Russians expected themselves and their families to be better off economically in the following year, while 30.8 per cent expected to be worse off. Moreover, 55.4 per cent expected the Russian economy to improve in the next twelve months, while 29.3 per cent expected the economy to worsen, see www.romir.ru.

Putin's popularity was bound to have a negative effect on his potential presidential rivals, Primakov and Luzhkov and their electoral alliance, with the ORT and RTR attacks playing secondary role.

Unity was also a target of negative campaigning. NTV, actively supporting OVR, exposed the graft, corruption, and the dictatorial ruling style of such Unity supporters as Yevgeny Nazdratenko (Primorye), Leonid Gorbenko (Kaliningrad oblast), and Kirsan Ilyumzhimov (Kalmykia) in its programmes. Yet, these accusations could hardly compare to the accusations made against Luzhkov and Primakov.

The pro-presidential media heavily promoted Unity. ORT devoted 28 per cent of its campaign coverage to Unity, while RTR devoted 15 per cent of its election coverage to the alliance. Moreover, Shoigu, the movement leader, was shown virtually daily on these two channels under the pretext of covering his government functions as the minister for the emergency situations. Unity's own television ads said virtually nothing about the movement programme. Instead they heavily focused on the top three candidates on the list: Shoigu, Karelin, and Gurov. The purpose of focusing on personalities, rather than on policies, was to draw an implicit but clear distinction between Unity and OVR. Indeed, the ads emphasized that Unity's leaders were not regular politicians, like Luzhkov and Primakov, but were people of honesty and integrity whom voters could trust.

The state media's heavy promotion of Unity and the movement's own campaign strategy could hardly explain Unity's meteoric rise in the polls. The most dramatic increase in Unity's popularity took place between 15 November and 3 December. The timing is hardly surprising since Putin openly endorsed Unity on state television on 24 November. From this moment on, Unity was simply riding on the coat-tails of Putin's own popularity: 53 per cent of Unity's voters decided to vote for the movement after Putin's endorsement.

THE RESULTS OF THE PARTY-LIST VOTE

A comparison of the results of the party-list vote in the 1993, 1995, and 1999 Duma elections (see Table 11.3) reveals that the 1999 ballot both continued and reversed trends that emerged in previous ballots. Despite the ability of SPS to pass the threshold, the total liberal vote continued to decline. In fact, the liberal vote declined by 8.3 million between 1993 and 1999, and by 1.2 million between 1995 and 1999. This outcome reflects the failure of the economic reform to create a broad middle class that is the social base of Western liberal parties. At the other end of the political spectrum, KPRF's gains were rather modest: 1 per cent of the vote, for additional 762,000 voters. However, the party achieved one of its key electoral goals of establishing its domination of the left-wing electorate. If in the 1995 election votes for the KPRF constituted 72.8 per cent of the vote cast for leftist parties, in the 1999 ballot the KPRF share of the left-wing vote rose to 86.5 per cent.

Zhirinovsky's LDPR was able to enter the Duma with 6.1 per cent of the vote but continued its decline in the polls. In fact, from 1993 to 1999 Zhirinovsky lost 67.5 per cent of his electorate. Moreover, the nationalist electorate in general declined sharply in the 1999 elections. This decline (14.4 per cent, 10.2 million votes) is clearly a consequence of the co-optation of many issues on the nationalist agenda by Unity and OVR.

The largest increase in votes belongs to the parties at the centre of the Russian political spectrum. Altogether from 1993 to 1999, the centrist electorate grew by 25.6 per cent and 19.2 million voters. This growth of the centrist electorate does not represent growing voter

Table 11.3 **The 1993, 1995, and 1999 parliamentary elections: A comparison of the party-list vote**

12 December 1993		17 December 1995		19 December 1999	
Parties	% of Support	Parties	% of Support	Parties	% of Support
Liberals	*34.1*	*Liberals*	*16.1*	*Liberals*	*15.0*
RC	15.4	Yabloko	6.9	SPS	8.5
Yabloko	7.8	DVR	3.7	Yabloko	5.9
PRES	6.8	Others (9)	5.5	Others (1)	0.6
RDDR	4.1				
Centrists	*16.3*	*Centrists*	*24.8*	*Centrists*	*41.9*
WR	8.1	NDR	10.1	Unity	23.3
DPR	5.5	WR	4.6	OVR	13.3
Others (2)	2.7	PTS	4.0	WR	2.0
		Others (10)	6.1	Others (6)	3.3
Nationalists	*22.8*	*Nationalists*	*21.8*	*Nationalists*	*7.4*
LDPR	22.8	LDPR	11.2	LDPR	6.1
		KRO	4.3	Others (4)	1.3
		Others (7)	6.3		
Communists	*20.3*	*Communists*	*30.6*	*Communists*	*28.1*
KPRF	12.4	KPRF	22.3	KPRF	24.3
APR	7.9	APR	3.8	Workers' Russia	2.2
		Workers' Russia	4.5	Others (3)	1.6
Parties with no clear orientation (2)	*2.0*	*Parties with no clear orientation (7)*	*2.1*	*Parties with no clear orientation (4)*	*2.5*
Against all	*4.2*	*Against all*	*2.8*	*Against all*	*3.3*
% of the vote cast	54.8	*% of the vote cast*	64.4	*% of the vote cast*	61.9

Source: Acronyms: RC = Russia's Choice; RDDR = Russian Movement for Democratic Reforms; PRES = Party of Russian Unity and Accord; WR = Women of Russia; DPR = Democratic Party of Russia; LDPR = Liberal-Democratic Party of Russia; KPRF = Communist Party of the Russian Federation; APR = Agrarian Party of Russia; DVR = Russia's Democratic Choice; NDR = Our Home Russia; PTS = Party of Workers' Self-Government; KRO = Congress of Russian Communities; SPS = Union of Right Forces; OVR = Fatherland-All Russia Bloc.

disenchantment with both liberalism and communism. In fact, the centre of the Russian political spectrum becomes increasingly non-ideological due to the growing importance of parties created by the largely non-ideological ruling elites. If in the 1995 election, votes for the Our Home Russia and Ivan Rybkin Bloc, the two non-ideological parties created by the government, constituted 44.8 per cent of the centrist vote, in 1999 OVR and Unity voters constituted 87.4 per cent of the centrist electorate.

In clear contrast to the previous parliamentary elections, the 1999 elections were marked by the very aggressive intervention of regional leaders, who attempted to influence the outcome of the vote. The election showed the mixed results of this effort. OVR counted heavily on the ability of their regional leaders to influence the vote, yet, only in eight out of twenty cases was the support for OVR substantially stronger regionally than in Russia as a whole (13.3 per cent of the vote).[18] At first glance, regional leaders who openly or semi-openly endorsed Unity were far more effective in influencing the election than regional leaders supporting OVR. Out of thirteen regions with governors supporting Unity, only in one was the vote for the movement below its national average (23.3 per cent of the vote). The best result for Unity was in Tuva (70.8 per cent of the vote), a republic whose leaders always successfully produced the electoral results desired by the government. Yet, the fact that Unity did well in many regions without the governors' support indicates that their role in assuring the campaign success ability is highly contextual and is not be taken for granted.[19]

VOTER PROFILE AND ITS IMPLICATIONS

Table 11.4 provides us with a clear picture of the social profile of the electorate of the six main parties. The Communist voter is older, largely uneducated, lives in small towns or villages, barely survives economically, and believes that he will never adjust to the political and socio-economic changes experienced by Russia in the last ten years. This is clearly the profile of the social stratum that lost the most in the transition to capitalism. At the same time, this electorate is very sure of its political identity. While the electorate of the other parties indicates a high degree of uncertainty in defining itself ideologically, 89 per cent of the KPRF electorate defines itself as 'Communist'. With such a strong notion of political identity, these voters are likely to continue to support KPRF in future ballots.

The SPS and Yabloko electorate is not only at the opposite end of the political spectrum from KPRF's supporters but also at the opposite end socially and economically. A majority of the electorate of both parties is under the age of 40, well educated, living in the big cities, comfortable economically and well adjusted to the social and economic changes. It also has a fairly strong democratic political identity. The two issues that divide the liberal electorate

[18] The support was strongest in Ingushetia (88.0 per cent), Moscow (40.7 per cent), Tatarstan (40.7 per cent), Bashkortostan (35.2 per cent), Kabardino-Balkaria (34.7), Mordovia (32.6), and Moscow oblast (27.7 per cent), all regions with supportive leaders. At the same time, OVR did rather poorly in such regions with supportive leaders as Nizhny Novgorod (6.8 per cent), Novosibirsk (5.8 per cent), and Chelyabinsk (8.7 per cent). For the third person on the OVR list, Mayor Yakovlev of St Petersburg, his city's support for his own party (15.7 per cent) must have been well below his expectations.

[19] Among regions with strongest support for Unity were Magadan (43.0 per cent), Pskov (38.3 per cent), Udmurtia (36.6), Amur (36.2 per cent), Kostroma (35.0 per cent), and Voronezh (32.7 per cent). In none of these regions did the governor support the movement. In the case of SPS, Samara governor Titov campaigned hard for SPS and, as a result, the alliance received 22.1 per cent of the vote in his region, a major improvement on the 2.7 per cent of the vote cast for DVR in the 1995 election.

Table 11.4 **Social characteristics and political orientation of the Russian electorate**

	KPRF	Unity	OVR	Yabloko	SPS	LDPR
Gender						
Female	52.0	51	56	54	58	38
Male	48.0	50	44	47	42	62
Age						
18–24	5	10	10	12	25	18
25–39	17	38	29	40	37	42
40–54	26	24	25	29	23	23
55–99	53	28	36	19	15	18
Education						
Below secondary	51	32	34	21	20	36
Secondary	38	52	43	52	56	59
Higher	11	16	23	27	25	5
Size of Community						
Town population more than 100,000	31.5	30	47	51	55	30
Town population less than 100,000	36.8	41	29	34	31	38
Village	31.6	29	24	16	14	32
Economic Situation						
Barely makes ends meet	45	33	28	24	17	32
Enough for food	40	41	46	41	44	37
Enough for food and clothes	13	23	21	30	31	28
Can buy durable goods easily	2	3	5	6	8	3
How you identify yourself ideologically?						
'Communist'	89	6	17	3	5	12
'Democrat'	1	26	28	45	51	34
'Nationalist'	1	9	10	7	5	16
Difficult to answer	9	59	44	44	40	38
Did you and your family adjust to the changes Russia underwent in the last ten years?						
Did adjust	28	45	41	48	58	37
Would adjust in the near future	51	25	24	30	20	25
Would never adjust	53	27	31	18	18	33
Difficult to answer	4	3	3	4	3	5

Table 11.4 **continued**

	KPRF	Unity	OVR	Yabloko	SPS	LDPR
Do you think the present government would be able to improve the situation in the country in the near future?						
Yes	27	52	30	25	41	33
No	40	16	34	41	25	29
Difficult to answer	34	32	37	35	34	39
Do you think Putin's government is tackling Russia's problems better or worse than the past governments?						
Better than past governments	43	72	47	40	55	51
Same as past governments	43	21	39	46	35	32
Worse than past governments	4	1	6	6	1	2
Difficult to answer	9	6	8	8	8	9
* *Do you support the action of the Russian government in Chechnya?*						
Approve	70	86	70	85	75	74
Disapprove	30	14	30	15	25	26

Source: VTsIOM (23 Dec. 1999) at www.polit.ru/vciom and www.russiavotes.org *New Russia Barometer VIII (19–29 Jan. 2000) at www.russiavotes.org.

are the attitude towards Putin's government, with the SPS voters being significantly more supportive and optimistic than the Yabloko voters, and the attitude towards the Chechen war, with the Yabloko voters much more supportive than the SPS voters. In other words, the success of SPS was not a result of its fervent support for the all-out war, while Yabloko's failure had little to do with its call for a negotiated solution. It is clear that the liberal electorate valued other issues substantially more than their parties' stand on Chechnya.

With no clear ideological message besides calling themselves 'centrists', Unity and OVR essentially competed over the same portion of the electorate that regarded itself neither liberal nor Communist. The voter profile of both parties suggests that each party appealed to a different segment within this electorate. The voters of both parties were identical in their economic well-being (slightly worse off than the liberal voters of SPS and Yabloko but much better off than KPRF voters), and were fairly well adjusted to the political and socio-economic changes (although liberal voters were more so). At the same time, Unity's electorate was younger and less educated than that of OVR. And if the OVR electorate predominantly resided in the larger cities, Unity voters were mostly residents of small towns and villages.

The two most notable differences between the two electorates were on the issue of the assessment of the Putin government in general, and its policies towards Chechnya in particular. Unity voters were substantially more optimistic than OVR voters in assessing the Putin government's present and future ability to improve the situation within Russia. The

Unity voter had trusted Putin and his government above all other parties, and this supports our earlier claim that the alliance's electoral success was a direct consequence of the meteoric rise of Putin's own popularity and prevailing feeling of optimism. There was a sixteen-point difference in approval of the war in Chechnya between Unity and OVR's electorates (86 and 70 per cent, respectively). It is hardly surprising that Unity voters were more supportive of the Chechen war; after all it was the policy with which Putin was most identified. The fact that OVR voters were less supportive of the war than voters of all other parties is an indicator that ORT and RTR attempts to brand OVR as unpatriotic on the issue of Chechnya, indeed, cost the party the votes of people who strongly supported the war effort.

Finally, the electorates differed in terms of their political identity. Among OVR voters there were almost three times as many people who identified themselves as 'Communists' as among Unity voters. In fact, the percentage of OVR voters who identified themselves as 'Communists' was the highest among voters supporting any of the non-Communist parties and was probably a consequence of OVR's success in attracting a segment of the KPRF electorate. The Unity electorate, on the other hand, had the highest percentage of people who were unwilling or unable to define themselves politically. Unity's non-ideological message stressed that their leaders were not the 'same old' politicians and Putin himself emphasized that he was above parties and party politics and this appears to have resonated among voters who saw themselves as independent.

After the election, there was speculation that Unity 'stole' many of its voters from LDPR. An analysis of the social and ideological profile of the LDPR electorate indicates that both electorates have four common characteristics: a high percentage of people under the age of 40, residence in small towns and rural areas, a relatively good economic situation, and having adjusted to the current political and socio-economic conditions. However, they significantly differ in all other characteristics. LDPR was predominantly a male party (and had been so consistently since 1993), while support for Unity is even among men and women. LDPR also had a far less educated electorate than Unity. In terms of the ideological identity, LDPR attracted significantly more voters who identified themselves as Communists and nationalists than Unity. Zhirinovsky's electorate was also substantially less optimistic about Putin's government than the Unity electorate. All this suggests that Unity was probably able to attract a segment of the less nationalistic, better-educated and less anti-government LDPR constituency.

ELECTIONS IN THE SINGLE-MEMBER DISTRICTS

Alongside the party-list ballot, the 1999 elections also determined the fate of the 225 single-member district seats. Again, the election rules had a significant effect on the results of the single-member district vote. In the 1995 ballot candidates had to submit signatures of 1 per cent of the district's registered voters in order to secure a place on the ballot. This was a rather easy requirement that resulted in 2,628 candidates (11.7 candidates per district). For the 1999 elections, candidates were allowed to substitute the payment of a deposit of 83,500 roubles ($3,000) in place of signature-gathering. The addition of the deposit option had the potential of increasing the number of candidates on the ballot.

To reduce the number of candidates, the electoral law gave the district electoral committees a freer hand to disqualify candidates for submitting incorrect income and property holdings statements, for having too high a percentage of falsified signatures on their petitions, or for committing minor violations of the electoral law during the campaign. This had the desired effect of reducing the total number of candidates on the ballot to 2,226 (9.9 candidates per district). However, this increased the ability of local leaders to influence the single-member district races since district electoral committees were often under their control. In fact, in Bashkortostan, Komi, Ingushetia, Kemerovo, and Samara prominent political figures disliked by the regional authorities were either refused registration or removed from the ballot by district electoral committees during the campaign.[20]

The second major consequence of the electoral law was the preservation of the existing district boundaries.[21] This was tremendously helpful to the incumbent deputies since the 1995 redistricting resulted in a 33.5 per cent re-election rate. In the 1999 election the re-election of incumbents went up to 47.8 per cent and this was clearly influenced by the preservation of the existing district boundaries. The third innovation of the electoral law that had direct impact on the election was a ruling that annulled the results of an election in a district in which the number of votes cast against all candidates was higher than the number of votes cast for the winning candidate. In the 1999 election, this happened in eight districts. In the repeat elections of 26 March 2000, none of the December first-place finishers was able to repeat his success. Yabloko was the major victim of this rule since it lost three Duma seats.[22]

Another feature of the electoral law that has continued to influence the outcome of the ballot since its introduction in 1993 was its 'first past the post' structure. With no run-off option the candidates of ideologically similar parties had to join forces in order to maximize their chances of victory. However, this incentive did not motivate parties into national cooperation agreements in either 1993 or 1995. This was repeated in 1999 even though at the local level parties did cooperate in a small number of districts. Needless to say, as in previous elections, this lack of cooperation resulted in painful losses for both liberals and the Communists. Thus, the failure of Yabloko and SPS to agree on a joint candidate in St Petersburg district No. 208 led to the election of a little-known OVR candidate and defeat for Yabloko's incumbent. In Omsk district No. 130 KPRF won the party list vote with 27.5 per cent of the vote, 12.3 per cent more than the next party. Yet, in the single-member district race its candidate, Alexander Kravets, failed to win the seat because he and the incumbent deputy, nationalist deputy speaker of the Duma and the KPRF parliamentary ally, Sergei Baburin, could not agree on who should represent the anti-government forces on the ballot. As a result, the seat went to a pro-government independent businessman.

As we mentioned earlier, one of the consequences of the electoral law was to strengthen the ability of regional leaders to shape the outcome of single-member district races. This was significant since regional executives effectively controlled the local media, as well as other

[20] In Bashkortostan, a district electoral committee denied registration from the incumbent deputy, Alexander Arinin, a bitter foe of the republican president Rakhimov. In Samara, a district electoral committee removed from the ballot the incumbent deputy, a prominent opposition politician, Albert Makashov, for paying in cash for printing campaign material, a minor violation of the electoral law. The removal of Makashov cleared the way for the victory of the governor-supported SPS candidate in the district.

[21] The electoral law stipulated that the Duma had to publish new district boundaries at least 100 days before the elections. In case of failure to amend the boundaries within this time frame, the elections were to take place with the 1995 districts. The Duma failed to meet this 100 days deadline, forcing the elections to take place in the old districts.

[22] In addition to Yabloko, this rule cost KPRF, Unity, OVR, and Women of Russia one seat each.

resources needed for a successful campaign effort. In the 1999 elections, governors and presidents took active part not only in the party-list elections but also in the single-member district races. Luzhkov, Yakovlev, Shaimiev, and Rakhimov were especially aggressive in this regard. In these four regions, OVR won eighteen out of its total thirty-two single-member district seats. Of nine Unity winners, four were from regions where governors were sympathetic to the alliance. Those governors who did not have a partisan agenda in the election still actively campaigned for a variety of independent candidates in order to lobby their interests in the Duma. The liberal parties, who had virtually no support among the regional leaders, were victimized by this electoral activism: if in the 1995 election liberal parties on the ballot were able to elect thirty-three single-member district deputies, in 1999 this number had declined to nine. Only KPRF, with a strong regional organization and a stable constituency, could withstand this onslaught and won forty-seven single-member district seats.

Since the inception of the current electoral system, one of the main features of the single-member district races has been the significant presence of independent candidates. The 1999 ballot was no exception. Independents were often wealthy businessman or representatives of regional leaders and business lobbies who wanted direct access to the legislative process or parliamentary immunity from criminal investigations. Since 1993, all major parties also employed the strategy of placing their own candidates on the ballot as independents. This was largely done to win votes in a district that might not support a candidate should he run on the party ticket. As Table 11.5 shows, in 1999, various parties won an additional twenty-nine seats by using this strategy, with KPRF winning an additional fourteen seats and Unity eight.

Part Two: the 26 March 2000 presidential election

As soon as the results of the parliamentary elections were known, it was clear that Luzhkov and Primakov were the main losers and that Putin had the best chance of winning the presidency. The presidential elections, however, were six months away and, as the 1996

Table 11.5 **Duma seats**

Parties (1999)	PR seats	SM district seats	SM district seats (Independent)	Total seats (1999)	Total seats (1995)
SPS	24	5	2	31	–
Yabloko	16	4	1	21	45
Unity	64	9	8	81	–
OVR	36	32	3	71	–
LDPR	17	–	1	18	51
KPRF	67	47	14	127	158
NDR	–	7	–	7	55
Other parties	–	9	–	9	65
Independent	–	114	–	85	77

presidential election demonstrated, six months was sufficient time radically to improve a candidate's ratings in the polls. To prevent any possibility that Luzhkov or Primakov might regain the popularity they enjoyed in the early autumn of 1999, Yeltsin resigned his office on 31 December 1999, a move that in accordance with the Constitution made Putin acting president. This move not only gave Putin the important incumbency advantage but also forced a pre-term presidential election, since the Russian Constitution required that the presidential ballot be held within ninety days of the president's resignation from office. With the election moved forward to 26 March 2000, there was little chance that Primakov, Luzhkov, or any other candidate could seriously challenge Putin. In January 2000 both Primakov and Luzhkov withdrew from the race, leaving Putin with only one serious opponent, Zyuganov. Yet, if Zyuganov's popularity in January 1996 was 21 per cent of the vote, in January 2000 his rating stood at 11 per cent and every poll showed that he had no chance of winning the presidency.[23]

While the ultimate outcome of the presidential ballot was never in doubt, the margin of victory was. The electoral law required a run-off if the winning candidate did not receive 50 per cent of the vote. Putin wanted to avoid a run-off in order to have a stronger mandate for his policy agenda and to be less beholden to the media barons and regional leaders whose power he intended to undercut.

There were three possible factors that could cause a run-off. First, the emergence of a single candidate capable of unifying the liberal wing of the electorate, and thus securing the 15 per cent of the vote that the liberal parties received in the December 1999 election. Yet, no such candidate could have emerged in the political circumstances that prevailed in January–February 2000. The strong mutual antagonism between SPS leaders and Yavlinsky effectively eliminated his candidacy. Despite this, Yavlinsky was determined to run for the presidency in order to prove that he was still a major force in Russian politics. Moreover, the SPS leaders themselves could not make up their mind regarding the candidate to support in the presidential race. As we mentioned earlier, on the eve of the parliamentary election Kirienko openly endorsed Putin's forthcoming presidential bid and the party certainly owed at least some of its success to this endorsement. On the other hand, Titov, the only major regional leader to join the alliance, wanted to run as the SPS candidate on the presidential ballot. After a period of indecisiveness, SPS endorsed Putin's candidacy, forcing Titov to run as an independent candidate without any meaningful endorsement.

The two other factors capable of forcing Putin into a run-off were a poor campaign strategy or a shift in the mood of the electorate. The upbeat mood of the electorate, so crucial to Unity's success in December, continued. In the VTsIOM poll of 25–8 February 2000, 36 per cent of the participants said that they expected their family situation to improve within five years. In comparison, in January 1997 only 25 per cent said the same. Moreover, 58 per cent of the participants stated they were satisfied with their lives in general. In January 1997 only 40 per cent expressed such a feeling. Another VTsIOM poll (10–13 March 2000) revealed that 58 per cent of Russians thought Putin would take the country in the right direction.[24]

Like Zyuganov in 1996, Putin's choice of campaign strategy was influenced by his reading

---

[23] On the 2000 presidential election, see also McFaul, *Rossiya v izbiratel'nom tsikle*, 484–562.

[24] www.polit.ru/documents/188760.html; www.polit.ru/documents/198059.html.

of the preceding parliamentary election. In essence, it was a duplication of Unity's campaign strategy. As we pointed out earlier, Unity essentially presented itself as a non-political movement that was led not by ordinary career politicians, but by honest people who cared about Russia. Adapted to the reality of a presidential campaign this strategy attempted to show that Putin was not an ordinary politician who used ordinary campaign techniques to get elected. In essence, Putin campaigned by not campaigning. Unlike Yeltsin in 1996, he refused to make any campaign promises, to run any campaign ads, to hold rallies, or to attend rock music concerts. Since he did not want the election to be about ideas, Putin, in sharp contrast to Yeltsin in 1996, refused to turn the election into a referendum on Communism, even though his main opponent was the KPRF leader.

Putin never formally issued a programme during the campaign. The document that for all practical purposes functioned as his programme was his 25 February 2000 'Open Letter to Russian Voters'. This document perfectly fitted his strategy of dispelling the view that he was an ordinary politician by honestly describing the problems of poverty, crime, and corruption. The 'Open Letter' did not provide any concrete solutions to these problems but simply contained a pledge to tackle them and restore Russia to its greatness.[25] This document became the major campaign manifesto and giant posters of it decorated the central areas of all major Russian cities.

An integral part of this strategy was Putin's travels around the country. He rode in Moscow suburban trains chatting with the commuters or was a dinner guest of an ordinary family in Kazan to demonstrate his closeness to the problems of ordinary Russians. He made a special effort to appeal to women by meeting women textile workers in the city of Ivanovo, something Yeltsin never did. To show his credentials to be the commander-in-chief he spent a night on a nuclear submarine and flew on a fighter jet to Chechnya.

The state-controlled media carefully documented all his visits in order to promote the image of a non-political politician. In fact, Putin received as much coverage on Russian television as the three main challenges, Zyuganov, Yavlinsky, and Zhirinovsky, received together. In the crucial period between 3 and 21 March, ORT devoted over nine hours of coverage to Putin.[26]

At first sight, this campaign strategy appears to have achieved its goals. As Table 11.6 shows, Putin's rating continued to climb, reaching its peak of 58 per cent on 13 March. Yet, shortly thereafter his rating began to decline and by 20 March it had fallen to 53 per cent. His job approval rating as prime minister and acting president had declined to 67 per cent, the lowest since mid-October 1999.[27] With a margin of error of 3.8 per cent, the possibility of a run-off was suddenly very real. This decline in ratings was probably a consequence of what some voters saw as hypocrisy in the non-politician campaigning style that emphasized a rejection of politics as usual, and vicious personal attacks on Yavlinsky in ORT and RTR broadcasts in the last two weeks prior to the ballot.

On election day, Putin avoided a run-off by winning 52.9 per cent of the vote,

---

[25] 'Otkrytoe pis'mo Vladimira Putina k rossiiskim izbiratelyam', *Rossiiskaya gazeta*, 25 Feb. 2000.

[26] *Preliminary Report on Monitoring of Media Coverage during the Presidential Elections in the Russian Federation in March 2000* (Dusseldorf: The European Institute for the Media, 2000) at www.eim.org.

[27] www.polit.ru/documents/198772.html.

Table 11.6 **Ratings of major presidential contenders (August 1999–March 2000)**

Candidate	Aug.	Sept.	18 Oct.	9 Nov.	6 Dec.	4 Jan.	7 Feb	13 March	20 March	Actual result
Putin	2	4	21	36	45	48	57	58	53	52.9
Zyuganov	26	27	20	21	19	11	17	21	21	29.2
Primakov	19	19	16	10	8	8	–	–	–	–
Yavlinsky	9	9	7	5	5	3	2	5	6	5.8
Zhirinovsky	7	3	3	2	3	2	2	3	3	2.7
Luzhkov	9	10	8	4	1	1	–	–	–	–
Others	8	8	5	5	3	3	5	3	3	3.5
Tuleev	–	–	–	–	–	–	–	2	3	3.0
Refuse to answer	7	13	11	10	9	12	7	6	NA	–

Source: VTsIOM at www.polit.ru/vciom.html

approximately 500,000 votes less than Yeltsin received in the second round of the 1996 elections.[28] Zyuganov finished second with 29.2 per cent of the vote, 8.2 million votes less than in his performance in the 1996 run-off but 3.2 million votes more than all the Communist parties received in the December 1999 poll. This result reaffirmed Zyuganov's position as the undisputed leader of the left. Despite heavy television advertisement in the last weeks of the campaign, Yavlinsky finished third with 5.8 per cent of the vote, 1.2 million votes less than in 1996 but 400,000 votes more than Yabloko in December 1999, making the results not totally disappointing from his perspective. Zhirinovsky finished fifth with 2.7 per cent of the vote, 3.7 million votes less than in 1996 and 1.9 million votes less than LDPR in 1999. This result probably brings to an end his remarkable ride in Russian politics that started with the surprising third place finish in the 1991 presidential election.

While Putin's victory in 2000 very closely mirrors Yeltsin in the 1996 run-off, the geography of the vote is hardly identical. A comparison of the Yeltsin and Putin vote in Russian cities with a population of 500,000 and above reveals that support for Putin was substantially weaker than for Yeltsin (66.3 per cent for Yeltsin, 50.7 per cent for Putin). The gap was especially large in those cities with a population of 1,000,000 and above (70.3 per cent for Yeltsin, 51.1 per cent for Putin). Moreover, if the share of the big cities in the total vote for Yeltsin was 32 per cent, it was only 25 per cent of the total vote for Putin. This finding suggests that Putin owes less to big city voters than Yeltsin and therefore can be less attentive to the political moods prevailing in the big cities. Since liberal causes and parties were always

[28] An investigation by the *Moscow Times* found evidence for the falsification of at least 551,000 votes in Dagestan, 51 per cent of the entire vote cast in the republic, and listed complaints of fraud in many other regions. The paper also highlighted the fact the number of registered voters inexplicably grew by 1.3 million from December 1999 to March 2000. All this led the paper to a conclusion that Putin did not receive the required 50 per cent of the vote on 26 March 2000. This is certainly possible in the light of VTsIOM's last pre-election poll cited earlier. See Yevgeniya Borisova, 'And the Winner Is?' *Moscow Times*, 9 Sept. 2000.

stronger in the big cities, these results are not promising for the future of liberalism in Russia.

Zyuganov did not do well in the big cities in the 1996 run-off (27.9 per cent of the vote vs. 40.3 in Russia as a whole) and again in 1999 (24.4 per cent of the vote). In fact, he received 586,000 fewer votes in big cities than in 1996. Yet, if in 1996 the total share of the big cities in his electorate was 18 per cent, in 2000 this share grew to 22 per cent. This evidence suggests that Zyuganov's popularity outside the big cities declined more sharply than in the big cities. If this trend continues, the Communists could be in danger of losing their traditional strength in smaller cities and the countryside.

As the VTsIOM post-election poll revealed, 77 per cent of Unity voters, 54 per cent of OVR and SPS voters, 32 per cent of Yavlinsky and Zhirinovsky voters, and 12 per cent of the KPRF voters cast their ballots for Putin. This cross-political spectrum support constitutes indirect proof that Putin's campaign strategy allowed voters of all ideological persuasions to see in him what they wanted to see. These expectations, however, may not survive in the long term. As president, Putin will have to make choices that will inevitably alienate one or another segment of the electorate.

Zyuganov received support from 75 per cent of the KPRF electorate. Moreover, 73 per cent of his voters supported his candidacy in the 1996 elections (see Table 11.7), a reaffirmation of the strong sense of loyalty of the Communist electorate. At the same time, he received 13 per cent of the LDPR electorate, 11 per cent of the OVR electorate, and 6 per cent of the Unity electorate. It is interesting to note that the degree of Zyuganov's support among the LDPR, OVR, and Unity electorates closely matches the percentage of voters in these parties who identify themselves as 'Communists.' All this suggests that should LDPR, OVR, and Unity disappear by the next election, these voters might embrace the KPRF as their party of choice.

In terms of age, gender, and economic well-being, Zyuganov's electorate was virtually identical to that of KPRF. However, there are some notable differences as well. While Zyuganov's electorate was the least adjusted to the political and socio-economic changes than the electorate of other candidates, it was substantially better adjusted than the KPRF electorate. Moreover, Zyuganov's electorate was substantially better educated than KPRF's. Finally, while 89 per cent of KPRF voters defined themselves as 'Communists,' only 53 per cent of Zyuganov's voters did so. Since Zyuganov could hardly appeal to economically better off and non-Communist voters, this finding suggests that the vote for Zyuganov was for some a protest vote against Putin and his policies.[29]

A comparison of the Yavlinsky and Yabloko electorate reveals striking similarities in the areas of age, gender, political identity, economic well-being, present and anticipated, as well as an easier adjustment to the political and socio-economic changes. Two striking differences between the two electorates are the levels of educational attainment and support for the war in Chechnya. Yavlinsky's voter was far better educated and far less supportive of the Chechen war than Yabloko's voter. In fact, while the Yabloko electorate was among the strongest group of supporters of the war in Chechnya, Yavlinsky's electorate had the lowest level of support. This finding suggests that Yavlinsky lost some of the least educated and the most ardent Chechen war supporters to Putin, while gaining the

---

[29] McFaul came to the same conclusion analysing the aggregate results of the election; see Michael McFaul, 'One Step Forward, Two Steps Back', *Journal of Democracy*, 11/3 (July 2000), 26–7.

Table 11.7 **Social characteristics and political orientation of the Russian electorate at the 2000 presidential elections**

	Voted for:			Non-voter	All replies
	Putin	Zyuganov	Yavlinsky		
Gender					
Male	39	49	51	50	46
Female	61	51	49	50	54
Education					
Less than secondary	31	35	8	23	28
Secondary	54	55	60	61	58
Higher	15	9	32	15	14
Age					
Mean	46	54	39	39	45
Standard deviation	18	16	13	16	18
Vote in 1996 presidential election					
Voted for Yeltsin	60	10	63	32	39
Voted for Zyuganov	15	73	2	11	26
Voted for neither	25	17	35	58	35
Support for actions of the Russian Government in Chechnya					
Strongly disapprove	3	6	8	5	4
Somewhat disapprove	10	12	23	16	13
Somewhat approve	45	46	53	45	46
Strongly approve	42	36	16	34	37
Extent of the party identification					
Identifies with a party	39	82	73	28	46
Does not	61	18	27	72	54
Broad political outlook					
Pro-market	38	8	46	22	26
Communist	9	53	2	8	18
Nationalist	10	7	7	6	8
Green	2	4	7	4	3
Other	4	4	5	5	5
None	37	25	34	55	40

Table 11.7 **continued**

	Voted for:			Non-voter	All replies
	Putin	Zyuganov	Yavlinsky		

Current family economic situation
All in all, how do you rate the economic situation of your family today?

Very bad	17	30	21	31	25
Not so good	53	51	48	44	49
Fairly good	29	19	32	24	25
Very good	2	0	0	1	1

Past family economic situation
How would you compare your family's economic situation with what it was before perestroika?

Past much worse	9	12	16	15	12
Past somewhat worse	18	4	24	17	15
Same	20	9	21	17	16
Past somewhat better	22	26	19	22	23
Past much better	31	50	21	30	34

Future family economic situation
What do you think the economic situation of your family will be in five years compared to now?

Future much worse	3	4	0	6	4
Future somewhat worse	6	15	7	9	9
Same	43	53	44	38	43
Future somewhat better	41	25	40	40	37
Future much better	7	3	9	8	7

Adaptation to change
How have the big changes that have occurred since Soviet times affected you?

Adapted	46	33	35	42	41
Hope to adapt	28	28	46	32	30
Live as before, no change	9	7	5	8	8
Can never adapt	16	32	14	19	20

Source: New Russia Barometer IX (14–18 April 2000); at www.russiavotes.org.

support of the better-educated voters and the least supportive of the Chechen war voters of SPS and OVR.

As one could expect, Putin's electorate shared many similarities to the electorate of Unity. Both electorates were strikingly similar in terms of their age, education, economic well-being, as well as being supportive of the Chechen war. However, while Unity's electorate was evenly divided between men and women, Putin's electorate was predominantly female. His strategy of appealing to female voters clearly achieved its goal. Putin's electorate also indicated a much better adaptation to the political and socio-economic changes and higher levels of political identity. These differences clearly corroborate VTsIOM's post-election survey finding that significant numbers of the SPS and OVR supporters voted for Putin.

Conclusions

In 1999 and 2000 Russians went to the polls to chose a new parliament and new president. These elections marked the end of the Yeltsin era in Russian politics, a politics that was defined by confrontation between Yeltsin and his allies in the ruling elite and the liberal movement and the Communist and nationalist opposition. Both the 1999 and 2000 elections were neither a referendum on Communism or on radical economic reforms. The parliamentary election functioned as a presidential primary for the two competing wings of the ruling elite. Unity's electoral success and OVR's failure made Putin the winner of the primaries and a president within three months. To all the other parties, the parliamentary election constituted an opportunity to consolidate their position on the political map or demonstrate their ability to survive. To scholars who study elections, the 1999 Duma elections provided additional evidence that institutional design, campaign strategies, organizational resources, and the mood of the electorate substantially matter for the final outcome. The Duma elections also showed us that parties have distinct social bases and that such factors as age, education, residence, gender, economic conditions, and adaptability to socio-economic changes play an important role in the choices Russians make at the ballot box.

The presidential elections showed that the front runners tend to adopt the campaign strategy that essentially worked for their parties during the parliamentary elections. In this sense, Putin in 2000 was no different from Zyuganov in 1996. However, what works in the parliamentary elections may not be effective in the presidential ballot. Zyuganov lost in 1996 and Putin might have avoided a run-off only due to a ballot falsification (see n. 28).

The presidential elections also showed us that while the electorates of the main presidential candidates shared some similarities with the electorates of their parties, there were also significant differences in such areas as gender, educational achievements, political identity, and support for the Chechen war. Finally, we also noted that there was a major difference in the voting patterns of the electorate of the big cities between the 1996 and the 2000 presidential elections.

The main feature of both elections was the great appeal of parties and politicians who pretended to be above politics. Moreover, two parties—OVR and Unity—parties that gained 37 per cent of the vote and had not existed six months before the vote, had no real ideology, and could disappear into the dustbin of history before the next scheduled elections. The rejection of politics and the rise and fall of parties created by various segments of the ruling elite in order to perpetuate their hold on power are unlikely to contribute to the consolidation of democracy in Russia. While negative campaigning is a permanent feature of campaigning in developed democracies, the negative campaign used by the Russia state-controlled media in both the 1999 and 2000 elections would never be accepted in the West as a legitimate part of democratic process. Moreover, these two elections taught the ruling elite how it could use the electoral process to perpetuate its hold on power and destroy political opponents. As such, these elections might have pulled Russia further away from Western-style democracy than pushed closer to it.

12 The Iceberg of Russian Political Finance

Vladimir Gelman

On 19 June 1996, just three days after the first round of the Russian presidential elections and only two weeks before the run-off between Russian President Boris Yeltsin and his Communist rival Gennadii Zyuganov, the President's security service arrested two men at the exit gate of the Russian White House. Those arrested, Arkadii Yevstafiev (an assistant to Anatolii Chubais, one of the key figures in Yeltsin's election campaign) and Sergei Lisovskii (who was in showbusiness but who also played an important role in Yeltsin's campaign), were carrying a Xerox-paper box containing $538,000 in cash; the money was to be used as payments to pop stars involved in pro-Yeltsin propaganda. According to their account, Yevstafiev and Lisovskii had been handed the box by Boris Lavrov, a commercial bank officer, who, in turn, had received the money personally from the Russian Deputy Minister of Finance. Yevstafiev and Lisovskii were released the following morning. However, the consequences of their arrest were far more far-reaching than those of a normal criminal incident. On 20 June Yeltsin signed decrees for the resignations of Alexander Korzhakov (his Security Service chief), Mikhail Barsukov (the Director of the Federal Security Service) and Oleg Soskovets (a First Deputy Prime Minister); the former two were among Yelstin's closest allies.[1] Then, following his victory in the run-off election, Yeltsin assigned Chubais as his Chief of Staff.

But what of the $538,000 in the box? In his public speeches Chubais referred to a 'provocation' by Korzhakov, allegedly aimed at disrupting the run-off election, and Chubais denied that there had been any intention of using that money for campaign purposes. However, almost five months later a popular newspaper, *Moskovskii Komsomolets*, published what it claimed to be the transcript of a meeting in June between Chubais, Viktor Ilyushin, a senior presidential aide, and one more person, still unknown, in which ways to cover up the use of the money in the campaign were discussed. This alleged meeting took place after the arrest of Lisovskii and Yevstafiev; in what is alleged to be its transcript Ilyushin was quoted as saying that he had told President Yeltsin they could catch fifteen to twenty men leaving the President Hotel (Yeltsin's campaign headquarters) with sports bags full of cash.[2] Since both Chubais and Ilyushin deny that this conversation ever took place, it is hard to be sure that Ilyushin was the man at the alleged meeting. But whoever that man was, he was absolutely correct in the main point he made: men with such sports bags could be caught

This chapter was first published in Peter Burnell and Alan Ware, eds., *Funding Democratization* (Manchester: Manchester University Press, 1998). Reproduced by kind permission of the author and Manchester University Press.

[1] A. Politkovskaya and E. Dikun, 'Natsional'naya tragediya na prokhodnoi pravitel'stva', *Obshchaya gazeta*, 25/8 (1996).

[2] A. Khinstein, 'Golosui, a to . . . ', *Moskovskii komsomolets*, 15 Nov. 1996, p. 3.

near all candidates' campaign headquarters—during campaigns almost every party and almost every candidate running for office in Russia used extra-legal (though not always illegal) payments of cash of, to put it mildly, either doubtful origin, or so-called 'black cash' (chernyi nal).[3]

Thus, the incident involving the cash in the Xerox-paper box was not an isolated incident in Russian political life. Even Communist rivals of Yeltsin's used similar methods in their campaigns; although one hard-line Communist, Viktor llyukhin, the Chairman of Duma Committee for Security, touched upon this topic in a press conference, that was his own private initiative. Before the run-off election all the media, except for Obshchaya gazeta, a moderate opposition newspaper, remained silent on the issue and almost all politicians followed suit.

What does this story suggest about Russian political finance and Russian politics more generally? Does money play the central role in campaigning and in day-to-day political affairs? What legal and political controls over political finance, if any, have been created so far, and how do they function? Last, but certainly not least, can the outcomes of elections and other aspects of Russian politics be bought? An attempt will be made in this chapter to answer these questions.

The institutional framework and the resources of the political game

Anyone who tries to analyse Russian (or post-Soviet) politics, is faced first with the problem of understanding the relevant institutions. The constitutional framework might be thought to be based on western models, because it includes institutions such as a presidency and a Constitutional Court that are borrowed from the experience of democratic (or, in Russian slang, 'civilised') countries. However, the functioning of these institutions often has little in common with the western prototypes. For instance, the absence of censors does not yet mean there is complete freedom of speech; again, although there may be competitive elections, the regimes are not always truly democratic—the Lukashenka regime in Belarus being the clearest example of this. This general point can also be made with respect to specific aspects of electoral and party politics. For example, the electoral law in Russia would seem in principle to conform with several liberal principles, such as judicial defence of electoral rights or the banning of the use by civil servants of their official status for the purpose of campaigning. While these objectives were laudable, they did not work in practice because the penalties for violations provided for in the law were of a purely symbolic kind.

Because of this, applying to post-Soviet politics notions such as 'democratic consolidation'[4] or 'post-communist authoritarianism'[5] should be undertaken with caution. When analysing the emerging political regime in Russia, models of a 'halfway house', like 'delegative democracy'[6] seem to be more helpful in trying to understand political affairs in

---

[3] E. Dikun and L. Sigal, 'Milliardy dlya diktatury elektorata', Obshchaya gazeta, 24/8 (1996); D. Skillen, 'Media coverage in the elections', in P. Lentini (ed.), Elections and Political Order in Russia: The Implications of the 1993 Elections to the Federal Assembly (Budapest: Central European University Press, 1995), 97–123.

[4] R. Orttung, From Leningrad to St Petersburg: Democratization in a Russian City (Basingstoke and London: Macmillan, 1995).

[5] P. Roeder, 'Varieties of post-Soviet authoritarian regimes', Post-Soviet Affairs, 10/1 (1994), 61–101.

[6] G. O'Donnell, 'Delegative democracy', Journal of Democracy, 5/1(1994), 55–69.

Russia.[7] On the one hand, elections under the communist regime could be described as neither free nor fair. That is, there was neither free competition between parties and candidates, nor fair access to the means of campaigning, nor, indeed, equal legal guarantees for electoral contestants. On the other hand, the ideal of liberal democracy is free and fair elections: a fully competitive contest between parties and candidates for the voters' support, with equal opportunities for all contestants. If elections under communism and those in an ideal liberal democracy represent the two ends of a continuum, then the practices of post-Soviet transitional regimes are far from either end. Russian elections may be described as free but not fair. They are free with respect to the level of competition; after December 1993 no single influential party or candidate at the national level could be stopped from participating in elections. Consequently, moves by the Central Electoral Commission (CEC) aimed at barring two opposition parties—Yabloko and Derzhava—during the 1995 parliamentary elections were halted by a decision of the Supreme Court.[8] But not all of the post-communist electoral process in Russia may be recognized as fair, since the competitors do not enjoy equal access to resources.[9]

Similar points can be made when considering aspects of party organization. The Soviet Union was a one-party state, while the ideal of liberal democracy is that of a multi-party system with organized parties competing for public offices. But what is 'a party' in post-communist Russia? Could the forty-three so-called 'electoral associations' that competed in the 1995 parliamentary elections be regarded as parties? Certainly, some of them were real political organizations based on popular leadership (such as the Liberal Democrats led by Vladimir Zhirinovskii, or Yabloko led by Grigorii Yavlinskii); some had an ideological label (like, the free-market-liberal Democratic Choice of Russia (DCR), led by Yegor Gaidar, or the hard-line 'Communists—Working Russia—for the Soviet Union', led by Viktor Anpilov). However, when using some kind of organizational definition of a political party,[10] only the Communist Party of the Russian Federation (CPRF), which claims to be the heir of the banned Communist Party of the Soviet Union, could be taken for a party. With the exception of the CPRF, Russian parties are not yet 'fully-fledged parties' on the local and regional levels as far as organizational development is concerned.[11]

At the same time, decision-making processes in Russian politics (including decision-making within the parties) are based mostly on patron–client relationships.[12] This has no legal recognition, but it is important—an example being the so-called 'party of power' which

[7] S. Fish, 'The advent of multipartism in Russia, 1993–1995', *Post-Soviet Affairs*, 11/4 (1995), 340–83; V. Gel'man, 'Regional'nye rezhimy: zavershenie transformatsii?', *Svobodnaya mysl'*, 9 (1996), 13–22.

[8] V. Gel'man, 'Vybory deputatov Gosudarstvennoi Dumy: pravila igry, zakonodatel'naya politika i pravoprimenitel'naya praktika', *Konstitutsionnoe pravo: vostochnoevropeiskoe obozrenie*, 1 (1996), 20–34.

[9] P. Lentini, 'Overview of the campaign', in Lentini, *Elections and Political Order in Russia*; R. Sakwa, 'The Russian Elections of December 1993', *Europe-Asia Studies*, 47/2 (1995), 195–227; Skillen, 'Media coverage'; M. Urban, 'December 1993 as a replication of late-Soviet electoral practices', *Post-Soviet Affairs*, 10/2 (1994), 127–58.

[10] J. La Palombara and M. Weiner, 'The origins and developments of political parties', in La Palombara and Weiner (eds.), *Political Parties and Political Development* (Princeton: Princeton University Press, 1966), 3–42.

[11] S. Fish, *Democracy from Scratch: Opposition and Regime in the New Russian Revolution* (Princeton: Princeton University Press, 1995); Fish, 'The advent of multipartism'; V. Kolosov (ed.), *Rossiya na vyborakh: uroki i perspektivy* (Moscow: CPT, 1995).

[12] M. Afanas'ev, *Pravyyashchie elity i gosudarstvennost' posttotalitarnoi Rossii* (Moscow: Institut Prakticheskoi Psikhologii, 1996).

includes officials of the executive branch of the government and their allies.[13] Since 1991 there have been several attempts in Russia to institutionalize this quasi-party but none have been fully successful. 'The party of power' phenomenon is based partly on the use of informal networks in the making of political decisions. This defines their mobilization strategy which could be understood as administrative mobilization. Administrative mobilization, which is especially effective in small towns and rural areas, includes the use of state or municipal resources for the purposes of executive officials and their allies, but sometimes, especially in ethnic republics, it looks more like some kind of informal contract of mutual loyalty between the elite and civil society.[14]

As far as ideology is concerned, the Russian party system is highly developed and embraces a vast spectrum—from libertarians to hard-line Stalinists.[15] With respect to organization, however, the Russian party system is underdeveloped. Operating in a 'delegative democracy' regime, where the government is not accountable to the parliament—either at national or sub-national levels—and without responsibility on the part of parties for the governmental agenda, it can be argued that the party system may be 'frozen' in its present form and may continue without much variation for many years.[16]

Sometimes the 'halfway house' state of party politics, as well as the political system as a whole, is understood as a temporary or 'unclear' stage of the transitional period. However, the argument being made here is that it may not necessarily be a phase of development of a standard model during a 'transition to democracy'.[17] Even at the micro level, such as in the case of political finance, much may remain unchanged. As the Russian political experience shows clearly, informal mechanisms of political practices have become embedded and they survive—at least in the form they have taken since 1993. An analysis of the structures of political parties, as well as electoral campaigning, does not reveal any tendency towards a transition to democracy, but, instead, there seems to be a stable form of politics with its own, written and unwritten, rules of the game, and with no tendency towards permanent change.

So what kind of strategies are deployed and resources used by parties and/or individual politicians in their competitive game, either during their day-to-day work or in seeking support during elections? There is no single model. Some, like the 'party of power', are using institutional resources. Others, like Zhirinovskii, for instance, are exploiting personal charisma. Still others, mainly communists, rely partly on their membership and partly on financial resources. However, as is shown below, the use of financial resources is usually ineffective unless it is combined with other resources which, in their turn, cannot be used effectively in the absence of money. If the former seems to be like eating salt without food, the latter is like eating food without salt.

[13] D. Badovskii, 'Tranformatsiya politicheskoi elity v Rossii: ot organizatsii professional"nykh revolutsionerov—k partii vlasti', *Polis*, 6 (1994), 42–58; A. Ryabov, ' "Partiya vlasti": popytka prevrashcheniya novoi rossiiskoi elity v veduschyu silu publichnoi politiki', in V. Kuvaldin *et al.* (eds.), *Partiino-politicheskie elity i elektoral'nye protsessy v Rossii* (Moscow: CKSIiM, 1996), 5–16.

[14] Afanas'ev, *Pravyaschie elity*; Badovskii, 'Transformatsiya politicheskoi'; Gel'man, 'Regional'nye rezhimy'.

[15] A. Salmin *et al.*, *Partiinaya sistema v Rossii v 1989–1993 gg: opyt stanovleniya* (Moscow: Nachala Press, 1994); Fish, 'The advent of multipartism'.

[16] A. Panebianco, *Political Parties: Organization and Power* (Cambridge: Cambridge University Press, 1988).

[17] G. O'Donnell and P. Schmitter, *Transitions from Authoritarian Rule: Tentative Conclusions about Uncertain Democracies* (Baltimore and London: Johns Hopkins University Press, 1986); S. Huntington, *The Third Wave: Democratizaton in the Late Twentieth Century* (Norman, Okla., and London: University of Oklahoma Press, 1991).

1. POWER RESOURCES, DIRECT AND INDIRECT

The advantage of incumbency (or being backed by incumbents) seems to be the most valuable resource. Incumbents, or incumbent-backed candidates, have the use of additional resources, from the support of the press (and free, indirect, 'advertising' in the media) to the use of civil servants in their own campaigns. The official support of a powerful official (from a governor to the President) is also very helpful in raising money for campaigning and the everyday needs of parties and politicians.

2. PERSONALITY RESOURCES

Some popular political figures rely on the sheer popularity of their names to start their campaigning without sufficient funds. For instance, the former Russian Vice-President, Alexander Rutskoi, who was born in Kursk, paid very little for the campaign he conducted there prior to the regional gubernatorial elections in October, 1996. Moreover, his campaign started just two days before the elections after Rutskoi had won a legal suit in the Supreme Court which allowed him to register as a candidate. Nevertheless, Rutskoi was supported by 78 per cent of voters. Some other charismatic leaders, quite popular in their constituencies, have also used personal popularity as the main resource in the political struggle.

Vladimir Zhirinovskii, the leader of the Liberal Democratic Party of Russia (LDPR), found another way to use personality resources. During the 1993 parliamentary elections he, as the party leader, used almost all the state-granted money to pay for air time when making more than twenty speeches on television. These speeches, aggressive but skilful, appealed to different social groups and were full of all kinds of promises (for instance, he promised a man to every woman).[18] However, the case of Zhirinovskii, who is such a good television campaigner, is somewhat exceptional in Russian politics.

3. CADRES

The myths of the 'gold of the Communist Party' must be ignored; Russian left wingers and their candidates (especially the CPRF) do not have 'big money' either for campaigning or for everyday needs. However, these parties are not poor either, and, especially before the 1996 presidential elections, they were busy establishing links with representatives of various sectors of Russian business.[19] But the main resource of the CPRF and its allies still lies in the significant number of local activists; they are well organized in local units based on old communist networks. (According to CPRF data, in January 1995 the number of party members was close to 500,000 which is more than the combined membership of all other Russian parties.) This resource provides opportunities for campaigning in different regions of the country, especially in rural areas. As the CPRF representatives noted themselves, they are using cadre resources for large-scale 'door-to-door' campaigning which, it seems, is more effective for their purposes than expensive advertising on a huge scale.[20]

---

[18] J. Hughes, 'The "Americanization" of Russian politics: Russia's first television election, December 1993', *Journal of Communist Studies and Transition Politics*, 10/2 (1994), 125–50; M. McFaul, 'Osmyslenie parlamentskikh vyborov 1993 g. v Rossi', *Polis*, 5 (1994), 124–6, Urban, 'December 1993'; Skillen, 'Media Coverage'.

[19] A. Zudin, 'Biznes i politika v prezidentskoi kampanii 1996 goda', *Pro et Contra*, 1/1 (1996), 46–60.

[20] Hughes, 'The "Americanization" of Russian politics'.

4. FINANCIAL RESOURCES

'Big money' as a single resource works badly in Russian politics. The candidacies in elections in the period between 1993 and 1996 of so-called 'New Russians' and 'traditional' business people were common, but also a failure in most cases. Vladimir Bryntsalov, the owner of the largest Russian pharmaceutical company, found himself in last place behind eleven other candidates in the 1996 presidential election. Vladimir Groshev, the Chairman of the board of one of the larger Russian banks, 'Inkombank', failed in the 1995 parliamentary election in a single-member district in Ryazanskaya oblast, despite the fact that his expenditures came to more than $200,000 (according to unofficial sources). The attempts of some 'New Russians' to create their own parties or 'blocks' were also unsuccessful. In 1993 the Party of Economic Freedom, led by Konstantin Borovoi, a self-proclaimed 'party of big business', was unable even to collect the 100,000 signatures of voters needed by a party in registering for the election. In fact, the 'New Russian' style of campaigning—including huge billboards, massive and expensive TV advertising, and a 'shocking' manner of delivering speeches—played a role in this failure: most Russian voters with their low standard of living, facing delays in the payment of wages and so on, instinctively disliked candidates who evidently had 'big money' backing their campaigns.

However, financial resources are necessary for both campaigning and everyday party needs. Money, if used in addition to power, personality, and cadre resources, can be effective in Russian politics. However, both the amounts and sources of the money used in politics remain somewhat mysterious.

The iceberg of political finance: the above-water and under-water elements

The electoral practices of the late-Soviet period give us clear examples of unfair campaigning. All the electoral costs were state-financed. The later amendments of the Constitution provided for the creation of a special 'common' electoral fund for the making of donations by individuals and companies. These donations were supposed to be distributed equally among all candidates. The same principle supposedly also guided access for all candidates to the media and to other means of campaigning.[21] However, the system proved unworkable. No one was committed to the idea of equal resources, and in many respects it also proved technically impossible to implement; for instance, it was supposed to provide for an equal number of public speeches by all candidates, and that was just not possible. At the same time, the state-owned resources (television, newspapers, other means of public address, and so on) were used to the advantage of those candidates supported by the Communist Party and their allies.[22] Their opponents, newly emerging political associations, had to resort to the use of illegal means of campaigning, using resources provided by the emerging private businesses and even some of the state-owned companies.[23] Although electoral commissions had the right to revoke the registrations of candidates who violated electoral law, legal

[21] A. Postnikov, 'Finansirovanie vyborov', in V. Vasil'ev (ed.), *Izbiratel'naya reforma: opyt, problemy, perspektivy* (Moscow: Manuscript, 1993), 95–8.
[22] V. Kolosov *et al.*, *Vesna-89: Geografiya i anatomiya palamentskikh vyborov* (Moscow: Progress, 1990); Orttung, *From Leningrad to St Petersburg*.
[23] Y. Brudny, 'The dynamics of "Democratic Russia", 1990–93', *Post-Soviet Affairs*, 9/2 (1993), 141–70.

sanctions during campaigning periods were not actually used because, as a legal analyst noted, events were moving too quickly for that to happen.[24] In the post-communist period, there was only a partial change in the situation: private funding was permitted, and the widely-proclaimed equal-access principle was abolished. Still, workable legal sanctions were never devised, nor did the use of state-owned resources for the benefit of incumbents disappear.

While institutional design, including electoral law, in the post-communist east European countries, was the result of national bargaining,[25] neither Russia's electoral system nor its constitutional arrangements were the result of any kind of round-table agreement; the same was also true with the decision on a constitutional assembly. Initially, it was the choice of a relatively narrow circle of free-market-liberal-orientated politicians and lawyers led by Dr Viktor Sheinis, a deputy of the Supreme Soviet of the Russian Federation. In the spring of 1993 this group drafted an electoral law which then was discussed by Russian politicians and experts.[26] However, almost all their comments concentrated on the electoral formula or on matters other than those of party finances. Moreover, according to one scholar, even the opponents of the reforms came up with no critique of the initial proposal.[27] Almost the entire draft was included in the set of electoral rules approved by Yeltsin's decree after the disbanding of the parliament in September 1993.[28]

The core of the reform of political finance was based on the principle of special 'electoral funds' to be used for the purposes of campaigning. According to Sheinis (in an interview given to the author in August 1994), he had borrowed this idea from the experience of political action committees in the United States. However, while in the United States such committees served as special organizations for campaigning, the electoral funds, according to the Russian law, were just bank accounts opened for donations. The sources of financing in Russia would vary between equal opportunity public funding approved by electoral commissions, donations from individuals and organizations, and the spending of candidates' own money or money from party funds. Donations from foreign nations and organizations, international institutions, state or local government institutions, military units, religious or charitable organizations, and companies whose capital contained more than a certain proportion of foreign capital were prohibited. (The latest rules have limited the permitted share of foreign capital in a donating company to 30 per cent of the total capital.) The maximum permitted size of funds was limited, by being tied to the kind of election involved and linked to the current level of minimum wage. For example, during the 1995

[24] Postnikov, 'Finansirovanie vyborov'.

[25] A. Lijphart, 'Democratization and constitutional choice in Czecho-Slovakia, Hungary and Poland, 1989–91', *Journal of Theoretical Politics*, 4/2 (1992), 207–23; B.Geddes, 'Initiation of new democratic institutions in Eastern Europe and Latin America', in A. Lijphart and C. Waisman (eds.), *Institutional Design in New Democracies: Eastern Europe and Latin America* (Boulder, Colo: Westview, 1996), 15–41.

[26] B. Strashun and V. Sheinis, 'Politicheskaya situatsiya v Rossii i novyi izbiratelnyizakon', *Polis*, 3 (1993), 65–9; D. Levchik, 'Osnovnye elementy elektoral'nogo prava i ikh primenenie v rossiiskom zakonodatel'stve 1992–1994', *Kentavr*, 5 (1994), 105–14; McFaul, 'Osmyslenie parlamentskikh vyborov'; Salmin *et al.*, *Partiinaya systema v Rossii*; Urban, 'December 1993'; A. Salmin, 'Vybory i izbiratel'nye sistemy: opyt Rossii v 1989–1993 godakh', *Sapere Aude*, 2 (1995), 8–27.

[27] Levchik, 'Osnovnye elementy'.

[28] 'Polozhenie o vyborakh deputatov Gosudarstvennoi Dumy Federal'nogo Sobraniya Rossiiskoi Federatsii v 1993 godu', *Bulleten Tsentral'noi Izbiratel'noi komissii*, 1 (1993).

elections the maximum amount a party (or 'electoral association' in Russian legal terms) could spend during any one campaign was 10.9 billion roubles (about $2.4 million) and spending by a candidate in a single-member district was limited to 437 million roubles ($95,000). Individuals could make donations of up to $188 to a single-member district candidate and $282 to an 'electoral association', while companies could donate as much as $1,880 and $18,800 respectively. By contrast, the public funding component of each party's funds came to just $25,500. So private funding was now the main source of campaign finances.

The regulations concerning the use of the media were based on a similar principle. The law provided for the right of each candidate or party to an equal number of speeches published free of charge. The electoral law and regulations issued by the Central Electoral Commission (CEC) applied only to the coverage provided by the so-called 'state' media, that is newspapers, television and radio stations either established, owned or sponsored by the state or municipal authorities, or financed from their budgets, or having some tax privileges.[29] This meant that the majority of TV and radio stations as well as some regional and local newspapers had to provide equal opportunities to all candidates and/or parties for pre-election campaigning. Indeed, candidates and parties did receive equally divided free newspaper space and air time. For instance, prior to the 1995 Duma elections each party was given thirty minutes of free air time on each of the nationwide television and radio stations. Additionally, they had the right to purchase more space or time, but the regulations required that the amount of purchased newspaper space or air time could not exceed the amount provided free. However, the cost of air time is high. During the presidential campaign in 1996 the price of a one-minute prime-time slot on the nationwide channels was $30,000. The distribution of air time and newspaper space (free or paid for) by state-owned or sponsored media was done by lot. As for non-state-owned media, the law remains silent as far as campaigning is concerned. The same is also true for editorial coverage of campaigns in state-owned media.

In making their initial proposals the reformers were informed by both their ideological preferences and their office-seeking interests. The ideological preferences were based on anti-state attitudes on the one hand, and on an overestimation of the virtues of entrepreneurship and private property, on the other. Their doctrine is based on the idea of a minimal state,[30] and the reformers rejected the idea of increasing the level of public financing for election campaigns and public financing of political parties in general. (The draft of the law on political parties, which included such a proposal, failed to pass in the parliament in 1994 and later was rewritten without any mention of public political financing. Eventually it passed in the lower chamber but was rejected by the upper chamber.) As Dr Sheinis said in an interview with the author in 1994: 'It is not quite so bad that some rich people buy votes and come to power. It is the state-owned redistribution that does the most harm to Russian democracy.'

Similar views are held by the leader of DCR, former Prime Minister Yegor Gaidar, who

---

[29] 'Federal'nyi zakon "Ob osnovnykh garantiyakh izbiratel'nykh prav grazhdan Rossiiskoi Federatsii"', *Rossiikaya gazeta*, 10 Dec. 1994, 4–5; 'Federal'nyi zakon "O vyborakh deputatov Gosudarstvennoi Dumy Federal'nogo sobraniya Rossiiskoi Federatsii"', *Rossiiskaya gazeta*, 28 June 1995, 4–6,

[30] Y. Gaidar, *Gosudarstvo i evolutsiya* (Moscow: Eurasia, 1995).

defined the social basis of his party as 'intelligentsia and entrepreneurs',[31] while one prominent DCR Duma deputy argued that the party 'would become the medium of interests of
large capital'. Alexey Ulyukaev, an ally of Gaidar's and the leader of the Moscow branch of
the DCR, says that the branches of a party should be established as commercial structures
for the sake of financial independence and the strengthening of the party's social basis.[32] In
practice, this can lead to criminal activity by local DCR activists. For instance, for six months
the DCR party structure was headed by Oleg Boiko, a businessman who owned a company
that turned out to be a pyramid-type scam. (Despite the fact that Sheinis has long been a
member of social-liberal Duma faction, Yabloko, his attitudes and political practices are
closer to those of the DCR.)

However, one reason above all other for 'institutional design'[33] taking this particular form
is the reformers' own interests in running for public office. While reformers are in favour of
supporting private business, they are also involved in taking control of state-owned
resources, including, in 1993, television. Democratic Russia (whose successor in the 1993
elections was the Russia's Choice block and, later still, the DCR) used both of these
resources in their campaigning.[34] The rules crafted for Russia's Choice (as well as for other
kinds of 'parties of power') facilitated various practices in relation to large-scale advertising
(television clips, billboards, colour posters, direct mail, and so on) and 'grey' propaganda—
that is, indirect advertising and comments on television and other state-owned media, and
the use of official status and privileges for electioneering.[35]

Generally speaking, all electoral procedures were constructed on this sort of basis. For
instance, the nomination of a candidate (or a party list) is controlled through the collection
of voters' signatures necessary for the registration (a minimum of 1 per cent of all voters in a
single-member district, or 100,000 signatures for a national list). Supposedly, to be able to
register a party needs to demonstrate at least a minimal level of popular support for its
candidates. In reality, two other ways of signature collection were developed. The first, or
'industrial', method involves coercion applied to signatories at state institutions, enterprises,
army and police barracks, universities and so on. The second method was a simple purchasing of signatures (during the 1993 campaign a signature could be purchased for between 100
and 500 roubles ($0.05 to $0.25)).[36] As a result the system of political finance created by the
more liberal reformers can be likened to an iceberg: there is the visible ('above-water')
portion of it consisting of electoral funds used for the purchasing of air time on TV and
radio. According to various sources this portion of political finance constitutes between 5
and 10 per cent of total expenditures in a campaign[37] and does not even come close to
covering day-to-day party expenses. Anyone analysing the official data on campaign
finances (that is, the amount donated by companies or individuals, the breakdown of party

[31] Y. Gaidar, 'Vystuplenie na uchreditl'nom s''ezde partii "Demokraticheskii vybor Rossii"', *Otkrytaya politika*, 2
(1994), 49–54.

[32] A. Ulyukaev, *Liberalizm i politika perekhodnogo perioda* (Moscow: Eurasia, 1995).

[33] Geddes, 'Initiation of new democratic institutions'.

[34] Y. Brudny, 'The dynamics of "Democratic Russia"'.

[35] Hughes, 'The "Americanization" of Russian politics'; Urban, 'December 1993'; Lentini, 'Overview of the
campaign'.

[36] Urban, 'December 1993'; Lentini, 'Overview of the campaign'; Gel'man, 'Vybory deputatov'; S. White *et al.*,
How Russia Votes (Chatham, NJ: Chatham House, 1997).

[37] Dikun and Sigal, 'Milliardy dlya diktatury'.

expenditures, and so on), provided by the financial department of the CEC (Vybory deputatov, 1996), will see only the 'above-water' portion of the iceberg. These data give no indication at all as to the resources forming the 'under-water' part of it.

Some techniques used in the area of hidden political finance have been described by two Russian political journalists, Elena Dikun and Lev Sigal.[38] Ironically, their article was published the very day that the two Yeltsin campaigners were arrested while carrying $538,000 in the Xerox-paper box. A number of ways of raising and spending money have been identified by Dikun and Sigal, and by other investigators as well, and some of the techniques used in the 'hidden' component of Russian political funding are indicated below.

1. DIRECT PAYMENTS IN 'BLACK CASH'

This method is never used when paying for the means of propaganda (such as air time), but is used mainly to cover other costs such as the salaries of campaign employees, the services of observers at polling stations, security guards, current office expenses, payments during signature collections, and, most of all, payoffs for 'grey propaganda'; these are payments to journalists who show a party's candidates in a favourable light (or the opponents in an unfavourable light) and to popular actors, singers, sports personalities and other popular figures who support publicly the candidate or party in question.[39] Then again, there are lottery sales, charitable acts in the name of the candidate or party, among other techniques.

2. CONCEALMENT OF PAYMENTS FROM 'BLACK CASH'

With this method some services, such as the making of posters and television clips containing pre-electoral promises such as the lowering of prices, are nominally paid for out of electoral funds, but this is a façade because the payments are actually made using 'black cash'.

3. PAYMENTS FOR STATE-CONTROLLED SERVICES BYPASSING OFFICIAL ELECTORAL FUNDS

Some banks and other companies either receive tax concessions or incur no penalties for tax underpayment in exchange for covering expenses in the election campaign of an incumbent candidate. At the same time, such companies often make simultaneous donations to the campaigns of opposing candidates as a form of insurance in case of political change. This kind of game can be dangerous. After the 1996 presidential elections one large and well-known Russian bank, Tveruniversalbank, which had close ties with the Communists—the former Soviet Prime Minister Nikolai Ryzhkov headed its board of directors—went bankrupt. This was a punishment from the 'Party of Power' for its contributions to the 'wrong' candidate. There were also rumours about the imminent bankruptcy of another bank, Inkombank, which supported Alexander Lebed. However, Inkombank, the fifth largest bank in Russia, still remains in business.

---

[38] Dikun and Sigal, 'Milliardy dlya diktatury'.
[39] Ibid.; Kas'yanenko, 'Protokoly kremlevskikh mudretsov', *Sovetskaya Rossiya*, 10 Oct. 1996, p. 2.

4. THE SELLING OF KEY POSITIONS IN THE PARTIES

During the 1995 parliamentary elections the seventh candidate on the LDPR party list was Mikhail Gutseriev, a businessman from the Ingush Republic (a Russian region on the Chechen border), who had, among others, sponsored 'invisible payments' to the party's campaign but who had never been a member of the party. After the elections, Gutseriev was nominated as a Deputy Chairman of the State Duma by the LDPR as a reward for his support. The same picture unfolds when looking at Yabloko, where, at the same elections, the number 8 position on the party list was held by Mikhail Yur'ev, an entrepreneur who also had never been known to be a member of the party. He had hardly any political experience at all but he too was nominated as a Deputy Chairman of Duma. The same practice has been observed in some regional and local elections (St Petersburg, Sverdlovskaya oblast).

However, the 1993 campaign clearly shows that the connection between the level of resources available and electoral successes is not always a straightforward one.[40] For example, even according to the official data, the most expensive campaign (that of Russia's Choice) cost the party 183 times as much as the total costs of the CPRF campaign, while the number of seats they obtained came only to 25 per cent of the total (forty as against the thirty-two won by the CPRF). Although there is only incomplete data on the financing of campaigns in sub-national elections, particular examples from that level of election show a similar picture.

Although almost every parliamentary faction condemned this system of political finance, the new electoral law (On Basic Guarantees of Electoral Rights of Citizens of the Russian Federation worked out in the Duma and passed in 1994) as well as the law relating to parliamentary elections passed in 1995 left the 1993 financial scheme intact, and it still remains largely unchanged. The new law simply limited the maximum permitted size of electoral funds and the amount of ('paid-for') time on television, and banned the use of 'black cash' as well as bribes to voters. However, the law failed to introduce any effective sanctions to deter these practices.

It is clear why the right wingers supported the status quo rules but the logic of the left wing in supporting it, to their own disadvantage, is still unclear. In all probability, the CPRF and its allies hoped for electoral success because of their massive membership, and in counting on door-to-door campaigning they paid little attention to the role of money. As is shown below, this approach has not been wholly successful, since traditional electioneering practices did not prove sufficient to produce successful outcomes in presidential elections.

Can elections be bought?

A crucial question should now be asked—can elections in Russia be bought? The answer to this question must be somewhat Delphic: 'no and at the same time—yes'! On the one hand, buying votes directly has usually produced little success. The best-known case of this sort goes back to the 1995 parliamentary elections in the 209th (single-member) district in St

---

[40] Hughes, 'The "Americanization" of Russian politics'; McFaul, 'Osmyslenie parlamentskikh vyborov'; Urban, 'December 1993'; Skillen, 'Media coverage'.

Petersburg, when Lev Konstantinov, the head of the company, Khoper-Invest, paid 15,000 roubles ($3.3) plus free food to every pensioner who voted for him. Konstantinov was prosecuted, but in any case he had received just 2 per cent of the vote, finishing ninth out of the twenty-four candidates.[41] In certain rare cases, when financial resources are supplementing personal popularity, greater success than this is possible. An example of this occurred during by-elections to the State Duma in the 109th (single-member) district in the Moscow region in October 1994. Sergei Mavrodi, a businessman, and the head of a pyramid-type company, MMM, was accused of having not paid taxes; he needed to get elected as a deputy, before a decision was made to prosecute him, in order to take advantage of immunity from prosecution that holding office would grant him. Mavrodi posed as a victim of tax investigators, and he paid cash and dispensed gifts to voters, including promising a donation of $100,000 to local development projects, supplements to pensions for all elderly people in the district, and so on. He was elected.

Buying votes, irrespective of the form of payment—beer, tea, cigarettes, promises of money from pension funds or insurance companies, lottery tickets, charitable donations, or whatever—does not usually help candidates, and it may have very little effect on the way the votes are cast. In contrast, however, buying votes indirectly, through various forms of implicit advertising and administrative mobilizations of voters is more effective, and this proved especially true during 1996 elections.

The campaigns of 1995–96 showed that the legal guarantees of access to the media for candidates and parties were observed to some degree, at least at the national level. This was not always so at local levels though. There were cases of damage thereby being done to some candidates' campaigns. For instance, the advertisements of one of the candidates in Kalmykia were stopped when he became critical of the Kalmykian President. In Moscow and the Moscow Region certain local television companies, such as MTK and Podmoskov´e, refused to guarantee free air time to candidates since there was no profit in it for them. This was important since, in general, television advertisements, both the free ones and those that are paid for, play an important role in campaigning.

The under-water component of the 'financial' iceberg, which is inaccessible to the law and to regulation, has given candidates ample opportunities to use indirect forms of campaigning and to employ resources such as air time and newspaper space, even on state-owned media. Non-political television and radio programmes were used for this. At the time of 1995 parliamentary elections Irina Khakamada, the leader of pre-electoral block Obshchee delo, appeared on the lottery show, Wonder Field, while before the elections in 1993 candidates from the pro-government block Russia's Choice showed up on television talking about tennis, theatre and similar topics. Then again, during the 1995 elections ORT, the so-called Russian Public Television, but in fact very much a supporter of the current government, kept showing films made by popular movie maker Nikita Mikhalkov who was second on the candidate list of the ruling party, Our Home—Russia (OHR).

In addition to pre-election advertisements in the 1995 and 1996 campaigns, ORT ran so-called 'social advertising clips'; these contained no electoral slogans but they were designed to create a psychological environment favourable to candidates of the ruling party.[42] Mikhalkov himself played the role of an aeronaut flying over Russia before returning home (which

---

[41] Gel'man, 'Vybory deputatov'.   [42] Ibid.

was meant to symbolize the electoral return of OHR). Officially this was not considered to be advertising but, clearly, it was understood that way by the viewers.

Since television news programmes are popular among voters, and therefore have strong effects on them, the candidates supported by the sponsors of television stations were shown in a favourable light, while their rivals were shown in an unfavourable light or were ignored. For instance, during the 1996 presidential election campaign three nationwide television channels ORT, RTR and NTV devoted 53 per cent of prime air time between 6 May and 3 July to coverage of Yeltsin while Zyuganov had only 18 per cent of the time, and the remaining candidates received a mere 11 per cent between them. More significantly, the positive references to Yeltsin outnumbered the negative ones to President Yeltsin by 492 while the negative references to Zyuganov outnumbered by 313 the positive references to him. Clearly, television stations were used for manipulating the media to the advantage of pro-government candidates.[43]

Analysis of press coverage undertaken by the European Institute for the Media, in Dusseldorf, revealed a similar picture. News and comments in general were described as 'strident, harsh and one-sided'.[44] The same style of news coverage was noted during the elections for regional governors.

Yeltsin's team used illegal methods without hesitation and with total impunity. As an official on the presidential staff stated: 'We are not about to give the Communists equal time or conditions. They don't deserve it.'[45] But what were the origins of this kind of one-sided coverage? Of course, several journalists had strong anti-Communist (or pro-government) attitudes and had personal reasons to engage in unfair campaigning. Nikolai Svanidze, a Russian Television Company commentator admitted: 'There is a political fight on here that has no rules. And should Communists win the media will lose independence. There is no choice.'[46] On the other hand, the use of administrative mobilization, especially at regional and local levels, was strong. During the elections for the Governor of St Petersburg in May 1996 all the local newspapers, even those not owned or sponsored by the state, broadcast news and comments favouring the incumbent, Anatolii Sobchak. When some journalists from the newspaper *Nevskoe vremya* expressed their independent views, they were forced to resign. In return for its loyalty to Sobchak this newspaper had been given a prestigious office at a low rent, and its editor-in-chief had been given a fashionable apartment in the centre of St Petersburg.[47] Opposing candidates were not mentioned and were totally excluded from both television and newspapers' news coverage, leaving these candidates with only their own air time and space in the newspapers. Again, during the 1996 presidential campaign, mentioning the name of one candidate, Grigorii Yavlinskii, was prohibited by television officials and governors in some areas.

Yeltsin's campaign in 1996 had no monetary problems. Since the legally permitted, 'above-water', portion of the financial 'iceberg' consisted of just $3 million, the under-water portion was many times the size of this—possibly hundreds of times its size. (There are

[43] White *et al.*, *How Russia Votes*.

[44] Quoted in White *et al.*, *How Russia Votes*.

[45] Ibid.

[46] Ibid.

[47] T. Drabkina, 'Sankt-Peterburg v mae 1996 goda', *Politicheskii monitoring*, 5/1 (1996); B. Vishnevskii, 'Nevezenie na nevskikh beregakh', *Rossiiskaya Federatsiya*, 21(1996), 18–20.

different evaluations of Yeltsin's 'under-water' component, ranging from $100 million to $500 million.) Covering the costs incurred in his campaign involved both state-controlled and other resources. One part of the state-owned resources used by the President in the campaign was the so-called 'executive vertical' which consisted of the whole hierarchy of civil servants, from the top down. The effects of administrative mobilization could be illustrated by the case of Novosibirskaya oblast. Here, the Regional Governor Vitalii Mukha (a former regional Communist Party leader who had been dismissed by Yeltsin, but then returned to power after election) rejected the idea of his participation in Yeltsin's campaign, on the grounds that that would be in violation of the law. In fact, Yeltsin's results in the first round of the elections in that area were much worse than in the neighbouring Omskaya oblast, while the levels of support for the Communists were almost the same. The President and his government then used every opportunity to delay paying wages and pensions in Novosibirskaya. Then there is the case of Nikolai Fedorov, the popularly elected President of Chuvashiya Republic where Yeltsin was defeated, who wrote a letter to the President after the election asking him not to punish the people of Chuvashiya by withholding budget transfers from Moscow in retaliation for their 'wrong' voting.

The campaign resources that did not come from the state budget were donated by large capitalist interests, mainly banks and the oil and gas industry.[48] This money was used primarily to pay for the means of propaganda. Pop and rock stars gave shows in the Russian provinces, under the title 'Golosui, a to proigraesch' ('Choose or lose'), which was paid for in 'black cash', including the cash from the notorious Xerox-paper box mentioned earlier. During the campaign an anti-Communist newspaper, *Ne dai Bog!* ('God Forbid'), circulated 10,000,000 copies through direct mail. According to personal messages addressed to top-level Yeltsin campaigners, the salaries of these people during the campaign were about $3,000 to $4,000 per month, paid in 'black cash' (the minimum monthly wage at that time was about $20). The installation of certain top businessmen at the highest levels of official hierarchy in the wake of the elections (Vladimir Potanin as the Deputy Prime Minister, Boris Berezovskii as the Deputy Secretary of Security Council), might also be interpreted as a kind of payment for their financial backing of the President in his campaign.

Four months after the elections, a Communist-backed newspaper, *Sovetskaya Rossiya*, published some records relating to the 'under-water' portion of the iceberg of Yeltsin's campaign finances.[49] According to these unofficial notes on the expenses incurred in Yeltsin's campaign, money had been paid for parties and public appearances at which public statements in support of Yeltsin had been made (for instance, the support of the Women of Russia movement had cost about $160,000). Payments were also made for the services of state-owned and 'independent' television and radio stations, information agencies, newspapers, and so on, which had presented the campaign from a 'correct' angle. Some actions on behalf of Yeltsin's campaign were paid for directly by business groups or business people who had been given substantial privileges by the President. For example, there is the National Sports Fund, which up to 1996 had held customs privileges with respect to the importation of tobacco and alcohol.

As a result, the CPRF and Yeltsin's other opponents were defeated. The Communists, being well organized, were able to compete against the administrative mobilization and

---

[48] Zudin, 'Biznes i politika'.   [49] Z. Kas'yanenko, 'Protokoly kremlevskikh mudretsov'.

financial domination of their opponents, but ultimately they were unable to overcome the combination of the latter's extraordinary financial resources and the full force of the state machine.

Conclusion

As the preceding observations show, the role of money in Russian political campaigning and day-to-day political affairs is relatively important, although not yet decisive. The anti-state attitudes and liberal reformers' interest in the support of business people resulted in the massive use of 'black cash' and other hidden resources—all of this happening in the absence of any effective degree of public control. These conditions created an environment of political corruption at all levels of Russian politics.

The iceberg-like system of political finance has, certainly, made many opponents. Scandals like the one involving the money in the Xerox-paper box erupt from time to time;[50] they resonate both in public opinion and among the political elite, but with no real consequences. In well-established democracies, such as Italy or Japan, scandals in the realm of political finance have forced some politicians to try to shift to 'clean hands' politics.[51] By contrast, in Russia's 'halfway house', not a single politician involved in corruption has ever left his or her post after being caught, although some of them may have been placed under investigation following their resignation from powerful positions. Situations like this sometimes look similar to the practices of the late-communist period when members of 'nomenklatura' could be prosecuted after leaving the Communist Party and powerful positions.

Since the Russian political elite has achieved an accord concerning the main policy-making issues, but not democracy,[52] this kind of 'elite settlement'[53] expresses the political society's own interests rather than the attitudes of their constituency. For instance, since 1994 there have been eight cases where prosecutors have applied to the deputies of both chambers of the Russian Parliament for permission to arrest Russian MPs, but only in one case (the above-mentioned Sergei Mavrodi) has the State Duma voted in favour of giving such permission. This makes the destruction of the iceberg unlikely to happen soon. On the one hand, the CEC declared in October 1996 that special legislation on political finance designed to end the 'financial iceberg' phenomenon was necessary, and that it was planning the drafting of a new law to this effect. However, having such a law approved by the Russian political elite—that is, by both chambers of the Parliament and the President—will be difficult.

Thinking in more general terms, the status of political finance depends entirely on the overall status of law and order in Russia. If extra-legal relationships continue to dominate over legality, it is unlikely that the system of political finance will function without violating

---

[50] Ibid; Khinstein, 'Golosui, a to . . . '; Politkovskaya and Dikun, 'Natsional'naya tragediya'.

[51] H. Alexander and R. Shiratori, 'Introduction', in H. Alexander and R. Shiratori (eds.), *Comparative Political Finance Among the Democracies* (Boulder, Colo: Westview, 1994), 1–11.

[52] A. Fadin, 'Obshchestvennoe soglasie v tselom dostignuto', *NG-scenarii*, 4 (1996), p. 1.

[53] M. Burton *et al.*, 'Introduction: elite transformations and democratic regimes', in J. Higley and R. Gunther (eds.), *Elites and Democratic Consolidation in Latin America and Southern Europe* (Cambridge: Cambridge University Press, 1992), 1–37.

the law. Certainly the key question is: how long can the 'halfway house' political regime in Russia last? If further steps are taken toward democratization and they become irreversible, then the political elite will be forced to shift towards a 'cleaner' set of rules of the game, and that should include political finance. But if the present sort of political regime becomes 'frozen' for the duration, then the 'iceberg' of political finance will not melt.

13 The Impact of Parliamentary Electoral Systems in Russia

Robert G. Moser

Giovanni Sartori has described the electoral system as 'the most specific manipulative instrument of politics.'[1] If this is true, then decisions involving the electoral arrangements of new democracies in the post-Communist world are among the most important decisions leaders of these new states will make. Among social scientists who study electoral engineering in general, there has emerged a broad consensus that elections based on proportional representation (PR) tend to foster multiparty systems, whereas 'plurality,' or winner-take-all, systems tend to produce two-party systems.[2] Moreover, proportional representation and multiparty systems are judged to be more representative, providing greater access to government office for more social groups, and more legitimate, providing greater correspondence between a party's proportion of the electoral vote and its proportion of seats in the legislature. Plurality systems are less representative but provide greater governmental stability by producing two-party systems and single-party majority government, rather than the less stable multiparty coalitions endemic in PR systems. Thus, the dilemma facing electoral engineers is whether to assign priority to the representativeness of PR and risk potential party proliferation and cabinet instability, or to opt for the stability of the two-party system and parliamentary majorities of the plurality system and give up some minority representation in the process.[3] Currently, one of the primary goals of electoral studies has become to

This chapter is an abbreviated version of an article which first appeared in *Post-Soviet Affairs*, 13/3 (July–Sept. 1997) 284–302. Reproduced by kind permission of the author and V. H. Winston (Bellwether Publishing).

[1] Giovanni Sartori, 'Political Development and Political Engineering', in John D. Montgomery and Albert O. Hirschman, eds., *Public Policy* (Cambridge, Mass: Harvard University Press, 1968), 273.

[2] See Maurice Duverger, *Political Parties: Their Organization and Activity in the Modern State* (London: Methuen, 1954), 226; Douglas W. Rae, *The Political Consequences of Electoral Laws*, 2nd edn, (New Haven: Yale University Press, 1971), 114–25; Giovanni Sartori, 'The Influence of Electoral Systems: Faulty Laws or Faulty Method?' in Bernard Grofman and Arend Lijphart, eds., *Electoral Laws and their Political Consequences* (New York: Agathon, 1986), 63–5; Rein Taagepera and Matthew S. Shugart, *Seats and Votes: The Effects and Determinants of Electoral Systems* (New Haven: Yale University Press, 1989), 112–25; Arend Lijphart, *Electoral Systems and Party Systems: A Study of Twenty-Seven Democracies, 1945–1990* (Oxford: Oxford University Press, 1994), 57–77. Plurality systems are also sometimes referred to as 'first-past-the-post' systems, for they award the contested seat to the candidate with the most votes, whether this total is a majority or not.

[3] See Guy Lardeyret, 'The Problem with PR', in Larry Diamond and Marc F. Plattner, eds., *The Global Resurgence of Democracy* (Baltimore: The Johns Hopkins University Press, 1993), 159–64; Quentin Quade, 'PR and Democratic Statecraft,' in ibid. 165–70; and Arend Lijphart, 'Double-Checking the Evidence,' in ibid 171–7.

design methods of fine-tuning electoral systems in ways that *combine* the best elements of PR and plurality systems.[4]

It is an open question, though, whether these generalizations, derived from research on established Western democracies, apply with equal force to the new democracies in the post-communist world. Indeed, in this chapter I contend that Russia's experience in her first two parliamentary elections (1993 and 1995) casts doubt on some of our most fundamental generalizations about electoral systems. Most importantly, winner-take-all elections in single-member districts did not produce two large parties, or even two-candidate races at the district level, as hypothesized in Sartori's modification of 'Duverger's law.'[5] Rather, party proliferation in the plurality race rivaled that of the PR portion of the 1993 election. In 1995, more parliamentary parties actually emerged from the plurality half of the election than from the PR contest. Moreover, dramatically different levels of disproportionality produced under the same PR rules in 1993 and 1995 suggest that the electoral system was not as influential on the disproportionality of votes to seats as the literature predicts it will be. While these findings contradict long-held hypotheses on the influence of electoral arrangements on party systems, I do not conclude that the electoral system has had no impact on the Russian party system. Rather, I argue that proportional representation has strengthened political parties, whereas plurality elections have fostered an influx of independent candidates that has undermined the role of parties. Moreover, each electoral system has encouraged the survival and success of different types of political parties.

Russia's mixed electoral system

Russia's post-Communist electoral system is a unique blend of PR and plurality electoral systems. Loosely modelled after the German system, Russia's lower house, the State Duma, consists of 450 deputies equally divided into two electoral arenas. Voters cast two ballots, one for an individual candidate and one for a party or electoral bloc. Half of the deputies are elected in 225 single-member plurality districts. The other half are elected in a party-list election, based on proportional representation, in one nationwide electoral district. Not only do the two portions differ in electoral formula but, more importantly, they differ dramatically in district magnitude.

Finally, the two halves of Russia's mixed electoral system are independent of one another. Unlike the German and other two-tiered, mixed electoral systems, Russia's two elections are not linked through a system of compensatory seats. The PR election is not designed to correct the disproportionality of the plurality elections. Rather, the two parts of Russia's electoral system are more like two separate elections occurring simultaneously for the same legislative body. Results for the two halves of the system are calculated separately and distribution of seats for the PR portion in no way affects the distribution of seats in the plurality portion, and *vice versa*. Such a dichotomy makes Russia a useful laboratory for studying electoral systems by isolating the consequences of dramatically different electoral

---

[4] See Lijphart, *Electoral Systems*, 139–52.
[5] Giovanni Sartori, *Comparative Constitutional Engineering* (London: Macmillan, 1994), 44.

Table 13.1 **Russia's mixed electoral system—two halves compared**

Electoral formula	District magnitude	Number of districts	Assembly size	Legal threshold
Plurality	1	225	225	–
PR, LR-Hanea	225	1	225	5%

Source: Election Law Compendium (1995), 293–4.

systems through their simultaneous use in a single country.[6] Table 13.1 shows graphically the key elements of the two halves of Russia's mixed electoral system.

This comparison of electoral systems within Russia is not without potential problems. The most severe is cross-contamination between the two cases compared. Unlike cross-national analysis or analysis across time, the electoral systems being compared in this test are not entirely independent of one another. They form two halves of one electoral system for the same legislative body in the same election. No matter how independently the two halves of the system operate, the separation of the Russian electoral system into two systems for the purposes of comparison remains artificial. Therefore, unlike comparisons of elections in different countries or elections in the same country taking place at different times, the results of the two electoral systems under investigation in this methodological scheme more than likely will influence one another to some extent. Parties that do well in one half of the election could be expected to have a coattail effect that improves their performance in the other half of the election. This could pollute the test of disproportionality and multipartism of the two contrasting systems. For example, if one or two large parties dominate the single-member plurality races, this may have coattail effects that produce greater vote shares in the PR contest. Consequently, the effective number of parties under PR rules would be lower than if the system had a purely PR electoral system. This is what is expected under conceptualization of Russia's system.[7] It corresponds to Sartori's argument that the plurality system is strong in its capacity to restrict the number of parties while PR systems are feeble and simply allow the number of social cleavages to be expressed as parties.[8] Conversely, the PR half of the election may allow for the establishment of a larger number of viable political parties that then go on to contest and win some plurality seats that would not survive under a purely plurality system.

While it is important to keep the danger of cross-contamination in mind, the comparison remains a useful one. Faulty conclusions should be easy to identify. If cross-contamination was significant, it should show up relatively clearly in the results of the analysis, such as a two-party configuration in both the PR and plurality contests, or a multiparty system under both electoral systems. Moreover, the same parties would be successful in both halves of the electoral system.

[6] For a contrasting viewpoint, see Matthew Shugart, *Building the Institutional Framework: Electoral Systems, Party Systems, and Presidents*, Working Paper 2.26 (Berkeley: Center for German and European Studies, University of California, 1994), 10–15.

[7] See Shugart, *Building the Institutional Framework*.

[8] Sartori, *Comparative Constitutional Engineering*, 54–8.

Such was not the case in Russia in 1993 and 1995. Results from the two halves of the Russian electoral system were remarkably different, suggesting very different consequences arising from the two electoral systems. This was particularly true in the first election (1993), in which partisan affiliations were not included on the ballot in the single-member district plurality races. The nonpartisan ballot greatly hindered 'straight-ticket voting' and substantially diminished the threat of cross-contamination between the PR and plurality portions of the election. Indeed, the winner in the PR half of the 1993 election, the Liberal Democratic Party of Russia (LDPR) led by ultranationalist Vladimir Zhirinovskiy, did miserably in the single-member plurality races. The introduction of a partisan ballot in 1995 witnessed greater correlation of results between the PR and plurality elections, although these elections also saw dramatic differences in results between the two parts of the election. Nowhere can there be found the expected dominance of plurality influence over PR. If anything, one could argue the opposite relationship: proportional representation may have overridden plurality effects in Russia. Regardless, parties experienced drastically different levels of success under the different systems. These facts suggest very limited cross-system contamination. The reason patterns of disproportionality and multipartism in Russia did not correspond to expectations had less to do with cross-contamination between the comparable cases and more to do with the particular social environment of post-communist development in Russia.

Proportional representation in Russia: 1993 and 1995

The PR half of Russia's mixed electoral system was conducted in a single nationwide electoral district; it thus had a very high district magnitude, similar to that found in the most proportional PR systems in the world, such as Israel and the Netherlands. However, its relatively high legal threshold of 5 percent significantly constrained the proportionality of the system, making it more similar to what Lijphart has called moderate PR systems, as found in Germany or Sweden.[9] If Russia follows the pattern of other democratic systems, one would expect her PR electoral process to produce more than two parties but not the severe party proliferation that could exist without the constraining filter of the 5-percent legal threshold.

Table 13.2 reports the major effects of the PR and plurality systems on Russian parties in the 1993 and 1995 parliamentary elections for the State Duma. The most striking difference between 1993 and 1995 was the number of parties contesting the two elections. In 1993, thirteen electoral blocs managed to collect the 100,000 signatures necessary for inclusion on the ballot. In 1995, authorities doubled the signature requirement to 200,000, yet 43 blocs were able to collect the signatures required to get onto the ballot. This difference in the number of parties contesting the election made for drastic differences in the effect of the 5-percent threshold on representation. In the relatively less crowded field of 1993, the distribution of the vote was such that eight electoral blocs managed to overcome the threshold and a relatively small proportion of the popular vote (about 9 percent) was wasted on unsuccessful parties. In 1995, the vote was so fractionalized across the field of 43 blocs that only four parties managed to cross the 5-percent barrier, while 49 percent of the vote was wasted on parties that received no legislative seats.

[9] Lijphart, *Electoral Systems*, 35–6.

The biggest reason for the large increase in the number of parties in 1995 was the nature and length of the signature-collection campaign. The 1993 election was a snap election, called without notice and having a much shorter period for collecting the signatures required to get on the ballot. Many aspiring parties and blocs did not have the time to establish the grass-roots organization necessary to collect 100,000 signatures distributed across Russia.[10] Moreover, signature collection was hindered by the tense conditions following the constitutional crisis of October, in which President Yeltsin dissolved the legislature and then violently rooted out the opposition holed up in the White House. Several parties were banned following these events; surely some citizens felt uncomfortable giving their signatures and passport numbers under such conditions, particularly to opposition organizations. By contrast, 1995 was a scheduled election. Electoral organizations had two years to build the organization necessary to overcome the signature requirement. Moreover, in those two years, private enterprise intervened in the form of private signature-collection firms that would collect the necessary signatures for a price. Hence, by 1995 parties had the time to build their own signature-gathering infrastructure or could simply purchase the necessary signatures if they had the money. In this way, it could be argued that the party fractionalization found in 1995 was the more accurate reflection of Russia's diverse ideological terrain than was the more limited number of parties in 1993.

Nevertheless, one could argue that the emergence of 43 electoral blocs in 1995 represented a failure of elites to heed the constraints of the electoral system. While it is true that the psychological effect of an electoral system takes time to develop, Russian party leaders appear to have been unusually oblivious to the built-in incentives for consolidation of parties. Why did so many blocs that clearly had no chance of overcoming the 5-percent barrier still spend the time and money to contest the election? In addition to the personal ambitions of certain leaders, the answer lies partly in conflicting incentives of the electoral system that encouraged party proliferation and partly in self-delusion as to the level of potential support within the electorate.

With respect to conflicting incentives, the PR contest provided more rewards for parties than simply legislative seats. Being on the PR ballot entitled an electoral bloc to government financing as well as free television and radio airtime. Thus, a party with little or no chance of winning legislative representation still had incentives to enter the race in order to get its name and message out, largely at the government's expense. This free access to mass media also produced an interesting interaction between the PR and plurality elections. Some blocs existed primarily to promote the chances of their leaders in the single-member district races. Leaders of the Pamfilova-Gurov-Vladimir Lysenko bloc, Common Cause, and the Party of Economic Freedom owed their victories in the plurality election partly to the name recognition and exposure they received as leaders of a PR bloc.[11]

The other part of the explanation for party proliferation in 1995 was the uncertainty

[10] The law stated that no more than 15 per cent of a bloc's signatures could come from any one region of the federation. This was meant to hinder the establishment of ethnically or regionally based electoral blocs; it apparently worked well in 1993 (*Rossiyskiye vesti*, 12 Oct. 1993). For a discussion of the impact of this aspect of the electoral law on party development in non-Russian regions see Robert Moser, 'The Impact of the Electoral System on Post-Communist Party Development: The Case of the 1993 Russian Parliamentary Election,' *Electoral Studies*, 14/4/1995, 383–7.

[11] Michael McFaul, *Russia Between Elections: What the December 1995 Results Really Mean* (Washington: Carnegie Endowment for International Peace, 1996), 17.

about the level of support parties might garner. In 1993, no one imagined that Vladimir Zhirinovskiy would win the PR contest with 23 percent of the vote. Russian opinion polls, while steadily improving, still produced conflicting and often inaccurate predictions. Thus, many parties using their own survey research or impressions of the electorate clung to the belief that they would defy the odds and overcome the 5-percent barrier.

Although the legal threshold did not have a noticeable psychological effect on the number of parties in Russia, it did have a substantial mechanical effect. The 5-percent barrier did indeed lessen the number of parties entering the legislature by barring small parties from representation. In 1993, the mechanical effect of the 5-percent barrier was to reduce the number of effective parties from 7.58 elective parties to 6.40 parliamentary parties (see Table 13.2). Such a restraining effect is about what one might expect from this relatively high legal threshold, given Russia's fractionalized party system. The parties denied representation were quite minor, with the exception of the Russian Movement for Democratic Reforms (RDDR), which narrowly missed the 5-percent cut-off. In all, parties denied access to the State Duma due to the 5-percent barrier enjoyed less than 9 percent of the vote. Moreover, the index of disproportionality for the PR system in 1993 was 4.94, which was actually higher than that in the 1993 plurality election but much lower than the disproportionality found in both the PR and plurality elections of 1995 (see Table 13.2). Compared to other countries, the 1993 Russian PR system produced quite a large number of effective parties and an above-average amount of disproportionality for a PR system with a moderate effective threshold.[12] Such a combination suggests that the emerging Russian party system possessed an underlying basis for relatively severe party fractionalization that a 5-percent barrier could not control.

However, 1995 produced an entirely different situation. With 43 electoral blocs competing, the 5-percent barrier would have a much different impact than in 1993, when 13 blocs competed. Clearly, a majority of parties on the ballot would not achieve the necessary 5 percent for representation. Consequently, many more votes would be wasted and the disproportionality of the system would increase dramatically relative to 1993. Indeed, in 1995,

Table 13.2 **Effects of Russian PR and plurality elections**[a]

Election	Effective number of elective parties	Effective number of parliamentary parties	Least-squares index of disproportionality
1993 PR	7.58	6.40	4.94
1995 PR	10.68	3.32	20.56
1993 Plurality	2.78	2.45	4.27
1995 Plurality	5.53	4.95	11.09

Note: [a] Calculated from data in *Byulleten'* (1993), 67; Colton (forthcoming); *Rossiyskaya gazeta* (17 Jan. 1996, pp. 1–16 and 24 Jan. 1996, pp. 2–14); *Svedeniya* (1995).

[12] Russia's figure of 6.40 effective parliamentary parties was higher than that in any other electoral system studied in Lijphart's large cross-national study. The level of disproportionality was higher than in Germany's electoral systems, which had similar effective thresholds, but lower than in several other systems. See Lijphart, *Electoral Systems*, 160–2.

nearly 50 percent of the popular vote went to parties that did not overcome the 5-percent barrier, once again showing that the legal threshold of 5 percent did not deter most parties from competing nor many voters from casting their vote for a 'sure loser.' Given this increased party proliferation, the mechanical effect of the 5-percent threshold was enormous. The four parties that did receive over 5 percent of the vote received roughly twice as large a share of seats as votes. The index of disproportionality of the PR system in 1995 was 20.56, far outstripping either system in 1993 and almost twice as high as the disproportionality produced by the 1995 plurality election. By international standards, only India's plurality system has produced similar levels of disproportionality.[13]

Proportional representation has had contradictory effects in Russia. It has allowed for the proliferation of parties in both 1993 and 1995. The 5-percent legal threshold designed to deter the proliferation of small parties seemed to have no impact, at least at the stage of elective parties. In the transformation of votes into seats, the 5-percent barrier had a constraining mechanical effect, as expected, but one that changed remarkably in degree of strength from 1993 to 1995. The 5-percent barrier trimmed the effective number of parties in the legislature by more than one in 1993 but produced a drop from over 10 effective elective parties to just over 3 effective parliamentary parties in 1995.

Clearly, the effects of Russia's PR system are not independent of the environment in which the electoral system operates. When party proliferation was high, but not outrageous, in 1993, the 5-percent barrier allowed this party proliferation to be reflected in both the electoral arena and parliament. But when the number of electoral blocs competing in the PR party-list race exploded from 13 to 43 in 1995, the effects of the electoral system changed. Party proliferation was again reflected in the electoral arena, as the increased number of effective electoral parties in 1995 attests. However, since the greatly increased party proliferation meant that many small parties would receive minuscule shares of the vote, the 5-percent barrier greatly restricted the number of parties represented in parliament, producing an extremely high degree of disproportionality between votes and seats. This suggests that effective thresholds behave differently after a certain level of party proliferation has been reached.

Plurality elections in Russia, 1993 and 1995

It is Russia's plurality elections that provide the greatest surprise for electoral studies. The first-past-the-post plurality system is considered the electoral system with the strongest effect on party systems. Elsewhere, this system invariably has produced roughly two large parties and a high incidence of parliamentary majorities, even in social conditions of high pluralism such as in India. However, in Russia the plurality system did not have this expected effect. In 1993, plurality elections produced a plethora of independent candidates, overwhelming nascent parties that had little organization and few well-known local candidates. By 1995, parties had gained a stronger foothold in the single-member districts, with the total vote for partisan candidates surpassing the total vote for independents although independents still greatly outnumbered any single party's support.

According to Table 13.2, the plurality system in 1993 did produce something of a two-party

---

[13] See Lijphart, ibid. 161.

configuration. However, this is a mirage. In reality the 1993 plurality election produced a predominance of independent candidates and what is better understood as a no party system since over half the deputies elected were nonpartisan. According to convention independents are treated as a single party when calculating the effective number of parties. In reality, independents represented every point across Russia's vast ideological spectrum and subsequently splintered into three parliamentary factions. If one calculates the effective number of parliamentary parties on the basis of the legislative *factions* that emerged after the 1993 elections, one gets a more accurate picture of the effect of the high number of independents on party proliferation in the State Duma. In the 225 plurality seats, the effective number of legislative factions produced was 5.79, a far cry from the 2–3-party system suggested by the standard effective number of parties index.

The 1995 plurality election provides a more accurate representation of the impact (or lack thereof) of the plurality electoral system on Russian parties. With the decline of independent candidates, a clear multiparty configuration emerges. In terms of both elective and parliamentary parties, the number of parties emerging from Russia's 1995 plurality election is much larger than that in any plurality system in the West; indeed, it is larger than in most PR systems as well. One could argue that the psychological effect attributed to plurality systems has not had time to take effect, and that, over time, Russia's plurality elections will produce two large parties. This may prove to be the case. However, not only did the plurality system fail to have a psychological effect, it also lacked the mechanical effect expected. In 1995, the plurality system brought the effective number of parties down by slightly more than one-half a party (from 5.53 to 4.95). This pales in comparison to the supposedly weaker PR system, which drastically curtailed the number of parties with its 5-percent legal barrier. The level of disproportionality, which has been shown to be even more strongly influenced by the electoral system, was also much lower than in the supposedly more proportional PR system.

In fact, in 1995, the plurality election allowed for the representation of small parties to a much greater extent than did the PR system. Had a 5-percent national-legal threshold been applied to the plurality election in 1995, only four parties would have gained representation. But with only the effective threshold in each district as a barrier to representation, more parties managed to make it into the legislature. The result was a multiparty system arising out of a plurality system in Russia.

This phenomenon has been addressed in the electoral systems literature. Douglas Rae argued that the absolute threshold for representation was actually lower in plurality systems than in PR, since only a plurality in any one district was necessary to win at least one legislative seat, whereas representation under PR required a percentage of the national vote.[14] Moreover, Rein Taagepera and Matthew Shugart[15] note that a common exception to the two-party effect of plurality systems has been party systems in which nationally marginalized parties enjoy concentrated geographical support. Under such circumstances, third parties are possible under plurality systems if they appeal to a geographically concentrated minority able to produce district-level pluralities, as is the case, for example, in Canada. Finally, Sartori has argued that even the strong plurality system cannot produce a two-party system when a country's party system is unstructured, which is clearly the case in Russia and other

[14] Rae, *Political Consequences*, 78.   [15] Taagepera and Shugart, *Seats and Votes*, 192–3.

post-communist states.[16] Sartori claimed that the plurality system retains a restraining effect in unstructured party systems, but only on the constituency level, meaning that single-member plurality elections encourage two-person contests, but an unstructured party system does not ensure that the two persons in each district will be from the same two parties.

Do these hypotheses account for Russia's multipartism despite its plurality election? Judging by the number of candidates fielded by each party, Russia has yet to see a truly nationwide party emerge, with the possible exception of the Communist Party, which showed impressive strength in the single-member districts. The Communist Party and the LDPR were the only parties to run candidates in more than half of Russia's 225 electoral districts. The LDPR is particularly interesting because it was the only party to be seriously under-represented in the plurality election, gaining over 6 percent of the vote but less than 1 percent of the seats. Under normal conditions, the fate of the LDPR should have been shared by the rest of the field of parties, even the Communists, since no party received even 15 percent of the national vote and most parties received less than 3 percent. Geographically concentrated support does seem to provide part of the explanation for the disproportionate success of the Agrarian Party. A stable constituency in rural areas still dominated by state farms provided the Agrarians with a reliable reservoir of district pluralities in rural Russia. The question remains why the Agrarian Party could not use this same constituency to overcome the 5-percent legal threshold of the PR election, since it provided the party over 6 percent of the national vote in single-member districts. As I will argue below, perhaps electoral arrangements have more fundamental effects regarding party identification and support, in addition to the mechanical effects commonly attributed to them.

However, it is not accurate to depict the Russian electorate as possessing geographically concentrated minorities analogous to the linguistic cleavages found in Canada. Rather, personality played the largest role in the success of small parties in the single-member districts. Most parties simply managed to elect their only well-known member, typically their leader. Thus, the Party of Economic Freedom had Konstantin Borovoy, PRES had Sergey Shakhray, and Common Cause had Irina Khakamada, all national luminaries, as their single winning candidates. The votes for these single individuals represented 22, 31, and 70 percent of their party's nationwide vote, respectively. Thus, Sartori's concept of an unstructured party system, in which personality rather than party identification and ideology determines electoral results, better explains the results observed in 1995.[17]

However, Sartori also argued that, even with an unstructured party system, the plurality system would have a constraining effect at the district level, producing a series of two-person races. A closer look at the district-level races in 1995 shows that this was definitely not the case in Russia. We counted the number of candidates per district,[18] taking into consideration the size of each candidate's vote and using the same mathematical technique as the 'effective number of parties' index. We found that Russian politics was thoroughly fractionalized even at the district level. According to this 'effective number of candidates' measure, the average number of significant candidates per district was not two, as projected by Sartori, but 6.53.

[16] Sartori, *Comparative Constitutional Engineering*, 44.
[17] Sartori, *Comparative Constitutional Engineering*.
[18] As listed in *Rossiyskaya gazeta*, 17 Jan. 1996, and in *Svedeniya o zaregistrirovannykh kandidatakh v deputaty Gosudarstvennoy Dumy Federal'nogo Sobraniya Rossiyskoy Federatsii po odnomandatnym izbiratel'nym okrugam* (Moscow: Central Electoral Commission, 1995).

Since, on average, there were 12 candidates that competed in each electoral district, slightly more than half could be considered competitive.

It is little wonder, then, that extremely small parties enjoyed more success in the plurality election. With the vote distributed among over six competitive candidates in each electoral district, the vote share necessary for victory in any one district was extremely low. Very many candidates made it to the State Duma with less than 100,000 votes. An electoral bloc such as Power to the People, which strategically ran well-known candidates, managed to parlay 2 percent of the nationwide plurality vote into nine parliamentary seats. With the addition of independents and others elected from small parties, and with a little help from the Communists, Power to the People qualified as a parliamentary faction with 35 members. That represents more than 15 percent of the legislature's seats, although the party garnered only 2 percent of the national vote! Under the fluid conditions of Russian politics, then, the usual constraints associated with plurality elections did not operate. Other factors overrode them.

Russia's plurality system of 1995 not only failed to reduce the number of nationwide parties to two, it also failed to have the most basic psychological effect of constraining the number of candidates at the district level. Because of its large number of effective candidates in each district (6.53), the 1995 plurality system had a relatively low effective threshold for plurality systems: on average, about 15 percent of a district's vote.[19] Even though this effective threshold for plurality districts was higher than the 5-percent legal threshold of the PR system, the fact that the latter was a national threshold (5 percent of the nationwide vote) made it a far more formidable barrier than 15 percent of a single district's vote. Given the geographical concentration of support for some parties (e.g., the Agrarians), and the notoriety of single leaders, each with their own parties, Russia's nascent party system made the plurality system a more proportional one than was its PR counterpart with a 5-percent national threshold.

The impact of electoral systems on Russia's parties

The discussion thus far would suggest that Russia's electoral system has had little systematic effect on its party structure. If one concentrates on the dependent variables commonly studied in the literature on electoral systems (number of parties and disproportionality), it is hard to escape this impression, since Russia seems to be an exception to the most well-supported hypotheses in the field. However, more broadly, the electoral system has had several fundamental effects on the Russian party system.

First, the electoral system has actually helped to establish or undermine the centrality of parties in the electoral arena. Just as creators of the electoral system had hoped, the PR system quickly established parties and electoral blocs as the central agents for structuring the electorate's voting choice. To get onto the ballot, elites were forced to form party lists. Voters then were forced to make a choice between party blocs. Nonpartisanship was not an option, even though the Bloc of Independents was created as one of the 43 blocs in 1995.

At the same time, plurality elections undermined this central position of parties by allowing independent candidates onto the ballot. In Russia's polarized political environ-

---

[19] The effective threshold was calculated simply by taking 100 (the total vote percent of the district) divided by 6.53 (the average effective number of candidates).

ment, nonpartisanship was a very attractive option, since adopting a party label identified with either the pro-reform or anti-reform political camps automatically alienated a large portion of voters on the other side. Moreover, the parochial (*i.e.*, localist) nature of the single-member district races worked against elite partisan affiliation given the need to portray oneself as a candidate willing and able to fight against Moscow on behalf of the district. Partisanship gave the impression that one was tied in with central authorities in Moscow and thus more likely to sell out the district's interests. Finally, the parties themselves were so organizationally weak that they had little to offer candidates in the form of material or symbolic benefits. The strongest candidates were still likely to run on their own name recognition and personal appeal as independents rather than risk the stigma of a partisan label.[20]

Secondly, the electoral system has had a significant influence on the level of support for specific parties in Russia. Figures 13.1 and 13.2 show a comparison of the number of seats gained from PR and plurality elections in 1993 and 1995. The LDPR provides the most dramatic example of how the electoral system shaped the distribution of power among parties. Without the PR half of Russia's electoral system the LDPR would not exist as a significant player in Russian politics. The Agrarian Party provides the opposite case. Its survival as a parliamentary party was sustained only because of its prowess in the plurality election. The largest parties coming out of both elections (Russia's Choice in 1993 and the Communist Party in 1995) distinguished themselves from the rest of the field as the only parties capable of achieving success in both electoral arenas. Russia's Choice actually lost the PR election to the LDPR but made up all of its deficit (and more) in the plurality election. The KPRF was the first party to combine victory in both the PR and plurality election and easily established itself as the dominant party in the 1995 Duma.

The electoral system has had a dramatic impact on the fortunes of individual parties because each system requires different resources for success. The PR election is national in scope. Success requires either a well-defined social constituency, such as the KPRF has among the older generation, or a charismatic leader who can appeal to the large group of undecided voters. Thus, the PR system has offered opportunities to political entrepreneurs, such as Vladimir Zhirinovskiy and Grigory Yavlinskiy as well as more organized interests, such as the Communists and the pro-reform 'party of power' (Russia's Choice in 1993 and Our Home is Russia in 1995). The plurality election cannot be won without some grass-roots organization and a cadre of well-known local politicians. The KPRF again has the advantage in this sphere, making it a formidable party despite its recent defeat in the presidential election. The Agrarian Party has shown how a strong sectoral tie can be effective in this system. Finally, the plurality system has opened the door for regional and personality-based parties to capture small numbers of seats. Transformation of the Fatherland, led by popular Sverdlovsk governor Eduard Rossel, can win seats in Sverdlovsk *oblast'*, and a host of personality-based parties can win one or two seats for their well-known leaders in their home districts. The party most left out in this context is the LDPR, with its relatively evenly distributed share of the opposition vote but lack of well-known local politicians.

---

[20] This may become less prevalent over time, as incumbents who were forced to join parliamentary factions to have any influence in the faction-dominated State Duma will have a hard time running for reelection as independents.

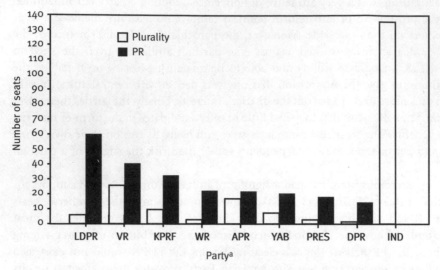

aLDPR = Liberal Democratic Party of Russia; VR = Russia's Choice; KPRF = Communist Party of the Russian Federation; WR = Women of Russia; APR = Agrarian Party of Russia; YAB = Yabloko; PRES = Party of Russian Unity and Accord; DPR = Democratic Party of Russia; IND = Independents.

Figure 13.1 **Seats in PR vs. plurality elections, 1993**

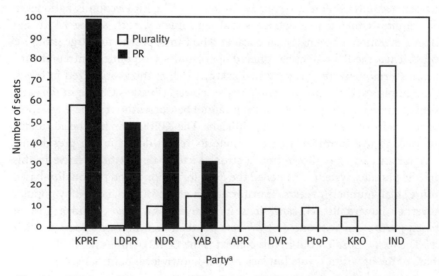

aFor abbreviations, see Figure 13.1; also, NDR = Our Home is Russia; DVR = Democratic Russia's Choice—United Democrats; PtoP = Power to the People; KRO = Congress of Russian Communities.

Figure 13.2 **Seats in PR vs. plurality elections 1995**

Conclusion

This study has used Russia's parliamentary contests of 1993 and 1995 as a laboratory for examining the effects of proportional representation and plurality systems. Since the two systems were used in the same elections within the same country, all other variables were held constant. We found that PR and plurality electoral systems had very different and important consequences, advantaging or undermining parties as the chief vehicle of electoral competition and helping to determine winners and losers. But the electoral systems did not have the effects commonly predicted by the Western literature on party systems. The failure of electoral systems to have the same effects in Russia that they have had in established democracies is not surprising, given the novelty of democratic practices and the fluidity of social life during Russia's turbulent transition from communism.

Section 5

Problems of Party Formation and Consolidation

Introduction

Archie Brown

While political parties are frequently given a bad name even in Western democracies and, still more, in Russia, no country-wide democratic polity has ever been sustained without the organizing and mediating role of parties. Russia had only limited experience of political parties before 1917 and these were accorded, at best, a tenuous legitimacy. Within a very few years after the establishment of a Soviet state all parties other than the Communists were ruthlessly eliminated. Thus, the territory that now constitutes the Russian Federation experienced seventy years of the monopoly of power of the Communist Party of the Soviet Union (CPSU). Increasingly, the 'leading role' of the Communist Party, as it was somewhat euphemistically known, was taken for granted. It was not until the late 1980s that the one-party state began to be widely and publicly questioned.

As the countries of Eastern Europe cast aside their Communist rulers in 1989, Russian citizens began, increasingly, to associate their misfortunes with the rule of the CPSU. Until the perestroika period, even dissidents had tended to argue that what was necessary was for Soviet rulers to take seriously, and abide by, their own Constitution—a Constitution which, in Article 6, enshrined the leading role of the CPSU within the political system. The radicalization of the public mood, in the light of glasnost and the free flow of information at home and from abroad, led many Russians to view the Communist Party in a far more critical light. Hitherto—unlike, for example, most Estonians, Latvians, and Lithuanians—a majority of Russians had been inclined to accept the CPSU as almost part of the natural order of things, and the limit of their aspirations in regard to it tended to be the hope for more, rather than less, enlightened leaders of that organization.

The first contested national elections of the Soviet era—those for the Congress of People's Deputies in 1989—were multi-candidate (in a majority of constituencies) rather than multi-party. Parties other than the CPSU had not yet been legalized, though the main political divisions in the country could, indeed, be seen within the ranks of that Communist Party. Joining the CPSU many decades after the years of revolutionary struggle had ended did not necessarily imply much, if anything, in the way of ideological commitment. People sought admittance to that party, or were invited to join it, for diverse reasons. The most common was that such membership was a necessary condition of advancement in the great majority of professions. What this meant was that the CPSU—in spite of the strict discipline which, until the late 1980s, prevented open political argument on basic issues—was far from being ideologically united. Behind the façade of unity there was actually a huge diversity of view—hardly surprisingly when the party had roughly one in ten Soviet adults in its ranks and when, by the end of the 1980s, this amounted to a membership of approximately twenty million people.

Between January 1990 and the August coup of 1991 more than four million people had left the party's ranks. By the end of that month the party had ceased to exist. In the wake of the coup, Yeltsin made it illegal for the CPSU to continue to operate on Russian soil. When a Communist Party of the Russian Federation was subsequently formed, only a small minority of the mass membership of the old CPSU signed up for it, even though throughout the post-Soviet period, the Communists have constituted what has been by far the largest of Russia's political parties.

For many Russians the idea of party was so intimately linked with *the* party which had been omnipresent throughout their lives, and which they had come to regard as responsible for most of what had gone wrong, that they had an aversion to the very concept and terminology of party. The movement which gathered a high level of support from radical critics of Communism in the last years of the Soviet Union, 'Democratic Russia', did not turn itself into a political party, and—partly as a result of remaining a looser formation—disintegrated in the post-Soviet era. Summarizing survey research on attitudes to parties, Timothy Colton has remarked that Russian citizens 'take a dim view of parties': 'They distrust them more than they distrust state institutions, believe they are far too numerous, and are nearly as likely to see the competition among them as harmful to the country as beneficial to it. And many do indeed float like driftwood from one party to another or into and out of political agnosticism.'[1] If many Russian citizens are floating voters, this is partly connected with a phenomenon which Richard Rose, in the opening chapter of this section, aptly terms *floating parties*. Although Yeltsin refused to identity himself with one party—while making it clear which parties he was *against*, above all the Communists—in the parliamentary elections of 1993, 1995, and 1999, the parties or movements which had the tacit support of the president were Russia's Choice in the first of these elections, Our Home is Russia in the second, and Unity in the third.[2] Parties, however, have come and gone over the past decade. By 1999 Russia's Choice was part of a coalition called the Union of Right Forces, Our Home is Russia had become a minor party and one no longer enjoying the support of the Kremlin, while a new 'party of power', Unity, had been created only in the autumn of 1999 to fight a nationwide election in December of that year. As Yitzhak Brudny writes in Chapter 11: 'As late as mid-September 1999, less than 100 days before the ballot, the government had no electoral alliance it could call its own.' Yet, in the 1999 parliamentary election Unity was able, with the key resources of the state behind it, to come a very close second to the Communists in terms of seats in the Duma.

The important point made by Rose is that it becomes extremely difficult, if not impossible, to hold a party responsible for its performance over the previous parliament when by the next election it has regrouped and changed its name. When a party or organization is formed at the behest of the executive and created out of the blue a few months before the country goes to the polls, this complicates still further movement towards democratic accountability. Thus, Unity (which, in keeping with the suspicion of *parties*, was not formally registered as a political party) did not exist at the start of the 1999 electoral *campaign*, never mind the *previous election*. Having attained substantial parliamentary representation, top-down parties, supplied from above rather than demanded from below, remain neither adequately constrained

[1] Timothy J. Colton, *Transitional Citizens: Voters and What Influences Them in the New Russia* (Cambridge, Mass.: Harvard University Press, 2000), 136.

[2] Yeltsin makes clear in his latest volume of memoirs that these were his preferences. See Boris Yeltsin, *Midnight Diaries* (London: Weidenfeld & Nicolson, 2000), 352–6.

by public opinion nor accountable to the electorate—particularly when they can reshape their formation and change their name before the next election comes round.

One of the most important functions a political party can play, especially in a multinational state, is to cut across ethnic and other cleavages and help to underpin citizen loyalty on an 'all-union' basis. Parties can foster identification with the democratic process and by taking account of, and aggregating, different interests, counteract an excessive particularism. In Russia, however, as Darrell Slider points out in Chapter 15, party development has not worked out like that. Even the larger Russian parties, with the principal exception of the Communists, have weak organizational bases outside Moscow. In numerous republics and regions, Slider observes, the successful candidates in regional legislative elections between 1997 and 1999 were not the nominees of a national political party or its regional branch. Moreover, when voters in the provinces are endorsing an apparently 'party' candidate, they may, in fact, be voting for a person whom the local president or governor has succeeded in putting in place. Even Communist governors, as Chapter 15 makes clear, have been willing to break with both the central and regional party authorities and to offer crucial support to a candidate of *their* choice. The case of Unity (Yedinstvo) is especially interesting, for most of its local heads are people chosen by the regional governor, though it has developed into a force within the State Duma backing the demands of the Putin administration to strengthen the federal authorities vis-à-vis the regions. Slider concludes: 'Yedinstvo's victory, while no threat to strengthening the federation, does not portend a consolidation of Russia's political party system'.

Stephen Whitefield, in Chapter 16, takes what is in some respects a more optimistic view of the prospects for party formation and consolidation in Russia. He accepts that governments are not formed on the basis of party allegiance, that the parties closest to power have been of a transitory character, and that neither of the two presidents the Russian people have elected thus far was chosen on the basis of party identification. Yet he elaborates on ideological and social divisions within Russian society which form a basis for partisanship and argues that, in so far as political parties are weak, this is not because voters do not know what they want. Nor, he contends, does the primary problem lie in Russian society. Whitefield, on the basis of extensive survey research replicated at regular intervals in the 1990s, points to a spectrum of opinion which at one end produces clusters of pro-market, pro-Western, and pro-liberal (both economically and socially) positions and at the other end substantially more numerous anti-market, anti-Western, and illiberal views. He also maintains that 'individual politicians do not appear to be able to manipulate the electorate to suit their interests but rather must respond to the socially determined concerns of Russians, at least when appealing for their votes'. Accordingly, he argues, Russian voters are able to find parties, even in a rapidly changing political context, which reflect their distinctive outlooks. Thus, he is able to conclude, if Russia's institutional framework were changed 'to allow parties more say in government', the proponents of such a change would find that 'the mass bases of parliamentary politics would already be in place'.

Whether institutionalizing pluralist democracy is a top priority for Russia's present rulers must, however, remain in doubt. Encouragement could be derived from the fact that Vladimir Putin identified himself more closely with one party, Unity, in public than Boris Yeltsin ever did during previous election campaigns. On one optimistic scenario, the success of Unity in the 1999 parliamentary election could pave the way for consolidation of something like a three-party system in Russia—with Unity in the Centre, the KPRF on the left, and an alliance of the

Union of Right Forces and the liberal Yabloko to the right of centre.[3] Other actions of Putin, though, indicate that while he is, indeed, a coalition-builder, his interest is in broadening the coalition in support of the executive rather than in fostering oppositional parties for the sake of democracy.

[3] See Timothy J. Colton and Michael McFaul, 'Reinventing Russia's Party of Power: "Unity" and the 1999 Duma Election', *Post-Soviet Affairs*, 16/3 (July–Sept. 2000), 201–24, esp. p. 222.

14   How Floating Parties Frustrate Democratic Accountability: A Supply-Side View of Russia's Elections

Richard Rose

The liberal theory of democracy is demand driven: voters decide what they want, and politicians compete to supply their demands. However, a realist theory is that the government reflects what elites choose to supply. This was very obvious in the 'Adam and Eve' era of Soviet elections when, as the story had it, God presented Eve to Adam and told him that this was the woman of his choice. Of course, supply-side influences can be found in every democracy, for elites write the election laws and take the initiative in organizing political parties—but these influences are peculiarly strong in the Russian Federation.[1]

The erratic and changing supply of parties in Russian elections has often worked against the possibility of holding elected leaders accountable; people cannot vote for a party that is not there. Nor can people vote against a party that has dissolved itself rather than give an account of its actions at the end of its term of office. Even though the Russian ballot gives the electorate the default choice of voting against all candidates, doing so is not an expression of a positive preference. Even though Boris Yeltsin and Vladimir Putin have favored some parties over others, neither has founded a party to mobilize support for members of parliament, as General de Gaulle did, let alone allowed themselves to be chosen by a party caucus that can hold them accountable, as is the case in Scandinavian and German parties. The party of the Kremlin is no more and no less than the party of power.

Supply and demand considerations are combined by Joseph Schumpeter into an elitist theory of democracy, where oligopolistic elites supply voters with parties among which they can choose. In its simplest form, the theory may be reduced to a duopolistic choice between the Governing Party and the Opposition. At an election, voters can vote for the In party; thus allowing the government of the day to remain in office or vote to turn the In party out, and put the Out party in. This was the choice offered in the second round of the 1996 Russian presidential election, when Boris Yeltsin and Gennady Zyuganov were the alternatives. In a proportional representation parliamentary system, voters may have a wider choice of parties, but decisions about who gets what in a coalition government emerge from interparty bargaining among the respective elites.

This chapter was first published in *East European Constitutional Review*, 9/1–2 (Winter–Spring 2000), 53–9. Reproduced by kind permssion of the author and the *East European Constitutional Review*.

[1] See, in this regard, Michael McFaul, 'Institutional Design, Uncertainty and Path Dependency during Transitions: Cases from Russia', *Constitutional Political Economy*, 10/1 (1999), 27–52.

To say that voters are free to decide who to vote for is meaningful, as Schumpeter noted, only in the sense that 'everyone is free to start another textile mill'.[2] In Russia, the deposit fee required for an individual to contest a single-member district is 1,000 times the minimum monthly wage, and for a party to qualify for the proportional representation list, it is 200,000 signatures or 25,000 times the minimum monthly wage. For the presidency, more signatures are required for a place on the ballot, costing upward of $1,000,000 to collect. In each instance, the costs of campaigning, including fighting legal and other actions launched by opponents, raise the financial threshold still higher.

In an established democracy, most of the expense of supplying parties and candidates represents an investment long since made. Major parties have existed for a half century or longer. Presidential candidates have usually devoted much of their adult life to politics, much of it in preparation for running for the nation's top political job. In the past decade, Russia has had three presidential elections and three for the Duma, but the supply of political parties has been erratic. This has not been due to a lack of political experience, for politicians as diverse as Boris Yeltsin, Yegor Gaidar, Gennady Zyuganov, and Vladimir Putin each served an apprenticeship in an extremely disciplined party organization, the Communist Party of the Soviet Union. Notwithstanding this, elites have shown too much skill in forming, breaking, and avoiding parties. While their actions may be explained in terms of self-interested rational-choice theories, the systemic consequences of their actions are counterproductive; the resulting free-floating party system destroys—or precludes—the central institutions necessary to create a representative and accountable democracy.[3]

The supply of parties in the Duma

The theory of parliamentary representation is that individuals vote for parties that best reflect their political outlook, whether pro- or antimarket, Slavophile or Western. This presupposes that most Russians identify with a set of political principles or ideology. But many still do not. When the eighth New Russia Barometer survey asked a nationwide sample of citizens what broad political outlook they most favored, 35 percent replied 'none.' The second largest group, 24 percent, identified with communist principles; 18 percent endorsed a market economy; 8 percent, social democracy; 7 percent, a great-power patriotic party; 5 percent, environmentalism; and the rest named other outlooks.[4]

With 26 parties on the Duma ballot in 1999, Russians had a plenitude of parties from which to choose. Some parties espoused a more or less clear political outlook, such as the Communist Party; the promarket Right Forces group, or the Zhirinovsky Bloc. Others, such as the Unity and Fatherland parties, were fuzzy-focus parties that claimed to represent everyone. In the event, many of the parties represented almost no one. For example, the Party of Women won the support of less than four percent of Russian women.

The supply-side initiatives of political elites are the primary cause of Duma seats chan-

---

[2] *Capitalism, Socialism and Democracy*, 4th edn. (London: George Allen & Unwin, 1952).

[3] See Herbert Kitschelt, Zdenka Mansfeldova, Radslaw Markowski, and Gabor Toka, *Post-Communist Party Systems* (New York: Cambridge University Press, 1999), 1 ff.

[4] Opinion data comes from New Russia Barometer VIII, a nationwide representative-sample survey conducted by VCIOM on behalf of the Centre for the Study of Public Policy, University of Strathclyde, interviewing 1,940 persons, 13–29 Jan. 2000.

ging hands. Just as mergers and acquisitions on Wall Street are driven by the ambitions and rewards available to financial elites, so shifts in representation within the Duma reflect initiatives by political elites. There is a big turnover in the number of parties on the ballot from one election to the next. In the 1993 Duma election, there were 13 parties on the proportional representation ballot; in 1995, there were 43; and in 1999, the number was down to 26.[5] In a new democracy, party formation invariably involves a certain amount of trial and error, but in Russia party turnover has been so abnormal that it has become an obstacle to accountable government. A necessary condition for voters to be able to hold politicians accountable is that the parties remain in business from one election to the next. If each election offers voters new choices, they have no basis for evaluating the past record and credibility of competing parties, or for rewarding or punishing parties on the basis of that past record.

When the deadline for the registration of political parties fell a year in advance of the 1999 Duma election, more than three hundred groups met registration requirements. At that time, the front-running party was Fatherland, the product of an alliance between Moscow mayor Yuri Luzhkov and his allies in the regions; it challenged the hold of Yeltsin and his entourage on the Kremlin. In reaction, those who had served Yeltsin, including Anatoly Chubais and Yegor Gaidar, began organizing groups that merged to become the Union of Right Forces. At the end of the summer, after Vladimir Putin had become prime minister, another pro-Kremlin party, Unity (also known as Medved), was formed.

In the Duma election of 1999, more than three-fifths of the vote in the proportional representation (PR) ballot was won by parties that had not contested the election four years earlier. The big winners were parties newly supplied by political elites to meet the demands of a post-Yeltsin market. The Unity party came in a close second to the Communist Party in the national PR ballot, and the ostensibly liberal Right Forces party was fourth; the anti-Yeltsin Fatherland party also did well. Duma seats were won by three parties that had won seats in the previous election—the Communists, Yabloko, as well as the Zhirinovsky Bloc, which was technically a new party but was offering the same old stuff as before. The Agrarians did not contest PR seats and Our Home is Russia, no longer the party of power, failed to win any seats.

Half the Duma seats are single-member districts. Whereas proportional representation requires politicians to compete on the basis of a party list, the single-member system encourages a supply of candidates representing local interests rather than parties. The winner is the person with the most positive votes, so long as the total is greater than the number of votes cast against all candidates (the default option printed on Russian ballots), and turnout is at least 25 percent. In the 1999 Duma election, the best-organized party, the Communists, contested almost two-thirds of the single-member districts, and two other parties, Yabloko and the right-wing Spiritual Heritage group, contested half the seats. The two parties closest to Vladimir Putin demonstrated that they were the party of power in Moscow by minimizing the number of seats contested nationwide. Unity nominated candidates in only one-sixth of the single-member districts, and Right Forces in less than a third of these seats.

---

[5] For details of results and voting behavior in previous Russian elections, see Stephen White, Richard Rose, and Ian McAllister, *How Russia Votes* (Chatham, NJ: Chatham House, 1997).

With an average of 10 candidates in each single-member district, some seats were won by candidates with less than a sixth of the popular vote. The median winner secured the endorsement of only 30 percent of the district's voters. Independents constituted the most successful category in contesting single-member districts, winning almost half the seats allocated last December.

Whereas an established democracy has floating voters, in Russia there is a floating party system. Between one Duma election and the next, major as well as minor parties may appear and disappear suddenly (Table 14.1). In 1993, eight parties won PR seats. The Liberal Democrats, led by Vladimir Zhirinovsky, was first in the popular vote, followed by Yegor Gaidar's Russia's Choice, then perceived as the party of power; the Communists came in third. In the 1995 election, seven of the eight major parties again appeared on the ballot; this gave their original supporters a chance to vote for or against them. In aggregate, about half the voters abandoned the parties they had supported two years earlier. (The gross number of voters abandoning their 1993 party was substantially higher, since the aggregate figures are net totals that cancel out individuals moving in opposite directions between parties.) In 1995, only four parties cleared the PR threshold (5 percent), including one new party, Our Home is Russia; it was, at that time, the party of power, led by the then-prime minister Viktor Chernomyrdin. In 1999, four parties, which had previously won PR seats in the Duma, did not contest the election, while newly invented parties won the most seats.

An election fixes the supply of Duma members, but not necessarily the parties to which

Table 14.1 **Russia's appearing and disappearing parties**

Parties	1993	1995	1999
Contesting three elections	(51.3)	(45.0)	(38.2)
Communist	12.4	22.3	24.3
Liberal Dem./Zhirinovsky	22.9	11.2	6.0
Yabloko	7.9	6.9	5.9
Women of Russia	8.1	4.6	2.0
Contesting two Elections	(30.3)	(18.2)	(1.2)
Russia's Choice	15.5	3.9	n.a.
Agrarian	8.0	3.8	n.a.
Russian Unity and Concord	6.8	0.4	n.a.
Our Home is Russia	n.a.	10.1	1.2
Contesting one election	(18.4)	(36.8)	(62.6)
Democratic Party of Russia	5.5	n.a.	n.a.
Unity (Medved)	n.a.	n.a.	23.3
Fatherland	n.a.	n.a.	13.3
Union of Right Forces	n.a.	n.a.	8.5
Others	12.9	36.8	17.5

Source: Stephen White, Richard Rose, and Ian McAllister, *How Russia Votes* (Chatham House, 1997), and www.RussiaVotes.org

they belong (Fig. 14.1). This is determined by politics within the *Koltsevaya Doroga* (Moscow Beltway). Once they have arrived in Moscow, Duma members elected as independents from single-member districts either come out in their true colors, as partisans, or join so-called convenience parties, offering office facilities and committee assignments to their nominal members. Three parties, which represent almost a third of the Duma's seats—People's Deputies, Russian Regions, and the Agro-Industrial bloc—are convenience parties that did not contest elections last December. Some Communist deputies also joined these new convenience parties in order to help them qualify as a Duma party. Fatherland immediately lost members as it become apparent that its future was less bright than that of the parties of power.

The distribution of leadership positions in the new Duma further attenuated the link between the voters and their representatives. Initially, the Kremlin endorsed concentrating committee chairs in the hands of parties that, together, had won barely two-fifths of the Duma seats in December—the Communists and Unity, plus a convenience party, the People's Deputies. After this led to a walkout by parties expecting to share committee chairs in proportion to their electoral (or at least, their Duma) numbers, committee chairs were reassigned to all parties except Yabloko. However, committee chairs were not supplied in proportion to a party's popular vote or seats in the Duma.

Whatever one makes of the Duma election, the losers are clear: they are the people who

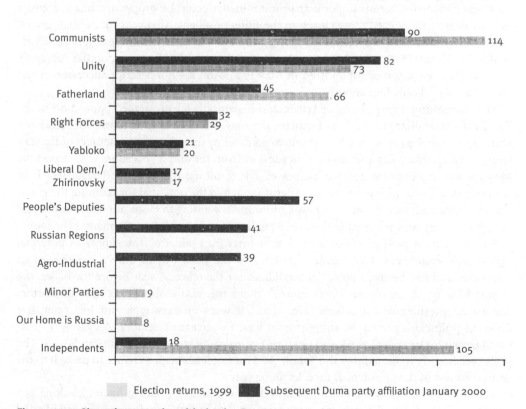

Election returns, 1999   Subsequent Duma party affiliation January 2000

Figure 14.1 **Changing membership in the Duma**
Sources: Central Electoral Commission (www.fci.ru); Duma (www.duma.gov.ru).

had hoped that the post-Yeltsin era would strengthen the development of representative and accountable government. While the Duma has been freely elected, its membership is not representative of public opinion in the way in which, for example, American members of Congress seek to be. The floating party system is thus an institutional obstacle to accountable government.

Supplying a president

The presidential election dramatically illustrates the importance of supply-side politics. As Boris Yeltsin's position deteriorated, the 'family,' that is, the complex of close relatives as well as political and economic leaders that had benefited from influence in the Kremlin, engaged in a frantic search for a candidate who might win the 2000 election. The most visible politician, Boris Yeltsin, was enormously unpopular and could not run for re-election because he had already served two terms. While rumors circulated in Moscow that the 'family' would suspend the election rather than risk defeat, Yeltsin was not in favor of such a high-risk strategy. In any event, his health made it very dangerous to assume he would live long enough to justify a seizure of power in his name.

The roll call of might-have-been presidents is lengthy. Between 1995 and the summer of 1998 a succession of Yeltsin prime ministers had gained temporary visibility. However, the post was dangerous, for an unpopular prime minister could be dropped, while a popular prime minister threatened those closest to the ailing president. After years of dogged service, Viktor Chernomyrdin was dismissed in March 1998. His youthful successor, Sergei Kiriyenko, was dropped after the August 1998 collapse of the ruble. His more popular successor, Yevgeny Primakov, was abruptly fired in May 1999. And his nondescript successor, Sergei Stepashin, lasted only four months.

The continuing unpopularity of Yeltsin and his entourage encouraged opposition to the 'family' to crystallize around Yuri Luzhkov, the mayor of Moscow, who was not associated with the national government. In addition to controlling the substantial resources of Russia's largest city, Luzhkov was able to draw on support from the oblast governors who shared the Moscow mayor's desire to decentralize power. The result was the Fatherland party, which, in forming an alliance with Primakov in August 1999, had the potential for winning the presidency by drawing votes from both non-Communists wanting to clean out the Kremlin and Communists by now resigned to the unelectability of their candidate, Gennady Zyuganov.

Public-opinion polls provided a market of sorts for evaluating the supply of potential presidential candidates. The standard practice of the polls was to offer a lengthy list of wannabes and has-beens as potential candidates for the office. A year before the ballot, the largest bloc of electors were 'don't knows'; there was also a significant bloc of electors against all presidential candidates (Fig. 14.2). Between January 1998 and July 1999, five different politicians gained the support of at least 10 percent of electors: Zyuganov, Primakov, Luzhkov, Alexander Lebed, and Grigory Yavlinsky. All were anti-Yeltsin candidates. The polls consistently indicated that the 'family' had no candidate with a chance to make it to the second round of the presidential race, let alone win it.

A year before his election Vladimir Putin did not exist as a political figure, let alone as a presidential candidate. Then in late summer 1999, two events transformed the presidential race. Yeltsin supplied a new face for the contest, naming the unknown Putin as prime

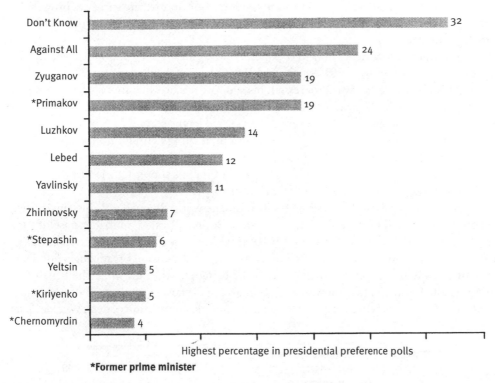

Figure 14.2 **Presidential front-runners before Second Chechen war.**
Source: VCIOM monthly surveys between January 1998 and July 1999.

minister. In the sense in which talented athletes are unexpectedly discovered, this ex-KGB agent was not a 'discovery'. It would be more apt to say that he was an 'invention'—supplied as an answer to the need of the Yeltsin entourage for a viable and secure presidential candidate.

A prime minister was ex officio a potential presidential candidate. But this does not make the incumbent a likely winner. The best showing of a prime minister in the opinion polls was the 15 percent support level given Primakov just before he was sacked. In VCIOM's August 1999 poll, only 2 percent favored Putin for president. This put him tenth in a list of ten potential candidates. Furthermore, all the front-runners—Zyuganov, Primakov, Luzhkov, Lebed, and Yavlinsky—were opponents of the 'family'. The following month Putin's support rose to 4 percent, but this still left him far behind four anti-Kremlin candidates.

The bombs that killed hundreds of Moscow residents a few weeks after Putin entered office added a new dimension to Russian politics. Whatever the source of the bombs—and there is far more speculation about the source than there is hard evidence—the destruction was blamed on the Chechens. After attacks on neighboring Dagestan by Chechen-based militants, the second Chechen war was launched with a strategy of saturation bombing that showed the Ministry of Defense had learned its lessons from Russia's ground losses in the first Chechen war, and also from the Pentagon's strategy in the war in Kosovo. Whatever their hesitations about volunteering to fight in Chechnya or the long-term consequences of the renewed war, a large majority of Russians endorsed the immediate successes brought by military action. (For details of public opinion, see the trend tables of VCIOM data, available at www.Russiavotes.org.)

Public opinion supported Putin in a popular war against a very unpopular enemy, the Chechens. By October 1999, VCIOM showed Putin the preferred presidential choice of 26 percent of Russians. As the war progressed, his support reached the unprecedented level of 42 percent, before the Duma vote, and passed the 58 percent mark at the beginning of January (Fig. 14.3). Concurrently the sentiments stirred by the second Chechen war reduced Zyuganov's support by a third. Even more important, it cut the ground from under Fatherland's potential candidates for the presidency, Primakov and Luzhkov. Whereas in August 1999, together, they had claimed ten times the level of Putin's support, by January 2000 that had dropped to one-sixth of the support for Putin.

The supply of candidates shrank as Putin's fortunes rose. By giving his blessing to two noncommunist parties before the Duma election, Putin cultivated a broader base of support; this also prevented the Fatherland party from seeming the primary anti-communist party. By the time nominations for the presidency closed, the cost of organizing a nominating petition was no longer worth the reward of being an also-ran, while the benefits of getting on the Putin bandwagon were real. Primakov, Luzhkov, and Lebed, all of whom had run ahead of previous Yeltsin prime ministers, did not file nomination papers. When official

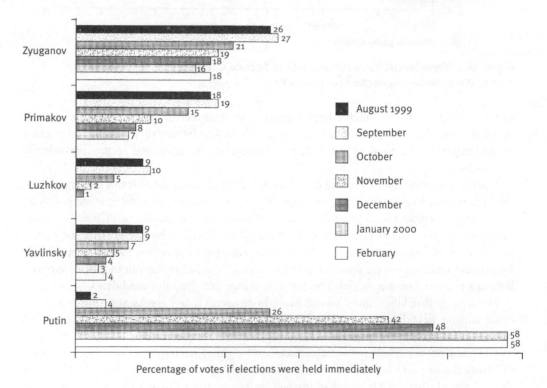

Percentage of votes if elections were held immediately

Figure 14.3 The rise of Vladimir Putin

Source: VCIOM representative-sample surveys: monthly figures from October 1999 average the results of two or more polls taken within the month. See also www.RussiaVotes.org.

nominations closed, only Zyuganov, Yavlinsky, and Zhirinovsky put themselves forward as candidates for Russians who wanted to oppose what Vladimir Putin represented without being so negative as to cast a default vote against everybody.

The importance of supply-side influence was rammed home on December 31, 1999, when a new president was supplied by an act of the Yeltsin entourage rather than by election or an act of God. Yeltsin's resignation gave the 'family' what they most demanded: amnesty for any and all acts committed by Yeltsin since the Russian Federation was launched on January 1, 1992. The blanket freedom from prosecution ensures Boris Yeltsin his permanent place in Russian history.

On the other hand, Yeltsin's resignation supplied Vladimir Putin with what he needed most, the power of an incumbent (albeit acting) president at the start of an election campaign. This gave Putin the most desirable position in the floating party system—the candidate of the party of power. Equally as important, Yeltsin's resignation provided a constitutional justification for moving the election date forward three months. The family's strategy worked. On March 26, Putin won the presidential election in the first round with 53.4 percent of the vote. Putin owes nothing to parties or Duma members; the only obligations he has are to the people who promoted him from obscurity.

Of necessity, the Russian elections have produced a government that other countries must do business with. But in dealing with it, foreigners should recognize that it no more represents the free choice of the Russian people than the Lada car was the choice of Soviet consumers. (People who have lived in a Gosplan economy are accustomed to 'choosing' what elites supply.) Moreover, the volatility of preelection support is a reminder that the winner's success is vulnerable to the dictum, 'easy come, easy go.' Putin's fuzzy-focus appeal drew support from many different sections of Russian society. The electorate has therefore given Putin an unclear mandate. This leaves Putin and his associates free to decide what policies to supply.

15   Russia's Governors and Party Formation

Darrell Slider

Ideally, political parties would form part of the federal 'glue' that would create cross-cutting ties and mutual interdependencies between federal and regional political elites. Political parties could play this role by linking national institutions to the regions on a number of dimensions: through ideological and personal loyalties, by mediating and focusing lobbying efforts for regional interests in the parliament, by creating mutually supporting organizational ties, and by raising and distributing funds needed to wage national and regional election campaigns. Party discipline would tend to punish defectors through the withholding of these valuable benefits. National parties could strengthen the federal system while encouraging regional leaders to adopt a broader perspective on national interests that link all the regions.

Since late 1993, elements of Russia's new political institutions have been designed with the purpose of encouraging the development of strong, national political parties.[1] Half the representatives in the State Duma, the lower house of the parliament, are chosen by party lists. Election rules also placed barriers in the way of regional parties: results would be determined on the basis of one national electoral district and a 5 per cent barrier excludes the smaller parties.[2] In the December 1995 elections, additional barriers to regionally based parties were put in place.

Despite these intentions, the development and institutionalization of national parties has been sporadic, at best. On the one hand, there has been an increase in the political importance of political parties and partisanship in Russian politics, particularly in comparing the 1993 and 1995 State Dumas.[3] But most parties remain small and highly personalized structures grouped around prominent personalities such as Gaidar, Zhirinovsky, Yavlinsky, Luzhkov, and others. While there are clear ideological differences among parties, organizational roots are weak, particularly outside the walls of the parliament. Indeed, the parliamentary fraction and its staff often constitute the core of the party organization. Few parties have significant regional structures, and their ties with leaders at the regional and local levels have been weak.[4]

Chapter specially commissioned for this volume.

[1] Interesting speculation on the institutional design flaws in Russia can be found in Peter C. Ordeshook, 'Russia's Party System: Is Russian Federalism Viable?', *Post-Soviet Affairs*, 12/3 (July–Sep. 1996), 195–217.

[2] The chief intellectual force behind the election law provisions on parties was Viktor Sheynis, long-time Duma member from Yabloko.

[3] On this aspect of Russian political development, see Robert G. Moser, 'Independents and Party Formation: Elite Partisanship as an Intervening Variable in Russian Politics', *Comparative Politics*, 31/2 (Jan. 1999), 147–65.

[4] For a number of useful studies on the development of Russia's political parties, see John Loewenhardt, ed., *Party Politics in Post-Communist Russia* (London: Frank Cass, 1998).

The aftermath of the Soviet experience left only one truly national party in the form of the Communist Party of the Russian Federation (KPRF), but, as we shall see, even its links to regional elites were tenuous. The KPRF, reconstituted in February 1993 on the remnants of the Communist Party of the RSFSR, gradually rebuilt its old organizational structure in the regions (though it is by law prohibited from organizing party cells at enterprises) and staked out a fairly reliable electoral base.[5]

Perhaps the most important indicator of political party penetration of the regions is the role played by political parties in nominating and supporting candidates for important political offices in the regions—regional legislatures and governors.

Political parties in regional assemblies

The first set of post-Soviet regional legislative elections took place in most regions between 1994 and 1995.[6] In these early elections, only about fifteen regions had assemblies with more than a small number of party-sponsored candidates. The second set of regional legislative elections took place in most regions between 1997 and 1999. There was a clear expansion in the number of regions with a party presence. National political parties are represented by at least a few deputies in fifty-six of seventy-eight regions for which information is available on the last set of assembly elections. In both the first and second set of post-Soviet elections, the KPRF was by far the most successful party, with the largest number of deputy groups in regional assemblies. In the most recent elections, the party won outright majorities in two regions, Krasnodar krai and Volgograd oblast, and had a strong presence in many assemblies. But there were also several regions where the KPRF suffered major reverses, going from majority party to minor faction in the republic of Chuvashia, and in Kamchatka, Vladimir, and Orel oblasts.

Apparent victories by national party-affiliated candidates in regional assemblies were often less than they seemed, however. One example was that of Yury Luzhkov's 'Otechestvo' in the Udmurtia republic elections of April 1999. This was in fact a victory by the head of the republic legislature Alexander Volkov. The Udmurt branch of this 'party' was created only four months before the election as a vehicle for increasing the share of Volkov supporters in the assembly. The organization did not nominate candidates, but endorsed a list. Two of the elected deputies were simultaneously members of Otechestvo and the KPRF.[7] Further proof of the tenuous nature of this party affiliation is that the Otechestvo deputies decided not to form their own fraction in the assembly, preferring instead to join 'branch' fractions geared towards industry, agriculture, or the social sphere.[8]

In examining the more recent elections, of equal interest is the fact that in ten oblasts and four republics not a single candidate was elected who had been nominated by a national political party or its regional branch.[9] This is not surprising in republics such as Kalmykia

---

[5] In many places the party has organized at the workplace without opposition from prosecutors; in Voronezh, for example, officials claimed the ban did not apply to privatized enterprises. For a discussion of how the party has been reconstituted, see Valery Vyzhutovich, 'Telo KPSS zhivet i pobezhdaet', *Izvestiya*, 12 Feb. 1999.

[6] Darrell Slider, 'Elections to Russia's Regional Assemblies', *Post-Soviet Affairs*, 12/3 (July–Sept. 1996), 243–64.

[7] The Otechestvo pre-election endorsements appeared in *Udmurtskaya pravda*, 2 Apr. 1999.

[8] *Udmurtskaya pravda*, 20 Apr. 1999.

[9] Of the smaller entities, the autonomous okrugs, eight of nine for which data were available had no parties represented.

and Bashkiria, where the political process is tightly controlled by authoritarian leaders Kirsan Ilyumzhinov and Murtaz Rakhimov. However, the list of party-less assemblies also includes Kemerovo oblast, where a prominent Communist, Aman Tuleev, is governor. Here, in the 1999 elections, Tuleev supporters won all but one seat in the assembly, but candidates ran as members of the 'Tuleev faction', not as candidates of the KPRF. Similarly, no party was represented as a result of the 1997 elections to the oblast duma in Novgorod, a region sometimes touted as a 'success story' in conducting political and economic reform, and whose governor, Mikhail Prusak, has been an active figure in NDR.[10]

A related measure of the lack of party penetration in the regions is the dearth of chairmen of regional assemblies who have a party affiliation. Chairmen of these bodies are important not only at the regional level, but because they along with governors form the Federation Council. The election of a party-affiliated chairman is an indicator that a political party had a working majority, often in combination with like-minded 'independent' deputies, at the first session of the assembly after the elections. Of Russian regional assembly chairmen, the largest number with a party affiliation come from the KPRF—at present Communists chair legislatures in Bryansk, Penza, Ryazan, Volgograd, and the Adygeya republic. More frequent than the election of party members as chairmen of assemblies were chairmen who represented the 'governor's party'—in other words, deputies who had been high-ranking officials in the oblast/republic administration or had been heads of local government. Both categories comprised officials who had been appointed by the governor.

Governors and political parties

In the initial period of post-independence politics, from late 1991 to 1995–6, governors and republic presidents tended to avoid attachments with national political movements. In this period, governors were appointed by the president and did not face an electoral test. Nevertheless, some governors did attempt to ally themselves with the so-called 'party of power' as a way to enhance their lobbying effectiveness with the central government. Indicative of the political fluidity of Russian politics, the party of power label was held by two different parties in succession, both linked to prime ministers. The attractiveness of these parties to governors was clear: they offered additional access to the corridors of power which would augment the ability of a governor to gain backing for the interests of his region.

The first party of power, the Democratic Choice of Russia (DVR was its Russian abbreviation), was headed by Yeltsin's first (acting) prime minister Yegor Gaidar. The party, contrary to expectations, did poorly in the December 1993 parliamentary elections, and in December 1995, now renamed Russia's Choice, it failed to meet the 5 per cent minimum. Yeltsin's decision to replace Gaidar in 1992 meant that the party's claim to influence on government decision-making dissipated quickly, and governors never had much incentive to seek an affiliation with the party.

The next 'party of power' was created as a vehicle for Gaidar's successor as prime minister, Viktor Chernomyrdin. Called 'Our Home is Russia' (abbreviated NDR in Russian) the party was organized in early 1995 and attracted a number of governors, including some who joined the party's board. With Yeltsin's sacking of Chernomyrdin in 1998, many of these

---

[10] Nicolai Petro, 'The Novgorod Region: A Russian Success Story', *Post-Soviet Affairs*, 15/3 (1999), 235–61.

governors distanced themselves from the NDR and/or sought other political affiliations. Of the thirty governors or republic presidents who were members of NDR's Political Council in 1997, only about half (sixteen) allowed their names to be used in this capacity in 1999. While many governors sought to change or diversify their political affiliations in 1999, an exception was Dmitry Ayatskov, the governor of Saratov oblast. He not only remained in NDR in late 1999, but was the number two candidate for the party on its national list for the Duma elections in December.

Starting in 1995, popular elections of governors represented a major change in the political landscape of post-Soviet Russia, one whose implications were poorly thought through by Yeltsin and his advisers. Elections made governors, as republic presidents before them, much less dependent on the centre. This increasing independence was also in part due to the fact that most governors won their elections without substantial assistance from national political organizations.[11] The fact that elections of governors took place on a schedule determined in the regions rather than simultaneously with national elections further undermined the role of national parties.[12]

There were a few instances, however, where a governor's victory appeared to depend on support from a national party. Most notable of these exceptions was Pskov oblast, where Yevgeny Mikhailov, a candidate supported by Zhirinovsky's Liberal Democratic Party of Russia, won election in 1996. He immediately brought outsiders from the LDPR into leadership posts in the oblast, virtually ignoring the local branch of the party.[13] Even this apparently strong tie between a governor and party did not last, however. After the December 1999 parliamentary elections, Mikhailov defected from the LDPR to the newest 'party of power'—Unity (Yedinstvo).

Electoral successes by governors relying on their own or locally generated resources further enhanced their independence, making them wary of exclusive ties with national political parties or movements. The lack of party connections of regional elites was most visible in the upper house of the Federal Assembly, the Federation Council. From 1996 to 2000, the Federation Council was made up of the top executive and legislative official from each of the Russian regions.[14] Its members did not form factions or ally themselves on party lines in conducting the business of the Council. In fact, on most issues, the regional leaders have demonstrated near unanimous agreement, usually going along with the recommendations of the Federation Council's committees and staff.

This pattern of party avoidance characterized even governors who had been aligned with the KPRF. This was in spite of the fact that the KPRF had by far the most developed network of regional party organizations and, therefore, the most advantages to offer party loyalists. Few 'red governors' were willing to associate closely with the national leadership of the KPRF. Of sitting governors, only Vassily Starodubtsev of Tula was on the party's Central Committee in November 1997.[15]

[11] See Steven Solnick, 'Gubernatorial elections in Russia, 1996–1997', *Post-Soviet Affairs*, 14 (1998).

[12] On the importance of sequencing of national and regional elections see Mark P. Jones, 'Federalism and the Number of Parties in Argentine Congressional Elections', *Journal of Politics*, 59/2 (May 1997), 538–50.

[13] See Darrell Slider, 'Pskov Under the LDPR: Dysfunctional Federalism in One Oblast', *Europe-Asia Studies* (formerly *Soviet Studies*), 51/5 (July 1999).

[14] In July 2000, at Putin's initiative, the law on forming the Federation Council was changed; henceforth it would be made up of representatives selected by regional legislatures and executives.

[15] The list of Central Committee members as of November 1997 appears on the KPRF website: www.kprf.ru.

Instructive in this regard is the case of another prominent Communist governor, Aman Tuleev. His base of support in Kemerovo oblast was highly personalized and independent of his party affiliation. Though Tuleev was and is a highly placed member of the KPRF and NPSR, he broke party ranks in August 1996 to become a member of Yeltsin's government as minister for cooperation with the Commonwealth of Independent States. He also ran on his own for president in 1996, withdrawing his candidacy in favour of Gennady Zyuganov only on the eve of the election. In June 1999 Tuleev founded his own political movement, 'Rebirth and Unity'. Members of the KPRF Central Committee Presidium refused to be present at the congress, which was attended by representatives from over fifty regions.[16] Perhaps proving that the party needs Tuleev more than vice versa, in October he was back in the KPRF fold as number four on the party list. But when the candidates for the four single-mandate districts in Kemerovo were nominated, Tuleev supported only one from the KPRF. Of the other three, one ran as an independent and two were nominated by the bloc Yedinstvo.[17]

As a rule, 'red governors' did not attempt to use the provincial party organization as an instrument of power. Conflicts with local Communist parties were common after the election was over. In Volgograd, shortly after Alexander Surikov was elected governor of Altai krai in 1997 with the support of the Communist-dominated movement 'For Real People's Power', he ordered all Communists appointed to government posts to cease their party activities.[18] When KPRF-member and Voronezh governor Ivan Shabanov was pressured by the party to appoint Communists to his administration, he responded 'as far as appointments based on party affiliation—forget it! . . . Excuse me, but as chief of executive power I am not subordinate to the obkom.'[19]

There are a number of reasons for the weak links between the KPRF and 'red governors'. First, despite the dominance of the Communist Party in the State Duma after the December 1995 elections, a Communist affiliation would not help in gaining access to the federal budget. Trumpeting one's Communist credentials would have been tantamount to waving a red flag in opposition to Yeltsin, and given the budgetary needs of most 'red belt' regions (which tended to be 'recipient' rather than 'donor' regions in relation to the federal budget), it could interfere with getting needed resources from the centre. Second, the KPRF was doctrinally hostile to strong governors and republic presidents. The Communist Party, both in statements by its leader, Gennady Zyuganov, and in the behaviour of its party fraction in the State Duma, has consistently favoured a strengthened role for the centre over the regions. In June 1997 Zyuganov published in *Nezavisimaya gazeta* a lengthy critique of Yeltsin's concessions to governors and republic presidents, arguing that they were undermining Russia as a unitary state. Zyuganov went on to lambast regional 'separatists, demagogues, and political hacks who have become used to catching fat gold fish in the clouded water of our current disorder'. Zyuganov also called for increasing the accountability of regional executives to legislative assemblies.[20] In February 1999 the KPRF leadership advocated

[16] 'Tuleev stal samostoyatel'nym igrokom', *Novye izvestiya*, 8 June 1999.

[17] All four candidates, of course, were Tuleev's people. 'Kommunisticheskie "Medvedi" Amana Tuleeva', *Nezavisimaya gazeta*, 12 Nov. 1999.

[18] 'Altaiskii gubernator trebuet ot kommunistov sdat' partbilety', *Kommersant-Daily*, 21 Mar. 1997.

[19] The obkom was the oblast committee of the Communist Party. Quoted by Vyzhutovich in *Izvestiya*, 12 Feb. 1999.

[20] Gennady Zyuganov, 'Muki tsentralizma', *Nezavisimaya gazeta*, supplement *NG-Stsenarii*, 13 Mar. 1997.

the end of popular elections of governors, allowing instead selection by legislative assemblies to choose the chief executive in the regions with the consent of the Russian president.[21]

The most recent national political movement to attract the interest of governors was Otechestvo (Fatherland). This was the political vehicle of Moscow mayor Yury Luzhkov, who had presidential aspirations. Both public opinion and the attitudes of regional leaders to Moscow presented immediate obstacles to Luzhkov's prospects. As the privileged capital, Moscow has long been an object of envy and hostility; the standard criticism was that any politician could do wonders if given the same advantages and resources as Moscow.

Luzhkov used his position as mayor of the richest administrative entity to develop the most extensive ties with regional leaders of any Russian political figure. As of June 1999, Moscow had agreements with seventy-three Russian regions.[22] Within the Moscow city government Luzhkov created a Committee for Public and Interregional Relations, headed by Lyudmila Shvetsova, that was responsible for developing and maintaining these relationships, and when former presidential spokesman Sergei Yastrzhemsky temporarily joined Luzhkov's team in mid-1999, he was given the responsibilty of co-ordinating the activities of this office.[23] In some cases, regional ties consisted of economic assistance from the city budget to poorer regions. In Kalmykia, for example, Luzhkov was a major force behind the construction of the republic president's dream project 'Chess City'. Briefly, Luzhkov's brother-in-law even served as prime minister of Kalmykia. For other regions, Luzhkov's regional policy was based on trading agreements, often on a barter basis. In other cases, such as the republic of Chuvashia, Luzhkov sent experienced specialists to staff top posts in the republic government.

When Otechestvo was founded in December 1998, Luzhkov called in a number of these political debts owed by regional leaders, and around thirty governors attended the founding congress.[24] Already at that time, Otechestvo reported having branches in eighty-eight regions (all except Chechnya), and in many regions governors reportedly commandeered what was left of the organizational structure of the party NDR.[25]

While attractive to many governors and republic presidents as a potential or alternative party of power, Otechestvo suffered from the hostile relationship that developed with the Yeltsin administration, and this led a number of regional leaders to hedge their bets. When the party held its second congress, in August 1999, a number of governors were no longer associated with the movement, and only eight regional leaders were included in the Otechestvo Central Council.

The rise of governors' parties

A new development in 1999 as part of the run-up to the December parliamentary elections was the creation of three political movements by coalitions of regional leaders in an attempt

[21] 'Kogo nado, togo i vyberem', *Segodnya*, 17 Feb. 1999.

[22] 'O razvitii mezhregional'nykh svyazey Moskvy', Pravitel'stvo Moskvy Postanovleniye ot 29 Junya 1999 goda N 578.

[23] Yastrzhemsky later joined Putin as the chief spokesman of the presidential administration. On his role in the Moscow administration, see 'O vnesenii dopolnenii v resporyazhenie Mera Moskvy ot 27 Maya 1998 N 519-RM "O respredelenii obyazannostei mezhdu chlenami Pravitel'stva Moskvy"' 20 July 1999.

[24] 'Regional'nyy desant v "Otechestvo"', *Izvestiya*, 19 Dec. 1998.

[25] Petr Akopov, 'Staryy dom dlya novogo Otechestvo', *Nezavisimaya gazeta*, 10 Mar. 1999.

to gain influence in the lower house of parliament. A constant refrain of Russian republic presidents and governors was that the State Duma was 'too politicized'. What this meant in practice was that its deputies were controlled by structures independent of regional leaders that were unresponsive to regional (that is, governors') concerns. In response to this and the governors' awareness of their own growing power, 1999 was marked by a flurry of party creating and party joining by regional leaders. Incidentally, the chairman of the Federation Council, Yegor Stroev, who is also governor of Orel oblast, strongly opposed the rise of governors' parties. He argued that the Federation Council in itself constituted what he called a 'political organization' for regional leaders, and that governors' parties are therefore not needed.[26] Stroev's fear is that the rise of governors' parties could undermine the cohesion of the Federation Council and perhaps threaten his own status as chairman.

It is fair to assume that one of the main purposes of this activity was to change the balance of forces in the State Duma so that governors and republic presidents could block the strengthening of federal institutions even more effectively than they could through the Federation Council. A veto by the Federation Council, after all, could be overridden by the Duma and the president. Success in the 1999 Duma elections would allow regional leaders to become multiple 'veto players'—permitting them to obstruct systemic reforms in both the upper and lower houses of the national parliament and in their regions.[27]

The parties chose different strategies to contest the 1999 elections. The first 'governors' party', the Voice of Russia (Golos Rossii), chose not to compete directly in the voting by party list and instead submerged itself within the bloc Union of Right Forces. The second group, Vsya Rossiya, allied itself with Otechestvo, in order to compete more effectively in the party-list vote. Only the third group, Yedinstvo, successfully registered its own party list.

All three groups attempted to influence the election of the other half of the Duma chosen in single-member districts. Because electoral districts are wholly within the territory of one region, there is a real opportunity for governors and republic presidents to influence the outcome of these elections. The instruments available to regional leaders include effective control over the media, access to the 'deep pockets' of local financial and industrial groups, and control over local governments and administrators—often including election commissions. In past elections to the Duma from single-member districts, republic presidents and governors have not attempted to determine the outcome in more than a few cases.[28] The administrative resources available to governors and republic presidents include numerous methods to commit vote fraud and thus change the results of elections.[29]

This new political activeness implied that governors themselves would seek seats in the Duma, and a number of governors did allow their names to be put on the party lists for

[26] Interview with Stroev in *Izvestiya*, 17 June 1999.

[27] The concept of 'veto players' is from George Tsebelis, 'Decision Making in Political Systems: Veto Players in Presidentialism, Parliamentarism, Multicameralism and Multipartyism', *British Journal of Political Science* 25/3 (July 1995), 289–316.

[28] One exception was the election of Yevgeny Zelenov to the 1995 Duma with massive support from the Novgorod oblast administration and local industrialists. Interview with Novgorod governor Mikhail Prusak in *Nezavisimaya gazeta*, 4 Mar. 1999.

[29] For evidence of Mintimer Shaimiev's capabilities in this area, used to deliver an apparent victory to Yeltsin in Tatarstan, see the article by John Loewenhardt, 'The 1996 Presidential Elections in Tatarstan', *Journal of Communist Studies and Transition Politics*, 13/1 (Mar. 1997), 132–44. A forthcoming article in the same journal by Loewenhardt details similar charges from 1999.

NDR, Otechestvo–Vsya Rossiya, and the KPRF. Yet it was obvious that no governor would give up the source of his power in order to become one of 450 members of the parliament's lower house. When Yedinstvo, the KPRF, and Otechestvo won seats in the Duma, sitting governors simply withdrew their names from the list and were replaced by less well-known candidates lower on the list.

GOLOS ROSSII (VOICE OF RUSSIA)

The first serious attempt to create a governors' party, Golos Rossii, was announced in January 1999, and formed in March 1999. Led by Samara governor Konstantin Titov, the movement included among its 'founders' a wide range of regional leaders, including controversial figures such as Ulyanovsk's Yury Goryachev and Primorye governor Yevgeny Nazdratenko. Titov, long a fixture in NDR, was joined by other former NDR leaders including Alexander Shokhin.[30] A number of analysts and political opponents considered Golos Rossii to be a creature of the Kremlin, designed to undermine the prospects of Luzhkov's Otechestvo.

Golos Rossii, however, never succeeded in establishing itself as a viable political structure. Titov himself contended in November 1999 that 'steps were taken to destroy the bloc on the part of the Kremlin and by several chiefs of subjects of the Federation'.[31] A more credible explanation for the failure of the movement lies in Titov's attempt to take the movement into the liberal, pro-market range of the political spectrum. In this, he quickly discovered that many (probably most) of the regional leaders who had co-founded the movement did not share his views. In August 1999 Titov united with Nemtsov and Kirienko in the bloc Union of Right Forces, and he was named the head of the political council of the movement. But the impact of Golos Rossii on the party list and the selection of candidates for single-member (majoritarian) districts was minimal at best. Most of the candidates were drawn from the ranks of Gaidar's Russia's Choice party.

VSYA ROSSIYA (ALL RUSSIA)

In April 1999 a larger grouping of regional leaders formed a second political bloc, ambitiously named 'All Russia'. Spearheaded by Mintimer Shaimiev, president of Tatarstan, early supporters included Ruslan Aushev, president of the North Caucasian Republic of Ingushetia, Bashkiria president Murtaz Rakhimov, and St Petersburg governor Vladimir Yakovlev.[32] Regional structures of the party appeared to be wholly the creatures of the regional leader; typically they did not even use the label 'All Russia'. In Tatarstan, for example, the organization was called 'Tatarstan—21st Century'.[33]

In part, Vsya Rossiya was formed as a counterweight to Golos Rossii. At the same time, according to the head of the presidential administration department for internal politics, the Yeltsin team actively facilitated the creation of Vsya Rossiya.[34] Contrary to Yeltsin's

---

[30] Shokhin drafted the movement's manifesto; he was interviewed in 'Okhota na provintsialov', *Segodnya*, 12 Mar. 1999; Titov is reported to have left NDR only in May 1999. *Izvestiya*, 6 May 1999.

[31] 'Kak zamanit' investorov na Volgu', *Nezavisimaya gazeta*, 6 Nov. 1999.

[32] 'Sozdaetsia vtoroy gubernatorskiy blok', *Nezavisimaya gazeta*, 20 Apr. 1999.

[33] See Ilya Malyakin, 'Gubernatorial Election Blocs: Russia Without Moscow or Moscow Without Russia?' *Prism*, 15 (Aug. 1999).

[34] See the interview with Andrei Loginov, in www.polit.ru. The interview took place in September 1999.

intentions, Vsya Rossiya later allied with Yury Luzhkov's political vehicle, Otechestvo, in August 1999.

In its programme Vsya Rossiya called for 'real federalism' in Russia, which would require increasing the power of the regions at the expense of the centre. While in practice regional leaders have already taken enormous powers from a weakened federal government, the programme claimed that 'not in a single democratic state is there such a concentration of power in the hands of a narrow group of people representing the federal centre, thus disregarding the interests of the regions and their inhabitants'.[35]

The Otechestvo–Vsya Rossiya coalition chose former prime minister Yevgeny Primakov as its chairman. Primakov, then the most popular Russian political figure, was a surprising choice in that his regional policy was in complete conflict with that of the leaders of the Vsya Rossiya bloc. Whereas Shaimiev and Aushev were among the staunchest advocates of giving the regions—particularly republics—increased autonomy from the centre, Primakov as prime minister called for a recentralization of control and the end of gubernatorial elections. (One Western analyst even viewed the creation of Vsya Rossiya as a reaction against Primakov's implied threats.[36]) A possible explanation is that both sides viewed the alliance as purely tactical and temporary, and the regional leaders agreed to accept Primakov for his vote-getting potential. In any event, the coalition of parties won over 13 per cent of the party-list vote and formed the third largest deputy fraction in the new Duma with forty-six members.

YEDINSTVO (UNITY)

The third bloc, created in late September 1999 as election deadlines were fast approaching, was Yedinstvo. The movement originated on the basis of a letter signed by thirty-nine regional leaders warning of the threats of destabilization in the pre-election period and calling for the election of 'honest and responsible people'. Yedinstvo (also sometimes referred to by the acronym 'Medved'' or 'bear') was seen by many observers as instigated by the Kremlin with the help of oligarch Boris Berezovsky to counter the Otechestvo–Vsya Rossiya bloc. One of the letter's signers, Murmansk governor Yury Yevdokimov, confirmed that the Russian Federation government (under then prime minister Vladimir Putin) 'acted as the initiator' of the movement.[37]

The bloc chose Sergei Shoigu to head both the organization and the party list. Shoigu, like Titov a member of the NDR Political Council, had developed a reputation as an honest and capable administrator as the government minister for emergencies. In contrast to, and in part as a reaction to, Golos Rossii and Vsya Rossiya, Yedinstvo studiously avoided any ideology.[38] It also initially avoided structure and organization. The main thrust of party strategy in late 1999 was to 'put the elections in the hands of the governors'. The Yedinstvo party list for the 1999 elections contained only one governor, Vladimir Platov of Tver oblast, and it appeared to be heavily controlled by a small subset of the original thirty-nine.

[35] The Vsya Rossiya 'Programmemnyye tezisy' were adopted at the founding congress in May 1999 and appear on the organization's web page, www.all-russia.ru.

[36] Floriana Fossato, 'New Political Bloc Finds Approval in Kazan', *RFE/RL Newsline*, 3/84 (30 Apr. 1999).

[37] 'Perekuem "Muzhikov" na "Medvedei"', *Segodnya*, 22 Sept. 1999.

[38] 'Ideologiia "yedinstva"—v otsutstvii ideologii', *Nezavisimaya gazeta*, 29 Sept. 1999.

Reported to be most influential in the movement were governors Rutskoi, Nazdratenko, and Platov.[39]

Just before the December 1999 elections, Yedinstvo received the endorsement of the popular prime minister (and soon to be president) Vladimir Putin. This provided an enormous boost to the party and its image, and it won an unexpected 23 per cent of the vote by party list and formed the second largest (after the Communists) Duma deputy fraction with eighty-nine members, including converts from the disbanded fraction of Our Home is Russia. The political significance of Putin's endorsement cannot be overestimated; what was initially a weak and little-known 'governors' party' was rapidly transformed into 'the president's party'.

Conclusion

A commonly voiced criticism of Russian economic reform efforts is that the problem of sequencing was inadequately considered; the order in which changes are introduced can have the effect of distorting or precluding future policies. A parallel argument can be made about political reforms and building a party system and an effective federation.

The strengthening and consolidation of regional elites prior to the establishment of federal institutions such as national political parties acts to inhibit the further development of those institutions. A major role was played here by the decision by the Yeltsin administration to extend popular elections to the post of governor. It both ratified and solidified the power of regional leaders, making them much less dependent on Moscow. The decision to allow elections for governors had a particularly negative impact on Russia's potential to develop national political parties, since the decision was made before such parties existed. This key modification in Russia's institutional framework was made in the heat of the political struggle going on in the centre, with little thought given to the consequences. In many ways, it was typical of Yeltsin's lack of attention to institutional design and development. His preferred pattern of action was crisis management, often exacerbating crises to enhance his ability to prevail.

In speculating about the direction in which Russia appears to be moving, one of the most instructive examples is Brazil. Brazil has, since the end of military rule, exhibited many institutional characteristics similar to those emerging in Russia: a strong presidential system, a federal structure, and strong elected (after 1982) governors with extensive patronage powers at the regional level. A shift of power to regions under the 1988 Brazil constitution gave them a strong economic and budgetary role which resulted in increasing governors' influence on representatives in the national assembly. In terms of party organization, Brazil's national parties have tended to be weak, decentralized, and poorly institutionalized; they tend to be dominated by a highly personalized type of politics. Scott Mainwaring has suggested that this mix of institutional and structural factors is a large part of the explanation for the dismal state of Brazilian politics, characterized by corruption, instability, and built-in obstacles to reform.[40]

---

[39] 'Legendy i mify bloka "Medved"-2' *Segodnya*, 21 Oct. 1999.

[40] Scott P. Mainwaring, *Rethinking Party Systems in the Third Wave of Democratization: The Case of Brazil* (Stanford, Calif.: Stanford University Press, 1999), esp. 190–7 and 264–6.

On the surface, it would appear that the increasing political activity of Russia's governors in 1999—manifested in the rise of governors' parties and political alliances—was a positive sign of involvement with national politics that could strengthen both democratic institutions and Russian federalism. It certainly provides evidence that, other than Chechnya, the regional elites of Russia have no interest in breaking up the country. Even the most intransigent of regional leaders, Mintimer Shaimiev of Tatarstan, took the lead in party and coalition building.

The potential for harm represented by these attempts should not be underestimated, however. The governors' blocs that were created in 1999 can be seen as an effort designed to prevent the growth of national political parties that could threaten the political dominance of regional elites. In effect the governors' blocs were 'anti-party parties' that sought to preclude national party building. The new, and often multiple, party affiliations of governors do not reflect a broadening of political perspective. As Viktor Ishaev, governor of Khabarovsk krai and member of the Political Council of Vsya Rossiya, put it when asked about the meaning of his party attachment, 'My party is Khabarovsk krai'.[41]

Once Putin became president, the most successful of the governors' parties, Yedinstvo, became the political vehicle for pushing through Putin's agenda in the Duma. Loyalties among Yedinstvo parliamentary deputies quickly shifted from the governors to Putin, who was able to dispense considerably more political and material benefits to the latest 'party of power' than were governors. Paradoxically, what began as a 'governors' party' became the core of a centralist, anti-governor coalition in the Duma. At the same time, because of its origins in the administrative resources of regional elites, the life-expectancy and strength of Yedinstvo as a political party is questionable. Most of the heads of local branches of the party remain people who were selected by the governor of that region. Yedinstvo's victory, while no threat to strengthening the federation, does not portend a consolidation of Russia's political party system.

In fact, one likely consequence of the new balance of forces in the Duma will be an attempt to amend the constitution to eliminate or substantially reduce the party-list element of Russian elections, a move that had already been endorsed by the Yeltsin adminstration after the repeated failure of pro-presidential parties. The effect of this change in the Russian political system would be to further hinder the rise of stable and institutionalized national political parties.

---

[41] 'Viktor Ishayev: Rossii nuzhna partiya razumnykh lyudei', *Nezavisimaya gazeta*, 13 Oct. 1999.

16 Partisan and Party Divisions in Post-Communist Russia

Stephen Whitefield

....

Introduction

Most commentators would accept that political parties in post-Communist Russia are weak on many dimensions. They do not govern: neither Yeltsin nor Putin were elected on the basis of their party attachments, nor are parties important sources for the recruitment of government ministers. In parliament, they are undisciplined and incoherent actors by comparison not only with parliamentary systems in the West but even with a number of presidential systems in Eastern Europe. Many parties, especially those most associated with power, have been transitory in character, and few have obtained representation in each of the three parliamentary elections since the collapse of the Soviet Union. In any case, a large number of deputies in the Duma consider themselves to be independents. Finally, parties tend to have weak organizations, little presence outside Moscow, and almost no ties to 'civil society'.[1]

This chapter addresses the implications of these problems of party development for our view of the relationship between parties and Russian society. Clearly, it is difficult to sort out cause and effect in the relationship between the party system and the partisan attachments of Russians. On the one hand, the institutional structure of Russia, in which parties play little role in governing, may give party leaders little incentive to work to attract voters based on differentiated social and ideological appeals and this may inhibit the development of the sort of bases of support for parties that underpin party systems in other societies.[2] On the other hand, it may be that lack of social divisions arising from civil society and a corresponding lack of ideological divisions within the electorate was the initial cause of weakly rooted parties or even, indeed, of pressures to design political institutions in which weakly rooted parties play little role.[3]

Chapter specially commissioned for this volume.

[1] Evidence for these assertions can be found in: Richard Rose, 'A Supply-Side View of Russia's Elections', *East European Constitutional Review*, 9/1–2, (Winter/Spring 2000), 53–59 (republished as Chapter 14 of this reader under the title, 'How Floating Parties Frustrate Democratic Accountability: A Supply-Side View of Russia's Elections'); Kathryn Stoner-Weiss, 'The Limited Reach of Russia's Party System: Under Institutionalization in Dual Transitions', Paper presented at Yale University, March 2000; Peter Reddaway, 'Instability and Fragmentation', *Journal of Democracy*, 5/2 (1994), 13–19; and Peter Rutland, 'Has Democracy Failed in Russia', *The National Interest*, 38 (Winter, 1994), 3–12.

[2] Cf., Herbert Kitschelt, Zdenka Mansfeldova, Radislaw Markowski, and Gabor Toka, *Post-Communist Party Systems* (Cambridge: Cambridge University Press, 1999).

[3] For a discussion of this point from a comparative institutional design perspective, see Matthew Shugart, 'Presidentialism, Parliamentarism, and the Provision of Collective Goods in Less-Developed Countries', *Constitutional Political Economy*, 10/1 (1999), 53–88. In Russian context, see Stephen White, Richard Rose, and Ian McAllister, *How Russia Votes* (London: Chatham House, 1997).

There is the third possibility, however. Despite evidence on many dimensions of party weakness, voters and parties in Russia may nonetheless have strong and stable relationships based on a correspondence between the programmes offered by parties and the social and ideological interests of voters. If this were the case, then it would tend to tell against the suggestion that the institutional design of the Russian political system was the result of societal limitations on the development of the party system or that the choice of institutions then led to a failure of parties to build important ties to the electorate. Moreover, it would give an indication of the possibilities for further party system development if elite interests or institutional incentives were to change to make parties more important for the governing process in Russia. Finally, it would put a different perspective on the development of the bases of democratic politics in Russia.

To consider these issues, the rest of the chapter looks at evidence, mainly derived from the author's own earlier and recent research (much of it conducted in collaboration with Geoffrey Evans) regarding the development of the mass bases of partisanship in Russia since 1993. To what extent is support for parties differentiated and by what social and ideological factors? Are the political divisions to party choice by voters stable or as volatile as the parties on offer? Do party elites and their voters share views about policies or are they cut off from one another?

The social bases of partisanship in Russia

Social bases to partisanship exist when voters sharing social characteristics tend to choose the same or similar parties. They admit of degree and may rise or fall (alignment and de-alignment) over time. The sources of social structuring of party choice may vary considerably across societies, including class, religion, ethnicity, gender, sector, etc., and there may be a number of distinct and independent social bases to party choice within a single country.

The existence of social bases to partisanship has often been held to be dependent on prior social organization or on party strategies themselves. For example, in some societies parties arose on the basis of a pre-existing civil society in which the public was already organized and differentiated on social lines by Church or trade union or by the state's treatment of ethnic groups.[4] Alternatively, parties may themselves seek to mobilize voters based on their social characteristics and only when they do so, regardless of the prior state of organization of civil society, will social divisions to partisanship emerge.[5] The problem with both of these approaches to social divisions in Russia is obvious; civil society is weak, and parties are also weak, and each of these might make it unlikely that social divisions will emerge.

The evidence regarding social divisions to partisanship in Russia, however, turns out to defy these expectations. Social groups have from the beginning shown divergent patterns of party choice and, moreover, these differences have tended to become more intense and varied over time.[6] Analysis of responses to surveys in 1993, for example, shows the existence

[4] The classic statement of the importance of prior organization for party formation and the creation of mass party linkages is found in Seymour Martin Lipset and Stein Rokkan, eds., *Party Systems and Voter Alignments* (New York: Free Press, 1967).

[5] Cf., Adam Przeworski, *Capitalism and Social Democracy* (Cambridge: Cambridge University Press, 1985).

[6] Stephen Whitefield, 'Social Responses to Reform in Russia', in David Lane, ed., *Russia in Transition* (London: Longman, 1995), 91–118; Stephen Whitefield and Geoffrey Evans, 'Class, Markets and Partisanship in Post-Soviet Russia: 1993–9', *Electoral Studies*, 18/2 (1999), 155–78.

of a single and rather weak social division based on essentially economic criteria: between those on high versus low incomes, the latter often older voters on pensions, and between urban and rural respondents. Over time, however, the strength of association between social characteristics and party choice grows and broadens; while remaining fixed principally in the economy, significant differences exist between urban and rural voters, and between the metropolitan centres of Moscow and St Petersburg where reform has been most advanced, and smaller cities and settlements. Divisions also exist between those reliant on state budgets and the rest of society. An especially clear division emerges oriented around age and pensions. The evidence over time also shows a very clear pattern of growth in the class bases to politics in Russia over time. These sorts of growing divisions are precisely what we expect in a society undergoing rapid marketization, in which there are also very difficult problems in the state budget. At the same time, non-economic alternative bases to social differentiation in Russia are also present though comparatively weak. Ethnic differences are there as, even more weakly, are those based on religious denomination in which the Orthodox differ from other members of society. Finally, there is a clear if relatively minor gender division to partisanship.[7]

The evidence, then, suggests that partisan division in Russia is not subject to multiple distinct types of social division but is mainly based on economic differences. Social division, however, is developed and has become increasingly complex as economic change resulting from the collapse of the command economy and the introduction of the Russian variant of the market has resulted in various social groups having both divergent economic experiences and, which is highly significant, developing clearer associations between their social interests and their choice of particular parties or presidential candidates.

The relationship between social interests and ideology, and between party divisions and the position of particular parties and candidates is discussed below. Before turning to these questions, however, a puzzle arising from the evidence needs to be addressed. Against either the first or second perspective on party development in Russia outlined in the introduction suggesting either that there were strong social impediments to the emergence of party division, or strong elite constraints because elites lacked incentives to build ties to the population, the reality appears to support the third position in which social divisions have emerged regardless. But how can it be, in the absence of either civil society or strong party organizations, that significant social divisions to partisanship have emerged at all in Russia? And what accounts for certain social characteristics being salient to partisan choices?

The emergence and growth of social divisions to partisanship even with weak parties and weak civil society says something very important about the possibilities of mass rational involvement in politics in Russia. Russians have had clearly differentiated social experiences since 1991 (and before this time of course), particularly in their economic experience, and this creates the basis for politically salient social divisions. But, while we should not exaggerate the weakness of parties, and some parties like the Communist Party of Russia do have social roots, in the main voters have been able on their own, with minimal help from parties or other organizational ties, and indeed in the face of great volatility of party labels, to find

---

[7] Stephen Whitefield and Geoffrey Evans, 'The Emerging Structure of Partisan Development in Post-Soviet Russia', in Matthew Wyman, Stephen White, and Sarah Oates, eds., *Elections and Voters in Post-Communist Russia* (Cheltenham: Edward Elgar, 1998), 68–99.

ways of relating their social identities and interests to partisan choices. The lesson of the Russian experience is that it may take much less information and organization for the social bases of partisanship to emerge than might have been expected.

The character of the social divisions follows from the sources of differentiated experience.[8] The evidence suggests that economic differences of various sorts are the main sources of division and this makes sense in the Russian context. While religion or ethnicity play important roles in other states, the fact is that in Russia these factors are not of widespread salience as bases of differentiation within the population. While Russians comprise about 80 per cent of the population, no minority constitutes more than approximately 3 per cent, and most minorities are both geographically dispersed and often linguistically Russified. Moreover, the electoral system with a 5 per cent threshold is not permissive of the establishment of ethnic parties. Ethnic questions do play a minor role in structuring ideological divisions, as we will see below, but given the ethnic composition of the population, ethnic identities should not, and do not, provide a basis for focused party choice by minorities and therefore distinct ethnic social bases to partisanship are absent. For a different reason, religion is not a politicized social division in Russia. While Catholicism, for example, has historically had a programmatic character on issues especially related to lifestyles and values, Orthodoxy has tended to avoid direct intervention in policy while allying itself with state power. Differences between the Orthodox and the secular, therefore, on policy questions tend to be very limited and so there is little in the experience of the political and social sphere that would translate into social divisions to partisanship in the Russian context. Economic differences are what remain and do sharply divide the population, though the extent of this should not be exaggerated.

The ideological bases of partisanship

Ideological divisions can take a number of forms and in Russia might be expected to, given the challenges facing the people of simultaneous and ongoing transitions from authoritarian rule to democracy, from plan to market, from empire to national state, and from autarkic power to an historically unparalleled integration into the international arena.

As was the case with social divisions, however, a number of possible patterns of ideological division might result from such potential. First, because of the sheer magnitude and complexity of the multiple challenges facing individuals, their families, and the country as a whole, voters might be expected to be confused and to lack a coherent set of attitudes or stable ideologies that might allow them to make sense of the transformation. Again, while civil society and parties might in other contexts aid the population in arriving at a coherent response to complex circumstances, and in this sense help to structure individuals' attitudes across a range of issues, their absence in Russia might compound the extent of ideological flux and confusion. However, given the fact that Russians are divided socially in their partisan choices, as we have just seen, it seems just as likely that ideological divisions will

---

[8] For a fuller discussion of the sources and forms of cleavage formation in post-Communist societies, see Geoffrey Evans and Stephen Whitefield, 'Explaining the Formation of Electoral Cleavages in Post-Communist Democracies', in Hans-Dieter Klingemann, Ekkehard Mochmann, and Kenneth Newton, eds., *Elections in Central and Eastern Europe: The First Wave*, (Berlin: Sigma, 2000), 36–70.

emerge based on coherent sets of attitudes derived from distinctive social interests and experiences.

But what form might ideological divisions to partisanship take? A second pattern might be to expect multiple ideological divisions along each of the lines of cleavage just mentioned, with some voters choosing parties based on their economic programmes, others on their relationship to democracy. Against this expectation of cross-cutting cleavages, finally, the pattern of ideological divisions might be essentially unidimensional, in which supporters of the market turned out to be also supporters of democracy, of the national state, and of integration with the West, while opponents of the market link this issue to a more general commitment to the old Soviet order comprised of an authoritarian, autarkic, and imperial state structure.

Evidence, however, for the existence of clear and significant ideological divisions to partisanship in Russia certainly does allow us to reject the first of these alternatives.[9] Despite the complexity of the experience of transition, and again without much help from political parties or civil society, Russians have been able to form relatively stable and coherent views of the world and have been able to relate these views to their choice of party. Moreover, the views that Russians tend to hold are strongly predicted by the social differences discussed in the previous section. People doing well tend to be economically liberal and to vote for similar parties. Indeed, although they always did so, the relationship appears to have strengthened over time, indicating considerable social learning.

The form of ideological division in Russia, however, is predominantly unidimensional rather than based on two or more cross-cutting cleavages. This means that for the most part voters are ranged from pro-market, pro-West, and pro-social and political liberal position at one end of the spectrum, to anti-market, anti-West and socially and politically illiberal views at the other. Each of these elements in turn is very strongly correlated with views of the former Soviet Union; those that identify with the USSR and regret its passing are much more likely to be committed to a set of illiberal policy positions. There is also some evidence that the part of the electorate most favourable to an independent Russia was also, at least for the first half of the 1990s, the most likely to be pro-Western and pro-market.[10] Ideological divisions in Russia, therefore, do not appear to be multi-dimensional. Moreover, within the main dimension, and consonant with the movement away from the old political order, there has also been a tendency for a growth in the relative importance of economic questions over the other elements of the dimension. As class and other economic social divisions to partisanship have grown, so too has the economic component of the ideological divide.

This is not to say, however, that the main ideological division has not at some point been cross-cut, though only to a minor degree. Some economic liberals are also politically authoritarian. More importantly, during the first Chechen war, many liberals as well as many supporters of the old order were opposed. Nonetheless, the evidence indicates that the Chechen division was relatively transient and essentially disappeared once the issue appeared in the short term to have been resolved. (We can surmise, however, that the revival of conflict may once again have divided the population, though on the basis of the limited

[9] Whitefield and Evans, 'The Emerging Structure of Partisan Development in Post-Soviet Russia'.

[10] Stephen Whitefield and Geoffrey Evans, 'The Russian Election of 1993: Public Opinion and the Transition Experience', *Post-Soviet Affairs*, 10/1 (1994), 38–60; Stephen Whitefield and Geoffrey Evans, 'Support for Democracy and Political Opposition in Russia, 1993–1995', *Post-Soviet Affairs*, 12/3 (1996), 218–42.

survey data available, public and party responses to the question appear to be much less divided during the second Chechen war than they were in the mid-1990s.)

Once again, the question arises as to why *ideological* divisions should be so essentially unidimensional in Russia, and the answer follows from the explanation for the mainly unidimensional and economic character of the *social* divisions in the country. In other post-Communist states, independent ideological bases to party choice form around distinct economic, value, and ethnic (including anti-Semitic) divisions because social experience and historico-cultural inheritances provide separate sources for their politicization. All countries tend to have strong economic differences that form a basis for differentiated views which translate into party choices. But some countries also have minorities, seen as socially distant at least by the majority, and which are sufficiently large and concentrated to obtain representation within the electoral rules; and some are divided by religious traditions that strongly differentiate value orientations. While Russia has the economic differences, it lacks the latter two, and in these conditions it is likely that other issues will become politically salient in so far as they connect to economic concerns. Economic losers in Russia are socially and politically illiberal, and anti-West, because each of these connects with the old Soviet order which they perceive as having provided more security, well-being and, connected to this, national pride. Opponents of the old order, conversely, have tended to do economically better and indeed stand to gain more by integration into the world economy. There is simply no other theoretical basis for the independent politicization of powerful ideological divisions in Russia and the evidence confirms this expectation.

Parties, presidential candidates, and voters

We have seen that socially differentiated Russians are able to relate their experiences to ideological programmes and in turn to link each of these to their choice of parties in ways that produce clear but growing political divisions. The evidence suggests, moreover, that the numbers of Russians able and willing to nominate a party with which they politically identify has grown considerably over time and now bears comparison with many established democracies.[11] These facts give rise to a number of further questions. First, does the choice of parties make sense given what we know about the social and ideological characteristics of their voters? Do parties, in other words, share a profile with their voters? Secondly, do we see significant differences in the extent to which parties connect with voters as opposed to the ways in which presidential candidates do? Is the character of the divisions underlying party support different from that underlying support for individual politicians?

Each of these questions is important to an appreciation of the significance of the findings in the previous two sections. If voters are not able to choose parties 'rationally' in the sense that the parties reflect their views, then the existence of social and ideological divisions is effectively spurious and voters are not making choices that effectively represent their social and ideological positions. By the same token, in the Russian system where the presidency is of much greater political significance than the parliament, the absence of social and

---

[11] See Arthur H. Miller, Gwyn Erb, William M. Reisinger, and Vicki L. Hesli, 'Emerging Party Systems in Post-Soviet Societies', *Journal of Politics*, 62/2 (2000), 455–90; Russell Dalton, Ian McAllister, and Martin P. Wattenberg, 'The Decline in Party Identification and the Consequences of Dealignment: The Evidence from 20 OECD Nations'. Paper presented at the Annual Meeting of the American Political Science Association, Washington DC, Sept. 2000.

ideological divisions for presidential choices or the existence of divisions of a quite different character from those discussed in the last two sections would indicate both greater instability than previously suggested and much greater influence of institutional and personal factors.

The evidence, however, appears to suggest a considerable and growing fit between voter positions and party profiles. In studies of political divisions in Russia between 1993 and 1998,[12] supporters of the Communist Party appear at the anti-market, anti-West, and politically illiberal end of the spectrum, with a social base that is mainly drawn from older and less-educated voters, pensioners and those with negative experience of economic reform, while Russia's Choice and Yabloko supporters were clearly the most liberal on a variety of measures and correspondingly drawn from the more educated and youthful parts of the population and disproportionately from residents of Moscow. Our Home is Russia and earlier the Democratic Party of Russia and Shakhrai's Party of Unity and Accord were found between these two ideological extremes and their voters were socially less distinctive as well. Supporters of Zhirinovsky's Liberal Democratic Party of Russia, as again might be expected, tended to be located towards the centre of the economic reform dimension but were more likely to favour authoritarian political positions and to support the Chechen war. Like supporters of reform parties, LPDR voters were often young, but also male and from smaller towns rather than the metropolitan areas. These results match the expectations that derive from the known positions of the parties on these issues.

Moreover, as Arthur H. Miller and his collaborators in the Iowa studies have shown from a number of surveys over the years in Russia (and elsewhere in the former Soviet Union),[13] party supporters are not only ideologically cohesive among themselves, but parallel studies of the positions of party elites has shown a strong correlation between these elites and their supporters. Not only do voters choose parties that nominally represent them, in other words, they even seem to choose parties in which the leaders share their view of the world. As Miller *et al.* conclude, the strong relationship between parties and their supporters is indicative of a party system that is in many ways strongly developed.

Presidential divisions also do not appear to be greatly different socially or ideologically from party ones. Of course, this point can only be pushed so far because the second-round run-off element of the presidential electoral system has the effect in itself of removing the possibility of multi-dimensionality of ideological divisions because voters are forced to choose among two competing candidates and not across a range of possible options. However, as was noted above, ideological divisions were essentially unidimensional in respect of party competition despite the existence of multiple party choices among the electorate in Russia arising from the party list and district system. The same outcome is also evident in the presidential contest when, as in the first round of the election, voter choice is considerable. In addition, the evidence shows that the nature of the dimension of ideological division is more or less the same whether voters are making presidential or party choices, from which we may infer both that the same structuring factors are in place for each case and that the

[12] Whitefield and Evans, 'The Emerging Structure of Partisan Development in Post-Soviet Russia'; Matthew Wyman, 'Elections and Voting Behaviour' in Stephen White, Alex Pravda, and Zvi Gitelman, eds., *Developments in Russian Politics 4* (London: Macmillan, 1997), 104–28; Miller, Erb, Reisinger, and Hesli, 'Emerging Party Systems in Post-Soviet Societies'.

[13] Ibid.

effects of personalities on the issue bases of politics are not highly significant. Considering the extent to which there is an association between the ideological characteristics of voters and their choice of party or candidate, neither does presidential competition appear to be less structured than is party competition. Moreover, when looking at analysis of the social bases of support for presidents, a very similar picture emerges to that shown earlier for parties. In other words, economic divisions (older voters, pensioners, poorer Russians versus younger, more educated and better off) characterize the social bases of presidential support, while ideologically voters are divided as they were when choosing parties by associated liberalisms and illiberalisms and views of the Soviet past. Finally, the relationship noted above between party profiles and the ideological and social characteristics of their supporters also applies to the fit between candidates and their voters: those nominating Gaidar, Yavlinsky, and Federov as their presidential choice are young, educated, and liberal; those nominating Zyuganov or earlier Rutskoi are older, less educated and less liberal; supporters of Yeltsin have moved over time from a more strongly reformist position towards the centre; and supporters of Zhirinovsky and of Lebed appeared in the centre on the economy while in an authoritarian position on political organization.

This evidence is important because the stability of divisions across presidential and party choices indicates that voters are able to relate their interests and commitments in similar ways to a variety of political conditions; indeed, it may be inferred that politicians, whether leading parties or competing as individuals, face the same electoral market. Against the claim made by Richard Rose that the 'supply side' of politics in Russia is decisive,[14] it appears more likely that the similarity of presidential and party divisions, in which supply conditions clearly vary, and of social and ideological divisions over time despite significant changes in the nominal parties on offer, is best explained by factors on the 'demand' side. Individual politicians do not appear able to manipulate the electorate to suit their interests but rather must respond to the socially determined concerns of Russians, at least when appealing for their votes. While institutions aggregate interests in particular ways and of course shape the way in which power and policy is made, they do not seem determinant of the social and ideological space in which democratic competition in Russia takes place.

Conclusion

The evidence discussed above points cumulatively to the strong development of partisan and party divisions in Russia, shaped by the social experiences and corresponding ideological interests of voters. Presidential competition during the 1990s matched rather than refuted this position and although Putin sought to present an image of broad appeal to Russians in the 2000 campaign, it is highly likely that his supporters divided socially and ideologically from those of Zyuganov, Yavlinsky, and other candidates in very similar ways to those described above. Growing partisanship in Russia should not be surprising given the capacity of voters to find parties that reflect their outlook. In many ways, the picture just described is indicative of a relatively developed party system. The sources of party weakness on the dimensions described in the opening paragraphs, therefore, are not to be found in

---

[14] Rose, 'A Supply-Side View of Russia's Elections'.

society even though it lacks the organizational forms of civil association, but rather in other aspects of the Russian transition.

The most obvious alternative explanation for some dimensions of party weakness is institutional: a powerful president who does not rely on the support of parliament does not stimulate party development in the legislature; the single member district portion of the electoral system has a similar effect on party organizational development and its reach into the provinces; federalism also has a negative effect on party formation and consolidation, particularly the indirectly elected representation of the regions; and the electoral cycle has led to Duma elections functioning as primaries for presidential elections to follow.

However, the analysis above points to the limited nature of institutional effects on partisan divisions. To return to the cause and effect questions raised in the introduction: *contra* Matthew Shugart,[15] institutional choice in Russia does not appear to be the result of the incapacity of Russians to arrive at socially and ideologically rooted partisan choices; and institutions do not appear to have a significant effect on the nature of the political divisions, either social or ideological. Despite the institutional context, voters appear to have converged with parties and presidential candidates on policy positions. If Russia were ever to change its institutional framework to allow parties more say in government then the mass bases of parliamentary politics would already be in place.

These conclusions are not intended to indicate that Russians get what they want politically. But they do suggest that the causes of weaknesses in political and economic performance in post-Communist Russia are not found in an incapacity of voters to know how to punish which leaders for failure to pursue their electorally expressed desires or that politicians in Russia are essentially demagogues moulding public opinion to their wills unconstrained by stable social and ideological divisions.

Governance problems in Russia no doubt have many contributing causes. The economic legacy of Communism and of the economic transition path is one; the weakness of the state and its enforcement capacity is another. But there is also a strong sense in which the character of the political divisions and of mass involvement in support for parties and presidential candidates is a significant contributor to the weakness of representative politics and good governance in Russia. Russians are highly divided on a single main ideological dimension, pitting the old order against the new. On this dimension, moreover, the distribution of ideological and party preferences has tended to be bi-polar.[16] Up to a third of the electorate are supportive of the old order and of the Communists; another roughly 10 per cent favour the market and authoritarianism and the LPDR and Zhirinovsky; the remainder are comparatively democratic and pro-market in principle, and do not wish a return to the past, despite considerable dissatisfaction with the course of political and economic transformation in practice. So long as Russians divide in this way and in these proportions, it is unlikely that political competition for the median voter will emerge or that the political and economic winners will face a strong and democratic political challenge. And as long as there is no credible democratic opposition in Russia, there is little incentive for the winners and their representatives to work for good government.

---

[15] Shugart, 'Presidentialism, Parliamentarism, and the Provision of Collective Goods in Less-Developed Countries'.

[16] Cf. Whitefield and Evans, 'Support for Democracy and Political Opposition in Russia, 1993–1995'.

Economic Reform: Politics, Interests, and Social Consequences

Section 6

Economic Reform, Politics,
Interests, and Social
Consequences

Introduction

Archie Brown

At various times in the first decade after the collapse of the Soviet Union, what is generally called 'economic reform' in the Russian Federation has been portrayed as a success story. The number of *Russians* who saw it in those terms constituted a small minority of the population, but Western governments, the IMF, and some economists who offered advice to the post-Soviet Russian government have tried hard to look on the bright side. This was reflected in the titles of books such as *How Russia Became a Market Economy* and *The Coming Russian Boom*, the latter published just two years before the Russian bust.[1] The crash of the Russian financial system, and the sharp, involuntary devaluation of August 1998, led, in the late 1990s, to more sombre assessments, though, in fact, by making imports more expensive, the crisis was a blessing in disguise for some sections of the Russian economy.[2] The public purse was also boosted by the substantial rise in oil prices. What was less clear when the Yeltsin era ended was whether much progress had been made in fundamental economic restructuring or in the creation of a legally regulated market economy.

In its 1999 *Transition Report*, the European Bank for Reconstruction and Development ranked twenty formerly Communist countries in terms of 'quality of governance'. Their criteria were those elements of governance (or failures of governance) with a particular bearing on the workings of the economy—for instance, tax collection and regulations, inflation and its control, policy stability or instability, corruption, and organized crime.[3] They ranked Russia seventeenth with only Romania, Kyrgyzstan, and Moldova faring worse. In particular, Russia exemplified many of the characteristics of 'state capture', whereby 'powerful vested interests in the economy have a tendency to side-step reforms that might improve governance while at the same time reducing distortions in the economy that work to the benefit of such interests'.[4]

Since the economic system was in limbo during most of the last two years of the Soviet system—no longer a 'planned' economy and not yet market-based—shortages, a perennial problem of the Communist command economy, had become worse. Yegor Gaidar's liberalization of prices in January 1992—a radical measure which wiped out the life savings of millions

---

[1] See Anders Åslund, *How Russia Became a Market Economy* (Washington: Brookings Institution, 1995); and Richard Layard and John Parker, *The Coming Russian Boom: A Guide to New Markets and Politics* (New York: The Free Press, 1996).

[2] Nevertheless, the most recent report of the European Bank for Reconstruction and Development points out that 'despite recent growth, average real incomes are still well below their pre-crisis level' (*Transition Report 2000: Employment, skills and transition* (EBRD, London, 2000), 203).

[3] EBRD, *Transition Report 1999: Ten years of transition* (European Bank of Reconstruction and Development, London, 1999), 116.

[4] Ibid., 117.

of people as prices rose precipitously—can be, and generally is, defended on the grounds that desperate times required desperate measures. There were, however, counter-arguments even from the ranks of those who accepted that price liberalization was, in principle, necessary and that prices fixed by the state were economic nonsense. The Yaboloko leader (and economist) Grigory Yavlinsky was among the more prominent critics who held that to free prices before demonopolization would enable monopolies to exploit their new opportunities and merely turn hidden inflation into overt and accelerated inflation. The response to that, most recently expressed by Gaidar's close associate, Vladimir Mau, is that institutional reforms take time to be implemented and that time was something Gaidar did not have.[5] Gaidar has himself put the point starkly in his memoirs:

Perhaps the main problem of adaptation to work in the government, especially in conditions of extreme crisis, is the radical change in the time dimension. Scholars plan their work in terms of years, months, or weeks. Advisers measure their time in hours and days. A head of government is forced to act within seconds, at best within minutes. To think quietly for a few hours, unhurriedly to seek advice, is almost a luxury.[6]

To the extent that Gaidar is right, it is all the clearer that the ideological predisposition a government head brings to his or her work will the more surely shape decisions that have to be taken with little time available for reflection. At any rate, Gaidar's price liberalization succeeded in its primary aim of filling up empty shelves in the shops, even if there was a growing gulf between those who could afford to buy the products and those who could not. Moving quickly to remove state-fixed prices was justified also on the grounds that difficult decisions would become even harder to take if they were postponed. Yeltsin's popular standing was still high at the beginning of 1992, and his backing for the 'young reformers' meant that it was possible to do things then which would have been politically dangerous later.

The early measures of the Gaidar government unquestionably improved the supply of goods and services. However, price liberalization did not lead to the more rational allocation of resources that might have been expected. What happened in a number of transitions from Communist economic systems, and conspicuously in Russia, has been summarized by Joel Hellman:

Rapid foreign trade liberalization with incomplete price liberalization has allowed state enterprise managers to sell their highly subsidized natural resource inputs (for example, oil and gas) to foreign buyers at world market prices. Price liberalization without concomitant progress in opening market entry or breaking up monopolies has created opportunities for some producers to earn monopoly rents. Privatization without reform of the credit mechanism has allowed managers to divert subsidized state credits earmarked to uphold production into short-term money markets at high interest rates.[7]

Whereas it had been widely assumed that the winners when an economy was partially

---

    [5] Vladimir Mau, *Russian Economic Reforms as Seen by an Insider: Success or Failure?* (London: Royal Institute of International Affairs, 2000), esp. pp. 9–15.

    [6] Yegor Gaidar, *Dni porazheniy i pobed* (Moscow: Vagrius, 1997), 125–6.

    [7] Joel Hellman, 'Winners Take All: The Politics of Partial Reform in Postcommunist Transitions', *World Politics*, 50/2 (Jan. 1998), 203–34, at p. 29.

marketized would form a constituency for more extensive reform, the reality has been that they constituted a formidable obstacle to it. As Hellman puts it:

Rising financial-industrial conglomerates, reconstituted on newly emerging securities markets, have used their power to block new market entry. New entrepreneurs-cum-mafiosi, who have gained tremendously from the liberalization of domestic and foreign trade, have undermined the formation of a viable legal system to support the market economy.[8]

Contrary, then, to the conventional wisdom whereby it was assumed—by, among others, many of Russia's economic advisers—that the losers, as marketizing reforms got underway, would be the main threat to 'the realization of the efficiency gains of a fully functioning market', the reality has been that this role has been played more influentially by the winners. This is very much at odds with the quite widespread view that democracy and far-reaching marketizing reforms are incompatible. The encouraging conclusion to be drawn from Hellman's comparative analysis is that 'postcommunist systems with a higher level of political participation and competition have been able to adopt and maintain more comprehensive economic reforms than states largely insulated from mass politics and electoral pressures'.[9] This suggests that those who have called for a 'Russian Pinochet' (and they have included people within the ranks of the self-proclaimed 'democrats' as well as more obvious authoritarians) are advocating a regime liable to be as retrogressive economically as it would be politically.

If an argument could be, and has been, made for rapid price liberalization in the difficult conditions of early 1992, there are now few scholars who would defend the form taken by privatization in Russia. In particular, that part of the privatization programme which from 1995 involved wealthy tycoons giving the government loans in return for shares in the most profitable parts of Russian industry, and in effect gaining ownership and control over Russia's most precious assets for a fraction of their true value, was insider dealing pure and simple.[10] There was no genuine competition among buyers and nothing could have been further removed from market principles than the sale of much of Russia's extractive industry at artificially low prices. That such a policy was given the blessing of people—among them, Anatoly Chubais—who were, in principle, committed free marketeers was paradoxical, to say the least.[11]

In the chapters which follow in this section, different perspectives are taken on how Russia's current economic system should be conceptualized. While no country has a completely free market economy—and Robert Dahl has argued persuasively that not only command economies but also strictly free market economies are incompatible with democracy[12]—Russian reformers, and a number of their international advisers, played down in the early post-Communist years the need for a regulatory role by the state. In principle, what was being urged upon Russia was a purer free market than was to be found anywhere in Western Europe. In

---

[8] Ibid. 233.

[9] Ibid. 234.

[10] For a particularly lively, and also well-informed, account of this process, see Chrystia Freeland, *Sale of the Century: The Inside Story of the Second Russian Revolution* (London: Little, Brown, 2000).

[11] Freeland credits Russian financier Vladimir Potanin with first coming up with the 'loans for shares' scheme. She suggests that Chubais was initially reluctant to compromise his reputation as a supporter of market principles, but that he was won over when Potanin promised to make the process look 'less egregiously corrupt' (ibid. 166–7).

[12] Robert A. Dahl, 'Why All Democratic Countries Have Mixed Economies', in John W. Chapman and Ian Shapiro (eds.), *Democratic Community* (New York: New York University Press, 1993), 259–82.

practice, what emerged was something much further removed from a market economy than that of any country within the European Union, even though it was a world away also from the Soviet-style command economy. On this, at least, Richard Ericson, Sergei Peregudov, and Nodari Simonia are agreed. For Ericson, the question is not 'how did Russia become a market economy?' but: is it even now 'in transition to a market economy'? He argues that 'a market system is non-hierarchical and functions within an established political and legal framework providing "rules of the game" constraining behaviour regardless of the political or social position of the agent' and that 'property and contractual rights in a market system are clearly defined and socially protected, regardless of the status of the agent'. While this may be more of an ideal type than a description of social and economic realities even in well-established market economies, the latter, hardly surprisingly, come far closer to it than does Russia. Thus, Ericson, though a firm supporter of brisk movement along the road to a market economy in Russia, sees the reassertion of state power over a variety of 'feudal' baronies as a precondition for 'a true market-based and market-driven economic system'.

Russia has, however, some particularly formidable obstacles standing between it and a viable market economy. It had a far longer period of Communist rule than the countries of East-Central Europe, it is much larger, has a climate and distances which impose additional costs on its producers, and has an economy (as Ericson notes) distorted by Soviet priorities. There are entire (Soviet-style) company towns and regions dominated by antiquated heavy industry. While purely market criteria might suggest the immediate closure of some of these gigantic plants, to shut down, in effect, a large city or a region would have social consequences so dire that politicians are obliged to take account of the human and political costs. Russian economic reforms have not amounted to 'shock therapy' in the strict sense, inasmuch as many uneconomic factories and coal-mines remain open, continuing to produce inefficiently, and with their workers paid intermittently.

The acute difficulty of transition from a Communist command economy to some kind of market system and the problem of maintaining even the inadequate levels of social welfare produced in the post-Stalin Soviet period have became abundantly evident in the course of the 1990s. Life expectancy for men in 1999 was only 59.8 years[13] (which, however, was an improvement on the post-Soviet low of 57.6 in 1994). Russia also has a very low birth rate and increasingly high death rates. In 1999 only 8.4 babies were born per thousand of population whereas the death rate (up from 1998) was 14.7 per thousand. The Russian Academy of Medical Sciences have blamed 'unfavourable social conditions' and extremely high use of alcohol and tobacco for what many Russian specialists view as a demographic catastrophe.[14]

Sergei Peregudov and Nodari Simonia, in Chapters 18 and 19, examine the role played by particular interests within the Russian economy and society. Peregudov provides a character-ization of what he sees as 'oligarchical corporatism', whose attributes include the hoarding by 'the commercial and entrepreneurial oligarchy' of 'all property relations that are worth any-thing' for themselves. The author of a book on 'Thatcher and Thatcherism',[15] Peregudov con-trasts the widening of share-ownership in Britain as a result of the privatization programme

---

[13] The average of 72 for women was very much higher and overall life expectancy in Russia in 1999 was 65.5 years.

[14] As reported by Reuters and RIA news agencies. See Johnson's Russia List, No. 4599, 25 Oct. 2000, items 1 and 2. For a much fuller analysis, see V. Shkol'nikov, E. Andreev, and T. Maleva (eds), *Neravenstvo i smertnost' v Rossii* (Moscow: Carnegie Centre, 2000).

[15] S. P. Peregudov, *Tetcher i Tetcherizm* (Moscow: Nauka, 1996).

carried out by the government headed by Margaret Thatcher with the high degree of concentration of ownership in post-Communist Russia. While critical of the oligarchical model of corporatism, Peregudov argues that a realistic way forward for Russia would be transition to different forms of corporatist relationships, whereby the widest possible spectrum of interest groups would be brought into the consultative process.[16]

Academician Nodari Simonia, who in the summer of 2000 became Director of a major Moscow think-tank—the Institute of World Economy and International Relations of the Russian Academy of Sciences (in succession to Alexander Yakovlev, Yevgeny Primakov and, most recently, Vladlen Martynov)—provides an especially detailed analysis in Chapter 19 of the role of particular interests in Russian economic and political life. Describing the system as one of 'bureaucratic capitalism', Simonia focuses on the linkages between economic interests and political power and argues that there is a need, in effect, for the state to become a more honest broker, so that senior state officials would no longer be the agents of particular commercial or defence sectors and engaged in factional struggle on behalf of these conflicting interests. Writing before the accession to the presidency of Vladimir Putin, he evaluates positively the prime ministership of Yevgeny Primakov which he sees as having been opposed both to 'unbridled liberalization' and 'centralized administration'. The role of the state under Putin is one of the themes addressed in the concluding section of this volume, and especially its final chapter.

---

[16] Grigory Yavlinsky comes close to the analysis of post-Soviet Russia offered by Peregudov, describing it as 'a quasi-democratic oligarchy with corporatist, criminal characteristics', but differs from him by not seeing a desirable future for Russia in any kind of corporatist terms (Yavlinsky, 'Russia's Phony Capitalism', *Foreign Affairs*, 77/33, (May–June 1998), 67–79.

17   Is Russia in Transition to a Market Economy?

Richard E. Ericson

Clifford Gaddy has raised serious questions about the reality of the apparent Russian economic revival in 1999.[1] In the same spirit, I would like to question the assumption of 'transition' as an appropriate characterization of the turbulent processes under way there. For, eight years into it, Russia seems nowhere near completing its transition to a modern market economy. Indeed, in terms of systemic change, little positive has occurred since the end of 1995, and the EBRD 'Transition Report 1999' notes significant regression in Russia, as well as in Kazakhstan, Kyrgizstan, Uzbekistan, and recidivist Belarus.[2] Further, the performance improvements in 1997 were more 'virtual' than real, while those in 1999, as Gaddy has so clearly indicated, may also be largely a statistical illusion. Indeed, what real 1999 increment in production, in monetization, and in fiscal balance has occurred is the result of massive devaluation coupled with a very fortuitous rise in energy and resource prices, and is unsustainable without massive investment and structural change.[3] So despite some indications of a market-like response to changes in the world economy in 1999, the Russian economy still seems far from a properly functioning market system.

This situation warrants, I believe, raising some questions. Is Russia in a 'transition'? Do we have our teleology right? Is it moving toward a market economy, or is another kind of system emerging from this 'great transformation'?

Increasingly it appears that economic institutions and interactions have settled into mutually consistent, self-reproducing expectations and patterns of behavior that are far from those consistent with a market economy. These patterns of expectations, understandings, and behavior have been adopted, or inherited, by 'those who matter,' by the elites who make the political and economic decisions that 'mold institutions' and 'move economic activity.' These patterns indeed are inimical to the proper functioning of markets as a system—to the systematic generation of normal market outcomes—even as they make use of, exploit, and extract rents from operating markets.

This suggests to me the possibility that the Russian transformation is not a 'market

This chapter is published, with minor abbreviations, from Richard E. Ericson's Ed Hewitt Panel contribution to *Post-Soviet Affairs*, 16/1 (2000), 18–25. Reproduced by kind permission of the author and V. H. Winston (Bellwether Publishing).

[1] C. Gaddy, 'Russia's Post-Devaluation Recovery: Real or Virtual?', *Post-Soviet Affairs*, 16/1 (2000): 12–18.

[2] *St. Petersburg Times*, 16 November, 1999.

[3] Structural barriers and investment needs are discussed in R. Ericson, 'How Real is Russian Economic Recovery?' *The Harriman Economic and Business Review*, 1/1 (Jan. 2000): 26–32.

transition,' despite destroying the foundations and pillars of the Soviet command economy.[4] The transformation, however, has built on their ruins, borrowing heavily from that Soviet legacy. Elites, institutional structures, patterns of economic interaction, attitudes, under-standings, and behaviors have all largely continued into the post-Soviet economy. Hence the transformation has developed a new systemic framework for economic activity that little resembles that of a modern market economy. Rather, it is a system whose structural charac-teristics remind one of a feudal-like economic system, albeit one built on a mid-20th-century industrial, rather than an agricultural, base. Such a system I call an 'Industrial Feudalism,' drawing an (imprecise) analogy whose foundations lie in a structural parallel-ism with the socioeconomic and political system that predominated in Western Europe in the early part of the second millennium of our era.

Let me outline several key characteristics of a 'feudal economic system' in terms that resonate with what I see in post-Soviet Russia.[5]

A 'feudal' economic system is part of an integrated political, economic, and social order. It is hierarchically structured, with members of a well-defined decision-making elite (the 'nobility') standing at the head of each structure. The bulk of the population (the 'laboring masses') is socially, politically, and economically subordinate and dependent, and there is only a weak and thin middle layer of specialists. Yet the system is substantially decentralized, with a weak center and strong local authorities, each with near-complete power over various limited domains. It is a system with no clear separation of political, economic, and social roles and/or powers, and hence without separation of public and private capacities and roles. The system is built on semi-autarchic socioeconomic units ('manors,' *aka* Soviet 'enterprises and associations') politically delimited as domains of personal authority. Indeed, in such a system all authority and discretion are personalized, as are all relations between domains, despite frequent appeal to a higher 'law' (the Church and God's, or Laws and Presidential Decrees, and Instructions). This generates a system composed of multiple, decentralized hierarchical structures of information and authority, including police and juridical (the interpretation and enforcement of 'laws'), with conflicting domains of influence and effect: a 'parcelization of sovereignty,' in the felicitous phrase of Anderson.[6]

In the more specifically economic sphere, it is important to note that such a system is characterized by:

- interaction based on traditional (inherited) patterns of coordination and control, implemented and enforced through overlapping networks of obligation;
- factor markets that are either degenerate or absent;
- ill-defined, diffuse, and traditionally circumscribed property rights, with multiple stakeholders and enforcement of such rights dependent largely on the power of the stakeholder;

---

[4] On those foundations and pillars see R. Ericson, 'The Classical Soviet-Type Economy: Nature of the System and Implications for Reform', *Journal of Economic Perspectives*, 5/4 (Fall 1991), 11–27; for a systematic, if early, account of their destruction, see A. Åslund, *How Russia Became a Market Economy* (Washington: The Brookings Institution, 1995).

[5] This argument is elaborated in my paper, 'The Post-Soviet Russian Economic System: An Industrial Feudal-ism?' available from my web site at: <http://www.columbia.edu/-ree3/>. The sources for the following characteriza-tion of feudalism are discussed there.

[6] P. Anderson, *Lineages of the Absolutist State* (London: N.L.B., 1974).

- the predominance of non-economic motivations, with wealth acquired, largely through transfer and seizure, for the power it gives over people.

In light of this, we might look to some of the key systemic characteristics of 'transformational' Russia. Four seem critical for accepting a 'non-market' characterization of the system:

- The conflation of economic and political actors and agents;
- The dis-integration of the state;
- A fragmentary market structure;
- The market non-viability of many economic and industrial structures.

The conflation of economic and political actors appears in the symbiosis of business and government, particularly at the local and regional levels. Indeed, the business and political roles of almost all leaders are closely intertwined, with these leaders often orchestrating personalized networks integrating business activities.[7] There is a continuing and indeed growing political 'management' of the local economy, protecting it from disruption through competitive challenge. This involves political control over privatizations, in particular over the allocation and management of real estate; local protectionism through restricting regional imports and exports and through licensing, inspections, and regulatory oversight; and both direct and indirect financial support through subsidies, barter, the acceptance of local scrip, and negotiated taxes (offsets).[8] It is also reflected in the recent wave of local 'renationalizations' through the manipulation of bankruptcy and tax offsets, and the political support of efforts to limit outside ownership and reverse acquisition of shares by inconvenient outsiders.

The lack of distinction between political and economic roles and agents is further reflected in the struggles among political units over business outcomes as well as policy. These include conflicts over land and property rights, the use and mobility of labor, and most particularly over tax collection and revenue sharing.[9] The latter often involves protecting local economies and the power and position of their elites through cutting off economic challenge by effectively demonetizing—turning to local scrip and barter systems, and the creative manipulation of offsets and arrears to exclude payment to outsiders, including the federal government.

This latter pattern sets the stage for the next general 'feudal' characteristic, the progressive dis-integration of the state. It begins with the insolvent federal fisc, leading to devolution of responsibilities to local elites who then control the content and provision of social services and financial transfers, and to the growing practice of 'tax farming' (Åslund, 1995, p. 321). This in turn supports negotiated, depending on status and power, social and tax obligations,

---

[7] A. Åslund has called this 'a negotiated economy with ample privilege for large and powerful enterprises regardless of their economic efficiency.' See his 'Russia's Financial Crisis: Causes and Possible Remedies', *Post-Soviet Geography and Economics*, 39/6 (1998), 319.

[8] The origins of the process are nicely laid out in D. Woodruff, *Money Unmade* (Ithaca, NY: Cornell University Press, 1999). For example, in December 1998, Krasnoyarsk and Kemerovo regions joined Tatarstan, Altay, and the Volgograd region in introducing new restrictions on food trade and grain transportation (*Moscow Times*, 12 Dec. 1998); on earlier actions, see S. Krayukhin and T. Zil'ber, in *Izvestiya* (12 Sept. 1998).

[9] Examples are ubiquitous in the Russian press. For a Western reflection, see P. Kranz, 'Is Moscow's Control Falling to Pieces?', *Business Week*, International Edition, 15 Feb. 1999.

making taxation severely regressive and penalizing, in particular, any independent (of political connections) economic agents. And it goes hand in hand with the increasing localization and 'privatization' of the provision of law, order, and justice, reflecting the lack of separation of 'the public' and 'the private'—the essence of corruption, which is naturally rampant in all areas of governance, both public and private.[10] The natural consequence is the substitution of political for economic objectives in decisionmaking, and the use of property and wealth for power over people, with government as a vehicle for rent extraction enhancing the leaders' property and wealth.

Third, we see a market structure that is fragmentary, fractured along political/administrative boundaries. Realms of interaction are limited by the withdrawal of local economies, supported by the political and economic decisions of their elites, from general monetized exchange. Rather localized quasi-monies, barter networks, and politically driven allocation and offset policies preserve incommensurate patterns of economic activity from competitive challenge. Thus the market structure reflects inherited patterns of interaction more than market opportunities. Only where there were no prior Soviet institutions—e.g., secondary financial markets; or where the market involves retailing simple products to final consumers; or where 'strong outsiders' such as Western firms and trading concerns must be dealt with, do we see more normally functioning markets, and even here they are often subject to considerable political manipulation and fraud.[11]

Most intermediate product and interindustry transactions still involve traditional, non-market, exchange relations among pre-existing entities and/or their offspring in networks that are largely inherited from the Soviet past.[12] This is particularly true with regard to critical industrial inputs such as energy, transportation, and basic materials, but is also the case for much of asset 'privatizations' and property transfers. This situation is supported not only by political action, as indicated above, but also by the growing re-demonetization of transactions (outside of retailing, finance, and foreign trade) from lack of legal protections, the weakness of banking, the rapacious nature of taxation, and tax collection through banks.[13]

The fragmented nature of the market structure is also reflected in the absence, or degeneracy, of effective factor markets. There is no market for productive land or real estate—production uses are tightly politically controlled, and the highly regulated urban

[10] There is a nice early discussion of this in V. Shlapentokh, 'Early Feudalism—The Best Parallel for Contemporary Russia', *Europe-Asia Studies*, 48/3 (May 1996): 393–411. The extent to which the use of force and nonjudicial dispute resolution in business has become institutionalized is emphasized in V. Radayev, 'On the Role of Force in Russian Business Relationships', *Voprosy Ekonomiki*, Oct. 1998.

[11] Indeed, the recent financial scandals and the collapse of many of the relatively 'modern' markets following the devaluation and default of 17 August 1998, show how fragile and conditional these markets were.

[12] Some 60–70 percent of all inter-industry transactions, and over half of all tax payments, involve barter or quasi-monies, and a substantial portion of remaining non-governmental payments is 'dollarized.' P. Karpov, 'On the Causes of Low Tax Collection (Arrears in the Fiscal System), General Causes of the "Arrears Crisis," And Opportunities for the Restoration of Solvency of Russian Enterprises', *Report of Interdepartmental Balance Commission*, Moscow, Dec. 1997. C. Gaddy and B. Ickes, *Russia's Virtual Economy* (Washington: The Brookings Institution, forthcoming).

[13] See the studies of industrial barter by S. Aukutsionek, 'Industrial Barter in Russia', *Communist Economies and Economic Transformation*, 10/2 (1998): 179–88, S. Commander and C. Mumssen. 'Understanding Barter in Russia', EBRD Working Paper #37. London: EBRD, December 1998; S. Guriev and B. Ickes, 'Barter in Russia,' preprocessed, Moscow, New Economic School, Sept. 1999.

real estate 'market' is a primary source of rents for local political powers.[14] Capital 'markets' are extremely thin and shallow, operating largely as a channel for financing governmental deficits and speculation by the elite. The banking system is also largely a mechanism of state finance through tax collection and the placement of government debt, and investment capital is generally unavailable.[15] Indeed, the budget is effectively bankrupt, firms are unwilling to give up significant equity and control for outside investment, and bosses engage in rent extraction for consumption and capital export purposes. Finally, the labor market is severely segmented and localized. Labor demand is restricted by the obsolete inherited Soviet industrial structure, and labor supply is restricted by production-based social services including housing, wage arrears and the lack of credit, and passport controls, tying workers to their inherited location.

A final critical structural characteristic undergirding the feudal nature of economic interaction is the market non-viability of much of the inherited Soviet industrial structure.[16] The Russian economy has preserved, albeit in increasingly dilapidated state, a large part of the distorted structure of capital, production, and interaction built over 60 years of economically irrational Soviet investment and development policies. This structure is only viable in a command economy, under arbitrary Soviet-type pricing that is unrelated to economic value or opportunity cost. Then necessary activity to maintain the structure is planned, commanded, and enforced, regardless of the costs and benefits to the agents involved.

When subject to uniform market valuations, many production operations, and much of the interaction within the structure as a whole, cease to be economically viable, to be able to cover the costs of even simple reproduction. Fundamental restructuring of technology, factor use, and market relations is necessary for market viability, requiring substantial investment and a radical change in management practices and personnel.[17] This would be seriously disruptive, indeed destructive, of inherited social and political relations, and hence is fought by the elite. Thus the structure is preserved in a 'virtual economy' where non-commensurate, idiosyncratic pricing—through the use of barter, quasi-monies, and tax offsets—creates a Soviet-like valuation environment, one politically protected in locally networked 'substantive economies.' This provides the industrial economic base for the feudal structure of power and interaction.

Thus we might draw a number of suggestive parallels between the contemporary Russian and a Medieval European system. In Russia we clearly see the 'parcelization of sovereignty' among the multiple, decentralized hierarchical structures exercising political, economic, and juridical authority over their own domains. The 'manors' and 'principalities' of the post-Soviet economy are its largely self-contained social-political and production entities. They include large industrial, agricultural, and construction enterprises, whether 'privatized' or not, new Financial-Industrial Groups and politically connected commercial structures ('oligarchs' and 'mafias'), and regional and local governments. The elite is largely inherited,

---

[14] This point is made well in A. Shleifer, 'Government in Transition', *European Economic Review*, 41/3–5 (1997): 385–410.

[15] See, for example, the discussion of the banking system in RECEP's *Russian Economic Trends* (11 Nov. 1998).

[16] This parallels the low productivity, generally only sufficient for simple reproduction, of the Medieval manor. See F. Pryor, 'Feudalism as an Economic System', *Journal of Comparative Economics*, 4/1 (Mar. 1980): 56–77.

[17] See, for example, the discussion In the McKinsey Global Institute Report on Russian Economic Performance, covering nine core Russian industries. It can be found at the McKinsey web site: www.mckinsey.com/mgi.html.

albeit not yet hereditary, deriving from the Soviet *nomenklatura*. They exercise personalized power through overlapping networks of personal ties and obligations.

The modern 'manors' maintain themselves through barter and network exchange in a virtual economy, through autarchic primitive production of food and primary products, and through the 'protection' provided by superior and outside entities in return for 'rents.' Competition is politically controlled, and property and contract rights are diffuse, encumbered, and often unenforceable through legal means. Thus traditional patterns of interaction naturally prevail.

Finally, we might view the Russian Presidency as a weak 'crown' with power exercised largely by 'the court'—advisors and 'the family.' The Federation Council can be seen as a Chamber of Lords, protecting regional privilege and prerogative, and fighting to extract as much as possible from the royal fisc, while the Duma appears as a chamber reflecting various elite special (corporate) interests. Finally, large integrative economic structures, such as UES, the railroads, Transneft and Gazprom, and perhaps some regions with 'reformist' policies (e.g., Veliki-Novgorod), fill the roles in a feudal structure of intermediaries and financial sources, much like Medieval towns and their ruling merchants and bankers, with personalized ties to the 'lords and nobles' of the System.[18]

Most of these characteristics stand in substantial opposition to essential aspects of a properly functioning market economic system. Although substantially decentralized and self-organizing, a market system is non-hierarchical and functions within an established political and legal framework providing 'rules of the game' constraining behavior regardless of the political or social position of the agent. In a market economy, 'sovereignty' resides in an autonomous state outside, and in some respects above, the market system, rather than being 'parcelized' among various political and economic actors. There is a clear separation of political and economic roles, of the public and private spheres, with rules and limits applicable equally to all regardless of rank or status. Similarly, property and contractual rights in a market system are clearly defined and socially protected, regardless of the status of the agent.

Interaction and networks in a market economy are thus primarily based on the perception of opportunity and mutual benefit from cooperation and/or exchange, and are perpetually changing in pursuit of new opportunity and/or cost avoidance. Ties are contractual, specific, and subject to voluntary renegotiation and third-party enforcement, rather than traditional, general, and based on personal commitment and obligation. And incentives derive from the rewards to meeting the needs and desires of other market participants, to creating new products, services, and wealth. Hence, investment in the pursuit of opportunity, and of the wealth to develop further opportunities, is a primary reflection of market economic motivation. In a market economy, economic power is clearly differentiated from political power and/or political/moral authority, and is based on success on markets rather than social or political legitimacy and power.

These 'modern' characteristics of a market system stand in sharp contrast to those of the coalescing Russian system outlined above. And they lie behind the growth of active, complex

---

[18] Indicative is the struggle of the 'family' to place 'its people' at the head of these 'cash cows.' See G. Peach in *Moscow Times* (23 Nov. 1999). The seven cash cows referred to are Gazprom, UES, the Railways Ministry, Sberbank, Transneft, Svyazinvest, and Rosvooruzheniye.

systems of factor, product, service, and financial markets, operating independently of direct political/social controls that are at the heart of a market economic system and provide the basis for investment and economic growth. In Russia, however, we see neither the deep structural characteristics of a modern market economy nor the functioning of an integrated system of complex markets fostering investment and growth. Rather, 'feudal' characteristics seem to be developing, without the foundation in agriculture and the restraining influence of a Church and its moral code, in the post-Soviet Russian industrial economy. Despite dramatic differences in technologies and capabilities for communication, for information processing, and for control of economic activity, a feudal 'parcelization of sovereignty,' a devolution of economic activity to quasi-autarchic networks, a fragmentation of markets, and a personalization of rule and interregional interaction seem to have taken hold.

The key question, and the one on which a true answer to the question posed at the beginning of this presentation hangs, is: 'How stable is this configuration of institutions and behaviors?' How long can the Russian economy remain stuck, as it seems to be, in a dimension outside of that containing the transition from 'plan to market'? Perhaps this configuration is only a brief phase, a perturbation, on the path followed by Europe to a real market economy. Once the current power struggles are resolved, and the state reasserts itself across all domains of political and economic activity, the rule of law may be established and stable market institutions allowed to form. And then we might see progress in transition toward a true market-based and market-driven economic system.

But how likely is that in the next generation? If the present system succeeds in maintaining stability in the face of the challenges of forgone outside economic opportunity for several generations, then we will be justified in considering it as much an alternative to a modern market economy as was its predecessor, the Soviet command economy.

18 The Oligarchical Model of Russian Corporatism

Sergei Peregudov

The model of oligarchical corporatism has already basically been realized on a 'micro-level'—on the level of individual financial and financial-industrial corporations and groups—and it has in fact largely come to define the essence of Russian corporatism as a national phenomenon in the second half of the 1990s. Taken together, the financial capital and the financial-industrial groups and conglomerates are the most influential part of the national economy and it is precisely their relations with the state that largely determine the present and future system of functional representation in Russia.

The term 'oligarchy' has entered firmly into the Russian political and scholarly lexicon and it requires little further explanation. In a sense it is equivalent to the term 'elite', although it is distinct from the latter in that it connotes not only membership of the 'select' part of society, but also an association with political power. In other words, it is not only an elite, but a 'powerful' elite.

The corporatist essence of the co-operation between the state and financial oligarchies lies, first, in the fact that resolutions amenable to both sides are worked out and taken through a process of mutual agreement. The second part of the corporatist model is also in operation: decisions taken are put into action again to the mutual benefit of both sides. However, this benefit materializes not through a process of compromise between group and state interests, but mostly through both sides' extraction of maximum political rents. According to the definitions of both Russian and Western political scientists, rent-seeking is linked primarily to the action of 'extracting monopolistic rights or any sort of privilege from the state' and also to the revision of 'existing property relations'.[1]

It is not hard to see that the current Russian reality displays conditions that particularly predispose the majority of interested groups to engage in rent-seeking. This is a far from complete process of de-statization and privatization, and also an extremely unpropitious set of conditions for normal productive activity as a consequence of most businesses' technological and organizational backwardness, and traditional consumer relations to the state.

The spring of 1995 can be thought of as the beginning of the new 'oligarchical' redistribution of state property, when several of the biggest banks came up with proposals for so-called securities privatization. Although both the presidential decree of 31 August 1995 and the agreements drawn up between participants in the negotiations envisaged credit secured by state property, this was in reality a barely concealed sale of shares. As is now universally

Chapter specially commissioned for this volume. Translated by Polly Jones.

[1] See e.g. *Politicheskaya renta v rynochnoy i perekhodnoy ekonomike* (Moscow: IMEMO, 1995), 5–7.

acknowledged, securities auctions were carried out with numerous blatant and covert violations, not at all brought about by a lack of experience, or by ignorance, but by a conscious attempt by both sides (banks and the functionaries entrusted with their implementation) to extract the maximum possible profit from the auctions. As a result, a whole heap of 'tasty morsels' of state property, mainly in oil and metallurgical companies, ended up in the clutches of several banks and financial groups, and their contacts with functionaries started to take on an essentially confidential and 'pally' character.

The special case of the securities auctions is interesting (and important) not only because they started off the new redistribution of state property to the benefit of the financial oligarchy, but also because this stage shaped the fundamental outline and characteristics of the new Russian corporatism. The specifically Russian peculiarities of this model include the following:

First, there is the absence of a centralized start to the process and the dispersal and even the chaotic nature of the interaction of the 'oligarchs' and oligarchical groups with the state. In so far as this peculiarity was predestined by the characteristics of the Russian oligarchy itself, which has been more fully researched in a number of specialized works, we limit ourselves here to this general observation.

Secondly, and no less important, is the fact that the commercial and entrepreneurial oligarchy has concentrated in its hands the overwhelming bulk of effective property resources, whereas the administrative and political oligarchy possesses the power and means of directly or indirectly contributing to its augmentation. Under conditions where both one and the other are chasing after political rents, such a distribution leads to an explosion of corruption and its penetration to the very heart of relations between representatives of power and the oligarchy.

The third factor, largely linked to the first two reasons, is the absence of any kind of agreement on a national or even 'class' idea or aim to be achieved as a result of corporatist cooperation. The fragmentation of elites and the dispersal of contacts between their corporate and administrative components provoke each of them into exploiting the current competition for their own essentially group and selfish aims. As for a national, 'state' idea, that is either completely lacking or ends up being relegated to the background.

With the arrival of the 'young reformers' in government in spring 1997, both they themselves and several of the 'oligarchs' started to promote widely the idea of a so-called universalist model of relations between business interest groups and the state, based on rules of the game binding on all participants. It is notable, however, that, as in 1992 after Gaidar was appointed the effective head of government, and this time as suggested by Chubais and Nemtsov, the model turned out to be unworkable. And this was not only to do with the fact that the powers of both first deputy prime ministers were rather substantially reduced. As is well known, their own activities and conduct departed rather drastically from the principles that they proclaimed.

The fourth feature of Russian oligarchical corporatism is the fact that, in spite of all its inner diversity, those who participate most directly in it hoard all the property relations that are worth anything 'for themselves', jealously guarding them from partition between other strata and groups of the population. The newly fashionable discussions of 'popular capitalism', and the necessity of forming an influential middle class are in reality empty words that are decisively discarded as soon as there seem to be any real steps in that direction. When in his time, the author explained the essence and particular features of the privatization pro-gramme carried out by Margaret Thatcher's government, the most striking feature was the attempt to use it in order to disperse property and to widen substantially the circle of shareholders. As a result, the slogans about 'a democracy of property-holders' and 'popular capitalism', proclaimed as one of the founding principles of Thatcherite policy, were not mere propaganda, for the proportion of shareholders in the population of the country went up from 7 per cent to 20 per cent over the course of the 1980s, reaching the impressive figure of 10 million people.[2]

Lastly, the final feature is the widespread use by both business and state oligarchies (including a very influential section of the old management) of various kinds of formalized procedures officially intended to ease the transition from a state-socialist economy to mar-ket capitalism and to achieve structural transformation of the economy. However, in many cases, these function merely as a kind of screen for the continuation of the same rent-seeking.

Also belonging in the list of similar procedures is the aforementioned securities auctions and the privatization and investment competitions that came after them. The latter were supposed to achieve not only the sale of packages of state property, but also to set in motion organizational-technical reforms and modernization of the privatized entities. This aim was particularly clearly stated during the carrying out of the so-called investment competitions, whose winners were obliged to plough a certain sum, fixed in negotiations, into the devel-opment of production and the revitalization of the company.

However, it is almost universally recognized, even officially, that the new owners, once they had acquired the necessary property rights (as a rule, after the price of the privatization package had been drastically cut) neglected the obligations that they had taken on and either completely or partially kept the sum earmarked for investment in their own pocket.

According to the data from the State Commission on Property, 74 per cent of 'new investors refuse to finance their property while the old management remains at the helm'.[3] The appeal to the conflict of new owners with old management is entirely justified in many cases. However, attributing all problems only to this conflict and, essentially, excusing the non-fulfilment of officially agreed obligations, as the workers at the State Committee on Property do, only encourages this kind of sabotage. Notably, neither that body itself nor the other competent organs of government have made any of these 'investors' answer for their actions, and have not demanded that the appropriate contracts be honoured. As a result, rent-seeking continues, especially where profitable companies and enterprises are con-cerned, and the enterprises themselves are being worn into the ground. As the president of the Union of Oil and Gas Industries, G. Medvedev, has privately stated, 'some new-fledged "property owners", once they've got hold of a profitable state oil company, reduce it to rack and ruin—and it's nothing, just water off a duck's back'.[4] L. Raketsky, governor of the Tyumen region, also mentioned this at a round table of oil-producers and Duma deputies.[5] This results above all in damage to the interests of the national economy and society. But the new owner himself will also lose in the long term if, while chasing after short-term profit, he

---

[2] For more details on this, see S. P. Peregudov, *Tetcher i Tetcherizm* (Moscow: Nauka, 1996), 157–66.

[3] *Rossiyskiy ekonomicheskiy zhurnal*, 2 (1999), 37.

[4] *Neft' Rossii*, 2 (1999), 8.

[5] *Neft' Rossii* (special supplement) (1999), 13.

lets slip the opportunity to transform the enterprise or company that he has acquired into a fully-fledged actor in the market economy.

An important channel for the acquisition of political rents on this contractual basis is entrusting the management of a packet of shares belonging to the state to a so-called trust. Yet again, the declared aim is the effective running of companies and businesses. However, the extent to which trusts are exploited for personal and group enrichment is shown in the fact that the state packets yield only 0.5 per cent profit annually to the treasury (according to 1997 figures), meaning that they contribute practically nothing to society.[6] In fact, that very 'mist' in which trust negotiations are shrouded—most clearly shown in 1997 and 1998 in the case of Gazprom—is highly symptomatic.

Those programmes and projects of reform and modernization of branches of industry and individual enterprises are often used as a formal cover. The fact that even the tiny portion of income (be it in the form of credits, different kinds of privilege, or guarantees) that *is* distributed among some of these projects is mostly not used as intended allows one to assert that we are dealing with a situation where practically the most important motivation is rent-seeking.

Another officially sanctioned channel for the 'privatization' of state means is the system of so-called authorized banks. Not for nothing has the principle of authorization been subjected to increasingly harsh criticism, and in 1997 the question of moving to a treasury system of maintaining state finances became acute. However, even if a decision is finally made about this exchange (which many specialists gravely doubt), the system of authorization will endure in the regions, carried out by branches of the leading banks and also by the most influential regional banks.

It would probably be possible to continue further this enumeration of 'legal' foundations for acquiring state property, income, and especially privileges. However, what has been said is already enough to lead to the following conclusion: the transitional state of the Russian economy in terms of property relations and of renewal of management and technology has meant that oligarchical corporatism in Russia in a great number (if not the majority) of cases is mixed and semi-formalized in nature. And in this lies the main distinction from those 'patrimonial', essentially informal relations, which have been formed, in, for example, the so-called triangles of growth in South-East Asia.

This circumstance, as well as the presence of fully formalized relations of a tripartite type in the centre and the regions, lends a particularly complicated and in many ways unique quality to Russian post-Soviet corporatism. Incidentally, this is unsurprising in view of the fact that nowhere in the world did the state penetrate more deeply into the economy and society than it did in the Soviet Union. Consequently, society's liberation from the clutches of the state is a uniquely painful process.

The August 1998 collapse of the financial markets and the severe crisis of the entire banking system of the country do not, apparently, fit with the opinions set out above about the enrichment of the oligarchy through the acquisition of political rents. However, in fact, this collapse was nothing but the logical outcome of the excessive dependence of banks and the banking community upon these rents, caused in part by the notorious government bonds (GKOs). Drawn into speculative 'games', and without having laid down any solid

---

[6] *Ekspert*, 20 Oct. 1997.

foundations in the real economic sphere, banks were essentially hostages to state finances. For this reason, it is not surprising that the collapse of the latter brought even the most seemingly powerful and reliable of commercial banks and financial-industrial groups to the brink of bankruptcy. The essentially corporatist link with the state turned out to be so tight that the collapse of its finances became the main reason for the general crisis of the banking system. The recently enormous power of the oligarchs turned to weakness when faced with the evolving situation and brought about their still great dependency on the state.

This raises a natural question about the means and mechanisms that might have been capable of placing relations between interests and the state on the sort of normative and moral basis that would have helped at least to minimize, if not to eliminate entirely, both the monopoly of the 'oligarchs' in business–state relations, and the predominance of their own selfish interests within them. To an extent, the resolution of the problem could lie in the introduction of the aforementioned 'universalist' model, which would really be capable of modifying, or even completely breaking up the current system. For in such a situation, the rules of the game would inevitably become stricter and the element of deals and 'agreements' kept hidden from society would recede into the background.

Paradoxical as it may sound, the oligarchical model itself generates certain preconditions for this kind of transformation. The 'pluralism' characteristic of the current Russian oligarchy and the increasingly brutal competition for various kinds of political rents, together with the growing interest of several of them in developing the 'real sector' permits the authorities not only to proclaim, but also to achieve this universalist step, especially when, for whatever reason, they feel a growing desire to stand up for the general state interest.

Also highly significant is the fact that, by staying on an informal basis, the interaction of state and business within the confines of oligarchical corporatism has enabled a whole series of procedures to be worked out, many of which are in principle capable of playing a significant role in the structural transformation and modernization of the economy and of economic development as a whole. Even the system of authorized banks, as shown in part by the experience of Moscow, can play a significant role in attracting investment in industry and can assist in bringing together the financial and industrial sectors of the economy. This could be yet more directly aided by more transparent investment competitions, programmes, and projects for the development of individual producers and production complexes, that are both more strictly supervised and founded on a qualitative professional expertise and effective societal and state oversight. It is, indeed, worth mentioning that certain steps in that direction are already being taken, both in the appropriate sub-departments of the Ministry for the Economy and the State Committee on Property and in a number of other departments.[7] This is also shown in the renewed interest in the budget for development and mechanisms to achieve it, demonstrated by both branches of power since the end of 1998.

Not everything is as clear-cut in the situation with trust management. By itself, the huge quantity of enterprises and companies with mixed forms of property, as well as of semi-autonomous state enterprises and firms, necessitate—if, of course, we exclude the possibility of nationalization—the widespread use of contractual (trust) relations in the foreseeable

[7] See e.g. the article prepared by the State Commission on Property about the outcomes of privatization and the basic directions of its further implementation in *Rossiyskiy ekonomicheskiy zhurnal*, 2 (1999), 38–40.

future.[8] And although the use of those relations for narrowly corporate and even personal ends will probably continue, this does not at all mean that state and society are powerless to reduce this to a minimum. And if the state can stand firm when dealing with such a powerful player as Gazprom, then in the vast majority of other cases it will be more a matter of technique and the need for a minimum of political will.

The question of the programmes and projects of modernization and the structural transformation of future production merits special discussion. Because of the deficit of state means, more and more significance—at times, primary significance—is being attached to the involvement of foreign capital in the realization of projects. But even in these cases, the role of the state is not reduced to being some sort of broker, in so far as it remains the most important player in an essentially corporatist agreement. The fact that projects agreed with the state are nearly always exploited in the name of narrow group and selfish interests does not mean that they are inherently bad. State programming and state support of special programmes and projects aiming to modernize specific branches of industry, manufacturing, and sectors of the economy are generally accepted practices throughout the world. Even countries with modern economies and industry have to resort to various forms of state involvement in working out high-technological projects in order to keep up with the competition in world markets, and often have to endow the state with principal responsibility for scientific and technological progress in the economy as a whole and in a series of key branches and production. When it comes to modern Russia, the state of her economy and industry is such that, even in the most propitious macro-economic conditions and market environment, it would be impossible to achieve any kind of breakthrough in technological or structural transformation without purposeful efforts on the part of the state.

But if this is the case and if the tendency to regulate the rules of the game in state–business relations is already present, will this of itself not lead to the 'natural' elimination of the oligarchical model? Russia, though, hardly has enough time to make it possible for us to trust solely to the goodwill of the 'oligarchs' and individual reformers. Moreover, in order to ensure that the general state interest becomes predominant, it is essential to have not only 'rules of the game', which will at best only yield results for the tip of the iceberg, but also political changes.

Lack of action, or anything resembling it, is dangerous not only because the oligarchical model, covered in a veil of 'transparency' and openness on the surface, will start to spread far and wide. Gathering strength on the regional, republican, and local levels, it will increase the threat of acute social and political crisis and of a total loss of governability. The other, no less serious danger lies in the consolidation—practically inevitable in this scenario—of the position of those forces who insist on the implementation of an authoritarian-bureaucratic type of economic policy.

In other words, Soviet and neo-liberal alternatives alike lead under the given conditions to the assertion of either bureaucratic or oligarchical corporatism. In the former case, it would be 'planned-market' ideology that would act as a cover, whilst in the latter, it would be neo-liberal and 'free' market economics.

The changes in Russia's economy and politics that began in the wake of the events of August 1998 have not yet been defined clearly enough to allow us to say with any certainty

---

[8] *Rossiyskiy ekonomicheskiy zhurnal*, 2 (1999).

what forms their interaction would take. It is evident, however, that although the positions of the financial oligarchy are seriously weakened, it would be premature to write off oligarchical corporatism altogether. What is more, the oligarchy has many faces, and, as shown above, its activities are not at all confined to the financial sphere. There is a danger, and a far from hypothetical one, that the oligarchy, revitalized at the expense of part of the old directorate and ministerial bureaucracy, would not fail to exploit the growth of state interference in the economy for their own selfish aims. In this case, oligarchical corporatism which continues to suck the blood out of the real sector of the economy will not only grow, but will be enriched at the expense of the bureaucratized forms that were already partly present in it earlier.

As the whole experience of relations between the state and the economy shows, attempts to limit corporatism to one type almost immediately give way to the expansion of one of its many other types, and result not in its reduction, but merely in a change of models. But is this situation in fact all that paradoxical? And is not this the kind of situation where it would be much more sensible to channel such relations in a profitable direction for society and, ultimately, for the business elite itself? One way of reaching this kind of resolution of the problem arises naturally and consists in subordinating already existing formalized relations of important financial-industrial capital and the state to the task of revitalizing the national economy and its scientific and technical potential. But it would be impossible to achieve a sudden transformation in a sphere where the arbitrary will of functionaries, encouraged by the financial oligarchy, reigns supreme. And, on all the evidence, this is starting to be felt more and more strongly by influential circles in both branches of power. After all the reshuffles of government, there are signs not only of good intentions and anti-demagogic feeling, but also of real political will aiming to bring order and to introduce effective control over the forms of corporatist agreement mentioned above. It is highly significant that objective tendencies towards the rationalization of corporatist relations are becoming more and more firmly underpinned by the authorities' subjective efforts, and by the oligarchy's acknowledgement of the destructive and futile nature of enrichment at any cost.

However, if reforms are confined only to these measures, medium and small business as well as other social organizations and groups will all be excluded from participation in the sphere of agreements between interests and the state. And this means that the whole system of functional representation will remain one-sided and elitist, and its potential possibilities will be only partially exploited. Therefore, in conjunction with the tasks of 'bringing order' into business–state relations, the development of forms of relations other than the elite is no less important and may be more so. By this we refer to the need to integrate the business elite into the wider process of corporatist agreement and at the same time to lend the entire system of functional representation a more balanced and democratic character.

As the experience of Western countries and Japan clearly demonstrates, this kind of alternative can be provided by the variants of the societal, or liberal, corporatism favoured in those countries, ranging from the national macro-system along Swedish lines and Austrian social partnership to schemes in which the participants are organizations of farmers, fishermen, and other comparatively narrow social-professional groups. However, by no means all of these variants are capable of yielding a quick and palpable result in Russia under current conditions. Thus, the development of tripartite systems involving the state, business, and trade unions is seriously hampered not only by the under-development of state and social institutions, but also by the absence of traditions of social partnership. This naturally does not mean that tripartite mechanisms and pacts have absolutely no future in Russia. The constant growth in societal interest in this kind of mechanism and co-operation rather suggests the opposite.

The main factor that motivates influential forces in the state and in businesses and trade unions to strive for the introduction of effective tripartism into the system of political bargaining is the seriousness of the social and economic problems needing to be resolved before Russia can get out of the essentially systemic crisis in which she currently finds herself. The huge disproportions existing in the economy and in incomes and wages, the threat of large-scale social conflicts, as well as the lamentable state of social services and the whole social sphere, force the state to try to draw all interested parties into an active and effective dialogue that will lead to consensual resolutions. Spontaneous, purely market mechanisms will clearly not work here, yet the post-Soviet state, even if it decided in favour of authoritarianism, is too weak to resolve those problems by violent means. Consequently, however ineffective their beginnings, tripartism will develop. One of the possible paths it may take is the creation of a mechanism of consultation with representatives of all interested and in any way influential groups functioning in the social-economic sphere. If there is even the slightest inclination towards consensus, the large number of these groups will compensate for deficiencies in representativeness and will ensure that decisions and recommendations made by them are endowed with a sufficient amount of authority.

A distinguishing characteristic of this kind of corporatist mode, if it materializes in real life, is a large component of pluralism and its hybrid nature. However, there is nothing particularly original in this model: Western political scientists have already identified various forms of 'corporatist pluralism' many years ago.[9] The round tables and other similar forums that are held in Russia from time to time with the president and government could in principle evolve into key links in this sort of mechanism. However, in all the manifestations of this in the 1990s, the representation of businessmen's associations and trade unions has been neglected, and only the financial and administrative-political oligarchy has ended up 'over-represented'.

In current Russian conditions, especially with a view to producing direct and more rapid results, mechanisms of formalized consultation (so-called administrative corporatism) have a much better chance of working; these have long played the most important role in the system of working out socio-economic resolutions, including in the law-making process. The main distinguishing characteristic of these mechanisms is the fact that they are basically created as an adjunct to particular ministries and departments, and the fact that participants are not chosen according to any formal criteria, but in the hope of including all significant organizations and groups with a direct relation to the sphere of competence of the organ to which the consultative structure is attached. Thus, in so far as each ministry and department is as a rule active in several directions and has several sub-departments responsible for each, the system of consultation is also correspondingly specialized. In certain instances, associations of business, firms, and trade unions active in a particular sector of the economy are drawn into the consultations, whilst in other cases, ecological associations, consumers' and

---

[9] See e.g. Gerhard Lehmbruch and Philippe C. Schmitter, eds., *Patterns of Corporatist Policy-Making* (London: Sage, 1982); A. Cawson, *Corporatism and Political Theory* (Oxford: Basil Blackwell, 1986), 12–44.

other organizations representing the interests of the general population play the major part, while in yet other cases a mixed criterion for representation is applied. In view of all this, the representatives of various circles and organizations of business and trade unions play a key role in consultative bodies.

According to recent data about the relations between organized interests and state institutions in Denmark and Norway,[10] the number of different councils, commissions, and committees attached to ministries and departments in Denmark and Norway came to 246 and 257 respectively over the second half of the 1990s. The author's own research into an earlier period shows that the number of consultative bodies attached to the central ministries and departments in a number of other, bigger Western countries approached several hundred, and in France they numbered around 5,000 at the end of the 1970s.[11] There are not noticeably fewer now.

The term 'administrative corporatism', used by several authors to describe these bodies, can hardly be considered fully adequate, as participation in the work of consultative bodies still does not place strict obligations on their members to put the agreed recommendations into practice, especially where their point of view was not fully taken into account, or was ignored. For this reason, it may be more appropriate to speak of a 'softened' form of corporatism, which many writers (including the author) prefer to term 'agreement'. Several scholars do not consider this kind of contact and relations corporatist at all, instead viewing them as only a 'potential opportunity to move towards corporatism'.[12]

Whichever category of state-interests relations in which we decide to place the system of consultative bodies, one thing is certain: this system is an organic part of the political mechanism of any democratic state and, in the same way as parliament, government, state service, and local administration, fulfils the functions belonging to it. It is the most important part of the entire system of functional representation and ensures (along with the party-parliamentary system) a basic complex of direct and two-way links between state and society.

As the experience of the countries mentioned shows, the inclusion of interest groups across the widest possible spectrum in constant co-operation with the state not only limits the influence of powerful economic structures upon it, but also in principle creates other rules of the game for relations with the authorities. As the interaction itself becomes more dispersed and specialized, important and powerful groups are obliged to enter into such a system on common foundations and become participants in it. At the same time, the effect of lobbying pressure applied outside the framework of consultative bodies is reduced. Accordingly, the role of entrepreneurial associations representing wide circles of business is increased.

We can state without exaggeration that the 'committee system'[13] is now one of the most important cogs in the mechanism of working out and making state decisions. It is precisely

---

[10] P. M. Christiansen and H. Rommetverdt, 'Parliament and Organized Interests in Denmark and Norway', *Paper prepared for the XVII IPSA world Congress* (Seoul, 1997), 10.

[11] See *Sovremenniy kapitalizm: politicheskie otnosheniya i instituty vlasty* (Moscow, 1984), 178–97.

[12] A. Yu. Zudin, 'Gosudarstvo i biznes: povorot vo vzaimootnosheniyakh?', *Politiya*, 3 (1997), 30.

[13] In using that term I am much indebted to the thorough research, published almost half a century ago by the Oxford professor, Kenneth Wheare, who reckoned the number of consultative committees attached to ministries in Great Britain to be at that time around 700. See K. S. Wheare, *Government by Committee* (Oxford: Clarendon Press, 1955).

this that is at the origin of the vast majority of resolutions and normative acts of executive power and also of the legislative projects that it introduces into parliament. This gives executive power the opportunity to put the necessary number of legislative projects on to the conveyor (on average, this constitutes over 90 per cent of their overall number), but also, particularly importantly, to ensure their high quality. Thus the participation in their preparation of the people charged with carrying them out makes them significantly more adequate to the needs of society and its constituent groups. The same naturally applies to the decisions taken by executive power itself.

As has already been noted, in contrast to the strict corporatist models, the second half of the formula (the participation of interest groups in the implementation of decisions taken) assumes a more flexible, less obligatory character in the committee system. But the proposed variant of the system of corporatist agreement will gain more than it loses from this. More accurately, it is not the variant itself that stands to gain, but the society where it functions satisfactorily.

As studies conducted over the course of the last few years by researchers at the Centre for Political Technologies show,[14] in Russia at present a multi-branched network of business organizations on national, branch, and regional levels has been created and is now up and running. And although they cannot yet compare in terms of 'maturity' with analogous organizations in the West (in particular, they cannot compete as employers' organizations), they are already entirely capable of acting as an adequate representative of the business community to the institutions of power. However, at the moment, they do not fulfil this, their most important function; more precisely, they fulfil it only to a very insignificant degree. And the main reason is that the state does not call upon them to do so, a fact that provokes increasingly sharp rebukes from the business community.

Of course, the committee system now existing in the West is not a model for slavish imitation. The experience of these countries themselves shows that it is impossible to create it in a single stroke. Yet, the question of the concrete path and forms of the creation of the committee system is not the main one. The main point is the acknowledgement on the part of the authorities and interest groups of the importance of this kind of channel of mutual relations, both for themselves and for society as a whole. When that is the case, the embryonic forms of this kind of representation that already exist[15] could 'mature' quite rapidly, multiply and develop into a worthwhile system.

---

[14] See *Sistema predstavitel'stva rossiyskogo biznesa: formy kollektivnogo deystviya* (research leader A. Yu. Zudin) (Moscow: TsPT, 1997) and N. V. Nazarova and Yu. V. Krasheninnikov, eds., *Obshchestvennye (nekommercheskie) ob"edieniya predpriyatiy i predprinimateley Rossii* (Moscow: TsPT, 1997).

[15] A. Yu. Zudin, *Gosudarstvo i biznes*, 29.

19 Economic Interests and Political Power in Post-Soviet Russia

Nodari Simonia

The nature of political power in Russia

There is a myth that after the unsuccessful August 1991 coup democracy was established in Russia. This myth is supported by the simplistic idea that the presence of such attributes as regular parliamentary and presidential elections, numerous political parties, and a press and other media representing different points of view means the existence of democracy itself. Outward appearances, however, hardly ever adequately reflect real content. The world has always had and still has dozens of states that have arrayed their traditional 'body' in a democratic 'suit' borrowed from the West. To prevent this suit from falling apart they have stitched it with strong authoritarian thread. That is exactly the case of Russia.

It is true that in 1990–91 a young democratic movement was at the vanguard of the struggle for the transformation of the USSR, but there was neither the social nor the economic basis necessary for it to establish itself in power; there were no appropriate traditions, no appropriate mass psychology or even a more or less developed civil society. That is why, objectively speaking, Russian democracy paved the way to power not for itself but for quite a different public force—the economic *nomenklatura* responsible for economic management.

Previously the ideological *nomenklatura* had held complete sway. The events of August 1991 eliminated it once and for all. During the short prime ministership of Yegor Gaidar in 1992, the economic *nomenklatura* was in confusion. When Viktor Chernomyrdin replaced Gaidar in December 1992 it began to recover from the shock and strengthen its position on the federal level. Its triumphant march into the Russian regions needed more time, entering its final stage only during the 1996–97 local elections, which were mostly won by pragmatic managers irrespective of party affiliation.

Russia's peculiarity and its trouble is that power which is democratic in its form and authoritarian in its essence is never strong. The power that emerged after the collapse of the Soviet Union has from the beginning been weak and unconsolidated. The society lacked social and political consensus both at the party level and in the very top power structures— between the executive and legislative branches and between factions and groups within the executive. Even President Boris Yeltsin, in spite of the deliberately cultivated image of a 'strong ruler', seemed unable to overcome the divisions within and between powers and the

This chapter is abbreviated from Nodari Simonia, 'Domestic Developments in Russia', in Gennady Chufrin, ed., *Russia and Asia: The Emerging Security Agenda* (Oxford: SIPRI and Oxford University Press, 1999), ch. 4, pp. 52–80. Reproduced by kind permission of the author and OUP.

political elite. Instead he manoeuvred and set different forces against each other. As a result a peculiar phenomenon developed or revived—the court cabal or 'shadow cabinet' familiar from pre-Revolutionary Russia. The composition of the shadow cabinet changed from time to time. In late 1997 and early 1998 Tatyana Dyachenko, the president's daughter, Valentin Yumashev, the head of the presidential administration, and some of his deputies obtained special influence in the presidential circle. Owing to their closeness to the president some of them achieved importance disproportionate with their real abilities, while the president's mood, sentiments, whims and state of health were becoming a critical factor of Russian domestic and foreign policy.

The initial euphoria following the 'victory of democracy' and the proclamation of radical economic and political reforms (the stage of 'romantic democratism') was evidence of the complete disregard for Russian realities, social forces and economic interests of the radical democrats and liberals in Russia and those Western circles who supported them.

The formation of bureaucratic capitalism

Bureaucratic capitalism is a specific form of capitalism during the catching-up phase. In fact it is a special version of 'primitive accumulation', initiated by the state bureaucracy and carried out with its active participation. It is especially typical for states with strong traditions of bureaucratic rule. The best-known examples in modern history were Kuomintang China (initially on the mainland and later on Taiwan), Indonesia from the mid-1950s and South Korea from the early 1960s. In the USSR the first elements of bureaucratic capital were already appearing at the end of the presidency of Mikhail Gorbachev[1] but the liberalization policies of Gaidar gave the impetus to the mass, practically unlimited formation of bureaucratic capitalism in all its manifestations. There was no malicious intent behind this. Most probably it was evidence of basic naivety and schoolboy dogmatism. Gaidar and his associates simply failed to take into account the obvious fact that no significant business stratum existed, so that only two social groupings could take advantage of the opportunities presented by a policy of unlimited liberalism in its classic form. The principal group was the economic *nomenklatura*, equipped with the necessary connections and know-how. The second included the representatives of illegal business (the 'shadow economy') who were already being widely cultivated during the period of Soviet General Secretary Leonid Brezhnev.

An important feature of the development of this form of capitalism in Russia was the fragmentation of bureaucratic capital resulting from the lack of a strong, consolidated state power. The serious antagonism between its various factions was in fact the essence of Russian politics in 1994–98 and found its reflection in changes and zigzags in foreign policy. It was typical that the presidential staff, the government and the media (both the pro-government media and most of the opposition) carefully disguised this fact, although for different reasons, deliberately overemphasizing the division between democracy and communism instead. For serious observers, however, it had become obvious long before that the process of commercialization of Russian society, including that of the greater part of the

---

[1] The author warned of the danger of this development already at the beginning of 1990. N. Simonia, 'Gosudarstvo, kooperatsiya i byurokraticheskiy kapital,' *Moskovskiye Novosti*, 9 (4 Mar. 1990).

left-wing opposition, had gone so far as to be irreversible and that the real choices now were not between communism and democracy but between different options for further capitalist development.

THE FACTIONS OF BUREAUCRATIC CAPITALISM

Initially the factions grouped according to economic sector. The three main sectors were export-oriented raw materials, financial-trading, and industrial.

The first was the richest and most influential as it included the oil and gas industries and other extractive industries such as non-ferrous metals. The oil industry alone provides about half of the country's foreign currency revenues and 40 per cent of budget receipts.[2] It had the strongest representation in the executive branch—Chernomyrdin, Prime Minister from December 1992 to March 1998, and Yury Shafrannik, Minister of Fuel and Energy from February 1993 to August 1996. This faction has its own commercial banks, created, like the corporations themselves, on the basis of former Soviet ministries and departments. Some corporations (Gazprom, Lukoil, Rosneft and others) came to act as autonomous foreign policy actors, first within the CIS framework, in both oil-importing and oil-extracting republics, but also in some more distant countries in Eastern and Southern Europe, the Middle East and South-East Asia.[3]

The financial-trading faction presents a more motley, less consolidated combination of commercial banks and large trading corporations. Initially it included commercial banks not connected with production financing. At most their ties with production amounted to purchasing, with the help of state officials, suitable enterprises at give-away prices to maximize their own profits or for further re-sale, mainly to foreign investors. In economics this is called the comprador function. The dominant role in this faction, however, was played by the 'authorized banks', 10 or 12 commercial banks chosen by the government to transfer budget allocations to state enterprises, organizations and so on, which enriched themselves mainly by using that money—for instance, foreign currency receipts of Rosvooruzheniye[4] and enterprises of the defence industry that export their own products—illegally to make a profit for themselves. A decisive role was played by the special connections those banks had with senior government officials. The base of this faction consisted of many medium-sized and small commercial banks engaged exclusively in financial speculation ('making money out of the air'). In 1995 there were 2,025 banks in Russia, but by 1997 numbers had been reduced to 1,697 by bankruptcies and the retraction of Central Bank licences from more than 300 banks.[5]

This faction of bureaucratic capital is more oriented to cooperation with the West than

[2] N. Lapina, *Rossiyskiye Elity i Natsionalnye Modeli Razvitiya* (Moscow: Institute of Scientific Information in the Social Sciences (INION), Russian Academy of Sciences, 1997), 6.

[3] For example, Lukoil and Gazprom are active in Azerbaijan, Iran, Iraq, Turkmenistan and even Africa. R. Narzikulov, 'Zimnyaya gazovaya politika,' *Nezavisimaya Gazeta*, 17 Feb.1998; S. Alison, 'Russian energy sector dismayed by strikes on Iraq', Reuters (Moscow), 17 Dec. 1998; A. Ivanov, 'Gazprom i Lukoil doplyli do Afriki,' *Finansovye Izvestiya*. 1 Dec. 1998; and *OGJ Newsletter*, 28 Dec. 1998.

[4] The state company for imports and exports of armaments and military technology, established in Nov. 1993 to coordinate arms export activity by absorbing most of the associations and enterprises that had the right to export arms.

[5] A. Sarkisyants, 'Sliyaniya i bankrotstva bankov: mirovoy opyt,' *Mirovaya Ekonomika i Mezhdunarodnye Otnosheniya (MEiMO)*, 10 (1998), 31.

the other two. It is second in wealth and influence to the raw materials faction. These two ruled Russia for six years and provided financial support to President Yeltsin in the 1996 elections. Yeltsin acted de facto as an exponent of their interests, granting them multiple advantages and privileges through his decrees and orders.

The core of the industrial faction was the defence industries, including their civilian production, which had suffered the greatest damage in the course of the reforms. Between 1990 and 1996, overall production of the defence industry was reduced by 53 per cent.[6] This does not mean that the director corps was starving. The scale of capital accumulation was smaller here than with the other two factions, but the process was intensive, primarily as a result of the notorious 'voucher privatization', which enabled the directors of the industry to concentrate the shares of their enterprises in their own hands.[7] Enriching themselves by 'eating through' fixed and current capital, they used state resources initially for their own profit and resorted to other machinations. Their prosperity contrasted seriously with the hardships of workers in manufacturing industry who had not been paid for many months. However, this faction also has separate branches and enterprises which managed to find their own niche on the world market and thus are in a better position.

It would be wrong to say that the industrial faction was not represented at all in the government and in circles close to the president. After the appointment of Oleg Soskovets in 1993 as deputy prime minister responsible for industrial policy, the defence industry, conversion, engineering, transport and metallurgy, an industrial lobby began to form and for the time being received the support of the man closest to Yeltsin—the head of the presidential security guard, Major-General Alexander Korzhakov. An intense struggle began, in the course of which the Soskovets–Korzhakov group tried to expand its influence to the areas of banking and oil, although with no visible success. The Communist Party also took upon itself the role of representative of the industrial faction's interests in the State Duma (the lower house of the Russian Parliament), but the Duma is hardly the body where real power is concentrated.

There were three stages in the emergence of bureaucratic capitalism: between 1992 and June 1996; from June 1996 to March 1997; and from March 1997 to March 1998.

In the first stage the raw materials and financial-trading factions dominated. They were united by the threat of opposition and by the fear that if a strong and patriotic personality came to power it might deprive them of their autonomy and impose on them a mechanism for the redistribution of their profits and incomes in the interests of the national economy. At the same time the contradictions between them were sometimes sharp and fundamental: for example, in 1993–94 they were engrossed in a stubborn struggle over the restructuring of the oil industry. Representatives of the industries engaged in raw materials production, headed by Chernomyrdin and Shafrannik, stood for the creation of a small number of vertically integrated companies, able to compete on world markets. The State Committee for the Management of State Property (Goskomimushchestvo) and the State Committee on Anti-Monopoly Policy, controlled by the Gaidar–Anatoly Chubais group, advocated a

---

[6] *Nezavisimaya Gazeta*, 5 Feb. 1996; and A. Ivanter, N. Kirichenko, and Yu. Beletskiy, 'Schastye v dolg ne voronesh,' *Expert*, 1–2 (Jan. 1999), 11.

[7] A detailed description of this process is given in J. R. Blasi, M. Kroumova, and D. Kruse, *Kremlin Capitalism: Privatizing the Russian Economy* (Ithaca, NY, and London: Cornell University Press, 1997).

subdivision of the industry into a multitude of smaller enterprises, supposedly to stimulate competition.

A tendency for the financial-trading faction to be squeezed out of leading positions in the government increased. The elections to the Duma at the end of 1993 clearly demonstrated the narrowness of the social base of the radical democrats and liberals, heralding the end of the short era of 'liberal romanticism'. In early 1994 Gaidar and many of his ministers lost their posts in the government and in February 1995 on the Security Council as well. Chubais remained as the only representative of the financial-trading faction in the executive. This may have been because of the president's tactics of checks and balances, but Chernomyrdin also needed a representative of the young reformers in the government in order to deter the onslaught of the industrial lobby and to maintain a reforming image for the West. In January 1996, however, Chubais was also removed from the government.

The oil and gas bloc sometimes acted not only autonomously but also contrary to the line of the Foreign Ministry, for instance, over the issue of the status of the Caspian Sea. In an attempt to block the creation of international consortia for the development of the oil deposits on the Caspian Sea shelf by Azerbaijan, Kazakhstan and other republics, the Russian Foreign Ministry came out with its own approach to the issue. However, the pragmatic Russian oil lobby (Lukoil, supported by Chernomyrdin and Shafrannik) correctly believed that it was better to have a share in the consortia to be created than to engage for years to come in long altercations between the foreign ministries of the republics involved, allowing the initiative to pass to the transnational corporations.

The turn to the CIS was also profitable for a considerable part of the industrial faction, as the breaking of many industrial links of the former integrated Soviet economic complex had been almost the main reason for a sharp decline of industrial production both in Russia and in many of the CIS republics.

The activity of the oil and gas and industrial complexes became apparent beyond the borders of the CIS, including in Middle Eastern countries (Iran and Iraq) towards which the USA was pursuing a policy of isolation. Here also it contrasted during the first half of the 1990s with the general line of the Foreign Ministry.[8] Their autonomy was, however, only relative because it was far from completely detached from the state in the financial and legal senses. To a great extent it depended on the benevolence of officials, primarily Chernomyrdin himself, and on various benefits and privileges (customs, taxation and so on).

After changes among the top Foreign Ministry officials in 1995, the first steps were taken to overcome the fragmentation and general unconcentrated nature of Russian foreign policy. Since then it has concentrated increasingly on defending the national interests of Russia. There was a slow turn in Russia's policy on Asia—an intensification of the Russian presence in the Middle East, the establishment of a strategic partnership with China in April 1996, the first steps towards a normalization of relations with Japan and the first serious efforts to create the preconditions for integration with individual CIS states.

The second stage of the struggle between the factions of bureaucratic capital and related political groups began between the first and the second stages of the presidential elections in June–July 1996. A serious, basic regrouping of the opposing forces took place. Yeltsin

---

[8] V. Razuvayev, 'Malenkaya neftyanaya voyna', *Segodnya*, 8 Sept. 1995; and V. Trofimov, 'Chem pakhnut kaspiyskii neftedollary', *Nezavisimaya Gazeta*, 10 Jan. 1996.

reintroduced Chubais into his administration and ousted the Soskovets–Korzhakov–Barsukov group from the presidential Olympus and the government. Seizing the opportunity, Chernomyrdin in his turn replaced active opponents from the industrial faction, headed by Soskovets, with more friendly and loyal ministers. This was accompanied by action to 'punish' those commercial banks that had supported the Communist Party or General Alexander Lebed in the election campaign or were too closely connected with Soskovets. The licence of Tveruniversalbank was revoked, while Unikombank, Inkombank and Kredobank faced difficulties. It is believed that Kredobank had something to do with pumping money into Chechnya under the 'flag' of the Committee for the Economic Reconstruction of Chechnya, headed by Soskovets.[9] However, Oneximbank, one of the largest banks that had been closely cooperating with Soskovets, suffered no damage. Chubais had always favoured this bank, repeatedly standing out, for instance, against the revision of the results of mortgage auctions where Oneximbank won. Chubais allied himself with the bank's president, Vladimir Potanin, and managed to achieve the appointment of Potanin to the post of deputy prime minister in August 1996.

Confrontations within the government structures between the two effectively ruling factions of Russian bureaucratic capital continued with variable success until the spring of 1997, when they resulted in another major reshuffle of government structures. However, one other important change in the structure of bureaucratic capitalism had begun, and was to develop later—the gradual fading away of the clear borders between the factions and the first signs of a restructuring of bureaucratic capital on a clan-group basis.

This was connected with two new elements. The first was the transition to a new phase of the division of state property—the putting up of the most valuable pieces of property for auction and tender, as a result of which the diversification of the large commercial banks' investment activity deepened. Some banks found interests in oil and other raw materials. Raw materials companies, in their turn, became owners or co-owners of certain industrial enterprises and commercial banks. Second, there appeared signs of a coalescence between financial and industrial capital in the shape of the establishment of financial-industrial groups. That process was to some extent initiated from above, that is, financial-industrial groups were created by the decision of the government, but they also developed spontaneously. Initially the commercial banks either bought enterprises that were already profitable (in order to maximize their own profits) or bought with the intention of reselling more profitably later. In any case they did not buy enterprises in order to invest in them seriously and expand production. This was a manifestation of the initial, rapacious stage of the primitive accumulation of capital, the separation of property from its traditional owner. The productive or creative function was still missing. Truly modern, vertically integrated corporations essentially appeared only in the oil and gas sector.

The beginning of the third stage was marked by a major victory of the 'financiers'—to be more exact, the group headed by Chubais. Chubais returned to the government as First Deputy Prime Minister and Minister of Finance. Boris Nemtsov, the liberal Governor of Nizhniy Novgorod Region, joined the government as the other First Deputy Prime Minister and Minister of Fuel and Energy. It was now possible to speak of a strong 'anti-raw materials' team of young reformers. Branch ministries were abolished, as were the positions

---

[9] See e.g. L. Galperin, 'Balans posle bitvy', *Moskovskiy Komsomolets*, 14 Aug. 1996.

of members of the industrial faction in the government. Chubais put Alfred Kokh at the head of the State Committee on the Management of State Property in order to gain control over further privatizations. Yevgeny Yasin, the Minister of the Economy, was replaced by his tougher deputy Yakov Urinson, one of whose main goals was the restructuring of the defence industry.

The new group of reformers set out under the banner of the fight with the natural monopolies. To suggest the size of the task they took upon themselves, it can be noted that these monopolies provide up to 70 per cent of Russia's budget revenues.[10] The task was ostensibly defined even more widely—to tackle 'nomenklatura capitalism'. Chubais stated that he wanted to break the union of privatized bureaucracy and bureaucratized capital.[11] Events were to show that he was the last person who could set himself such a task. He himself was one of those he intended to fight. In reality the idea was merely to ensure the victory of one faction over the other. Gazprom, of which Chernomyrdin had been chairman, was one of the first natural monopolies tackled by the reformers.

The odds in favour of the young reformers seemed so great that many newspapers began to write about one-party government and the forthcoming fall of Chernomyrdin.[12] The outcome was much more complicated. The reformers' bold but poorly considered actions encouraged a broad front to form against them, uniting a wide variety of forces from the raw materials producers and industrial factions to the power ministries. Chubais, moreover, probably relying on his powerful position in the government and on the goodwill of Yeltsin, almost stopped performing the function of a political representative. Before and immediately after the presidential election he publicly assured all those who had contributed to Yeltsin's victory that they would be appropriately rewarded; later he concentrated his efforts on close cooperation with one—Oneximbank and its International Financial Corporation (IFC)—and thus turned all other parties, including former allies, against himself. As a result the struggle then continued along new lines.

Major financiers (Boris Berezovsky, associated with a variety of businesses, including Logovaz and Aeroflot, and a television channel; Vladimir Gusinsky, owner of Mostbank and a great media empire; and others) virtually declared war on Chubais, using all the media resources they controlled. As a result of the 'book scandal', Chubais' position was seriously undermined and he lost many of his associates in key executive posts. The anti-Chubais coalition was later actively and effectively, but without fuss, supported by the Prime Minister himself. In late December 1997 and early 1998 he carried out another government reshuffle. Chubais and Nemtsov remained first deputy prime ministers but without their 'armies', that is, without their key ministries. Chubais lost control over the media and the State Committee on the Management of State Property. Chernomyrdin had been given control over the defence industry and Rosvooruzheniye in July 1997 (see below). The position of Chubais' group was thus seriously weakened and Chubais found himself once again in the situation he had been in in 1994–95, when he was a symbol of democratic reforms, but this time with a seriously tarnished reputation.[13]

[10] Intertax–AiF, 14–20 Apr. 1997.

[11] A. Kolesnikov, 'Yakov Urinson—razrushitel nomenklaturnogo kapitalizma' Segodnya, 8 Apr. 1997.

[12] See e.g. T. Koshkareva, and R. Narzikulov, 'Molodye reformatory gotovyat Nemtsova na zamenu Yeltsinu,' Nezavisimaya Gazeta, 8 Apr. 1997, and Y. Latynina, 'Chubais izgnal iz Minfina torgovtsev,' Izvestiya, 22 Apr. 1997.

[13] 'Politicheskiye kollizii v Rossi v dekabre–yanvare', Nezavismaya Gazeta—Scenarii, 2 (11 Feb. 1998), 9–10.

The armed forces and the defence industry

The demolition of the Soviet system of decision making also allowed the Russian armed forces and defence industry a degree of independence. General liberalization and commercialization did not leave the military sphere unaffected, but promoted unprecedented corruption and thus the formation of a military faction of bureaucratic capital. The 'honeymoon' of the democrats and liberals with the West had its negative side in the Russian Government's complete disregard for issues of military reform, reorganization and defence industry conversion. There was of course no lack of appropriate slogans and projects: only practical results were lacking. Besides, the new leadership of the armed forces found itself involved in the all-pervasive business of self-enrichment.

THE ARMED FORCES

One of the hotbeds of corruption and embezzlement of state property was the Western Group of the armed forces. The Russian and foreign press revealed scandalous abuse connected with illegal sale of cigarettes, liquor and so on, the sale of military property, technology and even some types of weapons, and illegal use of transport by top military for their personal possessions. For six years in succession in Russia information emerged about abuse by the senior military of the free labour force represented by their soldiers for the construction of luxury villas and about budget money allotted for the maintenance of armed forces personnel being diverted for personal use. A considerable source of enrichment for the military bureaucracy was the division of military property, equipment and weaponry between the CIS member states consequent on the break-up of the USSR. This was accompanied by illegal transfers of large quantities of weapons and ammunition.[14] The situation was especially piquant when military deliveries were made to both sides involved in regional or local conflicts.[15]

Independent action by the armed forces within the CIS framework was favoured by the fact that the Gaidar Government, and especially the Foreign Ministry, not only lacked a considered strategy in that area but consciously ignored it. Thus, the initiative, almost by natural process, passed to the armed forces and real problems between Russia and other CIS members and conflict situations inside those states served as a kind of springboard for the armed forces.

The armed forces during the first half of the 1990s were able to be a relatively independent actor in foreign policy. There were weighty reasons to justify this—concern for the security of Russia's new borders, Russia's need for a regional security system, and the preservation of old and acquisition of new military bases tracking stations and so on. In the CIS area, furthermore, many new foreign policy problems had important military implications. The only problem was that the solution of those problems had to be found within the framework and on the basis of state foreign policy, and not by the generals on their own.

[14] See e.g. I. Anthony, 'Illicit arms transfers', in I. Anthony, ed., SIPRI, *Russia and the Arms Trade* (Oxford: Oxford University Press, 1998), 217–32. According to one (unnamed) senior officer from the Office of the Chief Military Prosecutor, the value of the illicit arms trade is comparable to the legal income of Rosvooruzheniye. *Profil*, 42 (16 Nov. 1998), 31.

[15] Russia still recognizes the old government of Afghanistan. Nevertheless, it helped Ukraine to produce over 100 T-80 tanks which were delivered via Pakistan to the Taleban, N. Ivanov, '"Uspekhi" konversii,' *Nezavisimaya Gazeta*, 8 Sept. 1998.

Finally, there was another source of mass enrichment—the trade in arms and ammunition on the territory of Russia itself. In recent years this trade has become so extensive that it has produced the strange (at first sight) phenomenon of repeated major explosions in military stores, intended to prevent the detection of theft. That there have been no human casualties in these explosions demonstrates unambiguously that they were planned. In the Far East Military District they had become almost an annual tradition and in February 1998 there were explosions in military stores in the region of Volgograd and in the suburbs of Saratov.[16] An enormous 'contribution' was made by the protracted fighting in Chechnya after 1994. Unlike the Russian troops in Chechnya, local fighters never experienced any lack of modern Russian-made small or anti-tank arms.

There is a saying that 'a fish starts rotting from the head'. This was never more true than it is of the role of former Defence Minister Pavel Grachev. Grachev displayed a strong inclination for commercial diversions. As early as February 1992, when he was chairman of the State Committee on Defence and First Deputy Commander-in-Chief of the CIS Armed Forces, he joined a group of generals, founders of a limited-liability company called Aviakoninfo, set up to sell construction materials, buy timber, run cafés and restaurants, and so on. The business was not a success because of interference 'from the top'. Soon enough, however, Grachev became Defence Minister, and in October 1992 he created a state company, Voyentekh, for the sale of vast surpluses of arms, military technology and army property.[17] From 1993 'as an exception' Grachev allowed the air force to accept transport of commercial cargoes. Military transport aviation used to make several hundred such commercial flights a year. An approximate idea of the scale of that business can be given by the fact that for only three flights to Vietnam in 1997 the air force earned a net profit of about $300 000.[18] Stories also circulated about malpractice in the navy in the process of writing off ships, the use of nuclear submarines and other matters.

THE ARMS TRADE AND MILITARY–TECHNICAL COOPERATION

Perhaps the main part in the genesis of military bureaucratic capital was played by the official trade in arms and military technology within the framework programmes of military–technical cooperation with foreign countries.

In 1992, 12 special exporters were pursuing activities in that sphere. They worked very ineffectively, often breaking laws and regulations. Sometimes as many as 30 mediators circled around one serious contract. Then it was decided to reorganize the whole system of military–technical cooperation.[19] In November 1993 Rosvooruzheniye was created. Of the special exporters only MAPO (the Moscow Aircraft Production Organization) remained intact. At first Deputy Prime Minister Viktor Shumeiko tried to control Rosvooruzheniye and his nominee, Lieutenant-General Viktor Samoylov, was made Director-General. The initiative was joined by Soskovets, head of the Interdepartmental Coordinating Council for Military–Technical Policy (Koordinatsionny mezhvedomstvenny sovet

---

[16] A. Shafurkin, and A. Serenko, 'Novye vzryvy na armeyskikh skladakh,' *Nezavisimaya Gazeta*, 24 Feb. 1998.

[17] *Profil*, 1 (12 Jan. 1998), 12.

[18] *Kommersant-Vlast*, 2 (27 Jan. 1998), 25.

[19] On the organization of military–technical cooperation, see Anthony (n. 14), chs. 5, 6 and 7; and 'The management of arms transfers', in A. A. Sergounin and S. V. Subbotin, *Russian Arms Transfers to East Asia in the 1990s*, SIPRI Research Report no. 15 (Oxford: Oxford University Press, 1999), 44–69.

po voyenno-tekhnicheskogo politike). However, the whole military–technical cooperation programme was subordinated directly to the president in 1994 and Korzhakov placed his people in key posts. Boris Kuzyk was appointed special assistant to the president on military–technical cooperation while General Alexander Kotelkin became Director-General of Rosvooruzheniye in October 1994.

The stormy history of the expansion of Russian arms sales, mainly on Asian markets, and the equally controversial enrichment of the actors in the business now began. Rosvooruzheniye practically monopolized the arms trade (up to 90 per cent)[20] and when Grachev, who dreamed of bringing it once more under his own control, tried to intercept a contract with Malaysia for the sale of 18 MiG-29s in July 1997 Korzhakov immediately initiated a complex inspection of Voyentekh which exposed its participation in shady deals and brought it to the verge of collapse. Grachev was 'excommunicated' from the arms business.[21] From October 1995 Kotelkin virtually monopolized all cargo deliveries within the military–technical cooperation framework, having created a company, Cargotrans, on the basis of the transport department of Rosvooruzheniye.[22]

The leaders of Rosvooruzheniye often gave themselves the credit for the survival of the defence industry. In March 1997, for instance, they announced that in 1996 Rosvooruzheniye's investment in the defence industry amounted to more than $600 million.[23] Kotelkin interpreted the real contribution by Rosvooruzheniye to the defence industry rather differently: $250 million in investment plus attraction of $500 million in bank credits under the company's guarantees. A complex inspection of Rosvooruzheniye by the Attorney-General, Yury Skuratov, begun in the summer of 1996, revealed the scale of abuses by the company's leadership—enormous expenditure on the company itself against a background of debts to the defence industry totalling $200 million, concealment of profits, illegal foreign currency deals and so on.[24]

According to specialist observers, Rosvooruzheniye was by no means working as a charity in favour of the defence industry; rather it turned the latter into a source of enrichment. Valentin Trofimov, for instance, believes that its leadership chose to pay high rates of interest (20–25 per cent) to foreign agents' firms and 10 per cent more to a monopolistic transport company (in fact, to itself), and take between 7 and 10 per cent for 'services'. All this was a heavy burden for producers. Nevertheless, the narrow circle of lucky ones in the defence industry dared not grumble, as even the small sums they received from this trade were almost the only real money they could use to keep production and research and development (R&D) going. However, today the defence industry is dependent on external orders for 80 per cent of orders, instead of 20 per cent, as it was under the Soviet Union.[25]

---

[20] According to Kotelkin himself, the value of sales by Rosvooruzheniye increased from $1.7 billion in 1994 to $2.8 billion in 1995 (out of general sales by the defence industry as a whole of $3.05 billion), and up to $3.4 billion (of $3.5 billion) in 1996. Interview with Kotelkin, *Vek*, 27 (July 1997).

[21] *Profil*, 1 (12 Jan. 1998), 12.

[22] *Profil*, 3 (26 Jan. 1998), 62.

[23] *Delovye Lyudi*, 75 (Mar. 1997), 127.

[24] *Profil*, 3 (26 Jan. 1995), 59–60. The head of the Omsk local office of Rosvooruzheniye states that out of $230 million invested in production in 1996 and $190 million in credits (not $500 million) the Siberian military-industrial complex never received a single dollar. Interview with Vladimir Sosnin, *Moskovskiye Novosti*, 7–11 Sept 1997.

[25] M. Gabovich, 'Sekretnaya torgovlya,' *Moskovskiye Novosti*, 31 Aug.–7 Sept. 1997; and interview with Valentin Trofimov, *Moskovskiye Novosti*, 2–9 Oct. 1997, p. 12.

Following the removal of Korzhakov in the summer of 1996 a struggle started for his 'legacy'. In August 1997 the State Committee on Military–Technical Policy (Gosudarstvenny komitet po voyenno-tekhnicheskoy politike, GKVTP), which had served as a connecting link between the President and Rosvooruzheniye, was abolished and control over exports of arms and military technology handed over to the Ministry of Foreign Economic Relations.[26] The government even tried to establish direct control over Rosvooruzheniye, but at the time this proved impossible owing to the interference of General Lebed, head of the Security Council.[27] An attempt to abolish the monopoly of Rosvooruzheniye in 1996, when several other enterprises and organizations were allowed to act as special exporters, had failed. Lacking experience, connections, know-how and information on the state of foreign markets, those enterprises were helpless and had once again to turn to Rosvooruzheniye.[28]

THE DEFENCE INDUSTRY

Rosvooruzheniye was able to feed on the defence industry only thanks to the grievous state the industry had been in for six years. A sharp reduction in military expenditure—by 70 per cent over the two years 1991–92[29]—along with the government's neglect of the problems the defence industry was facing produced serious crisis. In the early 1990s the magic word 'conversion' was on everyone's lips. Scholars and statesmen vied with each other to explain to the public how enterprises would be able to preserve their high-technology potential and their production thanks to conversion, but they failed to understand the real problems and difficulties connected with conversion. With very rare exceptions all the hopes and projects for conversion turned out to be myths. Production at converted enterprises proved to be two or three times more labour-intensive than that of civilian enterprises and their products five or six times more expensive. By the beginning of 1996 two-thirds of such enterprises were unprofitable.[30]

The government more or less kept aloof from active assistance to conversion, as financing from the federal budget illustrates.[31]

As a result, after two or three years of unsuccessful efforts, the majority of enterprises stepped on to the road to deconversion. Naturally, this could not possibly succeed as the part of production that went to meet the state defence order was under-financed. The cumulative debt on the state defence order in 1992 totalled 7 billion roubles; in 1993, 920 billion roubles; in 1994, 4.2 trillion roubles; in 1995, 7.7 trillion roubles; and in 1997, 19.9 trillion roubles.[32]

There was a peculiar division of labour: the president signed appropriate decrees and projects pertinent to the defence industry, while the government did not execute them and did not apportion money. This is not surprising. The government was dominated by representatives of the raw materials producers and of the fuel and energy complex, and the relationship between the latter and the defence industry after the break-up of the Soviet

---

[26] Sergounin and Subbotin (n. 19), 57–60.

[27] *Profil*, 38 (19 Oct. 1998), 31.

[28] *Delovye Lyudi*, 75 (Mar. 1997), 124.

[29] E. Sköls *et al.*, 'Military expenditure and arms production'. *SIPRI Yearbook 1998: Armaments, Disarmament and International Security* (Oxford: Oxford University Press, 1998), 223.

[30] *Delovye Lyudi*, 75 (Mar. 1997), 124.

[31] Only a fraction of the amount budgeted for defence industry conversion was disbursed in 1993–4, and none in 1995–7. E. Titova, 'Byudzhetnye dolgi "oboronke" otlozheny na polgoda,' *Finansovye Izvestiya*, 30 Dec. 1997, p. iii.

[32] *Moskovskiye Novosti*, 1–8 Feb. 1998, 17.

Union had changed in principle. Formerly the defence industry had been at the top of the pyramid and the fuel and energy complex was its foundation, feeding the defence industry with cheap energy and necessary foreign currency. Now under conditions of relative autonomy the fuel and energy complex began to retain more of its profits, paying tax only with obvious reluctance and under severe pressure.

As a result of the abolition of the Soviet centralized management mechanism the defence industry turned into a chaotic set of different branches, open-type and limited joint-stock companies, separate enterprises and construction bureaux and organizations. Soon an elite group of enterprises and construction bureaux that had managed to find a niche in the world market stood out. They fell into two sub-groups, one which consolidated its position through cooperation with Western companies (for example, certain enterprises and construction bureaux in the aerospace industry) and one which consolidated its position with the help of military technical cooperation and in competition with Western companies. Both groups improved the situation in their business affairs because of the external factor. However, in the latter group especially favourable conditions were developing for the formation of bureaucratic capital.

Most non-elite enterprises were vegetating and living in poverty. However, some of them became the objects of the aspirations, with various motivations, of different bureaucratic capital factions and large Western corporations.[33]

The year 1997 was also the breaking-point in the struggle of different factions of bureaucratic capital for possession of the fattest pieces of the defence industry. The financial-trading faction delivered a weakening blow when the Ministry of the Defence Industry was abolished in March. However, by the summer of that year the initiative gradually began to pass to representatives of the raw materials producers. At the end of July a presidential decree gave the prime minister control of Rosvooruzheniye.[34] In August it was followed by a series of decrees that completely changed the defence industry system.[35] Rosvooruzheniye became a state unitary enterprise and two new intermediary organizations appeared on the stage—Promexport, which had to sell surplus Defence Ministry armaments, and Rossiyskiye Tekhnologii to deal in the sphere of military technologies. 'In a further effort to weaken the Company's [Rosvooruzheniye's] grip on the arms market ... [a] Kremlin decree granted the right to export weapons to two other state companies and to certain manufacturers ... allowing more of the revenues to go to the Ministry of Defence and to arms manufacturers'.[36]

One more exceptionally important aspect should be mentioned. In allowing two more intermediary organizations to be set up, Chernomyrdin acted as defender both of the interests of the defence industry and of the Defence Ministry (having granted them 'a piece

[33] Fairly typical examples of such intense opposition (in the course of 'repeated' privatizations, through sale of state shares of enterprises already incorporated) are the cases of Permskiye Motory in 1992 and Rybinskiye Motory in 1994. Municipal and regional authorities, arbitration courts at all levels, the Supreme Court, the government and the president found themselves involved in the struggle.

[34] 'On measures to improve the system of management of military-technical cooperation with foreign states', Presidential decree no. 792, 28 July 1997, reproduced in *Rossiyskaya Gazeta*, 2 Aug. 1997, p. 6.

[35] Sergounin and Subbotin (n. 19), 57–60.

[36] C. Freeland, 'Yeltsin reasserts Kremlin control over arms trade', *Financial Times*, 22 Aug. 1997; and *Expert*, 3 (26 Jan. 1998), 6.

each', not forgetting himself). The former head of the bank connected with MiG-MAPO, Yevgeny Ananyev, was made Director-General of Rosvooruzheniye in August 1997. *Delovye Lyudi* believes that this appointment was made thanks to the close ties of Ananyev with people from the presidential staff. As a result the people Oneximbank had long been counting on, such as Kotelkin, found themselves moved away from the direct management of the arms trade.[37] This is another angle on the developing 'anti-financiers' alliance. The positions of the financial faction were also considerably weakened by a scandal concerning deliveries (to be more exact, under-deliveries) of a batch of aircraft to India.[38]

The struggle around the creation of new corporations resumed with new strength at the end of 1997, revealing a range of old and new conflicts—between construction bureaux and producers; among producers for leadership of future business corporations; between enterprises and Moscow commercial banks; between the banks themselves (for instance, between Oneximbank and Inkombank): between the legislative and executive powers; and between the centre and the regions which were striving to get their share in future corporations. Since the end of 1997 even the Mayor of Moscow, Yury Luzhkov, has found himself involved in the struggle.[39]

1998: Crisis of the ultra-liberal model

In March 1998, when Chernomyrdin believed that he had concentrated almost all the levers of executive power in his hands and obviously anticipated becoming president in the near future, Yeltsin, displeased with Chernomyrdin's rapid rise and increasing independence, dismissed the entire government.

This marked the turning point in Russia's development. The structural crisis that had hitherto been semi-latent entered its open phase. In the following four or five months it became obvious that the model of development formed over the preceding six years was a blind alley. In the socio-political sphere the favourite method of the president, manoeuvring and playing colleagues off against one another, ceased to work. The illusory relative stability was broken even at the highest level of the executive power. There appeared signs of split and demoralization in the apparatus of the presidential administration and even in the narrow circle closest to Yeltsin. For instance, although Yumashev and Berezovsky had jointly initiated the removal of Chernomyrdin, they immediately split over the question of who was to become the next 'pocket' prime minister. Defying Berezovsky, Yumashev pressed for Sergey Kiriyenko.

Even more importantly, the spring and summer of 1998 revealed the complete exhaustion of the socio-economic model established as a result of the action of previous governments with the active cooperation of the IMF. A central element of that model was macroeconomic stabilization, interpreted as the fight against inflation at any cost. The result was a rather

---

[37] *Delovye Lyudi*, 84 (Dec. 1997), 25; and Yu. Ryazskiy, 'Proshchay oruzhiye,' *Moskovskiy Komsomolets*, 14 Jan. 1998.

[38] For the detailed story of this illegal operation, see L. Nikitinskiy, 'Samolety, obligatsii i korobka,' *Moskovskiye Novosti*, 20–7 Sept. 1998, p. 12.

[39] V. Zusmanov, and G. Mikhailov, 'Kto vyidet iz vody s "Sukhim",' *Profil*, 7 (28 Feb. 1998), 28–9; Interview with Mikhail Simonov, *Novaya Gazeta*, 2–8 Feb. 1998, p. 7; A. Onufriyev, 'MiG mezhdu proshlym i budushchim,' *Expert*, 12 (30 Mar. 1998), 30–1; M. Isayev, 'Krutoye pike VPK i MAPO,' *Nezavisimaya Gazeta*, 6 Feb. 1998; and E. Rato, 'Deputaty zadumalis o voyennoy aviatsii,' *Segodnya*, 25 Feb. 1998.

strange 'market economy' in which the greater part of industrial production appeared to be cut off from the system of monetary payment and moved into the shadow economy of barter, which even by the more modest estimates exceeded 50 per cent of the economy,[40] and the use of surrogate money. The credit system was isolated from the 'real', productive sectors of the economy and instead of performing its main function of serving those sectors it acted (together with the exchange markets) as a mechanism for pumping abroad a considerable part of the value added in production. This happened thanks to the ultra-liberal foreign currency market created with the assistance of Western experts. This situation meant that the state was unable to collect taxes, and as a consequence led to an increase of the budget deficit.

Meanwhile, as IMF instructions excluded the possibility of covering the budget deficit by printing money, starting from 1995 the government switched to financing the deficit exclusively by loan. A giant pyramid of treasury short-term bonds was built up, which very soon turned from being a means of patching holes in the budget to being a powerful means to take money, including that received from the international financial organizations, out of the budget. The growth of the pyramid was accelerated by the fact that in 1996–97 the Central Bank opened the treasury short-term bonds markets for foreign investors who had been previously acting through dummy Russian structures.

Kiriyenko became Prime Minister at the very moment when net returns from selling treasury short-term bonds came down to zero, and since then the net capital outflow has never let up, increasing monthly by 5 billion roubles. On the eve of the collapse of 17 August 1998 the treasury was paying out $1 billion per week on old bonds and had stopped the distribution of new bonds.[41] Oil prices remained depressed. The state found itself on the verge of bankruptcy.

Kiriyenko, calling his government a technocratic one, tried to be above the fight among the factions of bureaucratic capital, started to talk about industrial policy and began to create a ministry of industry and trade. However, the crisis had gone too far and the contradictions between the social and political forces in the country had been greatly aggravated. In this extreme situation another regrouping of forces took place. The representatives of big bureaucratic business separated into two camps, which had different views of the way out of the crisis.

One (relatively anti-Western) group consisted of those who were against the domineering role of the IMF and the Western transnational corporations in determining the tactics for Russia's way out of the crisis and the strategy for its future economic development. It was a large but ill-assorted group, including those 'oligarchs' who could not exist and flourish without the hot-house conditions created for them by previous governments and/or were reliant on corrupt ties with top officials, as well as those corporations (Lukoil and Gazprom) which had already obtained strong positions but which wanted to preserve them, including partnerships with foreign capital, and gain new privileges from the state.

Naturally, there could be no absolute cohesion within that group. For instance, the raw materials exporters were seriously interested in devaluation of the rouble as it could bring them considerable profit even while prices on the world market were low, but for the big financiers devaluation could be fatal as it would undermine their ability to settle credits

---

[40] Ivanter et al. (n. 6); and *Expert*, 1–2 (18 Jan. 1999), 11.   [41] Ivanter et al. (n. 6), 8.

received in the process of constructing the treasury short-term bonds pyramid, in which they had actively participated. Nevertheless, at that point in time they were united by the intention to prevent events developing according to the 'Western script'. Boris Berezovsky acted as their informal (and temporary) leader.

The second, more 'Western-oriented', group included those who believed it necessary to follow the recommendations of the IMF and were ready to play the role of junior partner of the Western transnational corporations. The undoubted leader of this group was and still is Anatoly Chubais.

Kiriyenko, although he had officially proclaimed a policy of neutrality, was in reality inclined to cooperate with the second group, which naturally caused great discontent among the first. Open riot seemed unavoidable. On 22 July 1998 the heads of six oil companies issued a sharp criticism of the conditions attached to the next IMF credit, calling the economic policy of the international financial organizations, which in particular involved an increase of fiscal pressure on the industries of the 'real economy', 'unreasonable and irresponsible'. *Nezavismaya Gazeta* (controlled by Berezovsky) did not hesitate to threaten to 'sweep away' the government of Kiriyenko.[42]

As the culmination of the crisis approached, Kiriyenko openly took the 'Western-oriented' course and the final decision on crisis measures proclaimed on 17 August was made with the direct participation of Chubais, preceded by consultations with Yegor Gaidar, the international financier George Soros and the leaders of the relevant US government agencies.[43]

On the face of it the decision on simultaneous default and devaluation had to satisfy both exporters and the commercial banks, which were forbidden to make payments on their foreign debts. In fact matters were more complicated and worse. First, the default was announced only for three months, which was too short a time for banks to solve the problem of their debt: by the end of the period the majority of them were expected to go bankrupt. Second and more importantly, Kiriyenko and Chubais prepared a 'Western version' of restructuring, putting the country's finances on a sound basis and allowing for bankruptcies. On the eve of the default Chubais openly called on foreign banks to participate in the restructuring of the Russian banking sector.[44] Not long after that, Nemtsov stated that Kiriyenko intended to apply a package of tough and radical reforms which Western leaders insisted on and which included the bankruptcy of politically influential but economically weak commercial banks and oil companies. It was envisaged that stronger companies, including Western creditors, could take control over weaker firms.[45]

The leaders of the opposite camp learned of those plans. With the help of the presidential administration Berezovsky made another 'upheaval' and secured the removal of Kiriyenko. Nevertheless, as in March 1998, the operation was only a partial success: the attempt to return Chernomyrdin to power was frustrated by the Duma.

The approval of Yevgeny Primakov as Prime Minister on 11 September brought

---

[42] 'Neft i politikantstvo,' *Nezavisimaya Gazeta*, 23 July 1998.

[43] Interview given by Kiriyenko and abstracts from G. Soros, [The end of capitalism], published in *Expert*, 1–2 (18 Jan. 1998), 8, 10 (in Russian).

[44] L. Krutakov, 'Chubais khotel sdat banki inostrantsam,' *Moskovskiy Komsomolets*, 26 Aug. 1998.

[45] Abstracts from an interview by Boris Nemtsov and comments on it, *Russkiy Telegraf*, 27 Aug. 1998; and *Expert*, 32 (31 Aug. 1998), 11 (in Russian).

immediate relative political stability. This was the first government to enjoy the support not only of the President and his administration but of the Duma and the Council of the Federation, as well as broad sympathy among the general public (as was more than once established by opinion polls). This may be connected with the fact that for the first time the executive power was led by a man who had no connections with any faction of bureaucratic capital and was a consistent statist.

The general features of the course taken by the Primakov Government were apparent— the gradual dismantling of the existing neo-colonial and neo-comprador model; the focusing of economic policy on solving the problems of the real economy; the restructuring of the banking system and industry in the interests of general economic development instead of self-enrichment; and the continuation of socially oriented economic reforms.

In order to develop this strategy fully, Primakov's Government had to solve the most complicated problem of debt, both foreign and domestic. The great difficulty here lay in the fact that the government was forced to solve this problem at the same time as developing a new strategy. For that purpose a number of long-term measures were undertaken.

The Russian Federal Property Fund established an Agency for the Restructuring of Credit Organizations, the goal of which was the creation of a new banking system, a return to normal working for the 18 largest banks, large regional banks, and the bankruptcy of approximately 720 banks which were beyond saving.[46] A new Russian Development Bank (RDB) was formed with capital from the 1999 development budget and the possibility of international financial groups participating in the bank's capital was envisaged. The RDB was created to accumulate means from foreign and home sources to provide credit for the 'real sector' regardless of forms of property—the main criterion was efficiency—using the mechanism of distribution of state investments on a competitive basis and provision of state guarantees.[47] In the course of setting up these two institutions the government resorted to consultations with the International Bank for Reconstruction and Development (IBRD) and the European Bank for Reconstruction and Development (EBRD). In its turn the Central Bank started to construct a post-crisis model of the home currency market instead of the former ultra-liberal one, with exporters being obliged to sell to the Central Bank 75 per cent of their foreign exchange earnings and with more effective regulation of exchange-rate fluctuations.[48]

In spite of another 'mutiny of the oil generals' in October 1998, the government increased its efforts to restructure this most important industry. The main directions of these efforts were: (*a*) a reduction of the number of companies through the merger of Rosneft, Slavneft, Onako (and then probably of Tyumenskaya), forming a large national oil company in which 75 per cent of shares would belong to the state; (*b*) the formation of a working group to control oil exports and related matters;[49] and (*c*) partial rationalization of those enterprises that were seized by the 'oligarchs' during the division of state property but which they failed to 'digest' and which had become a burden to them.

Foreign investment was another matter where Primakov did not support either of the

---

[46] For details, see *Kommersant-Vlast'*, 46 (1 Dec. 1998), 28; and *Segodnya*, 18 Dec. 1998.

[47] For details, see *Segodnya*, 23 Dec. 1998; and *Nezavisimaya Gazeta*, 30 Dec. 1998.

[48] For a more substantial analysis of these measures, see E. Makovskaya, 'Valutu tolko po nuzhdey,' *Expert*, 37 (5 Oct. 1998), 6.

[49] *Finansovye Izvestiya*, 22 Dec 1998; and *Moskovskiye Novosti*, 22–9 Nov. 1998.

opposing groups. Russia's interests and its national economy were his priority. He expressed a negative attitude to speculative portfolio investments and stood for promotion of direct private investments. Here a serious breakthrough has already been achieved: on 9 December 1998 the Duma passed legislation enabling production-sharing agreements (PSAs) and thereby promising to change the landscape of oil industry investment in Russia.[50] This added impetus to foreign investment in the already functioning Sakhalin-1 and Sakhalin-2 projects. Negotiations with Exxon on the Sakhalin-3 project became brisker. The Sakhalin-4 and Sakhalin-5 projects were next in turn. All this meant that the prospects for the development of the Russian far east and for energy cooperation with the Asia-Pacific countries could be regarded with more optimism. Immediately after the first breakthrough the government started preparing other important bills on foreign investments (for example, 'On concessions', 'On free economic zones' and 'On accounting') for introduction to the Duma.

The large part of industry that was excluded from the money circulation process was less affected by the recent financial shocks. Combined with a considerable weakening of the leading bureaucratic capital factions, this created favourable conditions for the government to concentrate on industrial expansion. Tight as the 1999 state budget was, the government put into the 'development' budget 21.6 billion roubles—five times more than in previous years.[51] However, it was not by any means planning to save industry in general. The approach was strictly selective. Only efficient industries were to be supported—those which were promising from the point of view of export and competitiveness on the home market or strategically important.

Naturally, the government proceeded from an understanding that foreign participation in this restructuring was necessary and was ready to allow foreign investors considerable financial privileges. Thus, while adopting at the end of January 1999 a plan of financial support for the Rosselmash joint-stock company (a monopoly in combine construction), it took into consideration the intention of the US company John Deare to participate in joint production, and was ready to give the plant a four-year debt postponement plus another four-year instalment on its main debt and a 10-year instalment on accumulated penalties.[52] In the defence industry the government started the process of centralization of production, coordination of research and creation of vertically integrated corporations. The creation of a large holding in Rossiyskiye Raketnye Dvigateli (Russian Rocket Engines), where it was decided to leave 51 per cent of shares to the state and grant 34 per cent to Russian and foreign investors, and the decision on the merger of the Sukhoi Construction Bureau with the MiG aviation complex[53] were examples.

In general the new government strategy was a resolute rejection of unbridled liberalization, but it was also almost as clear a rejection of a return to centralized administration.

[50] *OGJ Newsletter*, 4 Jan. 1999.   [51] *Nezavisimaya Gazeta*, 30 Dec. 1998; and *Segodnya*, 27 Jan. 1999.
[52] *Izvestiya*, 29 Jan. 1999.   [53] *Izvestiya*, 17 Dec 1998; and *Nezavisimaya Gazeta*, 20 Jan. 1999.

Public Opinion, Political Beliefs, and the Mass Media

Section 7

Public Opinion, Political
Beliefs, and the Mass Media

Public Opinion, Political

Introduction

Archie Brown

At a time of dramatic, and sometimes traumatic, political and economic change, it is hardly surprising that the attitudes of Russians should have shown great volatility. That may suggest that large conclusions should not be built on the basis of survey research. It can equally, without contradicting the first point, be a good reason why survey data should be constantly updated, with questions repeated at regular intervals. What is, at least, clear from precisely such replicated studies is that in the course of the 1990s levels of satisfaction with the political and economic changes which have occurred in Russia dropped significantly. The All-Russian Centre for the Study of Public Opinion (VTsIOM)—whose Director, Yury Levada, is the author of one of the chapters in this section—has kept track more assiduously than any other organization of changing Russian attitudes. In an article published in its house journal in 1999, Levada noted that the proportion of the population of Russia who agreed with the statement that 'it would have been better if the country had remained as it was before 1985' rose from 44 per cent in 1994 to 58 per cent in 1999.[1] The Brezhnev era was by 1999 viewed more positively than any other period of twentieth-century Russian history. Notwithstanding its hypocrisy and lack of freedom and democracy, that time is now seen through rose-tinted spectacles as people remember full employment, wages paid on schedule, the 'tranquillity' which Brezhnev-era spokesmen liked to emphasize,[2] and a Soviet Union enjoying 'super-power' status. The Gorbachev years, which—along with Gorbachev himself—were still evaluated very positively in 1989,[3] declined in popularity throughout the post-Soviet period, increasingly being seen as the start of a process whereby Russia and Russians become worse off.

That such perceptions of earlier Russian history were intimately linked to experience of the Yeltsin years was indicated by the rise in popularity of the Stalin era and the increase in negative evaluations of the Gorbachev period between 1994 and 1999. During that time the percentage of the population positively evaluating the Stalin years rose from 18 per cent to 26 per cent, while those taking a positive view of the perestroika era declined from 16 per cent to 9 per cent.[4] No new and positive revelations about Stalin's rule came to light in the second half of the 1990s and nothing new to the discredit of the Gorbachev years became known.

[1] Yury Levada, '"Chelovek sovetskiy" desyat' let spustya: 1989–1999', *Monitoring obshchestvennogo mneniya* (VTsIOM), 3 (41) (May–June 1999), 7–15, at p. 7.

[2] On 'tranquillity' as an official value in the Brezhnev era, see Archie Brown, 'The Power of the General Secretary of the CPSU', in T. H. Rigby, Archie Brown, and Peter Reddaway (eds), *Authority, Power and Policy in the USSR: Essays dedicated to Leonard Schapiro* (London: Macmillan, 1980), 135–157, at pp. 146–7.

[3] For a summary of the VTsIOM findings on Gorbachev's standing in 1989–90, as reported by Levada in those years, see Archie Brown, *The Gorbachev Factor* (Oxford: Oxford University Press, 1996), esp. pp. 6 and 10–11.

[4] Levada, '"Chelovek sovetskiy" desyat' let spustya: 1989–1999', 11.

Thus, it is evident that revised evaluations of these two very different Soviet epochs were highly dependent on changing attitudes to what was happening in Russia in the last decade of the twentieth century. Indeed, the post-Soviet period fared even worse in the same survey. In 1999 only 5 per cent viewed the Yeltsin years positively and 72 per cent of the population had a negative attitude to them.[5] Post-Soviet institutions fared little better. Asked in 1999 which social and political institutions merited trust, only 7 per cent of Russian citizens had full trust in parliament and only 5 per cent in political parties (as compared with 35 per cent having full trust in the Orthodox Church, 25 per cent in the army, and 13 per cent in the mass media).[6]

Two of the four chapters in this section, those by Richard Rose and Yury Levada, draw heavily on survey data (collecting information on behaviour as well as on attitudes), while the remaining two—by Oksana Gaman-Golutvina and Laura Belin—are more concerned with political and intellectual *elites* than with *mass* opinion. Rose (in Chapter 20) explores the ways in which both Soviet and post-Soviet organizations have unwittingly 'encouraged Russians to adopt antimodern tactics'. The use of connections, informal exchange of favours, and patron–client relationships—as well as, increasingly, in post-Communist Russia monetary bribes—substitute for reliance on the law or the willingness of public officials to act according to generally understood rules and procedures. Five-sixths of the respondents to a survey cited by Rose think that taxes can be evaded and differ only in their assessment of the best means of evasion. Consistent with that is an ambivalence about progress towards a law-governed state, since many citizens take comfort from the fact that the law is not enforced against them, however much they may wish to see its full rigours applied to the 'oligarchs', for instance.

Oksana Gaman-Golutvina, in the following chapter, also addresses the issue of modernity, but in the context of a loss of interest, as she sees it, on the part of the Russian elite in economic modernization. She points to a number of reasons for this—not least the heavy price which was paid both by the elite and the mass of the people for past economic development forced upon them by autocratic 'modernizers' from Peter the Great to Stalin. Moreover, she argues, instead of taking seriously economic modernization for the good of the country, the new elite has been obsessed with the acquisition of property for their personal benefit. Noting the dependence of even the most privileged of Soviet leaders on the party-state and their lack of property they could call their own, Gaman-Golutvina sees the determination of the Communist nomenklatura to remedy their property-less condition as a prime cause of the downfall of the old order. It was, she suggests, the absence of ownership rights which eventually turned 'the Soviet ruling class into the grave-diggers of the Soviet system'.

On one of Oksana Gaman-Golutvina's own illustrations of her point, however, a caveat must be entered. She quotes the late Raisa Gorbacheva remonstrating with her husband over the fact that he had not acquired even a tiny plot of land, although she had asked him many times to do so. In other words, for the Soviet leader who played a greater role than any other in the pluralization and subsequent dismantling of the Soviet *system*,[7] the pursuit of property was

---

[5] Levada, '"Chelovek sovetskiy" desyat' let spustya'.

[6] Leonid Sedov, 'Rol' SMI v izbiratel'noy kampanii', *Monitoring obshchestvennogo mneniya* (VTsIOM), 1 (45) (Jan.–Feb. 2000), 32–5, at p. 33. A further 38 per cent 'partly trusted' the legislature and 24 per cent partly trusted parties (as compared with an additional 20 per cent for the Church, 30 per cent for the army and 40 per cent for the mass media).

[7] As distinct from the disintegration of the Soviet *state* which was an unintended consequence of these transformative changes.

not a motivating force. More generally, it has become increasingly clear that in the last years of the Soviet Union politicians and political activists who were dismantling the old system were divided between those engaged in a scramble for property and those who were striving for greater freedom and democracy. In the post-Soviet period, some of those who had been in the latter camp joined the former. So, indeed, did some formerly hard-line Communists who, during the perestroika years, had been fighting ostensibly to preserve 'socialism'. Oksana Gaman-Golutvina's contribution to this volume is as much an impassioned plea for change as it is an analysis of the fate of the idea of modernization in recent (and more distant) Russian history. She appeals for more elite consensus, for a 'pact' between the financial-industrial groups and the state, and for an exercise of political will to advance the modernization of Russia.

The doyen of Russian survey research, Yury Levada, provides in Chapter 22 illuminating interpretations of Russian thinking about politics, based on a wealth of empirical data. He draws attention to the prevarication and ambivalence he finds in many contemporary Russian attitudes and even resorts to the Orwellian term, 'doublethink', to encapsulate the holding of two contradictory opinions simultaneously. Much of this he sees as a legacy of the Soviet period when self-deception facilitated self-preservation—both psychological and physical. Levada, on the basis of survey research, notes that a majority of the Russian population did not believe the pre-election pledges of candidates during the 1995–6 round of elections, but in the immediate aftermath of the elections did not hold non-fulfilment of promises against their favoured candidates. The recrimination came only later. Levada suggests that the rise and fall in public popularity of particular favourites has had little to do with knowledge of their activities, programmes, or aims. He credits the mass media with a high degree of success in manipulating Russian public opinion in recent years. Television has been an especially powerful influence, since 'what is not shown on the screen is effectively not shown to society'.

This links up with Laura Belin's final contribution in the section which, like Gaman-Golutvina's chapter, was specially written for this volume. A leading specialist on the Russian mass media, Belin concludes that they appeared distinctly less free by the end of the 1990s than they were in the early years of that decade. She points to new restrictions on the media and the selective attacks on media magnates whose television channels or newspapers had been among the more critical of the state authorities. This became especially evident during Putin's first year in office when first Vladimir Gusinsky and later Boris Berezovsky were targeted. Like most of Russia's new tycoons, Gusinsky and Berezovsky had much in their record which would not bear close scrutiny, but it was scarcely accidental that pressure was put on Gusinsky, in particular, since, as the president of Media Most, he headed the conglomerate which included the television channel, NTV. It had not supported Unity in the run-up to the 1999 parliamentary election or Vladimir Putin in the presidential election campaign. It had also conspicuously failed to report uncritically his activities once he was installed in office.

It was especially ominous, as Belin notes, that Mikhail Lesin, minister for the press, television and the means of mass communication since July 1999, personally signed an addendum to an 'agreement' which Gusinsky was pressurized into endorsing, whereby he would relinquish his controlling stake in Media Most to Gazprom in return for immunity from arrest. Berezovsky's case was different, since he had been supportive of Putin during the presidential election campaign, but the honeymoon did not last. By late 2000 the mass media owned or controlled by Gusinsky and Berezovsky were under threat of takeover or emasculation and their owners were domiciled abroad, declining invitations to come to Moscow to answer criminal charges. Compared with the Soviet Union before the reforms of the second half of the 1980s, the Russian media still exhibited substantial elements of pluralism, but—as Belin points out—the atmosphere had become such that old habits of self-censorship and obedience were reasserting themselves while attempts by the state authorities to use the media to their own advantage seemed increasingly successful.

20 Living in an Antimodern Society

Richard Rose

Modernization can refer to numerous forms of social change; for example, the replacement of religious faith with secular ways of thinking; replacing arbitrary rule with the rule of law; creating a money or an industrial economy; or bringing in democracy. The idea came to the fore in Central and West European societies because modernization occurred there first, long before it began in Russia. Before the Second World War, Europe could be divided along a north–south line between countries that were modern or modernizing in the social and economic sense, such as Britain, Sweden, Germany, and the Czech lands, and southern European countries, such as Portugal, Greece, and Bulgaria, countries that were premodern. The east–west divide was less important, for the Baltic states were more modern than the Iberian peninsula, and France had as many peasants as Hungary. Now we can see that the division between west and east is a successor to the north–south split, a distinction, roughly speaking, between modern and antimodern.

The culturalist approach to Russia argues for continuity between the Russia of today and the premodern folkways of unreformed czarist rule. Communist rule is seen as modifying patterns of behavior from the past century, adapting (and, in part, being transformed by) what was already there. From a cultural perspective, events of the past half-dozen decades, and even more so, of the past half-dozen years, are assumed to make little difference to the relationship that Russians have to life, nature, work, and vodka. While the truth of this culturalist perspective may be exaggerated, its relevance to us is clear: that the distinctly unmodern past of Russia still exists as an unacknowledged legacy, and one with which the country must still come to grips.

The Russian Revolution resulted in communist efforts to modernize a society that was premodern by any standard and thus produced a regime radically different from the communist regimes imposed in Central Europe after 1945. A lot was needed to introduce the attributes of a modern society into Russia. The communist goal, in attempting to transform society, was to create a New Soviet Man. The methods used to accomplish this, such as the mobilization of resources by the organizational weapon of the Communist Party, were radically different from the ways in which modernization had occurred in Western Europe. In Russia, the legacy of the modernization process is different, too.

When the Soviet Union collapsed, many fixed on a new goal: the transformation of Russia into a modern society with a market economy and democratic political institutions. The idea of 'plugging in' the market assumed that, if only one followed the appropriate

This chapter was first published in *East European Constitutional Review*, 8/1–2 (Winter/Spring, 1999), 68–75. Reproduced by kind permission of the author and the *East European Constitutional Review*.

macroeconomic policy and enacted the correct institutional structures for enterprise owner-ship, behavior would automatically be transformed. 'Market bolsheviks' sought to introduce capitalism into a country that had none of the prerequisites of a capitalist economy, as had England, for example, centuries earlier. In Russia, there was privatization without a private sector. Political parties were created as readily as a budding entrepreneur might print designer T-shirts—and with as little concern about what the logo on the T-shirt represented, as long as it caught the consumer's fancy. The voyage on which the Russian Federation was launched may now be seen for what it was, an attempt to 'rebuild the ship at sea.' And after the financial collapse of August 17, 1998, one might describe what is happening now as an attempt to 'relaunch a holed ship that has run aground'—without repairing the hull.

In the excitement of past and present upheavals, there was much talk about Russia being in transition. Unfortunately, less attention has been given to its starting point before 'transition' began. In parts of the former Soviet Union that have been going nowhere or altering only very slowly, the past remains important today, even though the Russian government is committed rhetorically to change. The governors of the Russian Federation cannot 'go home' to the Soviet Union, anymore than they (or their successors) can turn the clock back to the era of Stalinist purges or Russia before the introduction of electricity. But the actions of the new government show that 'the idea of Europe' is, once more, a minority taste in Russian politics, as it has been in turbulent times past.[1] Since Europe symbolizes a 'modern' form of governance and economy we ought to consider, then, to what extent Russians continue to live in an antimodern society.

Recognizing an antimodern society

The creation of the Soviet bloc split Europe between those countries that were modern in the Weberian sense and those that were modern in the Marxist-Leninist sense. The orthodox communist position was that late-capitalist industrial societies were not modern but deca-dent, and the more apparently developed they were, the sooner they were doomed to collapse. Marxism-Leninism was trumpeted as the truly modern doctrine, and the Soviet Union as its prime exponent. Even though the communist system had mass education, big cities, and jet airplanes, it was different because it created a nonmarket economy without private property and a party-state that administered affairs without regard for the principles of the *Rechtsstaat*.

A modern society is a knowledge-based society, rich in information. A modern society is transparent; everyone can observe relations of cause and effect and make rational calcula-tions about how to vote or spend money. A democratic government creates, as it were, a cybernetic system with continuing feedback between governors and governed. For all the prattle about cybernetics in the Soviet era, the communist system was opaque. Rulers ignored or repressed feedback. Ideology provided an a priori framework for predicting, prescribing, and interpreting events. To point to evidence contradicting Marxist-Leninist assumptions was to risk being branded an enemy of the state. Neither votes nor prices were used to determine what people wanted. Instead, party leaders and party committees decided what the people were supposed to want, and elections offering no choice meant the party-

---

[1] Iver B. Neumann, *Russia and the Idea of Europe: A Study in Identity and International Relations* (London, 1996).

state did not have to worry about the expression of popular dissatisfaction at the ballot box. A 99.9 percent vote for the party was intended to remind the electorate that they could enjoy only what Vaclav Havel has called 'the power of the powerless.'

Communist societies shared two attributes with modern Western societies: they were complex and, up to a point, effective (Table 20.1). A communist society was complex, because of the conflicting interests and ambitions within and between communist institutions, and because of the desire of the party-state to centralize control over the political, economic, and social institutions and their respective values. A communist system could also be effective, as was demonstrated by the capacity of the Soviet Union to put a man into space, to maintain an elaborate system of internal surveillance for the repression of political dissidents, or to manage ruthless border controls over thousands of kilometers.

To the casual observer of material phenomena, the subjects of communist systems appeared to be living in modern, if not yet 'postmodern,' societies. There were increasing numbers of cars on the streets, television sets in rural cottages as well as in high-rise flats, and more people could jet to the seaside for holidays—albeit in enterprise-controlled resorts within the Soviet bloc. Official statistics appeared to confirm modernization, for there was—in theory—a high level of investment, continuing economic growth, full employment, and little or no inflation. But the presence of some elements of a modern society—whether refrigerators or space satellites—does not mean that all materially prosperous societies are the same, much less that they are modern.

In Weberian terms, Russia was not just different, in some small ways, from conventional modern societies; it was antimodern. The rule of law had limited practical utility; in a system of socialist legality the demands of the party were of overriding importance. And given the absence of the rule of law, subjects could not rely on bureaucrats to deliver services to which they were, from another perspective, legally entitled. Without any sort of predictability, people who wanted things from the state either had to accept, fatalistically, what officials did or had to turn to an 'economy of favors' involving *blat*.[2] Money was neither necessary nor sufficient to secure valued goods, since bureaucratic commands allocated resources to enterprises and administered wages in what Janos Kornai characterized as a

Table 20.1 **Comparing modern and antimodern societies**

	Modern	Antimodern
Operation	Complex	Complex
Signals	Prices and laws	Rules, politics, bribes, and personal contacts
Openness	Transparent	Translucent, opaque
Lawful	Yes	Rigidity modified by waivers
Cause and effect	Calculable	Uncertain
Output	Efficient	Inefficient
Effective	Yes	Irregular

[2] See Alena V. Ledeneva, *Russia's Economy of Favours: Blat, Networking and Informal Exchange* (Cambridge, 1998).

command economy. In extreme cases, factories subtracted value instead of adding it, as their output could be worth less than the resources used to produce the goods. The unrealistic targets of five-year plans encouraged factory managers routinely to engage in deceit and exaggeration to give the appearance that everything was working all right—on paper.

In a developing country that is modernizing, by definition, a significant portion of the population lives outside the modern economy. Some lead the marginal existence of a first-generation urban underclass or follow a traditional lifestyle in rural areas. The movement of rural offspring to join the urban underclass is a collective step leading to a modern society. This is so because a developing country also has a modern sector. Modernization is a process of shifting people between sectors, increasing the proportion living in the modern sector while reducing the number of those living in the traditional rural areas virtually to nil.

The Soviet system was antimodern because the institutions it created to build its new civilization were intended as an alternative rather than as a prelude to 'bourgeois' norms and lifestyles. To get things done required much more time and energy than in Weber's paradigm of a modern bureaucracy working with the predictability of a vending machine. The communist system was a perverse example of Weber's dictum that 'power is in the administration of everyday things.' The power of the communist party-state was evident in the stress created by the maladministration of everyday things.[3]

The legacy of the Soviet era is that of social failure—and the consequences remain palpably evident. The institutions of a market economy have not yet been created by a few 'big bang' actions, such as the overnight creation of a stock market. Ironically, the supposedly smart institutions of Western societies, such as commercial banks and the IMF, have paid the biggest dollar price to learn this obvious lesson—of Russia's social failure—from the financial collapse of last August. Ordinary Russians did not need to lose dollars to learn this lesson, nor were they well enough off to have savings in foreign currencies. As John Earle of the Stockholm Institute of Transition Economies has pointed out, long before the Russian Federation defaulted on Western bankers it defaulted on its own citizens, failing to pay the wages and social benefits to which they were entitled.

Getting things done in an antimodern society

Even in an antimodern society there is no escape from organizations. The modern element of such a society is represented by the fact that most households depend on large organizations for education, health care, housing, and employment. The 'anti' element arises because these organizations do not work as they are supposed to. What do Russians do?

To determine the degree to which formal changes in society have made a difference in the way Russians get things done—and thus, the extent to which Russia is or is not an antimodern society—the seventh New Russia Barometer survey of the Centre for the Study of Public Policy, in 1998, collected data about how Russians deal with organizations that would be crucial to both large, complex, modern *and* antimodern societies. Unlike political-culture surveys, the Barometer study focused on behavior rather than attitudes and opinions. The behavior it emphasized is that required to get the goods and services individuals want, rather than voting behavior, which can produce a Duma or president that few people want.

---

[3] Max Weber, *Wirtschaft und Gesellschaft*, 5th edn. (Tubingen, 1972), 126.

The survey was part of the World Bank's 'Global Initiative on Defining, Monitoring, and Measuring Social Capital,' supported by overseas-development funding from the government of Denmark. (The author is solely responsible for the survey and for interpretation.[4])

Since institutions differ in how they work—doctors are much more personal than bureaucratic municipal landlords—the questionnaire covered various situations affecting a majority of households. The questionnaire thus treated relations between Russians and organizations as variable, rather than assuming that everything works in Russia as in a modern society or, the opposite error, that nobody knows how to get anything done. Second, the questionnaire dealt with situations in which various formal organizations are the major sources of welfare and income, such as hospital treatment, education, and employment. To focus on the delivery of goods and services that concern ordinary people yields more concrete evidence than questions about trust in distant national institutions, for which the television and press are the primary media of information.[5] Third, individuals were asked what they had done or would advise friends to do to obtain from organizations such things as admission to a university or a job.

The timing of the survey was particularly propitious: the Russian Centre for Public Opinion Research (VCIOM) undertook the actual fieldwork—asking the questions—between March 6 and April 13, 1998. The date was far enough distant from the old regime for evidence of change to have become evident. A total of 1,904 adult Russians were interviewed face to face in a multistage, randomly stratified sample covering the whole of the Russian Federation, urban and rural, with 191 widely dispersed primary sampling units. A big, nationwide sample avoids the trap of assuming that 'everyone's doing it,' however 'it' is defined. This is a big limitation of generalizations made by Westerners living in Moscow or anthropologists in rural villages.

Alternative tactics for getting things done

In a modern society, people do not require a repertoire of tactics for dealing with formal organizations. Bureaucratic organizations predictably deliver goods and services to individuals as citizens and customers. In a modern society a person claims a good or service, to which he or she is entitled by law or payment, and it is delivered, fairly and efficiently, by employees of a large, impersonal organization. In such a society no one thinks it unusual that electricity is supplied without interruption, and bills for payment are regularly received; an airline ticket booked by phone is ready to be picked up at the airport; and wages and pensions are routinely paid each month. If people use informal networks, it is to supplement or complement what is provided routinely by organizations; it is not a vote of no-confidence in the institutions of the state and market.

But what if modern organizations do not work in this way? Given the central importance of money, in a modern society, the inability of organizations to pay wages or pensions is a

---

[4] For full details of the survey sample, questionnaire, and answers, see Richard Rose, *Getting Things Done with Social Capital: New Russia Barometer VII*, University of Strathclyde Studies in Public Policy, No. 303 (Glasgow, 1998). On the Internet, see www.cspp.strath.ac.uk.

[5] For details about how Russians evaluate the institutions of society, such as political parties, the police, and private enterprise, see William Mishler and Richard Rose, *Trust in Untrustworthy Institutions*, University of Strathclyde Studies in Public Policy, No. 310 (Glasgow, 1998).

good indicator of the extent of organizational failure. The New Russia Barometer found that, in the early spring of 1998, three out of five Russians did not routinely receive the wages or pensions to which they were entitled; the proportion has undoubtedly increased since the financial collapse. Moreover, the state itself is more likely to pay wages late to employees of state enterprises, such as those in the military, teachers, and health workers, than the private sector is likely to pay its employees late. Pensions, a state responsibility that is easy to routinize in a modern society, are even more likely to be paid late than wages.

Confronted with organizational failure, individuals have a choice about how to respond. Informal networks can substitute for the failure of modern bureaucratic organizations. Or, for instance, if a landlord will not repair a broken window, you can fix it yourself—or freeze in the winter. In many developing countries, people who have grown up in a traditionally clientelistic culture can try the 'premodern' approach of personalizing relations with impersonal bureaucrats. (Similarly, a generation ago, in rural Ireland old people thought they needed a member of parliament to 'speak for them' in order to receive a pension to which they were entitled by law.)

Another alternative is the antimodern perversion of the rule of law, using connections or bribery to get bureaucrats to violate rules. In anticipation of frustration, people fatalistically assume that nothing can be done to make an unpredictable organization deliver as it should.

In each module of the questionnaire, respondents were asked what they had done or would advise a friend to do to get something done. For each situation, a multiplicity of tactics was offered in response. A majority of Russians assume that the organizations on which they depend for goods and services do not work with mechanistic predictability (Table 20.2). For example, only 35 percent think the social-security office will pay claimants the money to which they are entitled, and less than half think the police will protect their house from burglary. The percentage ready to rely on other types of organizations is lower still.

Whereas in a modern society, the market offers those with sufficient income an alternative to the failure of government organizations, in Russia choosing what you want from competing shops is a novelty. The great majority have sufficient money to pick and choose their food in the marketplace, and stores now regularly have stocks of food to sell. The 1998 New Russia Barometer survey also found that 86 percent of the households studied had a color-television set and 37 percent a videocassette recorder, both goods that can only be bought with 'hard' currencies. However, when more costly items are involved, the proportion able to turn to the market declines. Fewer than one in three ever expect to have sufficient financial resources to consider buying a house, and only one in six reckons they could borrow a week's wages from a bank (Table 20.2 [1]).

Individuals can end their reliance on organizations by substituting a nonmonetized production organized into a traditional informal network (Table 20.2 [2]). Past experience with food shortages and a desire to save money results in four-fifths of Russian households, including a large majority of city dwellers, continuing to grow some food for themselves. Informal networks are the most practical form of social security, too. While only one out of four Russians has any savings, and a big majority of the unemployed do not receive any state unemployment benefit, most can turn to family and friends for money if in need. Two-thirds report they could borrow a week's wage or pension payment from a friend or relative. In a developing society, such informal networks can be described as premodern, but in the

Table 20.2 **Alternative tactics for getting things done**

	Percent of respondents invoking tactic
Getting modern organizations to work (1)	
Public sector allocates services by law:	
Requesting police to help protect house from burglary	43
Asking social-security office to pay entitlement when claimed	35
Using market to allocate services to paying customers:	
Buy a flat if it is needed	30
Can borrow a week's wage from a bank	16
Informal alternatives (2)	
Nonmonetized production:	
Growing food	81
Can borrow a week's wage from a friend	66
Personalize (3)	
Beg or cajole officials controlling allocation:	
Keep demanding action at social-security office to get paid	32
Beg officials to admit person to hospital	22
Antimodern (4)	
Reallocate in contravention of the rules:	
Use connections to obtain a subsidized flat	24
Pay cash to doctor on the side	23
Passive, socially excluded (5)	
Nothing I can do to:	
Get into hospital quickly	16
Get pension paid on time (pensioners only)	24

Source: New Russia Barometer Survey VII (1998). Fieldwork by VCIOM; number of respondents; 1,904.

Russian context they are evidence of 'de-modernization'—reflecting the failure of large bureaucratic organizations to provide the social protection to which people are entitled.

When a formal organization does not deliver and the market or an informal network cannot be substituted, an individual can try to 'de-bureaucratize,' that is, find a way to make an organization produce goods and services. The relationship can be personalized (Table 20.2 [3]) by begging or cajoling officials to provide what is wanted or pestering officials until success is achieved. This is a stressful attempt to compensate for the inefficiencies of bureaucratic organizations by taking a step backward into a clientelistic relationship.

Organizations in Soviet times encouraged Russians to adopt antimodern tactics (Table 20.2 [4]); 68 percent of those interviewed said that to get anything done by a public agency in those days, you had to know party members, and it was even more widely assumed that you had to have connections through friends, friends of friends, or even friends of friends of friends. The Russian concept of *blat* often refers to using connections to misallocate benefits by 'bending' or breaking rules on behalf of people in a 'circle' (*svoim*). Connections continue to be seen as significant; for example, close to one-quarter of the respondents endorse connections as the way to get a government-subsidized flat.

The introduction of the market has increased opportunities for overt corruption, that is, paying cash to get officials to break the rules for personal benefit. Whereas one's party connections were most important in Soviet days, the average Russian thinks that dollars or deutsche marks now speak more loudly than a party card.

Taxation illustrates the way in which different defects of the Russian system combine to deprive the state of revenue that would be collected if Russia were modern. There are estimates that more than half the anticipated state revenue is not collected—and some of what is collected is 'levied' rather than paid by modern means. Among employed persons, only 41 percent say that taxes are deducted when their employer pays wages; 5 percent that no taxes are deducted; and a little over half (54 percent) do not know whether taxes are deducted. These replies leave open the question of what proportion of taxes deducted by employers are actually paid into the public purse, which institution controls the money, and what is done with it.

A majority of Russians say that there is no need to pay taxes if you do not want to do so, for the government will never find out, and three-quarters believe that a cash payment to a tax official will enable a person to evade payment of the taxes claimed. Altogether, five-sixths think taxes can be evaded; they differ only in whether the best tactic is not to pay at all or that a 'tip' to a tax official is needed to avoid legal problems.

The resources that individuals need to get things done are not equally distributed throughout a society. Networks are exclusive as well as inclusive; social exclusion (Table 20.2 [5]) describes the position of individuals lacking networks to secure everyday goods and services. In an antimodern society, vulnerability is greatest when the only network that an individual has is represented by public-sector organizations. When these fail, the vulnerable are effectively excluded from social services by an antimodern state.

To measure exclusion, for each situation the New Russia Barometer survey offered the statement: 'nothing can be done.' A great majority of Russians are not socially excluded, that is, unable to draw on some form of social capital when problems arise in everyday situations (Fig. 20.1). Depending on the situation, those able to rely on a network to get things done range from 60 percent to more than 90 percent. Similarly, when Russians are asked how much control they have over their lives, on a scale with 1 representing 'no control' and 10 'a great deal' the mean reply is almost exactly in the middle, 5.2. Only 7 percent place themselves at the bottom, feeling that they are without any control over their own lives.

Although only a minority are prepared to rely on the police, hardly any Russian thinks nothing can be done to protect his or her home from crime. People invoke alternatives, such as making sure there is always someone in the house, keeping a dog, or even getting a gun. The situation most likely to produce a sense of helplessness is the nonpayment of wages, because enterprises are so short of money that cajoling or bribing is of no avail.

While it is common to talk about categories of people as socially excluded (pensioners, unemployed persons, or women with children), social exclusion tends to be specific to a

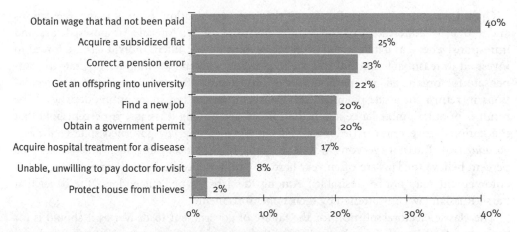

Figure 20.1 **Measures of social exclusion if organization fails**
(Those saying 'nothing can be done' to obtain services or goods as a measure of social exclusion)
Source: New Russia Barometer Survey (VII) 1998. Fieldwork by VCIOM; number of respondents: 1,904.

particular situation. Most Russians have a variety of networks on which they can rely. While very few have the social as well as economic resources to cope with all contingencies, relatively few are consistently without any network at all to fall back on. Across ten different situations, only 18 percent said that 'nothing can be done' in a majority of situations, and only 4 percent feel excluded in eight situations out of ten.

Implications

For Russians, organizational failure is not a sign that nothing works—but only that organizations do not work as in a modern society. When a formal organization fails to operate routinely, individuals have recourse to a variety of social-capital networks to get things done—informal do-it-yourself cooperation, personal cajoling of bureaucrats, the antimodern bending or breaking of rules, the market, or even—under the right circumstances—the state delivering goods and services.

How common is the Russian experience? Tianjian Shi's ironically titled *Political Participation in Beijing*[6] describes phenomena familiar to observers of Russia. Shi documents how the Chinese use cronyism, resistance, boycotts, adversarial activities, and personal appeals as standard operating procedures to spur officials to act. Chinese behavior is not a reflection of 'Asian' values, for empirical studies in the Republic of Korea show that, even though Korea has its share of elite corruption, there is much less corruption at the grass roots of Korean society, and the market is an effective modern alternative to state failure. In the Czech Republic, where the rule of law existed prior to the arrival of Soviet troops, and there was strong resistance to communist rule, the public today is much less inclined to turn to antimodern techniques to get things done.[7]

[6] Tianjian Shi, *Political Participation in Beijing* (Cambridge, Mass.: Harvard University Press, 1997).
[7] See Richard Rose and Don Chull Shin, *Democratization Backwards: The Problem of Third Wave Democracies*, University of Strathclyde Studies in Public Policy, No. 314 (Glasgow, 1999).

Organizational failure in Russia reflects the combination of too many regulations and too little adherence to bureaucratic norms. A surfeit of rules imposes delays and unresponsiveness, as different public agencies must be consulted. Individuals are forced to invest an unreasonable amount of time in pleading with and pushing bureaucrats to compensate for organizational inefficiencies. If bureaucrats offer to waive obstructive regulations in return for a side payment, this delivers a service but in an antimodern way. The result is popular ambivalence about the rule of law. Among Russians, 71 percent hold that the national government is a long way from the idea of a law-governed state (*pravovoye gosudarstvo*). But not everyone would welcome Russia's becoming such a state, since 62 percent believe the laws are often very hard on ordinary people. In such circumstances, law enforcement may not be desirable.[8] Among Russians, 73 percent endorse the belief that harsh Russian laws are softened by their nonenforcement.

The classic electoral solution for the failure of government to deliver as it should is for the voters to throw the rascals out, giving the opposition an opportunity to show what it can do. But what is to be done if a sequence of elections simply results in the 'circulation of rascals,' as one unpopular president or Duma representative is replaced by another who appears to be no better? At this point, a society has reached the limit of what elections can achieve.

Where antimodern practices are rampant—and that is the case in most of the successor states of the former Soviet Union—the result is a crisis of governability, such that the state is too weak both to collect taxes and to control its own expenditures. It delivers too much money to the few who are inside an elite *svoim*, and too little to the great majority. Recognizing this, there are those who argue for strengthening the capacity of the state to promote both welfare rights and classical liberal rights and are optimistic that this can be done. But one does not have to be Riga-born, as was Isaiah Berlin, to know that the paths that may be followed can involve great sacrifices (or a choice between sacrifices) in whichever direction one goes.

Russians, by contrast to the average Western adviser, understand how to survive by working with the system as it actually is. While people might desire better social services from the state, there is a high degree of skepticism about the capacity of the state to deliver the services available in a modern European society. For the time being, at least, the position appears to be a relatively stable, low-level equilibrium trap in which people cope with a system that is inefficient and corrupt. While one can argue that there is a better way, many Russians have also known worse.

Given a state in which bureaucrats, at best, break laws to help people and, at worst, break laws to popular disadvantage, what is to be done? Insofar as the selective enforcement in laws is a major problem in an antimodern society, a logical prescription would be to deregulate, repealing laws that create opportunities for extracting bribes and profiting from connections. A second policy would be to repeal taxes that otherwise can be evaded easily and to concentrate on those that can be collected, for example, on oil exports or on electricity supply. To the extent that public budgets would then have to be reduced, because of less expected revenue (though actual revenue could remain constant, given the current level

---

[8] Andras Sajo, 'Corruption, Clientelism, and the Future of the Constitutional State in Eastern Europe,' *East European Constitutional Review*, 7/2 (spring 1998), 37–46.

of tax evasion), cuts in spending should be targeted at nondelivered services and unpaid public employees. While this will reduce the services that individuals and households may rely on, the government could give vouchers so that those affected could make their own choices.

In the abstract, the above prescriptions would reduce the theoretical capacity of the government to behave like a modern Scandinavian or German social-welfare state. In reality such measures would move in the direction of matching the commitments of the Russian state to its actual capacity. Cutting back notional public services, an acknowledgement of government failure, might even stimulate the demand from ordinary Russians for government by the rule of law rather than forcing people to bend or break laws that have ceased to be relevant. This demand by the people is a precondition for the state's having the capacity to deliver, fairly and effectively, the benefits of a modern nation, whether it is a nightwatchman Hayekian state, which concentrates on the law of liberty and the market, or a social-democratic state, delivering a large number of welfare benefits—a goal that is conceivable but remote from the Russia of today.

21 Modernization and the Value System of the Russian Elite

Oksana Gaman-Golutvina

The changes in the political line-up that took place as a result of the 2000 presidential election and the accompanying generational shift in the political class naturally provoked avid discussion amongst experts as to the agenda of the future president—the contours of his strategies and policy directions, and also the aims and values that could constitute the basis for society's consolidation. Without a doubt, it would be most rational to base this strategy upon a system of universal values capable of consolidating society, for it is certain that any programme would be impossible to realize effectively without such consolidation. Over the course of the discussion, several different points of view emerged about the nature and character of the dominant values in society, and ways of optimizing their interaction.

However, there is one main problem which, if left unresolved, will mean that any value 'menus' and programmes based on them will run the risk of remaining pretty drawings on a backcloth of progressive degradation. By this I mean the necessity of rehabilitating the value of the notion of development in societal consciousness. The difficulty, though, is that, even when it has evoked theoretical devotion, in real life the idea of development in Russia has not been one of the unconditional basic values in either mass or elite thinking. That is because for the mass of the people the achievement of modernization in the country has always entailed pressure and exploitation from above, meaning violence (indispensable to compensate for the scarcity of other—financial, material, and temporal—resources for development). The Russian empire was constructed 'through a process of a genuinely inhuman fight for existence . . . The Russian Empire was built and defended by the people at a cost of unprecedented human sacrifice'.[1] Moreover, 'only through the use of extreme and all-encompassing pressure, iron discipline and terrible human losses could this . . . state exist'.[2] What were the reforms of Peter I or Stalinist industrialization worth if they were founded on 'the bones of Russians'? It is no accident that V. O. Klyuchevsky wrote that the decline in the overworked forces of the nation during Peter I's transformations was so great that it would not have been redeemed had Peter been fighting not only Karelia and Livonia, but all of Sweden, or even five Swedens.[3]

Chapter specially commissioned for this volume. Translated by Polly Jones.

[1] I. Solonevich, *Narodnaya monarkhiya* (Moscow: Feniks, 1991), 244.

[2] G. Fedotov, *Sud'ba i grekhi Rossii. Izbrannye stat'i po filosofii russkoy istorii i kul'tury*, vols. i–ii (St Petersburg: Sofia, 1992), 284–5.

[3] V. O. Klyuchevsky, *Russkaya istoriya. Polnyy kurs lektsii v trekh kniga*, vol. ii (Moscow: Musl', 1993), 579.

The political classes, for their part, were guarded on the subject of modernization because the achievement of development in Russia as a rule had entailed massive purges of the political classes themselves, aimed at ensuring the maximum efficiency of the administrative apparatus as an agent of modernization. The clearest example was the repressions of the 1930s, during which the 'old guard' was replaced by what Fedotov has called a 'military-athletic class'—'the iron people's commissars' and the 'iron secretaries', who were not versed in theory, but ready to build a 'new world' with the help of the means to hand, and sometimes without even them. The sources of the difficulties in rooting modernization projects in Russia traditionally lie in the weakness of internal impulses to development within the framework of the modernization model used to develop the country, and also in the fact that the aims and orientations of development were tasks that lay beyond the capabilities of the population. But these goals were not dictated by the whims of those in power, but by the national task of 'creating an Empire on a poor economic basis',[4] that is, the necessity of keeping society alive while competing with more successful geopolitical rivals. For this reason the authorities came out in favour of urging on development 'by the whip', albeit often against their own sympathies. An example of this is the fate of Alexander II who set in motion the great reforms of the 1860s and 1870s under pressure from the Crimean defeat, although they in many ways went against the political convictions of his youth.

How do things stand today? At present, the number of values common to the whole of society is minimal: there is a sizeable gulf between the aims and values of the elite and of the mass of the people. The value orientations of public opinion are largely determined by the priorities of individual survival, but their most common characteristic is an extreme eclecticism, which can be summed up by the immortal literary expression, 'I don't really know what I want: it could be a constitution, but then again, it could be sturgeon with horseradish'. As for the elite, their supreme values are power, prosperity, and success in the whole range of their parameters, but above all in the material sphere. But, in spite of the extent of the differences in value preferences, both the elite and the population at large have in common the fact that they are unreceptive to the value of development. Both the elites and the masses have contributed to the negative consensus on stagnation, 'each according to his abilities'—someone steals the factory, someone else the smokestack, but everyone is at it. The Third Rome ended up in the Third World. As for the consequences of this situation, the indifference of the masses to the idea of development as a value has only partly been a misfortune, as the position of mass groups these days determines little or nothing and public opinion is more easily swayed than ever before.

As far as the powerful groups go, the profound indifference of the modern elite to the idea of development is truly catastrophic, for it is precisely these groups, acting as a symbiosis between the higher levels of bureaucracy and the leading political-financial clans, who are destined to be key players in strategic agenda-setting as well as, de facto, the only agent in the formation of society's field of values. Analysis has shown that no external circumstances are as capable of wielding a steady influence over the decisions taken by the authorities as are their convictions and values, their meaningful ideas of the limits of the permissible in politics, the dominant norms governing interpersonal relations in the political-administrative sector and their goal orientations. While there are practically unlimited possibilities for the

[4] Ibid. 284.

powerful groups in our society to wield influence, given the significant degree to which they have 'privatized' the institutions and functions of civil society and the state, together with the total loss of authority of other participants (including the state) in the political process, these actors are deeply indifferent to problems of strategy.

Yet, notwithstanding the indifference of the leading political and financial groups to national interests and any strategy for development of the society and state, these same political-financial structures display an enviable talent for strategic thinking and action as soon as matters turn to narrow corporate interests. So, for example, the commentary to an Oneximbank official document and published a year after it was written, entitled 'Suggestions for the development of activity connected to the use of the financial market infrastructure',[5] noted that Onexim had managed to complete 50–60 per cent of the strategic tasks set over the year that the document had been prepared, which speaks not only to strategic thinking, but also to the ability to bring those tasks to fruition.

It is precisely the weakening in the function of agenda-setting that most threatens to erode the elite status of the leading groups. Over recent years, the contemporary political elite has increasingly frequently been reproached for immorality (this is shown by the numerous wars of *kompromat* in which a significant sector of influential groups in Russian society become entangled), which in the opinion of many experts robs its claims to elite status of any validity. However, in our view, the threat of erosion of elite status comes from another quarter. The modern political elite risks losing its elevated status not only because of declining levels of morality, but above all because the leading groups in modern Russian society are increasingly unable to fulfil their key function and therefore correspond less and less to the fundamental characteristic of the elite. That is to say: our national political class acts less and less often as an agent in the process of making the most important strategic decisions.

The strategic lack of agency stems from many factors. Above all, it results from the privatization of the institutions of the state and civil society: the achievement of historical and political agency is impossible without the presence of a state axis of identification. Moreover, the only real principle of identification for the political class today is the corporate (more accurately, the quasi-corporate), whilst for the population, it is the regional. The state interest as a tool for the articulation of universal aims and values has been destroyed as a value for most of society.

The high level of conflict in inter-elite relations, which more often comes to resemble the settling of scores between clans (for all that the political class consists of like-minded people), is yet another reason why the contemporary political elites have not become agents of development. However, the most important and profound reasons for the inefficacy of today's elite as an agent of development are largely determined by the significant political, psychological, and moral costs of the practice of forced modernization over previous historical periods and the deformations that arose over the course of that development. The indifference of today's elite towards questions of strategy is the flip side and consequence of the hypertrophy of utopian tendencies in the global historical project of forced modernization, with the primacy it places upon the value of the future and the instrumentalism of the present. Paraphrasing President John F. Kennedy's famous formula, it can be said that in

---

[5] *Nezavisimaya gazeta*, 18 Sept. 1997.

Russia, it has too long been asked, 'What can you do for your country?', so that *now* the majority of citizens are interested primarily in what their country can do for them.

In this lies the explanation for a notable paradox. The industrial modernization of the 1930s–1950s was achieved by the upwardly mobile offspring of peasant families, a first-generation intelligentsia. Yet the upshot of the political activity of the glittering constellation of intellectual leaders in the 1990s—and in terms of educational levels and occupations, the administration of Russia in the 1990s has no equal in the preceding history of the country—was a systemic crisis. And this had nothing to do with this generation's lack of administrative experience, as is sometimes supposed: from the start development never featured in the list of reform tasks. The slogan of the process was *distribution*. The force of the distributional charge (on a scale that merits the description *distributional obsession*) was determined by the colossal potential of the elite's discontent, built up from the psychological consequences of the constantly recurring contradiction between the functions of ownership and disposal peculiar to the Soviet nomenklatura, whose successors are today's elite. Although it disposed of colossal material state resources, the Soviet party nomenklatura itself was extremely poor, and by the standards of today, was destitute. The majority of the property belonging even to those high up in its ranks was public: furniture bore the stamps of the administration and property was subject to regular inventories. Stalin's daughter, Svetlana Allilueva, recalled how her father impressed upon her and her brother Vasily an understanding of the temporary nature of leaders' privileges: 'dachas, flats, cars—all these do not belong to you, and you shouldn't think of them as yours.'[6] Just how much this contradiction traumatized the generation of the late-Soviet nomenklatura is clear from the following episode. Andrei Grachev, the former aide to Mikhail Gorbachev in his time as general secretary, recalls a visit by the Gorbachev couple to France. When the French president's wife, Danielle Mitterrand suggested to Raisa Gorbacheva, who had praised the honey put on the table for breakfast, that she present her with several bee-hives for their country home, she clapped her hands and said reproachfully to Gorbachev: 'How many times have I asked you, Mikhail Sergeevich, to refuse state dachas and to get even a tiny plot of land! You see, right now, we have nothing to call our own—we'd have nowhere to put a beehive!'[7]

The Soviet nomenklatura were indeed the 'ruling class' of Soviet society, as Milovan Djilas and Mikhail Voslensky and other authors have defined it, but, unlike any other powerful elite, it was a servile class without rights. Receiving very little in the way of benefits even by comparison with the Western middle classes, the Soviet nomenklatura was constantly on the lookout for more, always fearing that what they got today could be snatched from them tomorrow. Even the highest placed functionaries in the proletarian state remained in their heart of hearts proletarians, for they had nothing and indeed were worth nothing, in spite of their abilities and merits, beyond the sum of privileges and benefits officially laid out by each successive leader. It was precisely the contradiction between the right to disposal—really large, and in certain periods, practically unlimited—and the right to ownership (more accurately, the absence of that right) which became the key contradiction in the mindset of the Soviet nomenklatura, and which eventually made the Soviet ruling class into the grave-diggers of the Soviet system. For this reason, it is not surprising that the dominant aim of the new elite became the striving to acquire everything here and now.

[6] S. Allilueva, *Dvadsat' pisem k drugu* (Moscow: Izvestiya, 1990), 159.
[7] A. Grachev, *Kremlevskaya Khronika* (Moscow: Eksmo, 1994), 74.

When thinking about the likelihood of a reorientation of the values of both the political class and mass groups in favour of a development strategy, it should be borne in mind that this kind of reorientation is not merely a matter of subjective preference, but is also determined to a large extent by the objective laws of the long waves of alternations between public opinion's attachment to universal values and to personal values. In this regard, it is worth noting that social life is subject to cyclical change. 'The change of landmarks'[8] can easily be found in materials relating to American history. It is well known that the characteristics of Americans noted by de Tocqueville in the first and second volumes of his famous work *Democracy in America*, even though a mere five years passed between the writing of the volumes (the first was written in 1835, the second in 1840), were very different. In the first volume, de Tocqueville, when assessing American society, noted energy, sympathy, civic activity, and an attachment to social interests. If the Americans had 'had to concern themselves only with their own affairs, their lives would lose half their meaning and would seem empty, and they would feel extremely unhappy'.[9] Yet in the second volume, which came out, as we have noted, only half a decade later, de Tocqueville depicts the American as weak, servile, and powerless, entirely absorbed in his own interests. The renowned American historian, Arthur M. Schlesinger Jr., after comparing such different characteristics, came to the conclusion that social activity and private interest swing, pendulum-like, between personal concerns (self-interest) and general interests (patriotism). 'The American can be so consumed by his own concerns that it is as if he is absolutely alone in this world, yet, the next moment, as though he had forgotten about them, he devotes himself to the common cause. At times it seems as though he is motivated by total greed, and at others, by whole-hearted patriotism'—it was on the basis of this reflection of de Tocqueville that Schlesinger rested his idea of the cycles of American history, defining a cycle as the perpetual movement between the application of the nation's efforts to the aims of the society, on the one hand, and to the interests of individual persons, on the other.[10]

Schlesinger's own research provides a convincing argument in favour of the notion that a society's strategy for development has to take into account the peculiarities of the cyclical nature of the public mood. To what extent can his concept serve as a basis to work out the development of Russia? The answer to this question is largely determined by the possibility of using the theory of cycles in the analysis of Russian society's development.

The last few years have been marked by the promotion of numerous concepts that have used the theory of cycles as a tool to interpret the peculiarities of Russian historical and political development.[11] The most developed conceptions of the cyclical nature of Russian history belong to Alexander Yanov[12] and Alexander Akhizer.[13] In Yanov's works, the cyclical

---

[8] Editor's note: The 'change of landmarks' refers to a school of thought among Russian intellectuals in the 1920s who criticized the bankruptcy, as they saw it, of political theory on both right and left.

[9] A. Tocqueville, *Demokratiya v Amerike* (Moscow: Progress, 1994), 191.

[10] A. Schlesinger, *Tsikly Amerikanskoy istorii* (Moscow: Progress, 1992).

[11] For an analysis of cyclical concepts, see V. Pashinsky, 'Tsiklichnost' v istorii Rossii (vzglyad s pozitsii sotsial'noy ekologii)', *Polis*, 4 (1994). However, the first work on this subject was probably that of E. E. Yashnov, *Osobennosti istorii i khozyaistva Kitaya* (Harbin, 1933).

[12] A. Yanov, *The Origins of Autocracy: Ivan the Terrible in Russian History* (Berkeley: University of California Press, 1981), and Yanov, *Russkaya ideya i 2000-g.* (New York, 1988).

[13] A. Akhizer, *Rossiya: kritika istoricheskogo opyta*, vols. 1–3 (Moscow: Philosophical Society, 1991).

nature of Russian history comes down to the regularity of a particular type of Russian power—autocracy, formed in the era of Ivan the Terrible. The automatic reproduction of autocracy's basic structures becomes a source of systemic crisis for the state, which, when challenged by reforms, results either in the system becoming stricter in response or stagnation. From the time of Ivan the Terrible to the mid-1980s, Yanov defines seven cycles, which each last between twelve and 125 years. However, such a significant chronological disparity can hardly serve as the basis for a theory that claims to be a verifiable, universal explanatory schema. Another detailed cyclical scheme of Russian history, put together by Akhizer, suffers from a similar disadvantage—the identification of historical periods of differing lengths as historical cycles. Thus, in his conception, the thousand years before the Revolution and the seventy-odd years of Soviet history are treated as equivalent periods.

As well as this, in recent years there have been attempts to use Nikolai Kondratev's theory of 'long waves'[14] as a heuristic tool for the study of the cyclical nature of Russian history.[15] However, in spite of the undoubtedly positive results achieved by this approach, it seems to us that Kondratev's theory of cycles as applied to the history of Russia is not a universal explanatory device, since it was worked out on the basis of materials gathered on Western, economically centred society (which, incidentally, does not throw into doubt the influence of global cycles on processes in Russia). Characteristically, it prioritizes economic factors of development—the impulse to modernization is caused by internal economic needs; the interests of the economic subjects coincide with state interests; the role of mechanisms of self-regulation in the regulation of social relations is great. In contrast, Russia is a politically centred social system, dominated by political aims and priorities, which renders modernization disorganized and forced. The use of production indicators as criteria for periodization can hardly be termed a reliable basis on which to construct a universal interpretative schema.

In this regard, cyclical theories as a heuristic and prognostic tool to analyse Russian reality can be utilized only in specific cases, although this is not to say that they are of no use. In part, it seems to us to be fruitful to use Schlesinger's characterization of changes in the public mood as pendulum-like, in spite of the substantial differences between the political culture and the popular mentality of Russia and the USA.[16] This is the case because the changes in public sentiments in Russia are to an even greater degree than in Europe or in the USA akin to a pendulum swing. The 'pendulum-like' nature of changes in the mass mood has been determined by the forced character of most of Russian modernization, combined—as we noted above—with the over-straining and over-exploitation of human resources, which necessitated a massive deployment of coercive and violent means over the course of modernization. The achievement of modernization, which bore the mark of a revolution in Russian conditions and demanded colossal expenditure of human energies, inevitably gave way to a decline in strength and to depression.

[14] Editor's note: Kondratev is generally known in the West to students of the history of economic thought as Kondratieff. A victim of Stalin's purges, he earlier received international renown as an economist for his discovery of 'long waves' or 'long cycles' in economic development.

[15] V. Umov and V. Lapkin, 'Kondratevskie tsikly i Rossiya: prognoz reform', *Polis*, (1992), V. Umov, 'Poselslovie k prognozu: kondratevskie tsikly v Rossii', *Polis* (1994), S. Dubovskii, 'Prognozirovanie katastrof (na primere tsiklov N. Kondrateva)', *ONS*, 5 (1993), V. I. Pantin, *Tsikly i ritmy istorii* (Moscow: Araks, 1996).

[16] O. V. Gaman-Golutvina, 'Politicheskaya kul'tura Rossiya i SshA v zerkale sravnitel'nogo analiza', *Vlast'*, 7 (1996).

This fatigue and exhaustion has to be taken into account by responsible statesmen, not only when working out electoral tactics, but also when making the choice in favour of one or other development strategies for the state. It is all the more necessary to take into account the phases of the public mood and the direction of public sympathies during work on Russia's development strategy because, in contrast to developed Western polities, characterized by effective articulation and aggregation of public interests which serve to regulate the definition of political behaviour of the appropriate social groups, in Russia the interests of mass groups are weakly articulated and are aggregated yet more poorly. For this reason, it is moods, not interests, that play the defining role in the formation of the position of many social strata.[17]

As for the concrete situation, it is certain that the current period of domination of 'short-term' personal aims and values, and likewise the popularity of 'easy money', will in the long term be replaced by universal strategic aims. But this will not happen in the near future—the periods of forced modernization, when the personal interests of the people were sacrificed to general aims, were of too long a historical duration. Thus it would hardly be reasonable today to appeal only to civic feeling. The exhaustion of the psychological resources of both the elites and the people, a 'cost of development' during the achievement of this global project, now limits the possibilities of using mobilizational methods of government and is largely responsible for today's problematic situation.

The means of resolving it lie in the realization of the most important potential for modernization—intellectual resources, which are ultimately the most important source of development (all the more relevant in view of the fact that, according to contemporary expert assessments, the economically profitable resources of useful raw materials are 30–70 per cent less than was earlier calculated).[18] This kind of strategy is also in line with the interests of national business, for the international experience of recent decades shows us that investments in the intellectual sphere yield the best results for national capital.[19] In the new geopolitical reality, the potential of the state is determined not only by its power, but above all by its ability to ensure the dynamism of the national innovative and economic system. Therefore, in order to survive in conditions of global competition, Russian elites have to ensure the development of society and the state through the use of progressive technologies. This is not the first time Russia has had to take on the task of advancing in leaps and bounds. As far as the technologies for creating modernizing motivation in the population are concerned, it would be much more rational to base the national development strategy upon aims that resonate with private interests than to call once again for a 'tightening of belts'. This necessitates a new version of the usual slogans in the national strategy: a nation for its citizens, and not the citizens for the nation, for these days the traditional Russian values of solidarity and justice are being replaced by the dignity of the citizen and his and her prosperity.

Moreover, the prospects for the achievement of societal and state development depend to a significant degree upon the chances of achieving elite consensus. In this regard, there are two possible variants of the evolution of the political process. The first depends on

---

[17] For more details, see O. V. Gaman-Golutvina, *Politicheskie elity Rossii: vekhi istoricheskoy evolyutsii* (Moscow: Intellekt, 1998), 371–4.

[18] A. Veber, 'Ekonomischeskiy rost—lyuboy tsenoy?', *Nezavisimaya gazeta*, 3 Apr. 1998.

[19] M. Ratz, 'Ot "revolyutsii sverkhu" k reformam i razvitiyu,' *Nezavisimaya gazeta*, 20 Mar. 1998.

influential Russian elite groups acknowledging that the potential of the (already relatively indifferent) relations to Russia of her global rivals—the major players in world politics—is close to running out. Having acknowledged this, the leading political-financial clans would enter into serious dialogue with the state to achieve a limited consensus on the principal aims of the country in the medium term. For this, the most important factor would be the ability to propose a concept of development and a strategy to achieve it. If the leading elite groups could reach a sort of 'pact' or consensus regarding the basic elements of a limited agreement on the main parameters of relations with the state, the principal aims of the state, and the probable means by which they might be achieved, it would be possible to maintain the territorial integrity of the Russian Federation as a subject of international law and to preserve the country as an historical and political entity.

The second variant would arise were it not possible to achieve such a consensus. In this case, the antagonism between elite clans, whose main rivals are the opposing Russian financial-industrial groups, would continue. As Raymond Aron wrote, if an elite is monolithic, that means the end of freedom, but if it is not only disunited but also antagonistic, that means the end of the state. In this case, inter-elite conflict provides the ideal situation for external division to occur, when any conflict between elites could be used to split up the Russian Federation into a new confederation 'of independent states'. This would mean the loss of territorial integrity and of the political and historical entity that is Russia.

But even if that elite consensus on the necessity of strategic consolidation were to be achieved, the fact of the consensus by itself would be a necessary, but not a sufficient condition to overcome stagnation. The main condition for the success of the modernization project is the presence of a political will to achieve this result. Until then, and so long as the power-holding class is not prepared to exercise the will to realize the idea of development, the fate of any strategy on the national political stage will be reminiscent of the plot of the famous play by Samuel Beckett, *Waiting for Godot*: this idea will remain like the great Godot, who is tensely awaited and whose arrival the actors only talk about. But who never appears on stage.

22 Homo Praevaricatus: Russian Doublethink

Yury Levada

According to the data published in '*Homo Sovieticus* Ten Years Later: 1989–1999'[1] only 3 per cent of those surveyed thought that elections in our country are won by 'the worthiest individuals'; 83 per cent think that the 'most cunning' win (and this distribution of opinion applies, with minor variations, to all social classes and political groupings without exception). Immediately after the elections to the State Duma, 50 per cent of those surveyed rated those elections as 'not very honest' or 'totally dishonest'. But nevertheless, in the same survey, the majority (55 per cent against 27 per cent) pronounced themselves satisfied with their results. It seems that the explanation for this clear—and entirely typical!—paradox of mass consciousness lies in the very characteristics of the criteria that they employ and their standards for the evaluation of social processes and events, that is, the normative field of human existence operating under current conditions.

As observations and investigations show, this field has multiple co-ordinates (or, in fashionable political terminology, is 'multipolar'); in it coexist different criteria, points of measurement, and systems of co-ordinates for normative evaluation—the permissible, the beneficial, the correct, and so on. As well as this, the very criteria are usually conditional and fuzzy, less fixed criteria than limits of the permissible or the relatively tolerable ('can be tolerated'; 'not the worst that could happen' and so on). This kind of normative field of human existence produces cunning types of behaviour and the characteristic traits of their exponent, the *homo praevaricatus* (or 'cunning person'). He adapts to social reality, seeking out loopholes in its normative system, or ways of turning the current rules of the game to his own advantage, whilst at the same time—no less importantly—constantly trying to find a way to get around those rules. This forces him constantly to justify his own conduct, whether by recourse to the necessity of self-preservation, taking 'others' as his example

With the permission of Professor Levada, this article from the official publication of the All-Russian Institute of Public Opinion (VTsIOM) has been adapted (and abbreviated) by the editor. Data from the tables are incorporated in the chapter, but the fullest version of them—in tabular form—is to be found in the original publication: Yury Levada, 'Chelovek lukavyy: dvoemyslie po-rossiyski', *Monitoring obshchestvennogo mneniya: ekonomicheskie i sotsial'nye peremeny* (VTsIOM, Moscow), 1 (Jan.–Feb. 2000), 19–27. The first part of the title literally translates as 'The Cunning Person', but the issue of the VTsIOM bulletin in which the article appears, and which lists the titles (only) in English, has rendered this as 'Homo Praevaricatus'. We have, accordingly, followed Professor Levada's own preferred (Latin) translation of the title, though 'lukavyy' is translated in more than one way in the chapter which follows, usually as 'cunning'.
Translated by Polly Jones.

[1] *Monitoring obshchestvennogo mneniya: ekonomicheskie i sotsial'nye peremeny* (VTsIOM, Moscow), 3 (May–June 1999), 7–15.

('you've got to live', 'all the same' and so on), or by appeals to normative systems of another order ('higher interests' and suchlike). The perpetual changes in social mood during the 'epoch of transformation'—the alternation of enthusiasm and disappointment, the rises and falls in personal ratings and so on—serve to indicate the notoriously lightweight nature of each election and the level of cunning self-deceit involved in each one of them ('perhaps we'll be lucky this time . . . ').

The results of this survey, and other mass survey data, generate a large amount of material for the analysis of various aspects of cunning behaviour. The empirically based investigation of this well-known stage in the evolution of the cunning behavioural type could also prove useful to the understanding of other types.

Universal traits and the Soviet peculiarities of the behavioural type

The cunning attempt to get around prohibition and to seek out convenient behavioural niches in normative systems on various—social, group, and personal—levels can of course be found amongst all peoples in all eras. For example, when a survey shows that, amongst contemporary Russians, only 11 per cent (7 per cent of men and 14 per cent of women) can say that 'they have never lied to anyone', and 32 per cent (27 per cent of men and 37 per cent of women) can say that 'they have never taken something that wasn't theirs without permission',[2] we are dealing with one of the most elementary and universally widespread types of human cunning (the scale and forms of the incidence of this behavioural phenomenon are of course linked to national, age, and gender behavioural structures). Its basis is the diversity of the normative fields themselves (societal, group, and role-playing) which determine the orientation and limits of human activity. In this case, we are concerned with more specific types and structures of cunning behaviour that are linked to the particular ways in which social norms themselves function in corresponding historical and national-state conditions—for example, the refusal to perform civic duties or to observe traffic rules.

The dominant variant of normative 'polycentric relativism' in Russian society arose as a result of the interaction of several successive breakdowns in regulatory structures. The unfinished process of modernization in Russia has fostered countless variants of normative conflicts on all levels of human existence and self-consciousness; out of this, in part, grew all the great literature of the last century, which expressed the conflicts between the two kinds of truth, *pravda* and *istina*, and that between truth (*pravda*) and justice, the rights of the 'little man' and the rights of 'supreme state power', the salvation of humanity and 'the tears of a child' and so on. In these scenarios, the cunning person almost invariably fell victim to misfortune.

The Soviet era ushered in a new system of norms and values, universal in significance and absolute in its sources (in the name of and for the sake of historical progress . . .), which was intended either to substitute for all existing systems, or subordinate them to itself. In fact, it merely changed around some of the signs and terms in a few normative fields and overlaid them with yet another formula. The formula 'what is right is useful' (in the rhetoric, useful

[2] *Monitoring obschestvennogo mneniya: ekonomicheskie i sotsial'nye peremeny* (VTsIOM, Moscow), 6 (Nov.–Dec. 1999), 6.

'to the working people', 'the cause of Communism' and so on; in reality, 'what suits the plans and orders from on high') led directly to a totally utilitarian normative system. The universally significant and all-embracing system of norms and values in reality revolved around a number of criteria—the 'big' and 'little' truth, the 'true' and the 'necessary', the 'long-term' and 'short-term' and so on.

From the very start, one of its most important characteristics was the fact that the demands placed upon people were mostly impossible to fulfil. It was impossible to interpret the twists and turns of political competition as the dictates of 'history'. No one succeeded in 'devoting all his strength to the fulfilment of the Five Year plan'. It was impossible to fulfil 'grandiose schemes' without additional instructions, the use of *blat*[3] and the overuse of deficient resources. All this gave rise to the emergence of the *homo praevaricatus*, Soviet-style. Total violence produced a total readiness to adapt in cunning ways to the system. Deprived of the possibility of protest, people either triumphantly or tacitly consented to imperative orders—and persistently sought out loopholes that would let them get around them. Most basically and most often, it was for the sake of eking out a living (the 'passive pledge' of cunning behaviour). Less often it was also used to exploit the possibilities of an ambivalent system for career or status advancement ('the active pledge' of cunning behaviour characteristic of the heroes of the day).

The success of this system (at least over long decades) would not have been possible had it relied merely upon mass coercion or mass deception. It has now become clear just how naive were the ideas circulating in the 1960s and even as late as the 1980s about the trickery of the public by the all-knowing and utterly cynical party-political authorities (along the lines of George Orwell's 'doublethink' mechanism). The cunning man—on all levels, in all his hypostases—not only tolerates deception, but is willing to be deceived, and, what is more, constantly requires self-deception for the sake of his own self-preservation (including the psychological) and for the sake of overcoming his own split personality and justifying his own cunning. 'Our noble lie' is not merely a clear poetic formula. The whole mechanism of the Soviet system created both 'cunning slaves' (to use Tatyana Zaslavskaya's very accurate expression) and no less cunning 'masters'. Both were cunning with each other and toward themselves.

Under conditions of ubiquitous cunning, the fulfilment of normative imperatives turns into a more or less cunning 'deal' (of the kind, 'let's pretend we're working—let's pretend we're paying them'), and this sort of imperative itself becomes totally personalized (the societal pact goes right down to the level of the 'pact' between the fare dodger and the tram conductor).

The co-existence and interaction of various normative fields with criteria for what is allowed and what is not, what is approved and what is not, are characteristic of different social systems in which there is a clear dividing line between work and leisure, between mine and yours, between the private and the official and so on. The distinctive feature of the Soviet system (which is entirely preserved to this day) consists in the fact that these dividing lines are blurred or erased. The cunning mind will easily surmount the literal barriers and

---

[3] Editor's note: *blat* is an ubiquitous Russian term which is difficult to translate, but can be rendered as mutual favours within informal networks. For a scholarly study of this phenomenon (which both oiled and subverted the machinery of Soviet institutions), see Alena V. Ledeneva, *Russia's Economy of Favours: Blat, Networking and Informal Exchange* (Cambridge: Cambridge University Press, 1998).

will find a multitude of loopholes in the given prescriptions—in a word, will play the game 'without rules' (or 'play games with the rules themselves').

After the breakdown of the system, the covert cunning on both sides simply came out in the open and became overt. In the post-Soviet situation, the breakdown of authoritarian normative structures created a scenario of corruption of all values and normative systems of society on a number of levels (including the personal)—this was no less serious and hazardous than the widely discussed corruption of the economic and political systems. At the same time, this situation of visible normative pluralism and 'lack of limits', as with any conflictual structure, has its own logic, that is, its own unwritten 'rules of the game'. The practical absence of universally binding authorities generates a multi-polar structure for the normative field, where diverse structures of influence coexist, compete with each other, and to a certain extent even cancel one another out. It is in this field that guidelines for behaviour operate and become embedded, creating a new national type of the *homo praevaricatus*.

The cunning behaviour of the epoch of stagnation consisted for the most part in adapting to stable structures and in careerism based on conformism. 'The epoch of transformations' alters the nature of that adaptation. The instability of all structures, including the ruling, shadowy groupings of opposition and support, create the ideal conditions for short-term 'pyramids' (not only financial-economic ones, but political ones, at different levels of the power hierarchy) and short-lived careers. This explains the calls for suitable human and personality types—above all, the 'flexible' person capable of turning a changing situation to his own advantage and of altering his opinions and allegiances to fit the changing state of affairs.

Let us now turn to the empirical material gathered in surveys.

'The limits of the permissible'

Our survey shows that there are no strict dividing lines between the spheres of acceptable and unacceptable behaviour. This applies to the fulfilment of various kinds of social obligations. In the case of military service, one can hypothesize that this is to do with the process of people's growing 'withdrawal from the state' over the last few years—the weakening of identification with state institutions and symbols. (This has led to recent calls to strengthen statehood through the regeneration of the army and military might in violent ventures and punitive expeditions. Our survey data show what ground those appeals would fall on.)

It is very noteworthy that the refusal of military service seems fully justifiable to age groups up to the age of 40—the younger the age group, that is, the nearer they are to call-up age, the more opinion will tend towards feeling that it is right to avoid this sacred duty. Amongst the youngest age group, under most immediate threat from being called up, the non-fulfilment of this obligation is more than twice as likely to be justified as it is to be condemned. In this case, those closest to the norm (as, incidentally, with other positions taken) are the oldest age group—people of pre-pension and pensionable age.

Education levels exert a similar influence on the indications of the acceptability of refusal of military service—the higher the level of education, the lower the normative index, and, amongst the highly educated, refusal is more often excused than condemned. The level of urbanization does not produce such a direct correlation. Military service is least likely to be considered obligatory by big-city dwellers, with these normative demands receiving a more favourable reception amongst village dwellers, in Moscow and (where approval is highest of all!) in small towns. True, amongst Muscovites, there is the highest share of cautious evaluations, such as 'partially reprehensible', and the lowest proportion of categorical opinions. In the urban sphere, there is a clash between enlightened tolerance and ideological intolerance of refusal to serve in the army.

The largest normative index for any of the positions comes in connection with the age-old problem of petty, 'professional' theft of materials, raw materials, tools, and so on from enterprises for personal use, as a sort of *'payment in kind'* (a half-forgotten term from collective farming). It could be that such a unanimous and massive condemnation of 'take home' is caused by the fact that in a deficit-free economy this habitual compensatory mechanism—which dates back to Chekhov's criminal—has lost much of its significance. But another explanation cannot be discounted—the Soviet-era worker's most widespread and, in fact, most tolerated means of receiving extra income is merely being hypocritically covered up, out of a cunning desire to look 'more respectable'.

The non-payment of taxes is the most modern of social 'misdemeanours'. In the era of a state-run economy, this kind of behaviour was practically impossible. It is categorically condemned by those over 40 years of age, but is thought to be more excusable by younger people. The upholders of the normative standard, as on other positions, are the elderly, for whom the normative index is significantly higher than for other groups. Evidently, the level of education is also now linked with the spread of 'market' cunning, meaning that those with low education levels condemn non-payment in far harsher terms than the highly educated.

It is possible to compare such data with the results of a later survey conducted in December 1999. Here, with another set of questions and a different sample, it is also evident that the 'most correct' groups are the oldest and that the youngest and the most well-off least often condemn non-payment of taxes. Businessmen are in fact the only group where the majority agree, or more or less agree, that it is not obligatory to pay taxes. This of course does not so much reflect these people's evil disposition as much as the ambivalence of the socio-economic system itself, which makes it impossible to conduct business without refusing state demands.

The population's most decisive condemnation, according to the data gathered in March 1999, is provoked by dereliction of personal duties (not paying off debts), not paying for purchases (shoplifting), and such an unlikely occurrence as the concealment of discovered treasure. The concealment of assets is condemned only moderately, whilst actions such as dealing on the black market only rarely receive condemnation.

'Contrary to truth and fairness'

Let us now turn to the set of data about the most complex form of cunning behaviour—when a person is obliged to dupe himself. We must first point out that people's cunning behaviour has on the whole increased over the course of the last decade.[4] Not 17 per cent, but a mere 12 per cent of those surveyed now say that they have never had to act 'against their own ideas of truth and fairness'. With the exception of the very young (which is, of course,

---

[4] Editor's note: All the comparisons are between 1989 and 1999.

important) and to some extent the very old, all remaining groups state that they now have to go against their own conscience more often. But there have been changes in the interrelations of factors forcing people to act in such a way.

In 1999, there was a significant reduction in the role of pressure from the 'bosses' as a factor predisposing to cunning (it was mentioned by only 13 per cent, down from 18 per cent in 1989). A notable exception to this are the bosses themselves, that is, leaders and the managerial corps: the extent to which they had to bargain with their own consciences under pressure from above has stayed the same (32 per cent to 31 per cent—the highest figures for any groups!). This figure has also stayed at the same level for elderly workers (18 per cent to 19 per cent) and amongst employees (17 per cent to 16 per cent). Specialists, workers, and pensioners refer less frequently to pressure from their employers. Students, like all young people, did not ever really have to answer to bosses' orders before, and now they do so even less (down from 8 per cent to 6 per cent).

At the same time, there has been a significant growth in the proportion of those who think that they have had to go against their conscience 'for the sake of business' (overall, from 24 per cent to 32 per cent)—as though the boss's will has turned into some kind of generalized corporate interest. This probably reflects the tendency for people to feel a growing identification with business and with their firm, that is, with a new player on the social playing field (and, correspondingly, a subject of cunning behaviour). There has been a particularly pronounced growth in the number of mentions of actions 'for the sake of business' amongst bosses (up from 31 per cent to 60 per cent), specialists (from 24 per cent to 37 per cent), students (from 23 per cent to 43 per cent) and also amongst the youngest respondents (from 23 per cent to 39 per cent)—and no change amongst pensioners and those with low education levels.

The process of 'withdrawing from the state' or 'privatization' is evidently linked for people to a growth in the proportion of appeals to pressure from the family (up from 5 per cent to 16 per cent on average). There are no noticeable differences between the groups, though the greatest significance is accorded to the family by the youngest respondents and by students, who are not yet entirely independent. Mentions of pressure from the collective remain fairly rare (from 4 per cent to 6 per cent), and mostly come from businessmen and employees—evidently meaning the corporate interests of the staff.

One somewhat unexpected and inexplicable phenomenon is the more frequent mention of the necessity of transgressing personal principles out of fear for one's relatives and loved ones (from 4 per cent to 9 per cent on average). This is characteristic of all the groups surveyed. To a certain extent, this is another consequence of the growth in 'family' pressures mentioned above; this also evidently speaks to a general atmosphere of exacerbated feelings of fear in society.[5] The percentage of those surveyed who said that they 'had constantly' to go against their conscience was small ten years ago, and has gone down further for all the groups under observation (on average for the samples down from 6 per cent to 4 per cent). However, over the same period, mentions of compromises made due to 'personal weakness' have gone up by about the same amount (only managers do not want to admit to them).

Amongst those voting in the 1996 presidential elections, those who most rarely stated that

---

[5] L. Gudkov, 'Strakh kak ramka ponimaniya proiskhodyashchego', *Monitoring obshchestvennogo mneniya: ekonomicheskie i sotsial'nye peremeny*, 6, (1999), 46–53.

they had never had to betray their own principles of truth and justice—strange as it may seem at first—were the most intelligent voters. Voters for Grigory Yavlinsky (in all, 7 per cent) most often, whilst those most convinced of their own infallibility were the electorate of Gennady Zyuganov (22 per cent) and Vladimir Zhirinovsky (17 per cent). Mentions of the necessity of going against conscience for 'occupational advantage' were notably higher than average amongst supporters of Yavlinksy (41 per cent) and Alexander Lebed (40 per cent). Voters who incline more towards such leaders as Zhirinovsky, Boris Yeltsin, and Lebed more frequently mention compromises made because of pressures from bosses. These data are of undoubted interest in characterizing the position and moods of Russian political society.

Which actions are not to our liking

The surveys of 'the Soviet person' in 1989 and 1999 allow us to compare the evaluations of 'unpleasant' tasks amongst different sectors of the population. There are noticeably important decreases in the rating of three tasks—'to order other people around' (from 30 per cent to 22 per cent), 'to convince other people of something I do not myself believe' (from 38 per cent to 26 per cent) and, to a lesser extent, 'to do something I do not understand' (from 59 per cent to 55 per cent). All three positions can be thought of as fully 'ideologically saturated' in the Soviet period, meaning that their repudiation clearly signals the departure of society from the old politicized, 'command' model of human conduct.

Almost all of the groups surveyed say that their power over others is much less of a burden now than it was before (all groups are down the same amount, about 1.5 times less). This state of affairs can be explained not so much by the fact that people like this kind of power more as much as by the fact that the very task of 'ordering people about' has become less widespread—yet another sign that mass behaviour is moving away from the Soviet model.

More than anything else, respondents say, the obligation to 'convince others of something I do not myself believe' was a burden to highly educated people and bosses—61 per cent and 59 per cent respectively. Incidentally, it is entirely possible that these groups were provoked into such a massive bout of self-criticism by the mood of society in 1989, especially the tendency to disassociate from the Soviet past. In these two groups there is also the most noticeable fall in the number of times the pressure to convince others is mentioned. It is also true that even now highly educated people and specialists lament the necessity of engaging in this unpleasant activity more than other groups (35 per cent and 37 per cent). The number of students who mention this is markedly less (44 per cent in 1989 and 21 per cent today—an indication of the end to 'Komsomol education'). But the remaining 25–30 per cent who find it distasteful (but, evidently, necessary) to convince others of the truth of dubious ideas still constitute a sizeable body. It is possible that these figures conceal the fact that many people now have to convince themselves and, to a lesser extent, others of the relative truth or moderate benefits of certain contemporary ideas or leaders. Yet again, equivocation continues to win out.

The necessity of undertaking 'social work' (or the current variant—'political' work) is disliked by people to about the same extent as it was ten years ago, even though the meaning of the term has undergone noticeable alteration. The young and the highly educated dislike this work the most, whilst the elderly and the uneducated find it least distasteful. It looks as though the political-oppositional activity that engages part of the older generations is a significant force.

And the necessity of 'being subservient to others' is on the whole as distasteful to people as it ever was. By comparison with the situation ten years ago, it irritates pensioners and those with little education more and young people a little less. About half of students, pensioners, specialists, highly educated people, and young workers find subservience unpleasant.

From gullibility to 'vengeance'

Observing the rise and fall of hopes for national leaders over recent years (Mikhail Gorbachev, Yeltsin, Yavlinsky, Lebed, Boris Nemtsov, Yevgeny Primakov, Vladimir Putin . . . further than that, the list remains open), Nikolai Berdyaev's famous expression about the 'eternal feminine' in the Russian soul—the readiness to trust in anyone who puts on a show of force and makes promises—constantly springs to mind, although by itself, this does not explain the phenomenon. The fascination with new idols (and the subsequent rather rapid disillusionment with them) is caused by society's lack of internal social organization. The deeper historical roots of this phenomenon evidently lie in relations between the state and the people in old 'pre-reform' Russia: until the social institutions of contemporary society (civil society) are in place, the masses are ready and indeed inclined to seek an external organizing force—from authoritarian power or another 'leading force'. For a sociological analysis, there is a wealth of material in the nation's history over the twentieth century, with all its revolutionary and post-revolutionary twists and turns. In this instance, we are interested in only one side of what went on—the ability of many people to be captivated by personalized symbols, only to be later disillusioned with them. Thus, if, initially, the leader figures in mass consciousness symbolized particular ideas—or at least, attractive slogans—then the subject of symbolic representation eventually becomes only power. Accordingly, promises to 'transform' the country evolve into the demand to 'bring order'.

Over the course of these regular alternations of enchantment and disillusionment, the mood of the masses in one way or another comes to be determined by the state of its 'thinking classes'—the more educated, politicized class who hold more influence and are capable of providing models of behaviour for the others to adopt. Throughout all the recent national disturbances, it was clear (in mass survey data as well) that changes in mass sympathies were notable above all in these strata. It is not the relatively 'dark masses' who suffer from gullibility, but the 'enlightened' few at the top. The absence of social organization and civil society is above all a feature of our intellectual and politically conscious elite (in the broad sense of the word; we do not mean the competing groups in the 'bearpit' around power).

Research into the electoral situation in the country (as far back as the 1995–6 round of elections) showed that the majority of the population did not believe the pre-election pledges of candidates for posts and did not believe that they would be honoured, and so did not bear any grudges towards their favourite candidates in the immediate aftermath of the elections. Grudges appeared only later—when favourites had ceased to be such. Here we have two connected questions which deserve special explanation—firstly, which factors get someone into power, turning an obscure functionary or provincial into the darling of public opinion, and, secondly, why public opinion so easily and rapidly abandons its favourites.

At least one explanation could lie in the kinds of thinking detailed above. Mass enthusiasm—especially when aroused by extremely important favourites—is from the outset ambivalent and ambiguous: the demonstrative excitement that is artificially whipped up (not only from outside, but also 'from within', through the mechanisms of self-delusion), is always combined with covert distrust, dark envy, and so on. At some point, this edifice will crumble, leaving that which was previously hidden to dominate and to become obvious. For this reason, each of these twists and turns has a minimal connection to real experience or rational assessment, for the public's fascination with the successive favourites has nothing to do with any mass experience of, or familiarity with, his activity, programme, or aims ('for we love and we hate randomly'). The main factor in these changes of sympathy is the contrast set up between the characteristics ascribed to the old and to the new candidates—for example, the image of a decisive and dynamic Gorbachev, set against the image of the indecisive and decrepit Leonid Brezhnev, then the decisiveness of Yeltsin set against the indecision of Gorbachev, and then the image of the younger and more resolute figures of Lebed, Nemtsov, and Putin set against the image of a decrepit Yeltsin (and there have been other contrasting pairings).

All this then generates the ever-present motor of all these changes—the shifting of blame on to the preceding era, authorities, or leader figure as a way of self-assertion (and as far as possible, self-justification), with each new change in the upper echelons—and it is difficult to see how this will not also feature in the socio-political processes following on Yeltsin's retirement. For the new ruling group can only use the procedure of 'shifting blame' because the masses are already ready for it and easily accept the transformation of a 'hero' into a 'villain' and the cause of all misfortune. This kind of transformation of a sacrosanct image into a cursed, infernal one is characteristic of any mythological system (for example, the medieval or totalitarian).

The ambivalence of all evaluations in the cunning consciousness allows demonstrative reassessments of events, eras, and participants to take place without involving any serious rethinking. Moreover, the explicit negativity in relation to political figures or structures often functions as a means of safeguarding one's own niche within these structures. And in exactly the same way, the widespread denunciation of the fact that 'everyone' in Russia (especially those in power or within the administration) is corrupt, takes bribes, uses 'murky' means and so on, is not merely a criticism, but also a cunning justification of one's personal conduct in at least tolerating, if not adapting to, a corrupt situation. The 'enemy complex', an eternal feature of public opinion, means that ambivalent meanings are ascribed to the categories 'our side'-'the enemy' and creates the possibility of the signs being switched around (although in an oppressed and frightened society, this will mostly go in one direction, that is, changing 'our side' into 'enemies').

The dynamic of public opinion in the last few months of 1999 produced a large body of material for analysis of the potential of the modern mass media to influence such transformations. These include most importantly the changes in reactions to the military actions in Chechnya over several months (from the significant support lent to the attempt to impeach Boris Yeltsin for unleashing the conflict between 1994 and 1996 to the larger support given to the new violent actions).

The unprecedentedly vulgar propaganda campaign against the Luzhkov–Primakov bloc was also highly effective. In the first stages, a significant proportion of those surveyed showed that the vicious attacks would have the opposite effect, but the pressure proved to be too strong.

Social diagnosis: solitude and the asthenic syndrome

In conditions of societal breakdown and weakness of traditional and group interpersonal structures, man with his worries and fears is constantly prey to feelings of solitude in relation to the authorities, social institutions, the powerful pressures of the mass media and public opinion. If he is called upon to behave 'like everyone else'—and to show that publicly, including in answers to public opinion surveys—he absolves himself of responsibility for individual positions, but at the same time cannot rid himself of feelings of isolation in relation to 'everyone else'. Only 13 per cent of those surveyed in 1999 (mostly young people) said that they had 'many close, reliable friends', whilst in 1989, 42 per cent said that this was true of them. Now 74 per cent of people say that they can totally rely on only one or two close friends.

The situation in Russia today inevitably increases the number of social and psychological barriers and distances, from the flat next door and one's neighbourhood, up to the level of the country, with its regions that are forever growing further and further apart. This leads to a growth in the social version of 'asthenic syndrome', the inability and the unwillingness to take on the misfortunes and sufferings of 'others', or, even worse, the persistent effort to shield oneself from them ('we live, unaware of the land beneath us' . . . these words have long served as a universal guide for conduct). Asthenic behaviour is equivocal because the actual situation of 'others' is familiar to every television viewer these days, much more than it ever was before, but the viewer remains a spectator, concerned above all with the danger that he himself will become a victim.

Another factor influencing the masses is the tendency to show 'far-off catastrophes'—the clear information about catastrophes, conflicts, and natural disasters that was novel ten years ago, but has now become everyday and usual.

The situation of political mobilization, mass conflict, and heavy human losses can all only exacerbate society's asthenic syndrome. When sufferings and victims are on a large scale, people can only feel their personal losses. Moreover, the scale of suffering and loss accessible to public opinion is to a significant degree defined by the powerful influence of the modern mass media (in particular TV, as what is not shown on the screen is effectively not shown to society). In an era of televisual 'mobilization', the treatment of mass misfortune is concentrated in the hands of the mass media and the political schemers linked to them—how viewers and voters react to those victims depends upon them.

It is for this reason that the asthenic syndrome of mass indifference and a mass unwillingness to take on board and understand, for example, the Chechen war, is so strong. As survey results show, the majority are worried mostly by reports of losses on the Russian side—everything else worries them to a far lesser degree.

'The vicious circle' of doublethink

In George Orwell's classic description, 'doublethink' is the ability to hold at one and the same time two contradictory opinions. The party intellectual knows how to change his own memories; consequently, he knows that he is playing around with reality; however, with the help of doublethink, he convinces himself that reality has remained untouched. To speak an utter lie and at the same time to believe in it is absolutely essential to this concept. Bringing such a fruitful term into the scientific and political realm requires looking into the internal mechanisms of combining contradictory positions. The situation presented here can be thought of as a deliberately simplified version of events for the sake of 'clarity' in the experiment. The Orwellian conception consciously and harshly demarcates the cynical and rational calculations of the all-powerful 'bosses' (in his terminology, the 'inner party') and the subservience of the political 'underlings' ('the outer party'). It clearly overestimates the ability of the ruling elite consciously and coherently to fulfil the role of the 'collective Grand Inquisitor'. In actual fact, as shown in a whole series of disillusionments and promises linked to changeovers in the make-up of the leading rulers and elites, there is practically no such demarcation. The coherence and rationality of actions 'from above' are in no way more significant than those amongst the lower levels of the socio-political pyramid of society. Those at the top live by the same rules of cunning doublethink as those typically subservient to them, deceive themselves in the same way, believing what they want to believe, and, if they are occasionally called upon to announce their decision to extricate themselves from the vicious circle, this only serves to entangle them still further within it. And for this reason, it is precisely the political elite (the top) that has been first to decay and become spiritually and morally corrupted. The experience of the last decade's changes and upheavals in Russia only confirm this once again. The sharpest of critiques of this position 'in retrospect' (meaning in effect the shifting of blame on to their predecessors) does not allow them to get outside the circle outlined by equivocal thinking. The calculation on the part of the 'new shift' of leaders that a military campaign, which is in the long term impossible to win, could bring much-needed benefits in the fight for power both before and during the presidential elections, is cynical and cunning. The hopes on the part of the former heroes of our radical democracy that they will remain close to power (or the mechanisms that serve it) if they carry on with this course of action relies to an even greater degree on cunning doublethink. Neither society nor its leaders have yet been able to move beyond it.

23 Political Bias and Self-Censorship in the Russian Media

Laura Belin

For much of the 1990s, the development of independent media was considered a clear success of the Russian political transformation. The end of the state monopoly on media ownership gave journalists unprecedented freedom to criticize the authorities. Privately owned media used this opportunity vigorously, especially during the first war in Chechnya, which began in late 1994. 'Alternative' coverage of that war forced state-controlled media to back away from false official versions of events.[1]

Journalists then made a tactical retreat during the 1996 presidential campaign. Privately owned media joined state-controlled outlets in supporting the re-election effort of President Boris Yeltsin. They did so in the belief that they were protecting media freedom from the consequences of a Communist return to power. After Yeltsin's victory, some announced their return to the opposition ranks and gradually resumed criticizing the Yeltsin regime.[2] Conventional wisdom held that having helped stave off the Communist threat, Russian journalists would be able to carry on as they had in 1995, relatively free from outside interference.

Yet by the end of the 1990s, the Russian media appeared markedly less free than they had in the early years of the decade, and Russian journalists were more gloomy about prospects for media independence. Strictly speaking, the state monopoly on media ownership was not restored, and government officials—at least at the federal level—did not frequently impose political censorship. However, a new financial dependence on industrial or banking groups led to a noticeable erosion of autonomy for Moscow-based media. Politicians and business leaders proved eager to use media under their control as weapons in political battles. During the 1999/2000 election cycle and the second war in Chechnya, government and law-enforcement officials stepped up attempts to intimidate some journalists and media that took the 'wrong' political position.

Owners attracted by power of media

The 1996 presidential campaign marked a turning-point for the Moscow-based media. Yeltsin's candidacy appeared hopeless just six months before the election. Opposition

Chapter specially commissioned for this volume.

[1] See report on media coverage of the Chechen war, 'Zhurnalistika i voina', published by the Russian-American Press and Information Centre, Moscow, 1995; Ellen Mickiewicz, *Changing Channels: Television and the Struggle for Power in Russia* (Oxford: Oxford University Press, 1997).

[2] Laura Belin, 'Private Media Comes Full Circle', *Transition*, 2/21 (18 Oct. 1996), 62–5.

parties did far better than pro-government groups in the December 1995 parliamentary elections. Wage and pension arrears continued to mount, and the unpopular Chechen war dragged on with no end in sight. In January 1996 opinion polls showed Yeltsin's approval rating in the single digits, and speculation was rife that the president would cancel the election rather than lose a fair contest.

Yeltsin recognized that he would need media support in order to overcome these obstacles. He set the tone for the campaign by replacing the chairman of state-run Russian Television (RTR) the same day he declared his candidacy in Ekaterinburg. The Kremlin also set about securing the loyalty of privately owned media. This task was less difficult than might have been expected, considering that most private media were highly critical of Yeltsin and his government throughout 1995. Eduard Sagalaev, who left the private network TV-6 to become the new chairman of RTR, later acknowledged that he was appointed after assuring Yeltsin that he was 'on the team'.[3] In the most remarkable turnaround of the campaign, Igor Malashenko, the president of the influential private network NTV, joined a team of Yeltsin strategists in March. NTV had earned a reputation for bold coverage during the Chechen war and was valued for its credibility with viewers. Before the campaign, NTV wore its opposition to the authorities as a badge of honour.[4] But Malashenko explained that if the private media provided 'unbiased, professional, and objective' campaign coverage, Zyuganov would win the election, and journalists would lose their freedom permanently. Better to become a temporary 'instrument of propaganda' in the hands of the Kremlin, he argued.[5]

The rapid and sweeping change in the media's coverage of Yeltsin was striking. Most criticism of the president disappeared. Yeltsin's promises to end the Chechen war and pay wage and pension arrears were treated unsceptically. Meanwhile, news reporting kept up an incessant anti-Communist drumbeat. Aside from a few opposition newspapers with relatively small circulations, the media presented Yeltsin and Zyuganov to readers and viewers only as the Kremlin wanted them to be seen.[6] The 51 per cent state-owned Russian Public Television (ORT) network even refused to air the final campaign advertisement produced by the Zyuganov campaign.[7]

Straightforward pro-Yeltsin, anti-Communist news coverage was merely one aspect of the self-censorship prevalent during the 1996 campaign. Between February and June, the media framed the campaign as a two-way contest between Yeltsin and Zyuganov, marginalizing all other aspirants. This coverage helped Kremlin strategists achieve their main objective: getting voters to view Yeltsin as the only barrier to a Communist return to power, rather than as an unpopular incumbent seeking re-election on his record.[8] During the final two weeks

[3] See interview with Sagalaev, *Izvestiya*, 18 July 1996, p. 6.

[4] In July 1995, criminal cases were opened against producers of the satirical puppet show *Kukly* and against NTV's celebrated journalist Yelena Maslyuk, who had interviewed a notorious Chechen field commander Shamil Basaev. Following a public outcry, both criminal cases were quietly closed in September 1995.

[5] Interview with Igor Malashenko in *Izvestiya*, 19 Apr. 1996, p. 6.

[6] The media bias was so pervasive that the European Institute for the Media concluded that the election was free, but not fair.

[7] A transcript of the never-aired video, featuring State Duma Culture Committee Chairman Stanislav Govorukhin, was published in *OMRI Special Report: Presidential Election Survey*, 10 July 1996.

[8] For more on Yeltsin's campaign strategy, see Michael McFaul, *Russia's 1996 Presidential Election: The End of Polarized Politics* (Stanford: Hoover Institution Press, 1997).

before the first round of the election, the media provided massive favourable exposure to Alexander Lebed.[9] Since Lebed had secretly agreed to back the president after the first round, and friendly interviews with Lebed often included anti-Communist material, such coverage worked indirectly for Yeltsin. The new tone of the reporting on Lebed was remarkable; journalists had often portrayed him as a dangerous nationalist in 1995. In between the first round of the election and the run-off two and a half weeks later, the media concentrated efforts on getting out the vote. Yeltsin's heart problems and disappearance during the last week of the campaign were almost entirely ignored in news reports, although journalists in Moscow were aware of (and worried about) the sudden decline in the president's health.[10]

Yeltsin's decisive victory in July—with 53.8 per cent of the vote to 40.3 per cent for Zyuganov—drove home to potential owners that the media were a powerful weapon for influencing public opinion, if harnessed effectively. It also demonstrated that Russian journalists could be mobilized to propagate a particular political viewpoint. Even though no experimental data have proved that media coverage was the decisive factor in the 1996 election, it is an axiom in Russia that Yeltsin would not have won without the media's support.

Media squeezed by market realities

Many journalists believed that they would regain their independence once the threat of a Communist election victory faded. They underestimated, however, the growing power of Russian financial groups. Most Bank founder, Vladimir Gusinsky, was the first to build a media empire, beginning in 1993. Boris Berezovsky soon followed Gusinsky's lead. Yeltsin's re-election encouraged other financial and industrial groups to expand their media holdings. The gas monopoly Gazprom, which had provided informal financial support to some newspapers in the early 1990s, began to acquire shares in various print and electronic media. Several other large banks and corporations sought opportunities to invest in the media market as well.[11]

The presidential election also prompted the Moscow city administration to expand its presence in the media world. In the early 1990s Mayor Yury Luzhkov's administration had secured friendly or at least neutral coverage by granting media based in the capital lower rates for taxes, rent, and utilities. A few publications, like the popular daily *Moskovskiy komsomolets*, had even closer ties to the city administration. After the 1996 election, Luzhkov's team began to acquire or create new vehicles to support the mayor, who was long considered a leading contender to succeed Yeltsin. The Moscow city administration financed the creation of the television network TV-Centre, which began broadcasting in June 1997. The following year, a corporation closely linked to the Moscow authorities purchased many publications, while the city authorities acquired from the federal government control over one of Russia's largest printing presses.

---

[9] See European Institute for the Media report on the presidential election; *OMRI Special Report: Presidential Election Survey*, 5 and 14 June 1996.

[10] Private conversations with numerous journalists in Moscow, June and July 1996.

[11] For a detailed picture of changing media ownership and financing in the late 1990s, see the series of reports on 'Russian Media Empires' by Floriana Fossato and Anna Kachkaeva. They can be found on the World Wide Web in English or Russian at www.rferl.org/nca/special.

Russian journalists did not expect or seek to become dependent on bankers, industrialists, or the Moscow city government. The 1991 law on the mass media contains no mention of media ownership or the rights and obligations of media owners. However, the shrinking Russian economy proved unable to support the vast majority of the country's media outlets. Since thriving businesses that could afford to advertise were in short supply, surviving on advertising revenue was a realistic option only for a few extremely popular publications.

The print media felt the squeeze most acutely. Once freed from state control, many Russian newspapers formed self-managing editorial collectives. But after the fall of Communism, production and distribution costs rose sharply. At the same time, newspapers became too expensive for many struggling citizens. In addition, the increased variety of television and radio entertainment eroded the appeal of newspapers.

Some publications were reluctant to seek financial aid or sell shares to businesses. A prime example was *Nezavisimaya gazeta*, whose editor, Vitaly Tretyakov, long refused to take any state subsidies or money from sponsors in order to protect his paper's independence. Only after insolvency forced the newspaper to suspend publication in May 1995 did Tretyakov relent. *Nezavisimaya gazeta* reappeared four months later, thanks to a substantial investment from Berezovsky's LogoVAZ group.[12] By the end of the 1990s, some Russian newspapers were formally still owned and managed by editorial collectives, but few managed to get by without any help from financial or industrial groups. Even the weekly *Obshchaya gazeta*, which gained a reputation for independence by supporting Grigory Yavlinsky during the 1996 presidential campaign, ultimately succumbed to financial constraints and sought support from investors in 1997. The respected business newspaper *Kommersant-Daily* avoided selling shares to investors for years, but it drew loans from some major banks, and the influence of its 'sponsors' was occasionally noticeable.[13] Financial difficulties eventually forced managers to sell a controlling stake in *Kommersant-Daily*, and the obscure company that purchased those shares in July 1999 resold them to Berezovsky within a month.

Self-managing journalists' collectives were not an option for most electronic media outlets: operating costs were too high and potential advertising revenues too limited. NTV could not have been created without the financial backing of Gusinsky's Most group. The network's satellite television project, launched in 1996, required capital investment from the Gazprom. The radio station Ekho Moskvy was managed by its journalists from 1990 until 1994, when Most became its sponsor. Managers of TV-6 sold small blocks of shares in the network over the course of the decade, but a desperate financial situation forced them to part with a controlling stake in June 1999. Berezovsky was the buyer.

Politically well-connected businessmen have gained sway even over nominally state-controlled Russian media. Berezovsky became the most influential figure at 51 per cent state-owned ORT while officially controlling a relatively small stake in the network. Even after resigning from the network's board of directors in late 1996, Berezovsky retained vast

---

[12] Over the next several years, Tretyakov acknowledged that *Nezavisimaya gazeta* was financially dependent on Berezovsky, although he denied that Berezovsky exercised editorial control. See Tretyakov's commentaries published in *Nezavisimaya gazeta* on 8 Apr. 1997 and 19 Dec. 1997.

[13] For instance, *Kommersant-Daily* devoted favourable coverage to a controversial May 1997 sale of a stake in the oil company Sibneft, which was won by a company linked to the SBS-Agro bank, a lender to the newspaper.

influence by paying the salaries of many of the network's top journalists and executives.[14] He routinely discussed the content of ORT's weekly analytical programme with its anchor, Sergei Dorenko.[15] Berezovsky also made key hiring decisions and negotiated ORT's contract with a leading advertising firm in late 1999.[16]

Another prominent figure in the media business gained strong influence over state television and eventually over Russian media policy as a whole. Mikhail Lesin, one of the founders of the Video-International advertising agency, became a Kremlin adviser soon after the 1996 election. (Video International produced the skilful television commercials for Yeltsin's campaign.) In 1997 Yeltsin appointed Lesin first deputy chairman of RTR, and Lesin soon gained considerable influence over the network's programming policy. He was reportedly behind the decision to cancel the politically sensitive programme *Moment Istiny* (Moment of Truth) in September 1997.[17]

Lesin's influence continued to grow as Yeltsin moved to centralize management of state-owned media.[18] Lesin was credited with helping draft a May 1998 presidential decree creating a huge state-owned media holding company. The new holding company included the All-Russian Television and Radio Company (the official name for RTR), nearly seventy state-owned regional television stations, and more than 100 facilities for transmitting television and radio signals. A July 1999 presidential decree created a ministry for the press, television, and radio broadcasting, and mass communications (hereafter referred to as the Media Ministry).[19] Yeltsin appointed Lesin to head the new ministry, which was given broad powers to develop state policy on advertising, telecommunications, licensing of television and radio, and production and distribution of audio and video materials. Russian journalists informally referred to Lesin's domain as the ministry of truth.

Having grown increasingly dependent on outside financing during the second half of the 1990s, Moscow-based media—at least media outlets engaged in hard news reporting—have poor prospects for becoming financially self-sufficient in the future. Tax breaks the media have enjoyed since the beginning of 1996 are scheduled to expire on 1 January 2002, making survival without sponsors even less likely. Those benefits include reductions in profit and value-added taxes, as well as exemptions from certain customs duties. Some journalists have warned that revoking the tax breaks will 'bury' the print media.[20]

Furthermore, there has been little sign of an economic boom that could provide media outlets with steady advertising revenues. On the contrary, the economic crisis that began with the rouble collapse of August 1998 caused severe financial difficulties for both Moscow-based and regional media. Printing and production costs rose as citizens' incomes dropped

[14] Special report by Anna Kachkaeva, *Ot Ostankino do ORT*, broadcast on Radio Free Europe/Radio Liberty's Russian Service, 5 Aug. 1997. See also Fossato and Kachkaeva, 'Russian Media Empires V,' www.rferl.org/nca/special/rumedia5/index.html.

[15] Dorenko confirmed the accuracy of a transcript of one such telephone conversation, which was published in *Novaya gazeta*, 16–19 Dec. 1999. Aleksandr Nevzorov, another frequent commentator on ORT, has claimed he speaks to Berezovsky almost daily. See *Vremya-MN*, 1 June 1999, p. 3.

[16] *Vremya-MN*, 7 Dec. 1999, p. 4.

[17] *Kommersant-Daily*, 11 Sept. 1997, p. 1.

[18] See profiles of Lesin published in *Obshchaya gazeta*, 20–6 Jan. 2000, p. 11, and *Novaya gazeta*, 20–3 Jan. 2000, p. 8.

[19] The decree simultaneously abolished the State Press Committee and Federal Service for Television and Radio Broadcasting, which had previously dealt with licensing matters.

[20] *Obshchaya gazeta*, 10 (9–15 Mar. 2000), 3.

sharply in real terms. The rouble crisis proved catastrophic for the advertising market. Combined revenues for advertising in Russia's print and electronic media in 1999 totalled just 43 per cent of the previous year's level. Nationwide television networks collected only one-tenth as much advertising revenue (in dollar terms) in 1999 as they had the previous year.[21] ORT, which had racked up debts even before the rouble crisis, narrowly escaped bankruptcy in December 1998 when Yeltsin signed a decree allowing the network to obtain a $100 million loan from a state-controlled bank.[22]

NTV had enjoyed healthy advertising revenues before the rouble devaluation, but in 1999 the network's parent company, Media-Most, had trouble repaying dollar loans taken out in earlier years. It was forced to seek new loans running into the hundreds of millions of dollars, guaranteed by Gazprom. In late 1999 it appeared possible that NTV assets would be seized to cover loans called in by state-controlled banks. Media-Most raised some cash in January 2000 by selling a 4.5 per cent stake in NTV and the TNT network to a US-based firm. But Gusinsky's media empire still appeared financially vulnerable. In January 2000, transmission fees for all three 'federal networks' (ORT, RTR and NTV) were more than doubled.[23]

The rouble crisis created upheaval in the Moscow-based media, as some banks and companies that had been major media investors fell on hard times. Most journalists took pay cuts, many lost their jobs, and some outlets were forced to seek new financial backers. However, it is striking that relatively few newspapers and magazines ceased publication. (The most prominent casualty was the year-old daily *Russkiy telegraf*.) In early 2000 one could find more than a dozen daily newspapers at Moscow kiosks—far more than a city the size of Moscow could support even in a prosperous country. Why did the number of media outlets not drop to a level corresponding to consumer demand and the size of the advertising market? The answer relates to the political uses of the media. In contrast to Western countries, where media have often been acquired as investments for profit, Russian corporate owners have been willing to subsidize loss-making media indefinitely.

How financial dependence slants news coverage

During the 1996 presidential campaign, it was difficult to discern to what extent media bias was caused by external pressure and to what extent by Russian journalists' own 'self-preservation instinct'. Neither journalists nor business interests wanted to return to Communist rule. Some journalists consequently failed to anticipate that editorial freedom could be threatened when their interests did not coincide with those of their financial backers.

The transformation of the newspaper *Izvestiya* during 1997 is instructive in this regard.[24]

[21] *Sreda*, 2, (Feb. 2000), 22–3.

[22] See Floriana Fossato, 'Media Face Dire Financial Straits', feature for Radio Free Europe/Radio Liberty, 6 Jan. 1999; *Teleskop*, 4 (3 Feb. 1999); *Novaya gazeta*, 6 (14–20 Feb. 2000), 1, 8–9.

[23] Since January 1996, NTV had been charged lower transmission fees than other private television networks. The policy shift in January 2000 simultaneously reduced transmission fees for other commercial broadcasters, which had previously paid far higher rates than ORT, RTR, and NTV. See *Rossiiskaya gazeta*, 1 Feb. 2000, p. 8; *Kommersant*, 18 Jan. 2000, p. 7; *Novaya gazeta*, 20–3 Jan. 2000, p. 8.

[24] See Laura Belin, 'Changes in Editorial Policy and Ownership at *Izvestiya*', www.rferl.org/nca/special/rumediapaper/appendix2.html.

When the loss-making paper sold a stake to the oil company LUKoil in late 1996, the editor-in-chief, Igor Golembiovsky, insisted that complete editorial independence would be preserved. But in April 1997 LUKoil managers and *Izvestiya* editors clashed over an article accusing Prime Minister Viktor Chernomyrdin of accumulating massive wealth while in office. As the conflict escalated, *Izvestiya* journalists first sought help from Yeltsin, then sold a major stake to Oneksimbank in the hope that the bank would fend off LUKoil. Instead, Oneksimbank and LUKoil joined forces to oust Golembiovsky, leading to a massive exodus of journalists. The newspaper's editorial line subsequently reflected the interests of the corporate shareholders.

The upheaval at *Izvestiya* signalled that financial dependence on corporations put real constraints on journalists' autonomy. But the extent to which corporate-funded media would become weapons in political and business disputes became apparent only after the coalition that helped re-elect Yeltsin fell out over privatization sales. The July 1997 auction of a 25 per cent stake in the telecommunications giant Svyazinvest sparked an 'information war' in competing media outlets. ORT and *Nezavisimaya gazeta*, under the influence of Berezovsky, unleashed furious attacks against the then first deputy prime ministers, Anatoly Chubais and Boris Nemtsov. They also attacked Oneksimbank, which led the winning consortium for Svyazinvest. NTV and the daily *Segodnya*, both owned by Gusinsky, did the same. Berezovsky and Gusinsky were involved in the losing bid for the Svyazinvest stake. Meanwhile, newspapers partly owned by Oneksimbank vigorously defended Chubais and Nemtsov and retaliated with attacks against Berezovsky and Prime Minister Chernomyrdin, who was considered close to him.

Although Yeltsin personally pleaded with bankers to stop 'slinging mud', the 'information war' did not subside. When Yeltsin removed Berezovsky from the Security Council in November 1997 of that year, state-controlled RTR and newspapers linked to Oneksimbank welcomed Berezovsky's ouster as a long-overdue step, but commentators on ORT and NTV depicted Berezovsky as a departing hero. Within ten days, media linked to Berezovsky and Gusinsky were flogging new allegations: Chubais and several associates each received $90,000 pay-offs from a publishing company linked to Oneksimbank. The fees were ostensibly paid for writing chapters for a book on Russian privatization—hardly a likely best-seller. Yeltsin sacked three high-ranking officials and reduced Chubais's duties in the government, but attacks on the 'young reformers' (code words for Chubais and Nemtsov) continued, as did selective reporting on both sides of the conflict.

Politically slanted news coverage continued after Yeltsin's sweeping March 1998 government reshuffle, suggesting that the use of the media to score political points could not be chalked up to one or two lightning rods in the cabinet. The short-lived government of Sergei Kirienko was incessantly attacked in media that had previously targeted Chubais, while those outlets that had defended Chubais stood firmly behind the new government.[25] When Kirienko's team adopted an aggressive stance to force Gazprom to pay its taxes in full, NTV responded with a torrent of hostile news reports and commentaries—all without informing viewers that Gazprom owned a minority stake in the network.

---

[25] Media coverage of the Kirienko government is analysed in greater detail in Laura Belin, with Floriana Fossato and Anna Kachkaeva, 'The Distorted Russian Media Market', in Peter Rutland, ed., *Business and the State in Russia* (Boulder, Colo.: Westview Press, 2000).

Bias and self-censorship in the Russian media extended beyond coverage of Kremlin power struggles or issues in which media owners had a direct stake, such as privatization. The coal miners' strikes of May and June 1998 appeared quite different depending on what newspaper one read and what television network one watched. The miners' blockades of major railroads could be seen as legitimate protests against the government's incompetence. But media sympathetic to the government framed the protests as a misguided attempt to blame ministers for mismanagement and corruption within the coal industry. Some even described the blockades as 'terrorist' acts threatening to drag down other sectors of the economy.

The influence of sponsors on media coverage can be subtle and difficult to detect. For instance, a newspaper report might criticize the government's proposed tax code on the grounds that it would hurt ordinary citizens or harm 'Russia's national interests.' In fact, the newspaper's sponsor may oppose the tax code for reasons that are not stated in the article; perhaps the code would raise taxes on oil exports or divert property tax revenues from the city of Moscow to regional governments.

The Duma campaign: enter 'information killers'

During the second half of the 1990s, 'information wars' were a continual presence in the Russian media. All political milestones, such as government reshuffles or allegations of high-level corruption, were accompanied by selective reporting in competing media outlets. It was, therefore, not surprising that the 1999/2000 election cycle was marked by politically slanted media coverage. Even so, the vehemence of the media attacks during the 1999 parliamentary campaign was startling, given that the Russian constitution grants far greater powers to the president than to the State Duma.

For Yeltsin's inner circle, the parliamentary election presented both a threat and an opportunity. The threat was the Fatherland–All Russia alliance, led by former Prime Minister Yevgeny Primakov and Moscow Mayor Luzhkov. After supporting Yeltsin for most of his presidency, Luzhkov became a vocal critic in 1998, saying Yeltsin was unfit to serve. In 1999, he sharpened his attacks on the president's so-called 'Family' (a key member of which was Luzhkov's long-time nemesis, Berezovsky) and it became clear that neither the 'Family' nor their property would be secure if the Moscow mayor gained power. As for Primakov, he had never been Yeltsin's first choice for prime minister but was picked as a compromise in the aftermath of the 1998 rouble devaluation. A campaign to remove him began after Procurator-General Yury Skuratov opened a criminal investigation of Berezovsky in early 1999, with Primakov's blessing. But throughout his tenure as prime minister, and even for several months after Yeltsin fired him in May 1999, Primakov was Russia's most popular politician by far.

A strong showing for Fatherland–All Russia in the Duma election would cement Primakov's position as the frontrunner in the race to succeed Yeltsin. For Kremlin advisers, the main tasks for the parliamentary campaign were to undermine Fatherland–All Russia and build support for Vladimir Putin, both in public opinion and in the future parliament. (Putin was virtually unknown to the public before Yeltsin appointed him prime minister in August 1999.) A new pro-government movement, Unity, was given plenty of favourable publicity on ORT and RTR, and in some newspapers, including *Nezavisimaya gazeta*.[26] Liberal Democratic Party of Russia leader Vladimir Zhirinovsky, who mouthed opposition rhetoric while supporting the government consistently in parliamentary votes, benefited from disproportionate media exposure as well. The main two television networks also supported the Union of Right Forces, a new alliance of old faces from various governments (including Sergei Kirienko, Boris Nemtsov, and Anatoly Chubais).

But the most striking development of the election season was the unprecedented media campaign to destroy Fatherland–All Russia. Newscasts on ORT and RTR relentlessly attacked the opposition alliance, and reports undermining Fatherland–All Russia leaders came to dominate the networks' 'analytical programmes'. The campaign against Fatherland–All Russia was so ruthless that a new term entered the political lexicon to describe hatchet men like television hosts Sergei Dorenko and Mikhail Leontiev: the 'information killer'. Primakov countered with a paid advertisement charging that the Kremlin clique feared a crackdown on corruption. However, ORT and RTR aired that commercial only alongside hastily produced copycat advertisements that dramatically reduced the impact of Primakov's words.

Thanks to the media policy of the Moscow city authorities, Fatherland–All Russia had some weapons at its disposal. Several newspapers defended Luzhkov and Primakov and attacked Unity as a front for Yeltsin's corrupt 'Family'. They also sought to undermine the credibility of the journalists leading the charge against Fatherland–All Russia.[27] TV-Centre newscasts lavished favourable coverage on Fatherland–All Russia, while the network's analytical programmes often publicized compromising information on the mayor's political rivals, especially Berezovsky and Chubais. But TV-Centre broadcast to a much smaller portion of the country than did ORT and RTR and had relatively poor ratings where it was on the air.

Coverage on the private network NTV was more balanced than on the other leading television networks, but news reports and commentaries were noticeably more sympathetic to Fatherland–All Russia and more sceptical about Unity. Grigory Yavlinsky's Yabloko party and the Union of Right Forces also received disproportionate exposure on NTV.

It is worth noting that the alignment of Russia's electronic media during the 1999 campaign was different from what emerged during the early stages of the 'information war'. With respect to many domestic political controversies from mid-1997 through August 1998, 51 per cent state-owned ORT and fully state-owned RTR were on opposite sides. The disparity suggests that formal ownership of Russian media is less important than the degree of the media's financial dependence. Slanted news coverage tends to reflect the interests of those paying the bills, and for that reason, Berezovsky's viewpoint (as opposed to the official 'state' position) came through more strongly on ORT's news and analytical programmes.

During late 1997 and much of 1998, Berezovsky and Gusinsky found themselves on the same side of many political disputes. The political slant of NTV's news coverage was similar

---

[26] Detailed analysis of media coverage of the campaign can be found in the series of *RFE/RL Russian Election Reports*, which are available at www.rferl.org/elections/russia99report/archives.html. Further details about air time and column space devoted to the leading electoral blocs can be found in the report compiled by the European Institute for the Media, which can be found at www.eim.org. The EIM concluded that Russian coverage of the 1999 campaign was in many ways 'considerably worse' than coverage of the previous parliamentary election and undermined the public's 'ability to come to a well-informed conclusion about who deserves their confidence'.

[27] For instance, *Moskovskiy komsomolets*, 24 Nov. 1999.

to that found on ORT (though NTV displayed a higher level of professionalism, and its bias was generally not as blatant as that found on ORT). But by the middle of 1999, relations between Gusinsky and Berezovsky had soured, and Berezovsky was back on good terms with the Kremlin. News coverage on ORT and RTR reflected a similar slant during the parliamentary campaign, while NTV was on the other side of the barricade. Coverage of Berezovsky and Gusinsky reflected the shift; in late 1999 and early 2000 media linked to Berezovsky publicized numerous reports discrediting Gusinsky and news coverage in outlets belonging to Media-Most. By the same token, many NTV reports lent credibility to corruption accusations against Berezovsky.

The 2000 presidential race

The parliamentary election results were heartening for the Kremlin. Unity far exceeded expectations and finished a close second to the Communist Party. Fatherland–All Russia was a distant third. Pro-government forces in the Duma commanded a plurality, if not a majority. Regional leaders who had supported Luzhkov and Primakov quickly began to gravitate towards Putin, and that trend accelerated after Yeltsin's surprise resignation on New Year's Eve. By the end of January 2000, it was clear that Putin would have no serious challengers in the early presidential election, set for late March.

Although the presidential election was in many respects a campaign without a contest, the media were by no means relegated to the sidelines. As during the Duma campaign, ORT and RTR spearheaded the effort to guide voters to the 'correct' choice. Newscasts provided glowing coverage of Putin, who was often shown surrounded by supporters.[28] Reports put a positive spin on his refusal to publish a programme or participate in televised debates. Although Putin was Yeltsin's hand-picked successor, correspondents on ORT and RTR depicted him as a new face and his opponents as relics of the Yeltsin era. As acting president, Putin received the lion's share of news coverage on other television networks as well. However, he granted interviews only to sympathetic journalists.

In contrast to the previous presidential race, the media did not demonize Communist Party leader Zyuganov, who had no chance of beating Putin. Although his daily activities received far less attention than Putin's, he appeared on many more interview programmes than in 1996. RTR even broadcast a lengthy documentary casting Zyuganov in a favourable light. However, all major television networks, including NTV, dealt a blow to Zyuganov by giving considerable publicity to a rival presidential candidate, Kemerovo oblast governor, Aman Tuleev. A former ally who supported Zyuganov in 1996, Tuleev repeatedly criticized the Communist Party leadership during the 2000 campaign.

The presidential race did not feature a smear campaign comparable to the one against Fatherland–All Russia until the final week. Its target was Yabloko leader Yavlinsky, who ranked a distant third in opinion polls but ran an aggressive campaign. He purchased numerous advertisements in large-circulation newspapers and appeared to benefit from some 'hidden advertising' (favourable exposure disguised as straight reporting) as well. He

---

[28] See the report by the European Institute for the Media at www.eim.org. For analysis of media coverage that aided Putin and hindered other candidates, see *RFE/RL Russian Election Report*, www.rferl.org/elections/russia00report/archives.html.

so often appeared on radio and television programmes that rival candidate Stanislav Gov-orukhin quipped that 'when you turn on your iron, you see Yavlinsky'.[29] Some analysts believed a strong showing for the Yabloko leader could prevent Putin from winning an outright majority in the first round of the election. During the last week of the campaign, ORT refused to air two interview programmes featuring Yavlinsky and aired a deluge of attacks on him, some of which were echoed on RTR. Correspondents accused him of breaking campaign spending rules, taking money from Israelis, Germans, and Americans, seeking to undermine Russian stability, and even having plastic surgery. Three days before the election, both networks gave prime-time news exposure to a phony press conference of flamboyant homosexuals expressing their support for the Yabloko leader. To a lesser degree, correspondents on ORT and RTR belittled the ousted procurator-general Skuratov, a mar-ginal presidential candidate who assailed high-level Kremlin corruption. ORT and RTR repeatedly reminded viewers of Skuratov's dalliance with prostitutes the previous year.

Further elements of the media campaign to help Putin included upbeat coverage of the fighting in Chechnya and reports aimed at boosting turn-out and dissuading people from voting against all candidates. There is no proof that Putin or his campaign staff ordered ORT and RTR employees to cover the campaign as they did. But news coverage on the two main networks conformed to Putin's campaign strategy, just as the networks had framed the 1996 election in a way that benefited Yeltsin.

Resurgence of state role

The use of the media as weapons to decimate Fatherland–All Russia and promote Putin's first-round election victory were part of a larger development in the late 1990s: an attempt to reassert the state's role in managing media coverage. Mikhail Lesin, appointed to head the new media ministry in July 1999, was a central figure in this process. He repeatedly demon-strated that he had a double standard when it came to evaluating the media's behaviour. For instance, in June 1999, while still first deputy chairman of RTR, Lesin defended the decision to cancel the programme *Sovershenno sekretno* (Top Secret), saying the show was axed for dealing in compromising information (*kompromat*).[30] Yet three months earlier, Lesin had supported—by some accounts engineered—the broadcast on RTR of a video showing Skuratov in bed with prostitutes. Producers of *Sovershenno sekretno* charged that the show was punished because powerful Kremlin figures were implicated in reports on corruption published in the related newspapers *Sovershenno sekretno* and *Versiya*.

Lesin's ministry was far from even-handed in ensuring the media's adherence to Russian law during the 1999/2000 election cycle. His ministry asked TV-Centre to cancel a weekly programme featuring the journalist Alexander Khinshtein, who was running for a seat in parliament. However, Lesin did not object to regular prime-time appearances on ORT by commentator Alexander Nevzorov, who was also running for a Duma seat. Moreover, Lesin criticized Fatherland–All Russia during an appearance on RTR two weeks before the election.

---

[29] See *RFE/RL Russian Election Report*, 17 Mar. 2000. Yavlinsky denied exceeding campaign spending limits or paying to be interviewed in the press or on television.

[30] Reuters, 22 June 1999.

Regarding coverage of the Duma campaign, Lesin's ministry issued two warnings to ORT and one to TV-Centre. Some independent experts argued that the violations committed by TV-Centre were less egregious than those committed by ORT (most of which were over-looked by the ministry) or by RTR, which received no warning or reprimand at all. A second warning issued later to TV-Centre concerned a technicality unrelated to the network's news coverage or programming—hardly deserving of sanctions from the Media Ministry.

Those warnings proved significant under a new procedure for granting and extending broadcast licences, developed by Lesin's ministry in 1999. (Licensing procedures were estab-lished by various presidential decrees and government directives throughout the 1990s as parliament failed to adopt a law on television and radio broadcasting.) The new rules stated that two warnings from the media ministry were sufficient to prompt a review on whether to extend an existing licence. That provoked protest from the National Association of Televi-sion and Radio Broadcasters, which held that licences should be automatically extended unless a court ruled that the broadcaster had not fulfilled programming obligations under which the licence was granted.[31]

The make-up of the newly created Federal Commission on Competitions for Television and Radio Broadcasting cast doubt on its potential objectivity. Lesin and other government bureaucrats held half the seats, and Lesin had the power to cast a tie-breaking vote. In February 2000 two radio stations controlled by the Moscow city authorities lost the use of their FM frequencies in an open tender, prompting cries of political discrimination by Luzhkov.[32] Lesin then dropped a bombshell less than a month before the presidential elec-tion, announcing that in light of the two warnings ORT and TV-Centre had received, the networks' broadcast licences would not be automatically extended when they expired that spring. Executives at the networks characterized the decision as 'blackmail' and 'the destruc-tion of politically displeasing mass media'.[33] In the journalistic community, Lesin's announcement was widely considered an attempt to coerce the networks into covering the presidential campaign 'correctly'. Few believed the financial or creative merits of various bids would determine the outcome of the May tender scheduled for the ORT and TV-Centre frequencies.

ORT won the tender for the Channel 1 licence without incident. As for TV-Centre, the decision appeared to be swayed by political rather than strictly legal considerations. The tender was postponed several times but not cancelled, despite a court ruling striking down the media ministry's second warning to the network (the justification for not extending the licence). After a series of private meetings between Lesin and Luzhkov, TV-Centre was allowed to retain the use of the frequency.[34]

Lesin topped a list of 'Enemies of the Press' released by Russia's Union of Journalists in July 2000, partly because of his handling of the TV-Centre controversy. Meanwhile, he has sought even more power for his ministry, advocating new requirements for licensing of print media.

---

[31] See *Vedomosti*, 10 Nov. 1999, p. A6, and *Rossiiskaya gazeta* on 26 Nov. 1999, p. 14.

[32] For the official defence of that decision, see *Kul'tura*, 4 (3–9 Feb. 2000), 1–2.

[33] ORT general director Konstantin Ernst was quoted in *Vek*, 9 (3–9 Mar. 2000), 1, 3; Oleg Poptsov, chief executive of TV-Centre, was quoted in *Kompaniya*, 8 (6 Mar. 2000), 5.

[34] Floriana Fossato, 'Luzhkov's TV Station Back in Favour', feature for Radio Free Europe/Radio Liberty, 7 July 2000.

Though not at risk of losing its licence, NTV and its parent company, Media-Most, came under increasing economic and political pressure beginning in June 1999, when state-controlled Vneshekombank demanded that Media-Most repay a huge loan in cash. Media-Most executives later charged that Yeltsin's chief of staff, Alexander Voloshin, indicated the loan would be extended if Media-Most agreed to support the Kremlin through the next parliamentary and presidential elections.[35] Although that loan was repaid following a court battle, more pressure followed from Media-Most investor Gazprom (in which the state is the largest shareholder). Shortly after meeting with Putin in February 2000, Gazprom chief executive Rem Vyakhirev criticized NTV's coverage of the war in Chechnya.[36] The following month, Gazprom demanded reimbursement for a $211 million loan it had repaid to a bank on Media-Most's behalf. In part Media-Most managers were to blame for their predicament, because of their earlier extensive borrowing. But a double standard was evident: ORT, which had borrowed at least $100 million from Vneshekombank in 1998, was not asked to repay that loan.

Worse was to come after Putin's inauguration. Media-Most's headquarters were searched in May 2000. Tax police were involved in the search, although officials initially said the raid was part of an investigation into illegal wiretapping. The following month, Gusinsky was arrested and charged with embezzlement in connection with the acquisition of a St Petersburg-based television company. Criminal charges were also filed against another senior Media-Most employee. Even if Gusinsky and his associates did commit crimes, politics appeared to be mixed up in his company's trouble with law enforcement officials. In June Russian border police blocked senior Media-Most executive Malashenko from attending an international conference in Salzburg, although Malashenko had neither been arrested nor charged with any crime. The criminal case against Gusinsky was abruptly closed in late July, after Gusinsky signed an agreement behind closed doors to sell a controlling stake in Media-Most to Gazprom. The extent of the official pressure to secure a management change at Media-Most became clear in September 2000. It emerged that Lesin had signed a secret addendum to the deal with Gazprom, promising that criminal charges against Gusinsky would be dropped if the sale went ahead.[37]

Although ORT dodged one bullet when its broadcast licence was renewed, officials moved to increase state control over the Channel 1 network. Relations between Berezovsky and Putin soured soon after the presidential election, as prosecutors investigated alleged embezzlement at companies linked to Berezovsky. The businessman criticized the president, as did newspapers under his financial control, but he also started negotiating a possible transfer to the state of his minority stake in ORT. Following the failed rescue of the Kursk submarine in August 2000, ORT star Dorenko's harsh assessment of the president brought matters to a head. In early September Berezovsky accused a senior Kremlin official of threatening him with prison unless he gave up his ORT shares. Within days, ORT's general

---

[35] Media-Most press release, issued on 10 Nov. 1999; NTV, *Itogi*, 14 Nov. 1999.

[36] *RFE/RL Newsline*, 16 Feb. 2000. Gazprom executives fearing a restructuring of the firm had incentive to curry favour with Putin.

[37] Shortly after the disclosure of Lesin's 'Protocol 6', Gazprom's media subsidiary sued Media-Most for non-repayment of loans and alleged breach of contract. Within days the Prosecutor-General's Office opened a new criminal investigation into whether Media-Most officials had illegally transferred property abroad. In early October, several state-controlled lending institutions announced plans to sue Media-Most for unpaid loans as well.

director cancelled Dorenko's programme and fired the two top executives in the network's news department, who had been hand-picked by Berezovsky.[38]

War inspires new restrictions on media

In 1995 the government had for the most part lost the battle to shape coverage of the fighting in Chechnya. However, the predominant media coverage at the beginning of the second war, which began in August 1999, was quite different. Rampant crime and kidnapping in Chechnya during the late 1990s alienated the Russian journalistic community. From August to October 1999, the vast majority of private as well as state-owned media devoted almost exclusively favourable or neutral coverage to the Russian military action. Many newspapers that had given Chechen fighters sympathetic coverage during the previous war condemned them as 'bandits' and 'terrorists' in 1999.[39]

Over time, though, the tone of Chechnya coverage in some media outlets began to change. ORT and RTR continued to broadcast almost exclusively optimistic or neutral reports about the 'anti-terrorist operation' (in keeping with the official lexicon, not a 'war'). Their correspondents' dispatches suggested that Russian forces were advancing steadily, and interviews with soldiers gave the impression that morale at the front was high. However, in November 1999 NTV and TV-Centre aired more 'pessimistic' reports and called into question official estimates of casualties.[40] Soon after the December parliamentary election, NTV enraged Russian officials by showing footage of Russian troops looting a 'liberated' village where an alleged massacre took place. Furthermore, in January 2000 several widely read Russian newspapers that had supported the military campaign began to question official strategy and casualty figures.

Officials responded by stepping up efforts to curb criticism of the war. In mid-January, Lesin summoned the head of Ekho Moskvy radio to his office to express his displeasure over an interview with Chechen spokesman Movladi Udugov.[41] Putin appointed Sergei Yastrzhembsky presidential aide in charge of managing information on Chechnya. A former press secretary for Yeltsin, Yastrzhembsky had crossed over to Luzhkov's team in 1998. New attempts to reverse the trend in media coverage came swiftly after the return of the prodigal spin doctor. In one interview, Yastrzhembsky implied that journalists had a duty to assist the war effort: 'When the nation mobilizes its forces to solve some task, that imposes obligations on everyone, including the media.'[42] Gaining access to the front lines was more difficult for journalists who did not fulfil their 'obligations'.

There were ways of getting around such barriers (mainly bribery), but the ordeal of Radio Free Europe/Radio Liberty correspondent Andrei Babitsky was a strong deterrent to those contemplating evasion of official restrictions. Babitsky disappeared in Chechnya in mid-January 2000. For two weeks, Russian officials denied having detained him, and soon after

---

[38] In an interview with Ekho Moskvy on 9 September 2000, Dorenko charged that ORT general director Ernst met daily with, and was directly subordinate to, Putin's chief of staff Alexander Voloshin.

[39] *Novaya gazeta* was one of the few consistent voices against the war. For monitoring of Chechnya coverage on major television networks from August to October 1999, see *Sreda*, 10 (Nov. 1999), 6–8.

[40] *Sreda*, 11 (Dec. 1999), 13–16.

[41] *Novaya gazeta*, 20–3 Jan. 2000, p. 8. Like NTV, Ekho Moskvy is part of Gusinsky's Media-Most empire.

[42] *Kommersant-Daily*, 21 Jan. 2000.

the Federal Security Service finally admitted Babitsky was under arrest, they ostensibly 'exchanged' him for Russian soldiers held prisoner by Chechen fighters, without having allowed him to call his family, his colleagues, or a lawyer. In fact, Babitsky was transferred to a pro-Moscow Chechen group, where he remained unable to contact the outside world. He was eventually given a false passport and taken to neighbouring Dagestan, then arrested for using the forged document. Putin defended the treatment of Babitsky, although he eventually gave his blessing to release the journalist from custody.[43] Even after Babitsky was allowed to return to Moscow, he was denied permission to travel abroad to speak about his experience in Chechnya. In July 2000 the Interior Ministry charged him with using false documents, a crime carrying a possible prison term.

What had particularly irked the authorities about Babitsky's dispatches was his tendency to quote Chechen military sources. Soon after Babitsky's release in March, Deputy Media Minister Mikhail Seslavinsky warned journalists that interviews with top-ranking Chechen officials would be considered violations of the law on terrorism. In the summer of 2000 it remained unclear how the law on terrorism would be applied against journalists or media outlets. In spring 2000 some media organizations received official warnings after broadcasting interviews with the Chechen president, Aslan Maskhadov, but the journalists involved were not charged with crimes.

Thought not as serious as the unlawful detention of Babitsky, another incident in early 2000 suggested that Russia's 'power ministries' felt newly emboldened to harass journalists. The interior ministry sought to transfer *Moskovskiy komsomolets* staffer Alexander Khinshtein to a mental health facility for psychiatric testing, based on the alleged crime of having a false driver's licence. The interior ministry dropped charges against Khinshtein after his case attracted attention from international watchdog groups, alarmed by the aggressive methods used while investigating him.[44]

Prospects for development

Some observers find grounds for optimism in Russia's media landscape. There is, after all, a degree of pluralism in the media, in contrast to the Soviet period (and to the current situation in several former Soviet republics). *Nezavisimaya gazeta* editor-in-chief Tretyakov has argued that 'nowhere in the world' will you find the pluralism of opinions that can be found in Russia.[45] Individual print or electronic media outlets may be biased, but since no one political or financial group has a media monopoly, there is, in the view of one Russian journalist, 'a peculiar freedom of information'. If one reads half a dozen newspapers a day and watches a variety of television networks, one gets a fairly accurate picture of the news.[46] However, few Russians watch the news on more than one television network or read several newspapers a day.

Leaving aside 'information killers' and journalists who take pay-offs for 'hidden advertising', there are clearly many Russian journalists who recognize the need for professionalism

[43] See the interview with Putin published in *Kommersant* on 10 Mar. 2000, pp. 1, 4. More details about the Babitsky case can be found at www.rferl.org.

[44] *Moskovskiy komsomolets*, 23 Feb. 2000, p. 1; *Kommersant*, 17 Feb. 2000, p. 3.

[45] *Nezavisimaya gazeta*, 18 Mar. 2000, p. 2.

[46] Andrei Fadin, 'In Russia, Private Doesn't Mean Independent', *Transitions*, 4/5 (Oct. 1997), 90–2.

and fair play. Some seek to protect their independence by avoiding contentious political or economic topics. Scores of Moscow journalists have changed jobs after facing editorial constraints. Many articles spiked at one newspaper have later appeared in a rival publication. The programme *Moment istiny* found a home on TV-Centre after being cancelled by RTR in 1997, and NTV picked up *Sovershenno sekretno* after RTR discontinued that programme in 1999. But journalists who leave one job to avoid censorship may quickly face similar constraints from their new employers. Leonid Krutakov left *Izvestiya* not long after he co-wrote a damaging article about Chubais. He went to work for *Novye izvestiya* but was soon fired from that paper for publishing an article elsewhere attacking Berezovsky.[47]

Some journalists were optimistic that media owners would come to value their assets as potentially profitable enterprises, favouring balanced reporting in order to gain the trust of readers and viewers. However, the latest parliamentary and presidential elections suggest that short-term goals of helping the 'right' candidates and undermining the 'wrong' ones outweigh long-term considerations about reputation or credibility. The impact of media coverage on public opinion and voting behaviour is notoriously difficult to assess. But given the apparent success of the campaign to destroy Fatherland–All Russia while promoting Unity and Putin, media sponsors are likely to continue to view their holdings as political rather than economic assets.

Furthermore, there is no consensus in Russia's journalistic community regarding professional standards. Even journalists with a good reputation often see 'educating' the public as a legitimate, even vital part of their jobs. NTV's long-time news director and later president, Oleg Dobrodeev, left NTV in early 2000 and was appointed by Putin to head state-owned RTR. Under his leadership, coverage of the war in Chechnya and the presidential campaign remained unswervingly loyal to the acting president. After the *Kursk* submarine sank, RTR correspondents with exclusive access to sites near the disaster lent credibility to official untruths about the accident and prospects for rescue. When Putin met with grieving relatives of *Kursk* crew members, only RTR's camera was allowed in the room, and Dobrodeev himself edited the footage to remove exchanges that might embarrass the president.

Collective resistance to state policies to manage media coverage has been thin on the ground; solidarity among Russian journalists has been an undisputed casualty of the 'information wars'. The secretary-general of the Union of Journalists, Igor Yakovenko, lamented in February 2000 that he has been unable to persuade editors of rival publications to sit at the same table to discuss problems affecting the entire journalistic community.[48] When some thirty media organizations of various political stripes sponsored a special issue of *Obshchaya gazeta* to protest against Babitsky's arrest and 'exchange', some of Russia's most prominent newspapers chose not to take part. *Moskovskiy komsomolets* editors complained in early 2000 that journalists did not unite to defend Khinshtein. Aleksei Simonov, president of the watchdog Glasnost Defense Foundation, spoke for many when he explained that he

---

[47] Krutakov's article for *Izvestiya* appeared on 1 July 1997, p. 1. He described his later experiences in an interview with *Komsomol'skaya pravda*, 29 Oct. 1997, p. 2.

[48] Yakovenko was speaking on 24 February 2000 at a Moscow seminar convened by the European Institute for the Media and Russia's Union of Journalists.

did not consider Khinshtein a journalist because of the latter's alleged cooperation with the special services.[49]

Alexander Minkin, who has brought several scandals to public attention, has argued that even if sources have ulterior motives for leaking compromising information to journalists, the public have the right to know. While few would claim that stories about bribery or insider privatization deals are not newsworthy, *kompromat* has a way of appearing at remarkably convenient times. Minkin's revelation that Chubais and others took $90,000 pay-offs received enormous media attention in November 1997. Yet four months earlier (before the Svyazinvest controversy), leading media outlets did not follow up on allegations that Chubais benefited from a suspicious $3 million loan from a bank that eventually won control of a coveted state property.[50] In fact, as long as privatization spoils were being distributed amicably, most Russian media did not accuse Chubais of favouring well-connected banks or presiding over crooked deals (the main exceptions being pro-Communist newspapers such as *Sovetskaya Rossiya*).[51]

When official misconduct was publicized in the late 1990s, speculation in Moscow circles often dwelled on Lenin's old question: 'who benefits from this?' The general disdain for Khinshtein reflects the fact that while muck-raking journalists win awards in some countries, Russian journalists who publicize official corruption are often assumed to be hired guns. Cynicism about investigative reporting thus undermined the media's ability to act as a watchdog. In 1999 and 2000 some astonishing allegations were barely acknowledged by other Russian media, except for outlets sharing the same political or financial patrons. In his final interview, the prominent journalist Artem Borovik remarked that it is frustrating to see a colleague pursue an investigative story and publish it at great personal risk, only to receive virtually no reaction.[52]

As of autumn 2000 it was too early to conclude that pluralism in the media would be sharply curtailed during the Putin presidency, but the cases involving Khinshtein, Babitsky, and Media-Most were not encouraging. The moves to distance Berezovsky from editorial policy at ORT came only after Berezovsky fell out with Putin. The political use of licensing procedures could limit diversity in the electronic media, making private networks more reluctant to give Kremlin opponents air time or pick up programmes cancelled by state television. By not objecting to the grossly biased coverage in his favour and refusing interview requests from media that criticize him, Putin has signalled that he values a friendly press more than a free press.

Another alarming development concerns efforts to make state funding for the media less transparent. In the draft 2001 budget proposed by the government, the paragraph on media subsidies was labelled 'top secret', even though normally only certain lines in the defence budget are classified. Whether intended to shield which media will receive state assistance, or to conceal what one unnamed official called 'special propaganda operations', or to provide

---

[49] *Kontinent*, 11 (Mar. 2000), 3. In *Sreda*, 2 (Feb. 2000), 5, Aleksei Pankin argued that it is cynical for Khinshtein to complain about the lack of solidarity given *Moskovskiy komsomolets'* pattern of defaming other journalists.

[50] Those allegations were the subject of a lengthy article in *Izvestiya* on 1 July 1997, p. 4.

[51] NTV and *Nezavisimaya gazeta* were among media that gave Chubais glowing coverage in 1996 but became his vocal critics later.

[52] Borovik appeared on NTV's *Antropologiya* in the early hours of 7 March 2000. He died in a plane crash two days later.

cover for the misuse of budget funds, the attempt to keep such information secret angered the Union of Journalists and watchdog groups. Furthermore, the draft budget calls for all subsidies to be disbursed to the Media Ministry and from there to media outlets' commercial bank accounts, a process that would not only increase Lesin's power, but would create more opportunities for misappropriation.

Regional media even less free

As a rule, media in the Russian regions face more restrictions than Moscow-based media. Although no formal monopoly on media ownership exists, there is a dearth of small and medium-sized businesses to support private media through advertising. According to a study carried out in 1999, regional leaders are often able to create a virtual 'political monopoly' in the media through uneven distribution of subsidies, and it is common for the leaders' relatives or close allies to own or manage nominally private media.[53]

The servility of journalists is especially pronounced during regional election campaigns. Local media in Orel oblast issued innumerable appeals to vote for Governor Yegor Stroev in 1997, while there was little media discussion of problems facing the oblast or of dirty tricks to keep opponents off the ballot.[54] In Bashkortostan, which ranks at or near the bottom in all measures of media freedom, the independent radio station Titan was shut down, and its director arrested, after broadcasting interviews with would-be challengers to President Murtaza Rakhimov in 1998. During the 1999 gubernatorial campaign in Primorsky Krai, the authorities cut the electricity to a private radio station, seized its building, and used political pressure to eliminate critical coverage from the local edition of *Moskovskiy komsomolets*.[55]

Restrictions on regional media accelerated during the 2000 presidential campaign, even though Putin faced no serious challengers. The Glasnost Defence Foundation, which monitors conflicts between journalists and authorities accross the Russian Federation, recorded sixty-three conflicts between journalists and authorities in January 2000. In February, that number rose to 123, and it rose again to 139 the following month.[56]

The media environment in some republics of the Russian Federation has been compared to that found in the extremely restrictive Central Asian regimes.[57] But despite a constitutional prohibition on censorship, the federal government did virtually nothing in the 1990s to protect press freedom in the regions. Federal officials intervened to combat censorship in Bashkortostan only in November 1999, when the republican authorities (who were supporting Fatherland–All Russia) shut down broadcasts of analytical programmes produced by ORT and RTR. The same month, the federal government did nothing to curb attacks on media freedom in Primorsky Krai, where Governor Yevgeny Nazdratenko supported the pro-Kremlin Unity bloc.

Correspondents who defy the authorities have suffered severe beatings in numerous

[53] Anna Kachkaeva wrote up the results of the study, which can be found on the website of the Moscow Media Law and Policy Centre at www.medialaw.ru/publications/books/conc1/index.html.

[54] Radio Free Europe/Radio Liberty's Russian Service, *Vybory-97*, 23 Oct. 1997. See also *RFE/RL Newsline*, 23 Oct. 1997.

[55] Julie Corwin, 'Looking Beyond the Ring Road', *RFE/RL Russian Federation Report*, 15 Dec. 1999.

[56] *Versiya*, 14 (11–17 Apr. 2000), 8.

[57] Radio Free Europe/Radio Liberty's Russian Service, *Kavkazskie khronniki*, 24 Sept. 1997.

regions, and several journalists, including the most prominent investigative reporter in the Republic of Kalmykia, have been murdered. But even where the governor or republican leader does not shut down media outlets or use violence to silence journalists, various carrots and sticks help keep the media in line. Access to government briefings is often denied to 'inconvenient' journalists. Print-runs or essential equipment are occasionally seized, and libel lawsuits are filed against journalists and newspapers that publish articles criticizing local authorities. (Since courts are rarely free from political pressure in the Russian regions, the authorities win the vast majority of such lawsuits.) Economic pressure takes several forms, from withholding subsidies to sending the tax or fire inspector to newsrooms. In addition, many regional leaders have used licensing bodies to punish or reward electronic media for political reasons. In all but a handful of regions, there are only one or two distribution networks for print media, making it easy for the authorities to block a publication from reaching the public.

The overall picture is bleak. 'Measuring Freedom of Speech', a study released in the autumn of 1999, examined freedom of access to information, freedom to report the news, and restrictions on distribution of the media. Although there was wide variation, the study found that none of the eighty-eight Russian regions studied (including the cities of Moscow and St Petersburg) had created conditions for genuine press freedom.[58] In January 2000 Putin signed a law mandating that subsidies to local print media be paid directly from the federal budget. The new law could somewhat reduce the print media's reliance on regional authorities, which previously had control over how federal funds were divided locally. But recipients of subsidies would then be at the mercy of the federal government's media ministry.[59]

Conclusion

Although the Russian media's independence from state control has not been reversed, editorial freedom remains limited. Most Russian journalists engaged in self-censorship to assist Yeltsin's re-election effort in 1996, fearing that they would lose their freedom if the Communists returned to power. Following Yeltsin's victory, business interests accelerated their media acquisitions in the hope of gaining political influence. Cash-strapped media outlets were not in a position to refuse help from 'sponsors', since the Russian economy could not support most print and electronic media. Financial dependence on banking and industrial groups led to biased coverage in many Russian media outlets in a way that few expected after the collapse of Communism in 1991.

While state-controlled media provided selective coverage of key political issues, the state's influence over private outlets grew with the creation of a new ministry to oversee the media. The second war in Chechnya brought with it further attempts to restrict coverage in private media. The tendentious reporting of the 1999 parliamentary election indicated that no punches would be pulled in using the media to destroy opposition movements and to

[58] Full results from the study can be found at www.freepress.ru/win/I.htm. A summary appeared in *Rossiyskaya gazeta*, 2 Nov. 1999, p. 3.

[59] In 1999 federal subsidies to print media totalled 60 million roubles (about $2.4 million), and the 2000 federal budget earmarked 150 million roubles (about $5.3 million) for such purposes. *Izvestiya*, 13 Jan. 2000, p. 1, and *Rossiyskaya gazeta*, 13 Jan. 2000, p. 5.

promote favourites of the Kremlin. Above all, the visible success of the biased coverage of the 2000 presidential race—in which Putin's victory became a foregone conclusion—suggested that attempts by state officials to use the media to shape public opinion are likely to remain part of the Russian political landscape for a long time to come.

Russian Statehood and the National Question

Section 8

Russian Statehood and the National Question

Introduction

Archie Brown

At a time when Boris Yeltsin was speaking on behalf of Russia against the 'centre', personified by Mikhail Gorbachev, during the last two years of existence of the Soviet Union, many Russians came to share his view that not only such republics as Estonia, Latvia, and Lithuania but also Russia was in need of independence. Yet, for a majority of citizens this did not mean a readiness to abandon a 'greater Russia'. With the exception of the public mood at the moment when the USSR ceased to exist, there was neither in the last years of the Soviet Union nor in the post-Soviet period majority support in Russia for the complete disintegration of the Soviet state. As Matthew Wyman has noted, on the basis of study of the survey data from the late Soviet and early post-Soviet years, 'only at one very specific time—the end of 1991—did this [unwillingness to use force] go as far as accepting the break-up of the Soviet Union itself'.[1] That mood of acquiescence did not survive long into the post-Communist era. Survey research has consistently shown that a majority of Russians regret the loss of the Soviet state, though there is also a majority who accept that it is unrealistic to believe that the old boundaries can be restored.

To seek the transformation of the Soviet system so that its politics became pluralistic and decision-making decentralized was one thing. But the paradox of seeking Russian 'independence' was that, historically, Russia and Russians had been the dominant partner within the Soviet Union. This was still more clearly the case in pre-revolutionary Russia which did not even pretend, as the Soviet Constitution did, to be a federation of nationally defined territories. (That neither regime was democratic meant, of course, that those who spoke for Russia had not been chosen to do so by the Russian people.) An additional major problem with seeking 'independence' was that the boundaries of what during the Communist period constituted the Russian Socialist Federative Soviet Republic (RSFSR) were not identical to the boundaries of Russia at any period of its pre-Soviet history. When Khrushchev, as a gesture to Ukraine, instigated the transfer of the Crimean peninsula from the RSFSR to the Ukrainian republic in 1954, this did not seem to be an especially momentous decision. Both the Russian republic and Ukraine were, after all, part of a centralized Soviet state in which Moscow had the last word. With the breakup of the Soviet Union, though, that became a highly contentious political issue. Most Russians, including those living in Crimea (who formed a majority of the Crimean population), regarded that territory as being part of Russia. At various times during the post-Soviet period such prominent Russian politicians as Alexander Rutskoy (when he was vice-president of Russia between 1991 and 1993), and the mayor of Moscow, Yury Luzhkov,

[1] Matthew Wyman, *Public Opinion in Postcommunist Russia* (Basingstoke and London: Macmillan, 1997), 172–3.

have asserted Russia's claim to Crimea. This brought a sharp reaction from the Ukrainian authorities in Kiev who were 'loath to see any territory removed from the control of their fragile new state'.[2]

Boris Yeltsin had contributed notably to the breakup of the Soviet Union by playing the Russian card against the Union. It was one thing for the Estonian political leadership to say that Estonian law took supremacy over Soviet law. It was putting the Union in far greater jeopardy for Yeltsin to assert that Russian law took precedence over Soviet legislation, since Russia occupied three-quarters of the territory of the USSR and contributed just over half of its population. As late as 1990 Yeltsin was saying it was 'unthinkable' for Russia to become independent from the Soviet Union.[3] Yet in that same year he insisted that the laws of the Union must not contravene those of Russia and that Russia was primary, the federal 'centre' secondary.[4]

Yeltsin, however, accepted the logic of his evolving position and subsequent actions when, along with Stanislav Shushkevich and Leonid Kravchuk, the presidents of Belarus and Ukraine, he announced the dissolution of the Soviet Union following their meeting at the Belavezhskaya Pushcha hunting resort near Brest in December 1991. He held that the boundaries of the Soviet successor states, Russia included, which existed at the end of the Soviet era, should be respected. There remained, nevertheless, a problem of reconciling Russian national identify with its new, weakened, and reduced statehood. From this the Russian president was not immune. Yitzhak Brudny has observed that in '1992 and 1993, Yeltsin did nothing to articulate a new democratic conception of the Russian nation' and that 'his rhetoric about the defense of the rights of ethnic Russians in the former Soviet republics legitimized the use of the nondemocratic ethnic definition of the Russian nation'.[5]

Even rhetorically, however, Yeltsin was no Milosević, and he sought peaceful relations with the other Soviet successor states. Preserving the territorial integrity of the new Russian state was another matter. To achieve this Yeltsin, on the one hand, made large concessions in a series of bilateral treaties to particular republics (most notably Tatarstan) and, on the other hand, gave his blessing to two fierce military onslaughts (in 1994–6 and again from 1999) on Chechnya. While Chechnya had become a barely governable republic and one in which a great deal of criminal activity was concentrated, the indiscriminate use of force by Russian troops, which brought about the deaths of tens of thousands of civilians (including many ethnic Russians during the bombardment of the Chechen capital of Grozny), pointed up the sharp distinction the Russian authorities made between what was permissible within the boundaries of their state and what was acceptable or prudent beyond them. The ruthlessness with which the two post-Soviet Chechen wars were conducted was at one and the same time counterproductive in terms of winning the hearts and minds of Chechens (and of promoting a harmonious future for Chechnya within the Russian Federation) and yet productive (because it illustrated the horrific potential costs) in discouraging any other republic from unilaterally asserting independence from the Russian state.

---

[2] Karen Dawisha and Bruce Parrott, *Russia and the New States of Eurasia: The Politics of Upheaval* (Cambridge: Cambridge University Press, 1994), 41.

[3] Leon Aron, *Boris Yeltsin: A Revolutionary Life* (London: HarperCollins, 2000), 375.

[4] Ibid. 377.

[5] Yitzhak Brudny, *Reinventing Russia: Russian Nationalism and the Soviet State 1953–1991* (Cambridge, Mass.: Harvard University Press, 1998), 264.

The problems of state building and rebuilding, of Russian elite perceptions of their nation-hood, and the identity crisis which the collapse of the Soviet Union provoked are analysed in the three chapters which follow in this section. Gail Lapidus, in Chapter 24, sees little evidence of serious political separatism in the Russian Federation with the significant exception of the Northern Caucasus where the conflict in Chechnya has the potential to cause instability in neighbouring republics, not least Dagestan. In contrast with the Soviet Union, Lapidus observes, Russians are not only much more dominant within the population of the country as a whole but they are also much more strongly represented within the republics of the Russian Federation, in fewer than half of which the titular nationality constitutes a majority of the inhabitants.

In the following chapter, Vera Tolz charts the variety of conceptions of the Russian nation to be found within the political elite. She notes the distinction which some, at least, among them make between the civic definition of Russian nationality and the ethnic (with the term, *rossiyskiy*, embracing all citizens of the Russian Federation regardless of their ethnicity, culture, language, and religion, and *russkiy* referring to ethnic Russians). The December 1993 Constitution, as Tolz observes, embraces the civic conception of the Russian people as 'a community of citizens' (*rossiyskiy narod*). But this notion remains essentially contested for, as Tolz also makes clear, there are important political actors in Russia for whom Russian identity is meaningful only within the context of a broader Union and others for whom it is either essentially Slavic or defined linguistically in terms of Russian speakers.

In the concluding chapter of the section, Ronald Suny likewise notes the lack of consensus on national and state identity in post-Soviet Russia and the difficulty the Russian Federation has had even on agreeing on the symbols of its statehood. In late 2000 (it is possible to add) it became clear that the Russian tricolour would survive as the national flag, but that it would be accompanied—in an interesting admixture of Soviet and Russian symbolism—by a return to the music of the national anthem of the USSR, albeit with new words. Notwithstanding the identity crisis, Suny sees evidence of a growing, if grudging, acceptance on the part of the Russian political elite of the continuing separate existence of the other successor states to the Soviet Union. Like the United States in the first half of the nineteenth century, he suggests, Russia is 'consolidating state authority over its own territory, defining its borders, and policing its neighborhood to prevent any rivals from establishing influence in its sphere of interest'.

24 State Building and State Breakdown in Russia

Gail W. Lapidus

In the seven years that have elapsed since the dissolution of the Soviet Union, the Russian Federation has been haunted by the specter of its own possible disintegration. Even before the demise of the USSR, a number of political actors and analysts had expressed their fear that by joining the struggle for sovereignty of other Union Republics, Russia had placed its own territorial integrity in jeopardy. Alarmed at the potential 'domino effect' of Russia's declaration of sovereignty, Aleksandr Tsipko warned at the time: 'the stronger the striving of the RSFSR to free itself from the center, the stronger will be the desire of the autonomous formations to free themselves from Yel'tsin . . . The relationship of "Russia to the autonomies" is constructed on the same principle as that of "the Union to the RSFSR".'[1] Similar views were echoed by Andranik Migranyan, who asserted: 'The bomb planted under the USSR by the declaration of Russian sovereignty is, it seems to me, facilitating not only the destruction of the USSR but also—to an even greater extent—the destruction of Russia itself . . . Where are the geographical boundaries of the republic that is supposed to represent ethnic Russians?'[2]

These widespread and continuing anxieties about the potential for separatism on the part of Russia's ethnic republics, which were fueled further by developments in Tatarstan and Chechnya in particular, were tersely captured in the title of a 1993 article by a leading Russian specialist on nationality issues: 'Will Russia Repeat the Path of the Union?'[3] Indeed, the conflict with Chechnya came to be viewed as a test of the Federation's viability, with advocates of the use of force insisting that unless Chechnya's secession-minded leadership were brought to heel it could trigger the unraveling of the entire Federation.

In retrospect, these anxieties regarding potential secessionism in the ethnic republics proved to be exaggerated. The demands for sovereignty on the part of Tatarstan were ultimately resolved through negotiations, and arguably a political solution could have been found to the conflict with Chechnya as well.[4] Although a comprehensive analysis of the reasons why the danger of ethnic separatism has not materialized lies beyond the scope of

This chapter was originally published as 'Asymmetrical Federalism and State Breakdown in Russia', in *Post-Soviet Affairs*, 15/1 (1999), 74–82. Reproduced by kind permission of the author and V. H. Winston (Bellwether Publishing).

[1] John Dunlop, *The Rise of Russia and the Fall of the Soviet Empire* (Princeton: Princeton University Press, 1993), 64.

[2] *Izvestiya*, 20 Sept. 1990.

[3] Leokadiya Drobizheva, 'Povtorit li Rossiya put' Soyuza,' in Liliya Shevtsova, ed., *Rossiya segodnya: Trudnyye poiski svobody* (Moscow: Institut mezhdunarodnykh ekonomicheskikh i politicheskikh issledovaniy, 1993).

[4] This argument is developed in Gail W. Lapidus, 'Contested Sovereignty: The Case of Chechnya,' *International Security*, 23/1 (1998): 5–49.

this article, several factors deserve to be mentioned here. First, the alleged structural parallels between the USSR and the Russian Federation (RF) that are believed conducive to ethno-national separatism do not stand up to closer examination. Despite the fact that the Russian Federation inherited key elements of the ethno-territorial structure of the Soviet Union, its structure is far less conducive to ethnic fragmentation than was that of the USSR. The USSR could be described as a Russian heartland surrounded, on its northwestern, western, and southern peripheries, by non-Russian republics; the 21 ethnically-defined republics of the Russian Federation, by contrast, are more like islands in an ethnically Russian sea, and most lack external borders.[5] Moreover, its demographic structure is strikingly different as well. Not only is the RF ethnically far more homogeneous than was the USSR, with an ethnic Russian population constituting almost 85 percent of the total, but within the ethnic republics of the Federation the titular nationality does not occupy the same dominating role, constituting a majority in fewer than half the republics. By contrast with the Union Republics of the USSR, Russia's republics never enjoyed the same broad panoply of political, economic, cultural, and foreign policy institutions, nor formal recognition of the right to secession. And unlike the Baltic states and Georgia, they lacked (with the possible exception of Tyva) any experience of independent statehood.

Not only is the institutional basis for mobilization weaker; so too is the political impetus. Although the process of national revival in the late Soviet period allowed a variety of grievances to be expressed, and gave voice to resentment against imperial conquest and exploitation, the government of post-Communist Russia was arguably less of a target for such grievances than had been the Soviet center. Moreover, by contrast with the national movements of the late Soviet era, in which anti-Russian sentiments were subsumed in a broader struggle for reform of the Soviet system and against Communist rule, national movements in the republics of post-Communist Russia were oriented toward ethnic rather than civic nationalism and were deprived of all but anti-Russian sentiments as the focus of mobilization. Indeed, Moscow's readiness to strike bargains with regional elites, and, with the notable exception of Chechnya, its effort to seek consensus rather than confrontation, also worked to defuse latent conflicts and antagonism.

Finally, although there continues to be a significant degree of support for the right of secession among the populations of a number of republics,[6] there has been little tendency to actually mobilize around it. Indeed, the past few years have been characterized by a notable degree of ethnic and political de-mobilization across the entire region of the former Soviet Union, as well as within the Russian Federation itself.[7] Recent analyses of popular attitudes

---

[5] The Russian Federation consists of eighty-nine subjects, divided into two broad categories: ethno-territorial units, which include twenty-one republics, and purely administrative territorial regions (oblasts and krays) populated mostly by Russians.

[6] A recent survey carried out by a team of researchers under the leadership of Leokadiya Drobizheva in several republics and regions of the Russian Federation in 1998 found strong support for the right of secession, with such a right being asserted by 54 percent of respondents in Tatarstan, 44.5 percent in Northern Ossetiya-Mania, and 60.4 percent in Sakha/Yakutiya. From 71 percent to 85 percent considered the use of Russian force in such circumstances to be unacceptable. See Leokadiya Drobizheva, 'Etnicheskiye i administrativnyye granitsy: Faktory stabil'nosti i konfliktov', Unpublished manuscript. Moscow: Institut etnologii i antropologii, Russian Academy of Sciences, 1998.

[7] Mark Beissinger, 'Event Analysis in Transitional Societies: Protest Mobilization in the Former Soviet Union,' in Dieter Rucht, Friedhelm Neidhardt, and Ruud Koopmans, eds., *Acts of Dissent: New Developments in the Study of Protest* (Berlin: Sigma Press, 1998).

suggest that the dissolution of the USSR, along with the catastrophic war in Chechnya, far from stimulating further separatism, have been sobering experiences; fears of disintegration and violence have turned out to play a moderating rather than a precipitating role. Although Moscow's use of force provoked harsh criticism and some countermeasures in a number of republics, the overall effect of the war was to dampen ethnonational separatism.

Moreover, as the war in Chechnya demonstrated once again, the international community is demonstrably unwilling to offer political support to secessionist movements. In view of its unequivocal support for the territorial integrity of the Russian Federation,[8] no republic elites could be under any illusion that foreign governments could be counted on to support their efforts. It is therefore reasonable to conclude that, barring unusual circumstances to be discussed later, ethnonational challenges to the federal center on the part of the constituent republics remain highly unlikely.

If separatist tendencies in the republics were earlier the main focus of concern, in the past few years it is the growing trends toward autarchy in the Russian regions that have increasingly attracted the attention, and the alarm, of analysts and political elites alike. While a healthy dose of decentralization was initially viewed as an important element of political democratization, given a long tradition of hyper-centralization of state power, Russia now faces an uncontrolled and seemingly uncontrollable unraveling of central power. It is above all the striking weakness of the Russian state, and the capricious and *ad hoc* quality of decision making, that are largely responsible for the growing assertiveness of regional elites, and that have encouraged the regions to act independently, and often in outright defiance, of central authority. This trend has given rise to fears that, at best, Russia is being progressively transformed from a federation to a confederation, and at worst that it will be thrown backward to the period of medieval chaos and conflict known as the era of 'appanage principalities.'

The economic and political crisis that came to a head in August 1998 dramatically accelerated these trends, as one regional leader after another announced radical measures to cope with the crisis by insulating his own region from its fallout. The heightened alarm generated by all these developments was dramatically expressed by newly-elected Prime Minister Yevgeniy Primakov in his first address to the Russian Duma on September 12, 1998. Voicing grave concern that Russia was in danger of breaking up, Primakov announced that the first priority of his new government would be the preservation of Russia's unity. 'This issue is far from theoretical at the moment, and far from hypothetical . . . We are facing a most serious danger, the most serious danger that our country will split into separate parts.'[9] In an effort to enhance the stake of regional elites in the fate of Russia as a whole, he announced that among his first initiatives would be an effort to give selected regional governors a more influential and visible role in national policy-making.

While a comprehensive examination of the sources and dynamics of center-periphery conflicts, and of the impact of the current political and economic crisis on them, is beyond the scope of this chapter, most of the issues at stake can be broadly grouped into two categories: political conflicts over issues of jurisdiction between center and periphery, and economic conflicts over the control and allocation of resources.[10] Indeed, the centrality of

---

[8] See Lapidus, 'Contested Sovereignty'.   [9] Quoted in *The Daily Telegraph*, 12 Sept. 1998, p. 17.

[10] This analysis excludes from consideration another category of conflicts, the 'horizontal' interethnic tensions and conflicts within and between republics.

these issues has dramatically altered the entire framework of discussion about federalism and center-periphery relations. To put it briefly, whereas much of the earlier discussions revolved around conflictual relations between the central government and the republics, and the relative status of republics compared to regions, in recent years, as much of the distinction between republics and regions has been eroded, other bases of cleavage have become more salient. In part this reflects the deliberate effort of the federal government to relativize the special privileges initially granted to the republics in the negotiations over the Federation Treaty of 1993 and in the bilateral treaties signed with individual republics. The resentment of the regions over what they considered their second-class status in an asymmetrical federation that granted what were, in their view, unjustified privileges to republics was partly defused by the Constitution of December 1993, which ignored the Federation Treaty and treated republics and regions as more or less equals.[11] Moreover, when the federal government effectively upgraded the status of the regions by proceeding to negotiate bilateral treaties with them as well, concerns over economic regionalism began to displace the focus on ethnic separatism. In the often chaotic and *ad hoc* bargaining process surrounding these negotiations, the demands of republic and regional elites tended to converge around similar issues: greater political and economic control over decisions affecting their regions or republics, and more favorable treatment with respect to taxation and resource allocation. Despite the widespread support for 'sovereignty,' there was in fact little expectation of or demand for separate monetary systems, military forces, foreign policies (as distinct from the development of economic ties with foreign partners), or other attributes of independent statehood. If the threat of secession once gave the republics a unique source of leverage in bargaining with the center, arguably the governors of key regions have available to them other assets that can be deployed.

These trends generated two broad types of conflict between federal authorities and regional elites. The first were largely conflicts over jurisdiction: over who has the right to make authoritative decisions over such issues as appointments of local officials, electoral rules, privatization, tax rates, the stationing of conscripts, or regulations concerning property rights. Despite a three-year-long effort to arrive at a demarcation of the respective powers of federal and regional authorities that would establish clear and transparent 'rules of the game,' their application continues to be highly contentious in practice. Some provisions of previously-signed treaties conflict with the Constitution or with other federal laws; others occupy ambiguous 'gray areas' whose status is contested. Consequently, center-periphery relations have been characterized by an ongoing 'war of laws' in which federal authorities seek to overturn decisions by local governments that are alleged to violate provisions of the Constitution or federal decrees, while local authorities retain considerable ability to block the implementation of these directives.

The federal government is not without instruments to enforce its will. At a high-level conference convened in January 1998 to discuss the problems and prospects of Russian federalism, Prosecutor-General (*Prokurator*) Yuriy Skuratov asserted that over the last two years, prosecutors at all levels had challenged and reversed over 2000 laws and resolutions

---

[11] For a more extensive treatment, see Gail W. Lapidus and Edward W. Walker, 'Nationalism, Regionalism and Federalism: Center-Periphery Relations in Post-Communist Russia,' in Gail W. Lapidus, ed., *The New Russia: Troubled Transformation* (Boulder, Colo.: Westview Press, 1995).

passed by regional legislatures that violated the Russian Constitution. Nonetheless, the report to the conference prepared by a commission of experts expressed concern over the 'contradictory and inconsistent nature of measures implemented to build a federal state in Russia,' and asserted that Russia was governed by methods characteristic of both unitary and confederal states.[12]

A second category of conflicts has centered on issues of resource allocation: (1) struggles over the level of federal taxes to be paid by regions and over the amount of subsidies to be returned to them; (2) struggles over the control and disposition of natural resources; (3) conflicts over the growing trend for regional authorities to issue their own currency equivalents; and (4) efforts to impose restrictions on the flow of goods into and out of regions, which violate the principle of a unified economic space across the Russian Federation.

While these conflicts reveal the chaotic and contradictory impulses that have shaped the development of federalism in Russia, given the enormity and variety of the challenges confronting the country the accommodationist thrust of central policies has on the whole served to defuse potential confrontations and provides a useful degree of flexibility in responding to the very divergent needs of extraordinarily diverse regions.

The economic and political crisis of August 1998 had immediate and far-reaching consequences in the regions, not only accelerating many of these trends but forcing the regions to become even more self-sufficient. With the ruble falling precipitously in value, bank accounts frozen, the price of consumer goods soaring and their availability shrinking, and panic spreading, regional elites were compelled to find their own ways to deal with the crisis. As one commentator put it, 'the collapse of the ruble and the banking system is nothing compared to the collapse of the Federation's political institutions. The central authorities' inactivity is forcing the regions to act on the principle of "every man for himself." The governors and presidents, realizing they can't expect any kind of specific guidelines from the center, much less any assistance, are taking extraordinary measures to keep the situation under control. The crisis management experience the regional elites have acquired and the additional powers they have assumed over the past few weeks will inevitably make Russia into a confederation.'[13] While this may well be an overstatement, the remarks speak to a serious set of problems.

The measures adopted by a number of regional leaders to cope with the crisis fell into several broad categories. A first set of measures were an effort to concentrate authority at the regional level for dealing with the crisis: the governor of Kaliningrad region declared an outright state of emergency, notwithstanding the fact that only the President of Russia is empowered to do so, while in other regions, including Nizhnyy Novgorod and Sverdlovsk, anti-crisis committees with virtually dictatorial powers were hastily established to ensure the continued functioning of economic and especially financial institutions. Secondly, a large number of regions and republics responded by introducing price controls on a range of basic foodstuffs and consumer goods in an effort to insulate their populations from the effects of inflation. Many regions imposed restrictions on the export of agricultural products from their territories, in violation of federal laws guaranteeing the free movement of goods and services throughout the Russian Federation. In some regions measures were adopted that sought to insulate local banks from the repercussions of the financial collapse

[12] Serebrennikov, in ITAR-TASS Moscow, English edn. 19 Jan. 1998.   [13] *Nezavisimaya gazeta*, 10 Sept. 1998, p. 2.

by halting the transfers of depositors' funds to Moscow or by organizing regional systems of internal and external settlements independent of the central banking system. And faced with little prospect of actually receiving the federal transfer payments to which they were nominally entitled, a growing number of regions either deducted those sums from tax revenues owed to Moscow or declined to transfer tax revenues altogether.[14]

These moves were described in highly alarmist terms in the national press. In the pages of *Izvestiya*, Valeriy Konovalov referred to 'food separatism' as even more powerful than political separatism, while a commentator on *Ekho Moskvy* declared August 17 to be the day when the regions began their existence as entities separate from Moscow.[15] While it is too early to judge the longer-term consequences of these developments, both the response of the federal authorities and the effects of market forces themselves acted to constrain and limit many of these trends. Restrictions on the export of goods prompted retaliation by neighboring regions; price controls reduced the willingness of suppliers to provide food and other staples; and the federal government acted swiftly, and in many instances successfully, to confront challenges to its authority. Alongside the more coercive measures available to it, the federal government also continued to wield a significant number of carrots: federal subsidies still play an important role in many regional budgets, and the large number of federally-owned properties in the regions—from military-industrial enterprises to the energy monopolies to the railroads—all employing large numbers of workers, depend on federal funding for their continued operation. Even the ability of regional leaders to attract the foreign investment and partners they count on to promote the development of their regions depends on the cooperation as well as the reputation of the federal government. It is not surprising, then, that by contrast with the situation that prevailed in the late 1980s no major political figures publicly advocate the further devolution of power in the Russian Federation; indeed all the leading candidates for the presidency have called rather for the strengthening of the state and a struggle against disintegrative tendencies.

What the above sketch suggests, however, is that the growing weakness of the federal center and its failure to meet the expectations once vested in it have had several longer-term consequences. They have multiplied the conflicts between center and periphery over jurisdictional and distributive issues, as the regions seek to assert greater control over power and resources. They have also contributed to a shift in focus away from a concentration on bargaining with Moscow to one of seeking regional strategies for survival as more self-sufficient entities, particularly in the case of wealthier and more resource-rich regions, or regions in the Far East with the potential for extensive foreign economic ties, such as the Amur and Sakhalin regions and the Maritime and Khabarovsk krays.[16] This tendency goes hand in hand with increasing public confidence in their own regional governments and a pervasive decline in confidence in the Moscow authorities. A survey commissioned by USIA and carried out in late 1997 confirmed that not only was confidence in regional governments

---

[14] Tatarstan, Bashkiriya, Kaliningrad, and Tomsk reduced or eliminated tax payments, while Kalmykiya planned to print rubles to replace tax revenues that had mysteriously disappeared from its National Bank, prompting federal authorities to liquidate the bank and shift its functions to the Volgograd region.

[15] Emil Pain, presentation at Stanford University, 6 Nov. 1998.

[16] For a discussion of these centrifugal trends, see Sergey Khenkhin, 'Separatizm v Rossii—pozadi ili vperedi?', *Pro et Contra*, 2/2 (1997): 5–19.

considerably higher than in the federal government, but it had grown from roughly 20 percent in 1992 to 44 percent by late 1997.[17]

A further notable trend is the growing diversity among the country's regions. Economic inequality has been accelerated by the weakening of the central government's redistributive capacity as well as by the diverse endowments of different regions, which give them differing potential to participate in the local as well as global economy. The traditional cleavage between 'donor' and 'subsidized' subjects of the federation has now been overlaid by the differences among raw-materials exporting regions, agricultural regions, and those with strong concentrations of heavy and military industry. According to one estimate, in 1990 the 10 most developed regions had a per capita industrial and agricultural output 2.3 times greater than that of the 10 least developed; in 1996 the gap had increased to 4.5.[18] The regions are also characterized by increasingly diverse leadership strategies and capacities, making the Russian federation a virtual laboratory for testing different developmental models.[19]

What does all this herald for center-periphery relations in the near term? The northern Caucasus constitutes a special case, with Chechnya effectively out of central control and a high potential for conflict and instability in neighboring republics, Dagestan in particular. A further contraction of Russian power in this region is not out of the question. Elsewhere in the Russian Federation we witness growing economic and political autarchy in regions and republics alike, but little evidence of serious political separatism. This picture could be altered significantly by two possible developments. The inability of the central government to provide for the welfare of military units across the territory of Russia has already made them increasingly dependent on local authorities. Were this trend to continue and intensify, the regionalization of the armed forces could significantly increase the capabilities of regional elites and create new temptations and dangers. The other potentially destabilizing trend would be the emergence of political actors promoting aggressive forms of Russian nationalism and chauvinism to advance their political ambitions. Actions that would threaten the autonomy and status of non-Russian populations and republics, or seek to mobilize Russian diasporas in neighboring states, could trigger an escalation of interethnic tensions and regional conflicts both within the Russian federation and along its periphery. But they would do little to address the more fundamental challenges of state-building in contemporary Russia.

---

[17] The survey also demonstrated considerable variations among regions in the level of public trust, ranging from highs of 81 percent in Oryol *oblast'*, 73 percent in Kemerovo, and 66 percent in Moscow city to a low of 21 percent in Vladimir *oblast'*. United States Information Agency, 'Russia's Regional Governments Are Gaining Public Confidence,' *USIA Opinion Analysis*. Washington, DC: USIA, 23 Jan. 1998.

[18] *Rabochaya tribuna*, 17 Jan. 1998, as translated in *FBIS Daily Report—Central Eurasia*, FBIS-SOV-98-019, 19 Jan. 1998.

[19] For a study explicitly focusing on such regional variations, see Mary McAuley, *Russia's Politics of Uncertainty* (Cambridge: Cambridge University Press, 1997).

25   Politicians' Conceptions of the Russian Nation

Vera Tolz

This extract from a longer article explores the views of Russia's politicians on what constitutes a Russian nation. It looks at the position of President Yeltsin and members of the presidential apparatus as well as at the views of the communist and nationalist opposition heavily represented in the Russian Congress of People's Deputies and the two subsequent Dumas. It also discusses the views of political elites in the ethnic autonomies of the Russian Federation (RF).

The executive branch

As far as the president and the executive branch are concerned we can identify the following approaches to nation building: attempts to define a nation in civic terms—as the nation of *Rossiyane*, i.e. a community of citizens of the RF regardless of their ethnicity; the definition of the Russian nation as RF citizens plus ethnic Russians and Russian speakers residing in the 'near abroad'; and finally, beliefs in the common eastern Slavic identity and in the continuing strength of the Union identity. These are exactly the same notions of a nation which are put forward in intellectual debates. All these visions have had an impact on Russia's policies towards the newly independent states, with one or the other vision prevailing at different times.

Between the autumn of 1991 and late 1992, Yeltsin's government demonstrated unequivocal commitment to de-ethnicised state building and to the strengthening of the civic identities of all citizens of the RF regardless of their ethnicity. This distinguished Russia from other newly independent states, whose governments' nation and state-building policies reflected a simultaneous reliance on both civic and ethnic identities. The majority of declarations of independence and new laws of the non-Russian states of the former Soviet Union described these states as territorial entities created on behalf of all the people residing there. But at the same time, the same legislation defined these new statehoods as a form of self-determination for dominant ethnic communities.

In contrast, no ethnonational doctrine was officially promoted in the RF in 1991–92. At the same time, the adherence to a common Union identity was stronger among politicians in Russia than among their counterparts in the non-Russian newly independent states. Both trends were reflected in the Russian citizenship law adopted on 28 November 1991, which calls a citizen of the RF not *russkii* (ethnic Russian), but *rossiyanin* (defined in civic terms

This chapter is adapted and substantially abbreviated from 'Forging the Nation: National Identity and Nation-Building in Post-Communist Russia', *Europe-Asia Studies*, 50/6 (1998), 993–1022. Reproduced by kind permission of the author and Carfax Publishers Ltd.

regardless of ethnicity). The law recognised all those living in RF territory at the time of its adoption as its citizens.[1] All other former union republics, with the exception of Estonia and Latvia, also adopted the territorial definition of citizenship. Yet the naturalisation process is more complicated in the non-Russian newly independent states than it is in the RF. The citizenship laws of the former make reference to what can be defined as an ethnic attribute—i.e. they state that to become a citizen by naturalisation one must have a knowledge of the state language. The RF citizenship law does not include this requirement. Instead, the only requirement for foreigners or stateless people who themselves and whose parents have never had Soviet or RF citizenship is to live in the territory of the RF for three years sequentially or for five years altogether, if the period of residence was interrupted. Moreover, in a manifestation of the belief in a common Union identity, the Russian citizenship law allowed all citizens of the USSR living outside the RF on 1 September 1991 to obtain RF citizenship by a simple process of registration, if they did not already possess citizenship of another newly independent state. This provision did not require former USSR citizens to move to Russia. Its termination in June 1994 was a response to protests from Estonia and Ukraine.[2] The law also allows all former citizens of the USSR to move into Russia to register automatically as RF citizens.

In sum, the RF citizenship law was explicitly lacking in any references to ethnic definitions of a nation compared with the laws of all the other newly independent states and did not give any preferential treatment to either ethnic Russians or Russian speakers compared with other citizens of the former USSR. Thus the law pointed to a mixture of RF civic and Union identities as the identities of the people whom the RF leadership believed it was governing. Russia's former foreign minister Andrei Kozyrev emphatically argued up until the autumn of 1992 that Russians and Russian speakers in the newly independent states did not constitute a specific problem for the Russian government.[3] At the time, as far as the majority in the executive branch of the government was concerned, Russian-speaking settlers in the 'near abroad' were not part of the Russian (*rossiiskaya*) nation, which was defined in territorial and political terms.

However, in 1993–94, largely under the influence of opposition forces in the Congress of People's Deputies and of some members within the executive branch, the attitude towards Russians and Russian speakers in the 'near abroad' on the part of Yeltsin and members of his government changed. In the discourse of Russian politicians, Russian speakers in the newly independent states started to be defined as an integral part of the Russian nation. In official speeches and various resolutions of the government, they began to be described as *Rossiiskaya diaspora*, for whom the RF was the homeland (*rodina*). It was in 1994 that the definition of the Russian nation as all citizens of the RF plus the communities of Russian speakers abroad seems to have had the greatest impact on the policies and official pronouncements of the Russian government. In his 1994 New Year Address to the nation Yeltsin specifically appealed to the diaspora by saying 'Dear compatriots (*sootechestvenniki*)! You are

[1] For the text of the law see *Vedomosti Rossiiskoi Federatsii*, 6 (1992), 308–20. See also 'Polozhenie o poryadke rassmotreniya voprosov grazhdanstva RF', *Rossiiskie vesti*, 23 Feb. 1994, p. 4.

[2] See article 18d of the citizenship law in its 1993 edition as quoted in Igor Zevelev, 'Russia and the Russian Diaspora', *Post-Soviet Affairs*, 12/3 (1996), 272.

[3] *Izvestiya*, 2 Jan. 1992, p. 3; *Nezavisimaya gazeta*, 20 Aug. 1992. See also Neil Melvin, *Russians Beyond Russia. The Politics of National Identity* (London, 1995), 11–12.

inseparable from us and we are inseparable from you. We were and we will be together'. A similar statement was repeated by Yeltsin in his annual address to the parliament that year.[4] This twist in Yeltsin's position was understandable. The notion of a civic nation was still very novel in Russia, whereas the definition of Russianness by language and culture had a long tradition.

It is sometimes assumed that all Russian politicians, including those who call themselves democrats, regard ethno-cultural (first of all language) characteristics as superior to citizenship in determining national identity and thereby overlook the fact that among 30 million Russians and Russian speakers in the 'near abroad' only 800 000 are RF citizens.[5] This is not true, however. Attempts to define Russian national identity in civic terms have never been fully abandoned by Yeltsin's government. In fact, even this broad definition of the Russian nation as a community of Russian speakers had an element of civic identity. That is why in 1993–late 1994 the Yeltsin government's policy towards the diaspora focused on persuading the governments of non-Russian newly independent states to grant dual citizenship to members of the diaspora.

Moreover, Yeltsin's address to the parliament in 1994 also mentioned a different (civic-territorial) definition of the Russian (*rossiiskaya*) nation as a co-citizenship (*sograzhdanstvo*) of people of the RF regardless of their ethnicity, culture, language and religion. Similarly, the Russian constitution adopted in December 1993 also defines the Russian people (*rossiiskii narod*) as a community of citizens.

The refusal of all the newly independent states, with the exception of Turkmenistan and Tajikistan (with the smallest Russian-speaking communities), to agree to the Russian proposal for dual citizenship meant a virtual collapse in 1995 of the Russian policy towards the 'near abroad' which took Russian speakers as the main focus of its attention.[6] The revision of Russian government policy had the following consequences: first, to return partially to the idea of a common Union identity; second, to try strengthening the common eastern Slavic identity; and finally (and simultaneously) to strengthen a new civic identity by searching for a unifying national idea, which could create a bond between all citizens of the RF and increase their loyalty to the new state.

Following the failure of the Russian government's policy of making newly independent states introduce dual citizenship for their Russian speakers, the Yeltsin leadership drastically increased efforts aimed at facilitating the reintegration of Russia and other newly independent states within the Commonwealth of Independent States (CIS). Instead of dual citizenship for Russians and Russian speakers, the Russian government began advocating CIS citizenship, which could strengthen a Union identity of Russians and other peoples of the former USSR. Even liberal members of the government began to refer cautiously to the possibility of reviving some form of union. In May 1996 *Nezavisimaya gazeta* published a working paper of the Council for Foreign and Defence Policy, a body staffed by moderate reformers, which claimed that the revival of the Union was feasible. The authors of the paper believed that the formation of a Russian national statehood was impossible, unless a full-fledged economic, political and military union was revived on the territory of the

---

[4] *Rossiiskaya gazeta*, 25 Feb. 1994. See also Melvin, *Russians Beyond Russia*, 18–24.

[5] P. Goble, 'Three Faces of Nationalism in the Former Soviet Union', in C. Kupchan (ed.), *Nationalism and Nationalities in the New Europe* (Ithaca, NY, 1995), 131.

[6] Zevelev, 'Russia and the Russian Diaspora', 272.

former USSR. The working paper also divided the former Soviet republics into categories, according to their importance for Russia. Ukraine and Belarus were regarded as those of the greatest importance.[7]

The view of the Council on the importance of Ukraine and Belarus for the formation of Russian national identity is shared by the majority in Yeltsin's government, although the president has never claimed that Ukrainians and Belarussians belong to the Russian nation. In May 1997 the presidents of Russia and Belarus signed a Charter on the Union between the two countries. The charter stipulated, among other things, that the two countries should introduce common citizenship. Yeltsin had even insisted that the charter include a provision to the effect that the two countries would eventually merge into a single state, but this was rejected by the Belarus side.[8] But even common citizenship, if indeed introduced, will have a significant impact on the formation of national identities of the citizens of the RF and Belarus. On numerous occasions, members of the Russian government have indicated their desire to have a similar arrangement with Ukraine. This is impossible, however, owing to the strong resistance of the Ukrainian leadership. It is noteworthy that efforts to facilitate CIS integration and secure a union with Belarus were most intensive during Yeltsin's presidential election campaign, as he apparently believed that most of his electorate had either Union or Slavic identities.

After the presidential election was over, the government returned to policies aimed at strengthening the civic identity of various peoples of the RF. Members of the government expressed a belief that the existence of such a compound civic identity could facilitate social mobilisation in support of government reforms. Largely in line with the Soviet and pre-revolutionary Russian traditions of a strong role of the state in forging national unity, the current Russian government believes in the supreme role of the state in a nation-building project. The underdevelopment of civil society has always been a justification for this approach. The question is how such a compound identity can be formed. According to the main advocate of civic nationalism in Russia, Tishkov, Yeltsin's government has not paid enough attention to the need to cultivate new symbols and values which would be meaningful to all citizens of the RF regardless of their ethnicity. It seems that, partly in response to this criticism, after his re-election as president in July 1996, in his address to the people Yeltsin urged society to search for a new 'Russian national idea'. *Rossiiskaya gazeta* was chosen as the vehicle to publicise the results of the search.[9] Most of the suggestions published in the newspaper spoke of the encouragement of state patriotism. This approach is not new. From the time of Peter the Great and Catherine the Great, Russian rulers have felt that it was up to them to unite society by promoting state patriotism—namely, people's unity around the tsar (or the Communist Party leadership) thanks to their pride in belonging to and serving a strong state. However, in 1917 and 1991 state patriotism could not prevent the disintegration of the country when it was in deep crisis. So, critics of Yeltsin's project of searching for a unifying idea say that the whole enterprise is futile because it is not the government's business to be a bearer of a nation-building project in the first place, and

---

[7] *Nezavisimaya gazeta*, 23 May 1996.

[8] *Moskovskie novosti*, 18–26 May 1997, p. 7; *Izvestiya*, 24 May 1997.

[9] *Rossiiskaya gazeta* began publishing various views on a new 'Russian idea' on 30 July 1996. See also *Rossiiskaya gazeta*, 11 Feb. 1997, p. 4, for the results of the search.

because especially now, when the weakness of the state is so apparent, the promotion of state patriotism cannot bring any results.[10]

The parliamentary opposition

Commitment towards encouraging a civic identity among citizens of the RF is not shared by the communist and nationalist opposition. Among the majority of opposition members, strongly represented in the legislative branch of government, three main visions of the Russian identity coexist. The first is that Russian identity has a meaning only within the framework of a broader Union identity; the second is that the Russian identity is a Slavic one, and the third is the definition of Russianness by the linguistic marker. The leader of the Communist Party of the RF (CPRF), Gennadii Zyuganov, argues that the Russian empire and the USSR constituted a unique Russian civilisation, all of whose members had a common identity. To support his views he refers primarily to the works by Danilevsky, Ilin and the Eurasianists. This position is, however, combined with his simultaneous belief that the Russian identity is actually Slavic. In his books *Derzhava* and *Za gorizontom*, Zyuganov unequivocally includes Ukrainians and Belarussians into the Russian nation, referring to nineteenth-century Russian historians to prove his point.[11] He also unequivocally regards all the Russians and Russian speakers abroad, regardless of their citizenship, as an integral part of the Russian nation and argues that 'without the reunification of the divided Russian people our state would never rise from its knees'.[12] Therefore, in using symbols and appealing to common values which could unite the people, the CPRF mixes those of the Soviet period (first of all the red flag) with those of the Russian empire, which would have a meaning only to ethnic Russians. For instance, nowadays many communists promote Orthodoxy as a key element of Russian national identity and argue in favour of state support for the Russian Orthodox Church, without considering what it would mean for non-Orthodox citizens of the RF. The position of ultra-nationalists, represented in the 1993 and 1995 Dumas by Vladimir Zhirinovsky's Liberal Democratic Party of Russia, is similar to that of Zyuganov, i.e. it is a mixture of the three main above-mentioned identities. In sum, to members of the radical communist-nationalist opposition, civic identity has no appeal, whereas a common Union identity has the overwhelming preference. However, the definitions of the Russian nation as a community of eastern Slavs or as the community of all Russian speakers in the former USSR are regarded as alternative possibilities, if the recreation of the Union fails.

More moderate nationalists, such as Stanislav Govorukhin, who leads a bloc bearing his name in the Duma, view the Russian nation as a community of eastern Slavs plus all Russian speakers in non-Slavic newly independent states. Despite the fact that in March 1996 the bloc voted in favour of the Duma resolution, put forward by the communists and the LDPR, which proclaimed the Belovezhe Accord null and void, Govorukhin is not in favour of the

---

[10]   See, for instance, D. Likhachev in *Novaya gazeta*, 9 Dec. 1996, p. 1; T. Uklyuchina in *Segodnya*, 1 Aug. 1995, p. 3; and Yu. Afanasev in *Delovoi mir*, 15 Apr. 1995.

[11]   G. Zyuganov, *Za gorizontom* (Moscow: Informpechat, 1995), 38. Zyuganov regularly singles out two figures whom he regards as the main authorities on Russian history—Danilevsky and Stalin. He praises the latter because he officially condemned Pokrovsky's theories and rehabilitated the views of nineteenth century Russian historians.

[12]   Quoted in *Nezavisimaya gazeta*, 15 Dec. 1995, p. 2.

restoration of the USSR as he does not view all former Soviet citizens as belonging to the Russian nation.[13]

Finally, in the Congress of People's Deputies and in the Duma from early 1992 onwards there have been moderate centrists who argue that Russian and Soviet identities have always been separate and they also do not include Ukrainians and Belarussians in the Russian nation. Nevertheless these centrists forcefully argue that all the Russians and Russian speakers in the 'near abroad' do belong to the Russian nation and view Russia as their homeland, and that therefore their defence should be the main priority of the Russian government. The question of the citizenship of members of the diaspora is of little importance to these politicians. Back in 1992–94 this position was represented by such otherwise moderate politicians as the chairmen of the parliamentary Committees for Foreign Affairs Evgenii Ambartsumov and Vladimir Lukin.

The opposition leaders devote much more space in their writings and public speeches to the question of what is the Russian nation than do the president and his supporters in the executive branch of government. For instance, Zyuganov's books dwell at length on the formation of the Russians as a nation. So did articles and speeches of Yeltsin's main critic in the executive branch in 1992–93, Vice-President Alexander Rutskoi, who published a series of articles on Russian nation building which were largely based on Ilin's notion of the Russian nation.[14] In contrast, Yeltsin's books focus mainly on his rise to power and on the struggle against his political opponents. The CPRF has even set up analytical centres, such as the RAU corporation and Spiritual Heritage, whose members are instructed to produce 'general theories' of Russia's post-communist nation building.[15] These institutes are staffed with former employees of the Academy of Sciences and former instructors of Marxism-Leninism, whose main sources of inspiration are conservative pre-revolutionary thinkers and Soviet theories of nationalities relations. Parliamentary deputies from communist and nationalist factions also organise joint conferences with intellectuals, such as Rogozin, on issues related to Russia's nation building.[16] It is these intellectuals who shape the views of the political opposition on what is the Russian nation. Finally, a number of intellectuals, among them the above-mentioned Lukin and Ambartsumov, were elected to the parliament, thus being able directly to integrate intellectual discourse into political debates.

In turn, the opposition heavily influences the position of members of the executive branch on nation building. Indeed, Yeltsin's policies that indicate shifts in his perception of what is the Russian nation usually come as a reaction to the pressure from the opposition. This was the case, at least in part, with Yeltsin's policies towards Russian speakers in the 'near abroad'. In turn, Yeltsin's decision in 1996 to increase his efforts to achieve CIS and Slavic integration came in response to the communist-sponsored resolution revoking the Belovezhe Accords.

The direct influence of intellectuals on shifts in the government's views on how the Russian nation should be defined is also noticeable. A number of intellectuals who are active participants in the debates on nation building have served as Yeltsin's aides, advisers and members of the Presidential Council; on rare occasions they have even occupied ministerial

---

[13] *Nezavisimaya gazeta*, 15 Dec. 1995, p. 2.

[14] See, for instance, *Pravda*, 30 Jan. 1992.

[15] V. Tishkov, *Ethnicity, Nationalism and Conflict in and after the Soviet Union. The Mind Aflame* (London, 1997), 247.

[16] *Megapolis-Express*, 7 Apr. 1993, p. 15.

positions. The best known of them are acting prime minister in 1992 Egor Gaidar, ethnographer and Yeltsin's adviser on inter-ethnic relations in 1992 Galina Starovoitova; Tishkov; historian and presidential counsellor in 1992–93 Sergei Stankevich; Karaganov; ethnographer Emil Pain and political scientist Georgii Satarov, both of whom became Yeltsin's aides in 1994. Gaidar, Starovoitova and Tishkov were instrumental in promoting the idea of de-ethnicised nation and state building in the RF in early 1992. In late 1992–93 Stankevich's influence was probably as important as the pressure from the opposition in convincing Yeltsin that Russian settlers in the 'near abroad' should be seen as an integral part of the Russian nation. Stankevich was the author of the first major Russian government policy document 'On urgent measures for the implementation of socio-cultural cooper- ation of citizens of the RF with Russian compatriots abroad', which he presented to Yeltsin in January 1993.[17] Such intellectuals as Karaganov and Migranyan also played their role in shaping the government's attitude towards Russian-speaking settlers thanks to their close ties to Stankevich and other members of the presidential apparatus. In 1996 Karaganov, as a member of the Presidential Council, exercised some influence on Yeltsin's decision to promote CIS integration during his election campaign.

In turn, a concept of a civic Russian nation, which Yeltsin still promotes, albeit inconsis- tently, has also emerged as a result of the efforts of intellectuals. This concept has been advocated by Tishkov—a scholar who continues to keep close ties with the president and his entourage thanks to his short-term position in the government in 1992. It is largely through his efforts that the definition of the Russian (*rossiiskaya*) nation as a community of citizens of the RF was introduced in the Russian constitution and appeared in presidential New Year and parliamentary addresses. These addresses were written by Yeltsin's advisers Pain and Satarov, both liberal intellectuals, who solicited Tishkov's help.[18]

Leaders of ethnic autonomies

The idea of creating a civic Russian (*rossiiskaya*) nation of citizens of the RF united by loyalty to the new political institutions and the constitution is challenged not only by the members of the national-communist opposition in Moscow but also by political elites of the non-Russian autonomies in the RF. The fact that 18% of RF citizens are non-Russians, the majority of whom are non-Slavs and even non-Christians, and the challenge that this situation presents to the unity of the RF are well recognised by Yeltsin and his advisers. Moscow's inability to find a solution to problems with Chechnya emphasised the magnitude of the challenge. Optimists in the Russian government think that the problem can be overcome. They argue that, although many non-Russians identify themselves first and fore- most with their autonomies rather than with the RF in general, regional/local and national identities do not have to be exclusive. Regional or local identities could peacefully co-exist with an all-embracing all-national one. The optimists reject parallels between the Union republics of the USSR and ethnic autonomies in the RF. First, they emphasise that in the RF a minority (33.4%) of non-Russians actually live in their autonomies. Moreover, non- Russians in the RF are far more russified and versed in Russian culture than was the case with the majority of non-Russians who were allotted Union republics in the USSR and who

---

[17] Melvin, *Russians Beyond Russia*, 15.   [18] Tishkov, *Ethnicity, Nationalism and Conflict*, 260.

lived in those republics.[19] However, Yeltsin himself and the majority of the advocates of civic nation building in his government nevertheless feel that the existence of administrative units in the RF whose borders are drawn according to ethnic principle is not desirable. The war in Chechnya intensified debates in the government about redividing Russia into regions whose borders would have nothing to do with historical settlements of non-Russians. Members of the opposition (Zhirinovsky being a prime example) fully support this plan.[20] However, such a position is rejected by political elites of the non-Russian autonomies.

Similarly to non-Russian intellectual elites, whose members often serve as advisers to political leaders of ethnic autonomies, these leaders argue that the notion of a civic nation amounts to imperialist russification in disguise. Citing the views of the ethnic political leaders, the deputy prime minister for ethnic relations, the Dagestani Ramazan Abdulatipov, argued in an open letter to Yeltsin that the view of the Russian (*Rossiiskaya*) nation as a community of citizens, as mentioned in Yeltsin's parliamentary addresses in 1994 and 1995, was similar to 'the Bolshevik idea of the fusion of people'. He also identified 'Western influences' in this concept and stated in this connection:

We should not copy a Western path of state building. It is based on assimilation, which has always been carried out by force. We are unique, because 150 different nationalities live in our country, and they preserve their ethnicity, culture and languages ... For the people of the RF collective rights have priority over individual human rights. It is only in the distant future that the latter could take priority. In the West, the supremacy [of individual rights] is achieved through the destruction of entire populations. Thank God, the Russian nation has never been historically that cynical.[21]

Therefore the Russian government not only has not yet implemented its plan of merging ethnic autonomies with predominantly Russian economic regions, but it has even preserved the nationality entry, which means ethnicity rather than citizenship, in Russian passports. This is a peculiar development, the only reason for which is concession to the pressure exercised on the federal government by the non-Russian political elites. Russian ethnic identity is weaker than that of the non-Russians of the former USSR. Yet the non-Russian newly independent states, when introducing new passports, abolished references to ethnicity in them.

[19] E. Pain, *Druzhba narodov*, 6 (1994), 156–64 and *Moskovskie novosti*, 5–12 June 1994, p. 5A.
[20] Vera Tolz, 'Unease Grips Moscow and the Ethnic Republics', *Transition*, 4 (1995).
[21] *Nezavisimava gazeta*, 14 Mar. 1995, p. 3.

26 Russia's Identity Crisis

Ronald Grigor Suny

....

Russia's post-Soviet 'identity crisis' has been interpreted by both authoritarian nationalist writers and more democratically oriented authors as the product of the radical, imposed turn from the 'natural' course of history by the Bolsheviks. The seventy years of Soviet power are imagined as a deviation, a distortion that must be reversed to restore Russia to its true and healthy path toward civilization. This interpretation both contributed to and was itself shaped by the truly revolutionary shift from the Soviet regime with its clearly articulated ideology to one that eschewed official imposition of ideological conformity. The nature of that shift, limply labeled a 'transition,' was extraordinarily abrupt, with a sharp rejection of the norms and values of Soviet society and its view of history and the political world, and, in the name of 'reform,' the establishment of a systemless system with which the majority of people were completely unfamiliar. A world that had been experienced, even with all its repression, mundane imperfections, and corruptions, as one of order, progress, and purpose, at least up through the mid-1970s, was abandoned by Russia's leaders and many intellectuals in favor of a world of unpredictability, embedded corruption and criminality, economic hardship, military weakness, and the precipitous decline of Russia from great power status to a wounded, humiliated, truncated state. As the liberal professor of philosophy Igor Chubais put it, 'The euphemism "reform" . . . is used in reality to explain the abolition of the old rules—often unacceptable but sometimes fair—and the failure to accept any new norms at all. In the current situation, the term "reform" has become a synonym of the concept "chaos."'[1]

The eradication of the Soviet value system did not result in a consensus on national or state identity, and though many democratic and Western values have gained greater acceptance among Russians in the 1990s, the country remains deeply divided between those who support the general direction of the economic and political changes initiated by Mikhail Gorbachev and Boris Yeltsin and those for whom the rejection of the Soviet past as an authentic part of Russia's history and tradition meant their ejection from the rebuilding of the nation. People who had fought for and suffered for that system were overnight rendered disgruntled, disoriented red-flag-waving marginals. The turn back to symbols and institutions of the pre-Soviet past—the double-headed eagle, the imperial flag, the Orthodox

Originally part of a much longer article entitled 'Provisional Stabilities: The Politics of Identities in Post-Soviet Eurasia', *International Security*, 24/3 (Winter 1999/2000), 139–73. Reproduced by kind permssion of the author and Harvard University.

[1] Igor Chubais, 'From the Russian Idea to the Idea of a New Russia: How We Must Overcome the Crisis of Ideas' (Cambridge, Mass.: Strengthening Democratic Institutions Project, Harvard University, July 1998), p. 1.

Church, the reburial of the last czar's family (though not [yet] the revival of the Romanov anthem, 'God Save the Czar')—resonates negatively among many former *sovki*, not to mention the 20 percent of Russia's population that is neither Orthodox nor ethnically Russian.[2]

Russian political elites as well as public opinion are deeply divided over the question of what constitutes the Russian nation and state. Russians remain uncertain about their state's boundaries, where its border guards ought to patrol (at the edge of the Russian Federation or the Confederation of Independent States [CIS]?), confused about its future shape (is Chechnya in or out?), its relations with its neighboring states (is Belarus in or out?), and even its internal structure as an asymmetrical federation.[3] In a masterful review of Russian thinking on these issues over the last decade, Vera Tolz argues that three incompatible views of legitimate Russian statehood contend for acceptance. Conservative nationalists, the most militant Communists, and the so-called Eurasianists believe that 'the Russian Federation should initiate the restoration of a union, which should be joined by as many of the former Soviet republics as possible.'[4] A second group adopts an idea of the Russian nation that was prevalent in the prerevolutionary period-Russia as the union of Great Russians, White Russians (Belarussians), and Little Russians (Ukrainians). This idea of Slavic unity, closely identified with Aleksandr Solzhenitsyn, involves ambitions to include other areas with Russian populations, such as northern Kazakhstan, within the new Russian state. A third vision is the formation of a republic of Russian speakers, integrating the Russian-speaking diaspora into the federation and, perhaps, allowing some non-Russian autonomies to separate from the Russian state. To Tolz's list of 'homeland myths' a fourth might be added: the generally operative one that Russia is a multinational state in which 'Russian' is both understood as ethnic Russian (*russkii*) and as citizen of the republic (*rossiiskii).* Within the Yeltsin administration, policy has gradually shifted from 'a vision of Russia as a kin state of all Russian speakers,' dominant from 1992 to 1994, to 'policies facilitating the re-creation of some form of union on the territory of the USSR' becoming more important from late 1994.[5] Polling data reveal that 'the idea that the new Russia should be primarily the state of Russian speakers who enjoy a legally defined dominant status, as well as the idea that the Slavic nucleus of the USSR should reunite, attracts the largest support within the Russian Federation.'[6] Tolz ominously concludes that 'the view that the borders of the Russian Federation are in urgent need of revision is more widespread among Russian intellectuals, politicians, and the public at large than is usually assumed in western scholarly literature.'[7]

The lack of a clear, coherent, widely accepted national identity lay at the core of Russia's foreign policy fluctuations in the 1990s. No matter how weak it was at the moment, Russia continued to identify itself to itself and others as a great power, and great powers seldom operate under the same rules and constraints as lesser powers. Though increasingly it became a purely symbolic issue, as a great power Russia continued to see the 'near abroad' as a sphere of interest and occasionally demanded a role in protecting those it considers its

[2] *Sovok* (plural, *sovki*) literally means 'dustpan,' but in the late Soviet period it referred negatively to something or someone 'Soviet.' It has come to be an ambivalent reference to a Soviet person.

[3] Ronald Grigor Suny, 'The State of Nations: The Ex-Soviet Union and Its Peoples,' *Dissent* (Summer 1996), 90–8.

[4] Vera Tolz, 'Conflicting "Homeland Myths" and Nation-State Building in Postcommunist Russia,' *Slavic Review*, 57/2 (Summer 1998), 268.

[5] Ibid. 289.

[6] Ibid. 293.

[7] Ibid. 294.

conationals (the so-called *russkoiazychnye* [Russian-language speaker]) in neighboring states. Like the United States in the Western Hemisphere, Russia sought to police its own neighborhood and reserved the ability to guard frontiers that impinge on its security. Though Yeltsin did not plan to reannex the states of South Caucasia[8] and Central Asia, he promoted a greater military and political presence, even hinting that the United Nations should give Russia exclusive rights as gendarme in the area. Russia also made clear it wanted partnership in the exploitation and development of the natural resources of the region, most important the offshore oil in Azerbaijan. Moscow repeatedly claimed the right to protect rail lines in Transcaucasia, for the major link from Russia to Armenia passes through Abkhazia and Georgia and the line to Baku passes through Chechnya. The government stated that it was not interested in the dismemberment of the republics of South Caucasia, which could set 'a most dangerous precedent' and lead to similar struggles in Russia, but was concerned about the spillover of unresolved ethnic conflicts into Russia. A reading of the Russian press reveals that opinion makers and decision makers shared a view of a Russia surrounded by dangers—from militant Islam, ethnic mafias, agents of foreign states, and drug traders. The question for the Southern Tier was not whether there would be a strong Russian presence but what kind of presence it would be. Some prominent observers in the West feared the rise of a new Russian imperialism, pointed to Russia's self-image as a great power, and rehearsed Russia's repeated interventions in the near abroad. At the end of 1994 and early in 1995, Boris Yeltsin and his foreign minister, Andrei Kozyrev, publicly declared their support for the reintegration of the countries of the former Soviet Union, first economically, but also militarily and possibly politically. But Russia's self-proclaimed status was a highly imaginative one that did not correspond to its actual power. Even if Russia wanted to reconstruct an empire, it was no longer capable of doing so. Moreover, the first war in Chechnya (1994–96) clearly demonstrated the heavy costs of empire, and Russian leaders hesitated to repeat that mistake. Rather than a sign of a pattern of Russian expansionism, the Chechnya adventure was a sign of state weakness, a product of the narrowing of political decisionmaking into the tight circle around Yeltsin. Chechens were presented by the authorities as bandits, vicious criminals, and drug dealers who presented a corrupting threat to the Russian state. Yet even though these images resonated among the population, a considerable and influential segment of the Russian public opposed war until in 1999 Chechen incursions into Daghestan and a mysterious series of apartment house bombings in Moscow licensed a second, brutal invasion of the rebel republic. This war is publicly justified as a fight against terrorism and to secure the territorial integrity of Russia.

Despite sometimes inflammatory rhetoric, particularly by Duma deputies, Russian foreign policy, notably toward the Southern Tier, tended to moderate over time. After almost a decade of independence there has been a grudging acceptance of the new constellation of states and the limits of Russian power. What might be called the 'Yeltsin Doctrine' can be interpreted as recognition of the independence and sovereignty of the existing states, combined with a reluctance to give up Russia's paramount role in the Southern Tier. Though Russian policymakers favored dominance in the realm of security and, perhaps, a special role in protecting Russians and other minorities, Russia appears at present to be a relatively

[8] The term 'South Caucasia' refers to the isthmus that lies between the Black and Caspian Seas and to the south of the range of the Great Caucasus Mountains. Traditionally, this region was called Transcaucasia, a reference that implied the view from Russia in the north.

benign hegemon in relationship to the Southern Tier rather than a neo-imperialist threat.[9] Moscow has progressively come to terms with the actual limits of its power and Russia's new status as a regional power. Like the United States in the first half of the nineteenth century, it is consolidating state authority over its own territory, defining its borders, and policing its neighborhood to prevent any rivals from establishing influence in its sphere of interest.

Russia may not yet be a fully democratic state, but its evolution over the last decade has involved the internal generation among many elite politicians, as well as younger members of society, of an identification with democratic values, satisfaction with its current state boundaries, and respect for the sovereignty and territorial integrity of its neighbors. An optimistic scenario for the future might envision strong republics in the south that would encourage more moderate policies on the part of Russia, and a democratic Russia limiting its major strategic interests in the region to maintaining stable, prosperous states on its southern border and a secure buffer against intrusions from Turkey, Iran, and China, not the full burden of colonizing a complexly mixed and resistant population. Yet because of its own internal confusion and corruption, its occasional pretensions to empire, and the insecurity it engenders among its neighbors, Russia has not been able to convince many of the former Soviet states that they ought to give up independence in decisionmaking in favor of Russian hegemony. Russia can no longer credibly claim to be filling a power vacuum or providing security or mediating conflict or aiding in economic development or building democracy. A crisis-ridden chaotic Russia cannot exercise the special role its pretensions to great power status want to play in the region. Russia's crisis of identity has left it without a clear justification for hegemony.

The Russian state is a state in flux, its 'interests' dependent on such contingent factors as the health of an ailing president, the international economy, and the somber mood of its impoverished and disgruntled people. There is one more identity tale to be told here, a particularly melancholy one. The West, with its own array of identities, holds out the prize of membership in the North Atlantic Treaty Organization (NATO) to those who come with the right democratic and market credentials. NATO expansion to a select number of East European states, perhaps later to the Baltic countries, is a clear message to Russia that it is not fit for membership in the 'West.' As the border of the Western alliance moves eastward, Russia and the Southern Tier are left unmanaged and undefined, and Russia is left to fend for itself with the specters of Islam, the drug trade, terrorists, and the dangerous opportunities created by the search for fossil fuels. With Russia more isolated and conflicted about its identity and role in the region, the Southern Tier remains one of the most unregulated and unpredictable security zones in the world.

---

[9] Menon and Spruyt make the point that a benign Russia is contingent on internal democratization and greater stability of Russia's neighboring states. Should Russia become politically authoritarian in combination with instability on its borders, the likely outcome would be a neo-imperial Russia. Rajan Menon and Hendrik Spruyt, 'The Limits of Neorealism: Understanding Security in Central Asia,' *Review of International Studies*, 25/1 (Jan. 1999), 96–7.

Federalism, Regionalism, and Local Government

Section 9

Federalism, Regionalism, and Local Government

Introduction

Archie Brown

All federal systems, whether in a democracy or a hybrid political system, impose constraints on majorities, even when (as is by no means always the case) a majority can be said to exist within the polity as a whole. If that point needed any underlining, the American presidential election of 2000 provided it. But it applies also to policy-making once a government is installed. As Alfred Stepan has put it, 'all democratic federal systems are to some extent center, majority and "demos-constraining"'.[1] Federations are also all asymmetrical in one way or another. Even the United States, which in constitutional terms is among the most symmetrical, is highly asymmetrical so far as the units that compose it are concerned as well as socio-economically. By according two seats in the Senate—which is, after all, the important upper chamber of an unusually powerful legislature—to each state, regardless of vast differences of population size and size of the economy between the largest and the smallest of the Federation's component parts, the Constitution disadvantages states such as California and New York, just as the electoral college aspect of American federalism, in a sense, devalued the votes of their electorates in the 2000 presidential election.

Where there are different nationalities within a state, there is a greater propensity for federations also to be *constitutionally* asymmetrical. This contradicts the majoritarian principle, but so, as we have already noted, does federalism generally. Viewing federalism as a possible antidote to nationalism, Graham Smith described 'federation as a peculiarly territorial and non-majoritarian form of organising the political and cultural life of citizens in multiethnic societies'.[2] That the will of the majority should generally prevail is, after all, only one element of a democracy—and may even on occasion, given the possibility of a 'tyranny of the majority', be anti-democratic. The Soviet 'federation' was largely symmetrical so far as its basic components—the fifteen union republics—were concerned,[3] but it was also

---

[1] Alfred Stepan, 'Russian Federalism in Comparative Perspective', *Post-Soviet Affairs*, Vol. 16/2, (Apr.–June 2000), 133–76, at p. 133.

[2] Graham Smith, ed., *Federalism: The Multiethnic Challenge* (London: Longman, 1995), 3.

[3] There was, however, a hierarchy of units. Nationalities, whose territory did not have a Soviet border or who were not deemed major enough to be granted a union republic, were in a substantial number of cases given so-called 'autonomous republic' status (which did *not* mean that in Soviet practice they had real autonomy) and below them were national units called autonomous oblasts and okrugs. The most common, large administrative unit (on average of similar size to an average American state) was the oblast (region). To complete the complex picture a unit very similar to the oblast, but distinguished, in principle, by greater ethnic diversity, was named the krai. In a striking instance of path-dependence all these units are to be found in the post-Soviet Russian Federation. The main terminological difference is that what were formerly 'autonomous republics' are now simply the 'republics' of Russia, since the union republics, to which in the USSR 'autonomous republics' had a subordinate status, are now independent states with a seat in the UN. All of these units, whether republics or oblasts, differ also in substance

fundamentally a sham. At one extreme it enshrined a right of secession, the *absence* of which has been regarded as one of a number of yardsticks of federalism,[4] even though in political practice the first secessionist moves would—prior to the Gorbachev reforms—have led to the immediate arrest of its proponents. At the other extreme, territory could be moved from one unit of the federation to another at the whim of the central party-state authorities. There was no independent judicial review in the hypothetical instance of a dispute between one of the units (or subjects) of the federation and the federal authorities. Still more crucially, the role played by the highly disciplined and centralized Communist Party of the Soviet Union meant that, in practice, there was *no* area of policy in which Moscow could not impose a decision from above on a union republic, whether one as large as Kazakhstan or Ukraine or as small (but nationally self-conscious) as Estonia. The strictly hierarchical party organization, in other words, cut across federal boundaries.

In one important element of asymmetry, the largest of all the Soviet republics, Russia (the RSFSR), did not have its own republican party organization. This meant that the Politburo and Secretariat of the Central Committee at an all-union level made decisions directly for Russia without having to go through the transmission belt of a republican Central Committee appar-atus. Given the size of Russia and the fact that Russians were overwhelmingly the predominant nationality in the central organs of the CPSU, it would have looked for most of the Soviet period like unnecessary duplication to have a separate republican-level party organization for the RSFSR. Yet, this was an important exception to the symmetrical rule of Soviet-style 'federal-ism', inasmuch as party organs were in reality—as distinct from Soviet constitutional precept—the highest institutions of state power. In the fourteen out of fifteen republics which did have a party organization, the first secretary for that republic could, within limits, defend the material interests of his domain, but if he (and it was always a *he*) took this too far, he was in danger of being arraigned for 'bourgeois nationalism'. In light of the absence of areas in which a republic had an absolute right to make policy, the non-existence of judicial review, and the encroach-ment into every area of political life of the centralized Communist Party, it is reasonable to conclude that the USSR was not a genuine example of a federal state.

Nevertheless, the fact that those national homelands known as union republics had their own Communist Party Central Committees (with the exception until 1990 of Russia) and overtly state institutions, such as republican Councils of Ministers and Supreme Soviets, meant that there were *potential* structural supports for political activity. For most of Soviet history that was of minimal practical significance, given the hierarchical and disciplined style of rule imposed by the Communist Party, but it became enormously important once a greater tolerance and de facto pluralism emerged in the second half of the 1980s. Those who struggled, in the first instance, to turn a pseudo-federation into a polity with genuinely federal relations were able to use structures which had previously been highly constrained (as well as constraining) as their institutional base. As Rogers Brubaker has observed of the demise of the Soviet Union:

That this paradigmatically massive state could disappear in so comparatively orderly a fashion, ceasing to exist as a subject of international law and withering away as a unit of administration, was possible chiefly

from what they were in the Soviet period (with the exception of its last years) in that they enjoyed during the Yeltsin era a significant element of autonomy.

[4] Ivo D. Duchacek, *Comparative Federalism: The Territorial Dimension of Politics* (New York: Holt, Rinehart and Winston, 1970), 207.

because the successor units already existed as internal quasi-nation-states, with fixed territories, names, legislatures, administrative staffs, cultural and political elites, and—not least—the constitutionally enshrined right to secede from the Soviet Union (it is one of the many ironies of the Soviet breakup that it was decisively facilitated by what regime leaders and Western commentators alike had long dismissed as a constitutional fiction).[5]

In the very last years of the Soviet Union, when the Communist Party could no longer play its 'leading role', federal forms acquired federal substance on their way to becoming staging-posts for secessionist movements.

In early *post*-Soviet Russia no political organization even purported to assume the role of a ruling party and in the absence of a strong vertical power structure, the units of the federation—especially the new (formerly 'autonomous') republics—acquired substantial autonomy in reality as distinct from mere terminology. However, the 1993 Constitution did not accord the right of secession, and—as suggested in the previous section of this book—it is highly unlikely that the Russian Federation will follow the fissiparous example of the USSR. The struggle between executive and legislature during the First Russian Republic (in 1992 and especially 1993) led to special deals being made with particular regions and republics. As the late Galina Starovoitova, a Duma deputy who was assassinated in St Petersburg in 1998, noted in a book published the year before her death:

This confrontation had a clear impact upon the development of Russian federalism, since republican and regional elites emerged as powerful political actors who could determine the balance between the two opposing forces. Both the president and the parliament vied for their favor by allocating subsidies and other economic privileges, to the detriment of the nation's financial stability. Under these circumstances, the problem of equality between republics and regions largely lost its importance as both republican and regional leaders, recruited mostly from the old party *nomenklatura*, asserted themselves as the supreme arbiters in the country.[6]

While there is much truth in this, the fact remains that *asymmetry* is the norm rather than the exception in federal systems and, indeed, even in multinational states which are not formally federal but have embarked on serious devolution of power. Thus, asymmetrical devolution in Spain began with the granting of autonomous community status in December 1979 to the Basque country and Catalonia, where there were distinct nationalities with their own traditions. But by the late 1990s there were seventeen autonomous communities, including some which did not previously have even a strong sense of regional, let alone national, identity. Their powers are asymmetrical, but there has been a tendency towards levelling up the legislative competence of the relative newcomers towards that enjoyed by the Basque country and Catalonia. Yet the Catalans and the Basques continue to hold out for 'a distinctive level of autonomy over and above that enjoyed by the other communities'.[7] In Britain

---

[5] Rogers Brubaker, *Nationalism Reframed: Nationhood and the National Question in the New Europe* (Cambridge: Cambridge University Press, 1996), 41–2.

[6] Galina Starovoitova, *National Self-Determination: Approaches and Case Studies* (Providence: Occasional Paper 27, Thomas J. Watson, Jr. Institute for International Studies, Brown University, 1997), 33–4.

[7] Paul Heywood, *The Government and Politics of Spain* (London: Macmillan, 1995), 142–64, esp. p. 163. See also Montserrat Guibernau, 'Spain: a Federation in the Making?', in Smith, ed., *Federalism: The Multiethnic Challenge*, 239–54.

asymmetrical devolution, reflecting the multinational character of the British state, has also occurred in the recent past, with the establishment of a Scottish parliament and Welsh and Northern Ireland assemblies. These bodies have powers that vary from one to the other, but all have substantially greater authority than any level of local government in England where regional assemblies have not (as yet, at least) been created.[8]

To speak of asymmetrical federalism in Russia is not, therefore, to say very much. It is more important to delineate the nature of the asymmetries. Towards that end, Alfred Stepan has very usefully distinguished three types of asymmetry in the contemporary Russian Federation—the constitutionally embedded, the extra-constitutionally negotiated, and the anticonstitutionally exercised.[9] Constitutionally embedded asymmetries include the fact that republics have a higher status than other units which make up the Federation, such as oblasts. The most important example of extra-constitutional asymmetry consists of the bilateral treaties signed between particular republics or regions and the federal authorities, giving the former special prerogatives not available to all 'subjects of the Federation'. More often than not, these did not receive legislative endorsement, but were, in a sense, private pacts between republican bosses and the presidential administration in Moscow. By anticonstitutional asymmetry Stepan has in mind the fact that a great many provisions in the constitutions or statutes of the eighty-nine subjects (units) of the Russian Federation contradict the federal constitution.

There is nothing necessarily damaging about the constitutionally embedded differences. As in the case of devolution in Spain or Britain, they may simply be a legitimate price of union. Even bilateral treaties or pacts could be justified if they were endorsed by both federal and republican legislatures—which, however, as Jeff Kahn makes clear in Chapter 27, has generally not been the case. No justification at all can be found for flat contradictions between federal and republican constitutional provisions or for discrepant federal and republican legislation, since this clearly is at odds with the rule of law of which Russia stands in need. In practical terms these particular asymmetries have worked against having a unified legal space and—until the Putin presidency—reflected appeasement on the part of Moscow of some of the republics and regions most prone to disregard the federal constitution and federal law. As Steven Solnick has remarked: 'Since 1991, Moscow has tended to reward, rather than punish, those regions that were most defiant; this suggests a weak center seeking to co-opt opponents, even at the expense of its allies among regional politicians.'[10]

In the first of the chapters in this section Jeff Kahn—the author of a doctoral thesis and forthcoming book on Russian federalism—notes that between 1994 and 1998 as many as forty-six of the eighty-nine subjects of the federation signed bilateral treaties with the federal executive. Not only were the treaties not ratified by the federal or regional legislatures, but they also sometimes included secret agreements which were not even published. These informal arrangements, extraconstitutional at best and frequently unconstitutional, were called more sharply into question after Putin succeeded Yeltsin in the presidency. The future of what is called 'the new Russian federalism' will depend, Kahn suggests, 'in large part on what

[8] See Archie Brown, 'Asymmetrical Devolution: The Scottish Case', *Political Quarterly*, 69/3 (July–Sept. 1998), 215–23.

[9] Stepan, 'Russian Federalism in Comparative Perspective', 145.

[10] Steven L. Solnick, 'The Political Economy of Russian Federalism: A Framework for Analysis', *Problems of Post-Communism*, 43/6 (Nov.–Dec. 1996), 13–25, at p. 20.

balance can be struck between valid assertions of regional autonomy and federal obligations to promote and protect democratic principles and a unified legal space throughout the country'.

Two of Russia's leading authorities on the regions of the Russian Federation, Alla Chirikova and Natalya Lapina, discuss (in Chapter 28) some of the numerous ways in which the centre can reimpose controls over the oblasts. For example, they note the cases in the Rostov region of a graduate of the Higher School of the KGB suddenly appearing as the new chairman of the main state bank in the regional capital, to be followed by another outsider who was close to the minister of internal affairs in the position of local police chief. Not coincidentally, the governor promptly thereafter announced his backing for the Putin-supporting parliamentary bloc, Yedinstvo, in the run-up to the Duma elections. Thereupon the region's serious problems with its debts, which the bank had raised, were resolved to the satisfaction of the governor. On the basis of extensive empirical research in the regions, Chirikova and Lapina conclude that 'talk of the weakness of the federal centre is largely untrue'—once, that is, the centre has shown that it has the political will to use the levers of power at its disposal.

Both Kahn and Chirikova and Lapina, in the chapters that follow, devote attention to the important decree Putin issued in May 2000 which divided Russia into seven federal districts, to each of which the president appointed a plenipotentiary representative. This new division of the Russian state was in itself an extra-constitutional act of potentially great significance, the more so since five of the seven heads appointed by Putin were generals, whether from the army, the ministry of interior, or the former KGB. The federal districts coincided exactly with the military districts into which Russia was already divided, but hitherto that had affected only the army, and not civilian administration. Chirikova and Lapina argue that reform of federal relations was long overdue, but they express concern that the creation of seven super-districts, part of the central authorities' policy of making the regions easier to govern and more dependent on Moscow, did not result from a negotiating process but was imposed unilaterally by the centre. More generally, they see the possibility of what they call 'guided democracy' or 'manipulated democracy', characteristic of many, though not all, of Russia's regions, being copied increasingly by the federal authorities. Thus, the latter appear to be borrowing from the regions an admixture of authoritarian and democratic elements even while they proceed to give tangible evidence of their disapproval of the actions of selected republican presidents and regional governors.

In the third of the three chapters in this section (all of them previously unpublished), Tomila Lankina focuses not so much on the relations between the regions and the federal authorities as on government at a lower rung in the hierarchy—local politics at the grass roots. She is particularly concerned with the relationship between the organs of government at the level of cities, towns, and districts, on the one hand, and the republics and regions, on the other. Lankina shows how the republican and regional authorities have been able to achieve dominance over the organs of 'local self-government'. The struggle which she sees ensuing is not so much one to enhance the power of government at the most local level as between the federal centre, on the one hand, and the republics and regions, on the other, for control of the localities.

27 What is the New Russian Federalism?

Jeff Kahn

Observers of Russia's stumbling transition to democracy might be forgiven for regarding successive promises of a 'new Russian federalism' with healthy scepticism. The centralizing legacies of so-called Soviet federalism still cast a shadow over the rubble of the former Soviet multinational state. Yeltsin's tightening grip on regional leaders following his violent but victorious battle with parliament in October 1993 suggested plans for more centralized rule. The new Constitution, the hard-fought prize of that battle, established tremendous powers for the federal executive and left the division of powers between centre and periphery purposefully ambiguous. The 'Parade of Sovereignties' that opened a new decade and closed the old Soviet era was overstopped in its tracks by its initiator, Boris Yeltsin.

Russia's first president did not create his powerful, 'unified' federal state. By the mid-1990s, federal and regional authorities alike bemoaned the failure to create a cohesive state system that could address mounting economic and social problems, although each side proposed very different solutions. Soon after the referendum that narrowly ratified his Constitution, Yeltsin launched a new parade. Signing treaties (*dogovory*) and agreements (*soglasheniya*) with the executive heads of ethnic republics (and soon thereafter with oblasts and krais), Yeltsin eroded the legal equality his Constitution proclaimed for different levels of centre–periphery relations. Savvy regional negotiators won budget privileges, powers of appointment, exemption from various federal requirements, and a tacit understanding that federal officials—at least for the time being—would look away from glaring violations of the federal Constitution and basic democratic principles.

With the sudden rise of Vladimir Putin, Russian federalism made another volte-face. The ambiguous enforceability of Yeltsin's treaties—never ratified by legislatures—was made clear by Putin's disregard for executive promises that no longer suited his interests. One of Putin's first presidential decrees, signed days after his inauguration, divided Russia into seven federal districts, each encompassing several republics, oblasts, and okrugs, and each headed by a presidential enforcer tasked to maintain the supremacy of federal law. Lists were rumoured to circulate in the Kremlin of regional leaders to be brought to heel. Putin described his project as the 'dictatorship of law.'

What forces have influenced such sea-changes in Russian federal politics? How might political scientists approach the dynamic of centre–periphery relations in a post-Soviet, and now a post-Yeltsin, Russia?[1] Examination of the conceptual and political struggles to define

Chapter specially commissioned for this volume.

[1] Chechnya (Ichkeriya) is not analysed here. The two wars fought thus far (conservatively estimated to have killed tens of thousands of combatants and civilians) have largely removed the republic from federal politics. On 8 June 2000 Vladimir Putin issued an *ukaz* establishing direct presidential rule. Ukaz No 1071, *Rossiyskaya gazeta*, 10 June 2000, p. 3.

Russian federalism provides insights into the path of Russian federal development and Russia's difficult democratic transition.

The spectrum of federal choices

In a country as large and multinational as Russia, it is unsurprising that renewed debates about federalism coincided with systemic political reform in the late 1980s. Federal arrangements offer small polities the freedom of self-government combined with the economic and security advantages of a larger state. Federalism also appeals to large states struggling with various forms of internal disharmony, but which value accommodating their diversity within a more unitary framework. As A. V. Dicey expressed this 'very peculiar state of sentiment', the citizens of a federation 'must desire union, and must not desire unity'.[2] Ethnic or religious minorities may consider federalism the best available means of cultural self-preservation, less risky than secession. There is seldom a single motivation; many factors co-determine the prospects for federal governance.

Federalism is best viewed as a spectrum of possible ways to divide jurisdiction over the same population between different levels of government. One of the best definitions of federalism captures its dynamic: '[The federal principle is] the method of dividing powers so that the general and regional governments are each, within a sphere, co-ordinate and independent.'[3] But federalism is more than the sum of its definitional parts; indeed, that is the very real goal a federal system is designed to achieve. Ivo Duchacek noted the importance of a 'federal political culture', a form of citizen loyalty to the federal polity that extends above and beyond regional allegiances. Acceptance of the inevitability of multiple, overlapping political identities and the importance of ensuring their complementarity is crucial in a federal system.

All federal systems rest upon a written, formal document, usually called a constitution, that is the supreme law of the land, overriding all other legislation or executive acts. As Dicey observed, federalism does away with the principle of the supreme sovereignty of parliament, which is subordinated in a federal system to a written constitution. This is one important distinction between federalism and the mere *devolution* of power, under which a parliament granting greater authority to lower levels of government retains the legal right (though not always the political ability) to revoke those powers later. An important difference between federal and *confederal* systems lies in this sovereign power accorded constitutional law. In confederations, established by treaty, the constituent units retain a far greater portion of their sovereignty and give up far fewer areas of jurisdiction to the union government. At its most extreme, a confederal programme may assert that the union government's proper role is only as agent of the component states. Thus, states might selectively reject federal laws or agency when they conflict with local laws and interests. This historically unstable 'doctrine of nullification' interprets a constitution not as a founding legal document against which a

---

[2] A. V. Dicey, *Introduction to the Study of the Law of the Constitution*, 10th edn. (London: Macmillan, 1967), 141.

[3] K. C. Wheare, *Federal Government*, 4th edn. (London: Oxford University Press, 1963), 10. Compare William H. Riker, *Federalism: Origin, Operation Significance* (Boston: Little, Brown & Co., 1964), 11. For an excellent and detailed comparative analysis of federal systems, see Alfred Stepan, 'Russian Federalism in Comparative Perspective', *Post-Soviet Affairs*, 16/2 (2000).

constitutional court may adjudicate disputes impartially, but as a political compact always open to political renegotiation.[4]

In many ways, the doctrine of nullification, notions of federal political culture, and the emphasis on a written constitution are different facets of a common theme: the problem of establishing an agreed framework of federal objectives. These three issues and the conceptual problems they raise are omnipresent in the development of the new Russian federalism. A consensus on the inherent value of the federal project is crucial for its success. In Russia, conceptual consensus has been conspicuous by its absence. This fundamental problem for the long-term stability of the Russian Federation can be traced back to debates about sovereignty and federalism reopened in the mid-1980s, underscored by the 'Parade of Sovereignties', and which continue today.

Conflict over the 'old' Russian federalism

The legacy of Soviet 'federalism' has exerted considerable influence on newer thinking. Lenin's and Stalin's early policies gave institutional privileges to ethnic elites in order to win allegiance to the Soviet state. The regime created what one scholar called the 'institutionalised monopoly on the public expression of ethnic identity'.[5] The map of Russia was redrawn to create new nations with their own administrative regions—these political boundaries have remained virtually unchanged. Early Soviet constitutions combined the language of federalism with the reality of democratic centralism. Contrary to the federal principle that certain spheres of authority remain the exclusive jurisdiction of each level of government, early Soviet constitutions created the legal fiction of 'dual subordination': each executive body was accountable both to its electorate and to the executive body higher in the hierarchy of democratic centralism. As one constitutional scholar observed: '[W]hile centralism might conceivably be reconciled with democracy it was entirely incompatible with local autonomy. . . . By coupling "horizontal" with "vertical" subordination it [dual subordination] seemed to grant local authorities a measure of control over local affairs; by the same token, however, it ensured that no part of such control was truly autonomous'.[6] Notions of 'horizontal' and 'vertical' federal relations have lingered in the post-Soviet federal vocabulary.

The contradictory rhetoric of Soviet federalism obstructed Mikhail Gorbachev's reforms, in part through institutional structures that Zbigniew Brzezinski noted created 'institutional vessels' for nationalist sentiment.[7] Federal reform was relatively low on Gorbachev's agenda until too late in his tenure as general secretary and Soviet president. Notes of Politburo discussions show that Gorbachev often listed alternatives to federation but seldom suggested any detailed plan of federal reform.[8] Few of his Politburo colleagues gained even that level of enlightenment.

Outside the Politburo, *suverenitet, federalizm,* and *pravovoe gosudarstvo* (law-governed

---

[4] Keith E. Whittington, 'The Political Constitution of Federalism in Antebellum America: The Nullification Debate as an Illustration of Informal Mechanisms of Constitutional Change', *Publius*, 26/2 (1996).

[5] Philip G. Roeder, 'Soviet Federalism and Ethnic Mobilization', *World Politics*, 43/2 (1991), 205.

[6] Aryeh L. Unger, *Constitutional Development in the USSR: A Guide to the Soviet Constitutions* (New York: Pica Press, 1981), 19.

[7] Zbigniew Brzezinski, 'Post-Communist Nationalism', *Foreign Affairs*, 68/5 (1989/90), 6.

[8] A. B. Veber, V. T. Loginov, G. S. Ostroumov and A. S. Chernyaev, eds., *Soyuz mozhno bylo sokhranit'* (Moscow: Izdatel'stvo 'Aprel'-85', 1995), 95.

state) were much more popular terms. National movements discovered that such language resonated well with their demands for greater economic and cultural autonomy. The ethnographer Yulian Bromlei, the geographer Vladimir Sokolov, and others incautiously proposed territorial redivisions of between three and sixty separate republics.[9] Not everyone supported federal solutions. Vladimir Zhirinovsky: 'How can the nationalities crisis be solved under these conditions? Only through fear. We need fear and a strong patriotic government; political life in the country must be frozen, all political parties forbidden, and all representative organs of power disbanded, except for the president and his authorised local representatives (governors [*gubernatory*], viceregents [*namestniki*]—whatever). All the republics must be abolished.'[10]

The conflation of federal with confederal approaches corresponded to conflicting objectives held by regional and Moscow-centred political elites. Federal authorities invariably advocated 'unified' or 'vertical' approaches to federalism, viewing the system as a simple hierarchy or pyramid. Regional leaders naturally embraced those elements of federal theory that emphasized local control, exclusive jurisdictions, and protection from an intruding central authority. They advocated a very weak centre, while federal politicians rallied around the slogan 'a strong centre and strong republics'.[11]

Conflicting conceptions of the new Russian federalism

EXPECTATION: THE PARADE OF SOVEREIGNTIES

Debates on federalism took place in a highly charged political environment, in newly elected regional Supreme Soviets and the First Russian Congress of People's Deputies, where delegations of regional elites actively participated in debates over the Declaration of Sovereignty that was issued by the RSFSR (Russian Soviet Federated Socialist Republic, soon to be the Russian Federation) on 12 June 1990. This Declaration (especially Article Nine, which 'confirmed the need to broaden substantially' the rights of federal sub-units), combined with Yeltsin's political junket through key regions that summer, was an obvious invitation for regions to assert their own autonomy. Yeltsin's populist exhortation in Tatarstan to 'take as much independence as you can hold on to,'[12] one of the most quoted and inflammatory statements of his career, deliberately focused on the element of federalism that most appealed to regional elites—autonomy from centralized rule. Yeltsin deliberately sought to weaken Gorbachev's power and increase his own support by galvanizing opposition to the federal centre.

His plan worked, and the 'Parade of Sovereignties' played a key role in undermining late attempts to reform Soviet 'federalism.' Twenty-four of the forty declarations of sovereignty were made by constituent units of the RSFSR. Unlike union republics (Ukraine, Belarus,

[9] Stephan Kux, 'Soviet Federalism,' *Problems of Communism* (Mar.–Apr. 1990), 9. Nicholas J. Lynn and Alexei V. Novikov, 'Refederalizing Russia: Debates on the Idea of Federalism in Russia', *Publius*, 27/2 (1997), 193. Gavriil Popov, *What is to be Done?* (London: Centre for Research into Communist Economies, 1992), 26–8, 48–9.

[10] 'Interethnic Contradictions in Russia: The Strategy of Parties and Social Movements (A Roundtable)', *Russian Politics and Law*, 32/5 (1994), 11–12. This round table was held in Moscow on 9 June 1992.

[11] Draft 'General Principles' for self-government published by a Supreme Soviet working group, *Pravda*, 14 Mar. 1989, p. 2.

[12] Yelena Chernobrovkina, *Vechernaya kazan'*, 10 Aug. 1990, p. 1.

Moldova, and the Baltic, Caucasian, and Central Asian states), autonomous republics (ASSRs in Soviet parlance) within the RSFSR desired not *independence* as sovereign states but respect for *sovereignty* within a renewed federation. Their declarations, remarkably similar to one another, emphasized the supremacy of local over federal laws, and many went on to declare separate republican citizenship, language rights, and exclusive ownership and authority over economic resources on its territory. These documents contained the regional conception of what the new Russian Federation should look like: a polity that took its orders from its constituent members. Autonomy was to be privileged above all else. Yeltsin's gambit did little but foment antagonism towards *any* central authority. Rather than encourage compromise in the renegotiation of autonomy, Yeltsin encouraged a mindset which at the time strengthened him against Union authorities (particularly Gorbachev) but left him vulnerable to his own short-sighted exhortations when he became the embodiment of the new 'Centre.'

NEGOTIATION: THE FEDERATION TREATY AND FEDERAL CONSTITUTION

Unilateral declarations of sovereignty were of minor legal-constitutional significance within the pre-existing Soviet system, but of enormous political significance. All ASSR declarations shared at least one more clause in common: these declarations were the basis for negotiating the Union Treaty for a renewed USSR and the Federation Treaty within the RSFSR. From the regional perspective, particularly that of republics, the Federation Treaty was the next logical step—a means to achieve the objectives expounded in these declarations. Such objectives were not shared by federal elites, who acquiesced to republican assertions of sovereignty, self-determination and even rights to secession as tolerable 'transitional devices' to maintain territorial integrity as the system developed.[13] True to regional self-conceptions of sovereignty, the first founding document to be negotiated was a treaty, *not* a constitution.

Central and regional elite conceptions of their common federal project starkly diverged. One negotiator from Bashkortostan complained, 'Acquaintance with the draft Federation treaty creates the impression that the authors strove to create a centralised, unitary state under the pretext of the Russian Federation.' The role of the sovereign republics was 'not more than the former *guberniya* of tsarist Russia.'[14] The Federation Treaty that emerged was a patchwork of three separate treaties (one for each level of the envisaged tripartite federal hierarchy of republics, oblasts, and autonomous okrugs) and two protocols.[15] The signatory republics saw the document as the keystone of a new federal order, a point they collectively underscored by insisting on repeated references to it in the draft federal constitution. The Federation Treaty officially acknowledged republican sovereignty, the right to self-determination and expressly prohibited federal intrusion into regional affairs, a long list of jurisdictions and authorities. In addition, one protocol promised half of the seats in one of the chambers of the proposed federal parliament to representatives of the ethnically defined regions (republics and autonomous okrugs).[16]

[13] Lynn and Novikov, 'Refederalizing Russia' 191–2. Robert Sharlet, 'The Prospects for Federalism in Russian Constitutional Politics', *Publius*, 24 (1994), 119.

[14] Zufar Yenikeev, 'Proekt dogovora nas ne ustraivaet', *Leninets*, М2 138 (7644), 24 Nov. 1990, 2.

[15] R. G. Abdulatipov and L. F. Boltenkova, eds., *Federativniy dogovor. Dokumenty. Kommentarii* (Moscow: Izdatel'stvo 'Respublika', 1992).

[16] 'Protokol k Federativnomu dogovoru', rep. in B. A. Strashun, *Federal'noe konstitutsionnoe pravo Rossii: Osnovnye istochniki po sostoyaniyu na 15 sentyabrya 1996 goda* (Moscow: Izdatel'stvo NORMA, 1996), 198–9.

In addition to the protocols, a special appendix (*prilozhenie*) was signed exclusively for one republic: Bashkortostan. At the eleventh hour, Bashkortostan threatened to walk out on the negotiations, an act that would have collapsed the process given the refusal of two key republics (Tatarstan and Chechnya) to sign the Treaty. The appendix granted special exceptions and privileges exclusively to Bashkortostan: its legislative and judicial systems were declared to be independent, assertions of independent statehood and the right to certain foreign relations acknowledged, and certain statements about republican control of property were added.[17] While it could be said that these special dispensations were nominal and often merely a few shades different from powers provided by the Federation Treaty, the Appendix established a powerful precedent from the outset of the 'renewed' Russian Federation: the ink was not yet dry on the Treaty before parochial bilateral exceptions to it were being made.[18]

The October 1993 shelling of the White House and arrest of Yeltsin's parliamentary opponents left the Federation Treaty subordinated to Yeltsin's draft Constitution.[19] While Articles 71 and 72 of the Constitution were nearly exact duplications of Articles I and II of the Treaty (establishing exclusive federal and joint jurisdictions), Treaty Article III on exclusive republican powers was omitted from the Constitution. The presumption that republics possessed all powers not explicitly handed over to the Federation in the Treaty—a more confederal conception—was reversed by Article 73, which granted constituent units only those remaining powers not claimed by federal authorities. Republican sovereignty and separate citizenship were no longer acknowledged.

NULLIFICATION: THE PARADE OF TREATIES

The Parade of Sovereignties developed a vocabulary and a mindset of provincial autonomy well before attempts were made to develop sound federation-wide organizing principles. Federation Treaty negotiations quickly fell hostage to that mindset as republics realized that they could ignore the federal centre (Chechnya and Tatarstan) or make last-minute ultimatums (Bashkortostan and Sakha-Yakutia) with a fair degree of impunity. Republican elites spoke in terms of 'treaty-constitutional' federal relations, implying their prerogatives as sovereign subjects of international law. Federal actors insisted on 'constitution-treaty'-based federalism, by which they meant the strong central power that had always dominated centre–periphery relations in Russia. A vocabulary of federalism built on an interest in multilateral, transparent, and equal relations was not of particular interest to either side. Bilateralism, exceptionalism, and hierarchy were the emerging norms of Russian federal politics.

A new phrase increasingly dominated regional conceptions of federalism—*snizu vverkh*, 'from the bottom up.' At its core was the notion that a federation really was *not* more than the sum of its parts, each of which had an indissoluble sovereignty of its own. This principle

---

[17] M. A. Aiupov *et al.*, eds., *Stanovlenie dogovornykh otnoshenii Respubliki Bashkortostan i Rossiyskoy Federatsii* (Ufa: Izdatel'sko-poligraficheskiy kompleks pri Sekretariate Gosudarstevennogo Sobraniya Respubliki Bashkortostan, 1997).

[18] Bashkortostan was not the only republic to receive a special, long-term agreement in exchange for its signature. Between initialling the treaty on 14 March, and signing on 31 March 1992, the diamond-rich republic of Sakha-Yakutia signed a lucrative diamond output agreement with federal authorities.

[19] Section Two, Article 1, §4. *Konstitutsiya Rossiyskoy Federatsii* (Moscow: Izdatel'stvo 'Os'-89', 1998).

found expression at the highest levels of regional politics.[20] In Tatarstan, the phrase even influenced republican law, passed weeks after the acceptance of a fiercely independent republican Constitution, which appealed to the then Russian Federal Supreme Soviet to construct 'treaty-constitutional relations' with the republic.[21]

Republican constitutions based their legitimacy on many of the same principles found in declarations of sovereignty, foremost of which was the principle that republican laws (by virtue of state sovereignty) retained supremacy over federal legislation. A hierarchy implicit in the treaty-constitutional approach raised republics above the federal government in all matters save those explicitly transferred by the republics. This approach sounded less in federal solutions and more in confederal ones. The federal approach was the reverse, summarized in 1994 by Yeltsin's then chief-of-staff Sergei Filatov: 'The most general trends are the aspiration of the republic elites to represent the powers of the Russian Federation as the sum of powers delegated by the components (this is notably characteristic of the constitutions of Bashkortostan, Buryatia, Sakha, Tatarstan, and Tuva). However, the powers of the Russian Federation ensue from its own sovereignty as a single, integral federative state, and they do not depend on the components.'[22]

Yeltsin responded to regional assertions of sovereignty by beginning a new parade, the Parade of Treaties. 'I have not renounced my formula,' he declared in the spring of 1994, 'Take as much sovereignty as you can swallow.'[23] Tatarstan was the first republic to receive a bilateral treaty, signed in February 1994 (although negotiations had taken several years). Bilateral treaties were really several documents: a treaty (*dogovor*), establishing general principles, and a complement of agreements (*sovershenie*) that provided short-term (five-year) concrete arrangements for budgetary, tax, personnel, and other relationships. Between 1994 and 1998, forty-six of the eighty-nine subjects of the Federation signed bilateral treaties with the federal executive.

The Parade of Treaties raised a number of serious questions for the future of Russian federalism. First, the practice of overriding, supplementing, or amending centre–periphery relations established in the federal Constitution highlighted the controversy and confusion of 'treaty-constitutional' versus 'constitutional-treaty' approaches to federalism. How important was the Constitution compared to a bilateral treaty? Second, it was unclear where bilateral treaties should be placed in the hierarchy of laws established by the Constitution. Bilateral treaties were never ratified by either federal or regional legislatures; they were wholly executive-driven relationships, exclusively involving presidents, governors, and prime ministers. This question of legality was further aggravated by the suspicion shared by many regional leaders that, in addition to published treaties, secret agreements were also negotiated. Third, apart from the content of bilateral treaties, the process of negotiation entailed a certain brinkmanship: the best treaties were negotiated by regions with the power

[20] Rashit Vagizov, a committee chairman in the Tatarstan Parliament, insisted that the voluntary delegation of political power 'from the bottom up' was a core principle of federalism. Author's interview, 10 June 1997, Tatarstan State Soviet, Kazan.

[21] Tatar Law 'On the order introducing into action the Constitution of the Republic of Tatarstan', in Rafael' Khakimov, ed., *Belaya kniga Tatarstuna: put' k suverenitetu, 1990–1995* (Kazan: Tsentr gumanitarnykh proektov i issledovanii, 1996), 23–4.

[22] 'Filatov on Center-Region Constitutional Issues', *FBIS Daily Report: Central Eurasia*, 2 Sept. 1994, p. 19.

[23] Elena Tregubova, 'Boris Yel'tsin v Tatarii', *Segodnya*, 31 May 1994, p. 1.

and nerve to withhold tax payments, boycott federal elections or otherwise exempt themselves from the federal polity.

The proliferation of treaties was accompanied by the adoption by republics and regions of their own constitutions and charters. The so-called 'War of Laws,' coincident with the parade of treaties, produced thousands of laws and constitutional clauses that contradicted the federal constitution and federal law. The Russian Federation Ministry of Justice announced in late 1996 that nineteen out of twenty-one republican constitutions violated the federal Constitution.[24] Article Seven of the Constitution of the Republic of Ingushetia announced that a federal law was 'lawful' only to the extent that it did not violate the 'sovereign rights' of the republic. Article 41 of the Constitution of Sakha-Yakutia required federal legislation to pass a vote in the lower chamber of the republican parliament before its jurisdiction would be accepted in the republic. Other republics, for example Adygeya and Dagestan, reserved the right to suspend federal legislation, subject to varying degrees of arbitration.[25] Despite the strong language of the federal Constitution and the small but growing number of high court cases denouncing regional non-compliance and malfeasance, republics continued to seek alternatives to the federal framework, often openly defying it.[26]

These are extraordinary claims for component states in a federal system, for they call into question the very unified legal space that is both a hallmark and a fundamental advantage of federation. The perils of nullification and the potential for the destruction of a federal civic identity are very real.

Putin's way: towards a 'dictatorship of law'?

Yeltsin made weak attempts to restructure increasingly difficult relations. On 30 July 1999 a new federal law came into force to regulate the bilateral treaty process.[27] The law re-emphasized the supremacy of federal laws and Constitution in the legal hierarchy, categorically stated the principle of glasnost in treaty promulgation, and gave regions three years to bring existing treaties into conformity with federal law. However, the law stopped short of establishing the ratification of treaties by federal and regional legislatures, requiring only examination (*rassmotreniya*) by the legislature prior to adoption. Given that no treaty had been signed since June 1998, the law seemed conspicuously late.

The inauguration of Vladimir Putin led to substantial change for Russian federalism. Less than a week after taking his oath of office, Putin issued a presidential decree (*ukaz*) on 'The Status of the Plenipotentiary Representative of the President in a Federal District'.[28] The

---

[24] Irina Nagornykh, 'Regiony staviat na konfrontatsiyu', *Segodnya*, 22 Nov. 1996, p. 2.

[25] *Konstitutsii Respublik v sostave Rossiyskoy Federatsii*, Vypusk 1 (Moscow: Izdanie Gosudarstvennoy Dumy, Izvestiia, 1995).

[26] See e.g. 'Postanovlenie Konstitutsionnogo Suda Rossiiskoy Federatsii po delu o proverke konstitutsionnosti statey 80, 92, 93 i 94 Konstitutsii Respubliki Komi i stat'i 31 Zakona Respubliki Komi ot 31 oktiabrya 1994 goda "Ob organakh ispolnitel'noy vlasti v Respublike Komi"', *Rossiiskaya gazeta*, 31 Jan. 1998, p. 4; Alexander Blankenagel, 'Local Self-Government vs. State Administration: The Udmurtiia Decision', *East European Constitutional Review*, 6/1 (1997), 51.

[27] Zakon 'O printsipakh i poriadke razgranicheniya predmetov vedeniya i polnomochii mezhdu organami gosudarstvennoy vlasti Rossiyskoy Federatsii i organami gosudarstvennoy vlasti sub"ektov Rossiyskoy Federatsii', *Sobranie zakonodatel'stva Rossiyskoy Federatsii*, 26 (28 June 1999), item 3176, pp. 5685–92.

[28] *Rossiyskaya gazeta*, 16 May 2000, p. 5.

decree divided Russia into seven federal districts to which Putin appointed plenipotentiary representatives to coordinate the activity of federal organs, ensure the observance of federal laws and the conformity of regional laws to the federal Constitution, and to suggest to the president the suspension of non-conforming legislation and executive normative acts. More *ukazy* soon followed, declaring laws or executive orders of some regions in violation of federal law and therefore null and void.[29] Boris Nemtsov, a former governor and leader of the Union of Right Forces, recognized the key to the decrees would lie in the calibre and standing of the people appointed to head the new districts. If they were just 'run-of-the-mill bureaucrats', then the whole new system would be 'nothing other than decorative'.[30] Putin's choices indicated his resolve: five of the seven representatives were generals (including Viktor Cherkesov, former deputy director of the FSB, and Petr Latyshev, former deputy minister of the MVD).[31]

Putin followed his *ukaz* with a salvo of proposals to reform the Federation Council and give him the power to dismiss recalcitrant executives, legislatures, and local government officials throughout the Federation.[32] Eugene Huskey, earlier in this volume (Chapter 6), analyses these bills, all three of which were signed into law after difficult passage through the Federal Assembly.[33] Putin's apparent victory, however, presents serious concerns of executive overreach, tipping an already fragile balance of the separation of powers (not only between branches of government but also between federal and regional levels of government). Although the Constitution is vague regarding who constitutes the 'representatives' that compose the upper chamber, many politicians and lawyers protested that such extensive reforms required full-blown constitutional amendment, not mere legislation.[34] A transfer of power from the Federation Council to a proposed 'State Council' under the executive branch would almost certainly require such amendment. Nikolai Fedorov, president of the republic of Chuvashia and an outspoken critic of the reforms, led other senators to begin an appeal to the Constitutional Court, contending that 'all honest lawyers admit that these reforms and laws are essentially revising the existing constitutional structure of the Russian Federation . . .'.[35]

One month after Putin's initial reform package, the federal Constitutional Court issued a Determination (*Opredelenie*) on the constitutions of Adygeya, Bashkortostan, Ingushetia, Komi, N. Ossetia, and Tatarstan.[36] This highly critical document rejected the claims to sovereignty (several bordering on the doctrine of nullification) made by these republics over the past decade. The decision of the Court—a court of discretionary jurisdiction—at such a

---

[29] See e.g. an *ukaz* of 15 May suspending a resolution levying fines by the head of Smolensk oblast as a violation of federal law. *Rossiyskaya gazeta*, 18 May 2000, p. 4. Other early decrees targeted alleged violations by Adygeya, Ingushetia, Amur, and Tver.

[30] *Segodnya*, 16 May 2000, p. 4.

[31] *Current Digest of the Post-Soviet Press*, 52/20 (2000): 2–4. *Rossiyskaya gazeta*, 20 May 2000, p. 3. *Segodnya*, 31 May 2000, pp. 1–2.

[32] Original proposals published in *Nezavisimaya gazeta*, 20 May 2000, pp. 4–5.

[33] The Federation Council predictably vetoed its own proposed dissolution and the federal executive power to dismiss governors. While in the latter case, the Duma overrode that veto with a 2:3 majority, a special conciliation commission was necessary to pass the amended Federation Council reform. Local government reform, Putin's third prong, provoked comparatively less controversy.

[34] RF Constitution, Art. 95, ss 2.

[35] *Radio Free Europe/Radio Liberty Newsline*, 4/148 Part 1, 3 Aug. 2000, 36.

[36] Opredelenie Konstitutsionnogo Suda Rossyskoy Federatsii, 27 June 2000.

charged moment in Russian politics was viewed by some as a political warning as much as a legal ruling. To others the Court's decision was unimportant. A senior official of the Permanent Mission of the Republic of Bashkortostan in Moscow observed (on condition of anonymity): 'In Russia, the political process is more important than the law itself. So the agreements of our president with the Russian Federation president are more important than the law. The Constitutional Court of Russia is just a body, highly respected, but just a body of the Russian Federation. It has nothing to do with the Republic of Bashkortostan—we have our own Constitutional Court.'[37] In Tatarstan, Tatar nationalists presented that republic's parliament and president with a bill declaring the decision invalid on its territory.[38]

Of course, such thinking is not new, but part of the ongoing, sometimes schizophrenic, conceptual battle over basic principles of federalism. The latest attempt at reform draws from that legacy as much as it continues it. The future of the 'new Russian federalism' depends in large part on what balance can be struck between valid assertions of regional autonomy and federal obligations to promote and protect democratic principles and a unified legal space throughout the country. As one respected legal scholar observed, Putin's federal reforms 'unwittingly unleashed a war', the resolution of which will not be quick and the outcome of which is impossible to predict.[39]

---

[37] Author's interview, Moscow, 14 July 2000.

[38] Boris Bronshtein, 'Vosstanovit' nezavisimost'', *Izvestiya* (online), 9 Aug. 2000.

[39] William Smirnov, prominent political scientist and lawyer, Institute of State and Law. Author's interview, Moscow, 13 July 2000.

28 Political Power and Political Stability in the Russian Regions

Alla Chirikova and Natalya Lapina

In recent years, there has been an increase in the influence of the regional authorities on the political situation in their areas. That influence becomes particularly noticeable when election campaigns are being prepared and carried out. The strategies adopted in the regions for controlling the political situation can be classed as 'overt' and 'covert'. This account of them is based especially on case-studies of the Perm and Rostov regions of Russia.[1]

The authorities in the Perm oblast operate *overt organizational and legal supervision*. This administrative strategy consists in the establishment of organizational structures within the administration that are capable of coordinating relations between the parties and ensuring equal conditions and opportunities for all. The creation of these means of monitoring the political situation has led in Perm to the emergence of a new set of links among the vice-governor for political affairs, the head of the public relations department, and the head of the political and national relations department.

In March 2000 a Consultative Political Council (CPC) attached to the head of the Perm region was created in Prikamye. The idea behind it was to maintain a political balance in the region. According to the Perm governor's assistant, Stepan Kiselev, the new body was created to work out a set of rules binding on all. The council has incorporated the region's most influential politicians—deputies, representatives of big business, and heads of the local and district administration.

The formation of these new administrative structures on the eve of the 1999–2000 elections showed that the regional administration intended to be active in analysing the political situation of the region so that it could accurately forecast possible changes in electoral behaviour, form information channels and supervise the legality of the various parties' conduct. For its part, the creation of the CPC is an important indication of the consolidation of the regional political elite around the head of the oblast, Gennady Igumnov, on the eve of the gubernatorial elections. The creation of legal structures responsible for political work was a new step on the part of the governor, but not all regional bosses were in agreement about it. The oblast administration's entry into the political sphere revealed the serious efforts on the part of the regional authorities to increase their role in the electoral process.

Chapter specially commissioned for this volume. Translated by Polly Jones.

[1] The research was conducted in the summer of 1999 with the support of the Ebert Foundation (Germany). Most of the writing of this chapter was completed in April 2000, with some minor updating in September of that year.

Round tables are becoming another means of overt supervision; they are organized on the initiative of the administration at the district and city levels alike. This practice has been widely adopted in both of the regions studied. As a rule, round tables are summoned to discuss the region's most pressing political problems. The majority (70 per cent) of round table participants give a positive assessment of this kind of mutual cooperation, saying that it allows them to get to know their political rivals better through establishing both inter-party and interpersonal relations with them. The round tables also allow the regional administration, in turn, to keep their finger on the pulse of the political processes in their region, to observe the development of parties and movements, and to establish working relations with them.

Yet another means of supervising the development of the political situation is the model of *information management*, developed in the Rostov oblast. This essentially consists of the transmission of essential information to the governor from his first deputies, each of whom controls individual territories and who are obliged not only to inform the regional author-ities about processes happening in their district, but also actively to resolve the most serious problems that arise there. This technique not only ensures reliability of information, but also allows the supervision of the local administration's conduct and the efficacy of its policies. In this case, the authorities replace the institutions of civil society, such as parties and social movements, and bring in 'direct rule'.

The methods of dominating local politics mentioned above can be classed as 'overt.' Another type of administration, which can be termed *selective patronage*, belongs in a different category. In this case, the authority establishes privileged relations with, and gives significant support to, several parties and movements without advertising its political con-tacts. The local authority's choice of parties and allies depends on several factors, including the political preferences of the authority's leader, the personal relationships formed between party leaders and the leader of the authority and, finally, the policies of the federal centre in party formation. Despite the fact that those representatives of power interviewed by us emphasize their equal relations with all democratic movements, information we received leads us to assert that each region has evolved its own system of preferential support for certain movements. Thus, in the Perm oblast in summer 1999, parties and movements were 'shared out' between the governor and the mayor: the mayor patronized Yabloko and Otechestvo (Fatherland), whilst the governor supported NDR, DPR, and Vsya Rossiya (All Russia). In the Rostov district during the same period there were noticeably warm relations between the regional and city administrations and the Fatherland party.

'Selective patronage' presupposes a different form of administrative support for political parties and movements than that observed in the case of overt control. The form of cooper-ation between the authorities and political actors that we describe above is based upon the personal relations between leaders of the authorities and the bosses of political parties, is private in nature, and is not amenable to regulation by society. This type of control over the political situation can be classed as semi-legal, without saying that it clearly contravenes Russian laws banning public servants from participating in electoral campaigns.

The methods of cooperation between authorities and parties and the means of control-ling the political situation that are evolving in the regions and that we survey above guaran-tee the stability and predictability of the political process. The role of administrative control over the sphere of regional politics increased in the run-up to the parliamentary elections.

This was particularly perceptible during the creation of the regional departments of the Yedintsvo (Unity). Before November 1999, the Rostov oblast authorities made no efforts to form a pre-election staff for Yedinstvo, although at the start of October, a group of thirty-eight deputies including the governor Vladimir Chub had proclaimed its support for the formation of a pro-government movement. However, just after the eruption of the region's serious energy crisis (October 1999), the authorities became actively involved in party formation. The administrative forces with the largest potential influence on voters were activated for Yedinstvo: the head of the district pensions fund, the district minister for education, the deputy minister for industry, the vice-governor for Cossack affairs, the vice-mayor of Rostov for social affairs/security, and the head of the city medical insurance fund. This method of mobilizing informational and administrative-political resources produced the expected result—in the Rostov oblast the pro-government party Yedinstvo was the undisputed winner in the elections, polling 30.7 per cent of votes in the region.

The strength and influence of regional power is an indisputable fact. Nonetheless, however strong the regional power, political and economic stability in any given region depends on the politics of the federal centre. Hitherto we have noted factors of internal regional stability and controls. Let us now turn to the analysis of external factors in the stability of the region—the relations between the Federation and its subjects.

The federal centre and the political stability of the Russian regions

The interaction of the regions with the federal centre and the influence of the latter on the political stability of the regions is a complex system. On the centre's side, the main players are the president of the Russian Federation, the presidential administration, and the head of the cabinet of ministers whilst on the side of the federal subjects, they are the head of executive power in the regions—presidents of the republics and the governors of the territories (*krai*) and regions (*oblast'*). Over the course of the 1990s, relations between the federal centre and the subjects of the Russian Federation have had their ups and downs. Experts have divided these relations into 'liberal' and 'centralistic' periods.[2] Liberal policies, associated with Viktor Chernomyrdin, were essentially aimed at expanding the power of regional authorities. Moves towards centralization, typified by such figures as Anatoly Chubais and Yevgeny Primakov, envisaged tougher control over regional processes and local authorities by the federal centre. Federal policies have swung from one extreme to the other, but neither has come to dominate.

In recent years, many regional leaders have achieved national recognition, with significant influence over the situation in their own regions, and in particular over the results of elections on their territories. However, these advances have not led in turn to an improvement in relations within the federation. The interaction of the centre with its subjects continues to operate not according to universal rules that are equally binding on all, but according to the personal relations between the powers in Moscow and regional leaders.

So what exactly are the interests of the federal centre and the regions and how should relations be constituted between them in order to ensure stability in both the country as a

[2] P. Turovskiy, ed., *Politicheskie protsessy v regionakh Rossii* (Moscow: Centre for Political Technology, 1998), 17–26.

whole and its individual parts? We have attempted to determine answers to these questions in the course of our interviews conducted in the Perm and Rostov regions.

What do the regional elites expect from the federal centre?

Data from our interviews allow us to discern those tendencies in the policies of the centre that regional elites consider in need of the most urgent change, with a view to making the situation in the country and in individual regions more manageable. These include (opinions given in percentages):

- The introduction of strict supervision of the use of state funds by the federal centre (70 per cent).
- The curtailment of the centre's strict control over currency flows within the territory and the introduction of rational and predictable rules to govern the distribution of transfers according to the situation in the region (60 per cent).
- The implementation on the part of the federal centre of differentiated policies toward donor regions and recipient regions (60 per cent).
- The coordination of the efforts of the centre and the regional authorities in matters of property privatization in the regions (50 per cent).
- A guarantee from the centre of the essential conditions for the reinforcement of territorial independence (40 per cent).
- A review of taxation policies imposed by the centre on the territories (40 per cent).

The suggestions that we received from the regional elites also include a variety of personal positions, but one tendency stands out particularly clearly: regional elites insist upon the redistribution of power between the centre and the regions, and demand that the centre's policies towards the subjects of the federation be well thought out and rational rather than arbitrary. This position was most consistently espoused by the vice-governor of the Rostov oblast, Gennady Kuznetsov, in his interview with us: 'The centre has to maintain its rightful functions. The centre must maintain all those federal functions and the necessary amount of federal funds for the upkeep of federal structures like the army, the police, and the organs of administration. That much is essential. The centre should also keep supervisory powers over fundamental issues, including control over the distribution of financial resources in the territories. But the centre has to present to the regions a clear outline of where it is directing our resources. If we agree to supervision, the centre must also be accountable to the regions.'

His sentiments are echoed by the other vice-governor of the Rostov region, and now a Duma deputy, Vladimir Averchenko: 'I think that the more federal power tries to limit the regions, the worse the outcome will be. The rule of law can only be built on the basis of reasonable compromise. If that doesn't happen, if there's just more ambition, shouting, and rebellion, then the growth of separatism will be unavoidable. You can't keep on playing around, saying what's possible for one person is impossible for someone else. They have to understand that each territory must live according to how well it works. At the moment ten Russian territories are donors. Let them live better. There has to be a system where it's profitable for regions to work better. At the moment we see the opposite happening—regions which don't work live better.'

The governor of the Perm oblast, Gennady Igumnov, also mentions the necessity of reforming the centre's policies towards the donor regions: 'Why should donors like us have the same budget provision as all the rest? Why does the federal centre only remember about us when it needs to take away piles of our money? Why do I have to be treated the same as any territory on 80 per cent subsidies? I'm earning money, you see, and that money is going straight from me to the territories. I shouldn't be living like they are.'

The emotional charge echoing in the words of the Perm governor, who has consistently shown loyalty to the centre, shows that the potential of the regional elites' unrealized expectations is running out inexorably, even for moderate and reasonable leaders. All this shows that the previous strategy adopted by the centre to deal with the regions cannot continue to be applied into the future. As the political situation stabilizes in individual regions, as power becomes stronger and the economic crisis is overcome, the desire for greater symmetry and partnership in relations with the centre will become more and more widespread. And one other interesting detail should be mentioned. The regional elites are no longer satisfied merely to demand an expansion of their own independence, but also now call for supervision of the centre by the federal subjects.

It is not only the oblast authorities who mention the necessity of rationalizing the system of centre-region relations, but also the heads of local administration, who are subject to twofold pressures from those above them. The head of the city administration in Novocher-kassk, Nikolai Pristyazhnyuk, has this to say: 'I support the transfer of power to the subjects of the federation. Even the simplest of questions, which could be solved on the town or regional level, takes half a year to be decided at the centre. It takes a lot of time for all the papers to get all the way across Russia. The idea of granting greater rights to the subjects of the federation is being voiced more and more clearly. But there's no question of giving up the main, financial lever. There has to be full independence. I don't think that the regional elites are going to get so angry that they start harming Russia. The vast majority of governors are normal folk.'

At the moment, the economy is developing into the regional elites' biggest priority. Governors are becoming more and more vocal about the need for a transfer of some federal property into the hands of the regional authorities. The economic elites are as concerned for this to be achieved as are the heads of regional administration. Local businessmen and directors think that the governor would be more efficient at managing the property that has until now been handled by the federal authorities and the Moscow banks. The disagreement between the federal centre and the regions over the question of economic development and regulation of property rights was felt by respondents to be a serious problem for the Russian Federation. 'You can't hope for anything financially from the centre,' says the former speaker of the Perm regional legislative assembly (now a Duma deputy), Yury Medvedev, 'All they do is take, take, take. We try to stand up to them, but there's nothing we can do about it. We can only demand of the centre that our powers be increased. As far as that goes, they have something to give, to share out. The main thing is to get more independence in managing property within the regional territory. That would make things better, not worse for the state. We're talking about major enterprises. The centre has to consult the regions when it comes to privatization.'

The elites also consider as long overdue the transfer of regional property, i.e. the sale of federal enterprises to private buyers, who could ensure the effective running of those enter-prises. 'If there's a federal enterprise, it should be an example of how things should work, something to strive for,' says one of our respondents. 'If not, then it's better to sell off that enterprise, put it up for auction. Maybe someone else will be able to sort things out. That's better than to pilfer it or to kill it off financially. It's all part of this market economy that we love to talk about.'

Our respondents also consider that a large degree of independence should be granted to the regions to form external economic links. That demand was voiced most frequently by representatives of the elite in Prikamye, a region aiming to expand its economic links with the outside world.

The evaluations that we received in the course of our investigation in 1999 diverge somewhat from the list of expectations formulated by representatives of the elite in our survey of 1996–8. The main indications of strain in centre–region relations appear in economic-legal matters. The past two years have intensified demands from regional elites to regulate financial relations between the centre and the regions and questions relating to the redistribution of property and to the (law-bound) improvement of property rights. Yet more intense is the demand for regulation of the legality of federal behaviour. New demands are also being formulated for the expansion of regions' rights in the formation of external economic contacts. Demands for increased independence for the regions and for the implementation of rational taxation policies at the centre have stayed at the same level. However, at the same time as criticizing the centre's policies and putting forward their suggestions and demands, the regional elites clearly acknowledged that they did not expect any rapid changes in federal relations. Their scepticism was entirely understandable. In 1999 and early 2000, the federal centre had other issues to resolve, connected to the parliamentary and presidential elections. Only after the resolution of these questions could the federal centre make serious decisions about the regions.

Power and the New Federalism: the centre's resources and its influence on political stability in the regions

In this section we will look in more detail at the interaction of the regions with the centre in an attempt to determine whether there is differentiation in the relations between different subjects of the Federation and the centre and where those differences lie, whether it can be deemed justified in the current conditions and how it impacts on the political situation in the regions.

Relations between central power and the subjects of the federation largely depend upon the type of political power developing in the region and upon the level of popular support for the local administration. Thus, the centre's relations with regions where authoritarian-national power has developed have always been complex. A section of regional leaders of this type—the presidents of North Ossetia, Yakutia, and Kalmykia—have not made political demands of the federal centre, preferring not to enter into conflict with the president of the Russian Federation. They have supported the centre on condition of non-interference by federal authorities in the internal affairs of their regions. Other authoritarian-national leaders have had more complex relations with the centre. The presidents of the prosperous republics of Tatarstan and Bashkortostan first chose to oppose the centre (1991–3) and only after achieving recognition of the special status of their republics started to cooperate with the federal authorities in a more or less peaceful fashion.

Leaders of regions which have developed the authoritarian-Communist type of regime have varying relations with the federal centre. Some sharply criticize federal power whilst others, in spite of their ideological convictions, acknowledge the benefits of collaboration with the federal authorities. Important examples include the governor of the Orlov oblast who is also chairman of the Federation council, Yegor Stroev, and the governor of the Kemerevo region, Aman Tuleev. Others choose the middle road: in their own regions, they engage in sharp criticism of the federal authorities, but remain emphatically loyal and well behaved in their dealings with state leaders. Alexander Surikov, boss of the Altai territory, exemplifies this kind of behaviour.

The authoritarian-bureaucratic Moscow authorities also rest on a knife-edge between conflict and reconciliation in their dealings with the federal centre. Over many years of Russian reform, the Moscow mayor, Yury Luzhkov, supported the president of the Russian Federation. However, after the personal political ambitions of the Moscow mayor became apparent, relations between the two centres of power underwent an acute deterioration. The decision by Luzhkov to create his own political movement, Fatherland, was taken by the presidential administration to be a blatant insult. After Primakov joined Fatherland, the situation further deteriorated. The conflict reached its peak during the electoral campaign at the end of 1999. However, the failure of Fatherland in the 1999 parliamentary elections (polling 13.3 per cent) forced Luzhkov to change tack. From the start of 2000 he regularly proclaimed his loyalty to Vladimir Putin and tried to regain lost trust.

The relations of the federal centre with leaders of the regions where elements of democracy have been observable have been for the most part quite good, albeit not without conflict, especially over such issues as unpaid taxes for the federal budget, the size of central transfers to the regions, or local enterprise debt.

Those leaders who have formulated their own individual style of leadership and have been capable of cooperating with the centre for the most part belong in the category of strong leaders. Their regions, for all the complexities of attaining consensus with the centre, depend less upon the conduct of the latter, although this is conditional on a number of factors. As well as those regional leaders who have managed to create an individual style of leadership and to establish relative independence from the centre, the federation also has many subjects with weak leaders who are entirely dependent on the decisions taken by the federal authorities. At times this dependency has turned them into the most overt opponents of the federal centre. Our interviews in one of the depressed regions showed that more than 80 per cent of the regional leaders surveyed consider the conduct of the central elites as 'inadequate' and 'chaotic', leading to destabilization in the regional situation. In saying this, they admit that the centre wields a large influence over the region, and that without its support, the local authorities would lose the ability to control the situation. The view of those surveyed is that the inconsistency of the federal centre forces regional elites to operate under 'emergency conditions', which has a negative impact on their influence over the region. The data from our interviews show that it is precisely weak regions characterized by political instability that resort to a chaotic set of rules of the game in conditions of uncertainty. The federal authorities find it difficult to engage in dialogue with weak regional leaders since the latter, in their search for new allies, frequently switch direction.

When discussing relations between the federal and regional authorities, contemporary Russian analysts often mention regional separatism and the potential disintegration of the

Russian Federation.[3] The authors of the current study are sceptical about scenarios of the breakup of Russia and hold that the factors favourable to integration outweigh tendencies towards disintegration. The federal centre, in spite of the fact that it lost many of its levers of controls over the regions during the 1990s, still maintains means of influencing the federal subjects, namely the powerful political-administrative and economic resources that the centre controls and is prepared to use if necessary. These are usually forgotten at times of liberal policies from the centre towards the regions, and are only recalled when centralizing tendencies gain ground.

The political-administrative means of influence possessed by the centre include: the activities of the federal authorities on the territory of the subjects of the federation, the policies carried out by the Moscow authorities in the regions, and the appointment of cadres. Federal services have lately become more active on the regions' territory. Prosecutors are bringing criminal actions against the representatives of the regional power elites. Also at work on the regions' territory is the free trade and anti-monopoly ministry. In many regions this organization has curbed arbitrary behaviour on the part of the regional authorities and has helped to ensure the universal observance of market rules. There is also growing success in bringing laws of the subjects of the federation into line with the Russian Constitution. The unification of laws is extremely significant in view of the fact that, according to the Federal ministry of justice, 20 per cent of the normative acts passed in the regions contravene the laws of the Russian Federation. There is much still to be done in this regard, in so far as the subjects of the federation illegally appropriate to themselves the plenary powers of the centre.

On the eve of the parliamentary and presidential elections, the centre again reminded the regional authorities of who decides the key questions in the Russian Federation. From the second half of 1999 onwards, new—and already well-known—mechanisms of control over the regions were put in place. Thus, in February 2000 it became clear that the ministry for the press was intending to broadcast state television regional campaigns under the full supervision of the state holding, VGTRK (the All-Russian State Television and Radio Company). In accordance with this resolution, the heads of local TV companies will be appointed without the regional authorities being consulted, which contravenes the agreements on the limitation of plenary powers signed between the regions and the federal centre.

The official aim of Moscow politicians is to carry out universal policies on the media and to stand up to the commercial media owned by the financial-industrial groups. But it is also no secret that the policies of the federal authorities are aimed against 'obstinate' regional leaders. The first victim of these policies was Moscow mayor, Yury Luzhkov. The outcome of a winter 2000 competition for the use of radio frequencies deprived Luzhkov of two of 'his' radio stations—'Govorit Moskva' (Moscow Speaks) and 'Radio Sport'.

In the last months of 1999 and in early 2000, the federal centre's financial control over the regions became stricter. In the wake of an investigation into debts to the federal budget, the federal Finance Ministry took control of the budgets of Dagestan, Tuva, the Altai republic, and the Kemerovo region.

Aside from universal mechanisms of control and pressure, the centre also has at its disposal 'special measures' for use in individual regions. Over the summer of 1999 in the

---

[3] See Turovskiy, *Politicheskie protsessy*, for more details.

Rostov region there were significant alterations to personnel. In July, S. Kugaev, a manager from Novosibirsk and graduate of the Higher School of the KGB, was confirmed as the new chairman of the Rostov Savings Bank (Sberbank). Immediately after this, the Savings Bank issued demands to the Rostov authorities to pay off their debts. In September, a new police boss appeared on the scene—S. Shchadrin, previously unknown in Rostov, but nonetheless close to the minister of internal affairs. Right after these two events, the governor, Vladimir Chub, officially announced his support for the parliamentary bloc, Yedinstvo. Following that, the conflict between the district leadership and the Savings Bank came to an end, whilst the problems with debts were resolved in favour of the oblast.[4]

The federal centre also has at its disposal economic resources that allow it to exert pressure on the regions. It remains in a strong position thanks to its ownership and administration of federal property and to its direction of the Central Bank, the Finance Ministry, customs, the Exchequer and other federal organs operating/active on a regional level. Over the voucher (1992–3), money (which began in 1994), and security (the first securities auctions took place over autumn–winter 1995) phases of privatization, the federal authorities parted with its property with relative ease. However, as the number of resources that it controlled diminished, and in the absence of effective new owners, the federal centre started to reconsider its attitude towards privatization. The first person to signal the intention of the state to increase its economic functions was the former Prime Minister, Yevgeny Primakov. These days, the demand is being repeated by the new president, Vladimir Putin. All in all, it seems likely that, in the near future, the restructuring of industrial and financial capital in Russia will involve the active participation of the state.

Besides federal propery, the centre also maintains at its disposal the railroads, transport routes and the gas, oil, and energy supply systems. The political alliance formed between the state and natural monopolies such as Gazprom and EES ensures the maintenance of a single economic space. In conflicts with the regional authorities, the largest energy companies will often take the place of the state, effectively carrying out federal policies. The presence of unified systems of communication and the maintenance of territorial integrity are the most important conditions for extraction regions—especially oil- and gas-rich ones—to reach their full potential. This applies equally to the 'Russian' provinces and to the national republics (Tatarstan, Bashkortostan). On the strength of this, it seems to us that the threat of separation of these territories from the rest of the Russian Federation is without serious foundation. Yakutia is also in a similar situation. This republic, relying for its livelihood upon imports of food and consumer goods, depends no less than oil- or gas-rich republics upon unified Russian transport routes. And every year the quota established by the federal centre on the export of Yakut diamonds constitutes a further means of influencing the national elite.

As well as controls over property and the resources of basic livelihood, the federal centre also possesses one more powerful economic lever over the regions: state finances. The analysis of inter-budgetary relations lies beyond the scope of this study. Let us merely mention that the authorities have recently been attempting to regularize relations between the federal centre and its subjects, to establish transparency in this sphere of activity, and

---

[4] A. Miroshnichenko, 'Deregionalizatsiya, ili kak Rostovskoy oblasti pomogli proyti put' ot "Otechestva" k "Edinstvu"', *Rossiyskiy regional'nyy byulleten'*, 2 (31 Jan. 2000), 3–5.

also to establish supervision over the regions' distribution of resources received from the federal budget.

Already in 1998 and particularly in 1999, the federal centre started to deploy the economic resources at its disposal in order to exert pressure on the regions. The main centres for putting these centralizing policies into effect have been Gazprom and EES. The Rostov oblast has felt the effects of these policies. In October 1999 Russia sharply cut the levels of electrical energy supplied to the region. Rostov then fell victim to its worst energy crisis since perestroika: 'The power-cuts were totally unscheduled, enterprises suffered colossal losses and popular discontent increased. There never used to be any of these strange kind of cut-offs. Everyone secretly blamed the head of EES, Anatoly Chubais, but no one said anything about the political reasons behind what had happened.'[5] It should also be recalled that precisely under these conditions, three weeks before the elections, the Don contingent of the pro-government movement, Yedinstvo, started work in earnest in Rostov-on-Don.

In his analysis of centre–region relations in 1998, Nikolai Petrov noted that there was a reshuffle of structures that allowed real cooperation with the regions. If two years earlier the presidential administration played a leading role in such issues, then by 1998, its role in the life of the regions was negligible, whilst the main exponents of the policies of integration became the natural monopolies. In connection with this, it should be noted that relations between the forces who directly participate in the conceptualization and realization of regional policies do not remain unchanged. Indeed in 1998–9, the position of the presidential administration was noticeably weakened by the political crisis and the political and physical weakness of the former president, Boris Yeltsin. After the retirement of Yeltsin and the appointment to the post of acting president of Vladimir Putin, the situation changed and the role of the presidential administration in the preparation and implementation of policy decisions once again started to grow. In addition, just before the parliamentary and presidential elections, the federal authorities mobilized all available resources in the hope of achieving the necessary political results; administrative, political, and economic means of putting pressure on the regional authorities all came into play. All this clearly indicates that talk of the weakness of the federal centre is largely untrue. If the authorities in Moscow set themselves a task, they will certainly find a way to complete it.

In our view, the weakness of federal power consists not in the absence of mechanisms of influence over the regions, but in the absence of rational and consistent regional policies at the centre. Nonetheless, one tendency in the federal centre's policies over the last two years has become clear: Russian executive power as embodied in successive governments has been trying to rearrange to its own advantage the plenary powers of the centre and the regions. Although the practical realization of these intentions is difficult and requires constitutional change, the Russian establishment is actively discussing the outline of new regional policies. Its proponents place particular emphasis on the following factors in centre–region relations:

- The restoration and reinforcement of the vertical power hierarchy.
- Changes in the formation of the group of regional leaders.
- The consolidation of the constituent parts of the federation.

The restoration and reinforcement of the vertical line power hierarchy is envisaged in

[5] Ibid. 5.

terms of expanding the powers of the federal executive over territorial structures. To this end, all the cabinets of ministers that have succeeded one another in power since March 1998 have not proposed any innovations, but have rather moved towards the kind of centralization mentioned above. The government is creating inter-regional structures in the regions, some of which have become immediately operational in several areas. These include, for example, the representation of the pensions fund or the regional department for the prevention of organized crime on the territory of two or three oblasts. There is a lack of consensus amongst regional elites on this issue. As an example, the Leningrad oblast around St Petersburg has reacted positively to the idea of creating inter-regional structures of the federal organs.

The changes in procedures for forming the group of regional leaders propose an end to the practice of electing regional heads and leaders of local administration and a return to the principle of appointment by the president of the Russian Federation followed by approval from the local organs of self-government.

The question of a merging of subjects of the federation and the creation of twenty to twenty-five larger subjects in place of the current eighty-nine is, not for the first time, being discussed by the elite. As with other issues concerning the reorganization of the federation, this question has produced serious disputes. Moscow mayor, Yury Luzhkov, Kemerovo regional governor, Aman Tuleev and the leadership in St Petersburg and the Leningrad oblast are all in favour of the idea of turning the current inter-regional economic associations into fully-fledged subjects of the federation.

If in the past it was the federal centre that initiated moves towards centralization, these moves are now supported by individual representatives of the regional elite. In February 2000 *Nezavisimaya Gazeta* published a letter from governors Mikhail Prusak (Novgorod oblast), Yevgeny Savchenko (Belgorod oblast), and Oleg Bogomolov (Kurgan oblast) to the acting president, Vladimir Putin. The letter was essentially a programme for the reform of the system of state power in the country.[6] The governors' proposals included the reform of the organs of local self-government, in particular at the level of districts (*raion*) and micro-districts (*mikrorayony*) in towns, urban committees, settlements (*poselki*), and villages. Under this, 'the organs of power on the district and town level are incorporated into the system of the organs of state power'. The governors proposed that the heads of regional and town administrations be appointed with the approval of assemblies of representatives, trade unions, manufacturers' associations, and other civil organizations. The principle of appointment and dismissal would extend to the heads of the component parts of the federation. The president, subject to the approval of assemblies of representatives, would also make decisions on these appointments. The letter made it especially clear that heads of executive and judicial power in the subjects of the federation should not also be members of the Federation Council. Accordingly, it also proposed reform of the federal organs of state power and changes to the structure and mechanism of the formation of the Federation Council, either through making the Russian parliament unicameral or through retaining the bicameral form, but by changing the make-up of the upper house so that each federal subject is represented by one elected deputy.

---

[6] 'O reforme sistemy gosudarstvennoy vlasti i osnovnykh napravleniyakh ekonomicheskoy politiki', *Nezavisimaya gazeta*, 25 Feb. 2000, pp. 1 and 4.

The authors of the letter also propose reforms to the administrative-territorial arrangements in the country. The document makes it clear that this reform in its initial stages will not affect the republics that are part of the Russian Federation. 'In the long run', the document runs, 'it is essential to carry out reforms to the administrative-territorial arrangements in the country in order to consolidate the subjects of the federation, taking into account economic expediency and the demands for administrative efficiency.'[7]

It is difficult to judge the motives of those who wrote the letter. Let us not forget that they are governors, chosen in free elections in their regions where they can boast of widespread support. Evidently, these leaders have 'outgrown' the regional level and are trying to make a name for themselves on the federal stage. However, it seems extremely doubtful that the ideas they lay out in their letter will be put into practice. The majority of elected governors, not to mention heads of republics, will be extremely unwilling to give up their elected status and will do all they can to protect it from the encroachments of the federal centre.

The idea of the 'consolidation' of federal subjects may be supported by 'strong governors', for whom unification might mean the strengthening of their position. The most vociferous opponents of unifications are the 'weak' leaders of subsidized regions who will receive no political or economic dividends from the policy. In addition to them, opponents also include the heads of the republics who rightly consider that the unification of the Russian territories would put those larger territorial units on the same level as the national republics in terms of power.

Taking into account the disinclination of the authorities to provoke tension in relations with regional leaders in the near future, and also the growing competition between regional elites, it seems likely that these innovations will remain on paper for the time being. The publication of the letter had, however, concrete results, provoking a discussion on the future of the Russian Federation which made its way into the mass media.

The Kremlin did not instantly make its official position on this initiative known, unless one counts President Putin's announcement that the election of governors should not be stopped. In this regard, during the election campaign for the leadership of the Moscow oblast administration and for the mayor of St Petersburg, it became clear that the federal centre intended to play an active role in elections for the heads of federal subjects and in the formation of the gubernatorial body. The proposals being voiced already in early 2000 by politicians in Moscow and a few other regions can best be understood as an attempt to test the waters in order to ascertain who are the potential opponents and supporters of reform.

Conclusions

Regional power is now a consolidated force. The heads of the regions, having managed to reach a compromise with their economic actors and with the local administration, have eased the work of executive power and created a sufficiently effective chain of administrative command. In so doing, they have accumulated in their own hands sizeable resources of influence and can count on the necessary popular support in their regions. The ability of the regional authorities to find 'an area of consensus' with their elites allows them to sustain the necessary level of stability in the region. Thus, in this respect, the experience of politically

[7] Ibid. 4.

stable Russian regions could serve as a good example for the federal centre in its search for the optimal model of power for Russia.

However, in spite of this, it must be acknowledged that the power structure that has been crafted in the Russian regions is in many ways transient in nature. It has already moved on from the old party-state system of administration, with its entire dependence on the centre, but it is still far from democratic. The present transitional state of power can be defined as *guided democracy*. Within the framework of this model, democratic institutions are only just being formed, but they have not yet evolved into influential decision-making centres: the executive occupies almost all of the public sphere, taking over the fundamental powers and authority. The separation of powers is basically formalistic; parties, social organizations and the mass media have not become effective opponents of the existing authorities.

'Guided democracy' is essentially a quasi-democracy, within which authoritarian and democratic elements coexist. For the Russian regions, guided democracy has become a means of overcoming chaos and of strengthening the hierarchy of power. Paradoxical as it sounds, it is precisely the model of guided democracy that has allowed the Russian regions to achieve the necessary level of political stability. However, it must be acknowledged that this is a highly 'dependent' and shaky stability precisely because it is developed and achieved with the help of 'guided' or 'manipulated' democracy.[8] Many analysts maintain that such a regime will soon be established on the federal level.[9] And that means the federal centre will be putting into practice a scenario already approved by the regions.

The main component of 'guided democracy' is the regional authorities' control over political processes. This control is achieved in different ways, but it often takes the form of the authorities' direct intervention in the process of party formation. The means of directing the political situation in the region are not specific, but vary according to the regions' models of power. Leaders who tend towards administrative models of the monocentric type attempt to establish strict control over the entire political space. Leaders favouring polycentrism seek out more variable and flexible techniques of administration. But for all this, it is important to note that, whichever model of power leaders support, they have sought in all the regions that we investigated to set up a dialogue with the economic and political actors, thereby ensuring the necessary levels of political stability.

Thus, the political stability of the Russian regions is a complex and contradictory phenomenon. Intraregional factors for stability—the strength of the regional leader, the influence and strength of the local authorities, and the degree to which the regional elite is consolidated—all play an important role. Political stability is largely determined by economic stability, the success of economic reforms, the achievements of the regional economy, and the current levels of popular satisfaction with the regional authorities. But the region is not an autonomous body. It is a part of the federation and therefore its regional stability is unthinkable without, first, normal relations with the federal centre and, second, without a stable and well-thought-out system of inter-regional relations.

During the year 2000 the president of the Russia Federation, Vladimir Putin, has taken radical steps to redistribute powers between the federal centre and the regions. They aim to

---

[8] S. Markov, 'Manipulyativnaya demokratiya', *Nezavisimaya gazeta*, 2 March 2000, p. 8.

[9] See e.g. V. Tretyakov, 'Rossiya: posledniy pryzhkov v budushchee. Tezisy programmy dlya novogo prezidenta strany', *Nezavisimaya gazeta*, 24 Feb. 2000, p. 8.

make the the regions easier to govern and to increase the provincial leaders' dependence on Moscow. No one doubts that reform of federal relations is long overdue. However, the variant on new federalism that the Russian president proposes clearly tends towards a monocentric model of power. It is founded on the idea of a strong state, where the influence of social actors other than the authorities—particularly, the influence of the economic and regional elites—is reduced to nothing. Over and above this, it is a great shame that the process of centre–region relations has not resulted from a negotiating process in which all interested parties could have participated, but has been carried through, like so many other Russian transformations, 'from above'. At present the federal centre is certainly stronger than the federal subjects. However, only time will tell how completely the Kremlin will be able to push through reforms of federal relations in the shape that it envisages.

29 Local Government and Ethnic and Social Activism in Russia[1]

Tomila Lankina

Introduction

Local government at a grass-roots level has long been normatively accepted as one of the fundamental tenets of a healthy democracy.[2] Local governing institutions arguably foster participatory attitudes, civic spirit, and a sense of political efficacy.[3] In multi-ethnic settings they provide vehicles for communities to address cultural matters and provide checks against majority rule. In Russia, however, local government has come to be an instrument for the exercise of power by the regional regimes and of the suppression of civic and ethnic activism.

The focus of this contribution differs from the other studies of Russia's regional politics in a number of respects. Few works have specifically dealt with local government. Many of the insights on Russia's local politics have come from studies of regional level, rather than local politics. Studies explicitly concerned with local government have focused on the administrative, managerial, and fiscal aspects, rather than the political and social ones. Others have limited themselves to describing the relevant law-making or the political conflicts at the federal level over local government reform. Scholars who have dealt with the social and political aspects most extensively have come from the pluralist or political culture perspectives. Those who come from elitist perspectives have focused on an examination of the elite and how its changing composition affects local governance and politics. The question of how particular institutional arrangements are used to translate elite preferences into policies and social mobilization or control has not been dealt with in a systematic way. Although studies of both regional and local politics provide evidence of the manipulation of the political process by the local regimes,[4] they do not provide a complete picture of how the varying local government set-up makes it possible. One area that has been ignored is the

Chapter specially commissioned for this volume.

[1] I am grateful to Ian Bayley for comments on an earlier version of the chapter.

[2] The current Russian legislation defines it as 'local self-government', as a way of stressing its grass-roots make-up and its independence from executive authority. However, the term is misleading, since local bodies often continue to be subject to executive lines of accountability. Here the generic term 'local government' will be used except where I refer to specific legal provisions defining it otherwise.

[3] Robert Putnam, *Making Democracy Work: Civic Traditions in Modern Italy* (Princeton: Princeton University Press, 1993).

[4] Andrei Tsygankov, 'Manifestations of Delegative Democracy in Russian Local Politics: What Does it Mean for the Future of Russia?' *Communist and Post-Communist Studies* 31/4 (1998), 329–44.

importance of the changing formal jurisdictions of the local government as a whole and the institutions that comprise it.

The political role of local government in the Soviet system and Russia: a path-dependent view

Throughout the Soviet and much of the post-Soviet periods local government has been accorded a special *political*, as opposed to simply administrative, significance. In the Soviet system the local government organs were formally those below the union and autonomous republic levels, starting from the oblast and going all the way down to the village settlement unit. In post-Soviet Russia, in contrast, local self-government refers to municipalities *below* the regional level.

The Soviet state was founded and legitimized by the notion of popular grass-roots rule through the institution of the local soviet, or council, from the word *sovet* (advice). Originating in the worker uprisings of 1905, during which the soviets served as strike committees, these bodies' political and mobilization role was appreciated by Lenin, who likened them to the Paris Communes of 1871. From October 1917 onwards the slogan 'All power to the Soviets!' aided the Bolsheviks in capturing, establishing, and legitimizing power throughout much of the former empire. In addition to its general populist appeal, the slogan also blended well with the Bolshevik strategies to win the hearts of Russia's numerous minority ethnic groups. It fitted well with the generic conceptions of minority self-rule propagated by the Bolshevik ideologues. The soviets, including those at the lowest town and village levels, were to be popularly elected, and were to combine legislative, executive, and control functions. The system was thus ostensibly designed to ensure genuine representation of workers, peasants, and other 'progressive' social categories, as well as minority ethnic groups. At the inception of the Soviet Union, however, and during the maturation of the system, the soviets' role was reduced to that of rubber-stamp instruments of Communist Party dictatorship, while most of their internal decision-making had shifted from the representative bodies, the soviets, to their executive arms, the *ispolkomy*.[5]

Although the soviets' role changed throughout the Soviet period—from a stress on their ideological role in the early years of the Bolshevik state—to that on their administrative function later, the local bodies, particularly the *ispolkomy*, remained the Party's main instruments of political control and mobilization. In fact, their increasing administrative and micro-management functions served to consolidate their hold over local constituencies in ways that would not have been possible for local governing institutions in Western settings. In the context of a state-planned economy and in the absence of an autonomous self-aiding civil society, their responsibilities were enormous. 'The Soviet citizen,' wrote Theodore Friedgut, a scholar of local politics in the USSR, 'who changes his residence, wants his boots resoled, or wants to buy new clothing will most likely have to deal with an agency of his local soviet.'[6] The *administrative* role of the soviets as the providers of social services

---

[5] For a discussion of the soviets in the Soviet system, see Michael Urban, *More Power to the Soviets: The Democratic Revolution in the USSR* (Aldershot: Edward Elgar, 1990).

[6] Theodore H. Friedgut, 'Community Structure, Political Participation, and Soviet Local Government: The Case of Kutaisi', in *Soviet Politics and Society in the 1970's*, ed. Henry W. Morton and Rudolf L. Tőkés (New York: The Free Press 1974), 263.

served to create an over-dependence on the local soviet for the satisfaction of the most basic local needs. The *political* role of the local bodies served to further consolidate their hold over local societies. The soviets, whose fusion with the Party organs went very far, permeated the whole social fabric with the help of auxiliary 'volunteer' agencies, such as 'comrade courts', patrolling groups, neighbourhood societies, and so forth, whose primary function was social control.[7]

It is thus not by chance that Gorbachev's efforts to democratize the system started with the reform of the soviets. Yet Gorbachev's approach to the local governing institutions was also essentially a *political* one. The reforms were primarily aimed at rallying support in the local soviets for his programme of political liberalization and against a possible conservative backlash. The local councils—even at the lowest levels—were charged with the discussion of legislation and issues of 'state-wide significance'.[8] Gorbachev's institutional changes likewise served to politicize these bodies. The councils, which had lost or indeed never had any substantial power in the Soviet system, were now to be invigorated and the weight of decision-making was to shift to the representative bodies and their elected presidiums.[9] They were also made more independent from the higher-level soviets in what represented Gorbachev's effort to break the principle of 'democratic centralism'. The first country-wide democratic and contested elections to the local soviets, which were held in 1990 in further-ance of Gorbachev's goals, produced large, partisan, and unwieldy politicized assemblies.

While independent candidates were also able to get in, the soviets at lower levels were packed with low to middle level nomenklatura, that is, former Party officials who, in the circumstances of Party collapse, found refuge in the emerging power centres. In the context of the emerging competition over political and economic spoils, and, in the ethnic republics, over the redefinition of the rules of entry into power based on ethnic criteria, the lower soviets were used by the rival elites as resource bases for the mobilization of social support. Gorbachev's deliberate efforts to garner support for his reform thus provided the new counter-elite, unaccountable to the higher organs, with mobilization resources.

As a result, between 1990 and 1992, the lower-level sub-regional councils emerged as major political actors in the regions. In the context of Gorbachev's political reform, the rise of republic nationalism and the disintegration of the Union, the urban and lower-level regional soviets made a point of voicing their opinions on the major political issues of the day and openly allied themselves with societal movements, often in opposition to the regional regimes. In multi-ethnic settings, the lower-level soviets often challenged the sover-eignty, secessionist, and nationalizing policies of the titular ethnic groups. This role of the lower-level soviets in the areas of non-titular group concentration was evident in Moldova's Transdniestria, in Nagorno-Karabakh, in the Crimea, and in Russia's ethnically defined republics.

During the August 1991 coup, many local soviets, particularly in the liberal urban settings, opposed emergency rule and challenged the more conservative republic and regional-level legislatures who had supported the putschists. During the events leading up to the October 1993 crisis, many lower-level soviets likewise took Yeltsin's side in the conflict. This role,

[7] Robert G. Wesson, 'Volunteers and Soviets', *Soviet Studies*, 15/3 (1964), 231–49.

[8] 'O vsenarodnom obsuzhdenii vazhnykh voprosov gosudarstvennoy zhizni', *Svod zakonov SSSR*, vol. 1 (Moscow: 1987), Art. 8, 101.

[9] For a discussion of the relevant institutional reforms, see Urban, *More Power to the Soviets*.

however, was not appreciated by Yeltsin, who, in his struggle with the conservative RSFSR Supreme Soviet, had come to think of all soviets as bastions of conservatism. In the aftermath of the coup and the October crisis a series of Yeltsin's decrees and Supreme Soviet stipulations took power away from the representative bodies and granted it to the local executives, who now formed part of the general vertical of executive power on regional and republic levels and controlled local budgets and taxes.[10] The councils were thus penalized for their perceived failure to take political sides in a partisan conflict.

Yeltsin's institutional reforms were justified on the grounds that the new bodies would better enforce economic reforms and liberalization at a local level. Both federal and regional bodies now stressed the administrative as opposed to the political function of local government. Although Yeltsin's decrees mostly involved the regions, the republics quickly followed suit in the process of desovietization. Yeltsin's reforms were used as an excuse to centralize power internally as the republics were embarking on the processes of 'nation-building'. Where the non-titular localities challenged sovereignization, the old soviet chairs were removed and new loyal heads of administrations appointed in their place. The consolidation of republic power in this fashion allowed for the virtually uncontested implementation of frequently ethnically discriminatory legislation.

When the increasing sovereignization and 'legal separatism' started to be perceived as threatening to the federal interests, local government once again became the focus of federal attention. In 1995 a new law on local self-government was passed, which mandated the election of local executives and provided for stronger local councils.[11] It also made local self-government *de jure* separate from both the state and regional levels; it would now be referred to as the 'third level of authority'. Yeltsin made no secret of the fact that the primary goal behind the efforts to invigorate local government was once again in the country's history a *political* one. Against the background of the growing power of regional and republic regimes vis-à-vis the federal centre, the Yeltsin administration had come to regard local government as a political check against regional regimes, as a political machine to mobilize opposition to them, and as an agency that has in the past and could in the future deliver the pro-Yeltsin vote where the republic and regional regimes had failed to do so. Although also dressed up in discourse on the virtues of 'civic rule' and the 'schooling in civil society'[12] local government became referred to as a 'mechanism for ensuring the country's unity . . .', its 'most reliable guarantee', a 'cement that binds Russia's state integrity'.[13] Yet, while in accordance with the new law, elections were beginning to be held for executive posts and the councils from 1995 onwards, the regions, and the republics in particular, were slow to give up their firm grip over municipalities, which they had acquired in the aftermath of the August coup. Where they did, local bodies re-emerged as political power centres, often challenging

---

[10] See e.g. 'Postanovlenie Verkhovnogo soveta RSFSR O dopolnitelnykh polnomochiyakh Prezidenta RSFSR po obespecheniyu zakonnosti deyatel'nosti Sovetov narodnykh deputatov v usloviyakh likvidatsii posledstviy popytki gosudarstvennogo perevorota v SSSR', *Vedomosti Soveta narodnykh deputatov RSFSR*, 34 (22 Aug. 1991), 1403–4; Postanovlenie S"ezda narodnykh deputatov RSFSR Ob organizatsii ispolnitel'noy vlasti v period radikal'noy ekonomicheskoy reformy, *Vedomosti Soveta narodnykh deputatov RSFSR* (Nov. 1991), 1722.

[11] 'Federal'nyy zakon ob obschikh printsipakh organizatsii mestnogo samoupravleniya v Rossiyskoy federatsii', (Moscow: Sobranie Zakonodatel'stva Rossiyskoy Federatsii, 1995).

[12] Vladimir Kurnechevskiy, 'Who Dislikes a United Russia?' (Moscow: *Rossiyskaya gazeta*, 6 April 1995), 1–2.

[13] Boris Yeltsin, 'On the Effectiveness of State Power in Russia', in *Yeltsin's Annual Message to Russian Federation Federal Assembly* (Moscow: *Rossiyskaya gazeta*, 17 Feb. 1995), 1, 3–8.

regional and republic regimes.[14] Many regions, however, had successfully sought mechanisms of control over the local bodies even when they had become elected.[15]

The preceding discussion has suggested that throughout much of the Soviet and post-Soviet periods, local governing institutions have been accorded a special significance in federation-wide and regional politics. Since political mobilization was the primary goal of much of local reform, the changing political roles of local government and the relevant institutional changes fostered from above in the last decade were thus bound to have affected local community politics. The following section investigates in greater detail the impact of the institutional changes on the exercise of local power and on social and ethnic mobilization.

Changing jurisdictions over public life: from the local council to the executive

The political role accorded to local governing bodies endowed them with substantial resources crucial for influencing the local social processes and levels of political mobilization. The first set of resources is derived from the local bodies' formal jurisdictions over public life. The second, specific to post-Soviet Russia, stems from continued dominance of the public sphere over the private one and the material reliance of the social agencies on the state and its institutions. The latter is thus a path-dependent view of the relation of the institutional agencies to the social actors. As power shifted within the local governing institutions—from the executive to the representative bodies and back again—so did the jurisdictional prerogatives of the representative versus the executive branches of local government. This was in turn bound to affect whether and how the resources were used over time.

The soviets, which were elected during Gorbachev's reforms of the soviets and which lasted into the post-Soviet period, provided for the election of presidiums from amongst council deputies. These were arms of the representative bodies, as distinct from the *ispolkomy*, the executive bodies, and they tended to be packed with the most activist and vocal deputies. In the early post-Soviet period, it was the presidiums, rather than the *ispolkomy*, which exercised much of the decision-making over aspects of public life. They were in charge of reviewing applications for and sanctioning mass demonstrations, protest acts, pickets, and so forth. They also often decided on common policies with respect to public associations, such as the allocation of municipal office space for them. In practice, these bodies exercised a much more active role than the simple registration of the facts of public life. It was not uncommon for presidium members to be leaders, or indeed, founders of the very public associations whose activities they were supposed to adjudicate.

Take the republic of Adygeya. When in 1991 the republic bodies embarked on sovereignty policies and attempted to institutionalize the over-representation of the titular Adyge group in the republic legislature, a Russian speakers' 'public' association, the 'Union of Slavs of Adygeya' emerged and actively contested the proposed arrangements. The group's

[14] Leonid Smirnyagin, 'Mayors against Governors?', *East-West Institute*, 4 (Mar. 1999).

[15] See Peter Kirkow, 'Local Self-government in Russia: Awakening from Slumber?', *Europe-Asia Studies*, 49/1 (1997), 43–58, 47.

co-founder was Valentin Lednev, a trade union leader. Lednev was an activist deputy in the soviet of the capital city, Maikop, and had well-known democratic leanings. He also sat on the presidium, which controlled all aspects of public life in the city. According to both the independent activists of the Union of Slavs, and soviet deputies like Lednev, this fusion of the public and soviet actors was crucial for the opposition movement activities. The Union, with the help of the city soviet, was able to sponsor a series of acts of mass protest. It also enjoyed office space in the soviet and the legitimizing umbrella of an association with 'serious' establishment actors in the council. This legitimacy, whose importance has been noted by scholars of social movements in Western settings as well, is essential for success with the wider public.[16] In Ufa, the capital of Bashkortostan, the soviet's presidium members and deputies maintained strong links with the democratic and nationalist opposition. During the 1991 coup, the soviet and its social allies challenged the Republic Supreme Soviet's tacit support for the coup using the soviet's press organ, *Vechernyaya Ufa*.

The fusion of the social and state agencies stemmed from the continued reliance by public associations on the state for resources crucial for any social movement activity. The soviets and their activists also endowed the social agencies with legitimacy, which they otherwise lacked. They also provided material facilities, such as office space, and other resources like publicity in the newspapers that they controlled.[17] In the context of the deep political and, in the ethnic republics, ethnic cleavages, the allocation of these resources by partisan figures in the representative bodies was bound to be selective.

The institutional changes fostered by the federal centre and effected at the local level in early 1992 altered the balance of power between the executive and the representative bodies. Not only were the latter stripped of much of their legislative and decision-making prerogatives, but, most importantly, the jurisdiction over public life and key instruments for influencing it had passed on to the local executives. The local councils in many of the large liberal urban centres had also lost control over the local city newspaper, with its crucial potential to shape public opinion. After the soviets were disbanded, the jurisdiction over the paper tended to pass on to the local administrations. Thus, where partisan politicized representative bodies controlled public life in 1990–2, from then onwards, this control passed to the appointed executives, accountable not to the counter-elite, but to the dominant regional regimes.

The political activists who retained their positions in the new bodies now stressed administration over politics and tended publicly to distance themselves from the opposition. Their gate-keeping over public activism extended from failure to register opposition groups to influence over slogans presented at mass demonstrations based on the criteria of 'social and ethnic peace', to repression, making use of the administration's control over local police forces. Simultaneously, the administrations now supported or created apolitical 'safe' pro-regime public associations, in what may be described as civic corporatism. Their primary

---

[16] William A. Gamson and Andre Modigliani, 'Media Discourse and Public Opinion on Nuclear Power: A Constructionist Approach', *American Journal of Sociology*, 95/1 (1989), 1–37.

[17] For examples from Perm, see Mary McAuley, 'Politics, Economics, and Elite Realignment in Russia: A Regional Perspective', *Soviet Economy*, 8/1 (1992), 46–88; on Omsk, see Neil J. Melvin, 'The Consolidation of a New Regional Elite: The Case of Omsk 1987–1995', *Europe-Asia Studies* 50/4 (1998), 619–50.

function became 'fronting'[18] for the administrations and the legitimization of their policies as enjoying a 'civic' backing. The following section investigates the effects of the reforms on the make-up of the representative bodies and the resulting shift in their social roles.

The mechanisms of social control: from politics to 'administration'

The 'professionalization' of local government was reflected in the make-up of the post-1990 councils. The study of council make-up facilitates theoretical and comparative reflections on how power is exercised through particular institutional arrangements and what are the effects of the given local government institutions on community mobilization.

This section draws on the data from the Ufa council in the capital of the republic of Bashkortostan. Bashkortostan, one of Russia's twenty-one ethnically defined republics, lies in the Middle Volga geographical region. It is one of Russia's wealthiest entities. Bashkortostan's titular nationality comprises only slightly over 21.9 per cent of the population, the largest groups being Russians with 39.9 per cent and Tatars, with 28.4 per cent. Despite the proportionately small percentage of the titular group in the republic, Bashkortostan, together with Tatarstan, was in the forefront of the parade of sovereignties in 1990–1.[19] Since then, it has striven to institutionalize ethnic Bashkir predominance locally in the form of language and other laws which are deemed to be discriminatory towards the Tatars and Russians. These measures were possible thanks to the controlled nature of the republic political process, the restrictions on the freedom of the press and on the operation of nationalist and democratic political opposition. The curbs were rapidly introduced following a period of sustained democratic and non-titular nationalist opposition to the republic regime in 1990–2 and in which the local councils, particularly the Ufa soviet, played a key role. After 1992, however, local institutions were centralized and heads of administrations loyal to the republican authorities were appointed in the localities.

Bashkortostan's local government reforms are broadly parallel to those of the other republics and regions. It, however, is usually cited as an outlier, and an extreme case of centralization, repression, and the fusion of the executive and legislative branches at all levels, including the local one.[20] Can we then still generalize from the republic to the other cases, including the non-ethnically defined regions? The choice of the case is premised on the assumption that Bashkortostan represents the 'ideal-type' of a regime whose features are present in many regions. Heads of local administrations continue to be appointed in Tatarstan, Adygeya, and other republics and are known to perform local social control functions. While regions were more likely to comply with the federal requirement of election of heads of administrations, these heads tend to continue to be controlled by the regional bodies.

Even in the comparatively democratic Novgorod region, which has been a front runner in introducing progressive municipal reform,[21] some scholars have observed that . . . 'the

---

[18] The practice of 'fronting' has been noted in Western community politics as well. See Edward C. Banfield and James Wilson, *City Politics* (New York: Vintage Books, 1963). See also Robert Dahl, *Who Governs?* (New Haven: Yale University Press, 1961).

[19] For a discussion of this process, see Jeff Kahn, 'The Parade of Sovereignties: Establishing the Vocabulary of the New Russian Federalism', *Post-Soviet Affairs* 16/1 (2000), 58–89.

[20] For a discussion of Bashkortostan's regime, see Tsygankov, 'Manifestations of Delegative Democracy'.

[21] See Nicolai Petro, 'The Novgorod Region: A Russian Success Story.' *Post-Soviet Affairs* 15/3 (1999), 235–61.

Novgorod City Administration de facto has become a department of the Regional Adminis-tration.'[22] The boroughs of the city of Moscow are notoriously under the thumb of the mayor Luzhkov. Municipalities' control also extends to the private sector in what Gelman, using Moscow as an example, has called 'municipal capitalism',[23] one reason being the continued reliance of the privatized enterprises on subsidies.[24] The August 1998 financial and political crisis only served further to increase local control over production—private and public.[25] Local governments also continue to exercise control and influence over public associations, as was observed in Nizhny Novgorod.[26] In all these cases, it may be said that local bodies serve as instruments for the exercise of power by a given ruling elite. While the nature of the elite varies from region to region and could be a subject of much debate—be it the old nomenklatura, ethnocracy, clan, family, or business networks—of interest for this discussion is how particular institutional arrangements are used for the exercise of power by a ruling regime, whatever its make-up. As such, Bashkortostan represents a generic regime-type, the differences being those of degree of centralization and control.

THE EXERCISE OF POWER

The 'professionalization' of the overall local government began with the shift of authority and power from the popularly elected councils to the appointed local administrations. As a result of these reforms, the heads of administrations/mayors have become central players in the local political process. In Bashkortostan, on a local town level, no local issue is decided without the involvement of or explicit sanction of the head of administration. This author-ity is reminiscent of Friedgut's observations about the local soviets in the Soviet system, cited earlier. It ranges from the granting of permits to set up a local business, to allowing the collection of signatures for a political campaign, to the registration of public associations operating locally. Although formal jurisdiction over such 'force' agencies as the police and the prosecutors' offices lies with the federal ministries, until recently, heads of administrations have had a say in the approval of the local representatives and exercised control over them.[27]

Executive dominance also extends to and is channelled through the ostensibly representa-tive bodies to the institutional, social, and professional networks which the deputies control, in what has also become common for regional and republic level legislatures.[28] Council deputies are subject both to formal and informal lines of accountability to the executive. The formal lines of accountability stem from the fusion of executive and legislative power,

---

[22] Dmitri A. Zimine and Michael J. Bradshaw, 'Regional Adaptation to Economic Crisis in Russia: The Case of Novgorod Oblast', *Post-Soviet Geography and Economics* 40/5 (1999), 335–53, 341. Also, a form of corporatism exists in Novgorod with regard to public associations, which are part of the Social Chamber set up in the local govern-ment, and in each of the region's twenty-two districts. Nicolai Petro, 'The Novgorod Region', 246.

[23] Vladimir Gel'man, 'Regime Transition, Uncertainty and Prospects for Democratisation: The Politics of Rus-sia's Regions in a Comparative Perspective', *Europe-Asia Studies*, 51/6 (1999), 939–56; 'Regime Transition', 947.

[24] Jean-Charles Lallemand, 1999. 'Politics for the Few: Elites in Bryansk and Smolensk', *Post-Soviet Affairs* 15/4 (1999), 312–35, 324.

[25] Yaroslav Startsev, 'Gubernatorial Politics in Sverdlovsk Oblast', *Post-Soviet Affairs* 15/4 (1999), 336–61, 341.

[26] For example, in Nizhny Novgorod, Gelman observed the exercise of patronage over public associations in exchange for their loyalty. Gel'man, 'Regime Transition', 949.

[27] President Putin has tried to change this practice, but it remains to be seen whether the regions will completely give up their de facto influence over the local 'force' agencies.

[28] For examples from Orlovskaya Oblast, Bashkortostan, and Krasnoyarsky krai, see Tsygankov. 'Manifestations of Delegative Democracy', 342.

Bashkortostan being a particularly notorious example of this. Local councillors, as, indeed, members of the republic level legislature, can combine executive posts in local administrations with being a councillor in other areas. As full-time appointees in local administrations, their primary accountability is to the bodies that appointed them, rather than a result of their part-time council positions. Aside from those formally under direct control of the executives, one can distinguish several categories of those within the 'informal' control networks.[29]

In the Ufa city soviet of fifty-eight elected deputies elected in 1999,[30] the largest categories are as follows: five (8.6 per cent) of the deputies are directly connected to council administrations; 24.1 per cent or almost a quarter, are heads of medical establishments; seventeen are managers (29.3 per cent), mainly heads of enterprises; and eight (13.8 per cent) are heads of educational institutions, mostly schools. The council also has one head of administration of a lower region. Thus, although only six deputies are directly connected to the administration, and form part of the formal executive chain of command, on close scrutiny it becomes clear that the majority of the remaining deputies are in reality subject to less formal executive control.

The bulk of the deputy corps could be divided into five categories.[31] The first are those forming part of the common system of executive power, such as the head of administration

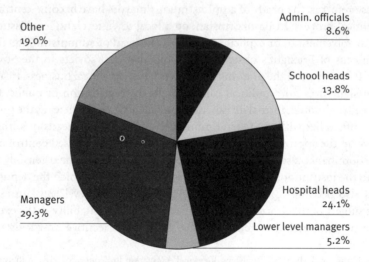

Figure 29.1 Composition of Ufa city soviet, 1999 (%)*
*Categories comprising below 4 per cent are collapsed into 'other'.

[29] For a discussion of local government's mobilizational role in Bashkortostan, see Tomila Lankina, '"Local Self-Government" or Local Political Control in Russia? The Case of Bashkortostan', *Russian Regional Report*, 4.28 (22 July 1999); and Tomila Lankina, 'Showcase of Manipulated Democracy: Shadow-Puppet Elections in Bashkortostan', *Transition*, 5/8 (1998), 62–4.

[30] Deputy lists obtained from *Vechernyaya Ufa*, 20 Mar. 1999, p. 1; and *Vechernyaya Ufa*, 3 July 1999, p. 1. Data on two deputies who were to be elected in August after the first two rounds are not available. The total number of council deputies is sixty. The data used here are based on the first rounds, in which a total of fifty-eight deputies were elected.

[31] Personal interview with Artur Asafyev, Ufa soviet deputy, Ufa, 3 June 1999. The remaining deputies are an engineer, a journalist, a teacher, a worker, a tram driver, a student, and two public association heads.

and other local executives. The second category is the directors of state enterprises. These tend to be appointed by the municipal administrations or the republic Cabinet of Ministers, or conclude contracts with it. This category is subject both to formal and less formal accountability. The informal one stems from their vulnerability to the tax inspectorate, the police, and other 'power' agencies, which may or may not be directly or *de jure* subordinate to the republic or local administrations, but are de facto under the control of local heads of administrations. The next category is the so-called 'business entrepreneurs', and there are several of those in the council. An examination of their activities and affiliations reveals that they tend to perform services vital to the city, and enjoy a certain status within the municipal services private contracts hierarchy. Take deputy Voropayev. He runs an enterprise for sanitary and technical works, and has an exclusive contract with the city to do so. His dependence on the administration is an informal one, as he is subject to material rewards, rather than direct accountability.

The two largest categories after 'managers' are heads of medical and educational establishments. The distinction between doctors and teachers on the one hand, and heads of the relevant establishments, on the other, is an important one, and prevents us from grouping the latter into the broader 'professional' or 'intelligentsia' category. The infiltration by these two groups, which has increased in the Ufa soviet from 1995 to 1999, and is observed in the councils in other regions as well,[32] is an interesting phenomenon. Scholars have noted that in the Soviet system too, hospital heads were part of the narrow local elite of 'notables.'[33] At present, hospital heads, as a local councillor maintained, are not mere doctors; they are 'entrepreneurs, tsars and gods within their institutions.'[34] Although school directors could not be described as entrepreneurs, they are the most powerful individuals within their institutions and enjoy status and prestige in the republic educational hierarchies. These two categories are both subject to formal and informal lines of accountability. The appointment of school heads is done by the local administrations, while hospital heads can be appointed by the local administrations as well as by the branches of the Ministry of Health.

What unites all the above categories is thus (1) their formal or less formal dependence on the executive chain of command; and (2) their key positions within organizations representing business, social, professional, and other networks.

THE CONTROL OVER SANCTIONS AND REWARDS AND LOCAL AGENDA-SETTING

The above discussion has been premised on an assumption that the administrations control enterprise managers and managers control their networks. While such an influence is a common feature of institutional politics, its role is particularly salient in the post-Soviet setting. Despite efforts to privatize local enterprises and services, the social agencies still massively depend on the state for the distribution of material rewards and services. Local administrations, like their predecessors, the soviets and their ispolkoms, are in charge of disbursing these benefits, which are in turn channelled from above. As Lallemand notes,

[32] Lallemand observes this phenomenon in the Bryansk and Smolensk provincial assemblies. Lallemand, 'Politics for the Few'.

[33] Kimitaka Matsuzato, 'Local Elites under transition: County and City Politics in Russia 1985–1996', *Europe-Asia Studies*, 51/8 (Dec. 1999). Matsuzato, based on his study of local elites, notes the 'continuity of elite structure' in the form of the continued predominance of the old notables in local politics.

[34] Artur Asafyev, personal interview, Ufa, 3 June 1999.

based on examples from Bryansk and Smolensk, 'municipalities have been expected to take upon themselves the social and communal expenses that many firms have been shedding'.[35] These prerogatives are substantially wider than those exercised by the municipalities in the West. The views of Anatoly Baranov, the deputy head of Ufa city administration, who frequently travels to Ufa's sister city in Germany, Halle, are typical of local administrators:

'When we are, say, in the West and ask a burgomaster or a mayor a question, what do you do if some food products are absent in the shop, he stares and says: what do I have to do with this? Not my problem. Here, in contrast, we are responsible for all now . . . in conditions when in our country the redistribution of property has not occurred, and when the main share of the property remains in state hands . . . In the West, he [the mayor] is not concerned with how enterprises are working . . . It is not his problem . . . Here in contrast we have a headache today about this too, because we don't have a real owner; it appears that everybody is the owner.'[36]

The republic bodies manipulate their control over local budgets as a means of political influence over the administrations: 'If the mayor shows independence towards the republic, the republic will say: deal with the salaries yourself'.[37] The administrations, in turn, manipulate the disbursal of funds to enterprises to achieve the same goal in what has been observed in other regions as well and has been described as 'pseudo-socialist activities'.[38] Enterprise managers in turn manipulate the issue of the payment of salaries to individual employees.

   The social expectations of the municipalities' role are likewise much greater than of those in the West. 'In contrast to the West,' maintains Baranov, 'when salaries are not paid here, even at privatised enterprises . . . workers come [to the local government bodies], criticising the administration: why don't you pay us salaries? We have to interfere.'[39] This view echoes the observations of scholars of local politics in other regions. In Sverdlovsk oblast, for example, during a student protest demonstration, 'the demands of the students concerning the reform of higher education were directed at the mayor and governor, even though these officials were not included in the formulation of that series of reforms'.[40] The social perceptions of the local governments as omni-powerful entities facilitate the manipulation of the issue of sanctions for deviating behaviour by the local bodies.

Theoretical reflections

It is now important to step back and reflect theoretically and comparatively on the information presented in the above sections. In many ways, the changes that were introduced into local government in 1992 were similar to those introduced in the context of the Reform Movement in America.[41] The councils were made less partisan, although not necessarily through the same system as they were in the USA. Banfield and Wilson define no-

[35] Lallemand, 'Politics for the Few', 321.   [36] Personal interview, Ufa, 4 June 1999.   [37] Ibid.
[38] Matsuzato, 'Local Elites under Transition'.   [39] Ibid.   [40] Startsev, 'Gubernatorial Politics', 349.
[41] For a discussion of the Movement, which was prominent in the early twentieth century, see Robert L. Lineberry and Edmund P. Fowler, 'Reformism and Public Policies in Amerian Cities', *American Political Science Review*, 61 (1967), 701–16.

partisanship as a 'system of elections . . . in which no candidate is identified on the ballot by party affiliation'.[42] No explicit provisions to this effect exist in the Russian federal law on the common principles of local self-government. In practice, however, the system of formal and informal sanctions over potential deviators within these bodies and the institutions that they control had the prima facie effect of depoliticizing local government and, therefore, community life as well. This ostensible depoliticization of local government is not due to the impartiality of the local administrators and their service to the community as a whole. Rather, their 'depoliticization' represents a legitimate way of squeezing potentially controversial political and social issues out of the public domain, lest they prejudice the exercise of elite power. Rather than simply crowding out the airing of opposing agendas, these bodies also serve as active means of channelling given preferences through their mechanisms of control.

Control can be exercised through both formal and informal mechanisms. Banfield refers to these mechanisms as 'structures of control'. He writes: 'When two or more actors come under the control of another on a continuing basis, i.e., from proposal to proposal, a *structure* of control exists.'[43] This would include the mayor's control over the city council, the newspaper's control over 'civic leadership' and the governor's control over the legislature. 'Centralization of control,' therefore, he writes, 'necessitates a linkage of structures where structures exist.'[44]

The preceding discussion has identified the formal lines of executive control that exist in Bashkortostan. Aside from control over individuals within large networks, the administrations possess jurisdictions over activities and functions crucial for the work of public and civic associations. These effectively allow for the suppression of potential activities in opposition to those of the most powerful actors. The direct executive control and jurisdiction over public life constitute *formal* lines of control.

The linkage of the structures of control is further exercised through the *informal* system of the manipulation of the distribution of 'private-regarding' and 'public-regarding' benefits.[45] The first is achieved through the tangible private benefits or costs that accrue to those who conform or deviate. A beneficiary is unlikely to challenge the administration or higher bodies on political grounds. Private-regarding benefits controlled by the local governments extend to large groups of people, although they are linked to public-regarding benefits, discussed below. The continued predominance of the state, as opposed to private, sector in the local economies and the reliance of local communities on local administrations for payment of salaries and employment makes the role of such control much greater than it is in the West. The threat of withdrawal of this benefit is widely practised in the localities. The subsidized local governments are often threatened with the withdrawal of subsidies by the regional bodies if they tolerate political opposition. The administrations, in turn, have an incentive to threaten individual enterprises and districts with the deprivation of these essential benefits should they deviate. The enterprise heads and those in control of other organizations do likewise within the professional networks that they control. Individual deviators within the networks, in turn, could be punished by the group for deviating, because

[42]   Banfield and Wilson, *City Politics*, 151.
[43]   Edward C. Banfield, *Political Influence* (New York: The Free Press, 1961), 311.
[44]   Ibid.
[45]   Distinctions made by Banfield, *Political Influence*, 315.

rewards could be withdrawn from the group as a whole if it becomes identified with the opposition.

Control over local agenda-setting is crucial for the fostering of public expectations about sanctions and rewards. Local governing bodies become media through which information about potential public sanctions gets spread. The heads of administrations, 'tsars and gods' within their locales, enjoy near monopoly control over the 'local newspaper',[46] and the information that appears in it; they also enjoy regular publicity and constituency contact in their areas. The control over agenda-setting allows for the framing of individual and group deviations as threatening the community at large in terms of material rewards. Deviations are also presented as posing a threat to such non-tangible value systems as 'ethnic peace' and 'social harmony'. Executive agenda-setting is furthered through the total institutional means of control over public life available to the local administrations, such as their influence over mass protest demonstrations and the slogans presented at them. This system, in turn, also allows for indirect control over the public associations, their public relations, and the resulting levels of social support they might get from those they purport to represent. Public agenda-setting represents the final 'linkage' of structures of control, because it consists of a daily reaffirmation of what actions would be tolerated and what would not. In such a system, the actual frequent exercise of sanctions and indeed coercion become redundant. This in turn fosters the perceptions of the legitimacy of the local bodies and their exercise of power.

Conclusion

The preceding discussion suggests that while local 'self-governing' bodies in most regions are not independent power centres in their own right, they have served as mechanisms for the exercise of power by the regional and republic level elites. As such, while lacking in authority and power vis-à-vis the higher power elites, they possess virtually unlimited power vis-à-vis the local societies they purport to represent and serve as transmission belts for the higher elite preferences into the grass roots.

The power elite itself varies in its composition from region to region and republic to republic, and the present discussion does not aim to identify the notables. Rather, it has sought to identify the institutional mechanisms, which allow the ruling elite—whatever its composition—to monopolize local decision-making by suppressing potential challenge from the grass roots or from the counter-elite. Since power tends to be concentrated at the regional, rather than local, level, the authorities in the localities become mechanisms for the exercise of regime power through the loyal appointed heads of administrations and their controlled councils. The exercise of power entails either social mobilization or its suppression, depending on elite preferences, the existence of elite cleavages,[47] and the degree of centralization of local government.

These institutional mechanisms for the exercise of power have been largely fostered by the Russian federal bodies, and, prior to that, by the Soviet Union, which accorded a special

---

[46] For the importance of the local newspaper in shaping public opinion in Western settings, see Banfield, *Political Influence*, 55, 239.

[47] See Vladimir Gel'man and Grigorii V. Golosov, 'Regional Party System Formation in Russia: The Deviant Case of Sverdlovsk Oblast', *Journal of Communist Studies and Transition Politics*, 14 (May/June 1998).

political and mobilizational, rather than narrowly administrative, significance to them. Mobilization peaked in 1990–2, when Gorbachev's institutional reforms created counter-elites and provided them with mobilizational powers. It subsided with Yeltsin's concentration of executive control at regional levels, a process which lasted at least until the passage of the 1995 law. The election of local mayors, which started after 1995, fostered the decentralization of local power and created an alternative counter-elite, as Yeltsin had hoped it would, as a counterweight to the regional regimes. These elected counter-elites have tended to foster, rather than constrain, local mobilization using their prerogatives over local agenda-setting in their struggle against the higher elites.[48] In both the centralized and decentralized regions, such control is possible due to (1) the broad institutional changes fostered by the federal centre, which weakened the councils and gave power to 'professional' administrations; (2) the endowment of these administrations, as opposed to the partisan representative bodies, with jurisdiction over public life; and (3) the continued predominance of the state, especially in provincial Russia, in the distribution of private benefits such as salaries, employment, education, healthcare. These factors make the local governing bodies powerful in their respective areas.

The ascent to power of the new president, Vladimir Putin, has prompted yet another stage in local government reform, but one that is still perceived through the prism of its *political* significance. Initially leaning towards Yeltsin's strategy of strengthening local government's independence to counter regionalism and separatism, Putin subsequently favoured the option of possible removal of local mayors by both the federal executive and the regional authorities. The latter option is doubtless a concession to the regions to lessen their obstruction of his efforts to curb their powers. These measures are likely to result in further executive centralization of control at local levels. Accordingly, local government will continue to serve as a mechanism for the exercise of federal or regional power but *not* that of the grass roots.

---

[48] The form of 'corporatism' that exists at regional levels tends to be practised by municipal elites in their struggle against higher organs. An example is the Yekaterinburg Mayor Chernetskii's establishment of the movement 'Our Home is Our City,' against Sverdlovsk oblast Governor Rossell's movement 'Transformation of the Urals'. Gel'man and Golosov. 'Regional Party System Formation', 38.

Section 10

Russia and the World

Introduction

Archie Brown

Russia is the largest country in the world and it is rich in natural resources. Both statements were even more true of the USSR, which also laid claim to being the world's first 'socialist' state and to be engaged in building communism. Yet the Soviet Union acquired 'superpower' status mainly because of its military might. Although it provided an example and source of support for some Third World revolutionaries, its political system was not found attractive by a majority of the electorate in any advanced country. In the 1930s, and subsequently during the Second World War, the Soviet state had acquired prestige, including misguided and uncritical respect for Stalin, in many European (and some American) intellectual and working-class circles as a bulwark against fascism. And, indeed, no country played as great a role in the defeat of Nazi Germany as did the USSR after its belated entry into the war in 1941. The Soviet Union was able, however, to extend Communism into East-Central Europe mainly thanks to the successes of its army and not through the free choice of the citizens of those countries. It was able subsequently to sustain those Communist regimes only by relying on the ultimate threat of use of force, and the occasional resort to it. Soviet political reach had been extended but its moral authority diminished by its acquisition of a clutch of satellites.

Economically, the story took a somewhat similar course. Soviet achievements impressed even American presidents and West European prime ministers for a time. First of all, there had been the rapid industrialization of the country under Stalin and the build-up of a huge and effective armaments industry. Then, in the Khrushchev era, President Kennedy and his European counterparts were much affected (and galvanized) by the first sputnik and Soviet primacy in putting a person into space. In the Stalin and Khrushchev years, these successes were accompanied also by impressive growth rates, at least on paper. Yet by the early 1980s the economic shine was well and truly off the USSR, as was its political glow, even for the significant minority in the West who had earlier imagined they had glimpsed a radiant future in Moscow. By the 1980s the international Communist movement was a dwindling and diminishing asset. Communist newspapers were freely on sale in Western countries, but outside Italy (where the Communist Party had enhanced its popularity by emphasizing its *differences* from, and with, its Soviet counterpart) and France, their circulations remained small.

Yet, there was some truth in the oft-repeated statement of the long-serving Soviet foreign minister, Andrei Gromyko, that no world problem could be resolved without the participation of the Soviet Union. In a bipolar world, the USSR had the capacity to make difficulties or ease them in virtually any of the areas of international tension, whether in Africa, Asia, Europe, or even Central America. Many non-aligned countries, while their preference, in principle, might be for a multipolar political universe, preferred bipolarity to a unipolar world and were content to play one 'superpower' off against another. Western policy-makers also, however unattractive they might have found the Soviet political system, could not fail to take seriously the brute facts that the USSR had achieved a rough military parity with the United States in the early 1970s and that it had (in common with the USA) enough nuclear weapons to destroy life on earth. Thus, a large part of Western diplomatic and military strategy during the post-war years was defined in relation to the Soviet Union. In the last years of the Soviet state Gorbachev's extraordinarily bold and innovative foreign policy, complementing a policy of liberalization and democratization at home, played a decisive role in ending the Cold War, but this scarcely rebounded to the advantage of Russia and the other Soviet successor states (with the notable exceptions of Estonia, Latvia, and Lithuania) in the way they could have hoped. The collapse of the Soviet Union, the most dramatic of the unintended consequences of Gorbachev's perestroika, produced such a rapid decline both of the Russian economy and of the Russian military machine that 'superpower' pretensions on the part of the Russian Federation could no longer be sustained. Yeltsin attempted to disguise this (and may even have succeeded in deceiving himself about the centrality of post-Soviet Russia's role in international affairs) by his ostentatious chumminess with Western leaders—in particular, with 'my friend Bill', otherwise known as President Clinton.

Vladimir Putin, who, unlike Yeltsin, displays some real nostalgia for the Soviet Union, clearly wishes to restore Russia as a great power—though not necessarily as a 'superpower'. His realistic starting point, though, is a recognition that, both economically and militarily, the country whose presidency he inherited in March 2000 was in dire straits. Moreover, he had to come to terms with a series of foreign policy failures. The fact that Russia was not able to prevent a NATO attack on Yugoslav strategic installations was one such failure, as was Russia's policy in Kosovo more generally. A former official in the Ministry of Foreign Affairs of the Russian Federation, Oleg Levitin, who was involved in Moscow's Balkan policies from 1990 to 1999 suggested, in a notably revisionist article, that these were not simply the result—as a more conventional Moscow view would have it—of insensitivity on the part of the West. As Levitin puts it:

Russia's Balkan policy has failed to accomplish any of its proclaimed or hidden goals. Moscow managed neither to become a genuine partner to the West, nor to create an effective anti-Western outpost in Yugoslavia. It did not do what it could to prevent the conflict in Kosovo. Russia remained indifferent to the sufferings of Kosovo Albanians and has failed to protect Kosovo Serbs.[1]

Moscow's worst-case scenario came true, Levitin adds: NATO troops entered Yugoslavia. His explanation for this failure links up with points made by Margot Light in Chapter 30 and has an applicability beyond the Balkans. For the failure there Levitin adduces three main reasons: first, Russia's general post-Soviet weakness; second, the inconsistency of its policies, partly stemming from 'the post-Soviet identity crisis'; and, third, uneven standards of Russian diplomacy, including 'a striking lack of geopolitical perspective and policy planning'.[2]

All three of these general points are borne out by Light's analysis of the first decade of post-Communist foreign policy. Until Russia's new identity was established it was, she notes,

---

[1] Oleg Levitin, 'Inside Moscow's Kosovo Muddle', *Survival*, 42/1 (Spring 2000), 130–40, at p. 130.
[2] Ibid.

difficult to decide what its foreign policy position should be. The international environment turned out to be less congenial than the Russian foreign policy elite felt they were entitled, following the collapse of the USSR, to expect. There was a growing discrepancy between declining Russian capabilities and its international aspirations. All this, and more, contributed to the incoherence of foreign policy during the Yeltsin years. Light sees the possibility of greater congruence between resources and aims under Putin. She observes, nevertheless, that while Putin seeks better relations with the outside world, Russia's relations with the West in general and the United States in particular could be damaged by NATO's enlargement, especially if this included countries which were formerly part of the Soviet Union. No less potentially damaging to Russian–US relations would be an American unilateral renunciation of the 1972 Anti-Ballistic Missile Treaty.

Vladimir Baranovsky, one of Russia's most astute analysts of foreign policy, raises (in Chapter 31) the perennial question of whether his country is 'a part of Europe or apart from Europe'. The geographical answer to this question is, he points out, mildly ambiguous and, politically, the ambiguity is far greater. While Russia's changed ideological position has brought it closer to Europe in terms of ideas, Baranovsky sees, none the less, a Cold War logic still operating in the West whose standpoint he portrays as 'how to prevent Russians from becoming disengaged, without however actually letting them in'. He notes that within Russia it is the United States which is made to shoulder most of the blame for a deteriorating relationship, even when the countries of Western Europe are pursuing a common policy with America. As Baranovsky observes:

it is quite remarkable that Russia's indignation with respect to NATO military operations in Yugoslavia was directed predominantly, indeed almost exclusively against the United States—as if the Europeans did not participate in them at all. The fact that the EU supported the war against Yugoslavia and even contributed to it, politically, economically and militarily, passed almost unnoticed in Russia . . . the European states involved in this campaign were basically viewed as operating under American pressure.

Interestingly, Baranovsky sees Vladimir Putin as having 'unambiguously positioned himself as a Europeanist' since becoming Russian president, and to be seeking closer links with Europe in particular as well as integration in the world economy in general.

Russia's relations with the new states which were at one time republics of the Soviet Union is the theme of Roy Allison's Chapter 32. He notes how the term, 'near abroad', which was much used in Russia in the first half of the 1990s to refer to the new Eurasian states, has gone out of fashion. It was resented within those countries where it was perceived as connoting that they were less than fully sovereign states, a feeling which was reinforced by the Russian desire to maintain the old borders of the Soviet Union as Russia's strategic border. As Allison shows, Russian policy has fluctuated since then but it has also differentiated between one region of the former Soviet Union and another. It was especially difficult, as he notes, for Russian politicians to accept that the break with Ukraine and Belarus was irrevocable, and many hoped for a political reconciliation and ultimate reunion of the three Slavic states. That seems a particularly unlikely prospect so far as Ukraine is concerned, less so in the case of Belarus. Alyaksandr Lukashenka, the president of Belarus, has actually sought close integration with Russia, and although that policy has been far from universally popular in Belarus, the most important hesitations have been on the Russian side. The interest in principle in Slavic reunion has been tempered by a lack of enthusiasm for taking on Belarus's economic problems and, at the democratic end of the Russian political spectrum, a distaste for the authoritarianism of Lukashenka and disinclination to see him accorded a role on a larger Russian stage. In common with other contributors to this volume, Allison stresses the limitation of the military and economic resources at President Putin's disposal. He notes that these are likely to be fully stretched by developments in the North Caucasus. Elsewhere in the CIS region Putin can be expected to pursue a policy of pragmatic persuasion and cooperation rather than attempt to re-establish a dominant relationship reminiscent of former times.

30 Post-Soviet Russian Foreign Policy: The First Decade

Margot Light

Introduction

The Russian Federation is by far the most powerful of the post-Soviet states in terms of size, military strength, and economic potential. It is also the recognized legal heir to the USSR, a permanent member of the UN Security Council and the only successor state with recognized nuclear status. As a result, after the disintegration of the USSR, Russia immediately occupied a more prominent role in the international system than any other Soviet successor state. Yet in the first decade of its existence as an independent state its foreign policy was characterized by a degree of incoherence which detracted from its effectiveness, diminished Russia's influence, and confused its international partners. This chapter will examine the reasons for this incoherence and reflect on how it affected Russian foreign policy, concentrating in particular on Russia's relations with the United States.

Incoherence is not an unusual feature of the foreign policies of new states, where the policy-making machinery is new and government departments have not yet established routine channels of communication and co-ordination. It was not entirely clear, however, that Russia belonged to the category of new states. After all, the Russian ministry of foreign affairs (MFA) took over the buildings and most of the personnel of the Soviet ministry of foreign affairs. Soviet embassies and trade missions abroad immediately began to represent the Russian Federation. In some ways, therefore, Russian policy appeared to be a continuation of Soviet foreign policy. Nevertheless, the constitution of the RSFSR in 1991 was very different from the 1977 Soviet Constitution and the Russian Federation adopted a new constitution in 1993. In institutional terms, therefore, Russia was a new state with all the attendant problems of establishing an efficient foreign policy bureaucracy, working out how institutions relate to one another in respect of foreign policy and deciding what the objectives of the state were in its relations with the outside world.

It is also not uncommon for the foreign policy of a country that has lost an empire to be erratic. Neither Britain nor France, for example, adapted easily to a post-imperial foreign policy. There was some ambivalence, however, about whether the Russian Federation *had* lost an empire. When the Soviet Union disintegrated in December 1991, most non-Russian Soviet citizens welcomed the simultaneous destruction of two empires, the Soviet and the Russian. Although their immediate concern was to free themselves from the shackles of the

Chapter specially commissioned for this volume.

USSR, they had bitter memories of the Russian empire as well as of the Soviet Union. Russians, however, were divided and ambivalent about the collapse of the Soviet Union. They believed that successive Soviet governments had exploited Russia in order to develop the other union republics. They certainly did not hold themselves responsible for the injustices of Soviet Communism. On the other hand, they did not mourn the loss of the pre-revolutionary Russian empire, because they did not identify themselves with it. Nevertheless, they soon became concerned that Russia had lost its identity when the Soviet Union collapsed. The complex process of redefining Russia's identity affected foreign policy. But even when agreement seemed to be reached about Russia's new identity, the mismatch between the foreign policy aims proclaimed by the leadership and the means available to implement them sometimes made Russian foreign policy seem incoherent.

It is not just domestic circumstances which determine a country's foreign policy. Foreign policy is, after all, a response to events in the outside world. And the external environment in the first post-Soviet decade proved less benevolent than Russians had expected. Western financial assistance to underwrite Russia's economic reform turned out to be far smaller than anticipated. Negotiations for multilateral aid were complex and long-winded, while the conditions attached to loans seemed unreasonably stringent and the means by which they were established unnecessarily intrusive. Moreover, the 'free' market espoused by the West did not mean that Russia had unrestricted access to the few markets where its goods enjoyed comparative advantage. Joining international organizations entailed delays and difficulties and this contributed to the perception that Western politicians patronized Russians, treating them as if Russia had been defeated in the Cold War. There was also a strong sense in Moscow that the West was indifferent to Russia's security interests. Working out how to respond to this surprisingly unsympathetic external environment also affected the coherence of Russian foreign policy.

Let us look in more detail at the domestic factors—the constitutional arrangements and identity problems—that affected the consistency of Russia's foreign policy.

Foreign policy decision-making in Russia

It is not surprising that foreign policy coordination was a problem in Russia. The Soviet-era constitution of the RSFSR had been amended to accommodate the new democratic institutions but it was vague about the division of power between the legislative bodies and the executive, on the one hand, and about the relationship between the functions of the government and the role of the executive president, on the other. The resulting fragmentation of foreign policy-making was exacerbated by the president's reliance on advisers who issued statements in his name, travelled abroad on his behalf, and rarely coordinated their activities with either the MFA or the Security Council, which was established in May 1992. President Yeltsin's unpredictability increased the confusion: he was given to making impromptu policy pronouncements, frequently taking both his own advisers and his interlocutors by surprise.

The constitution authorized the legislature to determine the general guidelines of policy. The Congress of People's Deputies and the Supreme Soviet struggled to maintain an effective voice in foreign policy and aspired to make the executive accountable. However, foreign policy soon became an instrument in the political conflict which beset Russia in 1993. The conflict permeated all aspects of policy-making, turning international affairs into an arena in which wider political battles were fought. Since no coordinating mechanisms had been established to integrate policy, it seemed at times that the legislature and the military each had its own, separate (and often contradictory) foreign policy which bore little relationship to the policy of the president which, in turn, sometimes seemed to differ from the policy of the MFA. As a result of these multiple voices, Russian foreign policy often appeared confused and confusing.

The 1993 constitution was clearer about the locus of decision-making: the president determined the basic guidelines of foreign policy, represented Russia in international relations, appointed diplomats and the Security Council, and conducted international negotiations. The Duma and the Federation Council retained the right to ratify international treaties. In addition, the Duma had the right to scrutinize foreign policy, while the Federation Council had to approve the use of Russian troops abroad. The new constitution did little to clarify the division of executive authority between the MFA and the president, however, and it encouraged a proliferation of presidential structures and advisers. Moreover, in 1995 the MFA and the 'power' ministries were made directly subordinate to the president rather than the prime minister. This increased the influence of the presidential executive on foreign policy. Although the MFA was charged with coordinating the foreign policy activities of other ministries, with a president whose preferred management style was to play advisers off against one another, the MFA often seemed to be sidelined, particularly while Andrei Kozyrev was foreign minister. Under Yevgeny Primakov, who was a stronger foreign minister, the status of the MFA rose. Although Primakov also improved the level of cooperation between institutions with foreign policy interests, the problem of coordination persisted.

Despite their limited foreign policy powers, the Federation Council has three committees which deal with international matters (for Security and Defence, for International Affairs, and for CIS Affairs), while the Duma has four committees (for Security, for Defence, for International Affairs, and for CIS affairs and Relations with Compatriots) and three commissions (on Geopolitics; 'Cooperation with Yugoslavia to overcome the consequences of NATO aggression'; and on Implementing the START 2, ABM, and Comprehensive Test Ban treaties and concluding a START 3 treaty).[1] The committees became more businesslike in their deliberations on foreign policy but, like their Supreme Soviet predecessors, Duma deputies used foreign policy debates and resolutions to express general opposition to the government and the president. Moreover, the Duma sometimes adopted resolutions which contradicted official foreign policy. Although they were not binding, the confusion they caused had damaging repercussions on perceptions of Russian foreign policy abroad. The Duma also postponed and delayed its ratification of treaties as a mark of disapproval of, and in an attempt to influence, government policy.

The poor constitutional division of foreign policy powers, the absence of established procedures for coordinating policy and the tendency of the Duma to use international issues for domestic political purposes all contributed to conveying the impression that Russian

---

[1] For the constitutional division of foreign policy responsibilities, see *Konstitutsiya Rossiyskoy Federatsii* (Moscow: Yuridicheskaya literatura, 1993). The names and members of the Federation Council and Duma committees are listed on their respective webpages. See <www.council.gov.ru/sostav/komitets/spis_kom.htm> and <www.duma.gov.ru/deputats/committe.htm> Retrieved 27 August 2000.

foreign policy was incoherent. A second important contributory factor was the general confusion as to the identity of Russia.

The problem of Russia's identity

Whether or not they believed that they had lost an empire, most Russians found it difficult to conceive of Russia as separate from the other successor states. As Roy Allison points out in a subsequent chapter, the Soviet system had been organized in such a way that it was difficult for the Russian leadership to relinquish control over the 'former Soviet space'. But forging a new identity was not just a question of accepting the loss of the empire and establishing normal diplomatic relationships with the new states of Eurasia. There was a dilemma about Russia's geopolitical identity. The disintegration of the Soviet Union and the existence of new, independent states to the west of Russia reinvoked an old question: was Russia part of Europe, or had the loss of empire turned it into an Asian or Eurasian power? The dilemma—which harked back to earlier debates about Russian identity—is graphically conveyed by the title of Vladimir Baranovsky's contribution to this book. Although Russia was further from Europe than it had been for 300 years, reform-minded politicians and commentators equated progress and prosperity with Europe and argued that Russia was European no matter how great the geographical distance separating it from the rest of the continent. Other, more nationalistically-minded, commentators claimed a unique Eurasian role for Russia. The vacillation between perceiving Russia as 'a part of Europe' and Russia 'apart from Europe' affected the coherence of Russian foreign policy.

There was also the question of status in the international system. Although Russia inherited the international role of the USSR, unlike the Soviet Union it was clearly not a superpower. Its economy was close to collapse and it was a continual supplicant for foreign aid. Indeed, it was doubtful that it should be considered a great power, given its economic predicament and the persistent political conflict which marked its first decade. The identity problem caused by loss of status was illustrated by the explanation of one Russian writer that although 'We are no longer one-sixth of the earth's surface . . . we continue to carry within ourselves one-sixth of the globe . . .'[2] The mismatch between the perception of great power status and the reality of Russia's declining power and capabilities was reflected in the gap that both Allison and Baranovsky identify between Russia's foreign policy rhetoric and its actions.

Until Russia's new identity had been defined, it was difficult to decide what its foreign policy stance should be. But international relations could not be suspended while the definition was reached; policy-makers had to respond to events in the external world even while the debate to clarify Russia's new role and status in the international system took place. The uncertainty about Russia's identity compounded the difficulty of formulating and implementing a consistent foreign policy without established procedures and effective channels of communication. Russian foreign policy specialists point out that policy-makers were themselves to blame for the fact that foreigners did not understand Russia's national interests: 'Through its incessant ideological, political and practical casting about, Russia frequently

---

[2] S. Razgonov, cited in I. Bremmer and R. Taras, eds., *Nations and Politics in the Soviet Successor States* (Cambridge: Cambridge University Press, 1993), 68.

creates difficulties for itself . . . In part this can be explained by financial and other material problems. But it is, to no small extent, the result of the absence of clear political direction . . . and the low level of coordination between departments'.[3]

How did these problems affect Russia's relations with the United States?

Russia and the United States

At first the new Russian leaders assumed that Russian foreign policy would be orientated towards the West. Somewhat naively, they believed that since Russia was in the process of establishing democracy and introducing a market economy, its national interests would coincide with those of the West. When it became clear that these hopes were misguided and when Russia began to assert its own interests, strains started to appear in Russian–Western relations. Russia turned its attention to other states, reviving relations with some of the USSR's former allies. This created further tensions in the relationship between Russia and the West. At the same time, the West, which had initially concentrated its attention on Russia, began to develop relations with the other successor states. This, in turn, triggered considerable anxiety in Russia about foreign influence in an area which, as Allison points out (in Chapter 32), Russians regarded as their sphere of influence. It was the issue of NATO expansion, however, and NATO's attack on Serbia, that created the greatest strain in Russian–Western relations. Before examining this issue in greater detail, however, let us look at the progress that was made in arms control.

BILATERAL AND MULTILATERAL ARMS CONTROL

In the 1980s, bilateral superpower nuclear arms control and multilateral conventional arms agreements marked the successive stages of East–West rapprochement that brought the Cold War to an end. In the first post-Soviet decade, by contrast, they provided evidence of the decline in mutual understanding. At first the circumstances seemed auspicious for further reductions in nuclear and conventional arms. In January 1993 the second Strategic Arms Reduction Treaty (START 2) was concluded by Russia and the United States. Each side would reduce its nuclear arsenals to 3,500 warheads and eliminate multiple warheads. Russia would eliminate its heavy land-based intercontinental missiles and the USA would reduce its submarine-launched nuclear warheads by 50 per cent. START 2 could not come into effect, however, before Belarus, Ukraine, and Kazakhstan (the three successor states in which nuclear weapons had been deployed in Soviet times) had completed the reductions agreed by the USSR in START 1. There was a further delay while both Russia and the USA tried to persuade a reluctant Ukraine to ratify START 1.

By then ratification of START 2 had become a controversial issue in Moscow, and the Duma refused to place the treaty on its agenda. One reason was the growing conviction described by Baranovsky that the Soviet leadership had made too many concessions to the West, and the belief that President Yeltsin was repeating this mistake. But refusing to ratify START 2 also served political purposes in the Duma's conflict with the president, as well as a means of signalling Russian opposition to US policies such as the proposal to expand NATO

[3] Pavel L'vovich Ivanov and Boris Mikhailovich Khalosha, 'Rossiya-NATO: Chto dal'she', *Mirovaya ekonomika i mezhdunarodnye otnosheniya*, 6 (1999), 5–15, quote on p. 9.

and attempts to modify the 1972 Anti-Ballistic Missile (ABM) Treaty. In the USA, however, the Duma's reluctance called into question Russia's commitment to arms control and President Clinton refused to begin negotiating a START 3 treaty until START 2 had been ratified. When Vladimir Putin was elected Russian president, he persuaded the Duma to change its mind about ratification. In April 2000 both START 2 and the multilateral Comprehensive Test Ban Treaty were ratified.[4] However, the Duma attached amendments to the START 2 ratification giving Russia the right to revoke it if the USA violated the 1972 ABM accord. Moreover, President Putin warned that if the United States abrogated the ABM treaty, Russia would cease to consider itself bound by any US–Russian arms control agreements.

The multilateral Conventional Forces in Europe (CFE) agreement which, when it was signed Paris in 1990, had symbolized the end of the Cold War, also faltered as mutual empathy declined. The CFE had limited the number of conventional forces that could be deployed in Europe by NATO and the Warsaw Treaty Organization. When the latter dissolved, the forces permitted it by CFE had to be divided up between the member countries. In 1991 the Soviet allocation had to be further subdivided among the European successor states. The Russian government soon realized that the forces it was permitted on its southern flank were inadequate to deal with the perceived threat to Russian security arising from the internal conflicts in the states on its southern perimeter. Since it had taken many years to achieve, NATO members were reluctant to renegotiate CFE. Their response was interpreted in Moscow as a refusal to recognize Russia's legitimate security interests. The issue had not been resolved by the deadline for full compliance with the treaty in November 1995. By then CFE, like START 2, had become hostage to NATO's expansion plans. The Russians had good grounds to argue that deploying conventional arms on the territory of an enlarged NATO would contravene CFE. NATO suddenly became more flexible about renegotiating the treaty and a new treaty was adopted at an OSCE summit in November 1999.

The future of the ABM treaty has dominated US–Russian relations in recent months. Invoking the threat of a nuclear attack by 'rogue states', the United States wants to develop a limited anti-missile system known as national missile defence (NMD). It can only do this by abrogating or renegotiating the ABM treaty which limits Russia and the United States to one anti-missile system each. The Russian government adamantly opposes both any modification of the ABM treaty and the development and deployment of NMD. Russian leaders and, less loudly, a number of European governments argue that the ABM treaty is the cornerstone of deterrence; modifying it will undermine the strategy which has kept the world safe from nuclear war. As for NMD, Russian defence specialists believe that the deployment of even a limited system would undermine Russian strategic nuclear deterrence. Russia would be forced to develop countermeasures such as increasing its stock of warheads.[5] A summit meeting between Presidents Putin and Clinton in June 2000 failed to resolve the impasse and it is likely to hinder negotiations for a START 3 treaty.

It is difficult to envisage future landmark arms control treaties of the kind that brought

---

[4] The Comprehensive Test Ban Treaty had been concluded in 1996. It should be noted that the US Congress is as reluctant to ratify the Comprehensive Test Ban Treaty as the Duma was to ratify START 2.

[5] See Alexander A. Pikayev, 'Moscow's Matrix', *Washington Quarterly*, 23/3(2000), 187–94 for the arguments against NMD. Some prominent defence specialists have a more flexible view of the ABM treaty than the official position. See, e.g. Aleksei Arbatov, 'Bezopasnost' dlya Rossiya i Zapada', *Mirovaya ekonomika i mezhdunarodnye otnosheniya*, 9 (1999), 8.

the Cold War to an end. According to Aleksei Arbatov, the problem is that Russia and the USA have different priorities. For the USA, the most pressing task is to prevent the proliferation of nuclear weapons, and of missile and dual-use technology. Russia's priorities, on the other hand, are reducing strategic missiles and conventional forces and preventing the deployment of tactical nuclear weapons in Eastern Europe, and any further NATO expansion.[6]

RUSSIA AND NATO

After the collapse of the Communist system, NATO undertook a series of measures to support the former Communist states without explicitly offering them security guarantees. The North Atlantic Cooperation Council (NACC), for example, offered consultation and cooperation with the alliance, first to the countries of Eastern Europe, and then when the USSR disintegrated, to all the former Soviet republics. The Russian government accepted the invitation with alacrity. In January 1994 NATO proposed a more active programme of cooperation: the Partnership for Peace (PfP). The Russian government was ambivalent, demanding special terms which reflected that it was a great power. It reached an individual Partnership agreement in June 1994. Neither NACC nor PfP was sufficient to allay the perception of the Eastern European former Communist states that Russian foreign policy was growing increasingly assertive. Their demands for full NATO membership became more insistent, particularly when Russian forces attacked Chechnya at the end of 1994. NATO politicians responded positively. Strong objections were voiced by the entire political spectrum in Russia: the eastward expansion of NATO was interpreted as a new version of containment, designed to exclude and isolate the Russian Federation.

NATO's invitation in July 1997 to the Czech Republic, Hungary, and Poland to join the Alliance might suggest that its members were indifferent to Russian objections. In fact, in an effort to ameliorate Russian anxiety, NATO had conducted intensive negotiations in the preceding months on a charter to formalize the relationship between the Russian Federation and the alliance. The NATO–Russian Founding Act on Mutual Relations, Cooperation and Security was signed in May 1997. It established a Permanent Joint Council which, in President Clinton's words, would give Russia 'a voice, but not a veto' in NATO affairs. To Russians, the Founding Act did not denote acceptance of NATO expansion and criticism of expansion did not abate. Nevertheless, Russians might have accepted the inevitable when the three countries formally became NATO members in March 1999. However, at its Fiftieth Anniversary conference in April 1999 NATO adopted a new strategic doctrine which envisaged 'out of area' military action (in other words, military operations in non-NATO member countries). The alliance also announced that its 'doors' would remain open to other countries seeking membership.

By then NATO had already put its new doctrine into action by launching an attack (without the approval of the UN Security Council) against Serbia in the face of strong and vocal Russian opposition. To most Russians the air attack on Serbia suggested that NATO's new doctrine could be applied to conflicts in the CIS or even within Russia itself. If NATO's eastward expansion was interpreted as a remote and indirect threat to Russian security, the threat represented by the new doctrine seemed far more direct and immediate. More

[6] Ibid. 8–9.

importantly, the attack on Serbia was perceived as portending a future in which NATO ignored Russia's interests, defied international law, and took upon itself the functions of the UN Security Council.[7]

NATO's conflict with Serbia came to an end, in large part as a result of Russian mediation, and Russia agreed to cooperate with NATO in supplying forces to police the peace in Kosovo. However, it has had a profound effect on Russia's perceptions of NATO and, since NATO and the USA are widely seen as synonymous, on Russia's relations with the United States.

POLITICAL RELATIONS

Arms control problems were symptomatic of divisions within Russia about what its foreign policy interests were and of a growing suspicion that the United States was intent on undermining Russian security. In part the suspicion arose from disillusionment with the outcome of economic reform and the perceived American role in dictating the course it took. There was irritation at the unexpected barriers to Russian exports and fear that relying on oil and natural gas exports would turn Russia into a commodity-producing economy of a type usually associated with the developing world. Attempts, particularly by the United States, to prevent Russia from selling arms, the one branch of manufacturing in which Russian goods were competitive on the world market, caused great resentment in the Russian Federation. But other differences had also appeared between Russian and American policy (towards Iraq, for example). Since other Western countries tended to follow the American lead, Russians became extremely bitter about the 'unipolarity' which, they believed, the United States wished to impose upon the international system.

Criticism of unipolarity was a persistent theme in Russian political discourse before the Kosovo crisis, but it became more insistent after the NATO intervention had taken place. Defined in the new Foreign Policy Concept as a world structured around 'the economic and power domination of the United States', unipolarity is contrasted to the multipolar system Russia seeks to achieve which 'reflects the diversity of the modern world with its great variety of interests'.[8] The Russian government has sought to canvass allies in its opposition to unipolarity. Joint Chinese–Russian communiqués and statements, for example, usually emphasize the commitment of the two countries to multipolarity and their resistance to a unipolar world order dominated by the United States.

Disapproval of American foreign policy is not, of course, unique to Russia, and it is by no means always unjustified. What is unusual, however, is that at the same time as using every available opportunity to criticize American attempts to dominate the international system, Russian leaders also speak warmly of the 'strategic partnership' between the United States and Russia.[9] Moreover, they count on the United States to intercede on Russia's

---

[7] Arbatov, 'Bezopasnost'', 6.

[8] 'Kontseptsiya vneshney politiki Rossiyskoy Federatsii', *Rossiyskaya gazeta*, 10 July 2000. For earlier references to the theme, see Yevgeny Primakov's address to the Foreign and Defence Policy Council, *Nezavisimaya gazeta*, 17 Mar. 1998 and Igor Ivanov's speech to UN General Assembly in 1998, Itar-Tass, 22 Sept. 1998.

[9] The term 'strategic partnership' was not reserved for the United States. Indeed, it was applied ubiquitously to almost every country with which the Russian Federation had active relations. At the press conference which ended the June 2000 US–Russian summit, the first of the new presidency, President Putin restricted himself to calling the United States one of Russia's 'main partners'.

behalf with the international financial institutions and are pleased to accept American economic assistance. The contradiction between the hostile rhetoric objecting to American unipolarity, on the one hand, and the friendly discourse in which the United States is Russia's strategic, or main, partner is one reason why Russian foreign policy sometimes seems confused.

In the following chapter Baranovsky explains Russia's ambivalence about Europe. It is no less ambivalent about the United States. However, whereas it is Russia's geopolitical and cultural identity that is the issue in relation to Europe, the source of its ambivalence about the United States is status. No matter how diminished their country is in the conventionally accepted dimensions of power, Russians regard their country as the equal of the United States—and they want to be treated as equal. And although they want this from everyone, it is particularly important for them that the United States regards Russia as an equal.[10] It is the perceived disregard for Russia's views, for example, in relation to air strikes on Iraq or NATO bombing in Serbia, that produces tension in US–Russian relations and accusations that the United States is intent on creating a unipolar world.

Status also causes problems in Russia's multilateral relationships. Russians, for example, want to be accepted as a member of what they like to call the G8 on a par with the advanced industrial nations that constitute the G7. The problem is that they also want the G7 to assist them to overcome their economic problems. The dilemma of being a supplicant for aid while also wanting to be accepted as a great power was well illustrated before the July meeting of the G7 in Okinawa. While President Putin maintained that Russia did not want any special benefits from its G8 partners, Prime Minister Kasyanov hoped that the G7 would engineer a write-off of Russia's Soviet-era debt. In the event, Putin did not ask for debt relief and Russia was treated as a great power.

Despite President Yeltsin's unpredictability, the reputedly warm personal relationship he enjoyed with President Clinton appeared strong enough to overcome the strains that developed in the political relationship between the two countries. If further strain is to be avoided, and if Russia and the United States are to reconcile their different priorities, President Putin will have to find his own modus vivendi with the new US president.

Future prospects

President Putin's manner is quite unlike that of President Yeltsin. In part this is because his background, his history, and his personality are very different. But his style also indicates something about his view of himself, of Russia, and of Russia's place in the world. There are further clues in his speeches and in the texts of the three new concepts—the National Security Concept, the Military Doctrine, and the Foreign Policy Concept—that have been published since he has been at the helm. He is realistic about the state of Russia's economy, he believes in a strong state, and he is a more overt nationalist (though he calls it patriotism) than his predecessor. Despite his view of Russia's economic decline, he believes that Russia is a great power. It is also a European power. The Foreign Policy Concept promises a consistent

---

[10] It should be emphasized that Russia is not unique in finding it difficult to accept its reduced status. Neither Britain nor France would contemplate giving up their permanent seats in the UN Security Council, for example, to states that are more powerful.

and predictable foreign policy, based on 'mutually advantageous pragmatism' and a reasonable balance between objectives and possibilities for attaining these objectives.[11]

It would seem, therefore, that Russian foreign policy will become more predictable since President Putin intends to deal with those factors that have made it appear incoherent in the past. In Russia's relations with the West, the optimism of the immediate post-Cold War period will not be recaptured. Nevertheless, despite the disillusionment in Russia about Western policy, the West will remain the focus of Russia's attention (with Europe taking precedence over the United States, judging by the order in which they are listed in the Foreign Policy Concept).

Although President Putin intends to improve relations, they are likely to remain uneasy without deteriorating to outright hostility. Just how tense they become, however, will depend on Western policy. According to Allison, Russia is determined to re-engage with the Caspian region, for example. Any attempt to exclude it from the area will cause tension. Nor will Russia find it easy to accept a closer relationship between Ukraine and NATO. Western criticism of the war in Chechnya has affected Russia's relations with the European Union (EU) and its membership of the Council of Europe, as Baranovsky points out. Russia's attitude to the enlargement of the EU has been positive, but if it turns out that enlargement damages Russia's economic interests, relations with the EU may deteriorate further. But the key to the future of Russia's relations with the West and, in particular, with the United States, is whether further NATO enlargement takes place. No Russian government can be expected to react with equanimity to a defence alliance which aims to include Russia's neighbours and from which it is excluded. While it is true that economic constraints will prevent an assertive response, the promise of a post-Cold War 'new world order' will be lost, if not irrevocably, then for the foreseeable future.

---

[11] For the Foreign Policy Concept, see n. 8. The National Security Concept is published in *Sobranie zakonodatel'-stva Rossiyskoy Federatsii*, No. 2, 2000, pp. 691–704 and the Military Doctrine can be found in *Nezavisimaya gazeta*, 22 Apr. 2000.

31   Russia: A Part of Europe or Apart from Europe?

Vladimir Baranovsky

....

The interaction of Russia and Europe is considerably affected by the changes currently under way in the international political landscape on the continent. In this regard, three issues have been of particular importance: the enlargement of NATO, the wars in the Balkans and the new agenda of the EU. At the same time, this interaction is inscribed into a more enduring framework consisting of various components—such as geographic realities, historic experiences, cultural characteristics, to name only a few of them. And Russia's domestic developments, whether the hostilities in Chechnya or the change of leadership in the Kremlin, are also a significant factor in relations between Russia and Europe.

Identity and geopolitics

Geographically, Europe and Russia are overlapping entities. Half of Europe *is* Russia; half of Russia is *in* Europe. However, politics, in contrast to geography, does not necessarily take this as axiomatic—either in Europe or in Russia.

It is true that geography contributes to this political ambivalence. Europe's western frontiers are clearly defined by the Atlantic coastal line; Europe's eastern limit, running southwards from the Urals, is more symbolic than natural. The fact that the Balkans is Europe's hot spot is undeniable. Whether the Caucasus is (or should be considered) *Europe's* headache is far less obvious.

Other foundations for drawing a dividing line between Europe and non-Europe are also confusing. If we use the civilization criterion, the question 'where does Europe end?' would bring about even more Kafkian answers: it ends thousands of miles away from Europe (somewhere in the southern hemisphere, in Australia) and at the same time within Europe itself (in some remote villages in the middle of Kosovo or Transylvania). In this regard, Europe is fluid. Whether Russia is a part of Europe may be debatable, but it is certainly a part of Europe's fluidity.

This goes in parallel with Russia's intellectual fluidity with respect to Europe. Debates on Europe have been part of Russia's history throughout the last thousand years. Moreover, they are an intrinsic part of Russia's search for self-identification—a search that continues now, on the threshold of the next millennium. What is really intriguing is the fact that the basic parameters of these debates are just the same now as they used to be centuries ago. The arguments have certainly become more elaborated, but they all point to the same range of conflicting, mutually exclusive conceptions. These belong to three basic groups.

First published in *International Affairs* (London), 76/3 (2000), 443–58. Reproduced by kind permission of the author and Blackwell Publishers.

Those in the first group assume that Russia *is* Europe, that it is genetically descended from the Christian civilization. There are several variations of this approach: Russia is *imperfect* Europe (that is, underdeveloped and lagging behind, or sick, or failed); or, Russia is *the best* Europe (with some European values being more adequately incarnated by intelligentsia and literature in Russia than anywhere else on the continent); or, Russia is *another* Europe, evolved in its eastern variant (via the Byzantine empire) and strongly influenced by external factors. But these are just segments of the larger fundamental idea: Russia and Europe belong to the same family.[1]

The second group of ideas underlines Russia's closeness to Asia, in opposition to Europe. The Byzantine empire which brought Christianity to Russia was itself a deviation from Europe and an increasingly Asian entity; the schism of 1054 made the division irreversible, and not only in religious terms. Furthermore, Russians lived for over two and a half centuries under the control of the Golden Horde, which irreversibly alienated Russia from Europe. In an alternative reading, this was a period of Russia's deliberate fundamental reorientation eastwards, a strategy which was essential to neutralize threats emanating from the West; even the Russian ethnicity is the result of the centuries-long amalgam of old Slavic and Turkic tribes. In any case, the historical destinies of Europe and Russia turned out differently, whereas the country's 'Asian predicament' was only reinforced by the subsequent expansion of the Russian state towards Siberia, Central Asia and the Far East.[2]

The third basic approach states that Russia is neither the West nor the East, neither Europe nor Asia. The Orthodox religion, its historical core element, stands opposed both to the Latin confession and to Islam. In contrast to European practice, Russia is not built upon the notion of ethnicity—it is a specific entity embracing over 100 various peoples and ethnic groups. As a civilization Russia represents a world in itself, a microcosm that follows its own destiny and develops its own rules. In other words, Russia is special; it should not and cannot follow exogenous standards.

Furthermore, possessing vast territory and huge natural resources, maintaining considerable cultural diversity and relatively high levels of education, cultivating meaningful social attitudes and ethical instincts, combining in a unique way a traditionalist mentality and an openness to innovative thinking—Russia may represent an ideal laboratory for developing a viable alternative to, or an organic amalgam of, values associated respectively with West and East. A messianic variation of this approach suggests that Russia may forge an attractive model to be followed by 'other worlds' in the light of a deepening crisis of global civilization.[3]

All these approaches appeal to historic developments, religious beliefs, normative values, psychological characteristics, behavioural patterns, cultural orientations and other fundamental factors that allegedly predetermine Russia's 'Europeanness' (or, alternatively, its absence). None of them could claim to have an upper hand in the intellectual evolution of

---

[1] For a comprehensive presentation of this argument, see Vladimir Kantor, '*Yest'* yevropeiskaya derzhava . . .'. *Rossiya: trudniy put' k tsivilizatsii* (Moscow: ROSSPEN, 1997).

[2] One of the most prominent proponents of the idea of Russia's Asian connections as the core element of the country's identity was the historian, ethnographer and philosopher Lev Gumilev, widely known in Russian intellectual circles for elaborating the theory of ethnogenesis. See e.g. his *Ot Rusi do Rossii* (Moscow: Svarog i K, 1998).

[3] See e.g. a recent article by Gavriil Popov, 'Russkiy kholokost', *Nezavisimaya gazeta*, 26 Apr. 2000, p. 8. Popov is a prominent politician of the 'first generation democrats' and a former mayor of Moscow.

the continent. All three pretend to influence its politics and policy. Each may evolve into a milder formula (Russia is a *specific* part of Europe—or it is the most European-oriented part of Europe's 'near abroad'). This is, so to say, the existential paradigm of Russia's thinking about itself and its external environment.

This existential ambivalence has marked Russia's attitudes to Europe for centuries. For Russia, Europe was always both charming and frightening, appealing and repulsive, radiating light and incarnating darkness. Russia was anxious to absorb Europe's vitality—and to ward off its contaminating effects; to become a fully fledged member of the European family of nations and to remain removed from it; to become an object of its courtesies and even its devotion—but at the same time to inspire fear and trepidation. Indeed, the whole history of Russia is cast in this contradictory feeling: its own centuries-long territorial expansion *towards* Europe—and memories of invasions *from* Europe; all the tormented searching of Russian sociological thought with its European-oriented 'Westernism' and the anti-European zeal of both the Orthodox church and the communal identity as negation of individualism. The 300-year-long record of social experiment from Peter the Great to this day is the most painful manifestation of this paradox, when models imported from the West (such as communism until recently or 'unrestrained' capitalism nowadays) evolved into such grotesque forms that even wider rifts opened between Russia and Europe.

It is true that Europe reciprocated with similar ambiguities. As a remote and almost exotic peripheral land with a significantly different lifestyle, Russia alienated the Europeans, and at the same time fascinated them. Its vast territorial space put Russia in a unique position in Europe—and generated fears about its expansionism. Its huge demographic potential inspired respect and consideration—as well as the feeling that the value of human life was significantly lower in Russia than in Europe. Russia was (and perhaps still is) regarded as possessing enormous resources which might eventually make it Europe's most important component—were it not for its anachronistic and corrupted economic system, incompatible with European ways of doing business. The impressive military might of Russia has been traditionally perceived as threatening Europe—although, eventually, redirecting other threats away from Europe and absorbing them.

This ambivalence persists nowadays, especially in Russian perceptions of European attitudes. Russia is no longer a military threat—but from a Russian perspective NATO intends to continue as the military alliance against an eventual re-emergence of threat emanating from Russia. The enlargement of NATO should not antagonize Russia—but Russia's involvement in this process is not considered even as a hypothetical possibility. The EU addresses its first 'common strategy' to Russia—and threatens it with sanctions. Russia's peacekeepers are welcomed to participate in KFOR—but, unlike leading Western countries, they do not get their own sector of responsibility. By and large the Cold War logic of 'keeping Russians out' seems to many of them to have mutated into a double-track task: how to prevent Russians from becoming disengaged, without however actually letting them in.

What many Russians see as a new European logic, as described above, does not make their choice of how to relate to Europe any easier. Certainly it does not promote the 'pro-European' trend in public consciousness; and the debate on Russia's European/non-European identity remains as fascinating as it is inconclusive. It is accompanied (and disoriented) by Russia's suddenly increased interest in geopolitics. In terms of culture and civilization, the distance between Russia and Europe is meaningless in comparison with what separates Russia from

Asia; but geopolitically Russia is undoubtedly in between the two. Russian 'Westernizers' criticize the concept of Russia's 'Eurasian identity' as an attempt to find a justification for consolidating the country's social and political backwardness, preventing modernization and undermining reforms. But they would hardly disagree that numerous external risks and challenges that Russia is facing are of a non-European origin—indeed, in terms of these challenges Russia *is* a Eurasian entity.

Thus Russia's cultural/civilizational and geopolitical identities are not necessarily the same. The failure to differentiate between them leads to confusion all the time. The European-oriented representatives of the intelligentsia want to see Russia moving westwards (focusing on its civilizational orientation), but they are blamed for making the country a hostage or satellite of the West (which is geopolitics). Similarly, failure in domestic trans-formations inspired (or believed to be inspired) by the West leads to a reappraisal of relations with the West and a significant cooling. The same logic (although with an opposite vector) created a serious risk that NATO air strikes against Yugoslavia might deliver a severe blow to Russia's fragile democracy.

Extrapolating geopolitical ideas into the realm of civilization is as wrong as making foreign policy only on the basis of cultural affinities. A Russian resident of Vladivostok would not feel himself less European than a Muscovite (although he lives 10 time-zones eastwards); but he would be much more sensitive, both positively and negatively, about China and Japan as his immediate neighbours.

In a broader sense, there is certainly a strong link between Russia's culture, mentality and historical legacy, on the one hand, and the country's national interests and ambitions in the international arena, on the other. But this link is not overriding; it does not necessarily determine Russia's attitudes and policies towards the external world. In this respect, Russia's Europeanness does not guarantee its *rapprochement* with the West, any more than "non-European" (or 'insufficiently European') characteristics of Russian civilization create insurmountable obstacles thereto.

Furthermore, even if Russia's geopolitical identification with Eurasia is recognized as different from its civilizational identification with Europe, what follows from this in terms of foreign policy implications may be a matter of serious controversy. The question is about choosing among the theoretically available strategies aimed at minimizing Asia-related risks. One approach would consist of promoting an 'Asia first' policy and developing preferential partnership with Russia's potential challengers in this area. Another, contrary, one would focus upon Europe, with the aim of consolidating Russia's European connection and secur-ing Russia's rear. In this case, it is assumed that Russia's Eurasian geopolitical status makes it imperative to promote *rapprochement* with Europe.

Russia's European uncertainties

Contrary to the expectations of the early post-Cold War period, the 1990s did not reduce the overall 'existential' ambivalence of Russia's perceptions of attitudes to, and policies towards Europe. It is worth recalling that post-Soviet Russia came on to the international scene with a strong pro-Western orientation (*ipso facto*, also a pro-European one). Destroying the old regime, getting rid of the communist past, proclaiming itself decisively in favour of democracy and a market economy—all this was considered to provide Russia with a ticket to the 'community of the civilized countries'. For a time, yesterday's foes were regarded as the most reliable friends. They were expected to welcome the new Russia with enthusiasm as an equal partner—both in Europe and elsewhere. Indeed, Russia's interests in the international arena were considered to be completely identical to those of the West. Operating together, they would constitute a nucleus of the 'new world order'.

Thus, Russia was both politically and psychologically ready to join the club of the international elite and to be recognized as a fully fledged participant of the emerging pan-European pattern that was to replace the bipolar organization of the continent. Such hopes, however, did not last long. Explanations differ as to what extent this was due to the initial excesses of the post-Cold War euphoria or, alternatively, to the mishandling of the emerging issues by various major international actors, including (or even beginning with) Russia itself. But one thing is obvious: in many respects Russia feels less at ease with Europe today than it did ten years ago.

Even Russia's ideological reorientation, bringing it closer to Europe on the level of some fundamental values, is not necessarily making the two more compatible. Ironically, even the contrary may prove true. Indeed, it was sufficient for the former Soviet Union simply to proclaim its 'Europeanness' to gain a sympathetic reaction from Europe. This is no longer the case for post-Soviet Russia: since it pretends to operate as a 'normal' member of the international community, the *quality* of the factors certifying its participation in the family of 'civilized' countries (democracy, human rights, market economy and so on) becomes a critical test. Serious difficulties that the country experiences in this regard represent a challenge for Russia first of all, but also for its European engagement. This might even lead to the paradoxical conclusion that Russia would have a better chance of interacting with Europe as an 'outsider' than as an 'insider', since the criteria for the latter status are more demanding and more difficult to fulfil.

The situation is even more depressing when geopolitics comes into the foreground. Here the fact of Russia's significantly reduced position in Europe is impossible to deny. Nevertheless, there are different explanations for this phenomenon. In fact, Russians began asking 'who lost Europe?' much earlier than Americans started to wonder 'who lost Russia?'

One explanatory theory attributes Russia's 'departure' from Europe to its badly conceived and inadequately implemented foreign policy, going back to the Soviet period of *perestroika*: the 'new political thinking' is blamed for unjustified concessions along the whole spectrum of Moscow's interaction with Europe and, in a broader sense, with the West as a whole. It is noteworthy that this criticism emanates not only from quarters professing communist orthodoxy and believing that Gorbachev and Shevardnadze betrayed the country's interests; the thesis that the *rapprochement* with the West was inadequately negotiated and poorly compensated seems to be shared by many professional analysts not associated with any particular ideology. From this perspective, the retreat of the Soviet armed forces from the centre of Europe, acceptance of the unification of Germany and dissolution of the 'outer empire' are all regarded as powerful bargaining chips that could have been traded for significant compensations to Moscow, but instead were simply given away.

A more liberal line of thinking suggests an alternative reading of this phenomenon, by which Russia's retreat is viewed predominantly as the logical course of events following on from the poor historical record of the Soviet Union. Moreover, the disengagement from Europe allowed Russia to get rid of unnecessary commitments and an excessive external burden—a burden, indeed, that is seen as one of the major causes of the strain that resulted in the collapse of the Soviet Union. Russia, according to this line of thinking, should regard its reduced position as an asset rather than as a loss.

Asset or loss, with the end of the bipolar division of Europe, Russia unexpectedly found itself pushed to the periphery of the continent. What used to be the immediate neighbour-hood of the country that controlled half of Europe is now separated from Russia by two territorial belts: the former Warsaw Pact allies and the former western republics of the Soviet Union. The problem here is not only that of becoming the most remote territory of Europe. A number of factors traditionally affecting the security status of the country, such as access to the high seas, availability of critical resources and so on, have significantly deteriorated with the disintegration of the USSR. Russia has also lost some important tools that were available to the former Soviet Union in terms of exercising influence on Europe. It will suffice to mention the redeployment of significant armed forces 1,000 miles eastwards, in the context of troop withdrawal from central Europe.

Looking at military developments in a broader sense, it is obvious that Russia's overall military might in Europe diminished dramatically during the 1990s. This is due to a number of factors: first of all, the collapse of the USSR; second, the unprecedented economic decline and financial crisis, making appropriate allocations of resources for military purposes impossible; third, the need to fulfil obligations according to international agreements and existing (or impending) arms control treaties. What remains at Russia's disposal can by no means be compared to former Soviet capabilities. Indeed, soon, for the first time since the mid-1930s, the scale of Russia's conventional forces will be reduced to that of just a large European nation; thus, the comfortable and secure feeling of being the pre-eminent military power on the continent is doomed to disappear. This is accompanied by similar trends on the level of strategic nuclear weapons: while at the moment it still possesses numerical parity with the United States, Russia is unlikely to be able to maintain it in the coming decades. Furthermore, Russia's forces are gravely weakened by the mass obsolescence of weapons and equipment and severe curtailment of procurement programmes. Since the mid-1980s, the scale of weapons procurement in Russia has dropped by as much as 80–90 per cent, in some cases by two orders of magnitude.

Such developments, alongside other factors, have significantly reduced Moscow's ability to affect developments in Europe. This new situation is recognized and basically accepted both by the country's political class and by public opinion. Moreover, it is by and large considered irreversible. Concerns about Russia's assertiveness with respect to what it has lost in Europe seem unfounded, or at least, highly exaggerated; even more so a possible re-emergence of a 'Russian threat' to Europe. There are no political forces in Russia today that believe that re-establishing the *status quo ante* is a practically achievable goal. In this sense, the rise of any significant revanchist trend in Russian foreign policy seems impossible, whatever domestic changes might occur.

At the same time, this basic acceptance of new realities by Russians is coloured with a certain bitterness, since retreat from Europe looked like a panicked flight rather than a result of a deliberate policy. Furthermore, Russia often regards itself as a victim of unfair treatment by other international players, who have taken advantage of its poor domestic situation. The predominant feeling is that even if Russia could not retain its position in Europe, it certainly did not deserve to be forced out ruthlessly and treated as a defeated country.

Justified or not, this complex of resentment does exist in Russia's thinking about Europe. It is reinforced by the increasingly uncomfortable feeling that Russia is being relegated to the sidelines of European developments. The debate over NATO enlargement has given additional weight to such a proposition. Even analysts without a hint of anti-Western feeling focused upon the argument that while NATO is gradually turning into the central element in the overall organization of the European political space, Russia is denied access to this structure. This can only exclude it further from decision-making with respect to crucial issues in Europe.[4]

Worse, Russia finds itself in the painful position of having lost all its old allies in Europe and being unable to attract any new ones. The rhetorical cordiality of the West is often overlaid by a watchfulness, suspicion and reluctance to take Russia's view into account. The former Warsaw Pact partners have all adopted a strong anti-Russian stand. The Baltic states are openly unfriendly. Even the reliability of the Commonwealth of Independent States (CIS) countries is doubtful. There is a strong sense that Moscow cannot realistically count on being supported by anyone in its international activities. Not surprisingly, Belarus has become the only possible partner for alliance bidding, all reservations with respect to President Lukashenko's regime notwithstanding.

This 'no allies' situation has another consequence, too: it draws Russia away from Europe, both geopolitically and ideologically. If allies are not available in Europe, they should be sought outside it; if Russia is considered as not meeting European standards, it should not regard them as 'sacred cows'; if the Europeans are unwilling (or unable) to accept Russia's right to be specific, there may be other less intrusive interlocutors. The most significant example of how this logic is translated into policy is Russian–Chinese *rapprochement*. Although Russia's connection with 'rogue states' should not be exaggerated, some of them may be predictably regarded as potential candidates for partnership 'by default', simply because alternative options, particularly in Europe, do not look available.

This syndrome of alienation from Europe is aggravated by strongly disappointing signals that the course of Russia's development is taking an opposite path to that of the majority of the continent. The economic performance of its western part is only one source of this perception, albeit a significant indicator in the light of the dramatic hardships and failures associated with the continuing transformation of Russia's economy. Another source of thinking along these lines is the significant breakthroughs in European integration achieved during the 1990s, while all of Russia's efforts towards CIS integration have dramatically failed. Moreover, while the EU states appear to be becoming closer to one another, Russia is in danger of losing its own territorial integrity.

Not only are Russia and the rest of Europe in different phases of their evolution, but the continent's centre of gravity is shifting westwards. The EU and NATO are expanding their activities and membership, their roles on the continent are increasing, the western core of Europe is becoming stronger and more consolidated, it is attracting and indeed absorbing practically all countries of the continent ... This is how Europe is viewed from Moscow nowadays: prosperous and strong, but not very reassuring as far as Russia is concerned.

It is true that there is much in this perception that is related to Russia's considerable

---

[4] See Alexei Arbatov, *Bezopasnost': rossiyskiy vybor* (Moscow: EPItsentr, 1999), 194–200.

difficulties in adapting itself to the country's radically changed situation—a phenomenon not unfamiliar to some former European colonial powers. Indeed, even in the most liberal-oriented circles the loss of superpower status continues (almost ten years after the event) to be a source of considerable unease and confusion, feelings often exploited by conservatives, nationalists, proponents of the restoration scenarios, those who believe that Russia is in an 'imperial predicament', and so on.

Certainly, this residual superpower/great power syndrome affects Russia's relations with Europe. They are damaged by Russia's frustration and irritation, by Russia's instinctive impulse towards re-establishing itself as a special player, 'not-like-the-others', by Russia's erratic attempts to position itself as a privileged partner of the United States and a complex (however ill-founded) of superiority towards the Europeans. Nevertheless, under certain circumstances, persisting elements of 'great power' psychological self-identification, mentality and historic memory could be helpful—for instance, to defuse grievances with respect to the challenging behaviour of some Europeans, such as former Warsaw Pact clients or Baltic states: the lack of respect on their part could be attributed to their feelings of inferiority and considered meaningless in terms of Russia's interests, not even deserving substantial reaction. But in general, having lost its superpower status, Russia is becoming more commensurate with European dimensions and scales, less frightening for the Europeans and more acceptable to them. On the other hand, if Russia's ambitions are to be downscaled to the level of 'regional great power', it is in Europe that Russia could perhaps most fruitfully play this role, to avoid excessively antagonizing other international actors and even to be recognized by them in this capacity.

Focus upon Europe

However ambivalent Russian thinking about Europe might be, it is by no means consistently anti-European, even less so in its policy-related implications. It is true that Russia may appear a hesitant, inconsistent or reluctant European. Nevertheless, the arguments for considering Europe by far the most important region in terms of Russia's fundamental interests in the international arena are compelling. Europe, according to this logic, is the main intended focus of Russia's long-term international strategy.

Since the end of the Cold War, Russia's relations with Europe have been directed by several fundamental factors. The ideological parameters of the classic Cold War pattern have become a thing of the past and are unlikely to re-emerge; traditional military-related considerations, based on the assumption of a major conflict on the continent, are no longer relevant; Russia's interest in economic links with Europe has considerably increased, due both to the imperatives of domestic reforms and to a desire to obtain better positions in the world market; and political interaction with Europe is essential if Russia is to achieve a respected international status. In addition, the centrality of Europe for Russia has only been reinforced by the failure of 'entente cordiale' with the United States. Russia has, moreover, every reason to believe that other international actors will consider its involvement in European affairs absolutely legitimate.

Russia's primary interest with respect to Europe consists in making it instrumental for the country's transformation. But within this overall paradigm (and to the extent to which 'high politics' still matter), Moscow aims at consolidating Russia's international role and preventing any developments that might marginalize Russia. Apart from that, some sub-regions in Europe are of special sensitivity for Russia: notably the Baltic Sea area, the Black Sea area, and the Transcaucasus.

Moscow has undertaken considerable political and diplomatic activity to promote a 'pan-European security architecture'. However, any temptations that may have existed to appeal for a totally new post-Cold War organizational pattern for the continent have been abandoned. Instead, Russia is trying to articulate its attitudes towards, interaction with, and eventual participation in the existing multilateral structures in Europe. In this context, it is worth outlining Russia's basic approaches to these.

Russia's nervous reaction to the prospect of NATO's enlargement eastwards has clearly revealed that the alliance is still perceived as a challenge to Russia's security interests. Another and even more significant motive is its wish to prevent the central security role in Europe being played by a structure to which Russia will not have direct access. Nevertheless, a 'special relationship' with NATO was considered a more practical strategy than promoting the re-emergence of the confrontational model; this was confirmed by the decision to sign the NATO–Russia Founding Act—a decision pushed through by the then Foreign Minister Yevgeny Primakov against considerable domestic opposition.

Moreover, Moscow seemed to be open to further *rapprochement* with NATO (albeit conditional upon a number of factors, first among them guarantees of non-expansion into former Soviet territory). However, this option was seriously undermined, first by the failure to provide the established Russia–NATO Permanent Joint Council with a substantial role, second (and most dramatically) by NATO's actions in Yugoslavia, and third by the adoption of a new strategic concept of NATO at its 50th anniversary summit in Washington. Re-establishing the cooperative pattern in Russia–NATO relations remains a formidable and challenging task.

The European Union is regarded as being the most powerful economic partner and important political actor in Europe. Russia–EU relations are considered to be developing successfully and to have good prospects. The Partnership and Cooperation Agreement between Russia and the EU has been complemented by two unilaterally adopted 'strategies' addressed by each side to the other. The overall positive image of the EU is well illustrated by Russia's attitude towards its forthcoming enlargement: paradoxically, for a time Moscow seemed to welcome this prospect even more enthusiastically than the EU's participants did—apparently, as a preferable alternative to the enlargement of NATO.

However, remaining outside the EU as it expands its territorial space and functional scope may exacerbate Russia's concerns about its own role in Europe. For the time being, these concerns have not been articulated in a very explicit way—supposedly due to Russia's obsession with the issue of NATO enlargement. But further consolidation of the EU will sooner or later make it clear that the dividing line between members and non-members might become much more fundamental than in the case of NATO. There is a growing understanding in Russia that this trend might damage its interests and its prospects in Europe, unless mitigated by significantly stronger incentives for further *rapprochement* with the EU.

The Organization for Security and Cooperation in Europe is—in terms of its genesis, composition and operational mode—by far the most attractive multilateral institution for Russia. It corresponds to many of Russia's concerns regarding the organization of the continental political space, and one would expect Russia to make consistent efforts to promote this institution. However, Russia's attempts to increase the role of the OSCE are often perceived as motivated by the intention to oppose it to NATO—an effort which cannot but discredit any pro-OSCE design. Furthermore, Russia seems to fear that the OSCE might limit its freedom of action within the post-Soviet space (particularly with respect to peace-keeping, as was manifested in the developments around the issue of Nagorno-Karabakh) or even within Russia proper (for instance, with respect to attempts to suppress separatism in the North Caucasus). Thus, while having a clear interest in upgrading the OSCE, Russia remains one of its 'difficult' participants.

When Russia became a member of the Council of Europe this was viewed as an important political gain attesting to the quality of the changes under way in Russia. It is feared, however, that failure to satisfy the Council's high standards regarding human rights and democracy would leave Russia vulnerable to severe criticism that might seriously damage its prestige. Within such a scenario, there is a risk of pushing Russia to reconsider the very idea of becoming internationally accountable. The recent condemnation of Russia's actions in Chechnya by the Parliamentary Assembly of the Council of Europe pushed some politicians and analysts to argue for withdrawal from this organization.

Moscow is involved in a number of sub-regional structures operating in Russia's immediate vicinity (such as the Baltic Sea States Council and the Black Sea Economic Cooperation); these are considered important for addressing some of Russia's immediate economic or political concerns. Strategically, they may contribute both to forging a more developed network of interdependence and to alleviating conflict-prone issues. Also important for Russia is its unquestioned right to be a fully fledged participant in these structures and even to count on a certain prominence as its due, as well as their potential for operating independently from the NATO-centred European system.

Russia's interest in developing a 'pan-European architecture' is accompanied by Moscow's orientation towards promoting bilateral relations with a number of key players in Europe. There seems, indeed, to be a deeply rooted conviction that the bilateral track is more promising than the multilateral one. By the end of Yeltsin's presidency, France and Germany were considered to be Russia's major partners on the European scene; Russia's new President, Vladimir Putin, has 'upgraded' the UK to this status. Each of these three is attractive for Russia in its own way: France on account of what is perceived as its independent policy and its reluctance to accept a submissive relationship with the United States, Germany on account of its crucial geopolitical position in Europe and its undeniable prominence in terms of economic might, and the UK on account of its role as one of the leading world political and financial centres, as well as through its expected ability to preside over the re-introduction of Russia, under its new leadership, into the international elite.

Russia's attitude towards American involvement in Europe has a contradictory character. Moscow's official policy line recognizes the essential role of the United States in European developments; Europe is traditionally one of the central issues discussed by Russians and Americans bilaterally. However, there is also a considerable amount of negativity in Russia's perceptions of, and reactions to, the actual and virtual US presence in Europe. This negativity is partly a residual legacy of the Cold War; but a kind of neo-anti-Americanism is also emerging, fuelled by the vision of the unipolar world in the making, with a single remaining superpower claiming to be the centre of the universe and operating in the international arena regardless of the legitimate interests of others (including those of the Europeans, allied and not with the United States). Related to this perception is a suspicion that the consolidation of transatlantic relations might damage Russia's interests and push it further away from the main paths of European development. These reservations run alongside sporadic attempts to play on what are perceived as American–west European contradictions and to promote 'pure European' approaches as a counterweight to excessive involvement of the Americans in the affairs of the continent.

All these trends were dramatically affected by developments in and around Kosovo since the end of 1998. In fact, the Kosovo phenomenon has influenced Russia's ideas on its relations with the outside world in a more fundamental way than most other events during the past decade. This episode could not but have a considerable impact on Russia's attitudes towards policies in Europe.

This 'European connection' of the Kosovo case for Russia might seem distressing if it were regarded only within the overall context of Russia's relations with the West. Indeed, NATO's military operation against Yugoslavia was assessed as a flagrant violation of international law, as a heavy blow against the existing UN-based international system, as an attempt to establish a 'new world order' by force, allowing arbitrary interference in the internal affairs of states (on 'humanitarian' or any other grounds). Also, Russia was strongly (and painfully) affected by the fact that the decision to use force was taken in spite of its objections; a decision interpreted as an additional manifestation of insulting disregard towards Russia and as one more attempt to disassociate it from crucial European issues.

The air strikes against Yugoslavia, as viewed by Russia, were the most convincing justification for its negativity with respect to the prospect of establishing a NATO-centred Europe. Indeed, the Kosovo phenomenon contributed more to the consolidation of Russia's anti-NATO stance than the whole vociferous campaign against the enlargement of NATO. For a while, Moscow's major concern seemed to consist in preventing the enthusiasts of a new Cold War from taking the upper hand in domestic debates on how to respond to NATO's aggression.

At the same time, it is quite remarkable that Russia's indignation with respect to NATO military operations in Yugoslavia was directed predominantly, indeed almost exclusively against the United States—as if the Europeans did not participate in them at all. The fact that the EU supported the war against Yugoslavia and even contributed to it, politically, economically and militarily, passed almost unnoticed in Russia. By and large, the European states involved in this campaign were basically viewed as operating under American pressure.

This perception, even if amounting to simplification or ignorance, redirected Russia's negativity away from the Europeans. Certainly, their record in Kosovo, as viewed by Russia, was very poor; their ability to operate independently from the United States turned out to be considerably less than it had expected. Moreover, the predominance of NATO in dealing with Kosovo was interpreted as undermining the process of building a strong 'European pole'.[5] At the same time, it was hoped that the Kosovo crisis would promote

---

[5] According to Nikolai Mikhailov, Secretary of State in the Russian Ministry of Defence, the strategic goal of the United States in Kosovo consisted in creating a long-term pole of instability for Europe as the main American competitor. See 'Yugoslaviya: god spustiya posle agressii NATO v Kosovo', *Kompas* (*ITAR–TASS*), 7 Mar. 2000. See also Dmitri Danilov, 'Eroziya struktur evropeyskoy bezopasnosti', in *Konflikt v Kosovo: noviy kontekst formirovaniya rossiyskikh natsionalnykh interesov* (Moscow: East–West Institute [Moscow Center]/IMEMO), June 1999, 18–21.

the self-identification of the Europeans and a more energetic search on their part for a more prominent (and more independent) international role.[6]

Thus, one of the side-effects of Kosovo has been increased Russian attention to Europe. Certainly, this is to a significant extent driven by an anti-NATO rationale. This is also true with respect to Russia's emerging attitude towards security- and military-related developments within the EU. This trend is promoting a diminution of the US role in security arrangements in the western part of the continent, and as such is attracting attention both in Moscow and in Washington; but Russia's attention seems to be primarily connected with its grievances against the United States. Meanwhile, the extent to which the Common European Defence and Security Policy (CEDSP) in the making has the potential to evolve into an 'extra-NATO' pattern may be a matter of some misperception and/or illusion in Moscow. Even if one posits a hypothetical model of a militarily strong and politically self-reliant 'united Europe', it is unclear whether this might alleviate Russia's NATO-related concerns or just refocus them (and, eventually, even reinforce them).

However, arguments in favour of developing interaction with a CEDSP might have some validity. By and large, any possibility of cooperating with the EU in this extremely sensitive area is regarded as deserving thorough consideration, and an eventual *rapprochement* might be a very significant contribution to Russian–European interaction.

On an even larger scale this prospect raises Russia's possible involvement in multilateral efforts aimed at organizing and consolidating the European security space: for example, in the form of Russian engagement in the modernization of the armed forces in east and central Europe. Another and even more promising project could be the development of the European tactical ballistic missile defence with Russian participation. This would be an essential step towards minimizing or even eliminating Russia's perception of a re-emerging threat associated with NATO (since joint air and missile defence is by definition possible only between non-enemies). Also significant is the fact that Russia's involvement in the project would be far more than simply symbolic—its superb S-300 and S-400 systems might eventually constitute its core.

New prospects?

The long-awaited transition to the post-Yeltsin era in Russia seems likely to affect the country's European perspectives in two ways.

On the one hand, the war in Chechnya that accompanies this transition has significantly worsened the background for relations with Europe. Not only are the excesses of the war strongly condemned by the Europeans, but their criticism is much more vociferous than that emanating from America. In addition, this criticism was energetically endorsed by some 'pure European' multilateral structures, including the EU and the Council of Europe. Meanwhile, at home, the war (at least during its initial stage) was supported by Russian public opinion as a tough, painful, but indispensable operation to re-establish control over this breakaway territory that had been turned by its separatist authorities into a nucleus of anarchy and terrorism threatening to expand throughout the whole country. Against this

---

[6] Comments substantiating this view include critical assessments of the US role in Kosovo made by some European political and military officials. See *Nezavisimaya gazeta*, 24 Mar. 2000, p. 6.

background, Europe appeared to be obstructing the fight against terrorists. Furthermore, its criticism was regarded as hypocritical, reflecting double standards, in the light of what had happened in Kosovo.

It would be hard to imagine a worse situation in which to promote Russia's *rapprochement* with Europe. In this context, it seems important to note that Moscow's new leadership has chosen to take a relatively moderate line in dealing with this issue in relations with outsiders, including the Europeans. Suffice it to mention Vladimir Putin's numerous meetings with European politicians and his patient (even if not very successful) attempts to explain to them Moscow's logic in dealing with Chechnya,[7] the spectacular absence of dramatic reaction to various statements and resolutions on this matter that could have easily been interpreted as scandalous interference in Russia's domestic affairs,[8] and even a certain degree of growing openness in the North Caucasus in response to Western demands.

It is true that there may be some simplification in what seems to be a prevailing expectation in the Kremlin: 'We'll finish with Chechnya, and the normalization of relations with the West will soon follow.' However, it is not hard to assume that Moscow's response to what it would see as 'intolerable interference in Russia's domestic affairs' might have been much more arrogant and irreconcilable with European viewpoints. Instead, whatever Russia's hypersensitivity on the issue of Chechnya, it is not considered to be an obstacle to 'business as usual' relations with the West, or even to their improvement.

This touches upon another (and by far the most important) aspect of the problem, namely the overall orientation of Russia's new presidency in the foreign policy area. In this respect, a number of key points deserve emphasis.

First, in the aforementioned never-ending debate about the European, Asian or Eurasian nature of Russia, Putin has unambiguously positioned himself as a Europeanist. His 'Westernism' looks more radical than the overall mood in the country (or even that of the political class) would lead one to expect.[9] The new version of the National Security Concept,[10] broadly (and inadequately) commented on as outlining a confrontational approach towards the West, points to an objective commonality of Russia's interests with 'leading states of the world', and particularly stresses cooperation 'first of all' with these countries. The message could not be more unambiguous: Russia wants to be *with* them and *among* them.

Second, Moscow seems ready to go far (and to go quickly) along this line in terms of practical policy. In this regard, Putin has sent very strong signals, such as the ratification of START II and CTBT, and the confirmation of Russia's readiness to develop arms control further. The decision (supposedly taken against considerable domestic resistance) to 'defreeze' relations with NATO is especially impressive after all that was said about this alliance in the aftermath of Kosovo.

---

[7] Thus, at the very beginning of his career as Acting President, Putin spent almost three hours discussing the issue of Chechnya with Lord Russell-Johnston from the Parliamentary Assembly of the Council of Europe: quite remarkable for the head of state, especially in comparison to the ten minutes that Yeltsin had devoted to talks with Chirac and Schröder at the OSCE summit in Istanbul.

[8] Putin refrained from over-reacting to the EU's position on Chechnya, adopted in December 1999 in Helsinki—although grounds could easily have been found to do so. Similarly, the presidential administration dampened the ardour of the State Duma when the idea of withdrawing from the Council of Europe was discussed.

[9] See Viacheslav Nikonov, 'Chego zhdat', *Nezavisimaya gazeta*, 7 May 2000, p. 8.

[10] This first comprehensive foreign and security policy document of the new administration was signed by Putin on 10 Jan. 2000.

Third, the foreign policy is to be inscribed into the new regime's broader 'philosophy', the core element of which is the idea of building a strong state—functional, viable and sustainable. Such a state has to be confident of itself but not necessarily assertive in the international arena. There is no doubt that the ability to resist external pressures is essential politically and has to be supported by adequate military potential; and in this respect Putin looks not in the slightest hesitant. However, in his own words, 'the power of a country is determined not so much by its military might, but rather by its ability to be a leader in developing and using modern technologies, to ensure high living standards to its population'.[11] Russia's integration into the world economy is by far the most important component of the state-building super-task.[12] Trivial as it might look, this thesis proceeds from a different orientation from those which put emphasis on military might as the country's major priority, and on nuclear weapons in particular as the only available guarantee of great power status.

From Russia's European perspective, this all looks too good to be true. One should certainly beware of taking a deterministic view of the substance of Russia's future foreign policy. Like any other political leadership, Putin and his administration will be subject to various pressures. These pressures will be generated by the different interest groups, ideological trends and political schools of thought operating in Russia: Westernizers and nationalists, moderates and extremists, communists and democrats, right-wing conservatives and left-wing liberals, proponents of international openness and protectionist-oriented business communities, and so on. Also, if Russia's emerging 'new course in international affairs' is to be consolidated, responsiveness on the part of Europe will be essential. Nevertheless, Russia seems to be entering the new millennium with encouraging signs of seeking to overcome the ambiguities of its European policy.

---

[11] Quoted from Putin's article on the eve of the year 2000 published on the Internet and then in *Nezavisimaya gazeta*, 30 Dec. 1999.

[12] This theme was highlighted, in particular, during Putin's short visit to London, the first that he paid to the West in his capacity as head of state.

32 Russia and the new states of Eurasia

Roy Allison

The creation of new states and the evolution of Russian policy

The dissolution of the Soviet Union at the end of 1991 led to the sudden creation of fifteen new states. However, the legacy of control over the union republics by Moscow could not be erased overnight. In fact it took years for the successor states of the USSR to consolidate their statehood and establish their identities on the international stage. In the cases of Central Asian states which found sovereignty thrust upon them it could be expected that this process would anyway be slow. But in the early 1990s the international statehood of the post-Soviet states and their search for legitimacy were also challenged by major internal conflicts which affected Tajikistan, all three Caucasus states, Moldova, and to a lesser extent Ukraine (in respect of Crimea). The outcome of these conflicts was complicated by the presence of Russian military forces, which were scattered over much of what Russian commentators often described as the 'former Soviet space'.

The Soviet legacy was also reflected in the economic infrastructure and trade arrangements which bound the region together. In addition, and crucially, the socialization of elites for over seventy years under Soviet rule left political networks and a cultural overlay in place which was only slowly displaced. Another strong political incentive for Russian involvement in the affairs of the post-Soviet states in the first half of the 1990s was the location within them of significant minorities of ethnic Russians, stranded outside Russia. Overall, the nature of the Soviet system and the existence of the former USSR geographically as a single Eurasian land mass meant that the interactions in this region had been more intense than those between former European colonial powers and their overseas colonies. It is not surprising that Russia has been slow to achieve normal state-to-state relations with the new states of Eurasia.

In the early 1990s Russian politicians and diplomats were reluctant to view the post-Soviet states as similar in status to other foreign states. They were described collectively as the 'near abroad'—a term with a presumption of limited sovereignty which was only dropped in the later 1990s. This kind of thinking was apparent in Moscow's effort to use Russian border troops to maintain the borders of the former USSR effectively as the Russian strategic border, to retain a geographical buffer between Russia and states further afield. It was also reflected in Russia's assumption or assertion of various 'responsibilities' outside its borders in the 'near abroad', such as in organizing peacekeeping operations or in protecting the rights of ethnic Russian minorities.[1] Russian politicians declared support for Russians

Chapter specially commissioned for this volume.

[1] For the Russian debate on these issues see Mohiaddin Mesbahi, 'Russia and the Geopolitics of the Muslim South', in Mohiaddin Mesbahi, ed., *Central Asia and the Caucasus after the Soviet Union: Domestic and International*

outside Russian borders and even for the rights of Russian speakers who were not ethnic Russians or Slavs. This was a potent issue in political debates in Moscow and a strong influence on the broad Russian psychological response to all the former Soviet republics, but it declined as an effective influence on Russian state policy in the second half of the 1990s.[2]

The formation of the Commonwealth of Independent States (CIS) created a structure, which Russian officials hoped could be used to exert strong influence or even dominance over the twelve member states (the Baltic States refused to enter this structure and Russian relations with them are not examined in this chapter). But Ukraine at least regarded the CIS as means for a 'civilized divorce' from the former metropolitan control of Moscow and other states expected that Russian views could be diluted in common discussions among so many participants.

As an organization to represent the common interests of its member states the CIS had a fatal flaw—while Russia could identify common interests in its policy towards the other Eurasian CIS states, these states themselves have had in common only their proximity to Russia and their Soviet legacy. The wide variations in the geographical locations and resources of the other CIS states have meant that the Russian-driven effort to pool their interests and important aspects of their sovereign decision-making—expressed in various forms of so-called 'CIS integration'—met growing resistance in the 1990s, except in the case of those states which have depended heavily economically or militarily on Russian support.[3]

The Russian commitment to broad multilateral CIS integration in the economic, trade, military, and political fields distorted the development of its foreign policy ties with the new Eurasian states and the effort was ultimately undermined by the weakened resource base of the Russian state. However, in effect Russian leaders developed an alternative strategy of developing ad hoc bilateral ties with key states along three basic axes: to the west with Belarus (since the real prize, Ukraine, distanced itself from Russia), to the south-west with Georgia and later with Armenia as Georgia became less tractable, and to the south with Kazakhstan.[4] The reinforcement of these strategic orientations in Russian policy has been a more manageable goal than CIS-wide ambitions, even if the nature of Russian political discourse has made it difficult for Russian officials to express this kind of realism on the record.

Several phases in the Russian policy debate influenced relations with the new states of

Dynamics (Gainesville: University of Florida Press, 1994). See also Roy Allison, 'The Network of New Security Policy Relations in Eurasia', and Pavel Baev, 'Peacekeeping and Conflict Management in Eurasia', both in Roy Allison and Christoph Bluth, *Security Dilemmas in Russia and Eurasia* (London, Royal Institute of International Affairs, 1998).

[2] See Neil Melvin, *Russians Beyond Russia: The Politics of National Identity* (London: Royal Institute of International Affairs/Pinter, 1995).

[3] Allison and Bluth, eds., *Security Dilemmas in Russia and Eurasia*, 1–3, 12–17, 281–300; Mark Webber, *CIS Integration Trends: Russia and the Former Soviet South* (London: Royal Institute of International Affairs, 1997); Richard Sakwa and Mark Webber, 'The Commonwealth of Independent States, 1991–1998: Stagnation and Survival', *Europe-Asia Studies*, 51/3, (1999), 379–415; Martha Brill Olcott, Anders Åslund, and Sherman Garnett, *Getting it Wrong: Regional Cooperation and the Commonwealth of Independent States* (Washington: Carnegie Endowment for International Peace, 1999).

[4] The prioritization of Russian policy along these axes was first proposed by the Council on Foreign and Defence Policy lobby in 'Strategiya dlya Rossii', *Nezavisimaya gazeta*, 19 Aug. 1992. The Council elaborated its views in 'Strategiya dlya Rossii II', *Nezavisimaya gazeta*, 27 May 1994, which reiterated the need for a differentiated Russian policy to the CIS countries.

Eurasia. Initially, in 1991–2 a period of confusion and withdrawal prevailed, during which economic priorities played a major role. The economic reformers around Prime Minister Yegor Gaidar had a primarily non-strategic and inward-looking perspective. At the same time Russia signed treaties of friendship and cooperation with many of its CIS neighbours, five of which joined Russia in May 1992 in an important collective security agreement. A second period, 1993–5, was characterized in contrast by 'great power rhetoric'; a growing consensus in Russian politics allowed Moscow to project a more outward-looking and strategic perspective. This was expressed in a determination to act as the leader on CIS territory and to prevent outsiders from filling a possible 'power vacuum'.[5] In spring 1994 President Yeltsin declared his intention to set up some thirty Russian bases in CIS states and the following September he issued a decree on 'Russian strategy with regard to CIS Member States' which called for a defence union based on common interests and military-political goals.[6]

In fact Russian capabilities did not support such ambitions and by 1996 Russian policy showed a more pragmatic search for solutions to conflicts in the region. By spring 1997 the influence in the Russian government of Anatoly Chubais and Boris Nemtsov was reflected in a priority on Russian economic growth and reforms as well as a search for geo-economic opportunities. This approach was slightly offset by the geopolitical priorities of Yevgeny Primakov in his capacity as foreign minister from January 1996 and later as prime minister. However, the late 1990s was characterized overall by Russia's reluctant disengagement from military-strategic commitments in the CIS states, a decline in mutual trade (despite the existence on paper of a Customs Union of Russia, Belarus, Kazakhstan, and Kyrgyzstan), the progressive diversification in the foreign relations of these states at the expense of ties with Russia, and the growth of new subregional organizations creating new kinds of attachments for CIS states. Some Russian officials referred to this phenomenon scathingly as 'geopolitical pluralism' in the CIS space.[7]

Russian policy was also confused by the influence of competing lobbies, including business and energy interests, and the failure by President Yeltsin to develop coherent, strategic lines of direction. However, beginning in autumn 1999 Prime Minister and then President Putin attempted to reverse some of the drift in Russian security and energy policies towards Central Asia and the South Caucasus through a focus on bilateral negotiations on a case-by-case basis with the leaders of states in the region (see below).

Russian interests and policy towards the South Caucasus

Military security interests historically dominated the imperial Russian and Soviet approach to the South Caucasus region and they continued to exert a strong influence in Russian

---

[5] This is expressed, for example, in President Yeltsin's decree 'Russian Strategy with regard to the Member States of the CIS', which defined the CIS as a Russian zone of interest and gave the region first priority for Russian national security and strategic interests, in *Rossiyskaya gazeta*, 23 Sept. 1995. The threat of foreign influence on CIS territory was elaborated in a report by the Federal Intelligence Service (SVR) under its then director Yevgeny Primakov, see 'Doklad federal'noy sluzhby vneshney razvedki', *Rossiyskaya gazeta*, 22 Sept. 1994.

[6] Decree in *Rossiyskaya gazeta*, 23 Sept. 1995.

[7] Russian ire was directed particularly against the geopolitical analysis of Zbigniew Brzezinski in his book *The Grand Chessboard: American Primacy and its Geostrategic Imperatives* (New York: Basic Books, 1997). The new subregionalism is analysed in Renata Dwan and Oleksandr Pavliuk, eds., *Subregional Cooperation in and around the CIS Space* (Armonk, NY: M.E. Sharpe, 2000).

policy towards Georgia, Armenia, and Azerbaijan in the 1990s. These interests were complicated by the Russian campaigns in Chechnya (1994–6 and from 1999), which have threatened a broader destabilization of the region. A growing interest in access to Caspian Sea energy resources and influence over pipeline routes has offered a new geoeconomic dimension to relations with the South Caucasus, especially with Azerbaijan and Georgia.[8]

A traditional Russian security objective in the South Caucasus has been the prevention of any large-scale strategic penetration or the formation of a perceived security vacuum. This could best be achieved by creating a 'belt of friendly states' and avoiding a full withdrawal of Russian military forces and bases established in the Soviet period. This is reflected in the conclusion of a Russian–Georgian treaty of friendship and cooperation and an agreement on Russian military bases on Georgian territory, which were reached in 1993 at a time when the Georgian state was weak. Russia has tried to retain these bases, although in autumn 1999 it committed itself to withdraw two of its four bases in Georgia, those at Vaziani and Gudauta.

Armenia, which has welcomed the continuation of Russian bases on its soil, has emerged as Russia's main strategic partner in the region as Russian influence in Azerbaijan and Georgia has waned. As early as May 1992 Armenia entered into a mutual defence pact with Russia, during 1994–6 there was a large-scale clandestine transfer of Russian arms to Armenia, and in August 1997 a bilateral treaty of friendship, cooperation, and mutual assistance was signed as well as a twenty-five year agreement on Russian military bases in Armenia. Despite the existence of this Moscow–Yerevan axis, Russian leaders have viewed the South Caucasus as a whole as within their natural sphere of interests and have strongly objected to the active development of Georgia's and Azerbaijan's relations with NATO, Western states, and Turkey.

In the first half of the 1990s Russia frequently displayed partisan support for local actors in the secessionist conflicts in the region—in Abkhazia, South Ossetia, and Nagorno-Karabakh. At times Russian political support appeared to shift between the conflicting parties. In this period the existence of these conflicts and the presence of local militias and fragile regimes gave Russia opportunities for political leverage on the local states. Russian-led peacekeeping forces in Abkhazia (like those in Moldova and Tajikistan) did not display the necessary impartiality or commitment to traditional principles of international peacekeeping.[9]

However, this policy of divide and rule was undermined by the first Russian military campaign in Chechnya (1994–6). This bitter struggle made it increasingly clear that there existed a 'complex' of security policy interactions in the wider Caucasus region: conflict in one part of this region, whether in the North Caucasian republics or the South Caucasus states, could easily spill over or catalyse conflict in another part of the region because of ethnic or cultural linkages. Such conflict could threaten the stability of the Russian Federation itself. Consequently, Russian leaders became more interested in dampening conflicts, preventing their resurgence, and building stability. But these goals were challenged from

---

[8] For a concise analysis see Pavel Baev, *Russia's Policies in the Caucasus* (London: Royal Institute of International Affairs, 1997).

[9] See Dov Lynch, *Russian Peacekeeping Strategies in the CIS Region* (London: Macmillan/Royal Institute of International Affairs, 1999); Lena Jonson, *Keeping the Peace in the CIS: The Evolution of Russian Policy* (London: Royal Institute of International Affairs, 1999).

autumn 1999 by Russia's prosecution of the second Chechnya campaign which, by relying heavily on military means to suppress insurgency, threatened to seriously destabilize the region. On the other hand the new war in Chechnya has led to a firmer Russian emphasis on the principle of territorial integrity, which offers more support to Georgia and Azerbaijan in their struggle against the breakaway regions on their territories.

Plans to develop Caspian Sea energy resources and large-scale investment in the energy sector of Caspian by Western states, the European Union, and Turkey depend on the development of an east–west trade and transport corridor in the South Caucasus. The prospect of Caspian energy resources being delivered westwards via Azerbaijan and Georgia has been viewed by most Russian leaders and business interests as a geopolitical challenge and as part of a broader Western drive to reorient these countries' foreign policies away from Russia. Russia has been unable to offer significant investments for the exploitation of Azerbaijan's oil and gas fields, but has actively promoted a northern oil pipeline route through the Russian North Caucasus regions as the key to exporting oil from Azerbaijan.

Russian interests and policy towards Central Asia

In the Soviet period the union republic of Kazakhstan was categorized separately from other republics of 'middle Asia', which reflected the close ties it had with Russian territories to the north. The Russian colonization of the territory of contemporary Kazakhstan was simply an extension of Siberian colonization—there were no natural barriers to the Russian advance like the Caucasus mountains to the Russian south-west. The importance of Kazakhstan to Russia has continued since it became independent and this is likely to remain the key relationship for Moscow in Central Asia, even if at different times Russian leaders have courted Uzbekistan, which vies for regional influence with Kazakhstan.

The fact that when Kazakhstan attained independence some 38 per cent of the Kazakh population were ethnic Russians has been a strong motivation for cooperative Russian–Kazakh state-to-state relations. Although Kazakhstan has adopted quite moderate laws on citizenship and the status of the Russian language, ethnic Russian and Cossack organizations in Kazakhstan have found supporters among Russian politicians and the possibility in the future of the secession of northern Kazakhstan to Russia has at times inflamed nationalist debate. These underlying currents have been glossed over by documents such as a 'Declaration of Eternal Friendship and Allied Understanding' signed by Presidents Yeltsin and Nazarbayev in July 1998.

Irrespective of the location of ethnic Russians, Moscow has core strategic interests in security relations with Kazakhstan. First, the stability of lines of communication to the southern border of the CIS region has been a core Russian strategic goal, and with the exception of limited access via the Caspian Sea and Turkmenistan, all surface routes from Russia to Central Asia pass through Kazakhstan. Second, Kazakhstan, with its long (and still not properly defined) border of over 6,000 kilometres with Russia, could become the last 'line of defence' against Central Asian instability. Thirdly, in the event of a future deterioration of Russian–Chinese security relations the Kazakh–Chinese border would assume greater strategic importance. All this has encouraged Russia to think of its southern neighbour as a strategic shield and to make it reluctant to withdraw from the military sites it has leased on Kazakh territory.

Despite these Russian priorities Kazakhstan has hardly been a client state of Moscow. Disputes between the two states have centred on high tariffs which Russia has imposed on Kazakh goods, which have undermined efforts to develop a free trade zone, on how to resolve interstate debt, on the status of the Baikonur space centre in Kazakhstan, on Kazakh determination to diversify its security policy, and on the terms of Kazakh access to the Russian oil and gas pipeline system.

The existence of the Soviet era pipeline system which links Russia and Kazakhstan has meant that Russia has had and is likely to retain a strong influence over the transport of Kazakh oil and gas wealth to markets further afield. The first large capacity new pipeline to be built from the Caspian region, by the Caspian Pipeline Consortium, will pass from the Tengiz oilfield through Russian regions to the port of Novorossiysk. The exploitation of Kazakh gas at the Karachaganak field and the find of a large new oilfield at East Kashagan in the Kazakh sector of the Caspian Sea (which could eventually be routed north via Russia) emphasizes the importance of the geo-economics of oil and gas for the long-term future of Russian–Kazakh relations. This may be a stabilizing factor. However, Russian leaders have tried to use Kazakhstan's need for access to Russian pipelines to extract concessions on other issues. At times Russian leaders have also argued that Russian energy companies should be given priority in acquiring the rights to exploit Kazakh blocs in the Caspian Sea. Despite this, by the end of the 1990s they seem to have accepted the Kazakh view that market competition should generally determine which companies should receive the rights to develop any given deposit.

By the late 1990s the main Russian interest in Turkmenistan was to benefit from its gas reserves or to prevent Turkmen gas from competing with Russian gas in Turkish or European markets. Such relations based on energy links have been used by Russia at times to pursue political ends in Central Asian states, but the increasing importance for Russia, and Russian companies, to gain financially from contracts with Central Asian partners has served to moderate Russian efforts to pursue geopolitical ends in this region which might jeopardize these economic gains.

Economic pragmatism has also gradually influenced Russian policy in the controversy over the delimitation of the Caspian Sea between the Caspian littoral states. Russia initially insisted on legal arrangements for the Caspian which would have made it very difficult for foreign investors to operate and therefore for anyone to benefit. While Russia has mooted the idea of a single Caspian Sea strategic authority (which would exclude non-Caspian states like Turkey or the United States) its position is likely to become more flexible. This has been encouraged by the various economic and financial benefits that Russian companies are likely to gain through their involvement in the consortiums to develop Caspian energy resources, and by the advantages of Caspian energy flowing north through Russian territory.

Russian relations with Uzbekistan have fluctuated considerably. In the period to 1995 close ties were achieved and the two countries signed far-reaching bilateral military agreements. In the following years Tashkent adopted an increasingly independent stand, developed close relations with Western states and limited its role in the CIS organization. Russia perceived Uzbekistan as a potential rival for regional influence in Tajikistan and more broadly in Central Asia. By autumn 1999, however, the deteriorating internal security situation in Central Asia and Uzbekistan's fears of destabilization by radical Islamic groups drew it into a renewed closer military relationship with Russia—Russia appeared as the only power capable of offering the military assistance required. This perception of internal vulnerability also drew Russia close to Kyrgyzstan, which earlier in the 1990s had drawn Russian criticism for its orientation to Western states and for independently negotiating its accession to the World Trade Organization, the first CIS state to do so.

The largest Russian security commitment in Central Asia has been to Tajikistan, through Moscow's leadership of the so-called 'collective peacekeeping forces contingent' in that state, its extensive commitment to defend Tajikistan's border with Afghanistan and its political support for President Rakhmonov. It was only in 1997 that Moscow reduced this support, as it realized that the unresolved civil war in Tajikistan threatened a broader destabilization of the region, and helped to broker a peace agreement for this protracted conflict. In wishing to keep a sizeable military force in Tajikistan Russian leaders seem to accept a domino theory according to which a military withdrawal from this country would make Russia unable to control the spread of 'Islamic fundamentalism' closer to the southern Russian borders or to control the spread of drug trafficking. However, despite this perception, it is not clear that Russia has the resources for an open-ended commitment to maintaining a major military outpost in Tajikistan. Russia's long term relationship with the new states of Central Asia will depend on the sophistication of its efforts to help them manage a variety of non-traditional security challenges arising in this region.

Russian interests and policy towards Ukraine and Belarus

It has been particularly difficult for Russian politicians to accept the irrevocable separation of Ukraine and Belarus from the Russian Federation. The expectation that these new states would revert eventually back to the fold—rejoin a Slavic core state—helps explain the reluctance of Russian leaders for many years to sign and ratify a Friendship Treaty with Ukraine. This treaty finally acknowledged the new Ukrainian state with its current borders (the former Soviet administrative borders), including the historic Russian region of Crimea. The Russian expectation of some grand Slavic reconciliation was considerably influenced by the existence of the eleven million strong Russian minority in Ukraine, some 20 percent of the population of the new state. Moreover, Russia had vital state interests in Ukraine arising from Ukraine's key strategic location on the Black Sea and partly astride Russia's links with Central and Western Europe. This location and Ukraine's industrial and other resources made it a pivotal state for an assertive Russian state to dominate.[10]

The psychological difficulty Russian politicians and diplomats had in accepting Ukrainian statehood was compounded by the complications of unravelling the Soviet legacy in Ukraine, which were greater than those in any other post-Soviet state. These wrangles explain much of the acrimony in Russian–Ukrainian relations during the early 1990s—over the division of the Black Sea Fleet, the control and eventual withdrawal of Soviet nuclear missiles from Ukraine, the terms of transit of oil and gas pipelines across Ukrainian territory, and the status of the city of Sevastopol and of Crimea. However, Russian leaders were cautious about trying to exploit the ethnic Russian population in Ukraine to exert pressure on the Ukrainian leadership. Strong support in Ukraine for reintegration with Russia could

[10] Sherman Garnett, *Keystone in the Arch: Ukraine in the Emerging Security Environment of Central and Eastern Europe* (Washington: Carnegie Endowment for International Peace, 1997), 49, and see chs. 2 and 3.

be found among Communist politicians and in eastern Ukraine. But President Yeltsin did not wish to support politicians of this kind who had links with opposition Communist forces in Russia or to risk sparking off major civil conflict in Ukraine, which would be destabilizing for Russia.[11]

On the other hand, Russian leaders were tempted at times to use Ukraine's energy dependence on Russia to bargain for other political objectives.[12] This has resulted in Ukrainian efforts to diversify its energy imports, including plans to gain access to Caspian energy reserves. However, it was not in the Russian interest to place at risk the transit of oil and gas through Ukraine until alternative Russian pipelines bypassing Ukraine could be constructed. In fact the Russian and Ukrainian economic systems have shown a significant degree of interdependence and complementarity, such as in the nature of goods traded and in links between defence enterprises. Even so Ukraine has been sensitive to Russia gaining influence over important Ukrainian economic assets. For example, it has been reluctant to accept Russian proposals to swap Ukrainian debt to Russia for Russian acquisition of equity stakes in the Ukrainian energy complex.

Russian leaders understood from the early days of the CIS that Ukraine's participation in or dissociation from this structure would largely determine the character of CIS integration overall. However, Russia has conspicuously failed in its efforts to draw Ukraine into a Russian-led CIS security structure. Nor has it managed to coordinate broader international security issues with Kiev on any regular basis. Instead, Ukraine has developed a close relationship with NATO and a 'Euro-Atlantic' foreign policy orientation. Ukraine casts itself as fully European (and views itself as not even geographically Eurasian).

Russian relations with Belarus offer a contrast. Russian leaders tended to view Belarus—or as they continued to term it Belorussia—even more than Ukraine as an artificial state. This view was strengthened by the weak sense of national identity in Belarus. After an initial period of neutrality, Belarus under the Russophile president Alyaksandr Lukashenka elected in 1994 has enthusiastically sought ever closer integration with the Russian patron state. In April 1996, to advance this integration agenda, Russia and Belarus founded an organization entitled the Community of Sovereign Republics, which was transformed into a Union a year later.[13]

For Russia these plans could help safeguard vital interests in Belarus, such as Russian pipelines passing through Belarusian territory, transport links towards the Kaliningrad region, and Russian military bases. Since Polish accession to NATO the position of Belarus as a crucial strategic buffer zone for Russia has been reinforced in the thinking of the Russian General Staff and the defence ties of the two countries within the 'Union' have become very close. Plans have been developed for a Russia–Belarus regional group of forces. However, by the late 1990s it was clear that Russian leaders did not wish any real merger of their economy with that of Belarus, even if Belarus remained a champion of Russian plans for CIS integration and of anti-NATO rhetoric. Russia could rely on verbal support from

---

[11] Tor Bukvoll, *Ukraine and European Security* (London: Royal Institute for International Affairs/Pinter, 1997), 43–4 and ch. 3 in general.

[12] Ibid. 80–3.

[13] See David Marples, *Belarus: A Denationalized Nation* (Amsterdam: Harwood Academic Publishers, 1999), ch. 6; 'The Place of Belarus on Russia's Foreign Policy Agenda', in Sherman Garnett and Robert Legvold, eds., *Belarus at the Crossroads* (Washington: Carnegie Endowment for International Peace, 1999).

Minsk for a variety of international security issues. However, this has become an alliance of convenience, where 'each partner wants to drag the other in his own direction while eyeing him suspiciously'.[14] Belarus is too erratic a partner and too alienated from mainstream international politics to be a real asset for Russia's developing foreign policy agenda.

Russian foreign policy directions under President Putin

President Putin's approach to the new states of Eurasia has appeared both attentive and assertive. His policy to this region, as his policy to Europe, is influenced by a search for economic advantage, but this may conflict with the continuation of more traditional geopolitical goals. For example, the Russia–Belarus Union is being actively promoted, even if the development of this entity would be a drain on the Russian economy. The new Russian Foreign Policy Concept approved by Putin in June 2000 rather blandly indicated the need 'to form a good-neighbour belt along the perimeter of Russia's borders' and to form a 'strategic partnership' with all CIS states. It also revived the theme that Russia's relations with these states should depend on their readiness to take account of Russian interests 'including in terms of the guarantees of rights of Russian compatriots'.[15] However, for such a document this was probably an obligatory reference and does not foreshadow any significant shift in Russian policy towards more assertive support of ethnic Russians abroad.

On the other hand an emphasis in the Concept on one aspect of military security cooperation with CIS states, 'combating international terrorism and extremism', has become a major theme in Russian policy statements. It represents a means for Russia to try to revive the closer coordination with the Central Asian states it had in the early to mid-1990s. The rising concern among Central Asian states over Islamic militancy and over threats arising from Afghanistan is accompanied by a perception of vulnerability. Russia responded to this in spring 2000 by gathering support for a CIS multilateral anti-terrorist treaty, by offering security commitments and by concluding bilateral defence agreements with Uzbekistan, which provide for the delivery of arms and joint air defence patrols.

There has been a similar Russian effort to rally the South Caucasus states behind a Russian-led anti-terrorist front, this time tied more specifically to the Russian campaign in Chechnya. This has been less successful since Georgia and Azerbaijan have perceived the main military danger as arising from possible Russian cross-border operations from Chechnya rather than from Chechen militants per se. It has been a priority of these states to avoid becoming drawn into the Russian military imbroglio in the North Caucasus. By spring 2000, however, Putin had improved the climate of Russian relations with Georgia and Azerbaijan, partly through his emphasis on the principle of territorial integrity and through exploring the prospects for creating some kind of regional security system in the Caucasus. Moscow might calculate that a more cooperative relationship with Azerbaijan would dissuade Baku

---

[14] Margartia Balmaceda, 'Myth and Reality in the Belarusian–Russian Relationship', *Problems of Post-Communism*, 46/3 (May/June 1999), 6, and see the argument pp. 3–13. For the evolution of the security relationship see Vyachaslau Paznyak, 'Belarus: in Search of a Security Identity', in Allison and Bluth, *Security Dilemmas in Russia and Eurasia*.

[15] This Foreign Policy Concept, approved by Putin on 28 June 2000, replaces a similar set of guidelines of 1993. See www.mid.ru/mid/eng/econcept.htm; retrieved on 11 July 2000.

from overly close relations with NATO. It might also assist Russian policy goals more broadly in the Caspian Sea region.

Putin appears determined to achieve a Russian re-engagement in the Caspian region, following Moscow's relative neglect of the area in the late 1990s and the lack of policy coordination under President Yeltsin. A new presidential envoy for the Caspian region has been active and a new structure for coordination of Caspian affairs has been set up in the Foreign Ministry. The discovery of a new offshore oilfield in the Russian part of the north Caspian by the Russian oil company Lukoil and the large Kazakh oil discovery in the East Kashagan sector (which could result in additional oil flowing north across Russia) are refocusing Russian attention on the economic gains to be had from this region and on the importance of Russian–Kazakh relations. But this geo-economic orientation probably coexists with more traditional geopolitical temptations, especially if the United States is perceived to be less committed to Central Asia than in previous years.

In contrast, Russian President Putin is unlikely to achieve a full rapprochement with Ukraine, despite references to a Russian–Ukrainian 'strategic partnership'. Putin's nationalist image serves to reaffirm Ukrainian determination to engage with 'Euro-Atlantic structures', including NATO. Various contentious issues between the two countries were left unresolved after Putin's first visit to Ukraine as president of Russia in April 2000, such as Ukrainian gas payment debts and Russian restrictions on trade with Ukraine. Putin's economic priorities were expressed in his call for Ukrainian arms manufacturers to join forces with their Russian counterparts on the international arms market. Russian–Ukrainian relations appear to have passed from a period of personalization, by former President Yeltsin and President Kuchma, to one of low-key pragmatism, in which protracted bargaining is likely over interests that are often difficult to reconcile.[16]

Ultimately Russian foreign and international security policy towards the new states of Eurasia under President Putin will be constrained as in the 1990s by the limited resources available to support an assertive policy and be influenced by the search for economic opportunities. Military resources and energies will be absorbed by the effort to manage Chechnya and to contain broader instabilities in the North Caucasus for years to come. The attempt to assert Russian interests and maintain a balanced foreign policy and security dialogue with Western states will also remain a priority and distract Russia from major military undertakings in the CIS region, even in Central Asia where closer cooperation is likely. The Putin presidency is likely to emphasize pragmatic coordination, cooperation, and alignments with certain key CIS states, rather than efforts to re-create some broader, more ambitious system to dominate the region.

---

[16] *Monitor*, Jamestown Foundation, 19 Apr. 2000, 6/78, pp. 5–6.

The Russian Transition in Comparative Perspective

Introduction

Archie Brown

The transition from Communism of almost thirty states, many of them acquiring independent statehood for the first time, provides enormous scope for comparison, even without taking into account the more general political science literature on transitions from authoritarian rule. That there has, indeed, been a transition *from* a particular form of political and economic system is almost beyond dispute.[1] Even the presence of former Communist rulers at the top of the political hierarchy in a number of the new states does not mean that there has been institutional or ideological continuity (as distinct from a slow turnover of political elites). It remains a much more open question what these states and societies are in transition *to*. In the former Soviet Central Asian republics, for example, it has been essentially to a different form of authoritarian rule. Where *Russia* is going remains an open question.

There are, therefore, good grounds for criticism of studies which make the assumption that all formerly authoritarian states are in transition both to a market economy and to democracy. There is ample evidence for the proposition that a market economy of one kind or another (and they come in different forms with diverse regulatory arrangements) has proved to be more efficient than the few known alternatives, including a command economy of the Communist type. A strong moral and political case can also be made for the superiority of democracy (which comes in an even wider variety of institutional forms) over authoritarianism. Yet it does not follow that all post-Communist countries are simply at different points of a predetermined path to the market and to democratic rule. Still less should it be assumed that the United States constitutes the ultimate model of the market and democracy and that all states in transition should, accordingly, be assessed in terms of their proximity to or distance from American norms. As the Russian political scientist Vladimir Gelman observes in Chapter 37, there are grounds for scepticism about 'teleological schemes of political development' which seem to amount to an 'iron law of democratization'. Gelman, however, finds useful insights both within the general 'transitological' literature and in the work of Western specialists on Russian politics, as is evident in his contributions to this volume and in his writings elsewhere. In his chapter in this section Gelman applies a number of concepts drawn from Western writing on transition to the Russian regions where he identifies different regime types and leadership strategies.[2]

---

[1] I say 'almost' for, as Valerie Bunce writes in a 1995 article which appears as Chapter 34 in this section of the Reader: 'One analyst's democratization is another's postcommunism—and a third might question whether post-communism is so "post".'

[2] It should be noted, especially in the context of his discussion of the relationship between the regions and Russia's national authorities, that Gelman—unlike the contributors to Section 9 of this volume—was writing prior to the 1999–2000 electoral cycle and the Putin presidency.

Other scholars have taken a much more negative view of transitology. A swingeing attack by Stephen Cohen, one of the minority of Sovietologists who showed keen awareness of different political tendencies within the Soviet Communist Party prior to perestroika, on (as he sees it) an American missionary crusade to transform post-Soviet Russia into a replica of the United States is combined with strong criticism of what he calls 'transitionology' (in preference to 'transitology').[3] Cohen is on target with a number of his specific criticisms. These include the propensity of many Western commentators in the 1990s to treat the plunder of Russia's natural resources, massive capital flight, insider dealing that had nothing in common with a free market, and symbiotic relations between leading politicians and those who acquired for derisory outlay Russia's mineral wealth as all part of the rich tapestry of 'reform' or 'transition'. Cohen is also right to regard as nonsense attempts to date the origins of 'transition' in Russia to 1991. He accurately points out that Communism as a system had largely been dismantled before then.[4] It does not follow, though, that Cohen's emphasis on Russia's specificities should lead to rejection, in essence, of comparative politics, including the area of study within it which focuses on transitions from authoritarian rule and problems of democratization. On that particular score there is much to be said for the contrary view well expressed by Charles King:

Postcommunist Europe and Eurasia are fertile ground for testing theories that were developed in other geographical contexts—theories of democratization, institutional design, interest-group interaction, and identity politics. The reinvigorated study of the region has also produced new work that promises to enrich the general study of the political economy of reform, federalism, transitional justice, and nationalism and interethnic relations. The one-lane dirt road that used to wend between area studies specialists and comparativists has, at last, become a multilane interstate.[5]

There is, in fact, a scholarly literature which is much more multifaceted than the conventional wisdom of many of Russia's foreign economic advisers in the early 1990s. Much of it brings to bear on the countries emerging from European Communism, including Russia, the insights of scholars who have studied the breakdown of authoritarian regimes in other parts of the world. It is worth noting that Gelman is but one of a substantial number of Russian students of politics who have found this literature to be of value in the analysis of post-Soviet developments. An important book by two scholars whose major specialist work has been on southern Europe and South America, Juan Linz and Alfred Stepan, and who have extended their enquiry into East-Central Europe and the former Soviet Union, is one of the most cited by political

³ Stephen F. Cohen, *Failed Crusade: America and the Tragedy of Post-Communist Russia* (New York: Norton, 2000). In Cohen's words: 'The basic premise of transitionology is that since 1991, however "rocky" the road, Russia has been in a reform process of "transition from Communism to free-market capitalism and democracy". Underlying that premise is another: Russia's "transition", no matter how painful and costly, is good, progressive, and necessary' (ibid. 21).

⁴ Ibid. 23–4. On this point see also Archie Brown, *The Gorbachev Factor* (Oxford: Oxford University Press, 1996), esp. 309–15.

⁵ Charles King, 'Post-Postcommunism: Transition, Comparison, and the End of "Eastern Europe"', *World Politics*, 53/1 (Oct. 2000), 143–72, at p. 145.

scientists in Russia itself.[6] Significant work within a transitological paradigm includes that of Andrei Melville, who heads the Political Science Faculty at one of Russia's most prestigious universities, MGIMO. In his 1999 book, *Democratic Transitions: Theoretical-Methodological and Applied Perspectives*,[7] Melville cites a very wide range of Western literature on comparative politics, particularly that relating to democratization, and draws also on empirical research by Russian social scientists, especially quantified data on public opinion.

A significant body of work by Western political scientists is now being read in Russia, among it comparative analyses that are found relevant by Russian scholars with a primary interest in understanding the vagaries of their own transition from Communism to what is thus far a hybrid polity and economy. Sometimes these Western political scientists have thrown light indirectly on post-Communists transitions and, in other instances, have written on them directly and illuminatingly, even though in notable cases they are not themselves specialists on the former Soviet Union, East Europe, or Communism.[8] At the Second All-Russian Congress of Political Scientists, held in Moscow in the Spring of 2000, there was plenty of evidence of a growing internationalization of the study of politics, with analytical categories, research agendas, and respect for empirical evidence in the East (as represented by Russia) and the West having more than ever in common.[9]

In the chapters that follow in this section, some sharp disagreements are expressed. All the contributors, in fact, accept the usefulness of comparative analysis, although they differ on

---

[6] The book is: Juan J. Linz and Alfred Stepan, *Problems of Democratic Transition and Consolidation: Southern Europe, South America, and Post-Communist Europe* (Baltimore and London: Johns Hopkins University Press, 1996). For citations, see, for example, the main Russian political science journal, the bimonthly *Polis: Politicheskie issledovaniya*, including their publication of an analysis by Linz and Stepan as the lead article in no. 5 (1997), ' "Gosudarstvennost'", natsionalizm i demokratizatsiya', 9–30—a translation of the chapter on ' "Stateness", Nationalism, and Democratization' in *Problems of Democratic Transition and Consolidation* (pp. 16–37). It is worth noting that the columns of *Polis* have been hospitable, more generally, to the writings of Western political scientists, including long-standing specialists on Communist and Russian politics.

[7] A.Yu. Melvil', *Demokraticheskie transity: Teoretiko-metodologicheskie i prikladnye aspekty* (Moscow: Moskovskiy obshchestvennyy nauchnyy fond, 1999).

[8] Apart from work cited elsewhere in this introduction, significant books in these categories include: Guillermo O'Donnell, Philippe Schmitter, and Laurence Whitehead, eds., *Transitions from Authoritarian Rule*, 4 vols. (Baltimore: Johns Hopkins University Press, 1986); Richard Rose, William Mishler, and Christian Haerpfer, *Democracy and its Alternatives: Understanding Post-Communist Societies* (Oxford: Polity Press, 1998); Giuseppe di Palma, *To Craft Democracies: An Essay on Democratic Transitions* (Berkeley: University of California Press, 1990); Larry Diamond, *Developing Democracy: Toward Consolidation* (Baltimore: Johns Hopkins University Press, 1999); and Laurence Whitehead, ed., *The International Dimensions of Democratization: Europe and the Americas* (Oxford: Oxford University Press, 1996). For a discussion of the literature on 'transitions from authoritarian rule', particularly that part of it emanating from Britain, see also my chapter, 'The Study of Totalitarianism and Authoritarianism', in Jack Hayward, Brian Barry, and Archie Brown, eds., *The British Study of Politics in the Twentieth Century* (Oxford: Oxford University Press, 1999), 345–94, esp. 385–93.

[9] Admittedly, that was viewed rather less benignly by someone who did much to try to develop a more objective study of politics in the hostile intellectual environment of the pre-perestroika Soviet Union, namely Georgy Shakhnazarov. For many years president of the Soviet Association of Political Sciences, Shakhnazarov, in his address to the opening session of the All-Russian Congress, 21–3 April 2000 (which I attended), questioned whether what was occurring was really 'the development of Russian political science' as distinct from 'the development of American political science in Russia'. Certainly, as with East-West 'convergence' more generally, it is Russian scholars in this field who have done most of the 'converging'. On what might be regarded as the 'pre-history' of contemporary political science in Russia, including Shakhnazarov's positive role in stretching the limits of the possible within a highly authoritarian regime, see Archie Brown, 'Political Science in the USSR', *International Political Science Review*, 7/4 (Oct. 1986), 443–81.

how much that is generalizable and valuable can be gained from transitology, not to mention 'consolidology'.[10] The main disagreement between, on the one hand, the two comparativists whose major work (like that of Linz and Stepan) has focused primarily on southern Europe and South America, Philippe Schmitter and Terry Lynn Karl, and, on the other, Valerie Bunce, who has written widely on Russian and East European politics, is on the relative value of intra-regional and broader comparisons. There are many bones of contention. Schmitter and Karl suggest that the 'eastern cases' of transition have been astonishingly rapid but that 'their consolidations promise to be lengthy, conflictual and inconclusive'. Bunce, however, questions the very concept of consolidation, viewing democracy as a process and an incomplete project (and *not only* in the former Communist countries) and holding that the notion of 'consolidation' implies 'democracy as an end state'.

The debate brings a number of issues into sharper focus, although quite a bit of common ground ultimately emerges. This includes a substantial measure of agreement on the complementarity of 'area studies', taken to mean specialist knowledge of particular countries and regions, and comparative politics, understood as involving a refinement of concepts and an interest in theory-building (although differences remain on the relative usefulness of attempts to construct 'general theory' as against more modest, 'middle-range' theorizing). Second, there is agreement, albeit from different perspectives, that the issue of how much the various trajectories of transition in the post-Communist states have in common with transition from authoritarian rule elsewhere (for example in southern Europe and Latin America) *is* important and worthy of serious study. Finally, and relatedly, notwithstanding the relative weighting attached by the protagonists, there is ultimate recognition that *both* comparisons of countries emerging from Communism (described in the chapters that follow as 'intra-regional', although Central Asia is a very different region from East-Central Europe) *and* cross-regional comparisons may be highly illuminating, depending largely on the questions one wishes to answer.

---

[10] 'Consolidology' is the name given to the study of the conditions that make for the successful consolidation of stable democracy.

33 The Conceptual Travels of Transitologists and Consolidologists: How Far to the East Should They Attempt to Go?

Philippe C. Schmitter with Terry Lynn Karl

The wave of democratization that began so unexpectedly in Portugal has not merely increased the number of attempted regime changes since 1974, it has distributed them over a much wider surface of the globe. No continent or geo-cultural area—no matter how 'peculiar' or 'backward' or 'remote'—seems completely immune from its effects.

This 'sea-change' in political life has been accompanied (somewhat belatedly) by the gradual and unobtrusive development of two proto-sciences: transitology and consolidology. The claim of these embryonic subdisciplines is that by applying a universalistic set of assumptions, concepts and hypotheses, they together can explain and hopefully help to guide the way from an autocratic to a democratic regime. The initial 'tentative conclusions' of transitology were limited to a small number of cases within a relatively homogenous cultural area: southern Europe and Latin America.[1] With the subsequent expansion in the number of transitions and the extension of democratization to other cultural areas, the founders of these two subdisciplines and their acolytes have had to confront the issue of 'conceptual stretching,' i.e., of the applicability of their propositions and assumptions to peoples and places never imagined initially.[2] Nowhere has the resistance to their pseudoscientific pretensions been greater than among North American specialists in the politics of the former Soviet Union and eastern Europe; hence, the subtitle of this chapter which invites reflection on whether it is safe to travel eastward with these allegedly universal and scientific concepts.

The founder and patron saint of transitology, if it were to choose one, would be Niccoló Machiavelli. For the 'wily Florentine' was the first great political theorist, not only to treat political outcomes as the artifactual and contingent product of human collective action, but

Republished, with some abbreviation, from *Slavic Review*, 54/1 (Spring 1994), 173–85, by kind permission of the authors and the American Association for the Advancement of Slavic Studies.

[1] The most blatant examples of 'early transitology' were Dankwart Rustow, 'Transitions to Democracy: Toward a Dynamic Model,' *Comparative Politics*, 2/3 (Apr. 1970): 337–63; and Guillermo O'Donnell and Philippe C. Schmitter, *Transitions from Authoritarian Rule: Tentative Conclusions about Uncertain Democracies* (Baltimore: Johns Hopkins University Press, 1986). The latter was based on southern European and Latin American case studies.

[2] The locus classicus for this discussion is Giovanni Sartori, 'Concept Misformation in Comparative Politics,' *American Political Science Review*, 64 (1971): 1033–53. For a recent updating and extension, see David Collier and James E. Mahon, 'Conceptual "Stretching" Revisited: Adapting Categories in Comparative Analysis,' *American Political Science Review*, 87/4 (Dec. 1993): 845–55.

also to recognize the specific problematics and dynamics of regime change. He, of course, was preoccupied with change in the inverse direction—from republican to 'princely' regimes—but his basic insights remain valid.

Machiavelli gave to transitology its fundamental principle, uncertainty, and its first and most important maxim:

There is nothing more difficult to execute, nor more dubious of success, nor more dangerous to administer than to introduce a new system of things: for he who introduces it has all those who profit from the old system as his enemies and he has only lukewarm allies in all those who might profit from the new system. (Niccoló Machiavelli, *The Prince*, VI)

Furthermore, he warned that the potential contribution of the discipline would always be modest. According to his estimate, 'in female times,' i.e., during periods when actors behaved capriciously, immorally and without benefit of shared rules, only 50 percent of political events were understandable. The other half was due to unpredictable events of *fortuna.*

Hence, transitology was born (and promptly forgotten) with limited scientific pretensions and marked practical concerns. At best, it was doomed to become a complex mixture of rules of invariant political behavior and maxims for prudential political choice—when it was revived almost 480 years later.

Consolidology has no such obvious a patron saint. It reflects a much more consistent preoccupation among students of politics with the conditions underlying regime stability. At least since Plato and Aristotle, theorists have sought to explain why—under the kaleido-scopic surface of events—stable patterns of authority and privilege manage to survive. While they have rarely devoted much explicit attention to the choices and processes that brought about such institutions in the first place—this would be, strictly speaking, the substantive domain of consolidology—they and their empirical acolytes have amassed verit-able libraries on the subject of how polities succeed in reproducing themselves over extended periods of time. It does not seem excessive to claim that American political science since World War II has been obsessed with the issue of 'democratic stability' in the face of class conflict, ideological polarization, Communist aggression, north–south tensions, and so forth.

The consolidologist, therefore, has a lot of 'orthodox' theoretical assumptions and 'well established' empirical material to draw upon. However, if he or she has previously been practicing transitology, it will be necessary to make some major, personal and professional, adjustments. The consolidation of democracy poses distinctive problems to political actors and, hence, to those who seek to understand (usually retrospectively) what they are doing. It is not just a prolongation of the transition from authoritarian rule. Consolidation engages different actors, behaviors, processes, values and resources. This is not to say that everything changes when a polity 'shifts' toward it. Many of the persons and collectivities will be the same but they will be facing different problems, making different calculations and (hopefully) behaving in different ways.

This suggests possible contradictions between stages of the regime-change process and the pseudosciences seeking to explain them. The 'enabling conditions' that were most con-ducive to reducing and mastering the uncertainty of the transition may turn into 'confining conditions' that can make consolidation more difficult.[3] The shift in the substance of politics tends to reduce the significance of actors who previously played a central role in the demise of autocracy and to enhance the role of others who by prudence or impotence were marginal to the demise of autocracy or the earlier phases of transition.

The transitologist who becomes a consolidologist must personally make an epistemological shift in order to follow the behavioral changes that the actors themselves are undergoing. During the early stage of regime transformation, an exaggerated form of 'political causality' tends to predominate in a situation of rapid change, high risk, shifting interests and indeterminate strategic reactions. Actors believe that they are engaged in a 'war of movement' where dramatic options are available and the outcome depends critically on their choices. They find it difficult to specify *ex ante* which classes, sectors, institutions or groups will support their efforts—indeed, most of these collectivities are likely to be divided or hesitant about what to do. Once this heady and dangerous moment has passed, some of the actors begin to 'settle into the trenches.' Hopefully they will be compelled to organize their internal structures more predictably, consult their constituencies more regularly, mobilize their resource bases more reliably and consider the long-term consequences of their actions more seriously. In so doing, they will inevitably experience the constraints imposed by deeply rooted material deficiencies and normative habits—most of which have not changed with the fall of the ancien régime.[4]

The consolidologist must shift from thinking in terms of a particularly exciting form of 'political causality,' in which unpredictable and often courageous individuals take singular risks and make unprecedented choices, and adjust to analyzing a much more settled form of 'bounded rationality' that is both conditioned by capitalist class relations, long-standing cultural and ethnic cleavages, persistent status conflicts and international antagonisms, and staffed by increasingly professional politicians filling more predictable and less risky roles. From the heady excitement and *under*determination of the transition from autocracy, he or she must adjust to the prosaic routine and *over*determination of consolidated democracy.

The likelihood that practitioners of this embryonic and possible pseudoscience can draw more confidently from previous scholarly work should be comforting, even if there remains a great deal of work still to do before we understand how the behavior of actors can become more predictable, how the rules of democracy can be made more mutually acceptable and how the interactions of power and influence can settle into more stable patterns. Apprentice consolidologists in the contemporary world also have two special problems:

1. they must sift through the experience of established liberal democracies in order to separate the idiosyncratic and contingent properties from the eventual outcomes;
2. they must decide to what extent lessons taken from these past experiences can be applied to the present dilemmas of neodemocracies.

The fallacies of 'retrospective determinism'—assuming that what did happen is what had to happen—and of 'presentism'—assuming that the motives and perceptions of the past are

---

[3] The idea and phraseology have been taken from the seminal article by Otto Kirchheimer, 'Confining Conditions and Revolutionary Breakthroughs,' *American Political Science Review*, 59 (1965): 964–74.

[4] Which implies that national differences in consolidation are likely to be greater than national differences in transition.

the same as those of the present—are all too tempting and could quite easily defeat the credibility of their efforts.

The neophyte practitioners of transitology and consolidology have tended to regard the implosion of the Soviet Union and the regime changes in eastern Europe with 'imperial intent.' These changes seem to offer a tempting opportunity to incorporate (at long last) the study of these countries within the general corpus of comparative analysis. Indeed, by adding post-communist regimes to their already greatly expanded case base, transitologists and consolidologists might even be able to bring the powerful instrumentarium of social statistics to bear on the study of contemporary democratization. For the first time, they could manipulate equations where the variables did not outnumber the cases and they could test their tentative conclusions in cultural and historical contexts quite different from those which generated them in the first place.

Specialists on the area, not surprisingly, have tended to react differently by stressing the cultural, ideological and national peculiarities of these cases—especially the distinctive historical legacy bequeathed by totalitarian as opposed to authoritarian anciens régimes. In their resistance to 'acultural extrapolation,' some former Sovietologists would bar all practicing transitologists from reducing their countries (now more numerous, diverse and autonomous in their behavior) to mere pinpoints on a scatterplot or frequencies in a crosstabulation. The lessons or generalizations already drawn from previous transitions and now being made about the difficulties of regime consolidation should *ex hypothesi* be rejected. Presumably, some (as yet unspecified) 'new science' of regime change must be invented and applied if one is to make any sense about the eventual political trajectory of ex-leninist or ex-stalinist systems.

This brief chapter is not the place to debate thoroughly such a contentious issue. My initial working assumption is that, provided the events or processes satisfy certain definitional requirements,[5] their occurrence in eastern Europe or the former Soviet Union should be considered, at least initially, analogous to events or processes happening elsewhere. More than that, they should be treated as part of the same 'wave of democratization' that began in 1974 in Portugal and has yet to dissipate its energy completely or to ebb back to autocracy.[6] Hence, all these cases of regime change—regardless of their geopolitical location or cultural context—should (at least hypothetically) be regarded as parts of a common process of diffusion and causal interaction. Only *after* (and not *before*) this effort at incorporation, mapping and analysis has been made, will it become possible to conclude whether concepts and hypotheses generated from the experiences of early comers should be regarded as 'overstretched' or 'underverified' when applied to late comers. Only then will we know whether the basins containing different world regions are really so interconnected and moved by such

[5] For example in some cases such as Romania, Bulgaria and Albania, it was at first unclear as to whether the ancien régime had indeed been deposed and whether the ensuing elections were conducted under fair enough conditions to consider that the winners were attempting to establish a different form of political domination. Subsequent events, especially in the process of government formation, have made it clear that a genuine regime change has taken place.

[6] Several authors seem to have independently picked up this notion of 'waves.' I explored it in 'The Consolidation of Democracy and the Choice of Institutions,' presented at the East–South Systems Transformation (FSST) Conference, 4–7 January 1992, Toledo, Spain. See also Sidney Tarrow, '"Aiming at a Moving Target": Social Science and the Recent Rebellions in Eastern Europe,' *PS* (Mar. 1991): 12–20; and Samuel B. Huntington, *The Third Wave: Democratization in the Late Twentieth Century* (Norman: University of Oklahoma Press, 1991).

similar forces. The particularity of any one region's cultural, historical or institutional matrix—if it is relevant to understanding the outcome of regime change—should emerge from systematic comparison, rather than be used as an excuse for not applying it.

This is not to say that one should deliberately ignore possible sources of variation across world regions. To the contrary, sensitivity to what is different about eastern Europe[7] may provide a useful corrective to the contemporary literature which is centered on southern Europe and Latin America. Most importantly, it may encourage comparativists to pay more attention to variables that have either been previously taken for granted, e.g. the existence of relatively established national identities or of relatively well functioning market mechanisms, or that have been examined and rejected as less important, e.g. the intromission of external powers. For the record, I propose to list without further elaboration the parametric conditions that seem most likely to affect differentially the outcome of regime change in the east as opposed to the south. They will, no doubt, disappoint area specialists since they focus on generic/structural, not particular/cultural or ideational properties.[8]

Condensing and simplifying, four contrasts stand out: in the point of departure, in the extent of collapse of the ancien régime, in the role of external actors, and in the sequence of transformative processes. Needless to say, these are all somewhat interconnected and could well be assembled under other rubrics.

1. Here the primary issue is not the 'classical' one of differences in level of development, literacy, urbanization and so forth. Nor, strictly speaking, is it the type of autocracy, i.e., totalitarian, 'leninist' or 'stalinist,' that has collapsed. On the first grounds, the eastern European countries and most of the republics of the ex-Soviet Union seem to overlap considerably with the previous cases in southern Europe and Latin America—certainly as far as human skills, social mobilization and productive capacity are concerned.[9] On the second, most of these political systems had degenerated already into some form of 'partialitarian' or authoritarian regime, not entirely removed from the ways in which their southern brethren were governed. Romania and Albania were obvious exceptions, although their high degree of personalization of power suggests a possible analogy with such cases of 'sultanism' as Somoza's Nicaragua, Trujillo's Dominican Republic and Stroessner's Paraguay. Nonetheless, we would readily concede that the peculiar monopolistic fusion of political and economic power into a party-state apparatus remained a distinctive attribute of the east.

But what is most striking are the differences in point of departure in socio-occupational structure as the result of many years of policy measures designed to compress class and

---

[7] The case of the ex-German Democratic Republic should be excluded from this universe. It was, however, equivalent, but only to the point at which the dynamics of reunification with the Federal Republic took over.

[8] It should also be noted that these parametric conditions do not radically juxtapose the eastern and southern cases, but overlap to some degree. For example, the Soviet Union, Yugoslavia and Czechoslovakia are not alone in having problems of national identity and borders that complicate the democratization process. Spain and, to a much lesser extent, Portugal had to deal with demands for greater regional autonomy, even secession. Similarly, countries in Latin America have had to cope with over-bloated state apparatuses and unproductive public enterprises, even if the issue did not approach the magnitude of the problem of privatization in ex-command economies. The Central American cases of Nicaragua and El Salvador, in particular, may have more in common generically with those of eastern Europe than with their regional brethren to the south.

[9] Although I would agree that there are important qualitative differences in the pattern and scale of development, especially with regard to production and distribution systems, that may make it much more difficult for the eastern countries to exploit these aggregate assets in a more open context of political or economic competition.

sectoral distinctions, equalize material rewards and, of course, eliminate the diversity of property relations. Except where a 'second economy' had emerged earlier and prospered commercially (i.e., Hungary), eastern social systems seem very 'amorphous' in their structures and it is difficult to imagine how the parties and interest associations that are characteristic of all types of 'western' democracy could emerge, stabilize their respective publics and contribute to the general consolidation of the regimes. At least until the twin shocks of marketization and privatization produce more substantial and more stable class and sectoral differences, the politics of these neodemocracies are likely to be driven by other, much less tractable, cleavages (i.e., ethnicity, locality, personality).[10]

2. In the extent of collapse of the previous regime, too, the contrast is striking. Not only were the regime changes less 'pre-announced' and the opposition forces less 'pre-prepared' to rule than in the south,[11] but once new governments were formed the role of previous power holders declined precipitously and significantly. There were a few exceptions where rebaptized (and possibly reformed) communists managed to do well in the initial 'founding elections' and to hold on as a group to key executive positions, but even then they often proved incapable of governing effectively and were displaced in relatively short order, *vide* Albania, Bulgaria and Estonia. By my calculation, only in Romania, Mongolia, Ukraine, Azerbaijan and Serbia are previous communists continuing to play a significant role either as a party governing alone or in alliance with others.[12] This contrasts with southern Europe and Latin America where neodemocracies were often governed initially by centrist or rightist parties which had important elements (and persons) from the previous regime in their ranks, and where de facto powers such as the armed forces, the police or the state apparatus retained very significant power to intervene in policy making and affect the choice of institutions. Spain, Brazil and Chile may be the most extreme cases, but almost everywhere (except Portugal and perhaps Argentina) the transition takes place in the shadow—if not under the auspices—of the ancien régime. Given the virtual abdication of their previous rulers, eastern Europeans could harbor the (momentary) illusion of a tabula rasa upon which to build new rules and practices.

3. One of the more confident generalizations of the previous literature emphasized the much greater importance of domestic forces and calculations as opposed to foreign influences and intromissions in determining the nature and timing of regime transition—hinting, however, at the likelihood that the latter would play a more significant role subsequently in

---

[10] My thinking on this matter has been influenced by the work of David Ost. See his 'Shaping the New Politics in Poland,' presented at the conference on 'Dilemmas of Transition from State Socialism in East Central Europe,' Center for European Studies, Harvard University, 15–17 Mar. 1991 and 'Labor in Post-Communist Transformations,' *Working Paper* 5.17, Center for German and European Studies, University of California, Berkeley, July 1993.

[11] Although it is hard to beat the initial Portuguese case for sheer surprise and unpreparedness to rule. Elsewhere in southern Europe and Latin America—except, most notably, in Nicaragua—opposition groups had much more time to anticipate coming to power and even to prepare elaborate contingency arrangements. On the unexpectedness of the eastern European transitions, see Timur Kuran, 'Now out of Never: The Element of Surprise in the East European Revolution of 1989,' *World Politics* (Oct. 1991): 7–48.

[12] No doubt, this generalization overlooks the possibility, even the likelihood, that forces from the ancien régime are still well entrenched in local units of governance and production and can, therefore, pose much more of an obstacle to democratic consolidation than would be apparent from the parties and persons governing at the national level. I am indebted to Steve Fish for this point. See his 'The Emergence of Independent Associations and the Transformation of Russian Political Society,' *Journal of Communist Studies*, 7/3 (Sept. 1991): 299–334 and his forthcoming *Democracy from Scratch: Opposition and Regime in the New Russian Revolution*.

the consolidation phase.[13] There seems to be virtual unanimity that this does not fit eastern Europe or Central America. Without a previously announced and credible shift in the foreign and security policies of the Soviet Union, neither the timing nor the occurrence of regime change would be explicable. In a few cases, e.g. Romania and the GDR, even active intromission by Gorbachev seems to have been necessary. Moreover, there is much more evidence of 'contagion' within the region, i.e., of events in one country triggering and accelerating a response in its neighbors. Unlike southern Europe and Latin America where democratization did not substantially alter long-standing commercial relations or international alliances,[14] the regime changes in eastern Europe triggered a major collapse in intraregional trade and the dissolution of the Warsaw Pact. Into this vacuum moved an extraordinary variety of western advisors and promoters—binational and multilateral. To a far greater extent than elsewhere, these external actors have imposed political 'conditionality' upon the process of consolidation, linking specific rewards explicitly to the meeting of specific norms or even to the selection of specific institutions.[15]

4. All of the above differences pale before the significance of the sequence of transformations, in my opinion. In none of the southern European or Latin American cases did the regime change from autocracy to democracy occur alone, in complete isolation from other needed social, economic, military and administrative transformations. However, except for Central America, it was usually possible to deal with these variegated demands sequentially. In some specially favored cases, major structural changes were accomplished under previous regimes. For example, most of these transitions 'inherited' acceptable national identities and boundaries—even if the degree of local or regional autonomy remained contested. In a few, the military had already been largely subordinated to civilian control or the economy had undergone substantial restructuring to make it more internationally competitive.

[13] For the initial observation, see Guillermo O'Donnell and Philippe C. Schmitter, *op.cit.*, 17–21. It should be noted that the cases upon which this generalization was based did not include those of Central America. In that subregion, external influence and intromission have been (and continue to be) much more significant. For a criticism with regard to southern Europe, see Geoffrey Pridham, ed., *Encouraging Democracy: The International Context of Regime Transition in Southern Europe* (Leicester: Leicester University Press, 1991).

[14] Greece's (temporary) withdrawal from NATO is a minor exception—counterbalanced by Spain's (contested) entry into NATO. The decision by all of the southern European countries to become full members of the EC did not as much alter existing patterns of economic dependence as intensify them. For an assessment of the impact of democratization upon regional security, cooperation and integration in the southern cone of Latin America, see Philippe C. Schmitter, 'Change in Regime Type and Progress in International Relations', in E. Alder and B. Crawford, eds., *Progress in Postwar International Relations* (New York: Columbia University Press, 1991), 89–127.

[15] This issue is discussed at greater length in Philippe C. Schmitter, 'The International Context for Contemporary Democratization,' *Stanford Journal of International Affairs* II, no. I (Fall/Winter 1993): 1–34. To the above general observations about the external context in eastern Europe, one could add another, more specific, condition: the sheer fact that it is located in such close geographic proximity to centers in western Europe of much greater prosperity and security. This makes the 'exit option,' especially for relatively skilled persons, much easier. On the one hand, this threatens to deprive these emergent democracies of some of their most highly motivated actors and to leave their consolidation in the hands of less talented ones; on the other hand, the very prospect of such a mass exodus increases the prospects for their extracting external resources intended precisely to prevent that from happening. Again, the parallel with Central America emerges. Here, too, the indirect influence and direct intromission of foreign agents has been of considerable importance, both in determining the timing and nature of their transitions from authoritarian rule and in 'conditioning' the consolidation of their respective democracies. These actions by the United States, in particular, are not unrelated to the region's geographical location and the threat that sizable flows of refugees could pose to its security. The present case of Haiti well illustrates the problem—and the difficulty of bringing effective external power to bear on an issue as complex and uncertain as regime change.

In eastern Europe not only are such major transformations all on the agenda for collective action and choice, but very little authoritative capacity exists for asserting priorities among them. There is a great deal more to do than in the south, and it seems as if it must be done at once. The codewords are *simultaneity* and *asynchrony*. Many decisions have to be made in the same time frame and their uncontrolled interactions tend to produce unanticipated (and usually unwanted) effects. Even within a given issue area, the absence of historical precedents makes it difficult to assert theoretically what should come first: holding elections or forming a provisional government? drafting a national constitution or encouraging local autonomy? releasing prices or controlling budget deficits? privatizing state industries or allowing collective bargaining? creating a capital market or sustaining a realistic exchange rate? and the list could continue ad nauseam. Even if 'transition theory' can offer a few generic insights strictly within the political domain, these risk being quite irrelevant given simultaneous—rather than sequential—demands for changes in major economic, social, cultural/national, military institutions. For example, one knows in the abstract that the formation of provisional governments can be a bad thing, especially before the configuration of national party systems is evident, but what if (as seems to have been the case in Czechoslovakia) it is necessary to head off a polarized conflict among nationalities? In retrospect, it seems to have been a crucial error for Gorbachev to have convoked (or tolerated) elections at the level of republics *before* holding a national election that would have legitimated his own position and, with it, the all-union framework of territorial authority, but presumably this reflected a correlation of forces within the CPSU and the military at the time.

One thing is becoming abundantly clear—and this was observed already in the classic article of Dankwart Rustow that lies at the origin of much of today's work on transition[16]— that without some prior consensus on overarching national identity and boundaries little or nothing can be accomplished to move the system out of the protracted uncertainty of transition into the relative calm (and boredom) of consolidation. This places the ex-Soviet Union and Yugoslavia in radically different sequences and it is not inconceivable that all of their 'inheritor republics' will be paralyzed by a similar imperative.

Having considered these four clusters and recognized that some of them do suggest significant 'inter-regional' differences, I would still argue that, as transitologists and consolidologists move from their more familiar haunts in the south to stranger (and, probably, less hospitable) ones in the east, they should stick to their initial operating assumptions.[17]

[16] 'Transitions to Democracy,' *Comparative Politics*, 2 (1970): 337–63.

[17] Since writing the above comments, we have read Sarah Meiklejohn Terry, 'Thinking about Post-communist Transitions: How Different Are They?' *Slavic Review*. 52/2 (Summer 1993): 333–7. While two of the points she raises concord easily with mine: the 'dual-track nature' of their transitions (my 'simultaneity'), the 'potential influence of the international environment' (my 'enhanced role of external actors'), on other grounds I would differ. For example, I would contest that all the earlier transitions took place at a lower level of socio-economic development and argue that the two sub-samples in fact overlap considerably—while conceding that certain qualitative aspects are significantly different. It may, in fact, be more difficult to dismantle an uncompetitive industrial apparatus *ex post*, than to create one *ex ante*, but that ignores the major effort that many capitalist neodemocracies have had to make in deregulation, privatization and industrial restructuring. On the issue of civil society, Guillermo O'Donnell and I argued not for their 'resilience' in southern Europe and Latin America, as she claims, but for their 'resurrection'—in most cases *after*, not *before* the transition. The unruliness, cacophony, political paralysis and demagogy she sees are by no means confined to post-communist civil societies. The only issue which does strike me as apposite is greater ethnic complexity. Several of the neodemocracies are exceedingly complex from any objective

These latter cases of regime change can be—at least initially—treated as conceptually and theoretically equivalent to those that preceded them.[18] Furthermore, it can be expected that they face the same range of possible outcomes—even if the probabilities of their attaining any particular one may vary considerably from their more fortunate predecessors.

My hunch is that the eastern cases may be lodged in the following paradox: *their transitions have been (astonishingly) rapid, non-violent and definitive*, i.e., new actors have come to power without using physical force to eject their predecessors and effectively eliminated the prospect of a return to the *statu quo ante*, in a relatively short period of time,[19] *but their consolidations promise to be lengthy, conflictual and inconclusive*. Compared to most (but not all) of the regime changes in southern Europe and Latin America, they will have more difficulty in selecting and settling into an 'appropriate' type of democracy. While it is by no means foreclosed that some of these countries will revert to some other form of autocracy than was previously practiced or that they will attempt to establish hybrid forms of *dictablanda* and *democradura*, the most probable outcome would seem to be protractedly 'unconsolidated democracy'—if only because some degree of obedience to the procedural minimum will be imposed by their dependence upon the European Community and other western countries.

ethnic perspective—Brazil and Peru, for example—but the subjective political consequences of this diversity seem less compelling. Spain successfully confronted the assertion of regional and linguistic demands during its transition—even if, I would admit, conflicts over national identity and national purpose played little or no role in the initial versions of transitology.

[18] The one thing that *cannot* be done is to take refuge in *empirie*—in the diligent collection of facts without any guidance from theories and models. Given the sheer volume of data, not to mention their frequently contradictory referents, without some sense of priorities and categories for classification no analyst is likely to be able to make much sense of what is going on—much less within a time frame that might be of some use to the actors themselves. Former Sovietologists converted to the new tasks of explaining transition and consolidation would be better advised to spend more effort on conceptualization—even an alternative conceptualization—than on diligent data gathering. Sarah Meiklejohn Terry's suggestion that former Soviet area specialists wait for ten to fifteen years before making their (presumptively) original contribution to transitology or consolidology strikes me as ill advised. Fortunately, there are those such as Laszlo Bruzst, David Stark, Grzegorz Ekiert, Andrew Janos, Russell Bova, Steve Fish, David Ost and Michael McFaul who have already begun such an effort.

[19] Romania and, more recently, Georgia are obvious exceptions to the generalization about non-violence, the (ex-)Soviet Union and (ex-)Yugoslavia to the relatively short transitional period.

34 Should Transitologists Be Grounded?

Valerie Bunce

The collapse of state socialism in eastern Europe[1] has led to a proliferation of studies analyzing aspects of democratization throughout the region. Central to many of these studies (particularly those by nonspecialists) is an assumption that postcommunism is but a variation on a larger theme, that is, recent transitions from authoritarian to democratic rule.

In a recent issue of *Slavic Review* (reprinted here as Chapter 33), Philippe C. Schmitter and Terry Lynn Karl provide a spirited defense of this assumption by arguing that democratization in eastern Europe can and should be compared with democratization in southern Europe and Latin America.[2] Their case rests on three points. First, they resurrect the old debate about comparative analysis versus area studies and argue in support of the former and against the latter. This is relevant to the question at hand, in their view, because: (1) many of the objections to comparing democratization in the east with democratization in the south are made on traditional area studies grounds; and (2) transitology, as a branch of comparative politics, features all the methodological advantages of comparative inquiry. They then turn to the 'difference debate.' Here, they argue that, while there are some differences between south and east, the differences do not by any means rule out a comparison among countries in Latin America, southern Europe and eastern Europe. Diversity is welcome, they contend, especially when, as with these cases, it involves variation around a common and unifying theme, that is, recent transitions from authoritarian rule. Finally, Schmitter and Karl argue that there is much to be learned from comparing democratization in Latin America, southern and eastern Europe. Such comparisons, they contend, help us define more clearly what is similar and what is different in recent transitions to democracy, sensitize us to new factors and new relationships, and allow us to test a wide range of hypotheses. As I shall argue below, their first claim is wrongheaded and irrelevant to the issue at hand; the second is debatable; and the third, while valid in some respects, nevertheless misrepresents both the costs and the benefits of adding eastern Europe to comparative studies of democratization.

Is the debate about the validity of comparing democratization, east and south, really a debate between area specialists and comparativists as Schmitter and Karl contend? I think

Republished, with minor abbreviations, from *Slavic Review*, 54/1 (Spring 1995), 111–27, by kind permission of the author and the American Association for the Advancement of Slavic Studies.

[1] In this commentary, the term 'eastern Europe' will be used to refer to all the postcommunist countries that during the cold-war era made up the Soviet Union and eastern Europe.

[2] *Slavic Review*, 53/1 (Spring 1994): 173–85. Their article is a response to criticisms not just by specialists in eastern Europe, but also by specialists in southern Europe and Latin America. However, this commentary will focus primarily on eastern Europe.

not, since those who question such comparisons do *not* do so on grounds of traditional area studies but rather on grounds familiar to any comparativist.[3] What is primarily at issue is comparability. For example, when Sally Terry catalogues the many differences between transitions to democracy in the south versus exits from state socialism in the east, she is *not* adopting what Schmitter and Karl have termed an area studies perspective. Instead, she is engaging *the* central question of comparative analysis. Are we comparing apples with apples, apples with oranges (which are at least varieties of fruit) or apples with, say, kangaroos? What Terry is arguing is that the many differences between eastern and southern transitions suggest that comparisons between the two involve at best apples and oranges (which would place important limits on comparison), and, at worst, apples and kangaroos (which would call the entire enterprise of comparison into question). Thus, Schmitter and Karl (and other transitologists) have a burden of proof. They cannot justify their comparisons of east and south by simply stating that these cases meet 'certain definitional requirements' or by arguing that we should compare first and worry about comparability second.[4]

If issues of comparability are a common theme in critiques of transitology, then so are other issues that lie at the heart of comparative inquiry—in particular, problems involving case selection, coding decisions and concept-indicator linkages. For example, in their investigations Schmitter and Karl include—for unspecified reasons—some postcommunist cases and exclude others. This is a problem. As every social scientist knows, sample selection determines which hypotheses can be tested and the kinds (as well as the quality) of the conclusions that can be drawn. To take another issue: on what grounds do Schmitter and Karl distinguish between pacted versus mass mobilization transitions (a distinction crucial to their investigations), given the considerable blurring between the two in the eastern European experience?[5] Finally, if the communists—now ex-communists—continue to occupy important posts in eastern Europe and if the media in most of these countries is still subject to undue control by the government in office, then is it accurate to argue, as Schmitter and Karl do, that these regimes have moved from the transition period to a period of democratic consolidation?

[3] This, at least, is how I read the literature questioning the validity of comparing east and south. See, for example, M. Steven Fish, *Democracy From Scratch: Opposition and Regime in the New Russian Revolution* (Princeton: Princeton University Press, 1994); David Bartlett and Wendy Hunter, 'Comparing Transitions from Authoritarian Rule in Latin America and Eastern Europe: What Have We Learned and Where Are We Going?' paper presented at the Annual Meeting of the American Political Science Association, 2–5 Sept. 1993, Washington, DC; Piotr Sztompka, 'Dilemmas of the Great Transition,' *Sisyphus*, 2 (1992): 9–27; Sarah Meiklejohn Terry, 'Thinking About Post-Communist Transitions: How Different Are They?' *Slavic Review*, 52/2 (Summer 1993): 333–7; Grzegorz Ekiert, 'Democratization Processes in East Central Europe: A Theoretical Reconsideration,' *British Journal of Political Science*, 21 (July 1991): 285–313; David Ost, 'Shaping a New Politics in Poland: Interests and Politics in Post-Communist Eastern Europe,' Program on Central and Eastern Europe Working Paper Series no. 8, Minde de Gunzburg Center, Harvard University, 1993; David Ost, 'Labor and Societal Transition,' *Problems of Communism*, 41/3 (May–June 1992): 22–4; Ken Jowitt, 'The New World Disorder,' *Journal of Democracy*, 2/2 (Winter 1991): 11–20; Valerie Bunce and Maria Csanadi, 'Uncertainty and the Transition: Post-Communism in Hungary,' *East European Politics and Societies*, 7/1 (Spring 1993): 240–75; Valerie Bunce, 'Can We Compare Democratization in the East Versus the South?' *Journal of Democracy*, forthcoming.

[4] This is the thrust of their discussion of sample selection in 'Modes of Transition in Latin America, Southern and Eastern Europe,' *International Social Science Journal*, 128 (May 1991): 269–84.

[5] This problem also emerges in some of the Latin American cases, where pacts were a consequence of mass mobilization. My thanks to Cynthia McLintock, Bela Greskovits and Hector Schamis for pointing this out.

All of this suggests, Schmitter and Karl to the contrary, that the debate about transitology is in fact a debate among comparativists about comparative methodology. To label critics area specialists, then, is to misrepresent the concerns that have been voiced about comparative studies of democratization, east and south. It is also, perhaps not accidentally, to skirt responsibility for answering some tough questions.

More generally, one can observe that it is a familiar rhetorical technique to reduce the issue at hand to a choice between positive and negative stereotypes. This is precisely what Schmitter and Karl do by juxtaposing comparative analysis to its 'other,' that is, area studies. In their rendition, comparativists emerge as 'the good gals.' They know what constitutes important questions and the data necessary to answer them, they strike the right balance between theory and empirics, and they are in the mainstream of their social science disciplines. Because transitology is a branch of comparative politics, moreover, it is innocent by association, that is, it features all of the positive traits of comparative study. By contrast, those who object to transitology are not comparativists—by definition. Instead, they are area scholars. This is a category which combines a number of undesirable characteristics. In their view, for example, area specialists take 'refuge in "empirie"'; they are allergic to theory; they only know one case and presume it to be unique;[6] they are isolated from their disciplines and 'clannish' in their behavior;[7] and they automatically privilege explanations that are 'particularistic,' 'cultural' and 'ideational' over explanations that are generic and structural.

Thus, one emerges from Schmitter and Karl's account with a sense that one can be no more 'for' area studies, 'against' comparative and, thus, 'against' transitology than be 'for,' say, crime, polio and war, or 'against' fatherhood and apple pie. In drawing a sharp and value-laden contrast between area studies and comparative analysis, they have tried to reduce the question at hand to a valence issue. However, it is not a valence issue. Some comparative studies are good and some are bad. Similarly, work by area specialists can be good or bad. The *quality* of the specific study in question, then, and not the genus to which it belongs, is what matters.

It is also important to recognize that the distinction between comparative and area studies, especially as drawn in sharp relief by Schmitter and Karl, is to a certain extent a false dichotomy. In practice, comparativists and area specialists often work hand in hand. For example, comparative studies can only be as good as their data bases and area specialists (by most definitions) are the ones that provide much of the data for comparative work (even for Schmitter and Karl). In addition, any list of the most influential theories in the social

---

[6] Schmitter and Karl seem to have misunderstood what their critics mean when they claim that state socialism and 'post-state socialism' are unique. The argument is *not* that each eastern European country is unique or that these unique characteristics are derived from, say, distinct national cultures. Rather the argument is a *structural* one. The focus is on the distinctive political, economic and social characteristics that all of these countries share as a consequence of state socialism.

[7] The use of the term 'clan' is reminiscent of the linguistic games the western imperial powers played when they decided in the nineteenth century to draw a clear line between the 'civilized' west—which had nations—and backward Africa—which no longer had nations, but, instead, had tribes, clans and the like (see Philip D. Curtin, *The Image of Africa* (Madison: University of Wisconsin Press, 1964)). Similar linguistic games—which allocate power, modernity and responsibility—characterize many of the recent western analyses of the former Yugoslavia and, more generally, the Balkans (see Maria Todorova, 'The Balkans: From Discovery to Invention,' *Slavic Review*, 53 (Summer 1994): 453–82).

sciences reveals that a good number of them were authored by area specialists and were based for the most part on extended field work in their particular countries, if not counties of expertise. Here, I am thinking, for instance, of work by Benedict Anderson, James Scott and Clifford Geertz, as well as by Guillermo O'Donnell, Robert Putnam and Philippe Schmitter.[8] Finally, it is by now well established that among the best studies in political science and sociology are those that combine comparative methodology with area studies expertise. Indeed, this is the strength of the recent volumes on transitions from authoritarian rule, edited by Guillermo O'Donnell, Philippe Schmitter and Laurence Whitehead.[9]

A final concern I have with framing the debate as one between area studies and comparative analysis is the tone adopted by Schmitter and Karl. What seems to be implied in their defense of comparative analysis in general and transitology in particular, as well as their attack on 'North American specialists' in eastern Europe, is that eastern European studies is a social science backwater. That is why, in their view, specialists in the region object to transitology and, just as importantly, why Schmitter and Karl feel it necessary to take on the burden of propagating the comparative message to the unconverted readers of *Slavic Review*. Their arrogance in this regard parallels the attitudes some western economists have taken when holding forth on the transition to capitalism in eastern Europe. Just as they have advocated 'designer capitalism,'[10] so Schmitter and Karl, and other transitologists, seem to be advocating 'designer democracy'—if not 'designer social science.'[11] What Schmitter and Karl do not seem to know is that the wall separating eastern European studies from

---

[8] See Benedict Anderson, *Imagined Communities* (London: Verso, 1991); James Scott, *Everyday Forms of Peasant Resistance in Southeast Asia* (London: Frank Cass, 1986); Clifford Geertz, *The Interpretation of Cultures: Selected Essays* (New York: Basic Books, 1973); Guillermo O'Donnell, *Modernization and Bureaucratic Authoritarianism* (Berkeley: University of California Press, 1973); Robert Putman, *Making Democracy Work: Civic Traditions in Modern Italy* (Princeton: Princeton University Press, 1993); Philippe C. Schmitter, 'Still the Century of Corporatism?' *The Review of Politics* 36 (Jan. 1974).

[9] See Guillermo O'Donnell, Philippe C. Schmitter and Laurence Whitehead, eds., *Transitions From Authoritarian Rule: Southern Europe* (Baltimore: Johns Hopkins University Press, 1986); *idem., Transitions From Authoritarian Rule: Latin America* (Baltimore: Johns Hopkins University Press, 1986); *idem., Transitions from Authoritarian Rule: Comparative Perspectives* (Baltimore: Johns Hopkins University Press, 1986); Guillermo O'Donnell and Philippe C. Schmitter, eds., *Transitions from Authoritarian Rule: Tentative Conclusions about Uncertain Democracies* (Baltimore: Johns Hopkins University Press, 1986).

[10] David Stark, 'A Sociologist's Perspective: Can Designer Capitalism Work in Central and Eastern Europe?' *Transition: The Newsletter about Reforming Economies*, 3 (May 1992): 1–4.

[11] Is this response to Schmitter and Karl just a matter of turf defense? There is an element of truth to their implied point that some eastern European area specialists are quite resentful of the recent reduced-entry costs to claiming expertise in eastern European studies. These feelings sometimes surface, for example, in discussions behind closed doors with rakija on the table. Just as obscurity had its costs, it appears so does notoriety. However, by 'designer social science' I mean something quite different and, I think, less contentious. First, empirical grounding is a necessary condition for conducting sound research and for offering sound advice. Second, social science is not so developed that it can predict what will happen in the future, let alone dictate what should happen. Third, postcommunist transitions are without historical precedent, yet social science theories are based in large measure on historical precedents. This, plus their multiple and interactive character, suggests that there are clear limits on the ability of social scientists to speak confidently about these transitions. Finally, there is a certain irony in the notion that, having rejected scientific socialism and thus the orchestration of social, political and economic developments 'from above,' the new regimes in the region are now being told by some from the west that there is 'scientific capitalism' and 'scientific democracy,' and that they can be imposed 'from above.' This is despite the purported virtues of regulation through the hidden hand in liberal orders. Humility, in short, and not arrogance should be the order of the day.

comparative politics came down long before the collapse of the wall separating eastern from western Europe[12]—and, thus, considerably before the arrival of 'democracy,' let alone transitology and consolidology, to the region.[13] Schmitter and Karl are unaware of this because they are new to this field. Moreover, their approach to democratization—which concentrates on elites and on the liberalized present and ignores other players, processes and the socialist past—automatically excludes from their purview most of the literature in eastern European studies. All of this testifies, more generally (if we may turn a common observation on its head), to the long and unfortunate isolation of many comparativists from the rich research tradition of eastern European studies.[14] Thus, by preaching the comparative message to eastern European specialists, Schmitter and Karl appear to be generals fighting the last war. Is it accidental, one might ask, that the academic battle they are waging happens to take place in a bipolar world?

Much more relevant to the question of democratization, east and south, is Schmitter and Karl's response to the 'difference' debate. Here, they do an excellent job of reviewing many of the differences between democratization in eastern Europe versus southern Europe and Latin America. They conclude that these differences do not rule out the incorporation of eastern Europe into comparative studies of recent democratization because: (1) the temporal clustering of these cases argues for cross-regional processes at work, which, in turn, suggest some commonalities across these regions; (2) comparative study benefits from variance; (3) the differences between east and south have been exaggerated (as have the similarities among the southern cases) and represent, in fact, variations on a common process of transition and consolidation; and, therefore (4) comparison among these countries is valid and valuable.

I have several responses to the first point. Let us accept for the moment the assumption that democratizations in the south and east occupy roughly the same temporal space and

---

[12] It is interesting to note in this regard that, prior to 1989, comparative analyses were more common in the eastern European field than in, say, Latin American studies. This is because of the homogenizing effects of state socialism and, thus, the extent to which eastern Europe—far more than Latin America—provided a natural laboratory for comparative study.

[13] This was less true for Soviet studies, where single-case analysis was more the norm, where comparative theories were not widely employed and where the assumption of studying a unique case was more widespread. This seems to have reflected the confluence of several factors: the sheer size and thus complexity of the former Soviet Union (which, after all, occupied nearly one fifth of the world's land mass); the difficulties of procuring data; the absence of a strong social science tradition within the Soviet Union (in contrast to, say, Poland, Hungary and the former Yugoslavia); and the academic politics of studying a super power (which led American studies in the same direction). At the same time, some Soviet specialists identified with the country they studied and thereby dismissed as irrelevant to their research all those little colonies to the west of the Soviet Union. However, these generalizations are less relevant to contemporary scholarship on Russia and the successor states. Comparative studies, expressed either as comparison of cases or utilization of comparative theory in single-case analysis, are now becoming the norm in post-Soviet studies.

[14] This isolation was expressed in many ways—some of which were imperial. Witness, for example, the pervasive practice during the cold-war period of western European specialists using the term 'Europe' in the titles of their books, articles, courses and even institutes, when the focus in virtually every case was only on the western half of Europe. To take another example: it has been common practice for courses surveying comparative politics to be not just Euro-centric (which is enough of a problem) but also western Eurocentric. This reflected the widespread assumptions within the discipline of political science that: (1) the only Europe that counted was western Europe and (2) western Europeanists were more scientific and more comparative in their analyses than their counterparts in other area studies.

that this speaks to the presence of similar dynamics of change. If this is so, then why should we employ approaches to the analysis of democratization (such as those offered by O'Donnell, Schmitter and Whitehead, as well as by Schmitter and Karl) that *ignore* the very explanatory factors that would seem to follow logically from these assumptions? Here, I refer to both international and economic variables that would appear to operate in virtually all these cases—for example, the development from the early 1970s onward of international norms supporting human rights and democracy,[15] the destabilizing consequences of the global debt crisis and structural adjustment policies,[16] and the political fallout from long term pursuit in the second and third worlds of import substitution policies. What I am suggesting, then, is that there is a contradiction between the rationale offered for comparing democratization, east and south, and the approaches transitologists take when carrying out their studies.

Second, did these transitions actually occur at roughly the same time and thus in roughly the same context? It is true that they are closer in time to each other than, say, democratization after Franco and democratization in Great Britain. However, it is also true that a few years can make a big difference in the causes and context of democratization. Let us take the examples of Spain and Hungary, two countries which share some similarities in the mode of transition. The transition in Spain occurred in a stable, bipolar international environment and Spain reaped enormous benefits from this (as well as its geographical location). In particular, the new regime had massive infusions of international economic aid, which allowed Spain to delay by ten years painful economic reforms. Moreover, Spain was assured of eventual entry into the European Community and NATO; the only question was whether Spanish political leaders and Spanish publics would support such actions. By contrast, Hungary has received far less international economic support and has had to deal immediately with destabilizing economic reforms. In addition, the end of the cold war, the Warsaw Pact and Comecon have created for Hungary (and its neighbors) a very uncertain international environment. Solutions to this problem, moreover, are slow in coming, given the many difficulties involved today in expanding membership of NATO and the European Union to include Hungary and other members of the former socialist world. What I am suggesting, then, is that the decade or so separating these two transitions made a significant difference in their international contexts. These differences, moreover, had direct domestic repercussions, creating very different processes of democratization in Spain and Hungary.

Schmitter and Karl's second point is more compelling. They are quite right in arguing that variety is the spice of comparative inquiry. Without variation, we cannot develop robust concepts, identify key explanatory factors or construct good explanations. However, there is a catch. Meaningful comparative study requires that differences be joined with similarities; otherwise, too much is in motion to trace relationships and to draw meaningful conclusions. Moreover, we can no longer assume in such circumstances that what we are analyzing in one context is the same as what we are analyzing in another. The key question, then, is whether

---

[15] See Dan Thomas, 'Norms, Politics and Human Rights: The Helsinki Process and the Decline of Communism in Eastern Europe,' Ph.D. dissertation in progress Cornell University.

[16] For an insightful analysis of how international economic pressures prefigured the outbreak of war in the former Yugoslavia, see Susan L. Woodward, *Balkan Tragedy: Chaos and Dissolution after the Cold War* (Washington: Brookings Institution, 1995).

the differences constitute variations on a common process—that is, transitions from dictatorship to democracy—or altogether different processes—that is, democratization versus what could be termed postcommunism. Schmitter and Karl take the first position and their critics the second.

It is not easy to reach a decision on this matter. Social science lacks the sophistication needed to distinguish between differences in degree and differences in kind. One analyst's democratization is another's postcommunism—and a third might question whether postcommunism is so 'post.' However, what can be concluded is that the differences between postcommunism and the transitions in the south are *far* more substantial than Schmitter and Karl's discussion seems to imply. Let me highlight just the most important of them.

First is the nature of authoritarian rule. What distinguished state socialism from bureaucratic authoritarianism and other forms of dictatorship in Latin America and southern Europe were its social structure, its ideology and ideological spectrum, its political economy, its configuration of political and economic elites, its pattern of civil-military relations and its position in the international hierarchy of power and privilege. Thus, state socialism was different along virtually every dimension that economists, sociologists and political scientists recognize as important.[17] If we reach further back in time, we find two more important contrasts: long-established states in southern Europe and Latin America versus ever-changing states in eastern Europe, and a historical tradition of democracy in Latin America and southern Europe versus the absence (save for Czechoslovakia) of any such tradition in the east. Nor can we assume—as is the tendency of many transitologists—that these factors are 'ancient history' insofar as democratization is concerned.[18] It is not just that they structure the agenda of transition, the interests and resources of major actors and, thus, the balance of forces supporting and opposing democratization, the transition to capitalism and the like. It is also that the boundary separating the authoritarian past from the liberalized present is a very porous one in eastern Europe.

There are also significant differences in the mode of transition. For instance, there is no equivalent in the southern cases either to the diffusion processes we saw in eastern Europe in 1989 or thus to the role of international factors in ending the Communist Party's political monopoly.[19] It is crucial as well to understand the end of state socialism as a process of national liberation—whether that was a consequence of the end of the Soviet bloc or the

[17] This was even true for 'deviant' Yugoslavia. See e.g. Vesna Pušic, 'Dictatorships with Democratic Legitimacy: Democracy Versus Nation,' *East European Politics and Societies*, 8 (Fall 1994): 383–401. Contrary to Schmitter and Karl, the distinctions between state socialism and other forms of dictatorship did not wither away when state socialism 'softened' (see, for instance, Maria Csanadi, *From Where to Where? The Party-State and the Transformation* (Budapest: T-Twins and Institute of Economics, Hungarian Academy of Sciences, 1995)).

[18] See, especially, Csanadi, *From Where to Where*. The key article giving rise to the 'proto-science' of transitology (aside from earlier works by Machiavelli, according to Schmitter and Karl) emphasized the importance of *historical context* in the process of democratization. See Dankwart Rustow 'Transitions to Democracy,' *Comparative Politics*, 2 (1970): 337–63. However, transitologists such as Schmitter and Karl have tended to delete the adjective 'historical' from this argument and concentrated, as a result, simply on current context.

[19] This is not to reduce the events of 1989 to the 'Gorbachev effect.' Rather it is to argue that the Gorbachev reforms were a necessary but not sufficient condition for the end of state socialism in eastern Europe. For an explanation—before the fact—of both the Gorbachev reforms and the collapse of state socialism in eastern Europe, see Valerie Bunce, 'The Empire Strikes Back: The Evolution of the Eastern Bloc From a Soviet Asset to a Soviet Liability,' *International Organization*, 39 (Winter 1984/5): 1–46.

end of an internal empire (as with the federal states of the Soviet Union, Yugoslavia and Czechoslovakia). In this sense, state, nation and identity were—and are—at the very center of these processes of change in eastern Europe.

Another difference is in the international context of transition. To summarize an earlier point: the eastern European transitions are taking place in an international system which is itself in transition. What needs to be added to this is the very different economic and strategic position in the international system of eastern Europe versus southern Europe and Latin America. At the time of transition, eastern European countries were not full members by any means of the international capitalist economy, and they were not allied in any institutional sense with the west.

The most striking contrast, and the one that bears most directly on the question of democracy, is in the transitional agenda. In southern Europe and Latin America, *the* issue was democratization; that is, a change in political regime.[20] Indeed, the circumscribed character of political change in southern Europe and Latin America is one reason why students of comparative democratization could reduce democratic transitions to a process involving interactions among a handful of political elites. By contrast, what is at stake in eastern Europe is nothing less than the creation of the very building blocks of the social order. What is open for negotiation is not just the character of the regime but also the very nature of the state itself,[21] not just citizenship but also identity, not just economic liberalization but also the foundations of a capitalist economy.[22] What is also at stake is not just amendment of the existing class structure but the creation of a new class system; not just a shift in the balance of interests, therefore, but something much more fundamental: the very creation of a range of new interests. Finally, what is involved in the eastern European transitions is not just modification of the state's foreign policies, but also a profound redefinition of the role of the state in the international system.

We can draw two conclusions from this brief summary. First, if we are interested in balancing similarities and differences, and in maintaining at the same time a reasonable number of cases, then we would not engage in comparisons between east and south. Rather, we would compare all or some of the 27 eastern European cases with each other. Second, we must be very cautious when comparing democratization, east and south: at best, such comparisons would produce a limited range of benefits; at worst, we could be placing

---

[20] See, especially, Robert Fishman, 'Rethinking State and Regime: Southern Europe's Transition to Democracy,' *World Politics*, 42 (Apr. 1990): 422–40.

[21] The centrality of state building in postcommunism reflects not just the inextricability of state and regime in state socialism and thus the powerful effects on the state of the end of communist party hegemony, but also two other factors: the presence in the region of so many new or newly liberated states and the necessarily powerful consequences for the state of a transition to capitalism. On the latter point, see Ivo Bicanic, 'The Economic Causes of New State Formation during Transition,' *East European Politics and Societies*, 9 (Winter 1995): 2–21.

[22] It is true that economic-liberalization and structural adjustment policies play an important role in the process of democratization, south as well as east. However, one cannot very easily equate economic reform in Latin America and southern Europe with economic transformation in the east. This is, first, because the issue in the south is amending a capitalist economy already in place, whereas the issue in the east (though Hungary provides a valuable middle case) is construction of a capitalist economy with state socialism—its virtual opposite—serving as the point of departure. There are, moreover, other key economic differences, all of which place unusual economic burdens on eastern Europe—for example, the collapse of the Soviet market, the primitive character of eastern European economies and the difficulties imposed by the process of building new national economies in so many cases.

ourselves in the unenviable and unviable position of sampling simultaneously on the independent and dependent variables.

This leads us to Schmitter and Karl's final set of arguments. What do we gain when we compare democratization, east and south? I agree with them that such comparisons can enrich our understanding of democracy. In particular, they remind us of the sheer diversity of ways young democracies come into being and evolve, and they help us define the essential characteristics of democratization by alerting us to differences, as well as to similarities, among democratic orders. Such comparisons also reveal a number of factors that were missing from prevailing theories of democratization.[23] All of these benefits flow quite naturally from a comparative project that is rich in cases and rich in diversity. What Schmitter and Karl do not mention, however, is a final advantage to such cross-regional comparisons. They can provide a powerful critique of prevailing understandings of democratization. They may not simply refine the common wisdom, they may overturn it.

When one looks more closely at transitology from the vantage point of eastern Europe, one is struck, first, by the fact that this is a literature rich in description but relatively poor in testable hypotheses. An example of this is constitutional design—an issue of great importance to many transitologists.[24] How can we test the relative benefits of parliamentary versus presidential systems if most of the systems in eastern Europe are in fact a combination of both, that is, a variation on the French Fifth Republic model? Moreover, how can we evaluate whether constitutional design matters if we have no measure of impact that differentiates among recent cases of democratization and if the purported consequences of constitutional developments could also be judged to be its causes? For instance, is it correct to argue that Hungarian democracy is more secure than Russian democracy because Hungary opted for a parliamentary system and Russia did not, and because the rules of the political game were formalized more clearly and earlier in Hungary than in Russia?[25] Or does it make more sense to argue that the problems surrounding the transition in Russia are far greater than in Hungary and that it is this fact that has produced both different constitutional trajectories and differences as well in the seeming prospects for democratic consolidation?

A second problem is that what is offered in transitions literature is not, in fact, a theory of democratization—a series of 'if, then' claims that can be tested—but rather an approach to the analysis of democratization—that is, a statement about what should be analyzed and how. All that this literature gives us is advice: we should look at strategic interactions among elites and treat democratization as a highly contingent process that is fraught with consider-

[23] This is evident, for instance, in some recent reflections on democratization by transitologists (see, for instance, Guillermo O'Donnell, 'On the State, Democratization and Some Conceptual Problems [A Latin American View with Glances at Some Post-Communist Countries],' *World Development* 21 [1993]: 1355–69; *idem.*, 'Delegative Democracy?' Working Paper No. 172, Helen Kellogg Institute of International Studies, Notre Dame, March 1992; Philippe Schmitter, 'Dangers and Dilemmas of Democracy,' *Journal of Democracy* 5 [April 1994]: 57–74).

[24] See e.g. Juan Linz, 'The Perils of Presidentialism,' *Journal of Democracy*, l (Winter 1990): 51–69; Arend Lijphart, 'Democratization and Constitutional Choices in Czecho-Slovakia, Hungary, and Poland, 1989–1991' in *Flying Blind*, ed. Gyorgy Szoboszlai (Budapest: Yearbook of the Hungarian Political Science Association, 1992): 99–113; Alfred Stepan and Cindy Skach, 'Constitutional Frameworks and Democratic Consolidation: Parliamentarism versus Presidentialism,' *World Politics*, 46 (Oct. 1993): 1–22.

[25] If the latter factor were so important, then how do we explain, for instance, the developmental trajectories of, say, Bulgaria and Romania (with their early settlement of constitutional issues) versus Poland and the Czech Republic (given their continuing problems with resolution of the rules of the political game)?

able uncertainty. What it does not give us is any explanation of why some authoritarian states democratize and others do not, why the process of democratization varies across cases, or why some democracies take root and others do not.

Since this literature is a series of claims about how we should approach the study of democratization, can we then argue at least that the approach offered is a sound one? Let me suggest one answer to this question by expanding on a point already mentioned: the addition of new variables to the equation. By joining eastern Europe with southern Europe and Latin America, we discover a number of crucial factors that are missing in the recent theories of transitologists—in particular, the interaction between economic and political transformation, the importance of the media in the process of democratization, the powerful influence of international factors, the key role of mass publics in transitions (as well as in consolidation),[26] the centrality of national identity and nationalism in the process of democratization, the importance of the left as well as the right in shaping democratic prospects and, finally, all those thorny issues having to do with the state, its boundaries, its strength and its place within the international order. This is a long list of missing variables, which focuses our attention on this question: at what point can we no longer tack on these factors to the prevailing approach to the study of democratization and should we decide instead, given the desire for parsimony and the considerable implications these additions hold for our very conception of democratization, that a completely different approach to the study of democratic transitions is required?

We can also judge the soundness of the prevailing approach by concentrating on what it includes rather than on what it lacks. Central to the approach of Schmitter, Karl, O'Donnell and their associates is the assertion that elites are central and publics peripheral. Thus, transitions to democracy are understood to be elite affairs and the more elitist, transitologists argue, the better. However, when we add eastern Europe to the equation, we begin to wonder about this emphasis since: (1) publics were important actors in ending communist party hegemony in many of these cases; (2) bargaining among elites is—especially before the fact—a very hard process to trace; (3) it is very difficult—again, especially before the fact—to determine elite interests and elite resources and (4) pacted versus mass mobilization modes of transition do *not* explain patterns of success in democratic consolidation in the postcommunist world. More generally, one has to wonder whether, in focusing so heavily on the machinations of elites, transitologists have not committed the very transgression they have lamented in the work of area scholars: the preference for a particularistic and voluntaristic understanding of social reality over one which is more general and structural.

Just as elites and their interactions are central to the approach developed by Schmitter, Karl and their associates, so are the core concepts of democratic transition, democratic consolidation and, finally, uncertainty. In each of these, once we add eastern Europe to the calculus we find a number of problems. Transition implies change that is circumscribed and directional, in these discussions, either towards or away from democratic governance. The first aspect does not fit the inherently revolutionary nature of postcommunism and the

[26] See e.g. Daniel V. Friedheim, 'Bringing Society Back into Democratic Transition Theory: Pact Making and Regime Collapse,' *East European Politics and Societies*, 7 (Fall 1993): 482–512; and Sidney Tarrow, 'Social Movements and Democratic Development,' forthcoming in *The Politics of Democratic Consolidation*, vol. 1, Richard Gunther, Nikiforos Diamandous and Hans-Jurgen Puhle, eds.

second leads to a misrepresentation of eastern European developments by forcing us: (1) to draw too sharp a distinction between the authoritarian past and the transitional present, (2) to privilege the democratic dimension over all other dimensions of change, (3) to assume that political change is separate from, say, economic and social change and (4) to code any and all major developments as factors necessarily affecting movement to or away from democracy.[27] Consolidation is also a problematic concept. First, it is unclear what 'consolidation' means in an empirical sense, aside from a vague notion that 'consolidated democracies' are those that, following transition, seem to promise longevity. Is democratic consolidation, then, just a matter of time? How do we factor in capacity to withstand crises? Is it the absence of democratic collapse or the presence of certain features, such as a demo-cratic political culture?[28] Does consolidation entail political stability and, if so, what does this mean? Is it the absence of such factors as significant anti-system protest, the govern-ment's loss of its coercive monopoly and sharp divisions among citizens and among polit-ical leaders, or is it the presence of such factors as relatively durable governing coalitions and widespread public support for the institutions and procedures of democracy? There is a final problem. If democracy is a process, not a result, and if the democratic project can never be completed, then how can we understand the term 'consolidation' with its implication of democracy as an end state?

The final member of the conceptual triumvirate in transitions literature is uncertainty. Here, again, we encounter a certain dissonance between concept and reality. On the one hand, transitologists have made a great deal of the uncertainties surrounding democratiza-tion. Indeed, this is the foundation for much of the theorizing about transitions from authoritarian rule. On the other hand, we see a clear pattern in the many new democracies that have come into being since the 1970s: an extremely high survival rate. If the democratic enterprise is so fraught with difficulties, as transitologists repeatedly assert,[29] then how do we explain this? It is not a sufficient response to argue either that these new democracies are still in the throes of consolidation or to presume that the durability of new democracies speaks in effect to a global bounty of 'heroic princes.' Rather the response should be to question whether democracy (today at least) might be easier than many have thought—or, at least, whether the imposition of authoritarian rule might be more difficult than many seemed to have assumed.[30]

All of these examples suggest that the addition of eastern Europe to comparative studies of democratization has one major benefit, aside from those outlined by Schmitter and Karl.

---

[27] Symptomatic of the pervasiveness of these assumptions has been the tendency of scholars (primarily on the Op-Ed page of *The New York Times*) to pronounce either that Russia has turned the corner on democracy or that democracy is finished in Russia.

[28] A survey of longstanding democracies would seem to suggest that: (1) there is great variety in what constitutes a democratic political culture; (2) it is very hard to distinguish between durable beliefs, values and behaviors and more short-term attitudes and the like; (3) some democracies feature by some standards a less than democratically minded public; and (4) the key to democracy might be mass culture but it also might be elite political culture. See e.g. Putnam, *Making Democracy Work*.

[29] See, especially, Philippe C. Schmitter, 'Dangers and Dilemmas of Democracy,' *Journal of Democracy*, 5 (Apr. 1994): 57–74.

[30] See, especially, Giuseppe Di Palma, 'Democratic Transitions: Puzzles and Surprises from West to East,' *Research on Democracy and Society*, 1 (New York: JAI Press, 1993): 27–50; Nancy Bermeo, 'Democracy and the Lessons of Dictatorship,' *Comparative Politics*, 24 (Apr. 1992): 273–91.

It introduces serious questions about the reigning paradigm of democratization. This leads us to the final point of this commentary. If Schmitter and Karl have been in some respects too conservative in estimating the value of comparing east and south (particularly when it involves '*samokritika*'), then they have been in other respects too liberal in their assessment of what can be learned from such comparisons. It is here that we must switch our discussion from the benefits of diversity to its costs.

The striking contrasts between transitions to democracy in the south and postcommunism in the east suggest that certain kinds of comparative exercises are highly suspect. First, there is a danger in presuming fundamental similarities when the similarities posited are in fact superficial and highly misleading. Ethnic diversity is a case in point. To equate Peruvian, Spanish and Portuguese ethnic diversity with that of the former Yugoslavia and the former Soviet Union (or even contemporary Russia, for that matter) is to skim over a number of distinctive features of ethno-politics in eastern Europe. Here, I refer, for instance, to the sheer magnitude of diversity in the region and its correlation with religious, political, socio-economic and spatial markers; the powerful historical meanings attached to ethnicity, nation, religion and state; the role played by state socialist regimes in developing national consciousness, as well as national elites, national institutions and proto-states within states; the central place of ethnicity, national identity and national movements in ending the communist experiment; the role of ethnicity in not just the process of nation and state building and democratization, but also in the transition to capitalism; the powerful impact of ethnicity on definitions and practices of citizenship; and the ways in which ethnicity in eastern Europe affects not just domestic politics and economics, but also interstate relations throughout the region. To be succinct: there is a former Yugoslavia, a former Czechoslovakia and a former Soviet Union, and there could be as well in the future a former Russia. There is, however, no 'former Peru' or 'former Spain.'

Another danger is to transplant onto eastern European soil arguments developed in response to the very different conditions existing in Latin America and southern Europe. Take, for instance, the argument developed in the southern context that publics are demobilized during transitions to democracy and that this contributes in positive ways to the democratization process. This argument makes little sense in eastern Europe, if only because of the pronounced role of average citizens as well as intellectuals in many of these transitions. Moreover, an argument can be made for the eastern European case, at least, that mobilized publics may very well be assets, not liabilities in the process of democratization. They may exert needed pressures on elites to adhere to the democratic rules of the game and they may provide the necessary political capital for the transition to capitalism.[31]

This leaves us with a final problem. If such different contexts call into question the transfer of concepts and arguments from south to east, then they most assuredly challenge the validity of using the southern experience to *predict* developments in eastern Europe. For instance, Guillermo O'Donnell, as well as Philippe Schmitter and Terry Karl, have voiced considerable pessimism about the future of democracy in eastern Europe. In particular, they have argued that many of the democracies in the region are incomplete and superficial, that

---

[31] See Valerie Bunce, 'Sequencing Economic and Political Reforms,' *East-Central European Economies in Transition* (Washington: Joint Economic Committee, 1994); Bela Greskovits, 'Is the East Becoming the South? Where May Threats to Reforms Come From?' paper presented at the XVI World Congress of the International Political Science Association, Berlin, 12–15 Aug. 1994.

these new democracies will take a long time to consolidate and that there are grounds for expecting at least some to revert back to authoritarian rule.[32] There are ample reasons, of course, to wonder about democracy's future in eastern Europe. However, one must ask whether transitologists are engaged in a careful reading of trends in eastern Europe, or whether their pessimistic conclusions are an artifact produced by measuring the east against the southern standard. Does eastern Europe have a problem with democracy or is it simply that eastern Europe is not Latin America or southern Europe?[33]

Thus, my arguments are four: first, the debate over comparisons between east and south cannot be reduced to the old debate between area studies and comparative analysis. Second, Schmitter and Karl are wrong when they portray comparative and area studies as polar opposites. Third, there are substantial differences between the east and the south, and this creates far more problems for comparing the two than Schmitter and Karl recognize. Finally, there are nonetheless some good reasons to engage in such comparisons. The most important reason, however, is not addressed by Schmitter and Karl: the ways in which the addition of eastern Europe to comparative studies of democratization alerts us to fundamental problems in how transitologists have understood and analyzed transitions from authoritarian rule—in the east and, one could argue, in the south as well.

---

[32] See Guillermo O'Donnell, 'On the State'; Schmitter and Karl, 'The Conceptual Travels'; Schmitter, 'Dangers and Dilemmas'; Schmitter and Karl, 'Modes of Transition'.

[33] To this must be added one more point. A major problem in theories of democracy (of older, as well as of more recent vintage) is that they under-predict the incidence of democratic government. There are in effect too many democracies, whether our theoretical perspective is that of, say, Seymour Martin Lipset; Barrington Moore; Dietrich Rueschemeyer, Evelyne Stephens and John Stephens; or Guillermo O'Donnell, Phillippe Schmitter and Laurence Whitehead. This suggests that: (1) our theories of democracy may be over-specified, (2) there may be no single path to a democratic order, (3) democratization may be best understood in highly voluntaristic terms and/or (4) democracy may not be as difficult a project as has been commonly assumed.

35 From an Iron Curtain to a Paper Curtain: Grounding Transitologists or Students of Postcommunism?

Terry Lynn Karl and Philippe C. Schmitter

Valerie Bunce, in her rejoinder[1] (here Chapter 34) to an article we published in *Slavic Review* (here Chapter 33),[2] seems to disagree with us in three regards: First, she claims that we pit area studies against comparative analyses and negatively stereotype the former in the process. Second, she contends that differences between regime transitions in the 'South' and the 'East' are so great that they prevent the making of meaningful comparisons, negating the value of such a cross-area enterprise. In a subsequent article, she writes: ' . . . the most logical comparison to be made is the comparison of the post communist countries with one another.'[3] Third, she argues that we misrepresent both the costs and the benefits of adding eastern Europe and the former Soviet Union to comparative studies of democratization. We shall concentrate on (re)examining and responding to each of these disagreements.

Comparative analysis versus area studies: a red herring

Before addressing the more serious analytical issues that Bunce raises, we wish to dispense with an imputation of hers that we found especially puzzling: that we are hostile to area studies per se.[4] Both of us are area specialists as well as comparativists. We have directed area studies centers, spent an extensive amount of time conducting field research on specific countries and subsets of countries, dedicated ourselves to training a new generation of area specialists and defended area studies against budgetary threats stemming from declining government and foundational support.[5] Bunce's claim that we engage in 'negative

Republished, with minor abbreviations, from *Slavic Review*, 54/4 (Winter 1995), 965–78, by kind permission of the authors and the American Association for the Advancement of Slavic Studies.

[1] Valerie Bunce, 'Should Transitologists Be Grounded?', *Slavic Review*, 54/1 (Spring 1995): 111–27.

[2] Philippe C. Schmitter with Terry Lynn Karl, 'The Conceptual Travels of Transitologists and Consolidologists: How Far to the East Should They Attempt to Go?' *Slavic Review*, 53/1 (Spring 1994): 173–85.

[3] Valerie Bunce, 'Comparing East and South,' *Journal of Democracy*, 6/3 (Fall 1994): 95.

[4] We will refrain from responding to the other misrepresentations of our work in Bunce's reply. Just to keep the record straight, however, we do want to answer her charge that our 'arrogance' is apparent from the fact that we felt it 'necessary to take on the burden of propagating the comparative message to the unconverted readers of *Slavic Review*.' Philippe Schmitter was approached (unsolicited) by the editor Elliott Mossman, who asked him if he would be willing to contribute a version of a talk he was invited to give at the 1993 annual convention of the AAASS to the very next issue of *Slavic Review*. Such was the proximity of the deadline that we were even unable to collaborate fully on the final draft—hence, the 'with' rather than 'and' connecting its two authors.

[5] See, for example, Terry Lynn Karl, 'In Defense of Area Studies,' *Enlace* (Stanford University, Fall 1992): 2.

stereotypes' of area studies, attack area expertise in order 'to skirt responsibility for answering some tough questions,' think area specialists are 'allergic to theory,' 'only know one case' and 'presume it to be unique,' or imply that eastern European studies is 'a social science backwater' is pure invention on her part. Our refusal to consider area studies and comparative analysis as mutually exclusive does not mean that we are reluctant to criticize certain practices often associated with area studies. What Bunce has wrongly cast as a basic hostility is, in fact, an appeal on our part for improvement in how area studies are conducted.

First, we observed that the field of communist studies—and especially its subfield of Sovietology—has long suffered a partially self-imposed isolation from the major social science disciplines. While this has also been true, to some extent, for other area study programs, it has been especially pronounced among US-based scholars who explicitly argued that communist systems were so distinctive as to preclude comparison.[6] We do not agree with those scholars steeped in this academic tradition who rely heavily (if not exclusively) on assumptions about the allegedly unique legacy of 'totalitarianism,' 'marxism-leninism-stalinism,' 'Soviet political culture,' etc. as an excuse for eschewing all comparison with other world regions—even though we fully agree that all countries and regions have some properties which are unique.[7] In our view, the position of those such as Bunce and others who a priori reject the application of theories generated elsewhere to 'post-communist transitions' would continue this unfortunate tradition of isolation.

Moreover, this rejection could well cut off US specialists from many eastern European and Russian scholars who are working on issues of regime change and democratization. If there is one major lesson that one can glean from area studies, it is that close contact and extensive exchanges between 'foreigners' and 'natives' are essential to producing high quality, creative and comparable work. Precisely because (for reasons that are enumerated by Bunce in her n. 13) US Sovietologists have generally had much less actual field experience within their region and much less close collaborative contact with their counterparts than, say, Latin Americanists in the United States, there tends to be a greater gap in conceptualization and research techniques.[8] Perhaps for this reason, many social scientists

[6] This is not a new observation. More than 25 years ago, some scholars of Soviet politics pointed out that the study of the Soviet political system and communist systems in general had proceeded in isolation from developments in social science concepts theory and methodology precisely because scholars had thought 'their' region to be so unique. See e.g. Frederic. J. Fleron, Jr., ed., *Communist Studies and the Social Sciences: Essays on Methodology and Empirical Theory* (Chicago: Rand McNally, 1969). For an overview of the history of the discipline of Soviet studies on this issue, see George Breslauer, 'In Defense of Sovietology,' *Post-Soviet Affairs*, (1992), 197–238, or Frederic J. Fleron, Jr. and Erik P. Hoffman, *Post-Communist Studies and Political Science: Methodology and Empirical Theory in Sovietology* (Boulder: Westview Press, 1993).

[7] For example, two scholars who otherwise differ quite substantially in their Sovietology agree most emphatically on the intrinsic peculiarity of 'its' legacy to eschew comparison: Martin Malia, 'Leninist Endgame,' *Daedalus* (Spring 1992): 57–75 and Ken Jowitt, *New World Disorder: The Leninist Extinctions* (Berkeley: University of Los Angeles: California Press, 1993), esp. 249–83.

[8] Bunce seems to have had access to an unspecified source that proves that 'comparative analyses were more common in the eastern European field than, say, Latin American studies'. Frankly, we doubt this and suspect that the opportunities to do research based on empirical field research, either individually or collaboratively, were limited, especially in the Soviet Union. For example, a comparison of the *Slavic Review* with its equivalent, the *Latin American Research Review*, would reveal, we suspect, many more articles in the latter that are co-authored by 'natives' and 'foreigners' (as well as many, many more authored by natives trained or resident in the US), and many more articles that deal with more than one polity or society within its respective region. Only since the regime changes in eastern Europe and the former Soviet Union has the opportunity to conduct comparative research

in eastern Europe and the former Soviet Union have eagerly seized upon a more generic and non-area-specific conceptualization of the processes of transformation that are engulfing them.

Second, exclusive concentration on intra-regional studies can restrict the ability of area specialists to understand their own region or particular country. There is no question, for example, that Latin Americanists have increased understanding of 'their' region through comparisons with east Asian experiences, which revealed a great deal about successful and unsuccessful development strategies as well as about the peculiarly predatory nature of many states in Latin America. It is highly unlikely that these same lessons would have emerged from intra-regional comparisons alone.[9]

Such efforts point to the following lesson: just because area studies were born in the untested notion that specific geocultural regions were somehow 'unique' does not mean this comfortable assumption should remain forever unexamined. Peter Smith's observation with regard to Latin America should hold true for eastern Europe and the former Soviet Union: 'The concept of "Latin America" is, in fact, a cultural construct, not a timeless verity.'[10] His call for questioning the logical foundations of the existing definitions and boundaries of Latin American studies may be even more compelling for eastern Europeanists. Given their relative isolation in the past, as well as their manifest unpreparedness for the advent of perestroika and regime change, it seems reasonable to suggest that a greater connection with scholars from other parts of the world who were studying topics like the decline of empire, the emergence of ethnic conflict, the transformation of one party systems, the transition from authoritarian rule, etc. might have served them well in preparing for what so unexpectedly occurred during the 1980s and early 1990s.

Third, and most important for our purposes, we argue that such a narrow insistence on intra-regional studies and the consequent exclusion of cross-regional comparisons could have a deleterious impact on the development of theory. It discourages area specialists from using data from 'their' region or country to confirm, refine or reject existing hypotheses in the larger field of comparative politics that have been generated by experiences elsewhere in the world. In this respect, we were most alarmed by the advice of Sarah Meiklejohn Terry for Slavic area specialists 'to take refuge in *empirie*' for ten years while deliberately ignoring

expanded considerably—and it is this opportunity that should not be missed. The issue we have posed is whether former Sovietologists and young scholars just entering this subfield will be better served by continuing to employ a particularistic, 'regionally specific' conceptualization of the problems of democratization or a more generic, 'inter-regional' one.

[9] See e.g. Gary Gereffi and Donald L. Wyman, eds., *Manufacturing Miracles: Paths of Industrialization in Latin America and East Asia* (Princeton: Princeton University Press, 1990); Fernando Fejnzylber, *Unavoidable Industrial Restructuring in Latin America* (Durham, NC: Duke University Press, 1990); or Stephen Haggard, *Pathways from the Periphery: The Politics of Growth in the Newly Industrializing Countries* (Ithaca, NY: Cornell University Press, 1990). In another example, Terry Karl's work demonstrates that the uniqueness of Venezuela's development patterns, which has always been a puzzle for Latin Americanists because it does not follow the same cycles of authoritarian rule and democratization as other countries in the southern cone, becomes more explicable through comparisons with other oil-exporting countries in Asia and Africa rather than through intra-regional comparisons alone (see Terry Lynn Karl, *The Paradox of Plenty* (Berkeley: University of California Press, forthcoming)).

[10] See Peter Smith, 'The Changing Agenda for Social Science Research on Latin America,' in Peter H. Smith, ed., *Latin America in Comparative Perspective: New Approaches to Methods and Analysis* (Boulder, Colo.: Westview Press, 1995), 23.

what was being written about transitions elsewhere.[11] How then can theorizing about transitions from autocracy or any other more general theorizing benefit from the experiences of eastern Europe and the former Soviet Union—even if the effort to include them only serves to prove such theories wrong?

Bunce seems to have several problems with this argument. She claims that 'transitology' is richer in description as well as concepts and assumptions than in testable hypotheses; therefore, she hints, it may not be worth the trouble to apply it elsewhere. But this should not come as a surprise to anyone familiar with this literature since its approach is quite explicitly possibilistic—not probabilistic or deterministic—in epistemology and design. She seems to accept without hesitation an orthodox positivist conception of what political science should be all about—and she is perfectly entitled to assume that the only valid form of thinking scientifically about politics is to reduce it to a series of discrete 'if, . . . then . . . ' hypotheses. We have argued that this is an excessively narrow conception of the role of theory and an especially inappropriate approach to the issue of contemporary democratization.[12]

Furthermore, she claims that some of the central concepts of 'transitions' literature are imprecise and that important factors or variables may be missing. Both points may very well be true but not for the reasons Bunce suggests. Regarding the former, for example, she misunderstands and hence misapplies the concept of 'uncertainty.' It does not mean that, because we (scholars looking after the fact) can now see that most transitions did in fact lead to some form of democracy, they must not have been so uncertain in the first place. What uncertainty does mean is that, at the time, 'normal politics' were no longer possible; actors no longer knew what their resources were, what their preferred strategies ought to be, who their appropriate allies were or even who their enemies should be. And all this was bound to have a major impact upon their calculations and behaviors, making the transition a quite different political process.

As for her second critique, there are undoubtedly 'missing' or 'undervalued' variables, but they are not the ones that Bunce lists. 'The interaction between economic and political transformations,' 'the powerful influence of international factors,' 'the centrality of national identity and nationalism in the process of democratization,' 'the importance of the Left as well as the Right in shaping democratic prospects' and 'all those thorny issues having to do with the state' are not 'missing variables.' They have all received some attention in our article in *Slavic Review* (and even more in our other publications), although the conclusions we draw and the weight we may give to each specific factor might not be satisfactory in her view. One missing item that we do acknowledge is 'the importance of the mass media in transitions (as well as consolidations),' although neither of us can understand why this should be peculiar to the east.

Bunce also gives the impression that scholars who use concepts or attempt to test hypotheses generated elsewhere must be 'imperialist' in intent. Advocates of 'designer democracy',

---

[11] Bunce quite mistakenly implies that we (not Meiklejohn Terry) advocated that all ex-Sovietologists should take 'refuge in *empirie*.'

[12] In order to illustrate her point about testable hypotheses, Bunce criticizes the works by Linz and by Stepan and Skach on the superiority of parliamentarism over presidentialism. This probabilistic argument, which is not even mentioned in our article in *Slavic Review*, is quite antithetic to the approach we have adopted and we agree with Bunce's skepticism about applying such seemingly empirical and universalistic findings to specific cases.

we stand accused of following in the steps of neo-liberal purveyors of 'designer capitalism'.[13] Our purpose, she implies, must be to impose an alien approach rather than to see how its application to a new area might modify and improve existing concepts and arguments. While there has certainly been a tradition of this sort in American political science, especially among those who seek to formulate or influence policy, this misreading of our intent should have been evident from our original article, where we argued:

One should not deliberately ignore possible sources of variation across world regions. To the contrary, sensitivity to what is different about eastern Europe (and the former Soviet Union) may provide a useful corrective to the contemporary literature which is so centered on southern Europe and Latin America. Most importantly, it may encourage comparativists to pay more attention to variables that have either been previously taken for granted, e.g. the existence of relatively established national identities or of relatively well functioning market mechanisms, or that have been examined and rejected as less important, e.g. the intromission of external powers.

Isn't it precisely this sort of juxtaposition of assumptions and hypotheses that is most likely to improve theory in both the original and subsequent areas? And if not, what is the alternative?

Cross-regional comparisons: comparing apples, oranges and, yes, even kangaroos

What the arguments above highlight is the central importance of engaging in cross-regional comparisons, i.e., for incorporating the experiences of the 'east' with those of the 'south' which have generated the original literature on transitions. Bunce claims that the differences between the two are so substantial that they cannot (and probably should not) be compared. What is at issue, she writes, is comparability: 'Are we comparing apples with apples, apples with oranges (which are at least varieties of fruit) or apples with, say, kangaroos?'

The problem is, however, that we do not know enough about these transitions to be able to assess just how distinctive they are. In other words, we don't yet know whether they are apples, oranges or kangaroos.[14] There may be just as much variation in event and outcome within a chosen 'region' as between it and any other region. Eastern Europe and the former Soviet Union may incorporate apples and oranges—and, who knows, even a kangaroo or two! Under these conditions it is simply premature to dismiss the possibility of comparison. If the peculiarity of one region's cultural, historical or institutional matrix is so essential to understanding the outcome, this should emerge from systematic comparison rather than be used as an excuse for not applying it.

Moreover, the fact that differences may be great is not a reason to jettison cross-regional comparison but could even be a strong argument in favor of carrying it out. There are many

---

[13] There is some irony in this label. In 1983 Terry Karl wrote the article 'Democracy by Design,' published in Giuseppe DiPalma and Laurence Whitehead, eds., *The Central American Impasse* (London: Croom Helm Publishers, 1985), in which she criticized US policymakers and international Christian Democrats for imposing an inappropriate model of democratization on El Salvador—a critique she has repeated in several subsequent articles. In the discussion of central America, the phrase 'designer democracy' originated with this article.

[14] We are grateful to Nora Bensahel for this point.

diverse forms of comparative analysis and, just because differences may be greater between the east and the south than within these respective groupings, it is not necessarily more reasonable or productive to compare 'all or some of the 27 eastern European cases with each other.' Maybe yes, maybe no. It all depends on the question being asked or, in Charles Tilly's words, 'on the intellectual task at hand.'[15]

In our case, we have hypothesized that the basic dynamics and patterns of transition from autocracy, which were first identified through both intra-regional comparative studies of Latin America and southern Europe and subsequently through cross-regional comparisons of these two regions, will also be found in the transitions from authoritarian rule in eastern Europe.[16] It is important to note that these arguments were generated by means of a 'most similar systems' research design because this strategy is especially suitable to the initial elaboration of plausible hypotheses. But today the task at hand is different. It involves testing, verifying, modifying and/or falsifying concepts and hypotheses that have been generated elsewhere. For this, the appropriate form of comparison is a more 'universalizing' one, that is, one which tests the argument that 'every instance of a phenomenon follows essentially the same rule.'[17] As a number of comparative methodologists have shown, this calls for a 'most different-systems' design, which purposely utilizes cases with similar outcomes on the dependent variable, e.g. 'a transition from autocracy,' but different values on a wide range of independent variables. This is the design that is tailor made for cross-regional comparisons since location within the different subsets permits one to introduce greater variation in a broader range of independent variables.[18]

Let us offer an example. Bunce and other former Sovietologists place a great deal of emphasis on the importance of 'identity politics' and on rising hostility (not to say, armed conflict) between ethnic groups as a key distinction between east and south. Presumptively, this makes processes of regime change in eastern Europe and the former Soviet Union so completely different that they should be conceptually and empirically segregated from southern Europe and Latin America. The kangaroos should be kept away from the fruits, so-to-speak! But this greatly underestimates the role that ethnic differences (and even violent struggles based on them) play in several southern transitions, e.g. Spain, Peru, Mexico and Guatemala, while overstating its role in some eastern cases, e.g. Poland, Hungary and Belarus. Instead, we suggest that what might be interesting is precisely to compare such ethnically diverse countries as Russia, Romania and Macedonia with a country such as Brazil which is at least as ethnically complex in its social formation but which has not experienced collective mobilization and conflict along these lines of cleavage. In other words, one might choose to compare kangaroos that jumped with those that have not!

To argue that a comparison of this sort 'at best . . . would produce a limited range of

[15]   Charles Tilly, *Big Structures, Large Processes, Huge Comparisons* (New York: Russell Sage, 1984), 145.

[16]   For the original elaboration of the theorizing about transitions from authoritarian rule, see the four-volume study of Guillermo O'Donnell, Philippe Schmitter and Laurence Whitehead, eds., *Transitions from Authoritarian Rule* (Baltimore: Johns Hopkins University Press, 1986). For a more recent 'inventory' of what these basic dynamics and patterns might be, see Philippe C. Schmitter, 'Transitology: The Science or the Art of Democratization?' in Joseph Tulchin, ed., *The Consolidation of Democracy in Latin America* (Boulder, Colo.: Lynne Rienner, 1995), 11–44.

[17]   The words are Tilly's, *Big Structures.*, 80.

[18]   See e.g. Adam Przeworski and Henry Teune, *The Logic of Comparative Social Inquiry* (New York: John Wiley and Sons, 1970); and Charles C. Ragin, *The Comparative Method: Moving Beyond Qualitative and Quantitative Strategies* (Berkeley: University of California Press, 1987).

benefits,' that it must be inferior to intraregional comparisons or perhaps that it should not even be attempted at all is to claim a priori (and without systematic evidence) that the arguments put forward about the breakdown of autocracy, the nature of transitions and their possibly democratic outcome elsewhere in the world are not applicable to eastern Europe and the former Soviet Union. Yet some specialists of the region have already explored this question with very interesting results.[19] Our own hunch is that, even if all of Bunce's points about the extensive differences between east and south were well taken, the sum of their impact would lead to a modification rather than a disgarding of the original 'transitology' paradigm.

The lessons of east–south comparisons: how much are they worth?

One of the best arguments for breaking the isolation of what has been known as communist studies and for carrying out cross-regional comparisons is evidenced by the work of Valerie Bunce herself. In order to develop her rationale for rejecting this type of comparative analysis, she had to engage in making the very comparisons she finds so suspect! And the results have been interesting. In both her rejoinder and a subsequent article cited earlier, she raises a number of important substantive issues. While her purpose was to demonstrate that these cannot be understood as variations on a common process of transition, what struck us about her 'catalogue of contrasts' is its close correspondence to our 'catalogue of similarities.' Since we have already made the general argument for the special utility of cross-regional comparisons and because we are in such substantial agreement about what constitutes the principal east–south differences, we will concentrate in the remaining space upon those substantive topics where we still disagree with Bunce.

1. The international political context. We had already stressed that the international political/strategic context was more significant in eastern Europe than in most of southern Europe or Latin America, although we would hesitate to place such a single-minded emphasis on the role of the Soviet Union as Bunce does. In our view, Adam Przeworski seems to have gotten it right: 'The constraint (in Eastern Europe) was external, but the impetus was internal.'[20] It is important to note that this same argument about the importance of the international political context is also true for central America, where US hegemony (though qualitatively different in form from that exercised by the former Soviet Union) circumscribed possibilities for democratization just as thoroughly.[21]

2. The international economic context. Bunce's implication that 'the destabilizing

---

[19] See e.g. M. Steven Fish, *Democracy from Scratch: Opposition and Regime in the New Russian Revolution* (Princeton: Princeton University Press, 1994); David Ost, 'Shaping a New Politics in Poland: Interests and Politics in Post-Communist Eastern Europe'; *Program on Central and Eastern Europe Working Paper Series*, no.8, Minde de Gunzburg Center, Harvard University 1993; and Grzegorz Ekiert, 'Democratization Processes in East Central Europe: A Theoretical Reconsideration,' *British Journal of Political Science*, 21 (July 1991): 285–313.

[20] Adam Przeworski, 'The "East" Becomes the "South"? The "Autumn of the People" and the Future of Eastern Europe,' *P.S. Political Science and Politics*, 24/1 (Mar. 1991): 21.

[21] Despite the fact that the US has not historically seen itself as an empire and has seldom chosen to rule another country directly, its actions in the Caribbean Basin have been those of a superpower. See Richard R. Fagen and Terry Karl, 'The Logics of Hegemony: The United States as a Superpower in Central America,' in Jan Triska, ed., *Dominant Powers and Subordinate States: The United States in Latin America and the Soviet Union in Eastern Europe* (Durham, NC: Duke University Press, 1986), 218–38.

consequences of the global debt crisis and structural adjustment policies' were uniform or even similar for all countries undergoing transition is false. They varied greatly in timing and importance from case to case, not only within regions but also between them. In our view, any effort to use this argument to explain either the occurrence or nature of regime transition is bound to fail empirically.

3. One wave of democratization or several? Bunce correctly points out that even if the transitions in southern Europe, Latin America and eastern Europe may have taken place in one democratic 'wave,' the years that separate different transitions make a significant difference in their international contexts. Her point that prospective membership in the EC played a role in southern Europe (and that there was no such attractive possibility for South America) has already been abundantly stressed. That the situation with respect to, say, Hungary is different from Spain is no doubt true, but it is not true that post-communist Hungary has received much less aid and assurances from its western neighbors than did post-Franco Spain before its negotiations for EC entry. Most of the Spanish adjustment to the EC (and inflows of foreign capital) came *before, not after* the transition to democracy— that is the real difference!

4. Differences in the nature of authoritarian rule. That the previous form of autocracy was different in eastern Europe and the former Soviet Union is not a novel assertion and we discussed it rather extensively in our initial article. What seems to be overlooked by Bunce is how much change had occurred in the practices—if not in the academic models—of 'state socialism' and 'totalitarianism' *before* the transition began. These internal changes in both political and economic relations were well observed by scholars in Poland and Hungary, but with some exceptions most US area specialists failed to conceptualize or monitor explicitly these alterations in the structure of underlying power and production relations prior to the change in regime—much less predict the magnitude of their impact upon regime persistence.

5. The presence or absence of a democratic tradition. That states in Latin America and southern Europe are 'long-established' and have more of a 'historical tradition of democracy' than states of eastern Europe and the former Soviet Union is an interesting point and one we also made in the article. But there is tremendous regional variation here between, say, Chile (which has a long tradition) and El Salvador (which doesn't have one at all). What is more controversial is to assume that the mere duration of a previous democracy is of major importance. Paraguay or Bolivia may have had a few more years of it than, say, Romania or Albania, but so what? 'Porous boundaries' between authoritarian pasts and liberalized presents are not a peculiarity of eastern Europe or the former Soviet Union.[22]

6. Modes of transition. That there have been significant differences in the modes of transition is something that we have written about rather extensively and does not bear repetition here.[23] It is not correct, however, to say that diffusion processes have been con-

---

[22] As for the assumption that transitologists do not pay attention to history, we can only assume that Bunce has not read what we and our collaborators have written about specific cases.

[23] 'Modes of Transition in Latin America, Southern and Eastern Europe,' *International Social Science Journal*, 128 (May 1991): 269–84. Bunce claims on unspecified grounds that we have miscoded Bulgaria. Fine, since we did indicate in the above article that all our codings of the eastern cases were tentative and subject to improvement by country specialists. The only reason that we are puzzled is because Schmitter gave a series of lectures in Sofia last year and all his respondents were fully agreed that the transition there unequivocally was in the 'imposed' category.

fined to eastern Europe. Spaniards were quite aware of what had just happened to Portugal, and there was an enormous feedback effect within and across regions in southern Europe, Latin America and, especially, central America. Admittedly, as we mentioned quite explicitly, the issues of national liberation/secession and geo-strategic location in the international system have had a quite different salience in the different regions—although there is some considerable overlap between central America and eastern Europe in these regards.

7. The transitional agenda. That the 'most striking contrast' is the simultaneity and asynchrony of transformation processes is precisely what we said in our original article. But we caution against assuming that change in southern Europe and Latin America (and central America, in particular) has been 'circumscribed' to the merely political. Although the timing has generally been more sequential, some of these countries have also grappled with major reforms in their industrial structures and export portfolios, role of the state, sectoral balances of interest, and even property rights and class structures. In central America, many of these issues have arisen simultaneously, just as in eastern Europe. Nicaragua, for example, has probably had to face almost the same range of problems as, say, Romania—with just as little success. In short, as in so many other aspects, the eastern and the southern cases, while obviously very different, are not so distinct as Bunce assumes. They overlap and that is precisely what provides such an interesting potential for interregional conceptualization and comparison.

8. The role of elites versus masses. Bunce claims: 'Central to the approach of Schmitter, Karl, O'Donnell and their associates is the assertion that elites are central and publics peripheral. Thus, transitions to democracy are understood to be elite affairs and the more elite the better.' But this is an oversimplification of the original O'Donnell/Schmitter argument; it does not take into account the work of other 'transitologists' who have a different view; and it falsely confuses an *observation* about the role of elites with a *preference* for this role.

O'Donnell and Schmitter argued that mass publics were essential at the start of a transition when 'the resurrection of civil society' was so often the major factor in forcing elites to go beyond their limited intentions of liberalization, but such publics tended to get demobilized as democratization proceeded—an observation born out in a number of case studies.[24] Karl subsequently claimed that the role of masses was greater in certain types of transitions (transition through 'reform' and transition through 'revolution') but that such transitions were both rare and generally unsuccessful in Latin America—largely due to the role of the US in circumscribing them during the cold war.[25] Once the external constraint of a hegemonic power is removed, it is reasonable to hypothesize that reformist transitions, characterized by a greater mass involvement, could become more likely.

Where we simply disagree is with Bunce's assertion (buttressed by a citation to Daniel Friedheim and Sidney Tarrow, footnote 30) concerning the allegedly key role of mass publics in the entire transition process. This is not a resolved issue; in fact, there is still a great deal of on-going controversy about it among scholars working on southern Europe and Latin America. Moreover, adding eastern Europe and the former Soviet Union to the sample does

[24] Guillermo O'Donnell and Philippe Schmitter, *op. cit.*

[25] See Terry Lynn Karl, 'Dilemmas of Democratization in Latin America,' *Comparative Politics*, 23/1 (Oct. 1990): 1–23.

not establish that masses were 'really' more important than elites.[26] Our impression is to the contrary: the more distance one gains from the eastern transitions, the more apparent it is becoming that key elements of the dominant elite within the ancien regime have not only survived the change in regime but may even have anticipated and contributed to it. If true (and Bunce hints in footnote 9 that it is so), this would bring at least some of these cases much more into line with those of the south—no matter how normatively distasteful this may be!

9. Predicting the future. Finally, we have been accused of being excessively pessimistic and of exaggerating the difficulties that neo-democracies in eastern Europe have to face—which is an 'artifact produced by measuring the east against the southern standard.' Since we doubt that this conclusion could be drawn exclusively from our article in *Slavic Review*, we assume that it must be based on Bunce's reading of some other literature on transitology.[27] We find this puzzling. On the one hand, our observation that some countries in the east are likely to survive the transition (that is, not revert back to the previous form of autocracy) but not be able to produce more than a 'hybrid' regime is not derived from applying southern standards of democracy to eastern Europe; indeed, the very notion of persistently 'unconsolidated democracies' was generated from observations concerning the southern countries.

On the other hand, the 'possibilistic' approach originating with O'Donnell and Schmitter, and Karl's subsequent claim that there may be no preconditions for democracy, has much more often been criticized as excessively 'voluntaristic' and hence optimistic. This is especially true because many of the countries of the south and the east lack one or more or all of the so-called 'structural requisites for democracy' that dominated the previous literature. It is, however, one thing to assert that most of these countries are 'condemned' to democracy for the foreseeable future because no other regime type seems to be credible and because so many international forces seem to be prepared to come to its aid. It is quite another to point out that very few of them will succeed in the short-run in consolidating a type of democracy whose benefits they will be able to enjoy. Whether this is being optimistic or pessimistic, or merely realistic is a judgement that we leave to the reader.

In sum, we have argued the following: first, the tactic of pitting comparative analysis against area studies was deployed by Bunce and not by us. It is a red herring. In principle there need not be any contradiction between area studies and the larger field of comparative politics, provided that both are firmly anchored in a common effort at theory-building, operationalization of concepts and solid empirical research. Second, both intra-regional and

---

[26] It is impossible to resist a comment on Bunce's assertion that in eastern Europe there has been no demobilization during the transition. If there is one theme that has repeatedly been mentioned to Schmitter during his trips to eastern Europe it is precisely this—not just the demobilization of various mass publics (women in particular) but, even more, of intellectuals! Whether this has been a good or a bad thing as far as the overall democratization process is concerned is another matter, although *pace* Bunce we have never argued that this contributes positively. We have simply pointed to the almost universal fact of demobilization and the ways in which this affects the choice of institutions, the outcome of elections and the advent of widespread *desencanto* with democracy. For a discussion of this point in Hungary, see Laszlo Bruszt and David Stark, 'Remaking the Political Field in Hungary,' *Journal of International Affairs*, 45/1 (Summer 1991): 201–45.

[27] Bunce does cite Schmitter's 'Dangers and Dilemmas of Democracy,' *Journal of Democracy*, 5/2 (Apr. 1994): 57–75, where it is specifically observed that very few neo-democracies have reverted to autocracy and that the real issue is not the survival but the consolidation of democracy.

cross-regional comparisons are essential to the process of theory building, but cross-regional comparisons which incorporate the experiences of eastern Europe have some distinct advantages for addressing many of the theoretical issues predominant in the study of democratization today. Such comparisons should be encouraged, not discouraged. Third, that interesting and, at times, novel lessons will emerge from this work seems already apparent through the efforts of so many eastern European and Russian specialists to apply the concepts, assumptions and hypotheses of 'transitology.'

The generic issue which remains—once the unnecessary polemics are over—is an important one. Which is the better strategy: should the scholars of post-communist transitions rely primarily on the unique cultural, structural or behavioral features inherited from the 'marxist-leninist-stalinist' past in their effort to understand what the outcomes of these momentous transformations will be? Or, should they focus on a more generic set of issues and utilize primarily non-area-specific concepts that presume a less historically constrained range of choices and hence a greater autonomy for actors? When and where the study of contemporary democratization is concerned, we still most emphatically favor the second strategy.

36 Paper Curtains and Paper Tigers

Valerie Bunce

I have three areas of disagreement with Schmitter and Karl. The first involves their interpretation[1] of what *I* argue in 'Should Transitologists Be Grounded?'[2] The second involves our different readings of what *they* argue in 'The Conceptual Travels of Transitologists and Consolidologists: How Far to the East Should They Attempt to Go?'[3] All of this leads in turn to a final area of disagreement. They see significant benefits in utilizing the transitological approach, whereas I am more skeptical.

What I do and don't argue

Do I reject cross-regional comparisons of transitions from authoritarian rule—as Karl and Schmitter repeatedly claim in this issue of *Slavic Review?* I do not. Let the final three sentences of 'Should Transitologists' serve to settle this matter:

Third, there are substantial differences between the east and the south, and this creates far more problems for comparing the two than Schmitter and Karl recognize. Finally, there are nonetheless some good reasons to engage in such comparisons. The most important reason, however, is not addressed by Schmitter and Karl: the ways in which the addition of eastern Europe to comparative studies of democratization alerts us to fundamental problems in how transitologists have understood and analyzed transitions from authoritarian rule—in the east and, one could argue, in the south as well.

What I argued, then, is that while such cross-regional comparisons evidence certain problems, they are, nonetheless, valuable precisely because they serve the very functions that Schmitter and Karl delineate; that is, hypothesis-testing, identification of new issues and new relationships and the like. Indeed, these functions, along with the more over-arching one of assessing the very worth of transitological approaches and large 'n' cross-regional studies of democratization, is precisely why I offered such a comparison myself. Moreover, as I argued in 'Should Transitologists,' this is the primary rationale for utilizing a different

Republished, with minor abbreviations, from *Slavic Review*, 54/4 (Winter 1995), 979–87, by kind permission of the author and the American Association for the Advancement of Slavic Studies.

[1] See previous chapter. In the text, this will be cited as 'From an Iron Curtain.'

[2] *Slavic Review*, 54/1 (Spring 1995): 11–127. Hereafter, this will be cited in the text as 'Should Transitologists.'

[3] See Philippe C. Schmitter with Terry Lynn Karl, 'The Conceptual Travels of Transitologists and Consolidologists: How Far to the East Should They Attempt to Go?' *Slavic Review*, 53/1 (Spring 1994): 173–85. In the discussion that follows, this article will be referred to as 'The Conceptual Travels.'

systems design—a rationale that I even recognized when imprisoned behind the veil of ignorance of Soviet studies.[4]

Why, then, in another recent article[5] do I state a preference for intra-regional comparisons of postcommunist transformations over cross-regional comparisons? There are four reasons. First, a different systems design is employed when: (1) there are strong reasons to argue that very different systems produce what seem to be similar outcomes; (2) the research question involves explaining the existence of these unexpected similarities, and (3) the explanation for these similarities can be presumed to lie outside system-level factors, given the existence of different systems, yet similar results. The problem with applying this logic to democratization in the east and the south—as I elaborated in 'Should Transitologists'—is that I have doubts about whether the first precondition is met. I am not convinced that we are safe in assuming that transitions from authoritarianism in the south produce the same outcome as the processes involved in leaving state socialism. If we cannot make such a claim, then the logic behind such comparisons is violated. The end result is that there will be too much variance—in independent *and* dependent variables—to narrow down the field of explanation to a reasonable number of plausible factors.

Second, there are some problems inherent to the exercise of carrying out comparative research involving a very large number of cases.[6] In particular, it becomes all too easy to make coding mistakes; to force diverse countries into predetermined categories that do not fit them; and/or to imbue coding categories with such flexibility that, while every case then fits, the imprecision of the categories is such that the meaning of observed relationships cannot be easily interpreted. Moreover, all of these problems, as I argued in 'Should Transitologists,' seem to surface in cross-regional comparisons of transitions from authoritarian rule that involve, in particular, a large number of cases. Thus, two problems present themselves when comparing the east and the south. One is the limits of comparability, and the other is the cost of working with large samples.[7]

Third, it might very well be the case that we have already reaped most of the benefits to be had from comparing a very large number of cases involving transitions from authoritarian rule. For example, such comparisons have already alerted us to the considerable differences between the east and the south; sensitized us to issues that need more attention in the analysis of the east and the south; and exposed the limitations of the transitions approach as developed by Philippe C. Schmitter, Guillermo O'Donnell, Laurence Whitehead, Terry Lynn Karl and others.

This leads us to the final reason: the advantages in general and in this situation in

---

[4] See Valerie Bunce, *Do New Leaders Make a Difference: Executive Succession Under Communism and Capitalism.* (Princeton University Press, 1981). This is why I find Karl and Schmitter's spirited defense of the value of cross-regional comparisons in general and their footnote 9 ('From An Iron Curtain') to be so puzzling.

[5] 'Comparing East and South,' *Journal of Democracy*, 6/3 (July 1995): 87–100.

[6] Karl and Schmitter, therefore, seem to conflate three issues in their response: cross-regional comparisons in general, large sample cross-regional comparisons dealing with democratization in the south and east and, finally, small sample cross-regional comparisons dealing with democratization in the south and east. My position on each of these three issues varies, as this reply will make clear.

[7] This is not to mention another problem—sample selection. As every social scientist knows, the conclusions we draw in our investigations rest heavily on the cases we select—and the cases we leave out. In large sample studies (which are not usually based in fact on sampling), the decisions to exclude some cases and include others can have enormous consequences for the arguments that can be and are made.

particular of engaging in intra-regional comparisons. Such comparisons allow us to get around the problems I have just noted. They allow us to strike a useful balance between the benefits of comparison—that is, the ability to control some factors while exploring variation—and the benefits of working with good data and precise categories. If done well (which depends, among other things, upon the questions addressed and their relationship to the selection of the cases), such comparisons can yield robust arguments. To this must be added the particular appeal of comparing the postcommunist countries with each other. They are of a sufficient number to allow for sophisticated sample construction (twenty-seven countries in all); they share a similar economic, political and social history as a consequence of the homogenizing effects of state socialism;[8] they evidence many similarities in their agendas of transformation; and they break down into useful clusters of similarities and differences with respect to a number of key variables (for instance, geopolitical and international economic location, level of social and economic development, patterns of politically relevant social cleavages, the degree of mass mobilization during the transitional period, degree of 'breakage' with the state socialist past, extent of economic and political liberalization prior to the end of communist party hegemony, ethnic diversity, approach to the economic transformation, age of the state and the like).

But does all this mean that there is no justification for engaging in either single case analysis or comparisons across regions when analyzing the process of democratization? The answer in both cases is obviously no. Single case studies have considerable value—in testing hypotheses, in tracing processes and in developing new concepts. Moreover, they can supply us with much-needed data, and they can help us make sense of a particularly puzzling situation. At the same time, there are some very good reasons to compare across regions—especially if the cases are selected for good reasons *and* if they are kept reasonably small in number.[9]

Thus, what I am arguing is that: (1) the question being posed should guide the research strategy (as I argued in 'Comparing East and South'); (2) good research can be conducted on an individual case, multiple cases within regions and multiple cases across regions; (3) the substantial differences between the east and the south render such comparisons, especially if conducted with a large number of countries, highly problematic, and (4) the post-communist cases represent an unusually optimal laboratory for controlled comparisons. To state a preference for intra-regional comparisons, therefore, is merely to argue that life is short, and these comparisons seem to promise the best payoffs.

There are several other issues where Schmitter and Karl seem to misread me. One is that I never argued that transitions in eastern Europe are without demobilization of the population. The other is that I do not reduce the collapse of state socialism in eastern Europe—in the articles in question or in any of my other work—to what they characterize in 'From an

---

[8] Indeed, this is why 'region' for eastern Europe is less a 'cultural construct' waiting to be deconstructed (as Karl and Schmitter argue in 'From an Iron Curtain') than a meaningful summary of an interwoven set of political, economic and social characteristics. By contrast, the diverse histories of countries in Latin America and southern Europe render the category, region, far less meaningful as a summary term.

[9] See, for example, Zoran Zic, 'Democratic Transition and Self-Determination in Multiethnic Societies: The Different Cases of Spain and the Former Yugoslavia.' Paper presented at the Nineteenth European Studies Conference, University of Nebraska at Omaha, October 5–7, 1994; Hector Schamis, 'Re-forming the State: The Politics of Privatization in Chile and Britain' (Ph.D. dissertation, Columbia University, 1994).

Iron Curtain' as ' . . . a single-minded emphasis on the role of the Soviet Union.' Instead, I see the Soviet role in 1989 as a necessary but not sufficient condition for the collapse of state socialism in 1989 (just as I see developments in eastern Europe in the 1970s and 1980s as a necessary but not sufficient condition for the event that preceded the end of communist regimes in eastern Europe; that is, the introduction of the Gorbachev reforms). Indeed, my understanding of the Soviet role in the collapse of state socialism is a good deal more subtle than Karl and Schmitter's portrayal of this 'international factor.' As I argued in 1984,[10] the very serious economic and political problems developing in the Soviet Union and eastern Europe (problems which *many* specialists in the field had been addressing for some years— as the voluminous footnotes in that article testify) reflected the interaction between the domestic political economy of these systems and the regional political economy—or the Soviet bloc. What this interaction did over time was to undercut legitimacy and stability, undermine economic performance, render eastern Europe an enormous burden on the Soviet Union, generate repeated pressures for major reforms at the domestic and regional levels and, as a result, undermine the very regimes and the bloc that these structures were supposed to support. State socialism, in short, was hoist on its own petard.

What they do and don't argue

In 'From an Iron Curtain,' Karl and Schmitter contend that it is 'pure invention' on my part to characterize them as hostile to area studies. My response is as follows. I am well aware of the fact that Schmitter and Karl are area specialists—as I duly noted in 'Should Transitologists' when I referred to the important contributions Schmitter, for example, has made as an area specialist to comparative theory. The same could also he said, of course, about Terry Lynn Karl. Moreover, I know that they have done a great deal to nurture their area studies. However, the issue at hand is not the position they have taken on area studies in their professional lives as a whole, but, rather, their position on this question as articulated in *Slavic Review*. What these two articles delineate is a position that: (1) points to a clear contrast between area and comparative scholarship (note, for instance, the divide they construct separating 'particular/cultural and ideational properties' as explanation in area scholarship versus 'generic/structural properties' as explanation in comparative politics; (2) states a clear preference for the latter mode of analysis over the former and, thus (given their definitions), for comparative work over area scholarship (see, for instance, their final paragraph in 'From An Iron Curtain'), and (3) makes the recommendation that area scholars give up their assumption that their country or their region is unique and, instead, embrace comparative theory and incorporate comparative cases (particularly those lying outside their region) into their studies.

As already noted in 'Should Transitologists,' I have a number of problems with each of these arguments. To reiterate briefly: the wall they construct separating area studies assumptions and approaches from those of comparative scholarship is in practice quite porous; area scholars for the most part merely assume that places matter and that scholars need expertise to understand what is going on in those places (and do not assume uniqueness—contrary to

[10] 'The Empire Strikes Back: The Transformation of the Eastern Bloc from a Soviet Asset to a Soviet Liability,' *International Organization*, 39 (Winter 1984/1985), 1–46. Also see my earlier article: 'The Political Economy of the Brezhnev Era: The Rise and Fall of Corporatism,' *British Journal of Political Science*, 13 (January 1983), 129–58.

what Karl and Schmitter argue in 'From an Iron Curtain' when they assert that 'area studies were born in the untested notion that specific geocultural regions were somehow "unique"'); each approach, even as they have defined it, has its strengths and weaknesses; and quite strong arguments can be made in support of area specialists teaching comparativists, as well as vice versa (the latter being their sole focus).

I suspect, however, that what is really at issue here—and what explains our different readings of the same text—is not so much the general question of area studies versus comparative analysis, but, rather, the specific case of communist and postcommunist area studies versus comparative analysis. What Schmitter and Karl seem to be arguing in fact is that area specialists working on the eastern half of Europe are the problem, and expanding their comparative horizons the solution. As they argue in this issue:

The field of communist studies . . . has long suffered a partially self-imposed isolation from the major social science disciplines. While this has also been true, to some extent, for other area study programs, it has been especially pronounced among US-based scholars who explicitly argued that communist systems were so distinctive as to preclude comparison.

They then go on (as they did in their earlier piece) to call on young and old specialists in the region to expand their comparative and theoretical horizons.

My response to this is: where is the evidence? Two citations are presented. One is a recent article by George Breslauer, where the focus is on the historical development of Soviet studies in the west, not the development of communist studies; where the concern is with what might have been done in terms of methods and theories versus what was done in the Soviet field; and where no systematic evidence is presented (because that is not his interest) on the differences between the evolution of Soviet studies versus the development of other area studies.[11] The other citation is a book edited by Frederic Fleron.[12] While Fleron does call for more methodological and theoretical sophistication (a call which is hardly unique to communist area studies), he does so, one must emphasize, in a book that: (1) was published in 1969, and (2) contains a large number of articles dealing with comparative theory and written by area specialists in the communist field. If one traces developments in the communist area field after 1969, moreover, one is struck by the fact that most of the scholars working in this field—particularly those who were trained from the late 1960s onward—defined themselves as comparativists and carried out research that testified to the accuracy of that self-designation.

The characterization of communist area studies as having been isolated from comparative politics, then, makes little sense, as does the conjoined claim that this was a problem for communist area studies in particular.[13] Perhaps Karl and Schmitter's argument needs to be

[11] 'In Defense of Sovietology,' *Post-Soviet Affairs*, 3 (1992), 197–238.

[12] See *Communist Studies and the Social Sciences: Essays on Methodology and Empirical Theory* (Chicago: Rand McNally, 1969).

[13] There is no definitive way to draw a conclusion as to whether communist area studies was more isolated from the comparative 'mainstream' than other area studies. At the very least, however, we cannot answer this question by comparing what was published in *Slavic Review* versus the *Latin American Research Review* (see footnote 8 in 'From an Iron Curtain'). This is because most of the major debates in the communist field and most of the comparative work done in this field was not published in *Slavic Review*. Moreover, for a variety of reasons, *Slavic Review* has tended to focus for the most part on Russia and the Soviet Union and not on eastern Europe.

reformulated to read: the major social science disciplines have long suffered a partially self-imposed isolation from communist studies.

Equally puzzling is their assertion that: 'What seems to be overlooked by Bunce is how much change had occurred in the practices—if not in the academic models—of "state socialism" and "totalitarianism" *before* (emphasis in the original) the transition began' ('From an Iron Curtain'). First, it would be highly surprising if I overlooked this, since I was one of the many in the field who was engaged from the 1970s onward in analyzing all those changes taking place in these systems—for instance, the decline of terror; conflict within the party, especially at the highest levels; the development of particular types of interest groups (even a version of corporatism!) and a particular type of civil society; the development of protest groupings; the expansion of trade and cultural contacts between east and west; and the introduction of economic reforms. Second, it is precisely these and other changes that led many of us to move from calling these systems totalitarian to using the more accurate term, state socialism—a term which Karl and Schmitter seem to misunderstand. Finally, if these changes were widely recognized and led to a proliferation of new studies (which they did), then why all the hubbub about the 'comparative backwardness'—so to speak—of communist area studies? After all, what this 'new thinking' did in practice was to build bridges between communist studies and comparative politics—bridges which, apparently, managed to run in only one direction.

If specialists in communist studies were for the most part comparativists as well by, say, 1975, then this is even more the case in 1995. Let me take as one example my experience over the past few years of reading book manuscripts by younger scholars in the field and working with a large number of students in this area in special seminars offered to advanced graduate students at the University of Toronto (on post-Soviet politics) and the Wilson Center (on eastern and central Europe and southeastern Europe). I cannot think of a single case where the graduate student or young scholar in question: (1) lacked training in comparative as well as in area studies; (2) wrote articles, dissertation chapters or books that were devoid of comparative theory, or (3) assumed a priori the uniqueness of the postcommunist experience.[14]

Thus, in misrepresenting the field, then and now, Karl and Schmitter have managed to identify problems and deficiencies which for the most part do not exist. At the same time, they have used this misrepresentation to manufacture dichotomous choices which also are hard to find in the real world; to treat certain scholars as exceptional when they are in fact representative of the field; and to proffer unneeded advice. It is for all these reasons that I characterized them in 'Should Transitologists' as hostile to communist area studies and patronizing in their tone.

---

[14] The key term here (which is used several times by Karl and Schmitter in 'From an Iron Curtain') is 'a priori.' First, the general tendency among scholars in the field has been to presume some similarities and some differences when comparing east and south, or east and west. Blanket statements about uniqueness, in short, are exceedingly rare. Second, while some established social scientists in the field might argue for uniqueness (such as Kenneth Jowitt—as remarked in footnote 7 in 'From an Iron Curtain'), they do so *in a bounded way, after* making some comparisons and, finally, *while* using comparative theory in order to pinpoint distinctive characteristics. Finally, my claim that eastern Europe has important differences from Latin America and southern Europe rests on a comparison of the three areas. It is simply incorrect, then, to characterize these arguments as either 'a priori' or blanket assertions of uniqueness.

The Merits of Transitology

This leads us to the final and most important issue: the merits of transitology. Here, we do not misread each other. Karl and Schmitter have a more positive evaluation of this approach than I do. I do not think that we need to repeat the arguments that each of us has made. The reader can render a judgment.

However, I would like to make the following points. First, in questioning the transitological approach I do not reject, by any means, all of the work that has been done on the south employing some notion of transitions from authoritarian rule. I, like many of my colleagues in the postcommunist field, have learned a great deal from this work and, no doubt, will continue to do so in the future. What concerns me, instead (as I discussed at length in 'Should Transitologists'), are the many problems I have with this approach, especially as it was most succinctly presented by Guillermo O'Donnell and Philippe C. Schmitter in *Transitions from Authoritarian Rule: Tentative Conclusions About Uncertain Democracies.*[15] One such problem that I did not mention in that article is the generation of arguments which appear to be major insights, but which are little more than common knowledge.

Second, Karl and Schmitter did not address in their response the criticisms I made with respect to: (1) the near absence of hypotheses in the transitological literature; (2) the problem of coding modes of transition as either popular mobilization or pacting; (3) the tension between seeing democracy as an outcome versus a process; (4) the problem of assuming interests in the postcommunist cases, and (5) the difficulties surrounding the concept of consolidation.

Third, what they see as variations on the same theme I still see as quite different—for example, the equation of the American empire in the Caribbean versus the Soviet empire in eastern Europe and the latter's manifestation as a hierarchical regional bloc or the equation of ethnic diversity in Brazil (an old state which is still standing and where ethnic mobilization is limited)[16] versus the nature of ethnic diversity in, say, the *former* Yugoslavia and the *former* Soviet Union.[17]

Fourth, I do not find their arguments about 'abnormal' politics in the transition period or about the 'possibilistic' character of transition dynamics to be a very convincing defense of the theoretical rigor of the transitological approach.[18]

Finally, I question the value of searching for a general theory of recent democratization. My sense is that we—like so many social scientists before us—are unlikely to get very far in such an endeavor. Moreover, to attempt to do so seems to me to have its costs. One such cost is designing arguments that are so theoretically flexible that they explain in fact very little, and the other is coding cases in such a way that they are crammed into ill-fitting categories. However, scholars differ on the relative pros and cons of constructing big theory. This is, ultimately, a matter of intellectual taste.

[15] Baltimore: Johns Hopkins University Press, 1986.

[16] See Rodolfo Stavenhagen, 'Challenging the Nation State in Latin America.' *Journal of International Affairs*, 45 (Winter 1992), 421–40.

[17] This does not mean, however, that such cases cannot be compared. What I am arguing is that such comparisons must be built around explicit recognition of the differences, as well as the existence of some relatively superficial similarities.

[18] This is particularly the case, since other cases of abnormal politics—for example, revolution and reform—have received quite sophisticated theoretical treatment.

37 Regime Transition, Uncertainty, and Prospects for Democratization: The Politics of Russia's Regions in a Comparative Perspective

Vladimir Gelman

....

Early in their seminal book on regime transition, O'Donnell and Schmitter raise the issue of transition from certain authoritarian rule to uncertain 'something else',[1] which could be democracy or a new authoritarian regime. Despite this degree of uncertainty, almost all works in this field are based on some kind of 'iron law of democratization'. Explicitly or implicitly, this type of research has been based on teleological schemes of political development. According to such an approach, all transitions will sooner or later achieve democracy (at least in Dahl's 'procedural' sense) as the final goal of political development. But there are no well-founded reasons why this should be so, save for macro-historical speculation. This kind of historical teleology seems similar to a pure Marxist-Leninist paradigm of historical materialism. In this article I choose an alternative paradigmatic approach to analysing regime transition—one that views it as a kind of open-ended process. At least, we know the point of departure (authoritarianism), but there is no way of knowing a priori the point of arrival.

Speaking purely in functional terms, the process of regime transition (i.e. the shift from one political regime to another), regardless of the regime type itself, includes several stages: (1) the decline of the previously existing 'ancien regime'; (2) its breakdown; (3) some kind of uncertainty in all components of the political regime; (4) the outcome of uncertainty, meaning the establishment of a new political regime; (5) institutionalisation of a new political regime (regardless of whether it is a 'democracy' or 'something else'). Paradigmatic differences between 'transition to democracy'[2] and an 'open-ended' transition are shown in Table 37.1.

The crucial points in the process of regime transition are stages 2 and 4—the breakdown of the 'ancien regime' (i.e. 'entry' into uncertainty) and the installation of the new regime (i.e. 'exit' from or 'outcome' of uncertainty). This 'gap' of uncertainty radically differs from the 'transition to democracy' model, where the installation of democracy results from the breakdown of the authoritarian regime 'by default'.

An abbreviated version of an article first published in *Europe-Asia Studies*, 51/6 (1999), 939–56. Reproduced by kind permission of the author and Carfax Publishers Ltd.

[1] Guillermo O'Donnell and Philippe Schmitter, *Transitions from Authoritarian Rule: Tentative Conclusions about Uncertain Democracies* (Baltimore and London: Johns Hopkins University Press, 1986), 3.

[2] See Dankwart Rustow, 'Transitions to Democracy: Toward a Dynamic Model,' *Comparative Politics*, 2/3 (1970), 337–63; O'Donnell and Schmitter, *Transitions from Authoritarian Rule*.

Table 37.1 **Stages of regime transition: 'transition to democracy' and 'open-ended' models**

Transition to democracy	Open-ended model
1. Liberalisation	1. Decline of ancien regime
2. Transition = installation of democracy	2. Breakdown of ancien regime
3. Consolidation	3. Uncertainty
	4. Outcome of uncertainty = installation of new regime
	5. Institutionalisation of new regime

Table 37.2 **Modes of transition (and degree of uncertainty)**

Actor/strategies	Compromise	Force
Elites	Pact (Low)	Imposition (Middle)
Masses	Reform (Middle)	Revolution (High)

Source: Terry Lynn Karl and Philippe Schmitter, 'Models of Transition in Latin America, Southern and Eastern Europe'. *International Social Science Journal,* 43/128 (1991), 275.

Uncertainty is a principal stage of transition, which is distinct from uncertainties in stable regimes. As Bunce noted, the distinction is that within authoritarian regimes the positions of actors are more or less certain, yet the institutions are ill-defined (or uncertain). In democratic polities, however, the institutions are defined (or certain), while the positions of actors are uncertain or, at least, not defined a priori. During the transition period, both these elements of political regimes—actors' positions and institutions—are uncertain to varying degrees.[3]

The variations of uncertainty are more clearly understood in connection with the use of different models of transition after the breakdown of the ancien regime employed by Karl and Schmitter.[4] They provide a four-cell matrix of ideal types of modes of transition, using as variables (1) types of actors who play a crucial role in the transition processes and (2) their use of strategies during the transition period.

As one can see in Table 37.2, these four modes of transition differ significantly in their degree of uncertainty. Pacts tend to be minimally uncertain, while revolutions provide large-scale (and, usually, long-run) uncertainty, connected with mass uprising and public violence.

The key characteristics of this uncertainty are the uncertain position of actors and the institution-free environment. Therefore, actors are free to fight for domination within the polity using all means for power maximisation, but not for the creation of democracy. The

---

[3] Valerie Bunce, 'Elementy neopredelennosti v perekhodnyi period', *Polis,* 1 (1993), 44–51.

[4] Terry Lynn Karl and Philippe Schmitter, 'Models of Transition in Latin America, Southern and Eastern Europe,' *International Social Science Journal,* 43/128 (1991), 275.

period of uncertainty in Russia's national politics gives clear evidence of this process. After the transition by imposition in August 1991, and until the violent outcome of uncertainty in October 1993, the struggle for the dominant position between rival actors—first between Gorbachev and Yeltsin, and then between Yeltsin and the Supreme Soviet—can hardly be regarded as a 'transition to democracy' in the sense of the normative theories. Even those politicians who call themselves 'democrats' have no intention of losing their positions and being replaced by other actors.

Such rational actors would reject the idea of competitive democracy, which needs the establishment of formal institutions for free and fair political competition, and threatens the loss (or at least limitation) of their powers. Indeed, the maximisation of one's own powers and the minimisation (or at least reduction) of the powers of any other actors who potentially could challenge one's position, fulfils a rational actor's strategy in a stage of uncertainty. For certain regimes, this strategy is limited either by institutions (in democratic regimes) or by other actors' opportunities, such as their positions or resources (in authoritarian regimes). During a period of uncertainty actors either have no institutional limitations or have insufficient information about other actors' resources. If one actor has enough resources to overwhelm others, it simply tries to assume the position of the dominant actor. This position means an absence of limitations on the 'leader' due to the relative weaknesses of other actors. If the resources of several actors are more or less equal, their struggle for survival could develop in the form of bargaining, if actors use a compromise strategy, or, in the case of the use of force, in the form of permanent violent conflict, such as Hobbes's 'war of all against all'.

A period of uncertainty—even large-scale and long-run—cannot exist forever, though. This stage inevitably comes to a conclusion in one way or another. The outcome (or exit) out of uncertainty could be regarded as a kind of reaction to the entry into uncertainty. Thus, partial use of the Karl and Schmitter schema of modes of transition engenders the development of a matrix similar to Table 37.2 that focuses on scenarios of outcomes of uncertainty. Variables in such a matrix include (1) the position of actors and (2) their use of strategies during the period of outcome of uncertainty (see Table 37.3).

The first of four possible outcomes of uncertainty, 'war of all against all', is an actor's decision about outcomes but does not yet qualify as a true 'exit' from uncertainty. If actors use force strategies when no one actor possesses overwhelming resources, the 'war of all against all' will continue, probably evolving into new forms. The 'warlordism' described by Kirkow in Primorsky *krai*[5] is the typical result of such a scenario. If in addition actors use

Table 37.3 **Scenarios of outcomes of uncertainty**

Positions of actors/strategies of actors	Compromise	Force
Dominant actor	Elite settlement	Winner takes all
Uncertainty or balance of forces	Struggle over the rules	War of all against all

[5] Peter Kirkow, 'Regional Warlordism in Russia: The Case of Primorskii Krai,' *Europe-Asia Studies*, 47/6 (1995), 923–47.

mass mobilisation or even external intervention as a weapon in such a struggle, this scenario tends to take the form of civil war. The case of the Chechen war is clearest in this respect. Nevertheless, from the viewpoint of new regime installation, this scenario of outcome of uncertainty cannot be regarded as a unit for future analysis. A second scenario could be realised if the one actor employed a force strategy better than others and achieved the position of dominant actor. The result of this scenario is a dominant actor victory in a zero-sum game based on the principle of 'winner takes all'.

The third possible scenario of outcome of uncertainty could be developed as a result of an explicit or implicit agreement between the dominant actor and other actors over the common acceptance of institutions that secured their current positions. This scenario is called an 'elite settlement', the term employed by Higley and other authors.[6] Finally, uncertainty or balance of force among actors, as well as danger of defeat in zero-sum conflict, incline them to use of formal institutions as 'weapons' in the struggle for survival. The regular use of democratic and/or legal institutions as such weapons makes them inevitable. This outcome could be regarded as a 'struggle over the rules', quite the opposite of 'war of all against all' (i.e. struggle without formal rules).

The matrix proposed is simply an analytical tool; in practice the outcome of uncertainty and installation of a new regime could combine features of the different scenarios. For instance, Russia's national political regime after the events of October 1993 was installed as a combination of the 'winner takes all' and 'elite settlement' scenarios. Yet, looking at some of Russia's regions clearly approaching some of these ideal-types facilitates exposing the logic of underlying different scenarios of outcomes of uncertainty and their impact on new political regimes. This brings us from theoretical considerations to the comparative analysis of Russia's regional political regimes.

Scenarios of outcomes of uncertainty

'WINNER TAKES ALL'

The causes for the emergence of a dominant actor which maximised its power through the use of force strategies could vary widely. A long duration of uncertainty tends to discredit all political actors. Thus, the opportunities for 'outsider' populists to seize all powers become more viable in cases of electoral contestation. The 1994 emergence of Lukashenka's regime in Belarus, as well as Kirsan Ilyumzhinov's regime in Kalmykia in 1993, are clear examples of this outcome (as to Russian national politics, Zhirinovsky's electoral successes in the 1993 parliamentary elections and Lebed's achievements in the 1996 presidential poll come close to such a scenario). Mass support easily solves any potential problems that might arise due to the abolition or elimination of any institutional limitations on arbitrary rule. The dissolution of parliaments, electoral fraud and limitations on the press elicit protests only from a narrow layer of groups of political activists, who maintain few resources in conditions of mass apathy. It is interesting to note that in the cases of Belarus and Kalmykia various forms of political opposition—i.e. liberals, communists and nationalists—created a negative con-

---

[6] See John Higley and Michael Burton 'Elite Variables in Democratic Transitions and Breakdowns', *American Sociological Review*, 54/1 (1989), 17–32; John Higley and Richard Gunther (eds.), *Elites and Democratic Consolidation in Latin America and Southern Europe* (Cambridge: Cambridge University Press, 1992).

sensus coalition. Without sufficient resistance, populist leaders are able to avoid political competition, even strengthening their positions through a biased set of formal institutions. For example, according to Kalmykia's electoral law, one-third of the deputies of the regional legislature were elected on a non-competitive basis from a list of nominations submitted by the President of Kalmykia; moreover, the election of these deputies was legally valid if this list of candidates passed a minimum threshold of 15 per cent of eligible votes.[7] As a result, populist leaders are able to assert control over the public sphere as a whole, based on traditional rather than rational-legal mechanisms of legitimacy.

The assertion of power by democratically elected executives in new democratic polities[8] is another option for the 'winner takes all' scenario. Political leaders who achieve top executive positions, even through the support of democratic parties or movements, attempt to avoid horizontal accountability[9] as well as avoid the danger of electoral defeat. Mass support in an environment without formal institutions is likely to result in power maximisation by the executive, using a combination of different strategies and institutions. The political regime in the city of Moscow is a case of such an assertion of executive power.[10] The emergence of this regime is based on mass support of the mayor (Gavriil Popov and then Yurii Luzhkov) in elections, and a strategy to minimise the influence of alternative actors through public discrediting, administrative damage, and the incorporation of a system of 'municipal capitalism' into the mayoral office. The political stability of this regime is enhanced by mass clientelism, making it easier to form a 'political machine' in the mayoral office, which penetrates all levels of city government and is secured through the electoral legitimacy of the dominant actor as well as the political regime as a whole.

Finally, the assertion of power may result from the decay of the previous political regime owing to long-run and large-scale uncertainty and 'war of all against all'. The case of Saratov *oblast'* is typical in this respect. Ryzhenkov evaluates the political struggle in this region during 1991–96 as 'aspiration for the (re)establishment and assertion of the *obkom* position. This position is characterised by total political, economic and ideological control over the state sector and public life through the establishment of a hierarchical system of government without any control over the governing group'.[11] However, none of the actors in Saratov achieved such a goal. Long-run conflict continued over a period of five years, and all actors' positions were weakened.[12] Under these conditions, most actors were forced to agree to a 'lesser evil' outcome. Since the former vice-mayor of Saratov Dmitrii Ayatskov came to occupy the position of Governor, political competition in Saratov *oblast'* has disappeared completely.

---

[7] Ol'ga Senatova, 'Regional'nyi avtoritarizm na stadii ego stanovleniya', in Tat'yana Zaslavskaya (ed.), *Kuda idet Rossiya? Sotsial'naya transformatsiya postsovetskogo prostranstva* (Moscow: Aspekt-Press, 1996), 150.

[8] See Samuel P. Huntington, 'Democracy for the Long Haul', *Journal of Democracy*, 7/2 (1996), 9–10.

[9] Guillermo O'Donnell, 'Horizontal Accountability in New Democracies,' *Journal of Democracy*, 9/3 (1998), 112–26; O'Donnell, 'Illusions about Consolidation,' *Journal of Democracy*, 7/2 (1996), 43–6.

[10] See Michael Brie, *The Political Regime of Moscow—Creation of a New Urban Machine?* (Berlin: Wissenschaftszentrum Berlin fur Sozialforschung Working Papers, 1997).

[11] Sergei Ryzhenkov, 'Saratovskaya oblast' (1986–1996): politika i politiki', in Kimitaka Matsuzato and Aleksandr Shatilov (eds.), *Regiony Rossii: khronika i rukovoditeli, Tom 2, Rostovskaya Oblast', Saratovskaya Oblast'* (Sapporo, Hokkaido University, Slavic Research Center, Occasional Papers in Slavic-Eurasian World, N34, 1997), 89.

[12] Petra Stykow, *Elite Transformation in the Saratov Region: From Hierarchical Rule of a Monolithic Power Elite to Strategic Interactions of Sectoral Elites* (Berlin: Max-Planck Gesellschaft Arbeitspapiere AG TRAP, N5 1995).

As one can see, despite different causes in the 'winner takes all' scenario of outcome of uncertainty, the outcomes are similar to those scenarios which do not envisage any breakdown of the ancien regime. These types of political regimes have emerged in some Russian republics, such as Tatarstan, where the ancien regime of the late-Soviet period was directly transformed during the post-Soviet period into a power monopoly of the governing elite. Referring to the political development in Brazil, Linz classified these regimes as an 'authoritarian situation' rather than 'authoritarian regime.'[13] The principal distinction here is that the formal institutions of a democratic regime still survive (such as the legislature, legislation, elections or political parties) but have little influence on the decision-making process. The dominant actor faces no obstacles to excluding other actors from the political process and securing direct or indirect control over political life and the media. Any expectations that the dominant actors will disappear in the future have little foundation: under conditions of an absence of real alternatives, successful governments can survive, secure popular support and minimise any evidence of uncontrolled political activity. The emergence of political alternatives through the influence of external actors seems, at the very least, doubtful. The Russian national authorities need stability, loyalty and predictability of regional political regimes more than open political competition with unclear consequences. Such mutual interest of external actors and the regional dominant actor tends to be institutionalised in the form of informal contracts between regional and national authorities (often confirmed by formal agreements). The scheme of 'exchange of loyalty for non-intervention' is the core of these contracts.

Overall, the 'winner takes all' scenario of outcome of uncertainty is likely to enhance the power monopoly of the dominant actor and the supremacy of informal institutions. The consequences of this scenario are the emergence of political regimes with numerous features of authoritarian rule. These regimes could be relatively stable, and the prospects of their democratisation are minimal.

'ELITE SETTLEMENT'

The scenario of 'elite settlement' is close to a 'pact'[14] which includes the reorganisation of elite interests and the achievement of substantial compromises among competing actors over crucial political issues. This perspective is commonly accepted by scholars of political transition who see 'pacts' as the most effective (fast and peaceful) means of democratisation.[15] However, 'pacts' which occur during the breakdown of the ancien regime are quite distinct from agreements achieved among actors simply for the sake of an end to uncertainty. The former (such as the classical Spanish Moncloa Pact) focused on defining formal institutions, such as the rules of public contestation during regime transition. Alternatively, the latter is based on the actors' intentions to secure their positions and thus to consolidate the new regime under conditions minimising competitiveness. In a framework

---

[13] Juan Linz, 'The Future of the Authoritarian Situation or Institutionalization of an Authoritarian Regime: The Case of Brazil', in Alfred Stepan (ed.), *Authoritarian Brazil: Origins, Policies and Future* (New Haven and London: Yale University Press, 1973), 233–54.

[14] See Karl and Schmitter, 'Models of Transition', 275.

[15] See Rustow, 'Transitions to Democracy'; O'Donnell and Schmitter, *Transitions from Authoritarian Rule*; Higley and Burton 'Elite Variables'; Samuel P. Huntington, *The Third Wave. Democratization in the Late Twentieth Century* (Norman, Okla., and London: University of Oklahoma Press, 1991).

of 'transition to democracy' pacts really serve as a mode of democratisation. But the outcome of uncertainty through pact serves to keep democratisation pending, or at least diminishes such unpleasant consequences of democracy as the threat of loss of power through public contestation.

This kind of 'elite settlement' is based on explicit or implicit agreements between the dominant actor and competitors over the sharing of powers, or the sharing of spheres of influence in a political market. Such a strategy is reasonable, even rational,[16] if the dominant actor has insufficient resources or faces other limitations on using a force strategy, while competitors have enough resources for survival but not enough for decisive steps toward their own ascent as dominant actor. Thus, both sides benefit from an 'elite settlement': the dominant actor secures its position, while its competitors receive access to subordinate positions within the governing group.[17] The formation of a 'minimum winning coalition' of dominant and subordinate actors is an immediate result of these pacts. The formation of this coalition has multiple goals, including protection against political outsiders (who are not included in the 'elite settlement') coming in and attaining powerful positions.

Among Russia's regions, the case of Nizhny Novgorod *oblast'* is typical of this scenario.[18] When appointed in 1991, Governor Boris Nemtsov had no influence on regional elites. Nemtsov had to rely on a force strategy, but later achieved several important informal agreements with the majority in the regional legislature, some enterprise directors, and parts of the administrative elite of the region. These subordinate actors were loyal to Nemtsov as the dominant actor, yet acquired greater security in their previous positions. Nemtsov used this strategy to establish more effective regional government performance[19] and for successful conflict resolution within and outside the region that worked to his own benefit. At the same time, political competition among actors was limited. In the 1995 gubernatorial election Nemtsov won easily with an overwhelming majority; his total vote was more than twice that of his closest challenger. In 1997, however, Nemtsov was appointed a first deputy prime minister in the Russian government and left Nizhny Novgorod, thereby undermining the basis of the regional 'elite settlement'.

A scholar in Nizhny Novgorod characterised the main features of the regional political regime under Nemtsov as follows: (1) prevalence of executive authority over the legislature; (2) an informal contract of mutual loyalty between regional and national authorities; (3) indirect control of regional authorities over the media; (4) neutralisation or limitation of real or potential centres of political opposition in the region; (5) patronage of regional executives over public associations—both political groups and 'third sector' non-governmental organisations (NGOs)—in exchange for their loyalty.[20] Although he referred

---

[16] See Gary Marks, 'Rational Sources of Chaos in Democratic Transition', *American Behavioral Scientist*, 35/4–5 (1992), 397–421.

[17] William Case, 'Can the "Halfway House" Stand? Semidemocracy and Elite Theory in Three Southeast Asian Countries', *Comparative Politics*, 28/4 (1996), 437–64.

[18] See Vladimir Gel'man, '"Soobshchestvo elit" i predely demokratizatsii'. Nizhegorodskaya Oblast,' *Polis*, 1 (1999), 79–97.

[19] See Kathryn Stoner-Weiss, *Local Heroes: The Political Economy of Russian Regional Governance* (Princeton: Princeton University Press, 1997), esp. pp. 90–130.

[20] Sergei Borisov, 'Postoyannye i peremennye velichiny regional'nogo politicheskogo protsessa do i posle vyborov', in Sergei Borisov (ed.), *Nizhegorodskie vybory-95: novye tendentsii i starye uroki* (Nizhny Novgorod: Izdatel'stvo VVAGS 1996) 37.

to these features as 'regional authoritarianism', the relative autonomy of the legislature and political parties and the absence of explicit violations of political and civil rights provided more grounds for classifying the impact of Nizhny Novgorod's 'elite settlement' on regional politics as a hybrid regime or 'semi-democracy'.[21]

The case of Nizhny Novgorod's 'elite settlement' is not unique among Russian regions. Similar features of elite consolidation and regime transition have been found in Tomsk *oblast'* by Mary McAuley.[22] In his study of elite developments in Omsk *oblast'* Neil Melvin has shown that the basis of an 'elite settlement' between governing groups and the left-patriotic opposition almost approached power sharing: the former won gubernatorial and city of Omsk mayoral elections, while the latter represented the region in the State Duma. As a result, elections did not challenge the positions of the governing group.[23]

The achievement of the 'elite settlement' does not mean, however, the sustainability of the political regime itself. It is challenged by an informal institutionalisation of arbitrary rule that undermines functioning democratic institutions. In the case of Nizhny Novgorod *oblast'*, core decisions about a regional programme of economic reform in 1992 were issued not by the legislature (or by any other formal institution) but by an informal Coordinating Council, which included the executive and legislative heads of the region and city of Nizhny Novgorod. The continuation of these informal practices of decision making provides a precondition for power assertion. An outsider populist, Andrei Kliment'ev, who has a criminal background and was under investigation during the 1998 election, won the mayoral race in the city of Nizhny Novgorod. Owing to victory of the 'wrong' candidate, the regional authorities cancelled the election and called for a new race. Thus, public contestation was limited. Nevertheless, in the next round another challenger won, finally breaking the 'elite settlement'.

This kind of 'elite settlement' is generally fragile, and changes in the balance of actors' resources easily undermine its stability. The breakdown of the 'elite settlement' either results in movement toward an 'authoritarian situation' (if the dominant actor strengthens its position) or 'entry' into a new cycle of uncertainty (if the dominant actor loses its position). For instance, President Murtaza Rakhimov of Bashkortostan remained in his post after a compromise decision among regional elites to increase opportunities for rent-seeking bargains with the Russian Centre. After this goal was achieved, Rakhimov—in one way or another—injured the chances of his political competitors and asserted a power monopoly in the region.[24] In St Petersburg an attempt to form an 'elite settlement' was unsuccessful for other reasons. Mayor Anatolii Sobchak had an informal agreement with a majority of the city's legislature to create for themselves favourable conditions for the mayoral and legislative elections. But those parties and interest groups which were not included in the 'elite settlement' established a negative consensus coalition, which presented a candidate in the

---

[21] See Case, 'Can the "Halfway House" Stand?'.

[22] See Mary McAuley, *Russia's Politics of Uncertainty* (Cambridge: Cambridge University Press, 1997), 156–220.

[23] See Neil Melvin, 'The Consolidation of a New Regional Elite: The Case of Omsk 1987–1995,' *Europe-Asia Studies*, 50/4 (1998), 643.

[24] Igor' Rabinovich and Sergei Fufaev 'Khozyain. Shtrikhi k politicheskomu portretu Murtazy Rakhimova', *Pro et Contra* , 2 (1997), 71–84.

1996 mayoral election. After the victory of the opposition-backed candidate, Sobchak lost his post and a new period of uncertainty had been launched.[25]

The 'elite settlement' scenario of outcome of uncertainty generally includes the sharing of powers between dominant and subordinate actors in order to limit public political contestation and establish the supremacy of informal, rather than formal, institutions. These regimes are fragile and very dependent on changes in the political situation. Speaking more generally, this scenario tends to act as a 'transition' between 'winner takes all' and the following scenario—'struggle over the rules'.

'STRUGGLE OVER THE RULES'

The third scenario of outcome of uncertainty could be described as a transition from 'war of all against all' to 'struggle over the rules'. When force strategies are exhausted, and the level of uncertainty is relatively high, the positions of political actors are threatened, as a result either of defeat in a 'war' or of unsuccessful bargaining over the 'elite settlement'. Therefore, installation of and adherence to formal institutions becomes the only opportunity for actors to survive within a regime. In such a situation, institutions become a 'weapon' for the actors.[26] Moreover, while supremacy of one actor tends to be fixed in the institutional design, uncertainty or balance of forces are likely to lead to the general acceptance of rules which allow actors to avoid the 'winner takes all' outcome.[27]

Political reform during 1994–97 in Udmurtia is a typical case of 'struggle over the rules'. As a local observer noted,

the constitution-making process in the republic was faced with contradictions . . . the compromise decision did not solve tensions between different groups of regional political elites. The prospects for establishing a presidency for the Republic of Udmurtia meant an opportunity for the full victory of one of these groups over its competitors. The outcome of this struggle was unclear, because the two main contenders had more or less equal political potential. Under this uncertainty, the Supreme Soviet of Udmurtia concluded that the rejection of the idea of a presidency would be the best solution of this political problem.[28]

Although one of these contenders, Aleksandr Volkov, was the elected chairman of the regional legislature, he was unable to monopolise power in the region. His attempt to gain control over local government in the region was terminated by a decision of the

---

[25] See Vladimir Gel'man, 'Konsolidatsiya regional'nykh elit i mestnaya demokratiya v Rossii: Sankt-Peterburg v sravnitel'noi perspektive', in Samuil Kugel' (ed.), *Sotsial'nye i politicheskie orientatsii Sankt-Peterburgskoi elity* (St Petersburg: Izdatel'stvo Sankt-Peterburgskogo Universiteta Ekonomiki i Finansov, 1998), 80–1.

[26] Barbara Geddes, 'Initiation of New Democratic Institutions in Eastern Europe and Latin America', in Arend Lijphart and Carlos Waisman (eds.), *Institutional Design in New Democracies. Eastern Europe and Latin America* (Boulder, Colo.: Westview, 1996), 18–19.

[27] See Adam Przeworski, 'Some Problems in the Study of Transition to Democracy', in Guillermo O'Donnell, Philippe Schmitter and Lawrence Whitehead (eds.), *Transitions from Authoritarian Rule: Comparative Perspectives* (Baltimore and London: Johns Hopkins University Press, 1986), 56–61; Adam Przeworski, *Democracy and the Market. Political and Economic Reforms in Eastern Europe and Latin America* (Cambridge: Cambridge University Press, 1991), 51–3.

[28] Igor' Egorov, 'Udmurtskaya Respublika', in Vladimir Gel'man *et al.* (eds.), *Organy gosudarstvennoi vlasti sub"ektov Rossiiskoi Federatsii* (Moscow: Mezhdunarodnyi Institut Gumanitarno-Politicheskikh Issledovanii, 1998), 80.

Constitutional Court of Russia. Therefore, the struggle of elites for power maximisation was 'forced to develop within the constitutional framework'.[29] As one can see, the use of this framework really limited opportunities for the assertion of individual power and preserved opportunities for contestation among actors.

The case of Sverdlovsk *oblast'* demonstrated a more advanced version in the development of the 'struggle over the rules' scenario. The use of formal institutions as 'weapons' here was accompanied by electoral competition among actors. Under the arbitrary rule of a dominant actor, mass politics were based on 'political machines' and administrative mobilisation. Alternatively, the 'struggle over the rules' scenario created an environment for the emergence of a competitive party system. After the 1993 dissolution of the 'Urals republic' and resignation of regional governor Eduard Rossel, regional elites in Sverdlovsk *oblast'* lost their unity, with no actors occupying a dominant position. On the one hand, having lost access to administrative resources, Rossel was forced to use alternative mechanisms of electoral mobilisation for his return to power; he headed his own political party, an organisation labelled a non-party movement, 'Transformation of the Urals'. On the other hand, it is likely that the use of formal rules/institutions underlay the legislative decisions to create political institutions which excluded a 'winner takes all' outcome (such as a PR electoral system and the autonomy of local government). Thus, even after his victory in the 1995 gubernatorial election, Rossel was still unable to monopolise power in the region. At the same time, his main contenders were forced to establish their own parties for elections to the regional legislature. After the 1995–98 series of electoral campaigns, the party system of Sverdlovsk *oblast'* became the basis for competition among political actors.[30]

Speaking more generally, limitations on political struggle imposed by formal institutions make the return of actors employing force strategies unlikely. Transferring this struggle into the field of electoral competition created an environment for contending with the various alternatives in the structure of a party system. In this sense, elite conflicts, rather than settlements, are more likely to limit the influence of informal institutions and aid in the growth of political society as a whole. In the end, the 'struggle over the rules' scenario of outcome of uncertainty is likely to provide an institutional framework as a precondition for democratisation in the sense of horizontal accountability through the institutional limitation on assertions of power. Nevertheless, this outcome has not yet achieved a full-fledged democratic regime as there has been no turnover of political actors within these institutions. Huntington's 'two-turnover' test of sustainable democratisation based on the achievement of a second shift of government due to electoral defeat[31] is helpful in this sense. Until the institutionalisation of the new regime through the second election of a chief executive, it is still quite fragile. In contrast with 'authoritarian situations', the consequences of the 'struggle over the rules' scenario may be a 'democratic situation'.[32] The different scenarios of

[29] Egorov, 'Udmurtskaya Respublika', 82.

[30] See Vladimir Gel'man and Grigorii V. Golosov, 'Regional Party System Formation in Russia: The Deviant Case of Sverdlovsk Oblast' in John Lowenhardt (ed.), *Party Politics in Post-Communist Russia* (London: Frank Cass, 1998), 31–53; Galina Luchterhandt and Ekaterina Rozina, 'Sverdlovskaya Oblast,' in Sergei Ryzhenkov et al. (eds.), *Stolitsy rossiiskoi provinsii. Portret chetyrekh regionov: istoriya, politika, kul'tura* (Moscow: Mezhdunarodnyi Institut Gumanitarno-Politicheskikh Issledovanii, forthcoming).

[31] Huntington, *The Third Wave*, 266–7.

[32] David Collier and Steven Levitsky, 'Democracy with Adjectives. Conceptual Innovation in Comparative Research', *World Politics*, 49/3 (1997), 446.

Table 37.4 **Scenarios of outcomes of uncertainty and characteristics of new regimes. The case of Russia's regions**

Scenario of outcome of uncertainty	Consequences of outcome of uncertainty	Characteristics of the new political regime	The cases of Russia's regions
Winner takes all	Authoritarian situation	Monopoly of a dominant actor, informal institutions	Saratov *oblast'*, Moscow, Kalmykia
Elite settlement	Hybrid regime	Sharing of powers between dominant and subordinated actors, informal institutions	Nizhny Novgorod, Tomsk *oblast'*, Omsk *oblast'*
Struggle over the rules	Democratic situation	Competition of actors, formal institutions, moving toward rule of law	Udmurtia, Sverdlovsk *oblast'*

outcome of uncertainty and characteristics of new regimes in Russia's regions are presented in Table 37.4.

Conclusion: actors, institutions and prospects

It is as yet unclear how this model of regime transition is applicable to the analysis of political developments in Russia as a whole. This issue is on the agenda for future research, however. At least three factors could challenge such a model: (1) the influence of external actors, (2) the influence of mass politics, (3) the dynamics of institutional changes. Until now, however, none of these factors has played a significant role in the changes of *regional* political regimes.

The influence of external actors—Russia's national authorities, as well as nationwide financial-industrial groups—affects persons who occupy powerful positions, but does not affect regional political regimes themselves. This lack of influence can be explained in two ways. First, state-building, which is based on the principle of rule of law, was not a priority task for Russian authorities. Second, the administrative resources of the Centre, as well as its capacity to employ force strategies, were exhausted after the 1994–96 Chechen war and the 1996–97 gubernatorial elections. Although the Centre has used some measures as substitutes for force strategies (such as pushing particular economic policies in the regions, the strengthening of presidential representatives as well as local governments vis-à-vis regional authorities), it has not been very successful. On the eve of the new wave of political struggles at the national level (especially during the 1999–2000 national elections), a compromise strategy of the Centre toward the regions—such as exchange of loyalty for non-intervention—seems the most rational.

The role of mass politics under conditions of widespread clientelism in Russia—which some consider to be a feature of Russia's political culture[33]—is limited. 'Political machines' as a tool of mass mobilisation are more effective than social cleavages, which could be transformed into forms of political competition only if they were supported by cleavages among elites.[34] There is no basis to connect these effects with the uncertainty of regime transition. In the long run, 'political machines' in American or Southern Italian cities have been undermined by modernisation processes; after the breakdown of a system of mass patronage, mass politics played a crucial role in political competition.[35] Yet, this perspective seems doubtful under conditions of arbitrary rule, which, pending the emergence of incentives to develop a party system in the regions, seems to be the only alternative to a clientelist elite-mass linkage, at least in the short term.

Finally, political institutionalisation in Russia strengthened rather than undermined authoritarian features of regional political regimes. Initially, arbitrary rule resulted from the decay of the ancien regime. Now it serves to strengthen actors in new political regimes, especially owing to their use of rent-seeking strategies. There are no actors yet who realise that it is in their interest to shift institutional frameworks from arbitrary rule towards the rule of law. The emergence of such actors could be connected either with the institutionalisation of democratic situations during the 'struggle over the rules' scenario or with the breakdown of those regimes, which would result in the 'winner takes all' and 'elite settlement' outcomes of uncertainty.

Speaking more broadly, democracy does not emerge 'by default' (or even 'by design'). It does not become inevitable because politicians who call themselves 'democrats' occupied power positions (even if they have good intentions). Democracy is a 'contingent outcome of conflict'[36]—and nothing else. If political competition among actors continues to develop, transitions to democracy may occur. In this sense, Churchill's well-known comment on democracy as a bad form of government, save for all others, means that political competition within the framework of formal institutions is simply the 'lesser evil' for actors. The question, however, is whether Russia's actors—on the national and regional levels—could choose the evil of democracy as really a 'lesser' one.

---

[33] See Mikhail Afanas'ev, *Klientelizm i rossiiskaya gosudarstvennost'* (Moscow: Moskovskii Obshchestvennyi Nauchnyi Fond, 1997).

[34] See Gel'man and Golosov, 'Regional Party System Formation'.

[35] See Brie, 'The Political Regime of Moscow', 13–21.

[36] Adam Przeworski, 'Democracy as a Contingent Outcome of Conflicts', in Jon Elster and Ruge Slagstag (eds.), *Constitutionalism and Democracy* (Cambridge: Cambridge University Press, 1988), 59.

Is Russia Becoming a Democracy?

Introduction

Archie Brown

The issue of democratization in Russia has emerged in many chapters of this volume—not only in the final section of the book which is explicitly devoted to it. It could hardly be otherwise. A country which had endured centuries of autocratic rule prior to the 1917 Revolutions, followed by a Communist regime which between the early 1930s and the early 1950s was totalitarian and for most of the remainder of the Soviet period never less than highly authoritarian, began in the second half of the 1980s to change dramatically. As the liberalization of 1986–7 gave way to pluralization and democratization in 1988–9, political struggle sharpened between conservatives who wished to turn back the clock to a time when the decisions of the Communist Party were unquestionable and radicals who wished to speed up the process of political transformation.

The Soviet system had been such that all efforts by dissidents to change it from below had ended in failure, and, given the sophisticated array of rewards and sanctions at the disposal of the regime, it was difficult to see how radical reform could be launched other than from above. Yet most observers believed that the system would remain equally effective at preventing anyone with radically reformist intent from climbing the greasy pole to the party leadership. Nikita Khrushchev, Soviet Communist Party leader from 1953 to 1964, had been, in his idiosyncratic way, a reformer and his attack on Stalin and Stalinism was, in the political context of the time, a bold and momentous breakthrough. Yet Khrushchev never for a moment questioned the superiority of the Communist system, believing that the removal of its Stalinist excrescences would reveal all the more clearly its advantages—economically, as compared with capitalism and, politically, over 'bourgeois democracy'. Even so, Khrushchev was ultimately overthrown by his more orthodox Communist Party colleagues and his fate served as a warning to his successors not to depart from the rules of the Soviet game. Yury Andropov, general secretary of the CPSU from November 1982 until his death in February 1984, was a reformer within narrow limits. He was at least implicitly critical of the economic slowdown, corruption, and cronyism of the Brezhnev years, but he never showed the slightest willingness to see the Communist Party relinquish any of its levers of power. Mikhail Gorbachev had from the outset more far-reaching changes in mind. Yet he initially believed that the existing system was reformable and could be significantly improved. Certainly, he did not reach the pinnacle of power with the intention of comprehensively dismantling the structures he had inherited. Nevertheless, three years after becoming general secretary he was taking the initiative in introducing changes which were to make the Soviet system different in kind—contested elections for a legislature with real powers, accompanied by a growing political and religious tolerance and a new openness (glasnost) that quite rapidly developed into freedom of speech.

The entire period from the radicalization of the Gorbachev reforms in 1988 until the beginning of the Putin presidency can be regarded as one of democratization, provided that it is borne in mind that democratization is not necessarily a unilinear process. In the Soviet and Russian case there have been many zigzags over those years. If, as Valerie Bunce suggests in the previous section of this volume, it is inappropriate to regard democracy as an 'end state', it *is*, nevertheless, something more than democratization. It is a *form of government*, albeit one which comes in many different institutional guises. It is also rather rare for established (or 'consolidated') democracies to return to authoritarian rule. The leading democratic theorist, Robert A. Dahl, after noting that pessimists at various times in the twentieth century were too ready to give up on democracy, goes on to observe:

Confounding their dire predictions, experience revealed that once democratic institutions were firmly established in a country, they would prove to be remarkably sturdy and resilient. Democracies revealed an unexpected capacity for coping with the problems they confronted—inelegantly and imperfectly, true, but satisfactorily.[1]

It would be difficult, of course, to find serious scholars who would argue that democratic institutions were already 'firmly established' in Russia. Indeed, in the three chapters that follow in this section, despite differences among the authors, none goes even so far as to argue that Russia is already a democracy. If the distinction is maintained between 'transition' and 'consolidation', the Russian Federation is still at a stage of transition with some uncertainty as to where it may be headed. But if democratization is, by definition, a more incomplete process than democracy, it was, nevertheless, a change of historic importance when the Soviet Union and Russia embarked on it. The initiator of the reforms, Gorbachev, used the term *demokratizatsiya* frequently (even as early as an important speech he made in December 1984, three months before he became general secretary), but in the mid-1980s what he meant by this was a reactivation of institutions which had become moribund, together with measures of liberalization, rather than democratization in a stricter sense of the term.[2] The reforms proposed by Gorbachev in 1988 for elections, first held in 1989, which were (*a*) by secret ballot, (*b*) multi-candidate and genuinely contested in a majority of constituencies, and (*c*) preceded by open debate, marked the real shift from liberalization to democratization and the beginning of a period when outcomes could be influenced from below as well as from above.

The transformation of the political life of the Soviet Union was of extraordinary importance since pluralizing and democratizing changes there, together with the conceptual revolution which was occurring in Moscow and the fundamental changes in Soviet foreign policy, opened the way for democratization throughout Central and Eastern Europe. In a number of the countries which in 1989 broke with Communism, the establishment of systems that can be called not merely 'democratizating' but *democratic* proceeded faster than in post-Soviet Russia. Yet, among the successor states of the former Soviet Union, democracy made far more progress in Russia than in a majority of the others. Of the fifteen countries which emerged from what had been the USSR, it is arguable that only the three Baltic states—Estonia, Latvia, and

---

[1] Robert A. Dahl, *On Democracy* (New Haven: Yale University Press, 1998), 188.

[2] See Archie Brown, *The Gorbachev Factor* (Oxford: Oxford University Press, 1996), 78–80 and 126.

Lithuania—have advanced further along a road of democratic transition than Russia (which is, not of course, to say that their transitions have been unproblematical, especially in the sphere of rights of ethnic minorities). Conventionally, these developments are incorporated in what is called the 'Third Wave' of democratization.[3] I would maintain, however, as I have argued elsewhere that:

What happened in Moscow . . . was of such decisive importance for the transition from Communism in Europe—and so interconnected are all those transitions—that it makes sense to see them as representing a discrete political phenomenon. If the notion of waves means anything more than a temporal bunching, and it is of limited use if that is *all* it means, then the changes in East and East-Central Europe constitute a Fourth Wave of democratization.[4]

Russia, however, lacked many of the incentives—such as the prospect of European Union membership—that encouraged political elites in East-Central Europe to construct strong democratic institutions and to respect democratic values. Moreover, what the Balts, Poles, or Czechs saw as a 'liberation'—from Soviet hegemony—most Russians perceived as a loss of their traditional statehood. Worries about national identity, as noted in Section 8 (and also by William Smirnov in the first chapter in this section), replaced pride in superpower status.

All things considered, what occurred in the first post-Soviet decade was better than what might have been feared. The expression, 'Weimar Russia', acquired a certain currency, reflecting the belief of a number of authors that the humiliations Russia had undergone could turn it into fertile ground for the ascendancy of ultra-nationalism or even fascism. The analogy was with Germany following its defeat in the First World War and its subsequent tribulations. Yet, in spite of the presence in the Russian political arena of some extremist political figures, none achieved a position of real power at the federal executive level. The Communist Party of the Russian Federation, with the nationalist tinge frequently to be found in the rhetoric of its leader, Gennady Zyuganov, siphoned off some of the support which might otherwise have gone to extremist parties of the right. Contrary to the pronouncements of Boris Yeltsin, the KPRF became, increasingly, a within-system party—especially in the second half of the 1990s—and a useful safety-valve for the discontent of many millions of Russian citizens.

William Smirnov (in Chapter 38) emphasizes the extent to which the changes associated with the names, first, of Gorbachev and, then, of Yeltsin were introduced from above, calling into question the strength of the social base for successful democratization. He also stresses the complexity of the threefold task which, as Smirnov sees it, faced post-Soviet Russia: first, the creation of a political market, i.e. advancing the process of democratization; second, creating an economic market; and, third, searching 'for a new nation-state

---

[3] See e.g. Samuel Huntington, *The Third Wave: Democratization in the Late Twentieth Century* (Norman: University of Oklahoma Press, 1991); Larry Diamond, Marc F. Plattner, Yan-han Chu, and Hung-mao Tien, eds., *Consolidating the Third Wave Democracies: Themes and Perspectives* (Baltimore: Johns Hopkins University Press, 1997); and Larry Diamond *et al.*, *Consolidating the Third Wave Democracies: Regional Challenges* (Baltimore: Johns Hopkins University Press, 1997).

[4] Archie Brown, 'Transnational Influences in the Transition from Communism', *Post-Soviet Affairs*, 16/2 (Apr.–June 2000), 177–200, at p. 182.

identity'.[5] While acknowledging the special difficulties confronting Russian democratization, Smirnov, in his chapter on the 'achievements and problems' of the ostensible attempt to build democracy, emphasizes the failures more than the successes. In an analysis congruent with that to be found in, for example, Section 6 of this volume, Smirnov observes:

An essentially neo-feudal, corporatist-oligarchical system has evolved in the country, in which republican and, to a lesser extent, regional princes and barons determine the rights, privileges, and rules of the game for their underlings. They will occasionally swear allegiance to the president of the country, but are ready to change camps at any sign of real or apparent weakness on his part.

Alexander Lukin (in Chapter 39) also takes a sceptical view of the extent to which Russian democratization has progressed. While rejecting stereotypes of Russian political culture, he brings the cultural dimension of politics into his analysis, remarking that what political actors deem to be rational varies radically from one cultural context to another. Whereas Smirnov was writing during Putin's first year in the presidency, Lukin's chapter is based on an article written at the end of the Yeltsin era. He is not optimistic about an early transition to democracy and argues, furthermore, that the pursuit of rapid democratization can do more harm than good. Lukin believes, on the contrary, that a long transition period is required.

It would be impossible to do justice to all of the diverse analyses contained in this volume in one final chapter and, in the concluding Chapter 40, I draw only selectively on the preceding contributions. My main concern is to sum up the relative success or failure of the democratization project in Russia in the context of examining the most basic requirements of a democracy. I touch also on the extent to which democracy may or may not still be a goal to which the post-Yeltsin political leadership attach a high priority.

---

[5] It was, indeed, the need for what I called a 'triple transformation' that made the *Soviet* transition so fiendishly difficult (Archie Brown, 'No Role Models for Soviet Transition', *Los Angeles Times*, 2 Apr. 1991, p. B7). The Soviet Union, if it were to make a successful transition, faced an even more daunting task than Russia. The first two elements of the required triple transformation were the same: movement to a market economy with a substantial private sector and transformation of the institutions and norms of a post-totalitarian authoritarian state into those supportive of democracy. But it was the third element, the need to transform relations between republics and the centre and of different ethnic groups within republics which, in combination with the first two sufficiently demanding tasks, made the Soviet transition uniquely difficult. Even Yugoslavia, which fared less well than the Soviet Union (inasmuch as the outcome was far more violent), had more experience over many years of significant market elements as well as of a more genuine federalism than the USSR had experienced up until Gorbachev's reforms.

38 Democratization in Russia: Achievements and Problems

William V. Smirnov

As Russia enters the third millennium after the three revolutions of the twentieth century, the last also being a counter-revolution, has she acquired a democratic organization of political social and economic life capable of ensuring her stable development? And has she risen above the conflict, dating back to the time of Peter I, between various, borrowed Western forms and, to put it neutrally, their Eurasian content?

Both within the country and abroad, the question of whether Russian civilization is compatible with democracy is raised more and more frequently. Could it be that thinkers as diverse in outlook, educational background, culture, and values as the Marquis de Custine and Petr Chaadaev, up to Richard Pipes and Zbigniew Brzezinski, who have all answered in the negative to this question, are not so wrong after all? The transformation of the country over the last fifteen years allows us to look for an answer to this 'eternal' question for Russia.

The historical-cultural context

In the theory of transitology—usually termed the 'Third Wave', though the transitions from Communism, as Archie Brown has argued, form a distinctive 'Fourth Wave'[1]—and in the practical experience of post-Communist development, amongst the most difficult problems is the attempt to find the optimal model for the formation of the democratic organization of political state power, civil society, and an effective market economy. The vast majority of Russian and foreign commentators investigate this problem from the point of view of the possibilities of the parallel creation of all three. In post-Communist Russia, only a few commentators, such as Gavriil Popov and Andranik Migranyan, originally came out in support of 'democratic dictatorship' or one of the variations on the idea of an authoritarian state as a form of political power that can ensure the realization of societal and economic transformations.

As well as this, the type and rate of democratization depend above all upon the historical peculiarities of the country under transformation, its dominant political and legal culture, the level of elite support for the reforms, and their consensus on the means and costs of achieving those reforms. This applies above all to Russia.

Chapter specially commissioned for this volume. Translated by Polly Jones

[1] Archie Brown, 'Transnational Influences in the Transition from Communism', *Post-Soviet Affairs*, 16 No. 2 (2000), 177–200, esp. 181–8.

All the previous attempts at modernization in Russian history, starting with pre-Petrine reforms, have been carried out 'from above', have been to varying degrees violent, and have aimed to change the state political and economic institutions of power and administration. Society, not only due to the relative lack of separation among political, economic, and social spheres characteristic of the pre-industrial era but also to the gulf, characteristic of the time, between the numerically insignificant ruling minority and the majority without civil rights, was effectively the passive object of this kind of Westernization.[2]

The Marxist-Bolshevik project to transform the country was, despite all of its populist rhetoric, itself a revolution of the avant-garde, whose proclaimed and actual aims could not be achieved without mass terror and total party-state control. Paradoxically enough, it was the state elite, almost more than anyone else, which was concerned to weaken this control, for though some of them were also executioners, as a category they were purged more consistently and ruthlessly than even intellectuals. As the Khrushchev thaw gave way to Brezhnev-era stagnation, party control weighed ever more heavily on the nomenklatura, since it hindered them in converting their almost unlimited power into property or in handing down at least some of that power as a legacy.[3]

For this reason, both perestroika and the attempt at a counter-coup in August 1991 and the 'coup' of December 1991 and the consequent radical-liberal reforms were all to a significant degree initiated and carried out 'from above' by competing groups of the old-new nomenklatura. Thus, for all the apparent, and indeed real, differences between the policies of Mikhail Sergeevich Gorbachev and Boris Nikolaevich Yeltsin, they are linked by the attempt to transform the country not so much on the basis of the dominant tendencies in public opinion or the readiness of society for such transformations, as on the basis of the ideas of those leaders and the elites surrounding them about the aims of the reform and the most effective ways of achieving them.

Strictly speaking, the collapse of the Soviet Union at the start of the 1990s was also not foreseen by Sovietologists because, objectively, the Communist system and the USSR could have gone on existing for far longer, modernizing an economy that was at that point far more developed than that in China, under strict party-police control, had it not been for the absence of political will in one part of the political elite, defeatism in another, a belief in the ideals of democracy and universal human values in a third, and the striving by the majority of elites to get rid of party-state limitations on the use of power in one's own interests.

The unchanging domination of leaders and elites over the course of almost all of Russian history can be partly explained by the fact that her political-legal culture is based upon paternalistic relations to political subjects. It is enough to point out that the overwhelming majority of the population in both tsarist and Soviet Russia valued equality over freedom and justice over legality. That is not to say that this culture has not undergone any changes. It should be borne in mind that the source of Leninist Bolshevism was Western Marxism. This explains the presence in Soviet ideology and rhetoric of such values as democracy (in truth,

---

[2] In the sevententh and nineteenth centuries, these were essentially two totally distinct cultural-linguistic and socio-economic communities.

[3] It is worth recalling that the children of high-ranking party-state workers never received important posts in this sphere, but their hopes revolved around finding work in the West. Incidentally, this latter circumstance played a role in generating pro-Western sentiments in reformist circles amongst the nomenklatura, which has not yet been fully appreciated.

'socialist'), political participation (in truth, compulsory-mobilizational), elections (in truth, without the right to choose), membership in numerous social organizations (in truth, entirely subservient to the CPSU). Formal legal attributes of political democracy such as a constitution with its many declarations of political and (partly real) social-economic rights and freedoms, legal principles, judicial independence, and so on also helped to foster democratic expectations in a part of Soviet society, in particular amongst the intelligentsia. However, right up to the end of the 1980s, the gulf between democratic rhetoric and authoritarian-totalitarian practice did not arouse any significant protests whatsoever in Soviet society.

The traditionally passive role of the overwhelming majority of Russian society is also shown in the fact that both the Revolution of 1917 and the outcomes of the conflicts in 1991 and 1993 were basically decided in the capital (St Petersburg in the first instance, and Moscow in the subsequent two). Dissidence and the intelligentsia protest movement were overwhelmingly concentrated in the Soviet period in Moscow and what was then Leningrad. Without wishing to doubt the courage and goodness of its participants' aims, it should be noted that they were after a certain point encouraged, supported, and exploited by certain groups of the power nomenklatura in their fight against other factions. This gives rise to the specific quality of anti-Communism and post-Communism in Russia as distinct from de-Communization in the countries of central and Eastern Europe. In Russia, to reiterate, the process was more the result of changes within the nomenklatura and the weakening of party-Soviet power than of the victory of an embryonic civil society over the previous system and its determined efforts to create a democratic system.

For this reason it seems almost paradoxical that the principal declared aim of 'perestroika' of the former Soviet Union and the subsequent reforms in post-Communist Russia was to create democracy. In no small part, this is linked to the figure of Gorbachev, who intuitively sensed that de Tocqueville's notion of the 'great democratic transformation', Woodrow Wilson's 'dissemination of democratic opinion and institutions' and 'the overthrow of all forms of state administration in favour of democracy', and Karl Marx's idea of the 'conquering of democracy' by the working classes and the replacement of 'the government machinery with genuine self-government' were at the core of the world system of values that developed over the last quarter of the twentieth century. Without any help from Samuel Huntington, Gorbachev became a disciple of the idea of 'the global democratic revolution'.[4]

The Gorbachev reforms ended with the failed coup attempt of August 1991, the banning of the CPSU, the dissolution of the USSR and the dismissal of the policies of its first and last president. These events were accompanied, and partly instigated, by the rapid increase of the power of Yeltsin—for example, when the enthusiastic deputies in the Supreme Soviet granted him exclusive authority to conduct economic reform through his own decrees over the course of one year.

[4] Alexis de Tocqueville, *O demokratii v Amerike* (Moscow: Progress 1997), 1; Woodrow Wilson, *The State*, quoted from: Gabriel A. Almond, 'The Intellectual History of the Civic Culture Concepts', in Gabriel A. Almond and Sidney Verba, eds. *The Civic Culture Revisited* (Boston and Toronto: Little, Brown, 1980), 7; Karl Marx, *Iz nabroskov 'Grazhdanskoi voiny vo Frantsii'* in Marx and Engels, *Collected Works*, 17. 601–2; and Samuel P. Huntington, *The Third Wave: Democratization in the Late Twentieth Century* (Norman, Okla., and London: University of Oklahoma Press, 1991).

Yeltsin's Russia: some results of the systemic transformation

The society and state that emerged in the 1990s resulted from the complex interaction of Russia's inherited historical-cultural characteristics, leaders' and elites' desire for transformation, the energetic and often avaricious exploitation by approximately 16–23 per cent of the adult population of the country of the economic and other possibilities that have arisen, the various forms of resistance offered to the reforms by the uncoordinated forces of opposition, and the passive adaptation to new conditions shown by the majority of Russians.

Post-Communist Russia has been confronted with a problem of unprecedented complexity, namely how to resolve simultaneously three historical tasks, which the transitional countries of Latin America, South-East Asia, and Eastern Europe dealt with in stages, albeit in different sequences: the creation of political and economic markets (democratization and the creation of a progressive and reliable economy respectively) and the search for a new nation-state identity. This last factor is linked to the outcome of the December 1991 Belovezh Accords between the leaders of Belarus, Russia, and Ukraine, whereby the Soviet Union was dissolved. Some specialists believe that this prevented the country from breaking up as Yugoslavia had done. However, the majority of Russian citizens, aided by the efforts of various nationalistic political parties, movements and groups, from Vladimir Zhirinovsky's Liberal Democratic Party down to the Communist Party of Gennady Zyuganov, deem the Belovezh Accords illegitimate, with some even holding them to be illegal. For these people, historical Russia had shrunk, whilst over 25 million Russians and other Russian-speaking peoples who identified with Russia had suddenly and against their will became inhabitants of foreign states (former Union republics).

The economic model chosen by Boris Yeltsin, conceptualized by Jeffrey Sachs and implemented by Yegor Gaidar, in conjunction with the model of privatization worked out by Anatoly Chubais, led to economic and socio-demographic collapse, if not catastrophe, according to numerous authoritative Russian and foreign experts. The amoralism and cynicism of those former Soviet leaders and elites—amongst them, intellectuals—who ended up in power in Russia, having for decades exploited slogans of 'socialist humanism', the right of every Soviet person to an equal and worthwhile education, medical and social provision, work, and a fulfilling life, were fully revealed in the cruel social-economic reforms of the 1990s, which brought fantastic riches to 3–4 per cent of the population whilst brutally impoverishing more than 70 per cent of Russians. This in turn means that 30 per cent of the population live below the poverty line, according even to official statistics that are calculated on the basis of the norms of the poorest countries in the world.

The selfish and avaricious behaviour of the old-new elite, who have—often through criminal means—accumulated at least $US300 billion since the start of privatization and channelled it out of the country, can also be seen in the fact that per capita GNP in 1998 was two times less than it had been in 1990, and unemployment levels have soared sixfold to 12 per cent of the economically active population.[5]

The combination of these basic factors has led, according to George Soros, to a 'system of

---

[5] Statistical data about the socio-economic indicators of the results of these reforms, presented in eloquent comparison with data from countries in Central and Eastern Europe, can be found in the magazine *Vlast'*, 2 (2000), 22–36.

bandit capitalism', which has grown to become a consolidated 'new oligarchy'. For all the sharp criticism intended by Soros's terminology, his words accurately reflect the distorted, unstable, and painfully transitional state of society and the political system and the highly conflictual and politicized interaction between the former and the latter. As Brown has observed: 'The absence of either an understanding of or legal sanctions against conflict of interest, the corruption that has pervaded the system from top to bottom, and the weaknesses of procedures for calling to account public officials, together with the lack of accountability of wealthy financiers wielding irresponsible power, have combined to frustrate the creation of civilized market relations as well as the building of democracy.'[6] Will it, then, be possible, given the current situation in the country, to transform these relationships into legal partnerships and will civil society, one of the necessary conditions for democratization and democratic consolidation, be created?

For all the diversity of opinion on civil society,[7] the main indications of its formation during the collapse of the Communist regime include the formation of social-political organizations and movements independent of the ruling Communist Party, the emergence of a middle class, the formation of a third sector consisting of non-commercial and non-political organizations, the assertion of the rights and freedoms of citizens within the framework of the rule of law, all underpinned by the embedding of the values of freedom, the market economy and representative democracy in mass consciousness. As far as the above are concerned, the results of the last decade of transformation in Russia are mixed and incomplete.

Notwithstanding the clamour surrounding the emergence of the first informal movement and informal groups and platforms, followed by proto-parties and political parties from the end of the 1980s, and despite the external indications of numerous social-political associations, in Russia today there are very few such well-organized active and influential pan-federal and inter-regional associations with steady numbers of members and followers. A genuine and effective multi-party system has not yet been established in the country. The majority of the many political associations formed during this period of 'political enterprise' have not, with the exception of the KPRF and the LDPR, gone beyond being social movement private gatherings, proto-parties, or parties based around a single leader. The weakness of political parties, their lack of firm foundations in Russian society and the absence of genuine popular support are all confirmed by the results of an empirical study of electoral-legal culture commissioned by the Central Electoral Commission of the Russian Federation (TsIKRF) and conducted by a team led by the author:

- Only 20.1 per cent of citizens consider themselves supporters of any political party.
- The fact that a candidate supports a given political party is seventh on the list of criteria taken into account by voters when deciding whom to vote for.
- Only a quarter (25.7 per cent) of voters taking part in the 1995 elections to the State

---

[6] Archie Brown, 'The Russian Crisis: Beginning of the End or End of the Beginning?', *Post-Soviet Affairs*, 15/1 (Jan.–Mar. 1999), 65–6.

[7] This diversity is shown in five articles in the first part of the book, ed., A. Yu. Sungurova, *Grazhdanskoe obshchestvo. V poiskakh puti* (St Petersburg: St Petersburg Humanitarian-Political Science Centre 'Strategy', as a supplement to the Magazine *Severnaga Palmira*, 1997); see also Yu. Zhilin, 'K evolyutsii ponyatiya grazhdanskoe obshchestvo', in ISPRAN, *Politicheskiy protsess i ego protivorechiya* (1997), 88–98.

Duma of the Russian Federation were chiefly motivated to participate by the desire to support a candidate or party, whilst 10 per cent had the opposite motive, namely to prevent a particular party or candidate from coming to power.

- Only 9 per cent of the adult population favour elections conducted solely on party lists, whilst only just over 13 per cent support a mixed electoral system that uses party lists to elect a section of deputies.[8]

One of the most serious obstacles to the development of democracy and civil society is the small size of the middle class, which, by the most optimistic estimates, did not constitute even 20 per cent of the population before the financial crisis of August 1998. This state of affairs can be explained primarily by the undeveloped state of small and medium business, itself caused by the criminal and oligarchical economy forming in the country and by the lack of any substantive support for that business from the authorities. This is compounded by the huge gap between the richest (top 10 per cent) and the poorest members of society, which is many times larger than in Western countries. This polarization of rich and poor, characteristic of weakly developed countries, is a constant source of social and political tension and conflict and creates fertile ground for political extremism of different hues.

The negative tendencies mentioned above are counter-balanced to a certain degree by the rapid development of the third sector, in particular charity, ecological, cultural, women's and more general human rights organizations, which collectively constitute significant channels for public participation and serve to protect human and citizen rights and freedoms. An incontestable proof of Russia's progress towards a civil society and a democratic state is the current constitution of the Russian Federation, which is the first in history to place the rights and freedoms of citizens beyond question and to guarantee them according to universal principles and the norms of international law. The constitution of the Russian Federation confirms nearly all the basic rights and freedoms laid out in international conventions. Nonetheless, the 1998 annual report by the Human Rights Commission attached to the president of the Russian Federation stated that 'Our country is still in the initial stages of the transition towards civil society and the creation of the rule of law . . . For the time being, both legislators and representatives of executive power do not consider themselves responsible for the protection of human rights. In a word, contemporary Russia has not yet overcome the centuries-old traditions of undervaluing man and denigrating his rights and freedoms.'[9]

In order to assess the results of Russia's democratization, it is equally important to look at its institutional aspects. The development of the current political system in Russia has passed through several stages since perestroika, each of which has left its mark, albeit to varying degrees. The system's basic features are laid out in the current Constitution of the Russian Federation, which was approved in a referendum held in December 1993 under conditions of profound social and state crisis in the wake of the presidential reform forces' victory in the tragic conflict of October 1993. This Constitution reflects the main differences in opinion that then existed between the majority of the population and the ruling elites

---

[8] For a more detailed account of the findings of this survey, see Yu.A. Vedeneev and V.V. Smirnov, eds., *Predstavitel'naya demokratiya i elektoral'no-pravovaya kul'tura* (Moscow: Ves' mir, 1997).

[9] 'On the observance of human and citizen rights in the Russian Federation, 1996–7', *Doklad kommissii po pravam cheloveka pri prezidente Rossiiskoy federatsii* (Moscow, 1998), 5.

over questions of the past and present of the country, the basic aims and values of society, and how to achieve them, and it suffers from many problems and contradictions. To illustrate these differences, it is worth recalling how insistently the liberal and anti-Communist elites, political groups, and movements identified themselves as leftist whilst calling the Communists and their allies rightists because up until the mid-1990s the term 'left' had a totally positive connotation for the majority of Russians, whilst 'right' was totally negative. Finally, the liberals fought the one-party regime of the CPSU under the banner 'All Power to the Soviets', which was subsequently abandoned by them at the end of 1993. But, if towards the end of the 1990s the ideological and political spectrum corresponded to world norms—the 'Union of Rightist Forces' as well as numerous other electoral associations and blocs calling themselves centre-rightists took part in the December 1999 Duma elections—then society itself and its economic and political systems continue to be essentially transitional.

For this reason, the liberal-democratic features of the political system in the Constitution of the Russian Federation, largely adopted from the French and US constitutions, coexist with personalist and authoritarian institutions that were included by the presidential entourage in order to ensure that the chosen economic reforms and privatization could be carried through without being reversed. Hence the fact that, in spite of the separation of powers laid out in the constitution, political-state power legally, and to an even greater extent in practice, is concentrated in the office of the president because of the weakness of other branches of state power. That is so much so that Western analysts often characterize the national political system as 'superpresidentialism' with only a 'fig leaf' parliament. This is corroborated by the fact that the Constitution does not directly envisage the right to parliamentary supervision over the conduct of the executive branch and does not view the right of deputies to ask probing questions as one of the most effective weapons in the arsenal of democracy.

In the effort to prevent any branch of power or any figure in authority from calling the president to account, not only has the office of vice-president been abolished, but the procedure for removing the president from office has also been made so complex that it is practically impossible to complete it. The president has also been endowed with plenary powers to form and alter the make-up of the government, including the prime minister and the cabinet's structures, and with rights to a delay veto on laws passed by the parliament and on the publication of their own normative legal acts. Thus the president can at any time paralyse the work of government by dissolving the Duma if it does not give the necessary consent to his appointed prime minister. This happened with remarkable speed in the case of the governments headed by Sergei Kirienko, Sergei Stepashin, and Yevgeny Primakov. As the conflict with the former prosecutor-general of the Russian Federation, Yury Skuratov, demonstrated, the president is in a position to overcome the opposition of the Federation Council where the removal of an inconvenient figure from other key posts in the political system is concerned. The judges of the three highest courts in the land—Constitutional, Supreme, and Arbitrage—are proposed by the president, whilst the other federal judges are directly appointed by him. In addition to this, it should be noted that the president also holds the purse strings. That is to say, the financial-material sustenance of the organs and employees of all three branches of government essentially depends upon the president and his business administration. The efficacy of this kind of power resource in a society with low incomes for the population and relatively high incomes and benefits for those in the higher echelons of political power and their counterparts in political-administrative and juridical-legal posts, who are also without the safeguards against arbitrary dismissal and appointments enjoyed by those in the West, was frequently emphasized during the Yeltsin presidency.

However, the enormous powers attached to the post of president at the same time make it a source of instability and conflicts. The winners in the presidential elections take almost all, whilst the losers stand to lose almost everything. The fight for total victory, haunted by the spectre of total defeat for the losing side, raises the stakes in any given contest so high that the competitors are prepared to use any means to win. Though the KPRF is, in many respects, much less critical of the Putin presidency than of his predecessor, it remains antagonistic to his declared economic policy.

In the spirit of the transformed dualism of the Soviet system, the president of the Russian Federation and his administration become the agenda-setting and powerful institution, whilst the government is an administrative-executive and subservient institution. Freeing itself of party control, the state apparatus successfully combats the establishment of any real parliamentary or societal supervision. The majority of fundamental state decisions are, as before, made 'behind closed doors', and the state apparatus concerns itself above all with the orders of the bosses and the preferences of certain favoured individuals and organizations, rather than with the interests and appeals of the general population. And, following the age-old tradition, the population responds to this by treating state functionaries and state organs with distrust, if not outright hatred.

By rejecting the previous model of all-encompassing regulation and control, and by hastily withdrawing from many spheres of economic, social, and cultural life, the state has ceased to be a socially consolidated political and administrative actor. It has effectively split up into a multitude of bodies and regional-feudal formations, which, if not privatized by corporations and industrial-financial groups and regional elites, are at least heavily dependent upon them. In spite of a certain reduction in the number of federal executive organs, there remains an unjustifiable duplication of their functions and competencies, and the activity of these organs often goes unsupervised and proves ineffective. The tight intertwining of business and politics, the almost unchecked conversion of power into property, the loss of society's levers of control over the state apparatus and the erosion of the former service ethics have created fertile grounds for enormous and pervasive corruption to flourish. The inability of the state and its administrative organs in any way to express and satisfy national and societal aspirations is an indication of the weakness of the state and the absence of a power hierarchy. Only the creation of a lawful, democratic, and hence strong, reliable, and properly functioning state can create the necessary conditions for the steady development of the country.

At present, the legislative 'rules of the game' in the economic and political spheres are incomplete and contradictory. For example, criminal groups have largely taken over the task of guaranteeing the fulfilment of economic contracts. Many legislative acts that the country needs, including the federal law 'On the Regulation of Lobbying Activity', come under great pressure from the representatives of financial and business interest lobbies not to be passed, or not to answer societal demands. The process of law-making, despite plans and programmes to guide it, is full of defects. As a result, numerous laws envisaged in the Russian Constitution that are essential for the development of the rule of law and for the mechanisms to ensure the political and legal security of the country and for a unified system of executive power are endlessly postponed.

These factors in conjunction with others, such as the peculiarities of Russian federalism and of the procuracy, the incompleteness of judicial reform, the unsatisfactory work carried out by many rights-protection organs, the weak control exercised by society over their activities and the low levels of law-abiding behaviour not only amongst the population as a whole, but also amongst state functionaries, all serve to undermine the efficacy of behaviour in accordance with the law.

Starting with the process of preparation of the Novo Ogarevo Accords,[10] the policies of trying to win the support of the republican and regional leaders by a mixture of advances and retreats continued through the stand-off between the Supreme Soviet and the President of the Russian Federation and the 1995 and 1996 federal elections, ultimately giving rise to an eclectic and paradoxical federative state arrangement for Russia that is partly inherited from the past. An example of this is the fact that Russians themselves, although they constitute 84 per cent of the nation's population, do not formally or legally have their own statehood. Moreover, Russians make up over 50 per cent of the population in sixteen out of the twenty-one republics, the single autonomous region (*oblast'*) and also the majority of autonomous okrugs that make up the Russian Federation. In total, 'rooted' ethnic groups make up a mere third of the republics' population and less than 11 per cent of the population of the autonomous okrugs.

The Russian federative system is hierarchical and asymmetrical, constructed on the basis of a fantastical mix of ethnic-national and territorial (national-state and territorial-administrative), contractual and constitutional principles, such that some federal subjects also belong in other federal categories. There is a clear imbalance in the interplay of centralization and decentralization. The current constitution of the Russian Federation also gives contradictory guidelines for the federative arrangements. Take, for instance, Article 5 of the Constitution. Its first line proclaims the equal rights of all federal subjects. In line 2, however, the article states that only republics can call themselves states and that only they possess the right to possess their own constitutions. The remaining sixty eight federal subjects are only allowed to have statutes. Moreover, in line 4 of this article, it is stated that 'all subjects of the Russian Federation are equal to one another' only 'in interrelations with the federal organs of state power'.

In the period of the 'parade of sovereignties', the elites of most of the titular nation-republics were able to secure special rights for their ethnic groups and for the republics that they had 'nationalized' in their constitutions and other normative acts passed in contravention of the federal constitution. Some of these rights were then confirmed in bilateral agreements between the federal and republican authorities. In response, the territorial subjects of the federation started to try to expand their own powers. The agreements brokered between the federal and regional authorities set in motion a twofold process:

1. A gradual, if selective, equalizing of the rights of nation-state and administrative-territorial federal subjects.

[10] Novo Ogarevo was the place, and refers to the process in which Gorbachev tried to work out a Union Treaty whereby a new division of powers between the federal authorities and the Union Republics would be voluntarily agreed. See Archie Brown, *The Gorbachev Factor* (Oxford: Oxford University Press, 1996), 285–93.

2. The creation of a new inequality owing to the fact that the administrative-territorial subjects had concluded agreements granting them extra rights and privileges.

One of the consequences of this, and of the incompleteness of judicial reform coupled with the weakness of judges and prosecutors, is not only that almost all republics have constitutions and normative acts that contravene the federal constitution and federal laws. There is also neither an effective legal mechanism nor the political will at the federal centre to bring the illegal normative acts passed by federal subjects into line with the provisions of the federal constitution and federal laws. The weakness of the federal centre and of the state as a whole and the absence of a universal power hierarchy have led to the emergence of effectively autonomous political-legal systems and diverse human rights regimes within the Russian state. Although the Russian Constitution supports almost all the human and citizen rights accepted by the international community, many of them, especially social and economic ones, are not fulfilled or are contravened.

In line with American doctrine, the constitution separates local self-government and state administration. However, in this instance, Western forms receive no legal, financial-economic, and organizational-political back-up. Suffice it to say that most local government budgets are still subsidized, and the republican-regional authorities are most unwilling to accord the decentralized power laid out in the law. As a result, local administrations have not become an independent link in the political system.

The formation of an effective and democratic political system in Russia is hampered not only by the economic crisis, poverty, and the consequent dissatisfaction with the authorities felt by a significant proportion of the population, the absence of an evolving civil society and of a national idea, but also by the weak and ineffective attempts to involve citizens in politics and administration, the low levels of political-legal culture amongst most of the population, and the selfishness and instability of an elite that is engaged in constant and uncontrollable in-fighting for power and property and their redistribution. The unprincipled behaviour and the use of 'dirty' means in fighting elections have not yet been eliminated, despite a constantly growing body of electoral, criminal, and administrative legislation.

Both the experiences of the world and of Russia herself show that leaders and elites play the decisive role 'from above' at times of transformation (including such diverse transformations as modernization, the transition from authoritarianism to democracy, etc.). This experience also shows that if a developed civil society, political and economic pluralism, and a system of institutional checks and balances do not all develop during a period of violent modernization from above, even if this is in the name of democracy and the free market, any dominant elites in society will evolve into a force independent of society. Whatever ideology they may proclaim, their concern will be to limit the potential for opposition and to prolong their own power. In such a situation, power-political processes, including elections, are characterized predominantly by in-fighting between leaders of various elites, reducing representative democracy to an elitist-dirigist or elitist-authoritarian regime. It is the elites and their perpetual in-fighting, the changes of coalition and political victories and defeats of one or other of those coalitions that determined much of Russian development in the Yeltsin era. An essentially neo-feudal, corporatist-oligarchical system has evolved in the country, in which republican and, to a lesser extent, regional princes and barons determine the rights, privileges, and rules of the game for their underlings. They will occasionally swear allegiance to the president of the country, but are ready to change camps at any sign of real or apparent weakness on his part.

One of a democratic system's main means of reining in egotism or megalomania on the part of elites and leaders (besides effective laws, courts, and police) are political parties and elections. The contextual and conjectural nature of the Russian constitution is revealed in these parts of the political system. For example, in contrast not only to most of the world's most recent constitutions, but also to the previous fundamental law, there is no separate chapter dealing with elections or the electoral system, and there is no constitutional regulation on the activity of political parties. Recall that in 1993, the only organized and influential political party was in opposition, and the first elections to the Russian parliament were not regulated by federal law, but by presidential decrees. Little has changed since that time. As before, the vast majority of political parties are effectively made up of Moscow-based leaders and their small entourage, and after them come several small groups all plagued by weak party organization, only coming to life during electoral campaigns. The under-development of political parties and the absence of a genuine multi-party system are in line with the interests of a significant proportion of the federal and regional elites. For example, it was for this reason that by the summer of 2000 a federal law on political parties had not yet been passed. Meanwhile, federal legislation on elections allows social organizations to participate in elections, so that there are other political organizations and movements taking part alongside the political parties. The Ministry of Justice of the Russian Federation registered 139 of these organizations in the 1999 elections to the Duma. It is difficult to think of a more effective way of fragmenting both the political system and society itself.

The elections to the State Duma are largely worthless, in so far as their results determine neither the composition of the country's government, nor the internal and external policies that it carries out. The absence of real plenary powers inevitably makes deputies more radical and irresponsible. The idea of the separation of powers is likewise contravened by the *ex officio* formation of the upper house of the Russian parliament, which has meant that the heads of executive power in the federal subjects have been at the same time members of the highest legislative body in the land.

In Russia people are not elected national or republican presidents, governors of the territorial subjects of the federation, or deputies (in an overwhelming majority of cases) as a consequence of the promotion and support of political parties. Electoral associations and blocs competing for these elected posts, with the exception of the KPRF, and, to some extent, Yabloko and the LDPR, represent not political parties, but organizations of leaders and groups of the elite. This explains the speed with which they form, change, shift from one to another, and fall apart. The majority of them are coalitions of the political-administrative and financial-industrial elites. The latter, after several failed attempts to create their own political parties, decided it would be more effective for them to subsidize already existing organizations. Considering the fact that it is practically impossible to conduct business in Russia without the support of the authorities, businessmen are obliged to give financial support to the federal and regional 'parties of power'.

A classic example of this kind of pseudo-party is 'Our Home is Russia' (Nash Dom Rossiya), which quickly fell apart after its leader, Viktor Chernomyrdin ceased to be prime minister, leaving the party unable to pass the 5 per cent party-list threshold for the 1999 State

Duma elections. 'Fatherland–All Russia' (Otechestvo–Vsya Rossiya) and 'Unity' (Yedinstvo) both aspired to take its place. The former was a motley conglomerate of Moscow and regional leaders and elites, united mostly in the hope that its leader, Primakov, would become president. As a result of the weak party identification felt by most Russians, of the information war conducted by the Kremlin with the help of the mass media and of the semi-legal and illegal actions of civil servants in the federal subjects, the bloc was relegated to third place. The republic and regional leaders in the bloc hastened to proclaim their allegiance to a more likely candidate for power.

'Unity', although hastily put together by that same Kremlin administration only three months before the elections from personalities who were relatively unknown, but quickly promoted by the mass media and 'sold' by regional functionaries, took second place in the ballot for seats in the lower house of the Russian parliament. As of mid-2000 it was turning into a political party adept at ensuring continuity of power and support for the president of the Russian Federation, Vladimir Putin, himself chosen by Yeltsin and his entourage through the use of these same technologies and resources.

The bitter rivalries between these elite-oligarchical groupings can be explained by the fact that they are not caused by a clash of ideas or values—the differences between them on that count are not large—but by the significant overlaps in their potential electorate and their aims of acquiring and retaining power and property. The lack of rules in political competition can also be explained by the specific character of Russian political-legal culture and the lack of elite consolidation. In addition, the history of many countries' transformations over the last few decades allows us to surmise that, without consolidation of the elite, neither social stability nor successful completion of reforms will be possible. This consolidation can be either voluntary or coerced. Voluntary consolidation is based upon shared values and aims or upon consensus on the rules and norms of social conduct, including political competition. At this point, neither the former nor the latter conditions for voluntary elite consolidation are being met in Russia. For that reason, it is likely that Russia will again see the coerced consolidation of the elite that has characterized so much of her history. This is instinctively sensed by the people, who are as usual turning to the search for a strong supporter of firm state authority who will 'bring order' to the country. The ruling elites are hoping to provide an answer to those hopes in the shape of Vladimir Putin.

As of today, the Russian political system continues to experience a prolonged period of transformation to democracy. It has to be said that the most recent experiment in adopting a few liberal-democratic forms of political-state power has thus far been mostly unsuccessful. Constitutional-political reforms are unavoidable for Russia. This is shown by the first steps of the president of the country to form seven federal okrugs and to initiate a project for laws to change both the way in which the Federation Council—the upper house of Parliament—is formed and also the balance of powers between local and regional authorities. But only time will tell whether a charismatic leader with the help of a reinforced state will be able to consolidate society and the elites without trampling on human rights and establishing an authoritarian regime that smothers the energy and freedom of its citizens. For the time being, both Russian citizens and observers abroad are trying to see whether the idea of 'a dictatorship of the law' that Vladimir Putin proclaims will in practice turn out to be a repudiation of the supremacy of the law, whether in the process of inevitable and justified efforts to limit the oligarchs' powers, freedoms—including freedom of information—will be preserved, and whether the conflict in the Chechen Republic will move on from armed conflict to political negotiation. Some wait with hope, others with trepidation, to see whether the fledgling Russian democracy can survive the experience of a 'strong' state.

39 Electoral Democracy or Electoral Clanism? Russian Democratization and Theories of Transition

Alexander Lukin

It seems clear that Russia's attempts at democratization and Westernization will not meet the expectations of Russia's democratic reformers. As happened in previous eras of Westernization, only some elements of Western liberal democracy have taken root in Russian soil, the most important of them being competitive elections. Other fundamental elements of liberalism have not only failed to flourish, but have degenerated since the late Soviet era. Compared with the late Gorbachev period of 1990–91, the mass media and courts in today's Russia are less independent, society's role is weaker, personal rights and freedoms are less secure, and even elections are less free and fair than they were in 1990. To understand this outcome of Russian democratization, the correlation between the electoral process and the development of liberalism should be examined.

Elections and liberal democracy

By the second half of the twentieth century, the belief that democracy is the ideal or at least the best possible organization of human society has become dominant among political scientists, and especially among the political elites of most countries of the world. There are virtually no discussions today of whether democracy is good or bad; opinions differ only on what kind of democracy is more democratic, or what kind of democracy is genuine. Some political scientists have pointed out that the desire of every leader and political movement in today's world to be seen as democratic led to such stretching of the term that it turned into 'not so much a term of restricted and specific meaning as a vague endorsement of a popular idea.'[1]

But the meaning of 'democracy' has not withered away completely. Authors of its numerous modern definitions can be divided into two major groups. Those who belong to the first, following Joseph Schumpeter, maintain that elections are the only practical criterion of

Reproduced, with minor abbreviations, from *Demokratizatsiya: The Journal of Post-Soviet Democratization*, 7/1 (Winter 1999), 93–110, by kind permission of the author and the Helen Dwight Reid Educational Foundation.

[1] Robert A. Dahl, *Democracy and Its Critics* (New Haven and London: Yale University Press, 1989), 2.

democracy.[2] The other group believes that democracy cannot be defined by elections alone. It can in turn be divided into two subgroups. The first consists of those who include the fundamentals of political liberalism in their definition of democracy. They argue that a democratic society should be characterized not only by the freedom and fairness of elections but also by a broadly defined pluralism. Thus, they identify democracy with its liberal-democratic form.[3] Others add social and economic democracy, guarantees of social equality, or at least of some level of social justice.[4]

Discussions about democracy are carried on almost exclusively among political theorists. In practical politics, however, Schumpeter's definition has prevailed. In today's world, governments and non-governmental groups in the West, and their supporters from the opposition forces advocating democracy and liberalization in non-democratic countries, call for immediate general elections according to the rules that exist in contemporary, developed liberal democracies. Regardless of whether it is Bosnia, Russia, Rwanda, China, or Nigeria, elections are promoted as the first and primary remedy for societal evils. In many cases, this approach has led to success, and using the criterion of elections alone, the number of democracies in the world is growing steadily. On these grounds, supporters of the electoral approach have begun to speak of the 'third wave' of democratization, which even led to the emergence of such bizarre concepts as Francis Fukuyama's 'end of history.'

At the same time, several theorists have observed that in many countries elections did not produce liberal democracy, with its widely accepted traits: a high level of freedom, the rule of law, secure rights and freedoms of individuals and minorities, and so forth.[5] In fact, in some cases they led to the reverse. Analysis of this phenomenon resulted in a new formulation that separated elections from liberalism and (when elections were still considered to be the essence of democracy) democracy from liberalism. The political systems that allow regular and relatively free elections but by all other dimensions do not meet the standards of liberal democracy were defined as 'electoral,' 'illiberal,' or 'delegative' democracies.[6]

According to the supporters of these new definitions, although the number of illiberal democracies in the world is growing fast, very few of them evolve into liberal democracies of the Western type. They warn that the formal electoral method of evaluation does not allow understanding of the more fundamental dimensions of a political system.[7] The experience

[2] Joseph A. Schumpeter, *Capitalism, Socialism and Democracy* (New York: Harper, 1942), 269. Among contemporary theorists this point of view is clearly shared by Samuel Huntington and Adam Przeworski with his colleagues. See Samuel P. Huntington, *The Third Wave: Democratization in the Late Twentieth Century* (Norman and London: University of Oklahoma Press, 1995), 7-10; Adam Przeworski, Michael Alvares Jose Antonio Cheibub, and Fernando Limongi, 'What Makes Democracies Endure?' *Journal of Democracy* , 1 (Jan. 1996): 50–1.

[3] See Robert A. Dahl, *Polyarchy: Participation and Opposition* (New Haven: Yale University Press, 1971), 2–3.

[4] For example, John Rawls, *A Theory of Justice* (Cambridge, Mass.: The Belknap Press of Harvard University Press, 1971), 75–83; Anthony Arblaster, *Democracy* (Buckingham: Open University Press, 1994), 98–9.

[5] For a comprehensive list of components of liberal democracy, see Larry Diamond, *The End of the Third Wave and the Global Future of Democracy* (Vienna: Institute for Advanced Studies, 1997), 8–10.

[6] Diamond, *The End of the Third Wave and the Global Future of Democracy*, 7; Daniel A. Bell, David Brown, Kanishka Jayasuriya, and David Martin Jones, *Towards Illiberal Democracy in Pacific Asia* (New York: St. Martin's Press, 1995); Fareed Zakaria, 'The Rise of Illiberal Democracy,' *Foreign Affairs*, 76 (Nov./Dec. 1997): 22–43; Guillermo O'Donnell, 'Delegative Democracy,' *Journal of Democracy* , 1 (Jan. 1994): 55–69.

[7] On the 'fallacy of electoralism' see, e.g. Diamond, *The End of the Third Wave and the Global Future of Democracy*, 5.

of democratization in such a vast country as Russia can provide important material for this discussion.

Russian democratization and theories of transition to democracy

There are two main approaches to the attempt at democratization in Russia. One employs popular theories of 'transition' and 'rational choice' and rejects cultural explanations. The other uses the traditional stereotypical view of the Russian political culture, according to which Russia's authoritarian cultural tradition rejects liberal democracy. The second approach is clearly simplistic and stunted, since it is static by definition and does not allow any significant change of political culture. The very fact that in some countries liberal democracy has finally stabilized suggests that preexisting culture is not an absolute and deterministic factor but can significantly change over time. This, however, does not mean that beliefs do not play a role in each specific period. As Larry Diamond put it, 'Whether changing or enduring, political culture does shape and constrain the possibilities for democracy.'[8]

Nevertheless, one often finds attempts to theorize about Russian democratization without employing the cultural factor. One of the most consistent attempts was undertaken by Michael McFaul. McFaul sees today's Russia as a country that has completed its transition to electoral democracy, where all major political actors have 'acquiesced to a new, albeit minimal, set of rules of political competition in which popular elections were recognized as the only legitimate means to political power.'[9] In his analysis, McFaul combines two approaches. According to one, 'rational choice' theory, the political process is determined by individuals who make rational decisions, pursuing their own interests and maximizing their own expected utility. Accordingly, political transition is seen as a struggle between the two groups: proponents of change and supporters of the *ancien regime*, the incumbents and the challengers. Sometimes these two groups come to an agreement on a new set of rules determining political behavior. In that case, the transition goes on smoothly and succeeds. In other cases, they do not agree and the transition fails. The second approach provided by the modern studies of transitions defines conditions under which a successful transition is possible: 'the narrower the contested agenda of change, the more likely that agreement will emerge.'[10]

McFaul divides the Russian transition into three periods. The first two attempts were unsuccessful: one ended in the putsch in August 1991 and the collapse of the Soviet Union; the next, in the armed conflict between the president and the Supreme Soviet in 1993. In both cases, 'agreement over new rules was not reached, pacts were not negotiated, and actors went outside of the existing rules of the game to pursue their interests. Opposing, polarized camps pursued zero-sum strategies until one side won because the contested agenda of change was wide and the balance of power between opposing actors ambiguous.' Thus, the reason for the failure is found in the excessive agenda of change, which included not only

---

[8] Larry Diamond, 'Introduction: Political Culture and Democracy,' in *Political Culture and Democracy in Developing Countries*, Larry Diamond, ed. (Boulder, Colo., and London: Lynne Rienner Publishers, 1993), 27.

[9] Michael McFaul, 'Democracy Unfolds in Russia,' *Current History* (Oct. 1997): 319.

[10] Michael McFaul, 'There Is a Charm? Explaining Success and Failure on Russia's Transition Road,' unpublished manuscript, Sept. 1997, 33. Courtesy of the author.

reform of political institutions, but also the introduction of new types of property relations, changes in sovereignty, and the need to redraw national and internal borders.

During the third stage, the number of issues on the agenda for change significantly narrowed. The questions of state sovereignty, borders, and property redistribution had already been largely settled, and the only important remaining problem was to find a new balance of political power. That is why, in McFaul's view, this problem was solved much more easily: the strongest actor imposed an explicit set of new rules and codified them in the new constitution of 1993, the distribution of power between actors changed, the balance of power was recognized by all significant actors, and the author of the new rules, Boris Yeltsin, although to a limited extent, 'submitted to self-binding mechanisms built into the new institutional order.'[11]

Explaining successful political change is in fact simply common sense: the less you change, the easier it is to achieve change. It does not, however, provide an answer to an important question: When the agenda of change is roughly the same, why in some cases does transition go much faster and easier and finally succeed, while in others it encounters great difficulties or even fails? Here one has to take into consideration the factor of culture and analyze the subjective understandings of goals, motives, and ideals of the actors. Let us compare, for example, former parts of one country: Estonia, Russia, Georgia, and Tadzhikistan. In all of them, the agenda for change was relatively the same: new borders, new sovereignty, redistribution of property, reconsideration of the internal political balance. Nevertheless, the results were quite different. The same can be said about Slovakia and the Czech republic, Serbia and Slovenia, or India, Pakistan, and Bangladesh. The failure of democratic institutions in some countries (especially in Asia and Africa where they were introduced by colonial powers) and their survival in others constituted a main reason for Gabriel Almond and Sidney Verba's introducing the concept of political culture in the first place.[12] Thus, a wider look at the Russian transition demands inclusion of the cultural factor into any theory of transition.

On the whole, one can agree with McFaul's 'rational choice' argument that 'the greater the consensus concerning the perception of the balance of power between major actors, the more likely a new set of rules can be accepted by all,'[13] but with one clarification: What exactly is considered rational (or irrational) behavior in a specific society at a specific time is determined by its culture. For example, a Japanese student who fails a university entrance exam may consider it rational to commit suicide by jumping out of a window because life without a university diploma in Japan might be widely believed to be disgraceful. A Russian student is likely to consider such an act irrational, even silly, and would rather drink a bottle of vodka to forget the failure and wait for another opportunity next year. That is not to say that no Russian student commits suicide under the given circumstances. However, statistics show that Japanese students commit suicide more often than students of any other nation. Cultural attitudes are not iron laws; individual behavior is determined by various factors. But knowledge of cultural attitudes allows one to speak of the most likely, typical behavior that is reflected by statistics. This is true of political behavior. A fighter for the rights of an

[11] Ibid. 34.

[12] Gabriel A. Almond and Sidney Verba, *The Civic Culture: Political Attitudes and Democracy in Five Nations* (Princeton: Princeton University Press, 1963).

[13] McFaul, 'There Is a Charm?' 33.

ethnic group in the United States is likely to consider it rational to engage in political lobbying and trying to influence public opinion using the mass media. To achieve a similar aim, a Muslim fundamentalist who believes that his soul will go directly to Heaven after he sacrifices himself for the just cause may believe it rational to blow himself up in an Israeli bus full of innocent people. In one political culture, it is thought rational to fight until final victory and give one's life for an idea; in another, it is thought rational to compromise in order to achieve what is practically possible.

Thus, explaining a choice of an individual or a political group is impossible without understanding what the actors themselves believe to be rational. The probability of achieving a consensus about the balance of power between major actors during a transition period has much to do with the subjective orientation toward consensus in general, the presence (or absence) of a wish to achieve it, and an understanding of its necessity. A balance of power is impossible or very difficult to achieve if such an understanding is alien to a given political culture, which might lack the custom, tradition, or desire to share power.

Soviet political culture and the collapse of the Soviet Union

Although many Russian political analysts and politicians, both in discourse and in theoretical writings, call for the separation of powers or a system of checks and balances, these democratic concepts have not yet penetrated Russian political culture in the post-Soviet era. These notions, borrowed from Western or pre-revolutionary Russian discourse, are usually seen in Russia today as instruments for achieving a higher political goal: an ideal and just society that would guarantee prosperity for all. If these instruments do not lead to a just society, they may be sacrificed and replaced by more effective ones. In this sense, the rule of law, rights of individuals and groups, and constitutional powers of different branches of government, although believed to be important and desirable, are valued less than other political goals.

The source of this instrumental approach to democratic procedures can be found in the political culture and political reality of the Soviet Union. There have been many attempts to theorize about post-Soviet Russian society. Most such attempts by political scientists, however, were superficial applications of Western political concepts to a very different Russian reality and, therefore, were inadequate. The most successful seems to be the anthropological approach of Janine Wedel, who sees the political process in today's Russia as a struggle between clans and cliques.[14] She, however, does not show the sources of the new Russian clan political system and the history of its development. To understand these sources one should look carefully at the last period of the history of the Soviet Union.

The political system of the classic USSR was characterized by an extreme concentration of power. That is why it was often defined as 'totalitarian.' However, the concentration of power did not manifest itself in the total control of the central Communist Party authority in Moscow (as it is often presented). Governmental authorities at various levels based on territorial or branch principles exercised power within their area of responsibility. The essence of Soviet totalitarianism was that all persons and institutions were co-opted by the

---

[14] Janine R. Wedel, 'Clique-Run Organization and U.S. Economic Aid: An Institutional Analysis,' *Demokratizatsiya*, 4 (Fall 1996): 571–97.

party structure. Every artist, writer, and actor, theoretically, was under a higher authority: a union of artists, writers, or actors. Those unions in turn had ministries above them, and the ministries had corresponding departments of the CPSU Central Committee. The structure went up to the Politburo of the CPSU Central Committee, which, in theory, had unlimited authority over everything. In practice, of course, the Politburo did not fire or employ every person in the country, it did not instruct every artist on what to paint, or every singer on what to sing, but it had the capability of doing so.

The highest authority sometimes allowed or in some cases even encouraged competition among various agencies (for example, between the KGB, the interior ministry, and the prosecutor's office, or between central ministries and local authorities), but there was always a higher level of authority above the competing ones that controlled all sides and was able to stop the rivalry if it had gone too far. Soviets were subordinate to their executive committees, and the executive committees to the CPSU committees of the corresponding level, and they all reported to the party committee of a higher level. On every building of the formally independent court one could read its official name: 'The Ministry of Justice of the RSFSR, People's Court of X District.' There were groups in the Soviet Union that promoted their interests and agenda. But until the very late years of Gorbachev's rule, any such groups had to act through official channels, recognizing a higher authority. They did not have a right simply to advertise their agenda, but could only submit it upward through the hierarchy.

This system naturally influenced beliefs of the population. And Russian democrats were no exception. They regarded the promotion of democratization as a tool that had to be used to destroy the system of absolute power of the corrupt, ineffective, brutal communist bureaucrats and to put in its place a similarly absolute power of democrats. They believed that only the absolute power of the 'good guys' could secure the creation of an ideal democratic society. The most important features of this society were believed to be justice, prosperity, and the realization of wishes and creative potential for all. The communist power and the government in general (since the Communist Party and the Soviet government made up a unified system of power) were understood to be the main obstacles to achieving this ideal. To remove this obstacle, it was thought necessary to destroy the whole pyramid of power from the top to bottom.

In 1991, the core of this pyramid disappeared and the whole structure crashed. It left behind numerous fragments: soviets, ministries, various government agencies, industries, research institutes, and other institutions that lost their leaders. After a short period of confusion, they began consolidating their bureaucratic power over those who had previously been under their command. In the absence of control from above and lacking the concept of separating power, these clans began fighting for absolute authority in their areas of competence. Some of them called themselves 'democratic,' some 'patriotic,' and some were politically neutral. Some were consolidating within a specific territory (as regional and republican power elites), and some according to the branch principle (as Gazprom, Lukoil, Russian Public Television, and other 'privatized' monopolies); some were formed of former friends and colleagues (as the influential St Petersburg clan led by Anatoliy Chubais), and others on the basis of former criminal connections. There were, of course, many mixed cases, and intermingling between new and old clans was also evident (or, to put it more precisely, those formed of formerly official and formerly unofficial structures). They had one thing in common: both old and new clans aimed not at negotiating to share power and responsibility with others, but at grabbing as much power and property as possible. In this sense, they all supported privatization of property and power and demanded 'sovereignty' over their resources.

Political differences played some role in this struggle, but they were not its determining factor. A vivid example is the struggle between Soviets and the executive branch that in 1992–93 paralyzed the government from district to federal level. This conflict was not as much over programs or ways of development, as between clan-type bureaucratic institutions whose former judge and boss, the CPSU, had left them to the mercy of fate. During that period, the supreme leader of the 'Soviet' clan, Ruslan Khasbulatov, saw his institution not as a parliament of the Western type, but as a Soviet-style department, and he was building it accordingly. He tried to introduce strict bureaucratic discipline from top to bottom not only within the Supreme Soviet, but to subordinate all lower level Soviets to those of a higher level (district Soviets reporting to regional, and regional to Khasbulatov himself). Khasbulatov, whose constitutional job was to preside over meetings of the Supreme Soviet and the Congress of People's Deputies, believed himself to be the head of the country's entire system of Soviets. And because, according to the constitution, the Congress of People's Deputies was the country's supreme authority, Khasbulatov saw himself as the supreme leader of the entire country. Likewise, President Boris Yeltsin saw himself as the supreme leader both as head of the country's executive branch, and as 'guarantor of the constitution' standing above all branches of power.

The fact that Yeltsin, unlike Khasbulatov, was elected by direct popular vote, made him confident that his authority was unlimited, regardless of any legal and constitutional formalities. The chairman of the Constitutional Court, Valeriy Zor'kin, also saw himself as the highest authority in the country, towering above both representative and executive branches and not limited to the field of interpreting the constitution. He often gave directions to the president and the parliament on how they should solve economic and political problems. Even Vice President Aleksandr Rutskoy demanded equal powers with the president based on the fact that they both were popularly elected on the same ballot.

'Democrats' and communist supporters, who were bitter enemies during the election campaign, soon joined forces to fight their former brothers-in-arms, who found themselves working for various branches of the executive—a clear indication of the bureaucratic (not ideological) character of the struggle for power, which began at the bottom level and only subsequently reached the federal center. Its first battle took place in the Oktyabr'skiy district in Moscow between the overwhelmingly democratic district soviet and its democratic chairman, Il'ya Zaslavsky. The war ended in October 1993 with the shelling of the building of the democratic Supreme Soviet by troops loyal to the democratic president. All sides accused the others of being totalitarian and nondemocratic, and of using old Soviet methods of suppressing opposition.

The proclamation of sovereignty by former Soviet and later Russian 'ethnic' republics, and even by some regions and districts, can also be understood as a bureaucratic struggle among fragments of a totalitarian system. Nationalist slogans (especially in the regions where the titular 'nationality' did not constitute a majority and ethnic problems were not acute) were often mere pretexts. Every minor regional government wanted to be sovereign at least over its small territory, and to control all property of value that happened to be there. Some cases were quite bizarre, such as the claim by the democratically dominated soviet of the Krasnopresnenskiy district in Moscow to sovereignty not only over all district property but also over the district air space. The fierce struggles for power among bureaucratic clans, even at the grassroots level, again argues against the theory that success of transition is determined exclusively by the scope of the agenda of change. The agenda at the district level was much narrower than at the national level, but the results were the same.

The so-called 'privatization' of state property also developed along the lines of bureaucratic-clan politics. Very rarely was state property transferred to genuinely private owners; as a rule, enterprises were grabbed by their former state managers, their families and friends, and groups otherwise connected to them, practically for free. The process was very different from examples of democratization in 'classic' autocratic regimes in Latin America or Southern Europe where major elements of the market structure and liberal politics were already in place. In the Soviet Union, it was part of the fragmentation of a totalitarian system into equally totalitarian parts. Before, everything belonged to one boss. Now that the boss was dead, everyone hurried to grab whatever they could: power, property, even air.

The essence of this struggle was poorly understood by most Western analysts, who stereotyped Russian political actors into two groups: the conservatives and the reformers, the supporters of the old and the promoters of the new, the democrats and the Reds. The honor of being included among the 'good guys' by influential forces in the West was often superficial. According to Wedel, the people of the St Petersburg clan came to be seen in the West as the only genuine reformers of the Russian economy largely because they spoke good English, could use economic terminology familiar to Western politicians, had previously studied at Western universities, were ready to call themselves 'reformers,' and had personal connections with influential Western economists. Granting full support to only one Gaidar-Chubais clan (which was not the only or even the most influential 'democratic' and 'reform-minded' group), the West committed a big mistake. Instead of promoting agreement, compromise, the separation of powers, and the division of authority, Western policy encouraged one clan to grab all of the power at the expense of others, to get around the official budget, to evade the constitutional control of the parliament and the government, and to disregard the existing law. The fallacy of this approach was, according to Wedel, based on 'thinking that lasting institutions can be built by supporting particular people, instead of helping to facilitate processes and the rule of law.'[15] There were, of course, supporters of the old and the new in Russia, but differences along those lines were disappearing fast. On the one hand, all actors wanted a change: to redistribute power and property in their favor. On the other, all acted within the framework and under the influence of old beliefs.

Elections played a peculiar role in this situation. At first, in the last years of Gorbachev's rule, they led to significant changes in the ruling elites. However, gradually, after the power was redistributed, the leadership of clans and groupings began to use elections to legitimize their claims to greater power at the expense of other clans. This stimulated the disintegration of the political system and led to dangerous conflicts that sometimes involved armed fighting. While the communist leaders were not elected and were not regarded as legitimate by the population, officials of every level in the new Russia were elected by popular vote and acquired legitimate status.

In this sense, the collapse of the Soviet Union and the following events should be

---

[15] Ibid. 595.

compared not with the death of authoritarianism in countries that experienced relatively long periods of limited liberalization (such as Spain, Portugal, or some Latin American countries) but with the breakup of another highly centralized monolith: the Chinese empire. In China, as in the Soviet Union, disintegration of the traditional, centralized, hierarchical system of government as a result of the revolution of 1911 was speeded by popular elections in 1913, leading to the creation of territorial militarist clans headed by warlords and of powerful oligarchic cliques with close ties to the government. The country was plunged into a period of ethnic and regional conflicts and wars until the strongest clan (which happened to be communist) took full control.

Democracy and the collapse of totalitarianism

Isaiah Berlin, in his classic *Two Concepts of Liberty*, pointed out that an enlightened and liberal autocracy could in theory secure more freedom than a democracy, where the majority brutally imposes its will on the minority. He stressed that 'freedom in this sense, at any rate logically, is not connected with democracy or self-government.'[16] But it is only recently that Western political scientists have begun to discuss the idea that democracy, if planted in unfertile soil, may fail to lead to greater freedom, and can even result in eliminating the small degree of liberalism already in place. Along with the classic cases of the democratic election of fascist regimes in Germany and Italy, several more recent examples are usually quoted in this respect: the near-victory of Muslim fundamentalists in Algeria, where a secular government had to cancel elections; elections in Yugoslavia that opened the way to power for nationalist extremists in each constituent republic and led to ethnic wars and the breakup of the federation, and so forth. Recently, in an intriguing article, Fareed Zakaria argued that in the contemporary world it is not liberalism, but illiberal democracy, where popularly elected leaders suppress civic liberties, that is on the rise. According to Zakaria, 'constitutional liberalism has led to democracy, but democracy does not seem to bring constitutional liberalism.' He pointed out that 'during the last two decades in Latin America, Africa, and parts of Asia, dictatorships with little background in constitutional liberalism have given way to democracy. The results are not encouraging.'[17]

Unfortunately, the possibility of a negative impact from the immediate introduction of democratic procedures in the Soviet Union has not been discussed by Western political scientists, or by Russian democrats. Both maintained that free elections would inevitably end communist domination and bring to power democrats who would create a Western-style, liberal constitutional democracy. Neither the role of popular beliefs nor the peculiarities of the structure of Russian society was taken into account.

There were, however, Russian authors who foresaw the coming threat. One of them was an émigré philosopher and political thinker, Ivan Il'in, who was exiled from Russia in 1922 by the Bolshevik government. Il'in believed that the failure of the first Russian democratization attempt in 1917 and the coming to power of fascist regimes in Europe constituted important lessons for those who were elaborating a strategy for Russia's post-totalitarian development. In his opinion, these historic disasters resulted from the dogmatic belief of

---

[16]   Isaiah Berlin, *Two Concepts of Liberty* (Oxford: Clarendon Press, 1958), 14.
[17]   Zakaria, 'The Rise of Illiberal Democracy,' 28.

democratic political activists in the necessity of introducing full-fledged democracy to unprepared societies. He predicted that if such an attempt failed in Russia in 1917, after a relatively long period of 'preparation,' the situation after the collapse of communism would be much less favorable. Writing in the late 1940s and early 1950s, Il'in argued that long years of totalitarianism changed the character of the people. In his view, 'if there is something that can deliver new, heaviest blows to Russia after communism, it is the stubborn attempts to introduce there a democratic system after totalitarian tyranny, because this tyranny had enough time to undermine all the necessary prerequisites of democracy in Russia, without which only mob riots, universal corruption and venality, and the surfacing of new ... tyrants are possible.' Il'in envisioned a real possibility of the disintegration of the country, its split into 'a system of small and powerless communities,' as a result of which 'the territory of Russia will be boiling with endless disputes, conflicts and *civil wars*'; a dismembered Russia will 'turn into a gigantic "Balkans," an eternal source of wars, a great breeding-ground of disturbances' and become 'an incurable plague for the entire world.'[18] As a way out, he proposed to introduce a strong authoritarian power that would educate the population and manage a return to normality by increasing the level of freedom, enriching the political experience of the population through a gradual introduction of elections and broadening electoral rights, guaranteeing rights of private property, and stimulating the development of independent education and information.

At the time, Il'in's ideas had very limited influence in the Soviet Union and among the émigré community. It was important, however, that among those echoing his views inside the country was the famous writer Aleksandr Solzhenitsyn. Beginning in the late 1960s, in articles and public addresses, Solzhenitsyn called for a careful, slow, and smooth way out of totalitarianism because 'if democracy is declared suddenly it would lead to an interethnic war in our country which would instantly wash away that very democracy.'[19] In his open letter to Soviet leaders, written in 1973 when he was still in the Soviet Union, Solzhenitsyn tried to persuade them that communist totalitarianism was doomed and therefore they should think about a reasonable way out. He suggested that they should reject the official ideology, allow religious and ideological pluralism, introduce the rule of law, cultivate the psychology of property owners in the population, and develop Siberia and Far Eastern regions of the country, while at the same time maintaining a monopoly on political power.[20] In 1990, in his analysis of Gorbachev's reforms, Solzhenitsyn again touched on the problems of democracy and transition from totalitarianism. After sharply criticizing the messy consequences of Gorbachev's perestroika, he explained that he did not mean 'to suggest that the future Russian Union will have no need for democracy. *It will need it very much*. But given our people's total lack of preparation for the intricacies of democratic life, democracy must be built from bottom up, gradually, patiently, and in a way designed to last rather than being proclaimed thunderously from above in its full-fledged form.'[21]

---

[18] Ivan Il'in, *O gryadushchey Rossii (Of Future Russia)* (Moscow: Voenizdat, 1993), 158, 172.

[19] A. Solzhenitsyn, 'Presskonferentsiya v Stokgol'me' (Press conference in Stockholm), 12 Dec. 1974. In A. Solzhenitsyn, *Publitsistika. Obshchestvennye zayavleniya, interv'yu, presskonferentsii* (Paris: YMCA-Press, 1989), 130.

[20] Aleksandr I. Solzhenitsyn, *Letter to Soviet Leaders* (New York, Evanston, San Francisco, London: Index on Censorship, 1974).

[21] Aleksandr Solzhenitsyn, *Rebuilding Russia: Reflections and Tentative Proposals* (New York: Farrar, Straus and Giroux, 1991), 82.

Il'in and Solzhenitsyn were ostracized by both Soviet and Western democrats, who blamed them for advocating autocracy and even fascism. The belief that immediate elections were the remedy for all of Russia's problems dominated both the Western political establishment and Russian opposition. A similar kind of criticism was recently aimed at Zakaria, whose only fault was to point to a well-known fact that authoritarian British colonial rule established the basis for relatively stable democracy in some former colonies. Zakaria was immediately blamed for advocating colonialism. Today, however, many experts acknowledge that one does not have to be an advocate of fascism or colonialism to doubt the role of premature elections, because 'if the ultimate objective is to encourage continuous development toward a well-functioning democracy, the *prerequisites* of democratic elections must not be ignored.'[22]

Political developments in post-Soviet Russia show that the pessimists were generally right. It is unreasonable to argue that those who spoke against an immediate introduction of a full-fledged democracy in the USSR were enemies of freedom and democracy in general and brought the disaster of new authoritarianism upon Russia. They were right in their analysis: liberal democracy on an unprepared soil is impossible, and elections under such circumstances inevitably lead either to anarchy or to a new authoritarianism legitimized by popular vote. The political predictions of Solzhenitsyn, who was accused by many 'professionals' of politics and political science of amateurism, idealism, and outdated traditionalism, turned out to be very realistic and practical. One should be glad that his darkest prophecies about a total ethnic war between the peoples of the Soviet Union have not yet been realized. Hitherto not millions (as the writer thought), but 'only' hundreds of thousands have died in such conflicts. But Solzhenitsyn's main conclusion that without a transition period, the way of democracy for Russia is 'false and premature' and that for the foreseeable future 'whether we like it or not, whether we intend it or not, Russia is nevertheless destined to have an authoritarian order' was correct.[23]

Already, the Russian political system is rather authoritarian. It is guarded from becoming an outright dictatorship not by its political culture or constitution, but by the weakness of the central authorities and by the personal respect of President Yeltsin for at least some democratic procedures and for the opinion of the West. At the same time, the weakness of central authority gives *carte blanche* to regional leaders. Those who care much less about democracy and the West have already created dictatorial regimes of various levels of repression (as in Primorskiy kray, republics of Bashkiria, Tatarstan, Kalmykia, and others).

As Zakaria rightly pointed out, for a transition to democracy to be successful the development of liberalism should precede the introduction of elections. The transitions in the countries of the former Soviet bloc provide proof for this conclusion. In countries with old, deep traditions of liberal politics, for example, the Czech Republic, the transition was peaceful and smooth. A comparison of the transition experiences in Hungary and Romania is revealing in this respect. Before entering the Soviet bloc, neither country had lived under democracy for any significant period of time, and their liberal traditions were equally weak. But the Hungarian communist leadership, already in the late 1950s, had begun liberalizing the regime, first in the sphere of economics and then in ideology and politics. By the time of

[22] Jorgen Elklit and Palle Svensson, 'What Makes Elections Free and Fair?' *Journal of Democracy*, 8 (July 1997): 34.
[23] Solzhenitsyn, *Letter to Soviet Leaders*, 53.

the collapse of the Soviet bloc, Hungary was arguably the freest of all its members, while Romania was ruled by the harshest dictatorship in the whole of Eastern Europe (with the possible exception of Albania). As a result, the transition to democracy in Hungary was entirely bloodless and much more successful than in Romania, which experienced a bloody popular revolt and a long period of instability. I would even express a seditious hypothesis: Hungary benefited not only from the readiness of its communist leadership under János Kádár to go ahead with serious reforms, but also from the fact that the threat of a new Soviet invasion contained democratization at the top level. As a result, the liberalization of the economy, ideology, and legislation and grass-roots democratization preceded free national elections. Full-fledged democracy came later to fertilized soil. The contrast with the situation of 1956 is only too evident. At that time, democratization was introduced quickly and without preparation, resulting in chaos, factional armed fighting, and lynchings (which events of course by no means justify the Soviet invasion).

In the Soviet Union, Hungarian-style liberal reforms under the guidance of a strong authoritarian power could have been undertaken by President Gorbachev. Several well-known Soviet political scientists, such as Andranik Migranyan and Igor Klyamkin, recommended such a policy to the Soviet leader in the late 1980s.[24] But such proposals were met with hostility by the majority of reformers, who demanded full-fledged democracy here and now. There was also no threat from the outside that would contain democratization. For internal political reasons, influenced by his advisors who were excessively good students of Western political thought but lacked a clear knowledge of their own country, Gorbachev tried to use free elections as a tool of liberalization to undermine the authority of the Communist Party apparatus (and was still criticized for being too slow by democratic dogmatists). At the same time, he did virtually nothing to reform the economy or to create a legal basis for liberalization. It soon became evident that the communist power structure, however stubborn and outdated it was, in fact constituted the only mechanism that governed the country. By destroying it and failing to substitute a new one, Gorbachev lost control over the political process, caused chaos in the system of government, and finally had to resign.

Despite this lesson, Yeltsin, who had even more confidence in Western-oriented advisors, committed the same mistake. Instead of consolidating his authority, legitimized by popular vote, and using his popularity for pushing forward a serious structural reform, he stressed elections and approved the kind of economic reform that would distribute the enormous resources under state ownership to a dozen clans of *nouveaux riches* without any significant benefit to the society. Yeltsin's political style matches well some elements of Guillermo O'Donnell's 'delegative democracy.' The Russian president believed that the people's trust, recorded in the verdict of the voters, gave him the right to unlimited power, while various formalities of liberalism, such as independent courts, were a nuisance (sometimes unavoidable in a democracy) that prevented him from doing what he was chosen to do: create the Great Democracy (as he saw it). This was a common belief among most democratic leaders in Russia on every level of authority. Not only president Yeltsin, but the mayors of Moscow and St Petersburg, Gavriil Popov and Anatoly Sobchak, the chairman of the Oktyabr'skiy

---

[24] For example, Andranik Migranyan, 'Dolgiy put' k yevropeyskomu domu' (The Long Road to the European Home), *Novyy Mir*, 7 (1989): 166–84; Igor Klyamkin, Interview in *Moskovskiy komsomolets*, 7 June 1990.

district soviet in Moscow, Il'ya Zaslavsky, and many of their supporters maintained: 'You elected us, now let us do whatever we think is right.' However, unlike leaders of 'delegative democracies,' Russian democratic leaders never stood above the struggle (although Yeltsin tried to create such an impression). In the public perception and in reality, they were leaders of one clan or an alliance of clans, and supported them against the others.

From the point of view of Russian democrats, the goal of building democracy justified the disregard of specific democratic procedures. One of the co-chairs of the Democratic Russia movement, Lev Ponomarev, for example, argued: 'Yes, a number of his [President Boris Yeltsin's] decrees, signed in a critical situation, were unconstitutional. But I would call them genius. They perfectly met political necessity.'[25] Moreover, at a certain stage Russian democrats, especially those who sided with the executive power, began to think that the enemies of reform used democratic procedures to the detriment of reform. The democrats who were elected to representative bodies thought the same of their former colleagues from the executive. As a result, in 1993 the country slid into chaos while power and property were divided among old and new clans and cliques. The power of the president remained strong only on paper, and his ability and will to promote liberal reforms almost came to naught.

The Russian experience

Despite a lengthy new attempt at democratization, today's Russia is still far from liberal democracy, perhaps farther even than in the last years of the Soviet Union. The new Russian experience shows that in a society where liberalization did not precede democratization and free elections were introduced hastily and spontaneously, a constitutional liberal-democratic system has few chances for survival. This does not mean that countries that lost stability as a result of excessively rapid democratization should be advised to reject all democratic achievements, forget about elections, and introduce an authoritarian dictatorship or invite the colonial rulers back. Such a recommendation is impossible in the contemporary world for both practical and ethical reasons. Obviously, there is no guarantee that an authoritarian or colonial regime is going to promote liberal democracy according to theoretical recommendations. Too many such regimes are preoccupied with maintaining power by any means, including severe repression, and such practice creates even more problems. In addition, the struggle for freedom and democracy, and sympathy for those who fall in this struggle, make it impossible for any person capable of humane feelings to recommend putting innocent people in jail and abolishing freedoms achieved by them in order to secure a theoretically superior path of transition. Nevertheless, Russia's experience, combined with failed or not extremely successful transitions to democracy in countries where hasty democratization led to anarchy or a new dictatorship (the Philippines, Algeria, Kazakhstan, Tadzhikistan, Georgia, Armenia, Croatia, Bosnia, and so forth), provides enough evidence to make different recommendations.

First, as Zakaria rightly argued, both scholars and politicians in the West should shift the focus of their support from those forces in countries with dictatorial regimes that call for immediate elections to those which may be capable of promoting consistent liberal reforms

---

[25] Quoted in V. Sogrin, *Politicheskaya istoriya sovremennoy Rossii* (Political History of Contemporary Russia) (Moscow: Progress-Akademia, 1994), 113.

while maintaining a certain level of stability and consolidation of state power. These reforms should not cover only the economy. The unique role of economic modernization as a basis for political democratization is often exaggerated. In fact, a market economy, which is impossible without a certain level of independence of economic actors, can stimulate the liberalization of politics only to a certain extent, by creating a system of new contractual relationships. However, recent studies show that new classes of entrepreneurs in some cultures may very well coexist with authoritarian power without demanding more independence or rights.[26] The development of a legal system and legal way of thinking is much more important. This should include the independence of the courts, the rule of law, separation of powers, development of independent civic organizations (not necessarily political, such as ecological or human rights groups), independence of mass media, and religious and ideological freedoms. These new phenomena are more important for creating the basis for liberal democracy. Equally important is maintaining effective government in the new, freer conditions, which implies a gradual reform of the work of police, courts, tax and customs agencies, ministries and departments of the central government, and local governments. Only in the process of these reforms of the political culture, of the ruling elites, and then of the entire population can respect for law and the concept of divided power become acceptable.

Second, it is necessary to recognize that the hasty introduction of free elections without previous political and economic liberalization is not only useless, but dangerous, having brought about near-anarchy on the vast territory of the former Soviet Union. Many in the West are beginning to understand how dangerous the anarchy is in Russia, a country with a huge arsenal of weapons of mass destruction that cannot secure proper storage of its nuclear materials. Recently worries have been expressed about free elections in Indonesia—another huge country with various complicated problems—where elections may destabilize the fragile ethnic and religious balance and bring to power ultranationalist leaders. One can only imagine what chaos free elections might bring to China—a country with a population of over one billion, with a significant nuclear arsenal and numerous economic, regional, ethnic, and ecological problems—if introduced before serious reforms of the legal system and of the entire mechanism of power.

Disregard for such reforms and overestimation of the role of elections are among the main reasons for Russia's condition today. Elections at various levels are held in Russia practically every month, but its political culture remains posttotalitarian. The elections do not create a new, effective system of government based on law and separation of powers, but are used by various clans in their struggle for power and even by criminal groups to evade justice. Therefore I do not consider the situation in Russia an irreversible triumph of democracy. The country's political culture has not fundamentally changed, and the absence of real liberal reforms does not augur well for such a change. The temporary balance of power, which came as result of forceful imposition of the will of one of the groups over others, is not based on new, stable rules of the game that are accepted by all. A new Russian president can easily ignore some provisions of the Yeltsin constitution or abolish it altogether. (Such an action would have solid legal grounds because the referendum on the adoption of the constitution was obviously fraudulent.) Therefore, Steven Fish's argument that many

---

[26] See Bell, Brown, Jayasuriya, and Jones, *Towards Illiberal Democracy in Pacific Asia.*

institutions in Russian politics, including democracy itself, survive by default, 'less because they function effectively than because no feasible alternatives seem to be at hand, or because the available alternatives do not enjoy the backing of forces that have sufficient power and resolve to alter the status quo,'[27] seems to be a more adequate description of the situation. With the aggravation of the economic crisis, alternatives will inevitably become more popular and the desire to alter the temporary balance will become stronger.

Under these circumstances, defining the current Russian political system as 'electoral democracy' is misleading. It manifests a common misperception that calls any country in which elections have been held without too many obvious irregularities a 'democracy.'[28] The term 'electoral clanism' describes Russia's reality more accurately. It is a political system where elections are not a means of selecting public officials according to law, within a framework of checks and balances (liberal democracy), or of directly selecting powerful charismatic authority that would occupy a position above the factional struggle and rule in the name of the majority (delegative or electoral democracy); rather they are merely the means of settling disputes among posttotalitarian clans that generally operate outside the law or in a situation of legal confusion.

All of this is not to say that liberal democracy can never take root in Russia. It is true that the liberal-democratic system was first formed in Europe under unique historic circumstances. But its later spread to many countries with different cultural traditions proves that the political culture of polyarchy can develop not only within a civilization based on Western Christianity. Nevertheless, a relatively long transition period is needed; in Europe itself the development of liberalism preceded the coming of the modern form of democracy by hundreds of years. Some think that in India, for example, this development occurred during the British colonial rule, when British respect for law was combined with indigenous Indian traditions of religious tolerance and peaceful coexistence of different cultural and ethnic groups and castes. In Greece, Japan, South Korea, Taiwan, Turkey, Poland, and Hungary, the consolidation of democratic regimes was preceded by lengthy periods when pluralistic elements of local traditions merged with the cultural and political influence of Western liberalism, creating a breeding ground for stable democracy with a unique national flavor.

Russian tradition also has some elements that may evolve into a liberal political culture. Russia's political system was already quite liberal in the nineteenth century, especially after the reforms of Alexander II, and after 1905 it became practically pluralist. Although the communist regime interrupted this development, some remnants of former liberalism survived. Some elements of real electoral practices (for example, in academic and professional organizations) and the tradition of moral independence were maintained during the Soviet period. Finally, at least one of the interpretations of the doctrine of the Orthodox Church, which is gaining more and more influence in today's Russia, stresses the importance of spiritual freedom. But these elements alone are an insufficient basis for a stable liberal-democratic regime. The most needed component—belief in the necessity to divide power—is still weak. Its further development is possible only if the Russian reforms fundamentally change their direction.

To become a democracy, Russia must develop the fundamentals of liberalism, a market

---

[27] M. Steven Fish, 'The Pitfalls of Russian Superpresidentialism.', *Current History* (Oct. 1997): 329.

[28] Elklit and Svensson, 'What Makes Elections Free and Fair?' 34.

economy, and the rule of law. Instead of an emphasis on elections and discussions of abstract monetarist schemes, it is important to develop respect for law and order, create a working system of separated and mutually controlling powers, and guarantee real independence of the courts and the mass media. At the same time, the system of government should be strengthened, so that decisions of all branches and levels of government are respected both by individual citizens and various groups. This can be achieved by a strong reform-oriented authority that would encourage necessary changes in the political culture. Alternatively, the country can slide into another circle of anarchy or produce a new totalitarian regime. This should be taken into consideration by those politicians whose goal is creating a liberal-democratic constitutional system in Russia.

40   Evaluating Russia's Democratization[1]

Archie Brown

Following a century in which Russia had more than its share of dictatorial rule, war, oppression, and suffering, it is appropriate to ask how far the high hopes for Russian democracy expressed at the beginning of the 1990s have been realized. Plenty of argument and a great deal of evidence relevant to that question are to be found among the preceding chapters of this volume. However, in order to evaluate the process of democratization in Russia more explicitly, a substantial part of this chapter will examine the extent to which contemporary Russia meets specific democratic criteria. In doing so I am partly following Robert Dahl's well-known eight 'requirements for a Democracy among a Large Number of People'.[2] However, I reduce Dahl's eight points to four (partly by amalgamation) and add two of my own which, I argue, are no less essential requirements of democracy than those whose central importance has been widely accepted.

The requirements of democracy which, in the pages that follow, form a basis for evaluation of the process of democratization in Russia are:

1. Freedom to form and join organizations
2. Freedom of expression and access to alternative sources of information
3. The right to vote in free and fair elections
4. The right to compete for public office
5. Political accountability
6. The rule of law[3]

---

[1] In the course of this chapter, I draw, with permission, from my article, 'Russia and Democratization', published in *Problems of Post-Communism*, 46/5 (Sept.–Oct. 1999), 3–13. The present chapter, however, is different both in structure and scope and, in contrast with the earlier article addressing a similar theme (written while Yeltsin was still Russia's president), takes account of developments up until December 2000. I am particularly grateful to Laura Belin, Yitzhak Brudny, and Paul Chaisty for their helpful comments on the draft chapter.

[2] These are: (1) freedom to form and join organizations; (2) freedom of expression; (3) right to vote; (4) eligibility for public office; (5) right of political leaders to compete for support; (6) alternative sources of information; (7) free and fair elections; and (8) institutions for making government policies depend on votes and other expressions of preference. See Robert A. Dahl, *Polyarchy: Participation and Opposition* (New Haven: Yale University Press, 1971), 3.

[3] The first four are those which draw upon (seven of) Dahl's points; the fifth and sixth requirements are those I add.

Six requirements for democracy

FREEDOM TO FORM AND JOIN ORGANIZATIONS

The freedom to join and form organizations, and other elements of freedom of association, emerged late in the Soviet period—from 1987–88 onwards—and many hundreds of thousands of people were actively involved in the new movements and organizations, especially during the last three years of the Soviet Union's existence.[4] At the beginning of the twenty-first century, the freedom to form an organization still exists, but belief in the efficacy of social movements and political association has declined. In formal terms, there was a growth in the number of groups in the Yeltsin era. Over 58,000 voluntary associations were registered by 1996, of which 3,000 had not only a local existence but operated also on a federal level.[5] By May 1999 the figure had grown to more than 100,000, of which 3,500 had an organization at the level of the federation.[6] Many of them existed largely or entirely on paper, and did not engage in any concrete activity. A majority of the groups were composed of only a handful of activists.[7] The most positive aspect of the post-Soviet growth in the absolute numbers of voluntary organizations was that this took place mainly outside Moscow, as compared with their disproportionate concentration (so far as the Russian republic was concerned) in the capital during the perestroika years.[8] In 1999 a federal law was passed whereby a re-registration process was required for all organized groups which would, according to the estimate of the then minister of justice, Pavel Krasheninnikov, 'liquidate about 50 per cent of the existing structures'.[9]

A case worthy of special attention is that of women's organized groups. In the post-Soviet period the social and political position of women has in a number of respects deteriorated, though not in all, for women bore by far the greater part of the burden of shortages and queuing characteristic of the Communist command economy. There are, however, far more women than male pensioners, given both the legacy of the Second World War and the fact that the death rates of men and women in Russia are so widely divergent. Many of them live in dire poverty, and for them the availability of produce in the shops is of little comfort. Women have not found it any harder than men to retain paid employment in post-Soviet Russia, but their presence in high politics declined in the course of the 1990s. (In the Communist era also, it should be added, women did not occupy the most influential political posts.) Sergei Peregudov, Natalya Lapina, and Irina Semenenko note that the movement, 'Women of Russia', successfully cleared the 5 per cent barrier for entry to the State Duma in the proportional representation part of the ballot in 1993, though it failed to do so in 1995. But they also argue that it would scarcely be correct to speak of a specific 'women's

---

[4] See M. Steven Fish, *Democracy from Scratch: Opposition and Regime in the New Russian Revolution* (Princeton: Princeton University Press, 1995); Geoffrey A. Hosking, Jonathan Aves, and Peter J. S. Duncan, *The Road to Post-Communism: Independent Movements in the Soviet Union, 1985–1991* (London: Pinter, 1992); and Alexander Lukin, *The Political Culture of the Russian 'Democrats'* (Oxford: Oxford University Press, 2000).

[5] Sergei Peregudov, Natalya Lapina, and Irina Semenenko, *Gruppy interesov i Rossiyskoe gosurdarstvo* (Moscow: Editorial URSS, 1999), 152.

[6] Ibid.

[7] Ibid. 151.

[8] Ibid. 152.

[9] Ibid.

movement' in Russia, for most of the women's organizations have not been concerned with gender-specific issues.[10]

Much that might be classified under the rubric of the women's movement involves multi-purpose associations as well as the institutionalization of very small (and often single-issue) groups. In this, women's associations differ little from the structure and focus of other social groups. The high political profile achieved for a time by 'Women of Russia', with its significant representation in the First Duma, was the exception that proved the rule, though its temporary success at a national level was not accompanied by much grass-roots political activity.[11] Moreover, that movement was less significant as a defender of women's distinctive interests than as a centrist and conditional ally of 'the party of power'. As befitted an organization which was an outgrowth of the Committee of Soviet Women, it did not, however, share Yeltsin's hostility to the Communist Party of the Russian Federation.[12] More than four-fifths of its voters were women, but even in 1993 five-sixths of Russian women supported other parties.[13] Following the December 1995 parliamentary election, the representation of women in high politics was significantly diminished. For example, in the Second Duma (1995–9) only 10 per cent of the deputies were women, and in the upper house of the legislature, the Federation Council, they constituted only 1 per cent.

During the Yeltsin years the kind of body carrying political weight and influencing public policy was very different from the mass movement, 'Democratic Russia', which helped to propel Boris Yeltsin to the Russian presidency in 1991. By the middle of the 1990s triangular relationships had developed within the political and economic elites, bringing together financiers, the profitable parts of Russian industry, and politicians or officials within the state structures. The term, 'financial-industrial groups' (or FIGs) which was coined for these golden triangles does not do justice to the scope of the interrelationships. Indeed, the most important of these groups took a quadrangular rather than triangular form. To the three-cornered linkage of political structures, banking, and industry was added a fourth dimension—ownership of a section of the mass media (both electronic and print).

The best known of these quadrangles are doubtless those associated with the names of Boris Berezovsky and Vladimir Gusinsky, both of whom have been summoned to answer criminal charges during the presidency of Vladimir Putin. The political significance of their changing relationship with state power in Russia is taken up later in the chapter. There have, however, been numerous other powerful groupings. One has centred on the giant gas company, Gazprom. It benefited from the patronage of Viktor Chernomyrdin who, conveniently, was Russia's longest-serving post-Soviet prime minister. The company's chief executive, Rem Viakhirev, has presided over a vastly rich source of revenue which enabled Gazprom to expand into banking and the mass media. It has partly owned Imperial Bank and has a substantial share in NTV and a smaller holding in Russian Public Television (ORT). Likewise, Moscow's mayor Yury Luzhkov has been not only the undisputed political boss of Russia's largest city, but has controlled property and industry in the capital, as well as several

---

[10] Peregudov, Lapina, and Semenenko, *Gruppy interesov*, 161–2.

[11] Ibid. 162.

[12] Stephen White, Richard Rose, and Ian McAllister, *How Russia Votes* (Chatham, NJ: Chatham House, 1997), 207; and Mary Buckley, 'Women and Public Life' in Stephen White, Alex Pravda, and Zvi Gitelman, eds, *Developments in Russian Politics 4* (Basingstoke: Macmillan, 1997), 189–207, esp. 198–202.

[13] White et al, *How Russia Votes*, 146.

newspapers, and cable networks. As noted by Laura Belin in Chapter 23, his television station, TV-Center, began broadcasting in June 1997. In many respects these conglomerates did not so much enhance democracy as the narrower interests of those with a stake in them. They did, however, help to sustain a flawed pluralism by providing alternative sources of information to those emanating from the Kremlin, a point which is elaborated below.

Political parties in the Second Russian Republic have been relatively weak and badly organized but by no means insignificant. The Communist Party, in particular, has country-wide support and a more solid organizational base than its rivals, though it has the problem that its strongest supporters are from the older generation and that its support is weakest among those under the age of 40.[14] Richard Rose, in Chapter 14, has pointed to the way in which parties have come and gone, making it difficult, if not impossible, to pinpoint accountability. Darrell Slider, in the following chapter, has shown how the move to election of regional governors before political parties had been established on a country-wide basis 'had a particularly negative impact on Russia's potential to develop national political parties', while Stephen Whitefield, in Chapter 16, observes that, notwithstanding the existence of partisan divisions in Russian society, parties have 'little presence outside Moscow' and, furthermore, 'play little role in governing' the country.

Yet, alongside a generally lower participatory rate in social and political organizations compared with the last years of the Soviet Union, there has been at least a very modest development and consolidation of political parties over the first post-Soviet decade. Russian parties may be top-down organizations but, with all their severe limitations, they have fared better than movements from below. Societal groups have played a much less salient role in post-Soviet political life than they did during the perestroika period. In the course of a detailed study of state–society relations in post-Communist Russia, Marcia Weigle writes:

The demobilization of Soviet Russia's nascent civil society after the demise of the Soviet Union meant that individuals and groups had no organized sphere in which they could articulate and reconcile their interests on the bases of established law and norms. . . . With no organizational or normative structures in place to shape the pursuit of personal and group interests, public life became a battleground of corruption, coercion, and crime, all in the name of the pursuit of personalistic, private interests that gave liberalism, with its emphasis on individual autonomy, a bad name.[15]

The official trade unions, inherited from Soviet times, have remained ineffectual in post-Soviet Russia.[16] Although there were miners' strikes and sit-ins in 1998, most action by Russian workers has been organized by small unofficial unions or movements. The government's assessment of union weakness became clear when it sent a bill to the State Duma in December 2000 which would revise the labour code by radically reducing workers' rights—at least on paper, for many of these rights had not meant much in practice. The bill proposed legalizing a twelve-hour working day, abolishing collective bargaining, and removing trade

---

[14] The survey evidence which supports that generalization is presented in Stephen Whitefield and Geoffrey Evans, 'Support for Democracy and Political Opposition in Russia, 1993–1995', *Post-Soviet Affairs*, 12/3 (July–Sept. 1996), 218–42, at p. 241.

[15] Marcia A. Weigle, *Russia's Liberal Project: State-Society Relations in the Transition from Communism* (University Park, Pa.: Pennsylvania State University Press, 2000), 335.

[16] Peregudov, Lapina, and Semenenko, *Gruppy interesov i Rossiyskoe gosudarstvo*, 164–74.

unions' rights to maintain offices and personnel on factory premises.[17] The small number of independent unions reacted more sharply than the official unions to the bill, and one activist in Zashchita, an alternative union claiming around 50,000 industrial and scientific workers, forecast that if the bill was passed, 'it will only succeed in giving a big impetus to genuine union organizing in Russia'.[18] On the government side, it was pointed out that by making it easier to dismiss workers, the bill would put an end to 'hidden unemployment', whereby people were nominally employed by a factory even if they were paid only irregularly (if at all). Duma deputies, however, who in general have been quick to endorse legislation emanating from the Putin administration, in this case responded cautiously, postponing their consideration of the bill until 2001.

Most movements from below have remained ineffective in post-Soviet Russia. During the Chechen war of 1994–6, an organization of Russian women, the Committee of Soldiers' Mothers, succeeded in getting access to the mass media and exercised some influence in mobilizing public opinion against the war. Earlier they had directed their attention to publicizing and combating the widespread and often brutal bullying of young conscripts in the Russian army.[19] But this association of soldiers' mothers has seen its influence and access decline, even though the launch of the second Chechen war in 1999 gave them more to worry about. The more general point is that the form of corporatism which has developed in Russia has given some financially powerful groups an inside track to, or even place within, the highest echelons of power and frozen others out, providing few incentives for citizens to participate in the organization of genuinely societal groups and even fewer opportunities for the groups to flourish and become influential.[20]

During the Putin presidency pressures from the state authorities on non-governmental organizations have become more overt. Already during Yeltsin's presidency there was, as noted above, a law requiring all NGOs to re-register with the ministry of justice or the regional authorities, and some human rights and religious groups have found it especially difficult to achieve registration. Among the organizations told that they could not include the phrase, 'the protection of citizens' rights' as part of their goals and objectives were Memorial,[21] the Glasnost Defence Foundation, and the St Petersburg-based Citizens' Watch.[22] The grounds for this decision were that only the state had the right to protect citizens. Re-registration has also been used highly selectively to delegitimize or put an end to the activities of religious groups not to the liking of the state authorities.[23] For example, the

[17] Fred Weir, 'The Kremlin Takes on Workers', *Christian Science Monitor*, 21 Dec. 2000.

[18] Weir, 'The Kremlin Takes on Workers'.

[19] Anatol Lieven, *Chechnya: Tombstone of Russian Power* (New Haven: Yale University Press, 1998), 201.

[20] For a useful guide to Russia's political parties, social movements, and organizations, see I. N. Bartygin, ed., *Politicheskie partii, dvizheniya i organizatsii sovremennoy Rossii na rubezhe vekov* (St Petersburg: izdatel'stvo V. A. Mikhaylova, 1999).

[21] Memorial began its existence as a pressure group in 1987, its initial aim being to have a memorial erected to the victims of Stalin. It developed into a movement concerned not only with investigating the political crimes of the past but also with advocacy of the rule of law. By the time it held a founding congress in January 1989 it had approximately 180 branches and some 20,000 active members. Its numbers are now much depleted. For the early years of Memorial's development, see Geoffrey A. Hosking, Jonathan Aves, and Peter J. S. Duncan, *The Road to Post-Communism: Independent Political Movements in the Soviet Union 1985–1991* (London: Pinter, 1992), esp. 13–19.

[22] Sarah E. Mendelson, 'The Putin Path: Civil Liberties and Human Rights in Retreat', *Problems of Post-Communism*, 47/5 (Sept.–Oct. 2000), 3–12, at p. 5.

[23] Ibid.

Salvation Army was told by a Moscow court in December 2000 that, since it had the word 'army' in its name, it was a 'militarized organization bent on the violent overthrow of the Russian government'.[24] In reality the Salvation Army had been operating community centres providing food, shelter, and clothing to the homeless and elderly poor in Moscow and thirteen other Russian cities.[25] The Russian human rights activist and Duma deputy Sergei Kovalev has taken an especially gloomy view of recent developments, saying: 'I fear, it is very likely that the year 2000 will someday be referred to as the "twilight of Russian freedom".'[26]

FREEDOM OF EXPRESSION AND ACCESS TO ALTERNATIVE SOURCES OF INFORMATION

The second requirement of democracy—freedom of expression and its essential counterpart, sources of information offering alternatives to the voice of officialdom—was achieved in the last few years of the Soviet Union's existence. A developing freedom of speech in private during the Khrushchev and Brezhnev years made a qualitative leap into freedom of speech in public in the late 1980s. After the proceedings of the First Congress of People's Deputies of the USSR in the spring of 1989 were broadcast live, and tens of millions of viewers heard deputies say with impunity things which would have earned them incarceration in a labour camp a mere five years earlier, freedom from fear replaced fear of freedom. The boundaries of glasnost were pushed wider, virtually from week to week, between 1986 and 1989, and by the end of that period had evolved into a genuine freedom of expression. Change in television came later than in the print media and was patchy, but even in 1989 not only did the live broadcasting of the First Congress of the new legislature have a huge impact, so also did the televised reporting of the anti-Communist demonstrations and the overthrow of Communist regimes throughout Eastern Europe that year.

In the post-Soviet period freedom of expression, in terms of people's ability to criticize as much as they like and to take part in demonstrations, has continued, and there has certainly been diversity in the print and electronic media, even if it is of varying reliability. There is also uninhibited access to foreign radio, satellite television, and now to the internet. The last of these additions to information technology is essentially a development of the post-Soviet period, although it follows logically from Russia's opening to the outside world which began in the second half of the 1980s. Communication both within the country and with foreigners by electronic mail is still an option available only to a fairly small minority of Russian citizens, but it has grown substantially in recent years. The FSB, successors to the KGB, are making strenuous efforts to monitor such activity, although thus far without impeding it.

In the *mass* media, the picture was mixed even before Putin succeeded Yeltsin in the presidency. The most independent television channel has been NTV, part of Vladimir Gusinsky's Media Most group. While its journalists engaged in a great deal of self-censorship and propaganda in 1996 to help ensure the re-election of Boris Yeltsin, at other times they have distanced themselves from the state authorities—in particular, with their

[24] As reported by Kenneth Baillie, the head of the Salvation Army's Russian activities (Paul Goble, 'Onward Christian Soldiers', *RFE/RL Security Watch*, 1/22 (18 Dec. 2000)).

[25] Ibid. That court decision is being contested by the Salvation Army, and it is possible that it may be reversed by a higher court (though at considerable legal expense), as has already been hinted by a Kremlin official.

[26] Cited by Mendelson, 'The Putin Path', 10.

reporting of the first Chechen war, and by *not* backing Vadim Putin in the run-up to the 2000 presidential election.

Neither in Russia nor in the West do limitations or pressures on journalistic freedom come entirely from the state. Newspaper proprietors, too, can restrict the range of critical comment and require deference to their own views and financial interests. While there has been some variety of opinion even within the newspapers owned by Boris Berezovsky and Gusinsky and the television channels controlled by them, the main advantage of this 'oligarchical corporatism' (a concept elaborated by Sergei Peregudov in Chapter 18) has been to provide alternative sources of information—different from that dispensed by other media groups and by the state. While the Berezovsky media have produced plenty of compromising information about business and political rivals, they have generally been more deferential to the state authorities than Gusinsky's Media Most. Berezovsky, indeed—until the Putin presidency—was very closely connected with the corridors of state power, not least through his excellent relations with Yeltsin's daughter, Tatyana Dyachenko.[27]

Some newspapers, it has to be said, would have ceased to exist altogether without the intervention of 'sponsors'. In the post-Soviet period the prices of the papers have risen sharply and their circulations have plummeted—in comparison with the last years of the Soviet Union. The newspaper, *Nezavisimaya gazeta*, run by a collective of journalists, had been a flagship of independence ever since it began publication in 1990, but, as Belin reports in Chapter 23, it ran into financial difficulties, and after disappearing altogether for several months in 1995, returned later that year under the financial control of Berezovsky. Although certainly much less independent than hitherto, it continued to publish a diversity of view in its opinion columns. It was, though, a definite setback for an independent press when the editor of *Nezavisimaya gazeta*, Vitaly Tretyakov, had, reluctantly, to accept funding from Berezovsky and, no less so, when the latter succeeded in the summer of 1999 in taking over *Kommersant*, a newspaper which had been particularly respected for its political news and analysis. Its independent editor, Raf Shakirov, was fired in August 1999, causing concern (which turned out to be justified) as to whether the paper would continue to be able to throw the same light on political skulduggery and economic malfeasance in high places.

For Gusinsky and Berezovsky, Putin's first year looked as if it would also be the last year in which they would hold sway over a large section of the Russian mass media. The former was charged with embezzlement and both, fearing arrest, chose to remain abroad. Financial irregularities, to put it mildly, have been massive and widespread in the post-Soviet era. It is difficult, therefore, to regard it as coincidental that while investigations against senior Kremlin officials which got under way during Yevgeny Primakov's prime ministership have been stopped, the sternest legal action has been taken against business tycoons who controlled sections of the mass media which divulged information or expressed views embarrassing for the state authorities. Gusinsky's NTV had long been a source of irritation to Yeltsin,[28] and, though he has departed, many of the senior ministers and presidential administration officials who came under the close scrutiny of NTV, particularly in 1999, are still in place. An example of NTV's breaking of previous taboos came on the evening of 30

---

[27] See Chrystia Freeland, *Sale of the Century: The Inside Story of the Second Russian Revolution* (London: Little, Brown, 2000); and Aleksandr Korzhakov, *Boris Yel'tsin: ot rassveta do zakata* (Moscow: Interbuk, 1997).

[28] Boris Yeltsin, *Midnight Diaries* (London: Weidenfeld & Nicolson, 2000), 295–6.

May 1999 when Yevgeny Kisilev, the presenter of the popular programme *Itogi*, alleged that there were close links between Nikolai Aksenenko, by that time first deputy prime minister and also minister of railways, and the oligarchs, Berezovsky and Roman Abramovich, on the one hand, and with Yeltsin's immediate entourage ('the Family'), on the other. Earlier that month Yeltsin had come close to appointing Aksenenko, rather than Sergei Stepashin, as prime minister in succession to Primakov. Only a late intervention by Anatoly Chubais, who subsequently went out of his way to lavish public praise on Stepashin, persuaded Yeltsin to nominate the minister of interior Stepashin rather than the minister for railways to the highest governmental office.[29]

While some moves were made against NTV in Yeltsin's time, the most decisive action came in Putin's first year, culminating in December 2000 when the Russian tax inspectorate issued four lawsuits against companies in the Media Most holding with a view to liquidating them as insolvent. These included NTV.[30] Kisilev, the director-general of NTV in addition to being its leading current affairs presenter, said that the aim of the authorities was clear: 'that is to destroy NTV and with it what is left of democracy in Russia'.[31] Gusinsky himself won at least a temporary reprieve on 27 December 2000 when a Moscow court dismissed the charges of fraud brought against him, but the procurator-general's office immediately announced that it would be appealing against that decision. Not unexpectedly, the Moscow City Court reversed the decision of the district court, leaving Gusinsky facing serious charges and his lawyers with the task of taking their case to the Russian Supreme Court.[32]

By the end of the year 2000 there were still alternative sources of information in the Russian Federation. A substantial freedom of expression, in public places as well as in private homes, also survived. However, self-censorship in the central mass media was becoming more prevalent, especially on television, and there were strong pressures, not excluding physical assaults, on journalists prepared to write about corruption in the Kremlin.[33] The attacks on Gusinsky's media empire, in particular, and on Berezovsky are an assertion of central state power against rich and unpopular businessmen who have wielded independent influence over public policy and the mass media. Vladimir Putin has both an institutional base in the central administration and the support of a majority of the public for cracking down on the best-known oligarchs. That in so doing the federal Russian authorities may also be reducing diversity in the mass media, curtailing the means of providing alternative sources of information, and, hence, retarding the process of democratization does not appear to worry the presidential administration. Indeed, the pressure from

---

[29] Interview with Igor Malashenko, *Kommersant Vlast'*, No. 23, 15 June 1999, pp. 18–20. The role of Chubais was also confirmed by Boris Nemtsov in a lecture at St Antony's College, Oxford, on 3 June 1999.

[30] BBC SWB, Russia: SU/4027/B2, 19 Dec. 2000.

[31] BBC SWB, Russia: SU/4026/B8, 18 Dec. 2000.

[32] *Financial Times*, 27 Dec. 2000, p. 6; *The Times*, 27 Dec. 2000, p. 16; and Reuters report by Andrei Shukshin, 'Russia Court Rules to Reinstate Media Boss Case', Johnson's Russia List, No. 5009, 5 Jan. 2001.

[33] Thus, for example, a journalist, Oleg Lurye, a correspondent of one of the most independent (albeit small-circulation) of Russian newspapers, *Novaya gazeta*, had his face slashed by attackers in the early hours of 17 December 2000. No attempt was made to steal his money, watch, or mobile phone. The newspaper's editor, Dmitry Muratov, connected the assault to articles by the journalist critical of senior Kremlin officials and their relations with businessmen (*Segodnya*, 18 Dec. 2000, reported on Johnson's Russia List, No. 4695, 18 Dec. 2000; and BBC SWB: Russia, SU/4027 B/4, 19 Dec. 2000). Six months earlier another *Novaya gazeta* journalist, Igor Domnik, was killed in the entrance to his block of flats.

the Kremlin is in the opposite direction—to enhance control over the flow of information to the public.

During the Yeltsin years the central media were, as a rule, significantly freer of state control than the local media in the republics and regions. In many localities it has been extremely dangerous for journalists to engage in investigative journalism not only into the activities of criminal networks but also into the machinations of the local mayor, governor, or president of the republic, and the latter bodies have not always been easily separable from the former. Even in the capital it was much easier in the specifically Moscow city newspapers to criticize President Yeltsin than to publish anything uncomplimentary about Mayor Yury Luzhkov. In many of the republics, regions, and cities of Russia unreconstructed local bosses have been no more tolerant of dissent or freedom of the press than they were in Soviet times before the Gorbachev reforms got under way. In Tatarstan, for example, President Mintimer Shaimiev has retained a tight grip on all levers of power, including the mass media—hardly surprisingly for one who actively supported the 'State Committee for the State of Emergency' and the August coup of 1991 and who immediately reintroduced censorship of the local mass media.[34] During the first decade of post-Soviet Russia some two hundred journalists have been murdered. In many cases the victims were especially intrepid reporters in the republics and regions who had investigated either organized crime or official corruption. In one of the worst cases, the most prominent independent journalist in Kalmykia, Larisa Yudina, who was also the local representative of the democratic political party, Yabloko, was stabbed to death in a political assassination in June 1998. She had been persecuted by the republican authorities for some time and her newspaper had to be printed outside Kalmykia.[35]

Freedom of expression has unquestionably been stronger at the federal centre of Russia than in most of the republics and regions, although the state-controlled media were used extremely tendentiously in the months preceding the 1999 Duma election in order to discredit two potential presidential candidates, Yury Luzhkov and Yevgeny Primakov. Even before then, journalists' dependence on those who were subsidizing their newspapers or television channels curtailed their freedoms, while in the republics and provincial Russia the controls exerted by presidents and governors tended to be much more direct and uncompromising. At best, then, this requirement of a democracy, which has already survived some turbulent times, remains a fragile growth.

THE RIGHT TO VOTE IN FREE AND FAIR ELECTIONS

Throughout the entire Soviet period Russians were able to vote. The trouble was that there was only one candidate. The right to vote began to be meaningful (other than as a demonstration of the regime's mobilizational capacity) only from 1989 onwards. It has remained a serious right, although the extent to which the elections have been fair, as distinct from free, is questionable. It is clear that neither the State Duma elected in 1993 nor its successor elected in 1995 are what President Yeltsin would have chosen had he possessed the power to determine the composition of the legislature. Yet, particularly in the first of these cases, the fairness was highly dubious. Lilia Shevtsova has noted that in the 1993 parliamentary elec-

---

[34] *Kto est' kto v Rossii* (Moscow: Olimp, 1997), 711–12.

[35] V. Rudnev, ed., *Delo No. 2; Respublika Kalmykiya protiv 'Sovetskoy Kalmykii'* (Moscow: Prava Cheloveka, 1997); and *Segodnya*, 10 June 1998, p. 7.

tion almost seven million ballots were mysteriously lost, the report of the Central Electoral Commission remained unpublished and was apparently destroyed, and 'even Yeltsin's closest allies later admitted that there had been electoral fraud'.[36]

Where unfairness comes in at the level of the presidential election, it is not primarily a matter of fraud—although that certainly occurred in some republics in both 1996 and 2000, it was not on a scale sufficient to have changed the outcome—but much more a question of access to money and the mass media. Thus, as Vladimir Gelman points out in Chapter 12, the sums spent on the Yeltsin campaign in 1996 were many times in excess of the permitted maximum. Furthermore, Yeltsin was given vast and extremely sympathetic coverage by television throughout the campaign, and General Alexander Lebed (who eventually came third) was also given a deliberate boost as the election drew near when it was believed that he would take votes away from the Communist leader Gennady Zyuganov. Yet, the election was sufficiently fair that Yeltsin had to play his part effectively. All the spin-doctoring and television coverage in the world could not, several years later, have brought Yeltsin victory in a remotely free election. Thus, the Constitutional Court was not required to display much civic courage to rule in 1998 that Yeltsin could not stand again. Those closest to Yeltsin, who were looking for security and continuity, had to find a candidate who, at a minimum, appeared capable of being a vigorous executive president for at least a four-year term. It seemed that they had found such a person in Vladimir Putin.

In a brilliantly orchestrated campaign, Putin was presented as a fresh face—as, indeed, he was, since until his elevation to the prime ministership a few months earlier he was little known to the average Russian—and an energetic candidate who had the great advantage of incumbency (as prime minister from August 1999 and as acting president from 1 January 2000) without the disadvantage of having been in the posts long enough to become unpopular. Moreover, by virtue of his high offices, Putin did not actually need to campaign in a conventional sense. He appeared on television as a man of action, combining his official duties with electoral needs as he travelled extensively throughout Russia. As Yitzhak Brudny notes in Chapter 11, he even spent a well-publicized night on a nuclear submarine and flew to Chechnya to greet the troops there at New Year. From the standpoint of democratization, a worrying feature of both the 1999 parliamentary election and the 2000 presidential election is that it brought victory to those who claimed to be above politics, while, nevertheless, condoning an exceptionally negative campaign on their behalf by the state-owned media. As Brudny puts it, 'these two elections taught the ruling elite how it could use the electoral process to perpetuate its hold on power and destroy political opponents'. In that sense the latest national elections, while better than no contest at all, did nothing to advance the cause of democratization in Russia.

Writing before the 1999 and 2000 elections, Michael McFaul has pointed to a more positive aspect of the experience of elections in Russia. He suggests that they have, at least, been a force making both for stability and moderation:

the actual process of elections has produced a moderating influence on Russian politics. Extreme nationalists and extreme communists failed to win representation in the 1995 parliamentary elections, while groups like [Zhirinovsky's] LPDR have lost support over time. Since its electoral defeat in the

---

[36] Lilia Shevtsova, *Yeltsin's Russia: Myths and Reality* (Washington: Carnegie Center, 1999), 96–7.

1996 presidential elections, the largest opposition group, the CPRF, has begun to creep toward the center and marginalize extremists within its ranks. In gubernatorial elections after the 1996 presidential vote, few communist candidates ran on militant platforms; none challenged the legitimacy of the political order.[37]

Moderation is certainly to be preferred to extremism, but as the 1999–2000 electoral cycle demonstrated, elections in which the institutions of the state, including the mass media controlled by them, are used to marginalize not just extremists, but legitimate opposition candidates and movements, can hardly qualify as fair.

THE RIGHT TO COMPETE FOR PUBLIC OFFICE

The rights of citizens to make themselves eligible for election and to compete for public office have been met up to a point in post-Soviet Russia—at least at the central level. Even there, the way in which the state-controlled media went out of their way to discredit Luzhkov and Primakov at a time in 1999 when both, and especially the latter, looked like serious potential presidential candidates, means that this 'right' was qualified in practice. Neither of these prominent politicians was legally debarred from competing, but their chances of success had been so reduced by artful use of the media that for either of them to embark on a presidential campaign would have carried with it a high risk of humiliation.

The great importance of raising vast sums of money to fight presidential elections has already been noted, especially by Gelman in Chapter 12. Although it has been argued that the importance of money in a Russian election can be exaggerated since 'the inability of candidates to commit themselves credibly reduces their ability to trade policy for either money or votes',[38] it is highly doubtful whether Yeltsin could have made the remarkable transition from single-digit popular support in January 1996 to presidential victory in the summer of that year without a wholly disproportionate share of financial resources behind his successful campaign. What is more, the favours extended by the Yeltsin administration in the aftermath of the election to those who had financed his campaign suggested that it *was* possible to trade money for influence over ministerial appointments, over the sale of natural resources, and over other policy outcomes.

At the republican level the right to stand for public office in contemporary Russia is sometimes crudely denied. Thus, for example, numerous obstacles were successfully put in the way of Ufa-born Alexander Arinin, a member of the State Duma, when he attempted to run in the 1998 presidential election in Bashkortostan against the incumbent, Murtaza Rakhimov. Ingushetia and Tatarstan have already had two uncontested presidential 'elections', even though that was against federal law. In Kalymkia, when Kirsan Ilyumzhinov was first elected in 1993, he had two opponents, whom he easily defeated—helped, no doubt, by his promise (not kept) to provide every inhabitant with $100 and every shepherd with a

[37] Michael McFaul, 'Lessons from Russia's Protracted Transition from Communist Rule', *Political Science Quarterly*, 114/1 (1999), 103–30, at p. 124.

[38] Daniel Treisman, 'Dollars and Democratization: The Role and Power of Money in Russia's Transitional Elections', *Comparative Politics*, 31/1 (Oct. 1998), 1–21, at p. 16. The power of money to influence votes, Treisman suggests, is limited by the fact that 'the existing institutional context renders hopes of achieving concrete aims through the electoral process somewhat naïve' (ibid.).

mobile phone.[39] By the following presidential election Ilyumzhinov—in flat contradiction of the federal legislation—had introduced a law establishing that elections could be held without alternative candidates. He himself was duly unopposed.[40]

POLITICAL ACCOUNTABILITY

Although Dahl does not explicitly include political accountability among the requirements of a democracy, some of what is implied by that concept is to be found in his stress on the importance of institutions for making government policies depend on votes and other expressions of popular preference.[41] However, one particularly concise definition of democracy, quite appositely, puts accountability at the heart of it. For Edward Friedman democracy should be 'understood as experientially fair rules by which citizens choose officials to run government in an accountable manner'.[42] Accountability is, indeed, as decisive a feature as any distinguishing democracy from varied forms of authoritarian rule.

The problem of accountability in Russia begins with the 1993 Constitution. The extent of the president's decree-issuing power is, by comparative standards, exceptional. Moreover, as Paul Chaisty notes in Chapter 7, the current Russian constitution not only restricts the legislature's ability to shape the composition of the government but also 'limits its powers to oversee and censure government officials'. The Constitutional Court which, during the period of constitutional struggle in 1993, attempted to act as a broker between the presidency and the legislature, fell into desuetude for fifteen months after the adoption of the Constitution. When it was resurrected in March 1995 it was a much less independent body. Graeme Gill and Roger Marwick have gone so far as to suggest that 'under the new constitutional arrangements, it was little more than a retainer for the President'.[43]

Notwithstanding a few exceptions in some republics of the Russian Federation, elections in post-Soviet Russia have generally been competitive. But contestation is not necessarily enough. Elections are important in Western democracies as a means of calling politicians to account and it is the threat of the next election which ensures their responsiveness to popular opinion. Politicians can be respected for giving a lead and for not slavishly following every public opinion poll, but in a democracy they have to select with care the areas in which they will defy or move ahead of public opinion. They cannot pursue a raft of major policies which are far removed from the outlook of a majority of the electorate. (The rise, fall, and rise of the Labour Party in Britain are illustrations of that point.)

Broadly speaking, however, Russia has had *elections with choice but without accountability*. Powerful political actors have pursued unpopular policies, regardless of election results, and there has been very little connection between votes cast and the composition of the government. As Timothy Colton has pithily put it: 'The insiders' party skippered by Prime Minister

---

[39] *The Economist*, 20 Dec. 1997, pp. 49–50. The anonymous author of the *Economist* article on Kalmykia observes: 'Strong government was one of Mr Ilyumzhinov's election promises–and perhaps the only one he kept in full.'

[40] Detailed discussion of these cases is to be found in Jeff Kahn, 'A Federal Façade: Problems in the Development of Russian Federalism', D.Phil. thesis (University of Oxford, 1999).

[41] Dahl, *Polyarchy*, 3.

[42] Edward Friedman, *The Politics of Democratization: Generalizing East Asian Experiences* (Boulder, Colo.: Westview, 1994), 2.

[43] Graeme Gill and Roger D. Marwick, *Russia's Stillborn Democracy? From Gorbachev to Yeltsin* (Oxford: Oxford University Press, 2000), 186.

Chernomyrdin, Our Home is Russia, was rejected by nine-tenths of the electorate in 1995, only to have Chernomyrdin linger in office and not be sent packing by Yeltsin until the spring of 1998, more than halfway through the Duma's term ...'.[44] Promises were made in the search for electoral support, not least by Yeltsin in 1996, which had no chance of being kept.[45] It could scarcely be claimed that Yeltsin even tried to fulfil all of his campaign promises. That many of them were, on the contrary, made in bad faith was indicated by the package of decrees he issued as early as August 1996—within two months of the presidential election. As Peter Rutland noted at the time: 'The decrees abolished all presidential privileges and tax breaks granted since the adoption of the 1996 federal budget, including most of Yeltsin's pre-election promises.'[46]

For Guillermo O'Donnell, drawing primarily on the experience of Latin America, this kind of behaviour is an integral part of what he calls 'delegative democracy'. O'Donnell himself tentatively suggests that this may be an appropriate concept for the Russian Federation in the 1990s and a number of specialists on Russia, including some of the contributors to this volume, have taken up the notion.[47] Voters, it is suggested, express confidence in a person and then leave that person, once elected to the presidency, free to decide what is best for the country, whether or not that entails the breaking of campaign promises.[48] Yury Levada, in Chapter 22, confirms, on the basis of survey research, that attitudes of this kind have been prevalent in Russia—at least in the short term until voters turn against a leader for reasons not necessarily connected with the breaking of promises. In O'Donnell's formulation of 'delegative democracy', a president is 'constrained only by the hard facts of existing power relations and by a constitutionally limited term of office'.[49] That may, indeed, be delegative rule, but is it delegated *democracy*? There is empirical evidence which, while not contradicting Levada's findings, at least casts doubt on whether Russians believe that what is encapsulated by the term, 'delegative democracy' really amounts to a form of democracy. The percentage of Russian respondents who believed that among the main meanings of elections is 'to choose among particular policies' went up from 27 per cent in 1993 to 45 per cent in 1995, while over the same period the proportion who thought that elections were 'to hold governments accountable for past actions' increased from 23 per cent to 33 per cent.[50]

[44] Timothy J. Colton, *Transitional Citizens: Voters and What Influences Them in the New Russia* (Cambridge, Mass.: Harvard University Press, 2000), 178.

[45] See e.g. Vladimir Brovkin, 'Time to Pay the Bills: Presidential Elections and Political Stabilization in Russia', *Problems of Post-Communism*, 44/6 (Nov.–Dec. 1998), 34–42.

[46] Open Media Research Institute (OMRI) Daily Digest, 20 Aug. 1996. A few spending promises were exempted from the freeze, among them payment of pensions arrears, but in practice many pensioners were still kept waiting.

[47] See Guillermo O'Donnell, 'Delegative Democracy', *Journal of Democracy*, 5/1 (1994), 55–69; O'Donnell, 'Horizontal Accountability in New Democracies', *Journal of Democracy*, 9/3 (1998), 112–26, esp. 117 and 120; M. Steven Fish, 'The Advent of Multipartism in Russia', *Post-Soviet Affairs*, 11/4 (Oct.-Dec. 1995), 340–83, at p. 358; and A. V. Lukin, 'Perekhodnyy period v Rossii: demokratizatsiya i liberal'nye reformy', *Polis*, 2 (1999), 134–54, esp. 150.

[48] It is worth noting, as Brudny does in Ch. 11, that, rather remarkably, Vladimir Putin did not make any campaign promises, nor did he run campaign advertisements or hold rallies. But, in a sense, he took 'delegative democracy' even further than did Yeltsin by not having a programme and justifying its absence on the grounds that if he issued one, people would immediately start picking holes in it.

[49] O'Donnell, 'Delegative Democracy', 59.

[50] See Jon H. Pammett, 'Elections and Democracy in Russia', *Communist and Post-Communist Studies*, 32/1 (Mar. 1999), 45–60, esp. 53–4. O'Donnell himself, it is worth stressing, is no apologist for what he calls 'delegative democracy'. On the contrary, in the same articles in which he discusses that concept, he emphasizes the paramount importance of enhancing accountability.

Yet, as Richard Rose has pointed out in Chapter 14, it is difficult to hold parties account-able when they have floated into existence and into obscurity with bewildering speed. It is equally difficult to hold prime ministers accountable when they can be changed at the whim of a president and, in Yeltsin's last years in power, frequently were. Although far more accountable to the people as a whole than was the top Communist Party leadership to the general public throughout almost the whole of the Soviet period, Russian politicians at the central level have been much less accountable than the existence of competitive elections should lead one to expect. The relative weakness of political parties, as noted by Rose, Darrell Slider, and Stephen Whitefield in Section 5 of this volume, is one major reason for that lack of accountability as compared with the ability, for example, of West European electorates to hold their governments responsible for their actions. The link between elec-tions and accountability is a stable and coherent party system which up to now Russia has largely lacked.

As the year 2000 ended, the weaknesses of the party system were being officially recog-nized, but some observers feared that the cure would be worse than the disease. President Putin submitted a new draft law on political parties to the State Duma in late December for the Duma to consider in 2001. It aimed to define a political party for the purpose of providing it with state financial support. An organization would have to have a minimum of 10,000 members, and at least a hundred members per branch in party organizations in more than half of the regions and republics composing the Russian Federation, to qualify for political party status. The Chairman of the Central Electoral Commission, Alexander Vesh-nyakov, made clear that the law was aimed at reducing the number of parties by encouraging amalgamations. The draft law immediately raised different concerns from those associated with the multiplicity of parties and the problem for the serious contenders of raising vast sums of money from private sources.

There are serious doubts as to whether, in contemporary Russian conditions, the state authorities can be relied upon to preserve a level playing-field between government-supporting parties and oppositional ones.[51] Yet, Vladimir Putin, in an interview on 25 December 2000, made many of the same apt criticisms of the post-Soviet party system that have been heard from Western political scientists, including those cited above. Observing that 'we don't have a well-defined structure of political life in the country', Putin attributed its absence to the fact that 'we don't have stable nationwide parties'. Currently, they were 'more like political clubs'. The law on political parties, which would bring about their consolida-tion, should allow them, he suggested, to spread their influence beyond the confines of the Moscow ring road. And if those parties emanated from the regions themselves and were able to extend their reach into Moscow, 'we will be able to say that we have a government ... formed on a purely party basis. And then it will be countered by some legal opposition which disagrees with the proposals, ideas and the policy line pursued by the government.'[52]

Boris Nemtsov, as leader of the Union of Right Forces, was quick to criticize the draft law, suggesting that 'the one who pays would have control' and adding: 'We already have prob-lems with our parties' independence, and funding them would simply end it altogether.'[53]

[51] 'Electoral Chief Outlines Draft Law on Political Parties', BBC SWB: Russia, SU/4027, B/3-B/4, 19 Dec. 2000.

[52] Interview with President Vladimir Putin broadcast on Russian TV on 25 Dec. 2000, reported in BBC SWB, SU/4032, B/3-B/8, at p. B/6, 29 Dec. 2000.

[53] AP report of 28 Dec. 2000, from Moscow, published in Johnson's Russia List, No. 4712, 29 Dec. 2000.

There are, however, many democracies in which funds are distributed by the state to sustain political parties according to clear and fair criteria. As Alan Ware has noted: 'By the late 1980s there was some form of public financing [of political parties] in nineteen liberal democracies, of which fifteen were long-established regimes that had been liberal democracies for over thirty years. In other words, about two-thirds of the well-established democracies had introduced state funding ...'.[54] Thus, there is nothing necessarily undemocratic about funding political parties from the public purse. Indeed, such state funding is supported in many countries on the basis that it prevents wealthy special interests from purchasing undue influence at the expense of the people as a whole and that, by supporting the cost of running a national political party, it is buttressing one of the most important parts of the democratic edifice. It is not, however, a panacea. As Ware observes:

even in those countries, such as Germany, where an extensive funding system has been set up, it has often failed to achieve one of its aims—the elimination of corruption. Financial scandals involving parties and interest groups have persisted in Germany. While public funding helped to bolster the parties as links between voters and politicians, at least until the early 1990s, it supplemented, rather than replaced, interest group money.[55]

In principle, the law on political parties, designed to reduce their number and increase their financial resources, could be a step forward in the democratization of Russia. Much will, however, depend both on the exact letter of the law ultimately adopted and on the spirit in which it is interpreted. The fear must be that it will be part of the 'guided democracy'—and, thus, not, strictly speaking, democracy at all—which, Alla Chirikova and Natalya Lapina suggest in Chapter 28, is already the dominant mode of government in a majority of republics and regions and which shows signs of prevailing also at the centre. The increasing tendency for Kremlin-approved candidates to be elected in the regions lends support to that view and raises the possibility that the new party system will turn out to be permeable and malleable.[56] At the same time, however, it will provide incentives to genuine democrats to put aside smaller differences in order to defend the values they hold in common. Thus, the eventual outcome of the law on political parties should not be prejudged, though it seems unlikely that the goal of those in the Kremlin who drafted it was to make life easier for the opposition.

THE RULE OF LAW

In most democracies—certainly in Western Europe and the United States—a rule of law preceded democracy. Law is far from being a sufficient condition for democracy but it is a necessary one. As is suggested by the notion of 'freedom under the law', which has a long lineage in English legal discourse, it is difficult even to envisage the various freedoms which

---

[54] Alan Ware, *Political Parties and Party Systems* (Oxford: Oxford University Press, 1996), 301–2.

[55] Ibid. 303.

[56] In November-December 2000 four regional governors were elected who were all in good standing with President Putin—Admiral Vladimir Yegorov (in Kaliningrad); the Sibneft oil tycoon, Roman Abramovich (in Chukotka); General Vladimir Shamanov, a former Russian army commander in Chechnya (who defeated the Communist incumbent, Yury Goryachev, in Ulyanovsk); and the head of the Federal Security Service in the Voronezh region, Vladimir Kulakov, who defeated the incumbent, Ivan Shabanov (who, like Goryachev, was a former Communist Party official).

are essential requirements of democracy without placing them in a legal framework.[57] Linz and Stepan rightly regard 'a clear hierarchy of laws, interpreted by an independent judicial system and supported by a strong legal culture in civil society' as a requirement of a consolidated democracy.[58] The crucial importance of a rule of law, both for the functioning of a 'civilized' market economy and for the advance of democratization has been stressed by a number of contributors to this book, among them John Dunlop, Eugene Huskey, Kathryn Hendley, Richard Ericson, William Smirnov, and Alexander Lukin. Whether Lukin is right to imply that in Russia's case the rule of law and democratization cannot be pursued simultaneously (as they have been, with a substantial measure of success, in a number of East-Central European countries) is another matter. It is arguable that those who would prefer to put further limits on such democratization as has occurred in Russia, rather than to advance that process are, in the main, the same individuals and groups who find it convenient to retain arbitrary sanctions and selective application of the law in preference to an impersonal rule of law.

While significant progress towards a rule of law was made in the last decades of imperial Russia, any lingering respect for legal norms did not long survive the Bolshevik Revolution. There were Soviet laws, some of them draconian, but—with the significant, albeit partial, exception of the Gorbachev era—law was always liable to be bent or swept aside if it got in the way of political convenience or of the interests of the Communist Party high command or the KGB. Moreover, connections (*svyazy*) and a system of mutual favours (*blat*) have been, and remain, more potent than law. In some ways they were more important in the Soviet shortage economy, as a means of getting scarce goods and services that even money could not buy, than they are today. Yet networks and informal rules are still of greater significance in public administration than formal law.[59] Kathryn Hendley, in Chapter 9, has shown why factory managers in economic disputes would rather rely on informal networks than risk resort to the law. They find it hard to believe that the administration of the law will be genuinely impartial and their 'law-averse trading partners could still appeal to political or other patrons'. Indeed, for a manager to resort to the law could be seen as an admission of the weakness of his connections, for why otherwise would he not seek the support of a powerful high official. To embark on legal action could, in other words, undermine both his credibility as a person of substance and his reputation for fair dealing, since the use of informal networks remains more socially acceptable than litigation.

Connections and *blat* were important to the new business class in Russia for their acquisition of capital assets in the first place. The number of formerly high Komsomol officials who, for example, are now among Russia's new rich may, perhaps, be attributed to a kind of Darwinian 'natural selection' which produced people of drive and ambition who would

---

[57] For elaboration of what that concept has meant in English law, see the classic work of A. V. Dicey (first published in 1885), *Introduction to the Study of the Law of the Constitution* (10th edn., London: Macmillan, 1961), 207–8.

[58] Juan J. Linz and Alfred Stepan, *Problems of Democratic Transition and Consolidation: Southern Europe, South America, and Post-Communist Europe* (Baltimore: Johns Hopkins University Press, 1996), 10.

[59] For the light they throw on informal networks see Alena Ledeneva, *Russia's Economy of Favours: Blat, Networking and Informal Exchange* (Cambridge: Cambridge University Press, 1998); and Janine R. Wedel, *Collision and Collusion: The Strange Case of Western Aid to Eastern Europe* (London: Macmillan, 1998). For a critique of post-Soviet public administration, together with proposals for its reform, see A. V. Obolonsky, 'Reforma rossiyskoy gosudarstvennoy sluzhby: kontseptsiya i strategiya', *Obshchestvennye nauki i sovremennost'*, 3 (1998), 5–15.

attain success in any system and rapidly learn the informal rules of a new game. But the fact that 'many of Russia's most powerful financiers' are the relatively young men 'who established commercial banks with the help of Komsomol assets in the late 1980s'[60] owes much also to the opportunities afforded by their institutional positions in the last years of the Soviet Union and the new incentives offered by economic transition. Not only Komsomol officials but many a Soviet economic manager was able to move almost seamlessly from managing assets to controlling them and, subsequently, to owning them—even if, given the ambiguities of the legal framework and the uncertainties in the administration of the law, their property rights remain insecure.

Ambiguity in the Russian law, while a potential long-term threat to Russian property, thus providing incentives for the massive capital flight which has been a feature of the post-Soviet era, could also, however, serve the interests of Russia's new business elite. So much so, that ambiguity was on occasion deliberately introduced into the design of the law. At the time of the 'loans-for-shares' privatizations, launched in 1995,[61] many of those who belonged to the new Russian business elite were anxious to avoid Western companies also getting their hands on the wealth of Russian extractive industry at knock-down prices. One way in which a Western corporation might, in principle, have achieved this would have been by forming an alliance with a Russian company. To prevent that from happening some of Russia's financiers and, in particular, the tycoon Mikhail Khodorkovsky, launched a legal and political campaign to keep foreigners out.[62] Their aim was to make the law so ambiguous that it would not be a question of Western companies finding a legal way of buying into Russia's mineral wealth, but rather one of whether they could compete with their Russian rivals for political influence: 'Did they have the domestic connections and savvy to outfox a powerful Russian company in a battle waged in the murky swamp of Russian legislation?'[63] Konstantin Kagalovsky, formerly Russia's representative to the International Monetary Fund, and by 1995 working for the Russian bank Menatep (part of a group headed by Khodorkovsky), was asked by the *Financial Times* journalist Chrystia Freeland how he had ensured that 'the laws were written in so precisely vague a fashion as to make it legally too risky for foreigners to participate'. To Freeland's surprise, Kagalovsky replied: 'Well, of course, I wrote the law myself, and I took special care with it.'[64]

Within the Yeltsin administration some officials took the law more seriously than others. The 1993 Constitution served, and even during the Putin presidency still serves, as a framework for political activity, but there have been numerous manifestations of an attitude to law which sees it as, above all, concerned with safeguarding the interests of the power-holders and their financial collaborators. Yury Skuratov (who had himself turned a blind eye to legal infractions in the presidential election year of 1996 and had failed to combat the introduction of legislation in the republics which contradicted federal law) was dismissed as

---

[60] Steven L. Solnick, *Stealing the State: Control and Collapse in Soviet Institutions* (Cambridge, Mass.: Harvard University Press, 1998), 251. See also Natalya Lapina, *Rossiyskie ekonomicheskie eliti i modeli natsional'nogo razvitiya* (Moscow: INION, 1997), 10.

[61] They are discussed briefly in the introduction to Section 6 of this volume and, in extensive and illuminating detail, in Freeland, *Sale of the Century*.

[62] Ibid. 175–7.

[63] Ibid. 176.

[64] Ibid.

procurator-general at the point (in 1999) at which he began to exercise his independence as a law officer. The case involved allegations that two Swiss firms, Mabetex and its affiliate Mercata Trading, paid bribes to the former manager of all the Kremlin properties, Pavel Borodin, in return for lucrative contracts to refurbish Russian state buildings. The Swiss authorities cooperated with the Russian procurator-general and expressed their disappointment when the case was finally dropped in December 2000, following months during which the post-Skuratov procuracy had shown a notable lack of enthusiasm for the investigation.[65]

Skuratov was not the first procurator-general to have to leave office because he attempted to enforce the law. When the State Duma exercised in 1994 its right of amnesty and chose to release from prison the leaders of the August coup of 1991 as well as those who led the resistance to Yeltsin when he forcibly dissolved the Russian legislature in September–October 1993, the Russian president instructed Aleksei Kazannik, who had been procurator-general for only a few months, to find a way of *not* releasing the prisoners. Kazannik, however, abided by what he understood to be the Duma's constitutional prerogative, even though he disagreed with their decision politically, and resigned his office immediately after authorizing the release.[66]

The procurator-general of Russia is nominated by the president but his appointment or dismissal has to be approved by the Federation Council. When Skuratov, as Laura Belin related in Chapter 23, was shown on Russian television in bed with two prostitutes—and the fact that cameras were in place indicated clearly enough that this was a case of entrapment—the Federation Council refused to endorse Yeltsin's dismissal order, though they acceded to Putin's demand in May 2000. In the intervening period Skuratov had been procurator-general in name only. Yeltsin devotes a chapter of his latest volume of memoirs to Skuratov and says that 'Yury Ilyich Skuratov managed to drag me, the Federation Council, and the whole country into a petty, sordid scandal'.[67] Yet, in writing about Skuratov and post-Soviet Russia's other procurators-general, Yeltsin accepts no responsibility for having appointed people whose term of office, on his own assessment, invariably ended in 'scandal', attributing this, rather, to bad luck:

People say Russia hasn't been lucky with its prosecutor generals. Stepankov, Kazannik, and Ilyushenko were Skuratov's predecessors. Stepankov left under a cloud during the White House rebellion of 1993; Kazannik released the 1991 coup plotters before the end of their sentences and then left, slamming the door behind him. Ilyushenko wound up in Lefortovo Prison (thanks to his successor, Skuratov). Each prosecutor departed amid scandal. And each one left behind a file cabinet of unsolved cases.[68]

When Pavel Krasheninnikov was dismissed as minister of justice in August 1999, he was told

[65] See 'Geneva Prosecutor Condemns Decision to Drop Mabetex Probe', *Jamestown Foundation Monitor*, 15 Dec. 2000, republished in Johnson's Russia List, No. 4692, 16 Dec. 2000; and Yury Skuratov, *Variant Drakona* (Moscow: Detektiv-Press, 2000), esp. 296–317. Borodin was, however, arrested in January 2001—on a Swiss warrant—while visiting the United States, and began a legal battle against his extradition to Switzerland.

[66] *Komosomol'skaya pravda*, 18 Mar. 1994, p. 7.

[67] Yeltsin, *Midnight Diaries*, 221.

[68] Ibid. 221–2.

by Kremlin officials: 'You have one problem: you always cite the law.'[69] However odd it may appear for this to be considered a defect in the holder of that particular office, the main functions of the procurator-general and the minister of justice, in the eyes of leading figures in the Yeltsin administration, were to find ways of bending or circumventing the law on behalf of the president and those closest to him.

Developing democracy or creeping authoritarianism?

For a time it was possible for well-wishers of democratization to take some modest comfort not from the practice of what has been called 'democracy' in post-Soviet Russia, but from the fact that Russians made a distinction between their self-proclaimed 'democrats' (for many of whom they developed a growing disdain) and the norms of democracy. The data collected since 1993 by Stephen Whitefield and Geoffrey Evans have been especially suggestive in this respect.[70] However, their findings from the last years of the Yeltsin presidency are less encouraging.[71] Whereas 1996, the year in which Yeltsin took to the hustings and won his second presidential election, saw a mild upsurge both of support for democratic principles and (albeit at much lower levels) for 'actually existing democracy' in Russia, the 1998 Whitefield and Evans survey showed identification with democratic norms down from 52.3 per cent in 1996 to 32.9 per cent, while positive evaluation for what passed for democracy in Russia was reduced within the same two-year period from 27.5 per cent to a mere 13 per cent.

Those, whether in Russia or the West, who have insisted on calling post-Soviet Russia a democracy have unwittingly undermined support for democracy, since the attitude of a majority of Russians has been: 'If *this* is democracy, we don't want it.' As noted above, however, many of them have consistently made a distinction between democratic principles, on the one hand, and the way Russia was governed under Yeltsin, on the other, with significantly more support for the principles than the political reality. Russia has, in fact, had a hybrid political system, or mixed polity, combining elements of democracy, arbitrariness, and kleptocracy. It has also been mixed government in the sense that there is a variety of political regimes within Russian borders—from some relatively democratic regions and republics to highly authoritarian ones, with the latter (particularly in the case of the republics) heavily outnumbering the former. Indeed, the centre—with all its faults—has tended to enjoy greater freedom and more democracy than the periphery. This may reflect the heavy concentration of countervailing powers and influences—of high-profile leaders of political parties, of well-educated professionals and the new commercial middle class,[72] and of political institutes and think-tanks—in Moscow.

There is one sense in which Russia under Putin is more 'democratic' than it was

---

John Thornhill, 'Opposition to Kremlin gets double boost', *Financial Times*, 18 Aug. 1999. As late as 1999 there were senior figures in the Kremlin, worried about the forthcoming 2000 presidential election, who were ready to provoke a crisis by reviving the notion of banning the Communist Party of the Russian Federation. As Thornhill reports, Krasheninnikov was publicly criticized by Yeltsin for not investigating the Communist Party rigorously enough, while behind the scenes he was blamed by others within the presidential entourage for finding no grounds for 'a decision to liquidate the party'.

[70] See e.g. Stephen Whitefield and Geoffrey Evans, 'Support for Democracy and Political Opposition in Russia, 1993–1995', *Post-Soviet Affairs*, 12/3 (July–Sept. 1996), 218–42.

[71] I am grateful to Stephen Whitefield for making these data available to me.

[72] The ranks of the latter were, however, much diminished by the August 1998 financial crash.

throughout most of the 1990s. He is in tune with public opinion to a degree which Yeltsin was not, except at the height of his popularity in the last year of the Soviet Union's existence. Of course, for a leader to be highly regarded by a majority of the population does not in itself imply that the form of government is democratic. Hitler and Stalin enjoyed adulation in their time and were, it would appear, popular with a majority of the German and Russian publics. Russia today, however, is very different, indeed, from Stalin's Soviet Union, not least in respect of the contrast between pluralism and totalitarianism. This means that we can, with greater confidence, write of Putin's popularity than that of any dictator. The assertion is based upon opinion polls, professionally conducted, and at a time when people are not afraid to answer honestly. (Had sample surveys, in which politically sensitive questions were asked, been conducted in the Soviet Union or Nazi Germany of the 1930s, the results would not have been worth the paper they were written on.) Of course, as noted above, there is more self-censorship in the Russian mass media today than there was throughout most of the 1990s and there is also more skilful effort devoted to projecting a favourable image of Russia's president. Yet enough freedom of expression remained, and enough diversity in the mass media still existed, at the end of 2000 to make it implausible to attribute Putin's high standing merely to manipulation of public opinion. In December 2000, 68 per cent of Russian citizens approved and only 23 per cent disapproved of his actions as president. That was only marginally down from Putin's 70 per cent approval rating the previous month and higher than his also impressive 64 per cent approval in October.[73]

A central feature of the Putin presidency—and one which appears to have contributed to his popularity—is the attempt to reassert central state power.[74] That in itself is not necessarily a backward step in terms of democratization. For behind post-Soviet Russia's democratic façade many of the most important decisions have owed much to the irresponsible power wielded by financiers who had discovered that high-level political contacts were the most cost-effective means of obtaining and protecting riches. Ironically, old Soviet propaganda about capitalist systems, which played down the significance of Western democratic institutions and overstated the power of bankers, would have been more apposite if it had been framed as a prediction about post-Communist Russia. Western writing about Russian 'reformers' has all too often blurred the distinction between transition to democracy and transition to a form of capitalism. There *are* Russian reformers who are quite sincere, albeit mistaken, in their belief that capitalism leads inevitably to democracy. For some of them that was sufficient justification for making an attempt to build it speedily and unscrupulously (as in the case of 'loans for shares')—with echoes, indeed, of the Soviet 'building of socialism'. There is, however, ample evidence of authoritarian regimes coexisting with predominantly market economies.[75]

Putin has used two levers, in particular, to reaffirm central state power vis-à-vis leading

---

[73] VTsIOM polls, conducted between 24 and 27 Nov. and on 18 Dec. 2000, reported in BBC SWB, Russia: SU/4011 B/4, 30 Nov. 2000; and in BBC SWB, Russia: SU/4030 B/2, 22 Dec. 2000.

[74] I have explored that theme in a forthcoming article, 'Vladimir Putin and the Reaffirmation of Central State Power' in *Post-Soviet Affairs*, 17/1 (2001).

[75] See e.g. Adam Przeworski, *Democracy and the Market: Political and Economic Reforms in Eastern Europe and Latin America* (Cambridge: Cambridge University Press, 1991); Przeworski *et al.*, *Sustainable Democracy* (Cambridge: Cambridge University Press, 1995); and Juan J. Linz and Alfred Stepan, *Problems of Democratic Transition and Consolidation: Southern Europe, South America, and Post-Communist Europe* (Baltimore: Johns Hopkins University Press, 1996).

'oligarchs' (or business tycoons), on the one hand, and the regions and republics, on the other. The first is the *selective application of the law;* the second is the *power of administrative reorganization.* As noted earlier, the law was selectively applied to Vladimir Gusinsky and Boris Berezovsky, each of whom controlled significant sections of the mass media and each of whom had aspired to exert independent influence over public policy. It was also applied to the former Russian vice-president, Alexander Rutskoy, when just twenty-four hours before the poll, he was disqualified from standing for re-election as governor of the Kursk region. Contravention of federal law has, however, been sufficiently widespread among Russia's business tycoons as well as among republican presidents and many of the regional governors that breach of law was scarcely the decisive factor in the decision to remove Gusinsky, Berezovsky, and Rutskoy as political players. Other tycoons continue to flourish and there are many republican and regional bosses whose records would no more stand up to rigorous legal examination than Rutskoy's. Selective application of the law is very different from the rule of law.

So far the indications are that any move away from oligarchical corporatism is not so much towards a law-bound market economy as towards state corporatism. That is to say, there remain business people as rich as those against whom criminal charges have been brought and who have benefited no less from insider deals and special privileges. Yet, at the end of the year 2000 their position seemed stronger rather than weaker, following the ousting of Berezovsky and Gusinsky. The price, however, of their continuing financial well-being and apparent security from prosecution has become political loyalty. What that means is that the disadvantages of privileged access to state officialdom and national resources are no longer counterbalanced, to some extent, by the benefit (in terms of democratization) of independent criticism of high officialdom in the mass media controlled by private rather than state capital. Most businessmen who have come to be known as 'oligarchs' have done little to modernize the real Russian economy. On the contrary, they are among those who have contributed hugely to the capital flight which has left Russia with a crumbling infrastructure and outdated technology. Their political influence has generally been self-serving and often malign, but at least a few of them (and Gusinsky most notably) made a contribution which was more positive than negative to one of the six requirements of democracy discussed earlier—freedom of expression and access to alternative sources of information.

If selective application of the law is the first major lever in the hands of the state—and, in particular, of the presidency—the second, as noted above, is the power which lies in the hands of the president to alter radically the country's administrative structure. The most striking example of that during the Putin presidency was, as noted by Jeff Kahn in Chapter 27 and Alla Chirikova and Natalya Lapina in Chapter 28, the presidential decree of May 2000 which established seven superdistricts, corresponding with the pre-existing military districts of the Russian Federation. One of the primary aims of this administrative change was the understandable one of seeking to ensure that the thousands of federal employees in the regions remained the agents of the federal centre and not, as so many of them had become, in the pockets of regional governors and republican presidents. It was, though, significant, as Chirikova and Lapina observe, that this adminstrative reform was foisted on the regions and republics unilaterally by the centre. It did not follow discussions, still less negotiations,

---

[76] Vladimir Putin, *First Person* (London: Hutchinson, 2000), 186.

between the centre and the regions. Putin's centralizing inclinations were indicated clearly enough when he declared: 'from the very beginning, Russia was created as a supercentralized state. That's practically laid down in its genetic code, its traditions, and the mentality of its people.'[76]

In the meantime, some regional governors and republican presidents continue to wield great power within their domains, but their continuing ability to do so looks likely to be heavily dependent on their loyalty to the federal presidency. Even Mayor Yury Luzhkov of Moscow, who has an independent power base in the form of strong support from the Moscow electorate and a solid financial underpinning inasmuch as new investment is heavily concentrated in the capital city, has been far less outspoken since the state-controlled mass media were turned against him in the second half of 1999. While he was sharply critical of Yeltsin on occasion, he has been uncharacteristically docile and deferential in his relationship with Putin. So far Putin's expectations of this relationship have been borne out. When he was asked before he was elected president how he thought Luzhkov would treat him, he responded: 'I think he will behave constructively. I don't think he will really have a choice.'[77]

During the Yeltsin presidency many observers came to underestimate the reserves of state power which could be called upon by a determined chief executive. Even in terms of democratization, a case can be made for significant reaffirmation of central state power, for there was nothing democratic about the way a handful of business people acquired control over Russia's greatest wealth-producing national assets. Nor has there been anything remotely democratic about the government of such republics of the Russian Federation as Bashkortostan, Kalmykia, or Tatarstan. But, thus far, most of the ill-gotten gains and most of the irresponsible power remain untouched. Much could still change in the course of the Putin presidency, for better or for worse, but on the evidence available it appears that financial tycoons and local dictators, provided they are politically circumspect and impeccably loyal to the federal president, will continue to enjoy their special privileges.

In a country the size of Russia, with its acute demographic and health problems, widespread poverty and absolute economic decline over the past decade, and with its potential, whether from weapons of mass destruction or ecological catastrophe,[78] to inflict incalculable suffering on itself and other countries, democratization is not the only criterion for judging its post-Soviet development. A case can be made that political stability, economic restructuring, and a firm legal order are no less important desiderata. That does not, however, mean that Western politicians, seeing relative stability, should misuse the term 'democracy'. By calling a hybrid regime, containing much arbitrariness, 'democratic', they devalue the very concept. Nor does it mean that these other desiderata need be in conflict with democracy. On the contrary, in the long run democracies are the most stable of political regimes as well as, typically, being more prosperous than countries with non-democratic governments.[79] Moreover, a rule of law, as has been argued above, is a *requirement* of democracy—a necessary, albeit not sufficient, condition of its existence.

This concluding chapter has not, obviously enough, taken up every theme developed in

[77] Ibid. 191.

[78] See Murray Feshbach and Alfred Friendly, Jr., *Ecocide in the USSR: Health and Nature under Siege* (New York: Basic Books, 1992). Since the Soviet Union ceased to exist, an already grim ecological situation has become much worse with environmental protection as a political issue further downgraded.

[79] Robert A. Dahl, *On Democracy* (New Haven: Yale University Press, 1998), 58–9.

the previous thirty-nine chapters. But no apology is required for ending a large volume on contemporary Russian politics with an evaluation of the democratization process. The issue is of central importance. To the extent that Russia becomes more genuinely democratic, it will by definition not only avoid a return to the cruel tyrannies which have plagued it so often in the past, but will also provide the best conditions for the autonomous self-development of its citizens and the economic development of that vast country. So far, notwithstanding remarks by Vladimir Putin on the need for a stable, coherent, and (by implication) competitive party system, which are remarkably congruent with much that has been said by Western political scientists, it does not appear that furthering democratization comes high on Putin's list of priorities. Re-establishing a strong state, consolidating central power against any possible rivals, whether entrepreneurial or regional, restoring national pride, and seeking to reverse the economic decline of the 1990s have been his main goals and preoccupations. Much of what is best about those aspirations is, however, in the long run more likely to find a solid foundation to the extent that their pursuit is combined with more serious democratization. To enter the cul-de-sac of creeping authoritarianism would do little for national pride or economic advance in the longer run. Alongside a revitalization of the office of president during Putin's first year which was in many ways positive, there were enough signs of old authoritarian habits of Russian officials reasserting themselves—not least a greater intolerance of critical voices in the mass media—to provide grounds for concern.

In contrast with almost the whole of the Soviet era, and indeed most of Russian history, the years since 1988 have been a short period of remarkable *democratization*, albeit in an extremely uneven process and one which has seen a transition from Communism but not yet a transition to *democracy*. It would, however, be a great mistake to imagine that authoritarianism is either culturally specific to or culturally predetermined in Russia. As Dahl has observed, 'the historical record tells us that democracy has been rare to human experience'.[80] All countries which today may firmly be counted as democratic were at one time under autocratic or oligarchic rule of one kind or another. The Russian polity over the past decade has contained elements of authoritarianism as well as elements of democracy, but it would be no less misleading to label the contemporary regime 'authoritarian' than to regard it as 'democratic'. While it is entirely possible that in the decade ahead, Russia will become more autocratic rather than more democratic, that is neither inevitable nor, contrary to some opinion within the Russian political establishment, desirable. As John Dunn has observed:

Human beings have done many more fetching and elegant things than invent and routinize the modern democratic republic. But, in face of their endlessly importunate, ludicrously indiscreet, inherently chaotic and always potentially murderous onrush of needs and longings, they have, even now, done very few things so solidly to their advantage.[81]

---

[80] Dahl, *On Democracy*, 180.
[81] John Dunn, *The Cunning of Unreason: Making Sense of Politics* (London: HarperCollins, 2000), 363.

Index of Names